Israel & the Palestinian Territories

THIS EDITION WRITTEN AND RESEARCHED BY

Daniel Robinson,

Orlando Crowcroft, Virginia Maxwell, Jenny Walker

PLAN YOUR TRIP

ON THE ROAD

THE DEAD SEA P285

ROEVIN /GETTY IMAGES ©

AKKO P175

LIOR FILSHTEINER /GETTY IMAGES ©

ELAN FLEISHER / LOOK-FOTO /GETTY

OLD PORT BO
TEL AVIV P11

Contents

SPECIAL FEATURES

Welcome to Israel & the Palestinian Territories

At the intersection of Asia, Europe and Africa – both geographically and culturally – Israel and the Palestinian Territories have been a meeting place of cultures, empires and religions since history began.

Holy Sites

Cradle of Judaism and Christianity and sacred to Muslims and Baha'is, the Holy Land invites visitors to immerse themselves in the richness and variety of the region's religious traditions. Ancient Jewish sites include Jerusalem's Western Wall and Byzantine-era synagogues adorned with sumptuous mosaics. The Roman-era synagogues around the Sea of Galilee may have been used by Jews and Christians before they diverged into separate faiths. Both Christian pilgrims and tourists can explore sites associated with Jesus's birth (in Bethlehem), ministry (in Nazareth and around the Sea of Galilee) and crucifixion (in Jerusalem). For Muslims, only Mecca and Medina are holier than Jerusalem's Al-Haram ash-Sharif, known to Jews as the Temple Mount – perhaps the most contested real estate on earth.

Tel Aviv

Brash, forward-looking and unabashedly secular, Tel Aviv is a multicultural swirl of skyscrapers, bike paths, atmospheric cafes, stylish bistros and buff bods tanning on the sand. One of the world's major centres of high-tech venture capital, the century-old city earned Unesco World Heritage status by virtue of its 1930s-style Bauhaus architecture.

Archaeology

Thanks to the painstaking work of generations of archaeologists, modern-day visitors can explore the 10,000-year-old mud-brick relics of Jericho, enter into the world of David and Solomon in Jerusalem's City of David, and twin a visit to Masada, with its dramatic tale of resistance to the mighty legions of Rome, with a tour of the thoroughfares and theatres of Beit She'an, still pulsing with Roman opulence. Many of the country's most extraordinary finds – including a 1st-century-BCE manuscript of the book of Isaiah (one of the Dead Sea Scrolls) – are on display in Jerusalem's Israel Museum.

Adventures in Nature

Few countries have so much geographic variety packed into such a small space. Distances are short, so you can relax on a Mediterranean beach one day, spend the next floating in the mineral-rich waters of the Dead Sea, and the day after that scuba diving in the Red Sea. Hikers can trek the length of the country on the Israel National Trail, splash through seasonal streams as they tumble towards the Jordan, explore spring-fed oases tucked into the arid bluffs above the Dead Sea, and explore the multi-coloured sandstone formations of Makhtesh Ramon. Many trails are ideal for mountain biking.

Why I Love Israel & the Palestinian Territories

By Daniel Robinson, Lonely Planet writer

One of the things I most enjoy about life in Israel is the exuberant diversity. Plenty of people look like characters in a Middle Eastern epic, but more interesting are the women and men who defy stereotypes and convention, crossing religious, cultural, artistic and culinary boundaries to bridge seemingly irreconcilable differences. The results – played out against a backdrop of desert wildflowers, sandy beaches, snowy peaks and cityscapes both modern and ancient – are inspiring, confounding, contradictory and, not infrequently, astonishingly delicious!

For more about our writers, see page 440

Above: Sunset over Tel Aviv (p105)

Israel & the Palestinian Territories

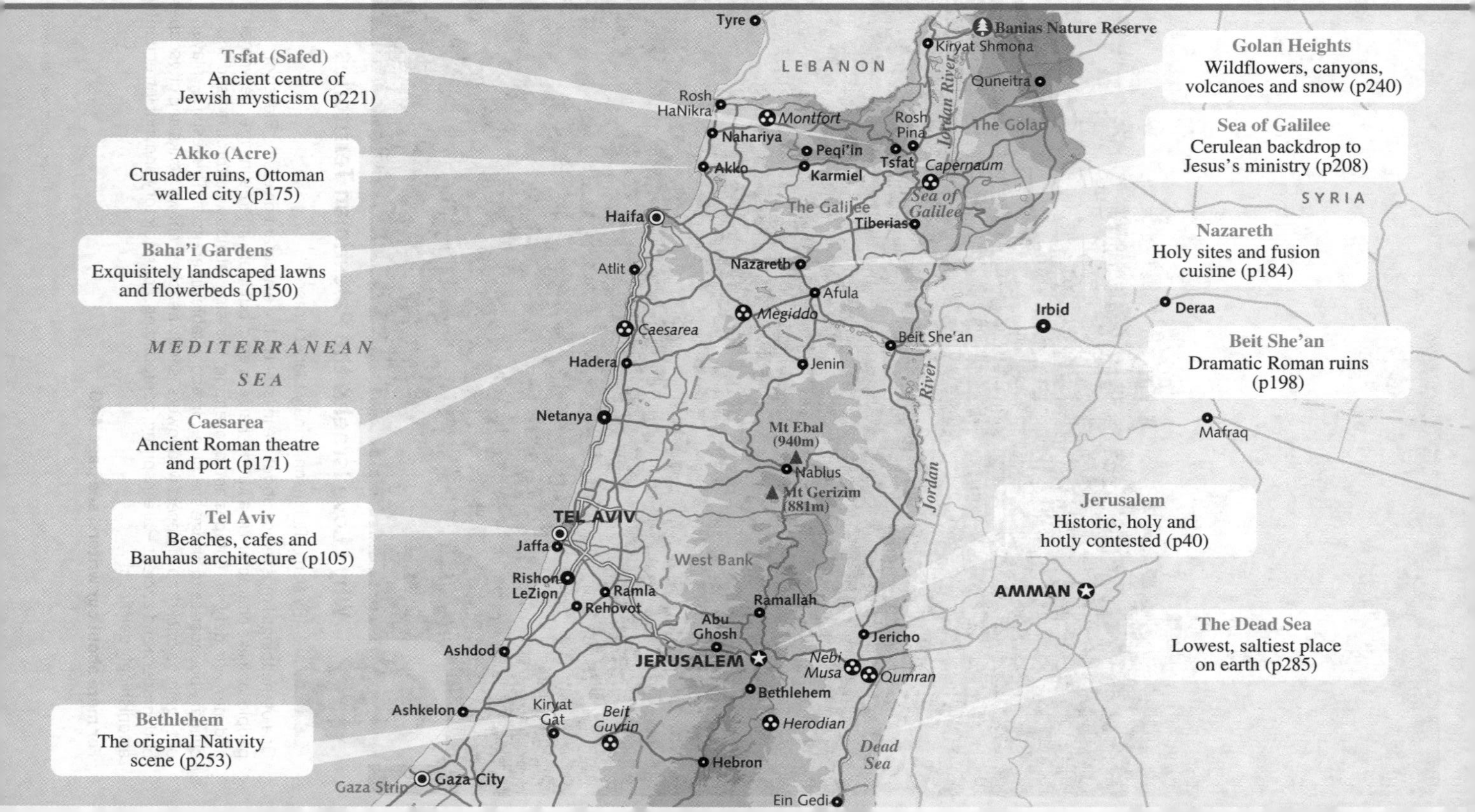

Tsfat (Safed)
Ancient centre of Jewish mysticism (p221)
Akko (Acre)
Crusader ruins, Ottoman walled city (p175)
Baha'i Gardens
Exquisitely landscaped lawns and flowerbeds (p150)
Caesarea
Ancient Roman theatre and port (p171)
Tel Aviv
Beaches, cafes and Bauhaus architecture (p105)
Bethlehem
The original Nativity scene (p253)
Golan Heights
Wildflowers, canyons, volcanoes and snow (p240)
Sea of Galilee
Cerulean backdrop to Jesus's ministry (p208)
Nazareth
Holy sites and fusion cuisine (p184)
Beit She'an
Dramatic Roman ruins (p198)
Jerusalem
Historic, holy and hotly contested (p40)
The Dead Sea
Lowest, saltiest place on earth (p285)
0 50 km
0 25 miles
MEDITERRANEAN SEA
LEBANON
SYRIA
Tyre
Banias Nature Reserve
Kiryat Shmona
Quneitra
Rosh HaNikra
Montfort
Nahariya
Peqi'in
Akko
Karmiel
Rosh Pina
Tsfat
Capernaum
The Golan
Jordan River
Sea of Galilee
The Galilee
Tiberias
Haifa
Atlit
Nazareth
Afula
Megiddo
Irbid
Deraa
Caesarea
Hadera
Beit She'an
Jenin
Netanya
Mt Ebal (940m)
Nablus
Mt Gerizim (881m)
Mafraq
Jordan River
TEL AVIV
Jaffa
West Bank
Rishon LeZion
Ramla
Rehovot
Ramallah
Abu Ghosh
AMMAN
Ashdod
JERUSALEM
Jericho
Nebi Musa
Qumran
Bethlehem
Ashkelon
Kiryat Gat
Beit Guvrin
Herodian
Hebron
Dead Sea
Gaza Strip
Gaza City
Ein Gedi

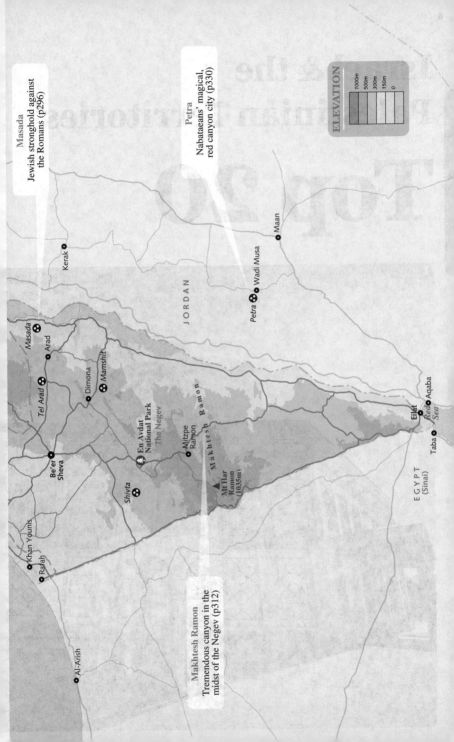

Masada
Jewish stronghold against the Romans (p296)

Petra
Nabataeans' magical, red canyon city (p330)

Makhtesh Ramon
Tremendous canyon in the midst of the Negev (p312)

ELEVATION

1000m
500m
300m
150m
0

Kerak

Maan

JORDAN

Masada
Arad
Tel Arad
Dimona
Mamshit
Petra
Wadi Musa

Be'er Sheva
En Avdat National Park
The Negev
Mitzpe Ramon
Shivta
Makhtesh Ramon
Mt Har Ramon (1035m)

Aqaba
Eilat
Red Sea
Taba

Khan Younis
Rafah

EGYPT (Sinai)

Al-Arish

Israel & the Palestinian Territories'
Top 20

Dome of the Rock

1 The first sight of Jerusalem's Dome of the Rock (p49) – its gold top shimmering above a turquoise-hued octagonal base – never fails to take your breath away. Perhaps that's what the unknown architects had in mind more than 1300 years ago when they set to work on this impossibly gorgeous building. The best view, some say, is from the Mount of Olives, but don't miss the chance to see it up close by taking an early-morning walk up to the Temple Mount/Al-Haram ash-Sharif.

The Dead Sea

2 You pass a sign reading 'Sea Level' and then keep driving downhill, eventually catching glimpses of the cobalt-blue waters of the Dead Sea (p285), outlined by snow-white salt deposits, reddish-tan cliffs and tufts of dark-green vegetation. At the oasis of Ein Gedi you can hike through steep canyons to crystal-clear pools and tumbling waterfalls before climbing to the Judean Desert plateau above – or heading down to the seashore for a briny, invigorating dip. To the south around Mt Sodom, outdoor options include adventure cycling along dry riverbeds.

KATERYNA NEGODA / GETTY IMAGES ©

KORD.COM / GETTY IMAGES ©

GRANT FAINT / GETTY IMAGES ©

ARTHUR TILLEY / GETTY IMAGES ©

Tel Aviv Beaches

3 A bit over a century ago, Tel Aviv was little more than sand dunes. Now it's a sprawling city bursting with bars, bistros and boutiques – but the beach (p121) is still the epicentre of life. Here, sunbathers bronze their bods while the more athletic swim, surf, sail and play intense games of *matkot* (beach tennis). Each Tel Aviv beach has its particular attractions – on-the-sand cafe tables, beach racquet-ball, shallow water for toddlers, a sex-segregated section for traditional Jews and Muslims – but all offer a sensual welcome to the warm, deep-blue waters of the Mediterranean.

Golan Heights

4 From towering Nimrod Fortress, the 'Galilee Panhandle' (p240) spreads out before you like a topographical map. But the looming flanks of Mt Hermon, snow capped well into spring, dwarf even this Crusader-era stronghold. Hikers can take on the alpine peaks of Mt Hermon or follow the cliff-lined wadis of the Banias and Yehudiya Nature Reserves on their way to the Jordan River and the Sea of Galilee. The Golan's basalt soils are ideal for growing grapes, so the local boutique wines are some of Israel's finest.

Above right: Nimrod Fortress (p246)

Western Wall

5 In Israel they say that every rock is holy in some way, but for Jews the holiest stones of all are those that make up the Western Wall (p59), the 2000-year-old western retaining wall of the Temple Mount. For centuries Jews have come here to pray and to mourn the destruction of the First and Second Temples. The wall's enormous stones, worn smooth by countless caresses, have an almost magnetic power, drawing close the hands and foreheads of the faithful, who come in search of a deep, direct connection with God.

JAMES L. STANFIELD / GETTY IMAGES ©

Church of the Holy Sepulchre

6 Built on what St Helena – Constantine the Great's mother – believed to be the site of Jesus's crucifixion and burial, Jerusalem's Church of the Holy Sepulchre (p54) is the holiest place in the world for many Christians. In darkened chambers infused with spirituality, a variety of Christian denominations keep alive here some of the oldest traditions of their faith. Visitors are welcome to join the parade of resplendently garbed clergy and simply dressed pilgrims as they shuffle reverently through candle-lit corridors redolent with incense.

GAVIN HELLIER / GETTY IMAGES ©

Baha'i Gardens

7 Fusing religious symbolism, breathtaking views and meticulous gardening, the 19 terraces of Haifa's Baha'i Gardens (p150) present visitors with a sublime expression of humankind's striving for beauty. The gold-domed Shrine of the Bab sits in the middle of the gardens, and tier after tier of geometric flower beds, immaculate lawns, sculptures and fountains cascade down the slopes of Mt Carmel, offering pilgrims and tourists alike a sense of incredible serenity.

Masada

8 The Romans had just destroyed Jerusalem when about a thousand Jewish Zealots took refuge on a remote mesa overlooking the Dead Sea. As you peer down from their towering redoubt (p296), you can still see the eight encircling Roman camps, connected by a siege wall, making it easy to imagine the dramatic, tragic events that unfolded here in early 73 CE. Eventually the Romans built a ramp and breached the walls, but all they found were a handful of survivors – everyone else had committed suicide rather than submit to slavery.

ANTHONY PIDGEON / GETTY IMAGES ©

DANITA DELIMONT / GETTY IMAGES ©

DANITA DELMONT / GETTY IMAGES ©

NEIL FARRIN / GETTY IMAGES ©

WENMIN LIU / GETTY IMAGES ©

Tsfat (Safed)

9 The spirit of the 16th-century rabbis who turned Tsfat (p221) into the world's most important centre of Kabbalah (Jewish mysticism) lingers in the alleyways and ancient synagogues of the Synagogue Quarter and in the nearby Artists' Quarter, where intimate galleries offer creative, joyous Judaica (Jewish ritual objects). A Kabbalistic vibe is also palpable in the hillside cemetery, where some of Judaism's greatest sages – the Ari, Yitzhak Luria, Yosef Caro – lie buried.

Above left: Market, Synagogue Quarter (p221)

Petra

10 Hidden deep in the red-rock mountains of southern Jordan, the ancient Nabataean capital of Petra (p330) is one of the world's most extraordinary archaeological treasures. Highlights include the Hellenistic-style Treasury, carved in its entirety out of the sandstone cliff face – and given heaps of free publicity thanks to Indiana Jones. The 'rose-red city half as old as time' and its modern neighbour, the tourist town of Wadi Musa, are just a two-hour drive from Eilat's Yitzhak Rabin border crossing.

Top right: The Treasury (Al-Khazneh; p332)

Caesarea

11 Hugely impressive Roman ruins make it easy to imagine city life here two millennia ago, when crowds in the amphitheatre cheered wildly as slaves fought wild animals and the theatre hosted top musical talent – as it still does today. The remains of Herod's vast port (p171), built to rival Alexandria, have been turned into one of the loveliest spots in Israel for a seaside meal or a cold beer. For a look underneath the harbour's turquoise waters, book an introductory scuba dive.

Above bottom right: Caesarea harbour

Nazareth

12 The village where Jesus grew up has also grown up and is now a bustling Arab city (p274). In the Old City, narrow alleyways are graced with churches commemorating New Testament events, and with Ottoman-era mansions. A new generation of restaurants has made Nazareth a star in Israel's gastronomic firmament. Alongside delicious old-time specialities, served with traditional Arab hospitality, you can sample East–West 'fusion' dishes – fresh local herbs with artichoke hearts, or wild Galilean pine nuts with beef.

Akko (Acre)

13 The alleys, mosques and colonnaded caravanserais of Akko's old city will transport you to the Ottoman era, but step underground and you're back in the time of the Crusaders, when this port city (p175) was the richest in the eastern Mediterranean and Marco Polo stopped here on his way to China. Wander through vast vaulted halls where Christian knights once dined, or follow in the footsteps of the Knights Templar through an amazing tunnel. The picturesque fishing port is a great spot to drink or dine.
Below bottom: Sea wall (p176) at Akko

JOHNNY STOCKSHOOTER / GETTY IMAGES ©

JULIAN KAESLER / GETTY IMAGES ©

Sea of Galilee

14 Before Judaism and Christianity became separate religions, Jesus and his earliest followers lived among the Jews of the Sea of Galilee (p208), in villages such as Capernaum – famed for its impressive synagogue – and Bethsaida. For breathtaking views of the area, head up to the Mount of the Beatitudes, where Jesus is believed to have delivered the Sermon on the Mount. A remarkably well-preserved wooden boat from the time of Jesus is on display at Kibbutz Ginosar. Swimming is possible at a variety of beaches, many linked by bike paths.

Above left: Mount of the Beatitudes (p209)

Beit She'an

15 For a taste of the decadence and grandeur of Roman life in the centuries after Jesus, stroll through the column-lined Cardo (main boulevard), stone-paved streets, elaborate bathhouses and public toilets of ancient Beit She'an (p198), destroyed – like Pompeii – by a sudden natural cataclysm, in this case the great earthquake of 749 CE. The 7000-seat theatre and its arched entrances look much as they did in the 2nd century, when dramatic performances were staged here (these days it's used for concerts).

Tel Aviv Architecture

16 Jewish architects fleeing 1930s Germany brought a radical new style to Tel Aviv: Bauhaus, also known as the International Style. Their legacy – some 4000 structures with clean lines, rounded balconies and 'thermometer' windows lighting the stairwells – constitutes the largest ensemble of Bauhaus buildings in the world, which is why the 'White City' (p105) was recognised as a Unesco World Heritage site in 2003. The preservation of Tel Aviv's Bauhaus gems is a work in progress – some have been restored, but many others await much-needed TLC.

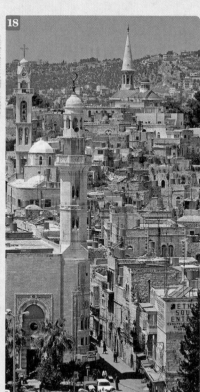

Makhtesh Ramon

17 Jerusalem is often described as 'ancient', but it's a veritable newcomer when compared with this geological phenomenon located in the midst of the Negev Desert. An asymmetrical canyon (p312) that owes its existence to 200 million years of erosion, this majestic gash in the landscape features pink rock formations, a multicoloured sandstone floor studded with fossils, and wildlife including oryx, gazelles, leopards, ibexes, vultures and onagers (wild horses). Sometimes windswept, always enigmatic, it's one of Israel's most underrated and compelling attractions. Above: Ibex

Bethlehem

18 For nearly two millennia, pilgrims have been making their way to what Christians believe to be the birthplace of Jesus. Walk the streets around the Church of the Nativity – a Unesco World Heritage site since 2012 – and Manger Sq and you'll see ancient stone buildings and narrow alleyways that look much as they did centuries ago. But Bethlehem isn't all about the past. The separation wall, which cuts the city off from Jerusalem, has become a vast canvas for street artists, from local Palestinians to British veteran Bansky, whose work remains a decade after he first visited the West Bank.

Israel Museum

19 Many museums claim to be 'world class', but here the accolade really does apply. Expanded in 2010, the Israel Museum (p79) is one of two extraordinary institutions in Jerusalem that owe their existence to an impressive program of international cultural philanthropy (the other is the Yad Vashem Holocaust museum, p80). Exhibits include the Dead Sea Scrolls, a superb archaeological collection, rooms chock-full of Judaica and Jewish ethnographic displays, art galleries (Van Gogh! Monet! Renoir!) and a sculpture garden replete with contemporary pieces.

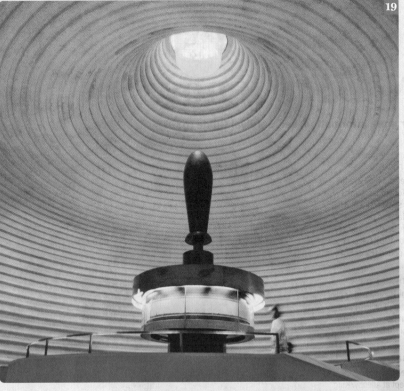

SHRINE OF THE BOOK BUILDING AT THE ISRAEL MUSEUM, DESIGNED BY ARMAND PHILLIP BARTOS, FREDERICK JOHN KIESLER AND GEZER HELLER

19

Nablus

20 The West Bank's second city (p274) sprawls between Mt Gerizim and Mt Ebal (known as the mountains of blessings and curses respectively). At its market, Palestinian shop-keepers shout the prices of everything from fruit and vegetables to perfume and spices. More sensory pleasure can be had eating *kunafeh* (warm, syrupy cheese-based pastry), Nablus' famous culinary delight, and at either of the city's tourist-friendly ham-mams. On Mt Gerizim are ruins that the Samaritans consider to be the first piece of land created by God, and an excellent museum.
Right: Stallholder, Nablus market

DAVID SUTHERLAND / GETTY IMAGES ©

20

Need to Know

For more information, see Survival Guide (p397)

Currency

Israel and the Palestinian Territories: Israeli new shekel (NIS or ILS); Jordan and the West Bank: Jordanian dinar (JD or JOD); Gaza: Egyptian pound (E£ or EGP)

Languages

Israel: Hebrew and Arabic (official), English; Palestinian Territories, Jordan: Arabic (official), English

Visas

Israel and Jordan (except at Allenby/King Hussein Bridge) grant on-arrival visas to most nationalities.

Money

ATMs widely available in Israel, less so in the Palestinian Territories, absent from Israel's border crossings with Jordan. Credit cards almost universally accepted in Israel.

Mobile Phones

All but the remotest areas have excellent 900/1800 MHz mobile-phone coverage. Local pre-paid SIM cards available.

Time

Two hours ahead of GMT/UTC.

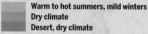

When to Go

Warm to hot summers, mild winters
Dry climate
Desert, dry climate

Tiberias
GO Oct–Jun

Tel Aviv
GO Oct–Jun

Jerusalem
GO Mar–Nov

Dead Sea
GO Oct–May

Eilat
GO Oct–Jun

High Season (Jul & Aug)

➡ Warm in Jerusalem, muggy in Tel Aviv, infernal in Eilat, Tiberias, Dead Sea

➡ Hotel prices spike and rooms are scarce

➡ Jewish holidays of Passover, Rosh HaShanah and Sukkot are also high season

Shoulder (Oct, Nov & Mar–Jun)

➡ Sometimes rainy but more often warm and sunny

➡ Spring wildflowers make March and April ideal for hiking

➡ Local tourist demand spikes during the week-long Jewish holidays of Passover and Sukkot

Low Season (Dec–Feb)

➡ Chilly or downright cold in the north, especially at higher elevations

➡ Popular time to head to the warmth of Eilat and the Dead Sea

Useful Websites

Israel Nature & Parks Authority (www.parks.org.il) Nature reserves and archaeological sites.

Israel Ministry of Tourism (www.goisrael.com) Background, events and a virtual tour.

ILH-Israel Hostels (www.hostels-israel.com) Independent hostels.

This Week in Palestine (www.thisweekinpalestine.com) Cultural goings-on.

Lonely Planet (www.lonelyplanet.com) Destination information, hotel bookings, traveller forum and more.

Important Numbers

Police/ ambulance/ fire	☑100/101/ 102
Israel country code	☑972
Palestinian Territories country code	☑972 or 970
Jordan country code	☑962

Exchange Rates

		NIS	JD
Australia	A$1	3.10	0.55
Canada	C$1	3.18	0.57
Euro zone	€1	4.45	0.79
Israel	1NIS	1.00	0.18
Japan	¥100	3.32	0.59
NZ	NZ$1	3.00	0.53
UK	UK£1	6.14	1.09
USA	US$1	3.98	0.71

For current exchange rates see www.xe.com.

Your Daily Budget

Budget: Less than 300NIS

➡ Dorm bed: 100NIS

➡ Meals of falafel or hummus, and supermarket picnics

➡ Travel by bus, train or sherut (shared taxi)

➡ Swim at free public beaches

Midrange: 500–600NIS

➡ Double room at midrange hotel (per person): 220NIS

➡ Meals at midrange restaurants

➡ Intercity travel by small rental car

Top End: More than 800NIS

➡ Luxury double room or B&B (per person): from 300NIS

➡ Meals at the finest restaurants

➡ Travel by midsize rental car or with guide

Opening Hours

Hours vary greatly by region and with religious holidays.

Banks 8.30am to between 12.30pm and 2pm Monday to Thursday, plus a couple of afternoons a week.

Bars and pubs Tend to be open until the wee hours.

Clubs After midnight till dawn seven days a week in Tel Aviv and Eilat, Thursday and Friday only in Haifa and Jerusalem.

Post offices 8am to 12.30pm and 3.30pm to 6pm Sunday to Thursday, to noon Friday.

Restaurants Highly variable.

Shopping malls 9.30am to 9.30pm Sunday to Thursday, until 2pm Friday.

Shops 9am to 6pm Sunday to Thursday, until 2pm Friday.

Arriving in Israel & the Palestinian Territories

Ben-Gurion airport (Tel Aviv; p412) Taxi to Jerusalem/Tel Aviv 280NIS/150NIS; sherut to Jerusalem 64NIS; train to Tel Aviv 18NIS.

Jordan River/Sheikh Hussein crossing (Jordan; p31) Taxi to Beit She'an 50NIS.

Allenby/King Hussein Bridge (Jordan; p32) Taxi to Jerusalem 200NIS.

Yitzhak Rabin/Wadi Araba crossing (Jordan; p31) Taxi to Eilat 35NIS.

Taba crossing (Sinai, p32) Bus to Eilat 4.90NIS.

See also Crossing Borders, p30

Getting Around

Israel and the West Bank have extensive public transport networks; for routes and schedules in Israel, head to www.bus.co.il. In Israel, buses and trains do not run on the Sabbath and Jewish holidays.

Car A great way to tour the countryside but parking can be a hassle in Tel Aviv and Jerusalem.

Bus Bus service is extensive.

Sherut Service taxis, which leave when full, are generally quicker than buses on major routes.

Train Intercity and commuter lines run along the coast, to Ben Gurion airport and up to Jerusalem.

For much more on **getting around**, see p413

If You Like...

Beaches

Hedonists bronze along the Mediterranean, while at the Dead Sea they float and apply mud packs. At the Red Sea the most colourful creatures are under the water. The Sea of Galilee offers old-fashioned family fun.

Metzitzim Beach A family-friendly half-bay just south of the Tel Aviv Port dining & nightlife area. (p121)

Coral Beach Nature Reserve Eilat's best beach is a utopia for snorkellers. (p322)

Ein Bokek Broad, clean and sandy – the Dead Sea's finest free beach. (p298)

Sea of Galilee Some are free, others come with fees and amenities, all are refreshing on a scorching summer's day.

Herzliya Pituach Fine Mediterranean sand between the marina and some of Israel's most expensive villas. (p144)

Akhziv About as far north as you can go along Israel's Mediterranean coast. (p182)

Hiking

Israel's hills and valleys burst into flower in spring, making it the ideal season to hit the hiking trails. Marked routes (p403) range from easy strolls for the whole family to multi-day treks requiring topographical maps (p406).

Israel National Trail Israel's longest footpath links the Lebanese border with the Red Sea.

Ein Gedi Two spring-fed canyon oases are home to a profusion of plant and animal life.

Makhtesh Ramon Hike through this vast desert crater, famous for its multicoloured sandstone.

Banias Cool spring water tumbles over waterfalls and nourishes Edenic vegetation.

Yehudiya Nature Reserve Canyons, waterfalls and pools on the western edge of the Golan.

Jesus Trail Walk from Nazareth to the Sea of Galilee.

En Avdat A hidden spring-fed oasis deep in the Negev Desert.

Wine Tasting

Grapes thrive in Israel's varied microclimates, producing wines of surprising richness and subtlety that have recently been winning international awards.

Golan Heights High altitudes, a cool climate, volcanic soils and top-rate savoir faire. (p233)

Dalton Plateau High in the Upper Galilee, 'Israel's Tuscany' produces some of the country's most highly regarded vintages. (p231)

Negev Highlands Hot daytime temperatures, cool nights, sandy soils, the latest drip-irrigation technology – and inspiration from the ancient Nabataeans. (p310)

Zichron Ya'acov A winemaking centre since the late 1800s, this town, overlooking the northern coastal plain, has a typically Mediterranean climate. (p169)

Ancient Synagogues

Impressive ancient synagogues, some adorned with ornate carvings and mosaics, have been unearthed all over the country.

Beit Alpha Famed for its extraordinary mosaics depicting a zodiac circle, a menorah, a shofar and a Torah ark.

Tiberias Mosaics here feature two seven-branched menorahs and a zodiac.

Korazim Decorated with exceptionally fine basalt carvings depicting floral and geometric designs.

Tzipori Byzantine-era synagogue with an exceptional mosaic floor.

Katzrin A Talmud-era synagogue made of dark basalt.

Gamla One of the world's oldest synagogues, believed to date from the 1st century BCE.

New Testament Sites

The historical Jesus was born in Bethlehem, grew up in Nazareth, preached in Galilee and was crucified in Jerusalem. Many sites associated with his life and ministry have become places of Christian pilgrimage.

Church of the Holy Sepulchre The site said to be of Jesus's crucifixion and resurrection is Christendom's holiest site. (p54)

Church of the Nativity Believed to be the site of Jesus's birth since at least the 4th century. (p255)

Basilica of the Annunciation Where many Christians believe the Annunciation took place. (p185)

Capernaum Jesus's home base during most of his Galilean ministry. (p214)

Mt Tabor Traditional hilltop site of Jesus's Transfiguration. (p196)

Mount of Temptation Where Jesus is said to have been tested by the Devil. (p267)

Nightlife

Sip Galilee wine on the seashore, nurse a local microbrew in a dark pub, watch live music under the beams of an old warehouse, or dance the night away on the beach or inside a disco.

Tel Aviv Port Seafront cafes, fine dining, music venues and all-night boogying. (p137)

Cameri Theatre Contemporary plays in Tel Aviv, with English subtitles on some nights. (p138)

Downtown Ramallah Home to some of the West Bank's liveliest cafes and bars. (p265)

Eilat Plenty of bars, pubs and clubs, some open till dawn. (p327)

Haifa Has nightlife centres up on Mt Carmel and down in the German Colony and Port Area. (p162)

Top: Interior of the Basilica of the Transfiguration (p196), Mt Tabor
Bottom: Nightlife at Tel Aviv Port (p137)

Month by Month

January

The coolest and wettest month of the year. Chilly in Jerusalem and the north; sometimes sunny along the coast; usually sunny at the Dead Sea and in Eilat. Occasional snow in Jerusalem and Tsfat. Low-season room prices.

☆☆ New Year's Day

An official holiday in the Palestinian Territories, a regular work day in Israel (1 January).

☆☆ Christmas (Orthodox)

Commemorates the birth of Jesus in Bethlehem (celebrated by Eastern Orthodox churches on 6 and 7 January and by Armenians in the Holy Land on 18 and 19 January).

☆☆ Tu Bishvat

(New Year of the Trees) Jews plant trees, and eat nuts and fresh and dried fruits (25 January 2016, 11 February 2017, 31 January 2018).

March

Thanks to the winter rains, hillsides and valleys are green and wildflowers are in bloom – a great time for hiking. Often rainy in the north. Low-season room prices.

☆☆ Purim

Celebrates the foiling of a plot to wipe out the Jews of ancient Persia. Children and adults put on costumes for a day of revelry (23 to 24 March 2016, 10 to 11 March 2017, 28 February to 1 March 2018; celebrated one day later in walled cities, including Jerusalem).

☆☆ Land Day

(Yom al-Ard in Arabic, Yom HaAdama in Hebrew) A Palestinian day of protest against Israel's expropriation of Palestinian land (30 March).

☆☆ Good Friday (Western)

Commemorates Jesus's crucifixion in Jerusalem. Falls on the Friday before Easter Sunday (for Protestants and Catholics, 25 March 2016, 14 April 2017, 30 March 2018).

April

Hillsides and valleys are alive with spring wildflowers – this is the best month for hiking. Accommodation prices spike during Passover and, near Christian sites, around Easter.

☆☆ Passover

(Pesach) Weeklong celebration of the liberation of the Israelites from slavery in Egypt. Jewish families hold a *seder* (ritual dinner) on the first night (in the Diaspora, on the first two nights). The sale of *chametz* (bread and other leavened products) is forbidden in Jewish areas (supermarkets hide such items behind plastic sheeting). Shabbat-like closures on the first and seventh days. Lots of Israelis go on holiday, so accommodation is scarce and room prices skyrocket (23 to 29 April

2016, 10 to 17 April 2017, 30 March to 6 April 2018).

✥ Mimouna

North African Jews celebrate the end of Passover with sweets, picnics and barbecues (29 to 30 April 2016, 17 to 18 April 2017, 6 to 7 April 2018).

✥ Good Friday (Orthodox)

Commemorates Jesus's crucifixion in Jerusalem (for Eastern Orthodox churches, 29 April 2016, 14 April 2017, 6 April 2018).

✥ Easter (Western)

Commemorates the resurrection of Jesus on the third day after the crucifixion; marks the end of Lent (40 days of penance and fasting). Catholic pilgrims throng Jerusalem's Via Dolorosa and the Church of the Holy Sepulchre, and many Protestants gather at the Garden Tomb (for Catholics and Protestants, 27 March 2016, 16 April 2017, 1 April 2018).

✥ Easter (Orthodox)

Commemorates the resurrection of Jesus (for Eastern Orthodox and Armenians, 1 May 2016, 16 April 2017, 8 April 2018).

✥ Holocaust Memorial Day

(Yom HaSho'ah) Solemn remembrance of the six million Jews, including 1.5 million children, who died in the Holocaust. Places of entertainment are closed. At 10am sirens sound and Israelis stand silently at attention wherever they happen to be (4 to 5 May 2016, 23 to 24 April 2017, 11 to 12 April 2018).

> ## RELIGIOUS CALENDARS
>
> Jewish holidays follow the lunisolar Hebrew calendar and fall somewhere within a four-week window relative to the Gregorian (Western) calendar. Some holidays are celebrated for two days in the Diaspora but just one day in Israel.
>
> The Islamic calendar is lunar, so each year festivals arrive 11 or 12 days earlier than the Gregorian dates. Final dates are determined according to the sighting of the moon and so may differ slightly from those cited below.
>
> Jewish and Muslim holidays begin at sundown and last until sundown of the following calendar day; the dates given here include the eve of the holiday.
>
> Eastern Orthodox churches use a combination of the Julian calendar and, for Easter, the Paschal cycle.
>
> To check the dates of religious holidays, go to www.bbc.co.uk/religion/tools/calendar.

✥ Yom HaZikaron

(Memorial Day) Commemorates soldiers who fell defending Israel and the victims of terrorism. Places of entertainment are closed. At 8pm and 11am sirens sound and Israelis stand silently at attention wherever they happen to be. Falls on the day before Israel Independence Day (10 to 11 May 2016, 30 April to 1 May 2017, 17 to 18 April 2018).

✥ Israel Independence Day

(Yom Ha'Atzma'ut) Celebrates Israel's declaration of independence in 1948. Marked with official ceremonies, public celebrations with live music, picnics and hikes (11 to 12 May 2016, 1 to 2 May 2017, 18 to 19 April 2018).

✥ Palestinian Prisoners Day

Palestinians remember their compatriots imprisoned in Israeli jails (17 April).

✥ Armenian Genocide Remembrance Day

Commemorates the genocide of Armenians by the Ottoman Turks during WWI (24 April).

May

Sunny but not too hot, with nice long days. School is in session in Israel, Europe and North America, so few families are travelling. The last rains often fall in early May.

✥ International Labour Day

An official holiday in both Israel and the Palestinian Territories (1 May).

✥ Leilat al-Mi'raj

(Al-Israa' wal-Mi'raj) Commemorates Mohammed's 'Night Journey' from Mecca to Jerusalem and from there to heaven (2 to 3 May 2016, 22 to 23 April 2017, 12 to 13 April 2018).

✿ Naqba Day

Palestinian commemoration of Al-Naqba (the catastrophe) of refugees' displacement in 1948 (15 May).

✿ Shavuot

(Pentecost) Jews celebrate the giving of the Torah at Mt Sinai. Dairy products are eaten and all-night study sessions held. Shabbat-like closure of shops and public transport. Popular time for domestic tourism, so accommodation is scarce and room prices are high (11 to 12 June 2016, 30 to 31 May 2017, 19 to 20 May 2018).

✿ Lag BaOmer

A break in the Jewish semimourning period between Passover and Shavuot. Celebrated with picnics, hikes, weddings and bonfires (25 to 26 May 2016, 13 to 14 May 2017, 2 to 3 May 2018).

June

Long days and sunny, warm weather. The coast is not as hot and humid as in July and August. Almost never rains. High-season room prices in some places.

✿ Ramadan

Holy month of dawn-to-dusk fasting by Muslims. Celebratory break-fast meals are held after dark. Offices may have shorter hours, and restaurants may close during daylight (6 June to 6 July 2016, 26 May to 25 June 2017, 15 May to 14 June 2018).

☆ Israel Festival

(www.israel-festival.org.il) Three weeks of music, theatre and dance performances, some of them free, in and around Jerusalem.

☆ Israeli Opera Festival

(www.opera-masada.com) Brings dazzling opera productions to Masada (early June).

✿ Naksa Day

Palestinian commemoration of the *naksa* (setback) of the 1967 Six Day War (5 June).

✿ Gay Pride Parade

Tel Aviv is bedecked with rainbow flags for Israel's biggest and most colourful gay and lesbian extravaganza.

July

Sweltering along the coast but pleasantly dry in Jerusalem. Sizzling hot at the Sea of Galilee, the Dead Sea and Eilat. Accommodation is pricey, especially in northern B&Bs and in cities popular with French tourists.

✿ Eid al-Fitr

(Festival of Fast-Breaking) The end of Ramadan is marked by one to three days of celebrations with family and friends (5 to 6 July 2016, 24 to 25 June 2017, 13 to 14 June 2018).

August

The hottest month of the year. Sweltering along the coast but pleasantly dry in Jerusalem; infernal at the Sea of Galilee, the Dead Sea and Eilat. Accommodation is expensive, especially in northern B&Bs and cities popular with French tourists.

✿ Tish'a B'Av

(Ninth of Av) Jews commemorate the destruction of the Temples in Jerusalem. In Jewish areas restaurants and places of entertainment are closed (13 to 14 August 2016, 31 July to 1 August 2017, 21 to 22 July 2018).

☆ Tsfat Klezmer Festival

Eastern European Jewish soul music high in the Galilee.

☆ Red Sea Jazz Festival

(www.redseajazzeilat.com) Eilat sizzles with the coolest jazz (last week of August).

September

Israeli schools are in session, so fewer families are travelling, though room prices skyrocket at Rosh HaShanah and during Sukkot. Flights are often full around Rosh HaShanah and Yom Kippur.

✿ Rosh HaShanah

(Jewish New Year) Shabbat-like closures last two days. Some Israelis go on holiday, so accommodation is scarce and room prices rise (13 to 15 September 2015, 2 to 4 October 2016, 20 to 22 September 2017, 9 to 11 September 2018).

🎆 Yom Kippur

(Jewish Day of Atonement) Solemn day of reflection and fasting – and cycling on the empty roads. In Jewish areas, all businesses shut and transportation (including by private car) completely ceases; Israel's airports and land borders close (22 to 23 September 2015, 11 to 12 October 2016, 29 to 30 September 2017, 18 to 19 September 2018).

🎆 Eid al-Adha

(Festival of the Sacrifice) Muslims commemorate the willingness of Ibrahim (Abraham) to sacrifice his son Ishmael. Marks the end of the hajj (annual pilgrimage to Mecca). Sheep are sacrificed (23 to 26 September 2015, 10 to 14 September 2016, 1 to 4 September 2017, 21 to 25 August 2018).

October

The start of the rainy season, though most days are dry and sunny. Accommodation prices skyrocket during the Sukkot holiday. Sites and activities that are only open in the warm season often close right after Sukkot.

🎆 Sukkot

(Feast of the Tabernacles) Week-long holiday that recollects the Israelites' 40 years of wandering in the desert. Jewish families build *sukkot* (foliage-roofed booths) in which they dine and sometimes sleep. The first and seventh day are Shabbat-like public holidays. Popular vacation

time for Israelis, so accommodation is scarce and room prices skyrocket (27 September to 3 October 2015, 16 to 22 October 2016, 1 to 10 October 2017, 23 to 29 September 2018).

🎆 Simhat Torah

Concludes and begins Jews' annual cycle of reading the Torah. Singing and dancing in synagogues (4 to 5 October 2015, 23 to 24 October 2016, 11 to 12 October 2017, 30 September to 1 October 2018).

🎆 Islamic New Year

(Hijri New Year) Marks the beginning of the Islamic year. Gifts and cards are exchanged (13 to 14 October 2015, 2 to 3 October 2016, 21 to 22 September 2017, 11 to 12 September 2018).

🍷 Oktoberfest

(www.taybehbeer.com) Pints, Palestinians and lederhosen at this beer festival in the pretty Palestinian village of Taybeh.

November

Sometimes rainy and chilly but frequently sunny. Often pleasantly warm along the coast, at the Dead Sea and in Eilat. Days are short. Low-season prices.

🎆 Yitzhak Rabin Memorial Day

Honours Prime Minister Yitzhak Rabin, assassinated on 4 November 1995. A national rally is held at Tel Aviv's Rabin Sq.

December

Sometimes rainy and chilly but not infrequently sunny and even warm. Low-season room prices except in Christian areas around Christmas. Days are short.

🎆 Holiday of the Holy Days

(HaChag shel HaChagim) Haifa's Wadi Nisnas neighbourhood celebrates Hanukkah, Christmas and the season's Muslim holidays with art and music (weekends in December).

🎆 Hanukkah

(Festival of Lights) Jews celebrate the re-dedication of the Temple after the Maccabean revolt. Families light candles over eight nights using a nine-branched candelabra; waistlines bulge due to jelly doughnuts (6 to 14 December 2015, 24 December 2016 to 1 January 2017, 12 to 20 December 2017).

🎆 Prophet's Birthday

(Mawlid al-Nabi) Celebrations mark the birthday of the Prophet Mohammed (22 to 23 December 2015, 11 to 12 December 2016, 31 November to 1 December 2017, 20 to 21 November 2018).

🎆 Christmas (Western)

Commemorates the birth of Jesus in Bethlehem. Midnight Catholic Mass is celebrated in the Church of the Nativity in Bethlehem. Christmas is a public holiday in the West Bank but not in Israel or Gaza (celebrated by Catholics and Protestants on 24 to 25 December).

Itineraries

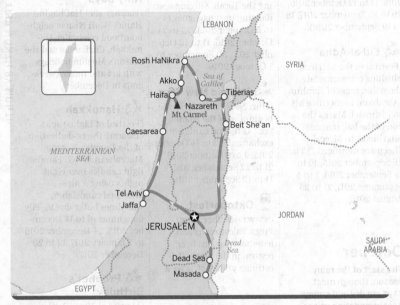

Best of Israel

2 WEEKS

Spend your first four days in and around **Jerusalem**, including a couple of days wandering the alleys of the Old City, exploring the Western Wall and the adjacent Temple Mount/Al-Haram ash-Sharif, and following the Via Dolorosa to the Church of the Holy Sepulchre. Break out your swimsuit and hiking shoes for a full-day excursion down to the **Dead Sea** and up the storied stronghold of **Masada**. Then head to the Mediterranean coast for three days around **Tel Aviv**, dividing your time between strolling, cycling, lounging on the beach, fine dining and watching the world go by. Next, head up the coast for a peek at Roman-era **Caesarea** before pushing on to **Haifa**. Check out the views from atop **Mt Carmel** and the Baha'i Gardens before a day trip to the walled city of **Akko (Acre)** and the grottoes of **Rosh HaNikra**. After a day in **Nazareth**, concluded with a tongue-tingling 'fusion' dinner, head to **Tiberias** for a day exploring the storied shores of the Sea of Galilee. On the drive back to Jerusalem, stop at the Roman ruins in **Beit She'an**.

Israeli Odyssey

After four or five days in and around **Jerusalem**, including a couple of days exploring the Old City and a half-day visit to the Israel Museum, take a trip down to the wondrous caves at **Beit Guvrin**, stopping at a winery on the way. Next, stir it up in **Tel Aviv** for a few days, strolling along the beachfront promenade to historic **Jaffa**, biking along the Yarkon River and working on your Mediterranean tan. On your way north to **Haifa**, stop at the Roman ruins of **Caesarea** and the quaint old town of **Zichron Ya'acov**, famed for its vintage winery. After touring Haifa's sublime Baha'i Gardens, visit **Mt Carmel** and the Druze village of **Daliyat al-Karmel**. The next day, continue north to **Akko (Acre)**, with its enchanting mixture of Crusader ruins and Ottoman relics. Then go as far north as politics permit, to the subterranean grottoes of **Rosh HaNikra**, before heading inland for a couple of days in **Nazareth**, exploring Christian sites and dining on traditional Arab delicacies and East–West fusion dishes. Based in **Tiberias** for a couple of days, relax around the Sea of Galilee, combining ancient synagogues and Christian sites with quiet beaches and, perhaps, white-water rafting on the Jordan River. Loop east to the Golan Heights, visiting the hilltop ruins of **Gamla**, the Golan Archaeological Museum in **Katzrin** and towering **Nimrod Fortress**. Circle west via the lush vegetation of **Banias Nature Reserve** to the wetlands of the Hula Valley, beloved by migrating birds; the quaint, cobbled streets of **Rosh Pina**; and **Tsfat (Safed)**, suffused with the spirituality of the Kabbalah (Jewish mysticism). Finally, head south through the Jordan Valley, strolling the colonnaded Roman thoroughfares of **Beit She'an** and visiting the Palestinian city of **Jericho**, whose ruins go back to the very beginning of civilisation. After a starlit night on the shores of the **Dead Sea**, rise early to catch the sunrise from high atop **Masada**. Continue south into the Negev Desert for a day or two around **Mitzpe Ramon**, including a hike into **Makhtesh Ramon**. Next stop, for a spot of sea, sun and snorkelling, is **Eilat**. Finally, cross into Jordan to visit the awe-inspiring 'red city' of **Petra**.

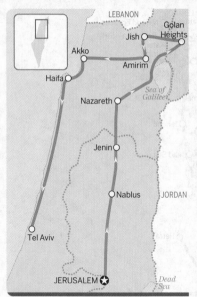

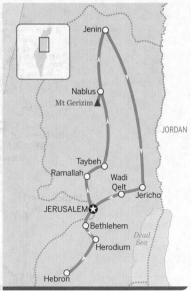

10 DAYS Culinary Trail

Start in **Jerusalem**, where contenders for the 'best hummus' title can be found in the Old City, and the foodie scene around the Mahane Yehuda produce market is worth exploring. For the country's best gooey-hot, cheesy-sweet *kunafeh* pastry, head north to the West Bank city of **Nablus** and then sample extra-virgin olive oil in **Jenin**. Make a beeline for **Nazareth**, where the buzzword is fusion, the culinary inspiration both Levantine and European. Continue your culinary pilgrimage on the shores of the **Sea of Galilee** with a lunch of St Peter's fish, and then head to the **Golan Heights** for perfectly aged steak – paired, of course, with Golan-grown red wines. Looping west, stop in **Jish** for Galilee-style Arab cuisine, or drop by the all-vegetarian settlement of **Amirim** for meat-free treats. Finally, head to the Mediterranean coast, sampling seafood and hummus in **Akko (Acre)**, creative Arab cuisine in **Haifa**, and modern Israeli cuisine in **Tel Aviv**, where glamorous restaurants run by celebrity chefs vie for attention with traditional eateries serving hummus, felafel and the local fast-food favourite, sabich.

1 WEEK Welcome to the West Bank

From the Arab bus station in **East Jerusalem**, hop on a bus to **Ramallah**, where you can drop in on the Muqata'a, last resting place of Yasser Arafat. Spend the afternoon sipping coffee, scooping hummus and clacking backgammon tiles, then get ready for a night on the town. The next day, drop by the only brewery in the Palestinian Territories, **Taybeh**, returning to Ramallah to catch a concert or theatre performance at one of the city's many arts venues. Next, head north – through olive orchards and terraced hills – to **Nablus** for a day of shopping in the enchanting market, scrubbing up at an ancient hammam and visiting the Samaritans atop **Mt Gerizim**. Then travel north to the Christian sites near **Jenin** and that city's renowned Freedom Theatre before looping east and south to **Jericho** for some extraordinary hiking in **Wadi Qelt**. Then slip southwestward to beautiful **Bethlehem**, with its winding lanes and ancient churches. Finally, stop off at Roman-era **Herodium** before heading down to the West Bank's troubled gem: the extraordinary city of **Hebron**, profoundly sacred to both Jews and Muslims.

Above: St Peter's fish, served grilled, at the Sea of Galilee

Right: Street vendor selling *nammoora* (squares of sweet semolina cake topped with nuts)

Plan Your Trip
Crossing Borders

Peaceful Borders

The borders between Israel and the two countries with which it has signed peace treaties, Egypt and Jordan, are open to both tourists and locals. (Note: most Western governments recommend avoiding all nonessential travel to the Sinai because of recent attacks against tourists by radical Islamists.)

Blue, Purple & Green Lines

The UN-certified international border between Israel and Lebanon is known as the Blue Line; the Israeli–Syrian ceasefire line of 1974 is known as the Purple Line; and the pre-1967 border between Israel and the then-Jordanian West Bank is known as the Green Line.

Border History

Britain and France determined the future borders of Palestine, Syria, Lebanon, Transjordan (Jordan) and Iraq in the secret Sykes-Picot Agreement of 1916.

West Bank Crossings

For tips on safe travel and what to expect at checkpoints, see p399 and p261.

Planning Your Crossing

Visas, Security & Entry Stamps

➡ For details on visas to Israel and Jordan, see p409.

➡ For tips on Israeli border control and security measures, see p33 and p398.

➡ Israel no longer stamps tourists' passports – instead, it issues you with a playing-card-sized slip of paper.

Land Crossings: Your Options

Israel–Jordan: Jordan River/Sheikh Hussein crossing, south of the Sea of Galilee; Yitzhak Rabin/Wadi Araba crossing, just north of Eilat/Aqaba

West Bank–Jordan: Allenby/King Hussein Bridge crossing, just east of Jericho (controlled by Israel)

Israel–Egypt: Taba crossing, on the Red Sea just south of Eilat

Gaza–Egypt: Rafah crossing (often closed)

Fees for land border crossings (not including visa fees, if applicable) are as follows:

COUNTRY	ARRIVAL	DEPARTURE
Israel	None	107NIS (182NIS at Allenby/ King Hussein Bridge)
Egypt	E£75	E£2
Jordan	JD5	JD10

Border Closings

Yom Kippur All Israeli land borders and airports closed.

Eid Al-Hijra/Muslim New Year Land crossings with Jordan closed.

Eid al-Adha Taba crossing with Egypt and Palestinian wing of the Allenby/King Hussein Bridge closed.

Ramadan All crossings may close early.

Northern Frontiers

Israel's borders with Syria and Lebanon are shut tight. Unless you're a UN peacekeeper, the only way to get to the other side is through Jordan – but if you've already been in Israel this can be tricky (see the boxed text p33).

To/from Jordan

While the two land crossings between Israel and Jordan are quick and efficient, the Allenby/King Hussein Bridge crossing between the Israeli-controlled West Bank and Jordan is not always as smooth.

Israeli exit fees can be paid at the border in a variety of currencies or by credit card. To save a handling fee of 5NIS, pay in advance at any Israeli post office (cash only) or online (https://borderpay.co.il).

Jordan River/Sheikh Hussein Crossing

Generally far less busy than Allenby/King Hussein Bridge, this **crossing** (☑04-609 3400; www.iaa.gov.il; ☻6.30am-9pm Sun-Thu, 8am-7pm Fri & Sat, closed Yom Kippur & Al-Hijra/Muslim New Year) is in the Jordan Valley 8km east of Beit She'an, 30km south of the Sea of Galilee, 135km northeast of Tel Aviv and 90km northeast of Amman. Jordan issues on-arrival visas (JD40) for many nationalities.

The Israeli side lacks an ATM, but you can get a cash advance at the currency-exchange window, open whenever the terminal is.

For travellers heading to Jordan, getting through Israeli border formalities usually takes no more than half an hour. You then have to take a bus (7NIS or JD1.50, twice an hour) to cross to the Jordanian side of the river (walking across is forbidden).

Getting There & Away

Taxis (☑052 328 8977), which wait at the border, can take you to Beit She'an (50NIS, plus 5NIS per suitcase) and destinations around Israel, including Tiberias (240NIS), Jerusalem (550NIS) and Tel Aviv (580NIS).

Kavim bus 16 connects Beit She'an with Kibbutz Ma'oz Haim (11 minutes, five or six daily Sunday to Friday), a walkable 1km west of the crossing.

On the Jordanian side, regular service taxis travel to/from Irbid's West Bus Station (JD1, 45 minutes). A taxi costs about JD20 to Irbid and JD40 to Amman.

Nazarene Tours (p194) links Nazareth with Amman (80NIS, 4½ to five hours), via the Jordan River/Sheikh Hussein crossing, on Sunday, Tuesday, Thursday and Saturday. Departures are at 8.30am from the company's Nazareth office, near the Bank of Jerusalem and the Nazareth Hotel (not to be confused with the office of Nazarene Transport & Tourism in the city centre) and at 2pm from Amman's Royal Hotel (University St). Reserve by phone at least two days ahead.

Yitzhak Rabin/Wadi Araba Crossing

Located just 3km northeast of Eilat, this **crossing** (☑08-630 0555, 08-630 0530; www.iaa.gov.il; ☻6.30am-8pm Sun-Thu, 8am-8pm Fri & Sat, closed Yom Kippur) is handy for trips to Aqaba, Petra and Wadi Rum. A bonus: thanks to the Aqaba Special Economic Zone, Jordanian visas issued here are free. Most hotels and hostels in Eilat offer day trips to Petra.

Getting There & Away

A taxi to/from Eilat (10 minutes) costs 45NIS. If you're coming by bus from the north (eg Jerusalem, Tel Aviv or the Dead Sea), it may be possible to get off on Rte 90 at the turn-off to the border or at Kibbutz Eilot, but from there it's 2km on foot through the desert (along Rte 109).

Once you're in Jordan, you can take a cab to Aqaba (JD10, 15 minutes), from where you can catch a minibus for the 120km ride to Petra (JD5, 2½ hours); minibuses leave when full between 6am and 7am and 11am and noon. Alternatively, bargain for a taxi all the way from the border to Petra (around JD50, two hours).

Allenby/King Hussein Bridge Crossing

Linking the Israeli-controlled West Bank with Jordan, this busy **crossing** (☎02-548 2600; www.iaa.gov.il; ⊗8am-midnight Sun-Thu, 8am-3pm Fri & Sat, closed Yom Kippur & Eid al-Adha, hours subject to change) is 46km east of Jerusalem, 8km east of Jericho and 60km west of Amman. It is the only crossing that people with Palestinian Authority travel documents, including West Bank Palestinians, can use to travel to and from Jordan and the outside world, so traffic can be heavy, especially on Sunday, around holidays and on weekdays from 11am to 3pm. Try to get to the border as early in the day as possible – times when tourists can cross may be limited and delays are common. Israeli citizens (including dual citizens) are not allowed to use this crossing.

Jordan does *not* issue on-arrival visas at the Allenby/King Hussein crossing – you'll have to arrange a visa in advance at a Jordanian embassy, such as the one in Ramat Gan, near Tel Aviv. However, if your visit to the Palestinian Territories and/or Israel started in Jordan, you won't need a new visa in order to cross back into Jordan through Allenby/King Hussein Bridge, provided you do so within the period of validity of your Jordanian visa – just show your stamped exit slip.

The bus across the frontier costs JD7, plus JD1.50 per piece of luggage.

Bring plenty of cash (Jordanian dinars are the most useful) and make sure you have small change. There are no ATMs, but both sides have exchange bureaux.

This crossing can be frustratingly delay-prone, especially if you're travelling into the West Bank and/or Israel. Chaotic queues, intrusive security, luggage X-rays (expect to be separated from your bags) and impatient officials are the norm; expect questions from Israeli security personnel if your passport has stamps from places such as Syria or Lebanon or you're headed to less touristed parts of the West Bank. There are separate processing areas for Palestinians and tourists.

Getting There & Away

Shared taxis run by **Abdo** (☎02-628 3281) and **Al-Nijmeh** (☎02-627 7466), most frequent before 11am, link the blue-and-white bus station opposite Jerusalem's Damascus Gate with the border (30 minutes, 40NIS);

the charge per suitcase is 5NIS. Private taxis can cost as much as 300NIS, with hotel pick-up as an option.

Egged buses 948, 961 and 966 from West Jerusalem's Central Bus Station to Beit She'an (and points north) stop on Rte 90 at the turn-off to Allenby Bridge (12.50NIS, 40 minutes, about hourly). Walking the last few kilometres to the crossing is forbidden, so you'll have to take a taxi (50NIS).

To get to/from Amman's Abdali or South bus stations, you can take a servees (shared taxi) or minibus (JD8, 45 minutes); a taxi costs about JD22. **JETT** (☎+962 6 566 4141; www.jett.com.jo) runs a daily bus to the border from Abdali (JD8.50, one hour, departure at 7am).

To/From Egypt

Taba Crossing

This **crossing** (☎08-636 0999; www.iaa.gov.il; ⊗24hr, closed Yom Kippur), on the Red Sea 10km south of Eilat, is the only border post between Israel and Egypt that's open to tourists. There's an exchange bureau on the Egyptian side. Check travel advisories before taking this route as the security situation in South Sinai is changeable.

You can get a 14-day Sinai-only entry permit at the border, allowing you to visit Red Sea resorts stretching from Taba to Sharm el-Sheikh, plus St Katherine's. If you're planning on going further into Egypt, you'll need to arrange an Egyptian visa in advance, eg at the Egyptian consulate in Eilat or the embassy in Tel Aviv.

Getting There & Away

Local bus 15 links Eilat's central bus station with the Taba crossing (4.90NIS, 30 minutes, hourly 8am to 9pm Sunday to Thursday, 8am to 3pm Friday and 9am to 7pm Saturday). On the way back to Eilat this line is known as bus 16; departures are 40 minutes later. A taxi costs about 30NIS.

Rafah Crossing

With a few exceptions, Egypt has kept the Rafah crossing between Gaza and Sinai closed since 2013. When or if it reopens, it is unlikely to be usable by leisure travellers.

BANNED: ISRAELI PASSPORT STAMPS

Arab and Muslim countries have widely varying policies on admitting travellers whose passports show evidence of their having visited Israel. Jordan and Egypt, with which Israel has peace treaties, have no problem at all, and the same goes for Turkey, Tunisia, Morocco and many of the Gulf emirates, as well as for Malaysia and Indonesia. Most of these places even allow in Israeli passport holders under certain circumstances.

On the other hand, Lebanon and Iran have been known to put travellers on the next plane out if they find even circumstantial evidence of travel to Israel, eg a passport freshly issued in Amman or a chewing-gum wrapper written in Hebrew. Saudi Arabia is also known to be very strict on occasion.

If there's any chance you'll be heading to Arab or Muslim lands during the life of your passport, your best bet is to make sure that it shows no indication that you've been to Israel. Simplifying matters is the fact that Israel no longer stamps tourists' passports, issuing instead a loose-leaf visa, and Jordanian officials generally do the same. Egypt, however, is not so flexible, and an Egyptian stamp from Taba is as much a testament to your having visited Israel as an Israeli one. If you need to get from Eilat to Sinai without a Taba stamp, one option is to cross to Jordan and then take a ferry from Aqaba.

Some countries, including the United States, allow their citizens to carry more than one passport: one for Israel, the other for the rest of the world.

Israeli Border Control

Israel's rigorous entrance procedures are a source of annoyance for some and a breeze for others. Don't be surprised if you are asked questions about your reasons for travelling, trips you've recently made, your occupation, your acquaintances in Israel and the Palestinian Territories, and possibly your religious or family background.

If you are meeting friends or family in Israel, you might want to have their full name, address and phone number handy (a letter confirming you're staying with them is ideal). If you have hotel reservations, a printout may help – or be completely superfluous.

If border officials suspect that you're coming to take part in pro-Palestinian political activities or if you have an Arab or Muslim name, they may ask some probing questions; on occasion they have even searched laptops. Sometimes they take an interest in passport stamps from

places such as Syria, Lebanon or Iran, but often they don't. The one sure way to get grilled is to sound evasive or to contradict yourself – the security screeners are trained to try to trip you up. Whatever happens, remain calm and polite.

Israeli airport security – whether you're flying in on an Israeli carrier or flying out on any airline – is the strictest in the business. It unabashedly uses profiling, but not necessarily in the way you think. In 1986, a pregnant Irish woman, Anne Mary Murphy, almost boarded an El Al 747 in London with Semtex explosive hidden in her luggage – it had been placed there without her knowledge by her Jordanian boyfriend, Nezar Hindawi, who is still in prison in the UK. Ever since then, Israeli security officials – at Ben-Gurion airport and at airports abroad – have been on the lookout for anyone who might unwittingly serve as a suicide bomber, with young, unmarried Western women near the top of the profiling list.

Plan Your Trip

Travel with Children

Travel with children in Israel and the Palestinian Territories is generally a breeze: the food's varied and tasty, the distances are short, there are child-friendly activities at every turn, and the locals absolutely love children. For general tips, see Lonely Planet's *Travel with Children*.

Top Activities for Kids

Underwater Red Sea Observatory
Take in scuba-quality reef views without getting wet; there's also a petting pool.

Rosh HaNikra
Kids will love the cliffside cable car and the deep blues of the sea-battered grottoes.

Water Hikes
A hike along – and through – a spring-fed stream is especially glorious during the hot, dry days of summer (try the Ein Gedi, Banias, Yehudiya and Majrase Nature Reserves).

Desert Cycling
Tweens and teens will enjoy mountain biking through the desert along a dry wadi bed.

Ya'ar HaAyalim
This animal park is in Odem, on the Golan.

Gangaroo
Pet kangaroos and feed lorikeets in the Jezreel Valley.

Mini Israel
Midway between Jerusalem and Tel Aviv, this park shrinks 350 of Israel's best-known attractions to scale-model size.

Israel for Kids

Israeli society is very family-oriented, so children are welcome pretty much everywhere. At every turn, your children will encounter local children out and about with their parents, especially on Saturday and Jewish holidays and in July and August.

Israel's **beaches** are usually clean and well equipped with cafes and even playgrounds. Make sure you slather on the sunblock, especially in summer, and stay out of the midday sun. (The Dead Sea, because it's so far below sea level, poses a lesser risk of sunburn, but kids have to be extra careful to keep the water out of their eyes.)

Most of Israel's **nature reserves** are fantastic for kids, and older children will enjoy the hikes – some gentle, some more challenging – on offer throughout the country. As park wheelchair access has improved in recent years, so has the ease of getting around with a stroller.

Tel Aviv (p125), **Jerusalem**, **Mitzpeh Ramon** and **Eilat** offer a wide variety of things kids will love, though the alleys of Jerusalem's Old City are tough for strollers.

Most shopping malls have a *meeschakiya* (play area) for babies and toddlers – a great place to meet local kids (and on occasion their colds), especially on rainy days.

Planning

Disposable nappies (diapers; *chitulim*), wet wipes *(magavonim)*, baby formula *(form-oola)*, baby bottles *(bakbukim l'tinok)* and pacifiers (dummies; *motzetzim*) are available in supermarkets and pharmacies, but prices are higher than in most Western countries. If your baby is picky, it pays to bring familiar powdered milk from home. Jars of baby food are also available, though in fewer flavours than in the UK or USA; organic baby food is available in some places. Medicines for children are easily obtained; almost all pharmacists speak English and are happy to assist.

A lightweight, collapsible (ie umbrella-style) stroller is convenient for travelling, but for the narrow cobblestone alleys and staircases in places such as Jerusalem's Old City, Akko, Safed and Bethlehem it's a good idea to bring a wearable kid-carrier.

Sleeping

With the exception of a few B&Bs *(tzimmerim)* that cater exclusively to couples (eg in Rosh Pina), children are welcome to stay almost everywhere. In the vast majority of hotels, guesthouses and B&Bs, babies and toddlers can sleep in their parents' room for free (let management know if you'll need a cot); older children sometimes incur an extra charge. Most rooms in HI hostels and SPNI field schools have at least four beds, making them ideal for families.

Eating

Virtually all restaurants welcome children, with both the servers and other diners taking the disruptions of kiddie mealtime in stride. Almost all have high chairs, and some also offer special kids' portions for child-sized prices. Most eateries, except the most upscale, are open all day long, so meal times can be flexible. Israeli breakfasts are famously copious and usually include at least a couple of breakfast cereals.

Many children take an instant liking to felafel, hummus, sabich (aubergine, boiled egg and potato, and salads in a pita) and shwarma, but as these fast foods (including their sauces and salads) are more likely than most meals to play host to microbes unknown back home, you might want to go easy, at least at first.

CHILDREN'S DISCOUNTS

At nature reserves, archaeological sites and museums, children generally get in free through age four, and receive significant discounts from age five through 17 or 18. Young children qualify for moderate discounts on buses and trains. Places whose main clients are children, such as amusement parks, tend to charge full price from age three.

Travelling by Car

➤ Babies up to one year old (recommended through age two) or who weigh less than 9kg must sit in a back-facing child seat (*moshav b'tichut*). A portable baby seat that can attach to both a car seat and a stroller is known in Hebrew as a *salkal*.

➤ For toddlers aged two and three (recommended through age four), a child seat (back or forward facing) is required.

➤ Children through age eight must sit on a booster seat.

➤ Car seats are not required for children who are riding in a taxi.

➤ A child seat must not be placed in any passenger seat equipped with an airbag.

The Palestinian Territories for Kids

Children receive a warm welcome in the West Bank and will often be whisked away to meet local children or treated to cakes and cookies. But travelling in the area has its own special challenges. Pushing a stroller around West Bank cities such as Ramallah, Nablus and Bethlehem can be laborious, and then there's the matter of getting through checkpoints. If you're travelling from Jerusalem to Ramallah, you might want to give the intimidating, prison-style turnstiles at Qalandia a miss, preferring instead a guided tour with a car and driver. In any case, remember to bring your kids' passports as well as your own.

Regions at a Glance

Jerusalem

History
Religion
Culture

Old City

Explore the Old City's Christian, Armenian, Jewish and Muslim quarters, including the Citadel (Tower of David) and the Via Dolorosa.

Sacred Sites

The Western Wall, the Church of the Holy Sepulchre, the Dome of the Rock: Jerusalem's many religious sites could keep you busy for weeks.

Diversity

Ultra-Orthodox Jews wearing *shtreimels* (fur hats), secular Jews in short shorts and tank tops, Palestinian Muslims on their way to Al-Aqsa Mosque, Christian clergy in long robes, feminist Orthodox Jews, gay-rights activists, free-spirited artists – you'll run into them all on Jerusalem's wonderfully diverse streets.

p40

Tel Aviv-Jaffa (Yafo)

Food
Shopping
Museums

Fine Dining

Yes, Tel Aviv has fantastic beaches, but the city's real passion is food. From felafel stalls and hummus joints to gelato parlours, European-style cafes, sushi bars and restaurants run by celebrity chefs, you won't go hungry here.

Boutiques

Tel Aviv has Israel's best shopping. Shop till your credit card groans in bazaars, modern malls and designer boutiques on Sheinken, Dizengoff and Shabazi Sts.

Exhibitions

Head to the Tel Aviv Museum of Art for Israeli and European art, Beit Hatfutsot and the Eretz Israel Museum for history and culture, and Design Museum Holon for contemporary exhibits.

p105

Haifa & the North Coast

History
Sacred Sites
Scenery

Ancient Ports

Caesarea was one of the great ports of antiquity and, 1000 years later, a walled Crusader stronghold. Akko (Acre), visited by Marco Polo on his way to China, is brimming with medieval and Ottoman history.

Spiritual Gardens

Haifa's incredible Baha'i Gardens are a spiritual highlight for people of all faiths. Elijah's Cave in Haifa is sacred to Jews, Christians and Muslims.

Sea Grottoes

The sea grottoes of Rosh HaNikra feature hues of blue you never knew existed. For stunning panoramas of the Mediterranean, head to Haifa's eagle's-eye promenade, high atop Mt Carmel.

p148

Lower Galilee & Sea of Galilee

Christianity
Archaeology
Food

Jesus's Ministry

Mary is said to have experienced the Annunciation in Nazareth, later Jesus's childhood home. It is believed that the Transfiguration took place at Mt Tabor, and Jesus spent much of his ministry around the Sea of Galilee.

Roman Sites

Top excavations include the Roman and Byzantine city of Beit She'an, ancient synagogues at Hamat Tverya, Korazim, Capernaum and Tzipori, and the Belvoir Crusader castle.

World Food

Nazareth is known for its East–West fusion cuisine; in Kfar Kisch you can dine the French way or sample delicious cheeses; in Kfar Kama you can try Circassian dishes from the Caucasus.

p183

Upper Galilee & Golan

Hiking
Bird Life
Wine

Wild Trails

Trails for all fitness levels abound, from the alpine summit of Mt Hermon (elevation more than 2000m) to the banks of the Jordan River (elevation less than 200m), and through the cliff-lined canyons of the Banias and Yehudiya Nature Reserves.

Migrations

Half a billion birds migrate through the Hula Valley – you can spot local and migrating species in the wetlands of the Hula Nature Reserve and Agamon Ha-Hula, especially in spring and autumn.

Winery Visits

Many of Israel's finest wineries, some of them boutique, can be visited at Katzrin, Ein Zivan and Odem on the Golan and on the Dalton Plateau northwest of Tsfat (Safed).

p220

West Bank

Shopping
Food
Religion

Bazaars

West Bank cities revolve around their lively bazaars. Shop for fresh fruit, taste sweets and haggle over handicrafts in the colourful markets of Hebron, Nablus and Bethlehem.

Local Food

Don't pass up any invitation for a home-cooked meal in the West Bank, where the dinner table overflows with spicy, tangy Middle Eastern delicacies. The best restaurants are in Ramallah.

Holy Sites

For Jews and Muslims the Cave of Machpelah is an important pilgrimage site. Christian sites include the Church of Nativity and the Mount of Temptation. No spiritual exploration of the West Bank is complete without a trip to the Samaritans of Mt Gerizim.

p249

The Gaza Strip

Inaccessible

Gaza is definitely not a tourism destination right now. Almost impossible to enter unless you're a journalist, aid worker or diplomat, this thin strip of land remains a danger zone. Although billions of dollars was pledged to reconstruct Gaza after the 2014 war with Israel, it is likely to be many years before the strip's heavily bombed cities and crippled infrastructure is capable of supporting its 1.8 million people – let alone tourists. Until then, its politically charged cities, beautiful beaches, historic sites and unique culture will remain off limits to all but a few.

p279

The Dead Sea

Beaches
Archaeology
Hiking

Dead Sea

Float on your back while reading the newspaper – a cliché but eminently doable in the hypersaline waters of the Dead Sea, which will relax your nerves and soothe your skin.

Masada

The Romans had already destroyed Jerusalem, but high atop Masada, 1000 Jews resisted the besieging might of Legion X, in the end preferring death to slavery.

Desert Oases

Year-round springs feed the dramatic desert oases of Ein Gedi and Ein Bokek, where hikers encounter cool streams, luxuriant vegetation, Edenic waterfalls and rare wildlife such as majestic Nubian ibexes.

p285

The Negev

Hiking
Diving
Archaeology

Desert Trails

The Negev Desert is filled with life. Hike through the wilderness of Makhtesh Ramon, Sde Boker or Ein Avdat and you'll likely spot camels, ibexes and soaring birds of prey.

Coral Reefs

Keen to explore coral reefs and swim with schools of tropical fish? Then come to the Red Sea to snorkel or dive. Just dip your head underwater and enjoy the show.

Nabataean Sites

Home to biblical ruins such as Tel Be'er Sheva and Tel Arad, plus the ancient Nabataean cities of Avdat, Shivta and Mamshit, the desert is slowly revealing its secrets.

p303

Petra

Ruins
Hiking
Scenery

Rose-Red City

The ancient city of Petra defies superlatives. Make sure you allow enough time to reach the Treasury in early morning, picnic at a 'high place' by noon, watch the sunset at the Monastery and walk the Siq by candlelight at night.

Desert Hikes

Petra has some great, accessible hikes. Engaging a local Bedouin guide will help bring the ruins to life.

Mountains

Colourful sandstone, wind-eroded escarpments and oleander-trimmed wadis make Petra's rose-pink landscape a suitable foil to the ancient architecture.

p330

On the
Road

Upper Galilee & Golan
p220

Haifa & the North Coast
p148

Lower Galilee & Sea of Galilee
p183

Tel Aviv
p105

West Bank
p249

Jerusalem ☆
p40

The Gaza Strip
p279

The Dead Sea
p285

The Negev
p303

○ **Petra (Jordan)**
p330

Jerusalem ירושלים القدس

Best Places to Eat

➡ Abu Shukri (p92)
➡ Machneyuda (p95)
➡ Modern (p96)
➡ Pinati (p93)
➡ Yudaleh (p94)

Best Places to Stay

➡ Abraham Hostel (p89)
➡ American Colony Hotel (p88)
➡ Arthur Hotel (p90)
➡ Austrian Hospice (p88)
➡ Christ Church Guesthouse (p88)

Why Go?

Holy to Jews, Christians and Muslims, Jerusalem's Old City is one of the world's foremost pilgrimage destinations. A repository of sacred buildings and relics, it is a place where the oft-abused descriptor 'living history' really does apply – here you can walk in the footsteps of prophets, pray in buildings constructed by order of caliphs and kings, and overnight in hospices where Crusaders and cardinals have slumbered. The soundtrack is of church bells, the muezzin's call and the shofar (ram's horn), and the streets smell of everything from church incense to the heady aromas of the spice souq (market). It's a sensory and spiritual experience unlike any other.

There's plenty to see outside the Old City, too, including the hugely impressive Israel Museum and the powerful Yad Vashem Holocaust memorial. They, together with the Old City's manifest attractions, make Jerusalem the number-one tourist destination in Israel for very good reason.

When to Go
Jerusalem

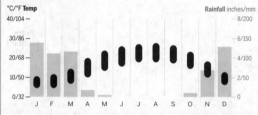

| **Apr** Pleasant temperatures, but be prepared for crowds and hefty hotel prices. | **Jul** The Old City is illuminated at night; shoulder-season hotel prices apply. | **Sep & Oct** Excellent weather, the Sacred Music Festival and relatively manageable crowds. |

History

First Temple

The first settlement on the site of Jerusalem was on the Ophel Ridge, immediately to the southeast of the present-day Jewish Quarter. A small Canaanite city mentioned in Egyptian texts of the 20th century BCE, it was conquered in 997 BCE by the Israelites under King David, who made the city his capital.

Under King Solomon (David's son), the boundaries of the city were extended north to enclose the spur of land that is now Temple Mount/Al-Haram ash-Sharif. The construction of the First Temple began in 950 BCE.

Some 17 years after Solomon's death, the 10 northern tribes of Israel split off to form the separate Kingdom of Israel and Jerusalem became the capital of the Kingdom of Judah. In 586 BCE Jerusalem fell to Nebuchadnezzar, king of Babylon, and both the city and the First Temple were destroyed; the people of Jerusalem were exiled to Babylonia. Three generations later, the king of Persia, Cyrus, allowed them to return.

Second Temple

The Second Temple was constructed around 520 BCE, and around 445 BCE the city walls were rebuilt under the leadership of Nehemiah, governor of Judah.

The next notable stage in the history of Jerusalem came with Alexander the Great's conquest of the city in 331 BCE. On his death in 323 BCE, the Seleucids eventually took over until the Maccabean Revolt 30 years later. This launched the Hasmonean dynasty, which resanctified the Temple in 164 BCE after it had been desecrated by the Seleucids.

Romans

Under the leadership of General Pompey, Jerusalem was conquered by the Romans around 63 BCE. Some 25 years later they installed Herod the Great to rule what would become the Roman province of Judaea (Iudaea). A tyrant's tyrant, Herod (often known as 'the Great') had his wife and children, as well as rabbis who opposed his rule, put to death. But he is also known for his ambitious construction and infrastructure projects, including expansion of the Temple Mount to its present form.

Upon the death of Herod, the Romans resumed direct control, installing a procurator to administer the city. Pontius Pilate, who is best known for ordering the crucifixion of Jesus around 30 CE, was the fifth procurator.

The Great Jewish Revolt against the Romans began in 66 CE, but after four years of conflict, the Roman general (and later emperor) Titus triumphed. Rome's Arch of Titus, with its famous frieze of Roman soldiers carrying off the contents of the Temple, was built to celebrate his victory.

With the Second Temple destroyed and Jerusalem burnt, many Jews became slaves and more fled into exile. The ruined city continued to serve as the administrative and military headquarters of the Roman province of Judea, but around 130 CE Emperor Hadrian decided to rebuild it – not as a Jewish city (he feared renewed Jewish national aspirations) but as a Roman city complete with pagan temples. This provoked the Jews' unsuccessful and bloody Bar Kochba Revolt (132–35 CE), led by Simon Bar Kochba. After the uprising was crushed, Jerusalem was renamed Aelia Capitolina and Judea became Syria Palaestina. The Romans rebuilt Jerusalem, but Jews were banned from the city.

Byzantines & Muslims

In 313 CE, the Western Roman Emperor, Constantine, and Eastern Roman Emperor, Licinius, met in Milan and agreed on an edict requiring tolerance of all previously persecuted religions. Eleven years after this, Constantine defeated Licinius in a civil war and became sole Emperor of the Roman Empire (later known as the Byzantine Empire). He legalised Christianity and his mother Helena visited the Holy Land in 326–28 CE searching for Christian holy places. This sparked off the building of basilicas and churches, and the city quickly grew to the size it had been under Herod the Great.

The Byzantine Empire was defeated by the Persians, who conquered Jerusalem in 614 CE. Their rule lasted just 15 years before the Byzantines succeeded in retaking the city. That victory, however, was short-lived, for within another 10 years an Arab army, led by Caliph Omar under the banner of Islam, swept through Palestine. In 688 CE the Dome of the Rock was constructed on the site of the destroyed Temple. Under the early Islamic leaders, Jerusalem was a protected centre of pilgrimage for Jews and Christians as well as Muslims, but this came to an end in the 10th century. Under the mercurial Fatimid Caliph al-Hakim, non-Muslims were persecuted and churches and synagogues were destroyed, actions that eventually helped provoke the Crusades.

Jerusalem Highlights

1 Feeling the spiritual power of the **Western Wall** (p59), Judaism's holiest place.

2 Visiting Christendom's most sacred sites, including the venerable **Church of the Holy Sepulchre** (p54).

3 Gazing at the architectural magnificence of the **Dome of the Rock** (p49), built on a site sacred to both Muslims and Jews.

4 Exploring the alleys of the **Mahane Yehuda Market** (p73), jam-packed with fresh-produce stalls, cafes and bars.

5 Going underground in the **City of David** (p66), the original settlement of Jerusalem.

6 Admiring the extraordinary art and artefacts at the **Israel Museum** (p79).

7 Pondering tragedy, evil, human resilience and reconciliation at the powerful **Yad Vashem memorial** (p80).

8 Learning about the city's long history at the Museum of the History of Jerusalem in the **Citadel** (Tower of David; p52).

9 Wandering through the colourful souqs of the Old City's **Muslim Quarter** (p62).

10 Following in Jesus's footsteps on the **Via Dolorosa** (p56) and **Mount of Olives** (p68).

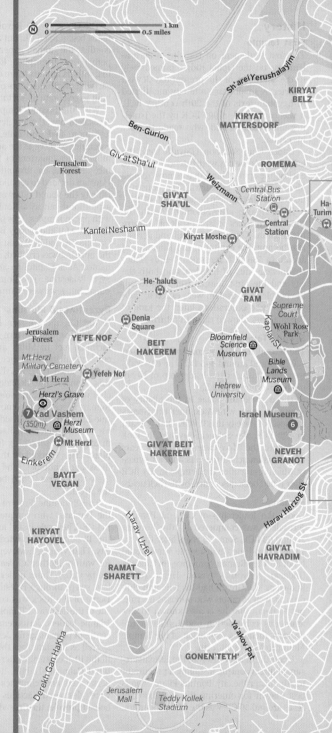

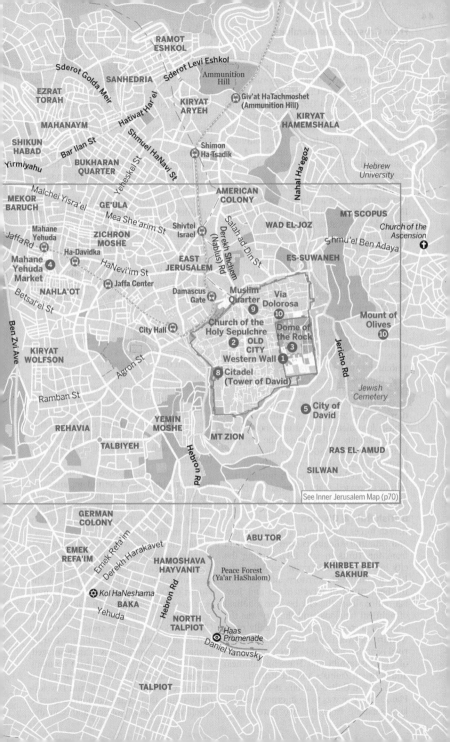

From Crusaders to Mamluks to Ottomans

The Crusaders took Jerusalem in 1099 from the Fatimids, who had only just regained control from the Seljuks. After ruling for almost 90 years, the Christians' Latin Kingdom was defeated in 1187 by Saladin (Salah ad-Din), whose efficient administration allowed Muslims and Jews to resettle in the city. From the 13th to the 16th centuries, the Mamluks constructed a number of outstanding buildings dedicated to religious study.

Although a Muslim academic centre, Jerusalem became a relative backwater. In 1517 the Ottoman Turks defeated the Mamluks, adding Palestine to their large empire. Yet although they too are remembered for their lack of efficiency in local administration, their initial impact on the city is still much admired today. The impressive Old City walls that were built in the mid-1500s by order of Sultan Süleyman, aka Süleyman the Magnificent, are still much admired today. But after Süleyman's reign, the city's rulers allowed the city, like the rest of the country, to decline. Buildings and streets were not maintained, and corruption among the authorities was rife.

In the wake of the Turkish sultan's 1856 Edict of Toleration for all religions, Jews – by this time a majority of the city's population of about 25,000 – were allowed to establish Jerusalem's earliest neighbourhoods beyond the city walls. Some of the first projects, begun in the 1860s, were inspired and financed by an Italian-born Englishman, Sir Moses Montefiore. As Jewish immigration rapidly increased, scattered neighbourhoods developed into what is now the New City.

British Rule & Division

British forces under the command of General Edmund Allenby captured Jerusalem from the Turks in late 1917, turning the city into the administrative capital of the British-mandated territory of Palestine. In these times of fervent Arab and Jewish nationalism, the city became a hotbed of political tensions, and the city was the stage for terrorism and, occasionally, open warfare, between Jews and Arabs, among rival Arab factions (eg between supporters of the Nashashibi and Husseini families) and between Zionists and the British.

Under the United Nation's 1947 Partition Plan, Jerusalem was to be internationalised, kept separate from the two states – one Jewish, the other Arab – that the United Nations proposed Palestine be divided into. Accepted in principle by the Zionist leadership and but rejected by the Arab and Palestinian leaderships, the Partition Plan was outpaced by events as the 1948 Arab–Israeli War engulfed the city and the country.

During the 1948 war, the Old City and East Jerusalem, along with the West Bank, were captured by Jordan, while the Jews held onto most of the New City. Patches of no-man's-land separated them, and the new State of Israel declared its part of Jerusalem as its capital.

For 19 years Jerusalem – like Berlin – was a divided city. Mandelbaum Gate, just north of the western edge of the Old City, served as the only official crossing point between East and West Jerusalem for the few who were permitted to move between them. In the Six Day War of 1967, Israel captured the Old City from Jordan and began a massive program of restoration, refurbishment, landscaping and construction.

Controversial Capital

Controversy continues to surround the status of Jerusalem, and as a result all countries maintain their embassies in Tel Aviv.

Both Israelis and Palestinians see Jerusalem as their capital. At present, the Palestinian Authority is based in nearby Ramallah, but it hopes one day to move to East Jerusalem. Israel is determined to never let that happen and has constructed a security fence that effectively seals the city off from the West Bank.

Israel has also massively expanded the municipal borders of Jerusalem, annexing parts of the West Bank to the city and developing 13 Jewish settlement neighborhoods in East Jerusalem. This annexation is widely seen as illegitimate.

Currently, approximately 275,000 Palestinian Jerusalemites live and work in East Jerusalem neighbourhoods and villages including the Old City; At-Tur on the Mount of Olives; Silwan and Ras al-Amud near the southern edge of the Old City; and Sheikh Jarrah and Shuafat north of the Old City. Some of these areas are modern and economically stable; others are traditional and economically disadvantaged. A 2013 report on the Palestinian economy in East Jerusalem compiled by the United Nations Conference on Trade and Development stated that Israeli authorities pursue a policy of physical, political and economic

JERUSALEM IN...

Four Days

This is the minimum amount of time you'll need to if you are to do the city justice – a week would be better.

Spend your first day in the Old City. Take the 9am **walking tour** conducted by Sandemans (p85) to get your bearings, and then head off to see **Temple Mount/Al Haram ash-Sharif** (p47), the **Church of the Holy Sepulchre** (p54) and the **Western Wall** (p59) (pre-book to take the Western Wall Tunnels tour; p59). Sample the city's best hummus at **Abu Shukri** (p92) for lunch and head to the city centre for dinner.

On day two, utilise Circle Line 99 (p86) to explore the major sights in West Jerusalem, including the **Israel Museum** (p79). Late in the afternoon head to the **Mahane Yehuda Market** (p73) to have a drink at one of its bars before heading off to sample some modern Israeli cuisine at nearby **Machneyuda** (p95) or **Yudaleh** (p94).

On day three, explore the **City of David** (p66) and visit **Mt Zion** and the **Citadel (Tower of David)** (p52). In the evening, attend the **sound-and-light show** at the Citadel (you'll need to pre-book).

On your last day, choose from the many remaining sights and activities on offer, including **Yad Vashem** (p80), the **Jerusalem Archaeological Park & Davidson Centre** (p59), the **Mount of Olives** (p68), the **Rockefeller Museum** (p72) and the **Museum on the Seam** (p70).

segregation of East Jerusalem from the rest of the occupied Palestinian territory and that its residents face official impediments with regard to housing, education, employment, taxation and representation. The report also stated that East Jerusalem receives a disproportionately small share of municipal services such as water, sewerage, road maintenance, postal services and garbage collection.

Various peace plans propose that the city be partitioned, with Jewish neighbourhoods in Israel and Arab neighbourhoods in Palestine. There is little agreement on exactly how to handle the Old City, especially Temple Mount/Al-Haram ash-Sharif, Judaism's holiest site and Islam's holiest site after Mecca and Medina.

As it stands, constructive and cordial interactions between Palestinian and Jewish Jerusalemites are few and far between, and the divide between East and West Jerusalem seems to be growing. Disturbingly, incidents of violent and sometimes fatal confrontation between extremist factions in both communities have been increasing in recent times.

◉ Sights

Jerusalem's major sights can be broken down geographically, with the highest concentration in the Old City. East Jerusalem,

the City of David and Mt Zion are all within easy walking distance of the Old City.

West Jerusalem contains a number of sights, including the Israel Museum, Mt Herzl, Yad Vashem and Ein Kerem, but these are spread out and are best reached by Jerusalem Light Rail (JLR), bus or taxi.

◉ Old City

In the late afternoon, as sunlight turns its ancient stone buildings golden, the Old City is a feast for the senses: church bells clang, the smell of spices and fresh herbs waft out of the souqs, the evocative strains of the call to prayer can be heard in the distance, and residents take to the narrow and winding alleyways on their way home to dinner. Mornings are different, crackling with energy as pilgrims from every corner of the globe arrive to worship at the Western Wall, Dome of the Rock or Church of the Holy Sepulchre; shop in the souqs; and explore the four fascinating quarters contained within the city's monumental walls.

Roads circle the Old City and there are four major entry points: Jaffa Gate, Damascus Gate, Dung Gate and St Stephen's (Lions) Gate. Most visitors enter through Jaffa Gate, which leads straight into the Christian and Armenian Quarters and from where the rest of the Old City is a short downhill walk. Damascus Gate leads

Old City

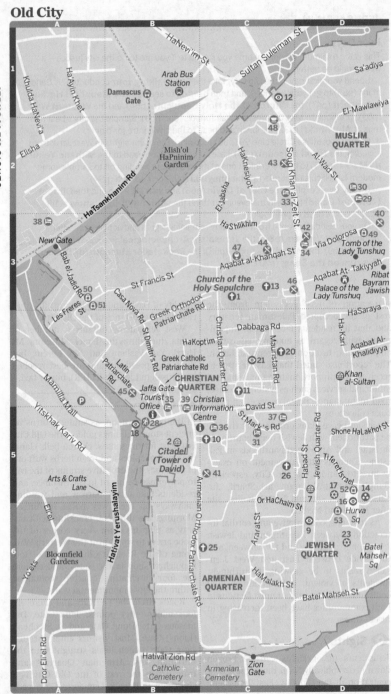

MUSLIM QUARTER

CHRISTIAN QUARTER

ARMENIAN QUARTER

JEWISH QUARTER

HaNevi'im St

Sultan Suleiman St

Khulda HaNevi'a

Ha'Ayin Khet

Elisha

Damascus Gate

Arab Bus Station

Mish'ol HaPninim Garden

HaTsankhanim Rd

New Gate

Bab el-Jadid Rd

Les Freres St.

St Francis St

Casa Nova Rd

St Dimitri's Rd

Greek Orthodox Patriarchate Rd

Latin Patriarchate Rd

Greek Catholic Patriarchate Rd

HaKoptim

Jaffa Gate Tourist Office

Christian Information Centre

Citadel (Tower of David)

Armenian Orthodox Patriarchate Rd

Mamilla Mall

Yitskhak Kariv Rd

Arts & Crafts Lane

Eli'el Rd

Yo'ets

Dror Eli'el Rd

Bloomfield Gardens

Hativat Yerushalayim

El Tapsir St

HaShlikhim

HaKnesiyot

Soug Khan al-Zeit St

Al-Wad St

Sa'adiya

El-Mawlawiya

Aqabat al-Khanqah St

Church of the Holy Sepulchre

Via Dolorosa

Tomb of the Lady Tunshuq

Aqabat At- Takiyyah

Palace of the Lady Tunshuq

Ribat Bayram Jawish

HaSaraya

Ha-Kari

Aqabat Al-Khalidiyya

Dabbaga Rd

Maristan Rd

Christian Quarter Rd

Khan al-Sultan

David St

St Mark's Rd

Shone HaLakhot St

Habad St

Jewish Quarter Rd

Tiferet Israel

Or HaChaim St

Ararat St

Hurva Sq

Batei Mahseh Sq

HaMalakh St

Batei Mahseh St

Hativat Zion Rd

Catholic Cemetery

Armenian Cemetery

Zion Gate

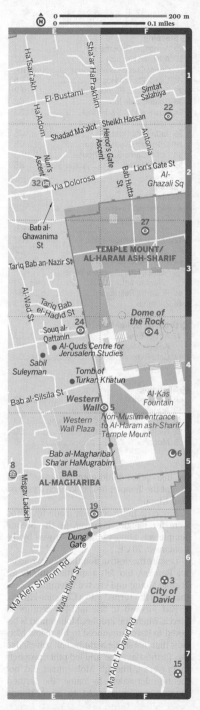

straight into the Muslim Quarter; Lions Gate to the start of the Via Dolorosa; and Dung Gate to the Jewish Quarter (Western Wall) and to the tourist entry for Temple Mount. Inside, most of the streets are pedestrian-only.

For a handy guide to church opening hours see www.cicts.org; for information about Jewish sites, see www.rova-yehudi.org.il.

⊙ Temple Mount/Al-Haram ash-Sharif

Temple Mount/
Al-Haram ash-Sharif   RELIGIOUS SITE
(Map p46; ⊘7.30-11am & 1.30-2.30pm Sun-Thu Apr-Sep, 7.30-10am & 12.30-1.30pm Sun-Thu Oct-Mar) **FREE** There are few patches of ground as holy – or as disputed – as this one. Known to Muslims as Al-Haram ash-Sharif (The Noble Sanctuary) and Jews as Har HaBayit (Temple Mount), this elevated cyprus-planted plaza in the southeastern corner of the Old City is home to two of Islam's most sacred buildings – the Dome of the Rock and Al-Aqsa Mosque – and is revered by Jews as the location of the First and Second Temples.

The Talmud states that it was here, on a large slab of rock protruding from the ridge of Mt Moriah, that God gathered the earth that was used to form Adam and that biblical figures such as Adam, Cain, Abel and Noah all performed ritual sacrifices. The most well-known account appears in Genesis (22:1-19): as a test of faith, Abraham was instructed by God to sacrifice his son Isaac but at the 11th hour an angel appeared and a ram was sacrificed instead. The Bible states that David later erected an altar here (Sam 24:18-25).

Although no archaeological traces have been found in situ (and are unlikely to ever be found, as archaeological excavations are out of the question due to religious sensitivities), Solomon is said to have erected the First Temple on the site of David's altar. The Talmud tells us that Solomon's temple took 7½ years to complete, but for reasons unknown it stood unused for 13 years. When it was finally consecrated, Solomon placed the Ark of the Covenant inside and celebrated with a seven-day feast.

After weathering a number of raids, the Temple was destroyed in 587 BCE by Nebuchadnezzar II of Babylon. Initially rebuilt by order of Zorobabel, who had been made

Old City

governor of Judea by Cyrus II after the Persian defeat of the Babylonians, it was then replaced by a largely new and much-extended Second Temple built by order of Herod the Great (r 39–4 BCE). Herod upgraded the site by building a wall around the mount and filling it with rubble, levelling off the enormous plaza we can see today. The biggest of the stones holding up Temple Mount (eg in the Western Wall) weigh over 500 tonnes.

Jews coming to Temple Mount approached from the south. Pilgrims were required to enter a mikveh (Jewish ritual bath) for purification purposes before ascending the steep steps; one of these has been preserved in the nearby Jerusalem Archaeological Park (p59). Inscriptions on stones warned that any Gentile entering the mount would do so on pain of death. Only

the high priest could enter the inner sanctum of the Temple; he did so once a year on Yom Kippur.

Any civic improvements made by Herod were for naught, however, as the Second Temple was almost totally destroyed by the Romans in 70 CE.

Despite the destruction they had wrought, the Romans, too, felt a spiritual affinity for Temple Mount and erected a temple to Zeus that was later turned into a Christian church.

Fast forward to the mid-7th century in Mecca, where the Prophet Mohammed is believed to have announced to his fellow Meccans that in a single night he had travelled to the 'farthest mosque' and led other prophets in prayers. Although Mohammed did not mention Jerusalem by name, the farthest mosque was interpreted to be Al-Haram ash-Sharif, thus making Jerusalem a holy place for Muslims (in fact, Temple Mount is considered Islam's third-holiest place after Mecca and Medina). When Caliph Omar accepted the surrender of the city from the Byzantines in 638 CE his interest in Temple Mount was immediately obvious, and he set about erecting a simple mosque. This was later replaced by the Dome of the Rock (c 691 CE) and the Al-Aqsa Mosque (c 705–15 CE).

Immediately following the 1967 Six Day War, Israeli commander Moshe Dayan handed control of Temple Mount to Jerusalem's Muslim leaders. Their control of the mount has never gone down well with fervently nationalist Jews and there have been a number of protests and incidents of violence, including failed plots to blow up Muslim holy sites in the early 1980s. Many Orthodox Jewish authorities forbid Jews from visiting Temple Mount because they may inadvertently tread on the sacred ground on which the Temple once stood.

For visitors uninvolved in the politics of the site, Temple Mount provides a relaxing contrast to the noise and congestion of the surrounding alleyways. It's a flat paved area the size of a couple of adjacent football fields, fringed with some attractive Mamluk buildings and with the Dome of the Rock positioned roughly in its centre. Below the surface of the pavement 19th-century explorers discovered more than 30 cisterns, some of them 15m to 20m deep and up to 50m long. Because of religious prohibitions, no-one is allowed into these today.

Al-Aqsa Mosque
MOSQUE

(Map p46) The name Al-Aqsa means 'farthest mosque' and is in reference to the journey Mohammed is believed to have made on his way to heaven to receive instructions from Allah. While the Dome of the Rock serves more as a shrine than a mosque, Al-Aqsa is a functioning house of worship, accommodating up to 5000 worshippers at a time.

Originally built by order of the Umayyad Caliph Al-Walid (r 709–15 CE), Al-Aqsa stands on what Crusaders believed to be the site of the First Temple and what others believe was a marketplace on the edge of the Temple. This might be where Jesus is said to have turned over the tables and driven out the moneychangers with a makeshift whip (Matthew 21:13).

Rebuilt at least twice after earthquakes razed it, Al-Aqsa was converted into the residence of the Kings of Jerusalem after the Crusaders took the city in 1099 CE. On the death of Baldwin II in 1131 CE the building was handed over to a 10-year-old order of soldier-monks whose members soon began referring to themselves as the Templars after their new headquarters. The order added extensions to the structure, including the still-remaining refectory along the south wall of the enclosure. The other Crusader structures were demolished by Saladin, who added the intricately carved mihrab (prayer niche indicating the direction of Mecca) to the mosque that can be seen today.

★ Dome of the Rock
RELIGIOUS SITE

(Qubbet al-Sakhra; Map p46) The jewel in the Temple Mount crown is the gold-plated Dome of the Rock, the enduring symbol of the city and undoubtedly one of the most photographed buildings on earth. As its name suggests, the dome covers a slab of stone sacred to both the Muslim and Jewish

---

❶ VISITING TEMPLE MOUNT/AL-HARAM ASH-SHARIF

There are nine gates connecting Temple Mount to the surrounding narrow streets, but non-Muslims are allowed to enter only at the Bab al-Magharibe/Sha'ar HaMugrabim (Gate of the Moors), reached via an ugly wooden walkway on the southern side of the Western Wall plaza. Line up early (if you don't, you're unlikely to get inside), and bear in mind that the site closes on Muslim holidays and is only open in the morning during Ramadan. You'll need to have your passport to make it through the security check. Note that it's possible to exit the enclosure by all open gates, not just Bab al-Magharibe.

Be aware that caretakers at the enclosure run a scam whereby they force any visitors deemed to be insufficiently clothed to purchase a shawl and wear it sarong-style. Needless to say, the sarongs are overpriced and receipts are unavailable. To avoid being subjected to this, both men and women should wear long pants or skirts (definitely no shorts) and have their shoulders, backs and decolletages covered.

It is not possible for non-Muslims to enter Al-Aqsa Mosque or the Dome of the Rock; trying to do so is both disrespectful and unwise.

Note that the enclosure is often closed to visitors during times of political unrest.

Al-Haram ash-Sharif/ Temple Mount

A TOUR OF THE TEMPLE MOUNT

The Temple Mount encompasses multiple sites that span an area the size of one or two city blocks. A visit requires a little planning and may need to be accomplished over a couple of days.

Ascend the rickety wooden ramp at the Western Wall plaza to reach the Temple Mount at the Bab al-Maghariba (Gate of the Moors). Passing through the gate, continue ahead to view the understated facade of the **Al-Aqsa Mosque 1** and the sumptuous detail of the **Dome of the Rock 2**. Take a slow turn around the Dome to admire its surrounding structures, including the curious **Dome of the Chain 3** and the elegant **Sabil of Qaitbay 4**. Don't miss the stunning view of the Mount of Olives seen through the stone arches known as the **Scales of Souls 5**.

Exit the Temple Mount at the **Bab al-Qattanin (Gate of Cotton Merchants) 6**; and return to the Western Wall plaza where you can spend some time at the **Western Wall 7** and visit the **Jerusalem Archaeological Park & Davidson Centre 8**.

MICHAEL KOHN

Scales of Souls
Muslims believe that scales will be hung from the column-supported arches to weigh the souls of the dead.

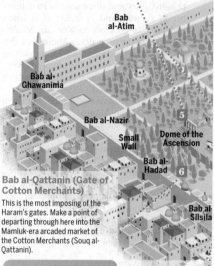

Bab al-Atim

Bab al-Ghawanima

Bab al-Nazir

Small Wall

Dome of the Ascension

Bab al-Hadad

5

6

Bab al-Silsila

Bab al-Qattanin (Gate of Cotton Merchants)
This is the most imposing of the Haram's gates. Make a point of departing through here into the Mamluk-era arcaded market of the Cotton Merchants (Souq al-Qattanin).

Sabil of Qaitbay
This three-tiered, 13m-high structure is one of the finest pieces of architecture on the Temple Mount. It was built by Egyptians in 1482 as a charitable act to please Allah and features the only carved-stone dome outside Cairo.

MICHAEL KOHN

MICHAEL KOHN

Dome of the Chain

Some believe this structure was built as a model for the Dome of the Rock. Legend has it that Solomon hung a chain from the dome and those who swore falsely while holding it were struck by lightning.

Dome of the Rock

The crown jewel of Jerusalem's architectural heritage, the Dome famously contains the enormous foundation stone that Jews believe is the centre of the earth and Muslims say is the spot where Mohammed made his ascent.

Al-Aqsa Mosque

One of the world's oldest mosques, Al-Aqsa (the Furthest Mosque) is 75m long and has a capacity for more than 5000 worshippers. The Crusaders called it Solomon's Temple and used it as a royal palace and stable for their horses.

Bab Hitta

Solomon's Throne

2

3

4

5

Summer Pulpit

Al-Kas Fountain

Musala Marwani Mosque (Solomon's Stables)

1

Dome of Learning

Mamluk Arcade

Bab al-Maghariba

7

Western Wall Plaza

8

Coming Clean

Al-Kas Fountain, located between Al-Aqsa Mosque and the Dome of the Rock, is used for ritual washing before prayers.

Western Wall

Today it's the holiest place on earth for Jews and an important cultural nexus on Shabbat, when Jews from around the city come to sing, dance and pray by the Wall.

Jerusalem Archaeological Park & Davidson Centre

This is the place to see Robinson's Arch, the steps that led up to the Temple Mount and ancient *mikveh* (Jewish ritual bath) where pilgrims washed prior to entering the holy temple.

TEMPLE MOUNT/AL-HARAM ASH-SHARIF: WHO'S IN CHARGE?

Administrative and security control of Temple Mount is a touchy subject with both Jews and Muslims. After the 1967 Six Day War, Israel ceded administrative control of the Temple Mount compound to the Jordanian-controlled Jerusalem Islamic Waqf, a trust overseen by the Grand Mufti of Jerusalem and the Supreme Muslim Council.

Then, in 1994, Israel and Jordan signed the Wadi Araba Peace Treaty, under which Jordan was given administrative control of all Muslim sites in Jerusalem. This agreement is still in force, although the Israelis maintain overall security in the Muslim Quarter and on the Temple Mount. Under Israeli rules, non-Muslims are unable to pray in the compound (something that infuriates ultranationalistic Jews) and Muslim men under the age of 45 are denied access when the security situation is judged to be unsettled. West Bank Palestinians are allowed access only during Islamic holidays, and even at these times only males aged over 35 and women of all ages may enter.

faiths. According to Jewish tradition, it was here that Abraham prepared to sacrifice his son. Islamic tradition has the Prophet Mohammed ascending to heaven from this spot.

The building was constructed between 688 and 691 CE under the patronage of the Umayyad caliph, Abd al-Malik. His motives were shrewd as well as pious – the caliph wanted to instil a sense of pride into the local Muslim population and keep them loyal to Islam. He also wanted to make a statement to Jews and Christians: Islam was both righteous and all-powerful, so it could build a structure more splendid than any Christian church on a location that was the location of the Jewish Holy of Holies, thus superceding both religions.

Abd al-Malik had his Byzantine architects take as their model the rotunda of the Holy Sepulchre. But not for the Muslims the dark, gloomy interiors or austere stone facades of the Christian structures; instead, their mosque was covered inside and out with a bright confection of mosaics and scrolled verses from the Quran, while the crowning dome was covered in solid gold that shone as a beacon for Islam.

A plaque was laid inside honouring Abd al-Malik and giving the date of construction. Two hundred years later the Abbasid caliph Al-Mamun altered it to claim credit for himself, neglecting to amend the original date. In 1545, Süleyman the Magnificent ordered that the much-weathered exterior mosaics be removed and replaced with tiles. These were again replaced during a major restoration in the 20th century. The original gold dome also disappeared long ago, melted down to pay off some caliph's debts, and is now covered with 1.3mm of gold donated by the late King Hussein of Jordan. The 80kg of gold cost the king US$8.2 million – he sold one of his homes in London to pay for it.

Essentially, however, what you see today is the building as conceived by Abd al-Malik. Inside, lying centrally under the 20m-high dome and ringed by a wooden fence, is the rock from which it is said Mohammed began his miraj (ascension to heaven). According to the Quran, the stone also wanted to join him in heaven and began to rise from the earth; Mohammed pushed the stone down with his foot, leaving a footprint on the rock (supposedly still visible in one corner). Jewish tradition also has it that this marks the centre of the world. Steps below the rock lead to a cave known as the Well of Souls, where the voices of the dead are said to be heard falling into the river of paradise and on to eternity. The mihrab in the sanctuary is said to be the the oldest in the Islamic world.

◉ Jaffa Gate

★ **Citadel (Tower of David)**   MUSEUM
(Map p46; ☑ 02-626 5333, 02-626 5325; www.towerofdavid.org.il; adult/student/child 40/30/18NIS; ⊙ 9am-4pm Sun-Thu, to 5pm Jul & Aug, 9am-2pm Fri & Sat, to 5pm Sat Jul & Aug) Commanding a prominent elevated location overlooking the Old City, the Citadel started life as the palace of Herod the Great. Also used as a palace by the Romans and Crusaders, the structure was extensively remodelled by the Mamluks and Ottomans and is now home to the impressive **Museum of the History of Jerusalam**, which tells the story of the city in a series of chronologically arranged exhibits starting in the second millenium BCE and finishing in 1948.

A megalomaniacal builder, Herod furnished his palace with three enormous towers, the largest of which was reputedly modelled on the Pharos of Alexandria, one of the Seven Wonders of the Ancient World. The chiselled-block remains of one of the lesser towers still serve as the base of the Citadel's main keep. Following Herod's death the palace was used by the Roman procurators; it was here that Pontius Pilate is said to have judged Jesus (John 18:28–19:16). The building was largely destroyed by Jewish rebels in 66 CE and the Byzantines, who came along some 250 years later, mistook the mound of ruins for Mt Zion and presumed that this was David's palace – hence the name Tower of David. They constructed a new fortress on the site.

As Jerusalem changed hands, so too did possession of the Citadel, passing to the Muslim armies and then to the Crusaders, who added the moat. It took on much of its present form in 1310 under the Mamluk Sultan Malik an-Nasir, with Süleyman the Magnificent making further additions between 1531 and 1538. Süleyman is responsible for the gate by which the Citadel is now entered, and it was on the steps here that General Allenby accepted the surrender of the city on 9 December 1917, ending 400 years of rule by the Ottoman Turks.

There is plenty to read and see in the museum, and a visit is highly recommended (try to come when you first arrive in the city, as the exhibits give an excellent introduction to its history and architecture). A useful audioguide is available at no charge on the museum website – download it before you arrive. There's a cafe in the garden courtyard and good views of the city can be enjoyed from the highest ramparts.

The popular **Night Spectacular** (adult/student & child 55/50NIS), a 45-minute sound-and-light show about the history of Jerusalem, is staged in the Citadel's internal courtyard twice per night, five nights per week; start times vary depending on what time the sun sets. See the website for details.

Jaffa Gate GATE
(Map p46) One of the six original gates built by order of Süleyman the Magnificent, Jaffa Gate is actually a dog-legged pedestrian tunnel passing through the city wall (the dog-leg was to slow down any charging enemy forces – you'll find the same arrangement at Damascus, Herod's and Zion Gates). The breach in the wall through which the road now passes was made in 1898 in order to permit the German Kaiser Wilhelm II to ride with full pomp into the city.

Inside the gate, on the left, is the Jaffa Gate Tourist Office. Be aware that the nearby shopfront with the 'Jerusalem Tourist Information Center' sign is a private tour operator, not the official office. The latter is on the corner of Latin Patriarchate Rd.

The Arabic name for the gate is Bab al-Khalil (Gate of the Friend), which refers to the holy city of Hebron (Al-Khalil in Arabic). In Hebrew it is Sha'ar Yafo (Jaffa Gate) because this was the start of the old road to the port city of Jaffa.

WALLS & GATES

Jerusalem's Old City walls are the legacy of the Ottoman emperor Süleyman the Magnificent, who oversaw their construction between 1537 and 1542. The northern wall, including Damascus Gate, was built first and then extended south, at which point it was delayed by a dispute over whether or not Mt Zion and the Franciscans' monastery should stand inside or outside the wall. To save time and expense the builders decided against looping the wall around the monastery, leaving the Franciscans out in the cold. Popular legend has it that when news reached Süleyman of the miserly cost-cutting exercise, he was furious and had the architects beheaded.

Five main gates were built as part of Süleyman's scheme (Jaffa, Damascus, Herod's, St Stephen's and Zion) and the Golden Gate on the southern side of Temple Mount/Al-Haram ash-Sharif was reworked from its original Ummayad version. New Gate was constructed in 1887 by order of Sultan Abdul Hamid to allow direct access from the newly built pilgrim hospices to the holy sites of the Old City's Christian Quarter. The unfortunately monikered Dung Gate (Sha'ar HaAshpot, or Refuse Gate, in Hebrew) was a secondary entrance in Ottoman times, only widened in the 1940s. The popular theory as to how its name came about is that at one time the area around the gate was the local rubbish dump.

All but Golden Gate are accessible today.

Christ Church
CHURCH

(Map p46; ☑02-627 7727; www.cmj-israel.org; Omar ibn al-Khattab Sq) This was the Holy Land's first Protestant church, consecrated in 1849. Located opposite the Citadel, it was built by the London Society for Promoting Christianity Among the Jews, whose founders were inspired by the belief that the Jews would be restored to what was then Turkish Palestine, and that many would acknowledge Jesus Christ as the Messiah before he returned. The first British consulate in Palestine was located in the compound, which now houses a guesthouse (p88).

In order to present Christianity as something not totally alien to Judaism, the church was built in the Protestant style with several similarities to a synagogue. Jewish symbols and Hebrew script figure prominently at the altar and in the stained-glass windows, and like all synagogues in Jerusalem, the church faces Temple Mount/Al-Haram ash-Sharif.

Ramparts Walk
HISTORIC SITE

(Map p46; ☑02-627 7550; www.pami.co.il; adult/child 16/8NIS; ◑9am-4pm Sat-Thu Oct-Mar, to 5pm Apr-Sep, 9am-2pm Fri) Truth be told, the idea of this 1km walk atop the ramparts is better than the reality. Views aren't all that impressive (they're better from the Citadel), and there's no shade, which makes it a real slog in high summer. Tickets are purchased from the Jerusalem Tourist Information Center tour operator near Jaffa Gate. Because the ramparts in Temple Mount are off-limits, there are two stretches: from Jaffa Gate south to Dung Gate, and from Jaffa Gate north to St Stephen's (Lions) Gate.

Note that the southern stretch is open until 10pm in July and August, and that the stretch between Jaffa Gate and St Stephen's (Lions) Gate is closed on Friday. The section between Jaffa and Damascus Gates provides the best views.

◉ Christian Quarter

The 18.2-hectare Christian Quarter is an attractive blend of narrow streets filled with souvenir shops, artisans' workshops, hospices, hostels and religious institutions belonging to 20 different Christian denominations. It has a resident population of 4500 people. At its centre stands the venerable Church of the Holy Sepulchre, one of the world's most important pilgrimage destinations.

If you enter the Old City through Jaffa Gate, the first two streets to the left – Latin Patriarchate Rd and Greek Catholic Patriarchate Rd – lead to a quiet area around New Gate where the local Christian hierarchy resides.

Heading straight across Omar ibn al-Khattab Sq from Jaffa Gate, you'll find a narrow passage that leads down David St, a tourist bazaar dedicated to filling up travellers' suitcases with overpriced tourist tat (bargain hard). About halfway down the street, to the left, is Christian Quarter Rd, another narrow passage lined with souvenir shops. Head down here to access the Church of the Holy Sepulchre.

David St ends at a chaotic intersection that leads on the left to Souq Khan al-Zeit St, one of the main thoroughfares of the Muslim Quarter, and on the right to the Cardo Maximus, which leads into the Jewish Quarter. Continuing downhill via a dogleg turn is Bab al-Silsila St, which leads to the Western Wall, Western Wall Tunnels and Al-Silsila entrance to Temple Mount.

On Friday, Franciscan fathers lead a cross-bearing procession along the route of the Via Dolorosa, leaving the Pilgrims Reception Centre 300m inside St Stephen's (Lions) Gate at 3pm (October to March) and 4pm (April to September). Unfortunately, crowds make the experience less than satisfying, so you will be better off following our walking tour (p56) at a different time.

★ Church of the Holy Sepulchre
CHURCH

(Map p46; ☑02-626 7000; ◑5am-9pm Easter-Sep, 4am-7pm Oct-Easter) Christendom's most important church huddles amidst souqs on the edge of the Christian and Muslim Quarters. For the past 16 centuries Christian pilgrims have arrived at this spot from every corner of the globe, and while the church building itself may not look particularly regal or attractive, the tears, laments and prayers of the pilgrims have done much to sanctify it. Be aware that the church can be hard to locate – the easiest access is via Christian Quarter Rd.

Built on a site considered by Christians to be the biblical Calvary or Golgotha where Jesus was nailed to the cross, died and was resurrected, the church incorporates the final five Stations of the Cross and is perennially packed with tourists and pilgrims. Those hoping to enjoy a period of quiet contemplation or worship will be sorely disappointed.

The decision to erect a church here is said to have been the result of lobbying on the part of Helena, the mother of Emperor Constantine, 300 years after the Crucifixion.

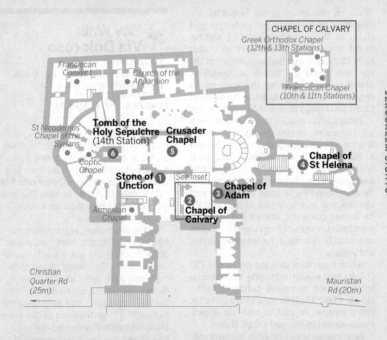

CHAPEL OF CALVARY
Greek Orthodox Chapel
(12th & 13th Stations)

Franciscan Chapel
(10th & 11th Stations)

Franciscan
Convent

Church of the
Apparition

St Nicodemus
Chapel of the
Syrians

Tomb of the
Holy Sepulchre
(14th Station)

Crusader
Chapel

Chapel of
St Helena

Coptic
Chapel

Stone of
Unction

See Inset

Chapel of
Adam

Armenian
Chapel

Chapel of
Calvary

Christian
Quarter Rd
(25m)

Mauristan
Rd (20m)

Church Tour
Church of the Holy Sepulchre

LENGTH ONE HOUR
START STONE OF UNCTION
FINISH TEMB OF HTE HOLY SEPULCHRE

On entering the church, you will see the ❶ **Stone of Unction** directly in front of you. This commemorates the place where the body of Jesus was annointed before burial. The current stone dates from 1810 and is often draped with pilgrims prostrating themselves on it or weeping over it.

Climb the steep staircase directly to the right of the front entrance. The ❷ **Chapel of Calvary** at the top is divided into two naves. The 10th Station of the Cross, where Jesus is said to have been stripped of his clothes, is at the entrance to the first (Franciscan) chapel, and the 11th Station, where it is said that Jesus was nailed to the cross, is also there. The 12th Station, in the second (Greek Orthodox) chapel, is said to be the site of Jesus's crucifixion; at its centre is the Rock of Calvary, on which an altar has been built (a hole in the altar allows pilgrims to touch

the rock below). The 13th Station, where the body of Jesus is said to have been taken down and handed to Mary, is located to the left of the altar.

Walk down the stairs beyond the Greek Orthodox chapel and then turn right. The ❸ **Chapel of Adam** to your right was the original burial place of the first two Crusader rulers, Godfrey de Bouillon and Baldwin I (their tombs were removed in 1809). Further on, down a staircase, is the ❹ **Chapel of St Helena**. Legend has it that it was here that Helena dug into the ground and discovered three crosses – the True Cross was identified after a sick man touched the crosses and was healed by one of them.

Continue around the eastern wall of the central ❺ **Crusader Chapel** and you will eventually reach a wooden rotunda housing the the 14th Station of the Cross, the ❻ **Tomb of the Holy Sepulchre**. Pilgrims queue to enter the tiny space and are given a few minutes inside before being hurried along by a priest on door duty.

While on pilgrimage in the Holy City, she took note of Hadrian's pagan temple and shrine to Venus (built in 135 CE), and believed it had been placed here to thwart early Christians who had worshipped at the site. She joined the Bishop of Jerusalem, Macarius, in petitioning the emperor to demolish the temple, excavate the tomb of Christ and build a church to house the tomb.

Excavations revealed three crosses, leading Helena to declare the site as Calvary. Work on Constantine's church commenced in 326 CE and it was dedicated nine years later. If you are a little confused as to why Jesus is said to have been crucified in the middle of the city, bear in mind that 2000 years ago this was an empty plot of land outside the former city walls. Shrines and churches were built on the site from the 4th century, occasionally destroyed by invading armies and rebuilt.

When his armies took the city in 638 CE, Caliph Omar was invited to pray in the church but he refused, generously noting that if he did his fellow Muslims would have turned it into a mosque. Instead, in 1009 the church was destroyed by the mad Caliph Hakim.

Restoration began in 1010 but proceeded slowly due to lack of funds. Eventually, the Byzantine Imperial Treasury provided a subsidy 20-odd years later. It wasn't enough to pay for a complete reconstruction of the original church, so a large part of the building was abandoned, but an upper gallery was introduced into the rotunda and an apse added to its eastern side as a sort of compensation. This was the church that the Crusaders entered on 15 July 1099 as the new rulers of the city. They made significant alterations and so the church as it exists today is more or less a Crusader structure of Byzantine origins. At this time the main entrance had two access points: the current entry door and another at the head of the Crusader-era staircase on the exterior, which led into a small chapel built to provide a ceremonial entrance to the site of Calvary. This chapel was walled up after the Crusaders' defeat in 1187; its carved lintel is now exhibited in the Rockefeller Museum (p72).

A fire in 1808 and an earthquake in 1927 caused extensive damage, and serial disagreements between the different Christian factions who share ownership (Catholics, Greek Orthodox, Armenian Orthodox, Syrians, Copts and Ethiopians) meant that it took until 1959 for a major repair program to be agreed upon. Due to the rivalries, the

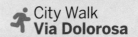

City Walk
Via Dolorosa

START VIA DOLOROSA, 1ST STATION
FINISH CHURCH OF THE HOLY SEPULCHRE
LENGTH 600M; 45 MINUTES

The Via Dolorosa ('Way of Sorrows') is the route that Jesus is believed to have taken as he carried his cross to Calvary. Its history goes back to the days of the earliest Byzantine pilgrims, who trod the path from Gethsemane to Calvary on Holy Thursday, although at the time there were no devotional stops en route.

By the 8th century, pilgrims were performing ritual stops to mark the Stations of the Cross (places where events associated with the Crucifixion occurred). In the Middle Ages, with Latin Christianity divided into eastern and western camps, the Via Dolorosa was split and each of the two factions forged different routes. In the 14th century, the Franciscans devised a walk of devotion that included some of the present-day stations but had as its starting point the Holy Sepulchre. This became the standard route for nearly two centuries, but it was eventually modified by the desire of European pilgrims to follow the order of events of the gospels, finishing at the believed site of the Crucifixion. Today, the popularly recognised stations are marked by round metal plaques.

The **1** **1st Station**, where Pontius Pilate is said to have condemned Jesus, is inside the working Islamic Al-Omariyeh school near St Stephen's (Lions) Gate. The entrance is the brown door at the top of the ramp on the southern side of the Via Dolorosa, next to the Ecce Homo Arch. Entry is not always permitted, so don't be surprised if you are asked to leave (your best chance is after school hours, from 3pm to 5pm).

The **2** **2nd Station** is located across the street in the Franciscan Church of the Condemnation, to the left after you enter the church compound. This is where it is believed Jesus received the cross; the Chapel of the Flagellation to the right is where he is said to have been flogged. Built in 1929, the design on the chapel's

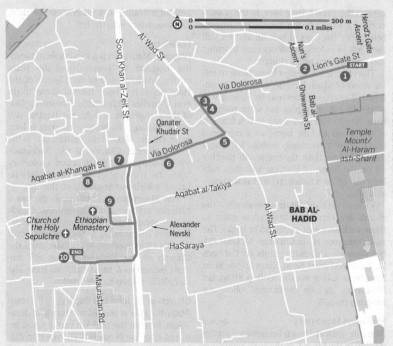

domed ceiling over the altar incorporates the crown of thorns, and the windows around the altar show the mob who witnessed the event.

Continue down a short hill until you reach Al-Wad St. Turn left on Al-Wad and walk just a few steps to the ③ **3rd Station**, where it is believed Jesus fell for the first time. The station is in the small chapel to the left of the entrance to the Armenian Catholic Patriarchate Hospice. The ④ **4th Station**, which marks the spot where Jesus is said to have faced his mother in the crowd of onlookers, is found at the entrance to the chapel.

As Al-Wad St continues south towards the Western Wall, the Via Dolorosa breaks off to climb to the west; right on the corner is the ⑤ **5th Station**, where it is said that the Romans ordered Simon the Cyrene to help Jesus carry the cross. The station is marked by signs around a door.

Further along the street, the ⑥ **6th Station** is marked by a brown wooden door on the left. This is where Veronica is believed to have wiped Jesus's face with a cloth.

A bit further along you'll enter bustling Souq Khan al-Zeit St. The ⑦ **7th Station**,

where it is believed Jesus fell for the second time, is a small chapel marked by signs on the wall of the souq. In the 1st century, this was the edge of the city and a gate led out to the countryside, a fact that supports the claim that the Church of the Holy Sepulchre is the genuine location of Jesus's crucifixion, burial and resurrection.

Cut straight across Souq Khan al-Zeit St and ascend Aqabat al-Khanqah St. A short distance up this street, on the left, is the stone and Latin cross marking the ⑧ **8th Station** where it is said Jesus told some women to cry for themselves and their children, not for him.

Backtrack to Souq Khan al-Zeit St and turn right (south). Head up the stairway on your right and follow the path around to the Coptic church. The remains of a column in its door mark the ⑨ **9th Station**, where it is believed Jesus fell for the third time.

Retrace your steps to the main street or head through the Ethiopian Monastery to reach the ⑩ **Church of the Holy Sepulchre** (p54), home to the remaining five stations.

keys to the church have been in the possession of a local Muslim family, the Nusseibehs, since the days of Saladin and it's still their job to unlock the doors each morning and secure them again at night.

The church has always been home to relics, many of which have been coveted by pilgrims. The cross discovered by Helena was originally put on display, but when pilgrims bent over to kiss it so many took a bite out of the wood to take home as a memento that there was eventually nothing left. These days, pilgrims limit themselves to pouring oil on the Stone of Unction and then rubbing this off on a handkerchief to take home as a relic.

Visitors here should dress modestly – the guards are very strict and refuse entry to those with bare legs, shoulders or backs. The main entrance is via Christian Quarter Rd, but there are also entry points via Dabbaga Rd (accessed from Souq Khan al-Zeit St or Mauristan Rd) or via the rooftop Ethiopian Monastery. To tour the church, follow our itinerary on p55.

Ethiopian Monastery CHURCH

(Map p46; ☉daylight hours) Sequestered on the rooftop of the Church of the Holy Sepulchre, this monastery houses a few monks from the Church of Ethiopia who live among the ruins of a medieval cloister erected by the Crusaders. The cupola in the middle of the roof section admits light to St Helena's crypt below. A door in the southeast corner leads through a chapel and downstairs to the courtyard of the Holy Sepulchre itself.

Around the cloister walls are paintings of Ethiopian saints, the Holy Family and the Queen of Sheba during her visit to Jerusalem. Ethiopian legend tells that it was during this visit that the Queen of Sheba, together with King Solomon, produced heirs to both royal houses, one of whom brought the Ark of the Covenant to Ethiopia.

The monastery is actually within the Coptic Patriarchate. When the Church of Ethiopia became a self-governing organisation in the early 20th century (previously, it was part of the Coptic Church), its monks were kicked out of the Coptic monastery and moved into huts here on the rooftop.

The monastery is reached via a staircase from Souq Khan al-Zeit St (look for a juice stand and the ramshackle entrance to famous pastry shop Zalatimo; p92). As you walk up the stairs you will see the patriarchate chapel straight in front of you

and an entrance to a cistern on the right. The monastery is to the left.

Mauristan HISTORIC SITE

(Map p46) Mauristan is a Persian word meaning 'hospital' or 'hospice', and this plaza on the southern side of the Church of the Holy Sepulchre once housed three medieval churches with attached hospices. One of these churches, St John the Baptist, still exists, although its hospice building is long gone. On the Mauristan's eastern side is the 1898 Lutheran Church of the Redeemer, which incorporates cloisters and a refectory from the 11th-century Church of Mary-la-Latine, which was originally on this site.

The Mauristan is lined by shops, has a 19th-century fountain in its centre and leads to two souqs (one full of butcher's shops) that link to David St. A fabulous view over the Old City's rooftops is available from the **Church of the Redeemer** (Map p46; museum, excavations & tower adult/child under 14yr 15/7.50NIS; ☉10am-5pm Mon-Sat).

Church of St John the Baptist CHURCH

(Map p46) This is the oldest church in Jerusalem, built in the mid-5th century and restored after the Persians destroyed it in 614. In the 11th century the merchants of Amalfi used the walls of the original building when constructing a new church, which became the cradle of the Knights Hospitaller. The present facade with the two small bell towers is a more recent addition. Now part of a Greek Orthodox monastery complex, it is accessed from Christian Quarter Rd.

⊙ Jewish Quarter

Unlike its more bustling neighbours to the north, the Jewish Quarter is predominantly residential, with 4500 inhabitants, modern stone buildings and a central square. The area was heavily shelled by the Arab Legion during the 1948 fighting and later demolished by the Jordanians, so most of the quarter had to be totally rebuilt after 1967.

While few historic monuments above ground are in evidence, there are a number of interesting archaeological finds below street level, some of which are said to date back to the time of the First Temple (around 1000 to 586 BCE).

The Jewish Quarter is the only part of the Old City that is fully equipped to accommodate wheelchair users. A designated route for wheelchair users begins at the car park south of Hurva Sq. Call ☎02-628 3415 for details.

★ **Western Wall** RELIGIOUS SITE

(Map p46) The builders of the Western Wall could never have fathomed that one day their massive creation would be an important religious shrine. Indeed, when it was built some 2000 years ago this most holy of all Jewish sites was merely a retaining wall supporting the outer portion of Temple Mount, upon which stood the Second Temple. Although the Temple was destroyed, its retaining structure remained and rabbinical texts maintain that the Shechina (divine presence) never deserted it.

Following the destruction of the Temple in 70 CE, Jews were sent into exile and the Temple's precise location was lost. Upon the Jews' return they purposely avoided Temple Mount, fearing that they might step on the Holy of Holies, the ancient inner sanctum of the Temple barred to all except the high priest. Instead they began praying at this remaining element of the original structure.

The Wall became a place of pilgrimage during the Ottoman period and Jews would come to mourn and lament the destruction of the Temple – that's why the site is also known as the Wailing Wall, a name that Jews tend to avoid. At this time, houses were pressed right up to it, leaving just a narrow alley for prayer.

In 1948 the Jews lost access to the Wall when the Old City was taken by the Jordanians and the population of the Jewish Quarter was expelled. Nineteen years later, when Israeli paratroopers stormed in during the Six Day War, they fought their way directly here and their first action on securing the Old City was to bulldoze the neighbouring Arab houses to create the sloping plaza that exists today.

The area immediately in front of the Wall now operates as a great open-air synagogue. It's divided into two areas: a small southern section for women and a larger northern section for men. Here, black-garbed ultra-Orthodox men rock backwards and forwards on their heels, bobbing their heads in prayer, occasionally breaking off to press themselves against the Wall and kiss the stones. To celebrate the arrival of Shabbat there is always a large crowd at sunset on Friday. The plaza is a popular site for bar mitzvahs, which are usually held on Shabbat or on Monday and Thursday mornings. This is a great time to visit as the area is alive with families singing and dancing as they approach.

Notice the different styles of stonework composing the Wall. The huge lower layers

BENEATH THE WALL

Western Wall Tunnels (⏰8.30am-5pm 02-627 1333; www.thekotel.org; adult/student & child 30/15NIS; ⏲7am-6pm Sun-Thu, to noon Fri) For a different perspective on the Western Wall, join a tour of the Western Wall Tunnels, a 488m passage that follows the northern extension of the wall. Dug out by archaeologists, the tunnel burrows down to the original street level (nicknamed Market St by tour guides because it was believed to have been a shopping area). The foundation stones here are enormous – one is a 5870-tonne monster the size of a small bus.

You can only visit the tunnels on guided tours (Hebrew and English all year, French in August only), which take about 75 minutes and must be booked in advance. These tours are very popular and fill up fast – try to book at least a week ahead of time.

are made up of Herodian-era stones, identifiable by their carved edges, while the stones above them, which are chiselled slightly differently, date from the time of the construction of Al-Aqsa Mosque. Also visible at close quarters are the wads of paper stuffed into the cracks in between the stones. Some Jews believe that prayers and petitions inserted between the stones have a better-than-average chance of being answered.

On the men's side of the Wall a narrow passage runs under Wilson's Arch, which was once used by priests to enter the Temple. Look down the two illuminated shafts to get an idea of the Wall's original height. Women are not permitted into this area.

The Wall is open to members of all faiths 24 hours a day, 365 days a year. Modest dress is recommended and head covering is required for men (paper kippot are available if you don't have one). Photography is prohibited.

Jerusalem Archaeological
Park & Davidson Centre HISTORIC SITE
(Map p46; ☎02-627 7550; www.archpark.org.il; adult/student & child 30/16NIS, guided tours 160NIS, audioguide 5NIS; ⏲8am-5pm Sun-Thu, to 2pm Fri) Offering a peek into the history of the Temple Mount area, this archaeological site near Dung Gate incorporates the remains of streets, columns, gates, walls, plazas and

JERUSALEM SYNDROME

Each year millions of tourists descend on Jerusalem to walk in the footsteps of the prophets, and a handful come away from the journey thinking they *are* the prophets. This medically recognised ailment, called Jerusalem Syndrome, occurs when visitors become overwhelmed by the metaphysical significance of the Holy City and come to the conclusion that they are biblical characters or that the Apocalypse is near.

The ailment was first documented in the 1930s by Jerusalem psychiatrist Dr Heinz Herman, who identified, for example, an English Christian woman who was so certain that Christ's Second Coming was imminent that she regularly climbed Mt Scopus to welcome him back to earth with a cup of tea.

In more recent times, there were reports of a Canadian Jew who, claiming to be Samson, decided to prove himself by smashing through the wall of his room to escape. Then there was the elderly American Christian woman who believed she was the Virgin Mary and went to Bethlehem to look for the baby Jesus.

In the most serious case so far, in 1969 an Australian Christian fanatic set fire to Al-Aqsa Mosque, causing considerable damage. He believed that he was on a mission from God to clear Temple Mount of non-Christian buildings to prepare for the Messiah's Second Coming.

Doctors estimate that Jerusalem Syndrome affects between 80 and 100 people per year, and although many have a recorded history of mental illness, about a quarter of recorded cases have no previous psychiatric record. You can occasionally see these people standing on city streets and holding placards that describe soon-to-be-occurring events of an apocalyptic nature.

Most sufferers are taken to the state psychiatric ward, Kfar Shaul, on the outskirts of West Jerusalem. Patients are monitored and then sent home. Doctors explain that the syndrome generally lasts a week and when the patient resumes his or her old self, they become extremely embarrassed and prefer not to speak of the incident. Doctors at Kfar Shaul have found it virtually pointless to try to persuade the deluded that they are not who they claim to be.

mikvehs exposed during archaeological digs in the 1970s. There's also a modern visitor centre where two video presentations – an interesting one about the excavations and another reconstructing the site as it looked 2000 years ago – are presented in both Hebrew and English.

As you enter the site you'll notice on your left the remains of what was once Jerusalem's main street, which ran the length of the Temple's Western Wall. Note the remains of an arch protruding from Herod's wall. This is Robinson's Arch (named after a 19th-century American explorer), once part of a bridge that connected the Temple Mount and the city's main commercial area. The piles of stones on the Herodian-era street below the arch are said to be part of the Western Wall, hurled down by Roman soldiers as they destructed the Temple in 70 CE. Nearby is a divided staircase leading down to a mikveh from the same period; one side was for bathers on the way to the bath and the other was for bathers who had been purified.

At the back of the site (ie closest to the Mount of Olives) are the Huldah Gates, also built in the Second Temple period. These originally gave access to tunnels that led up to the Temple Mount enclosure. Nearby is a largely reconstructed staircase that was once the main entry for pilgrims headed to the Temple Mount. Near the bottom of the steps you can spot more mikvehs.

Book in advance if you would like to take a guided tour.

Cardo Maximus
HISTORIC SITE

(Map p46) Cutting a broad north–south swath, the sunken Cardo Maximus is the reconstructed main street of Roman and Byzantine Jerusalem. At one time it would have run the whole breadth of the city, up to what's now Damascus Gate, but in its present form it starts just south of David St, the tourist souq, serving as the main entry into the Jewish Quarter from the Muslim and Christian areas.

Originally, the Cardo would have been a wide colonnaded avenue flanked by roofed arcades. Part of it to the south has been restored to something like its original appearance, while the rest has been reconstructed as an arcade of expensive souvenir and Judaica shops. There are wells to allow visitors to see down to the levels beneath the street, where there are strata of a wall from the days of the First Temple and the Second Temple.

Close to the large menorah (seven-branched candelabrum) near the southern end of the Cardo, the Alone on the Walls Museum (Map p46; ☑02-626 5923; adult/concession 25/12NIS; ⊙9am-5pm Sun-Thu, to 1pm Fri) documents the May 1948 campaign for control over the city through the stories of Jewish residents and fighters. The small but interesting exhibit includes a 15-minute video documentary and a gallery of photographs by photojournalist John Phillips, who worked with *Life* magazine and was in the quarter when it fell to the Arab Legion.

You can buy a combined ticket for this museum, the Burnt House and the Wohl Archaeological Museum for 45NIS at any of those venues.

Rabban Yokhanan Ben Zakai Synagogues
SYNAGOGUE

(Map p46; ☑054 665 5487; adult/child 10/7NIS; ⊙9am-4pm Sun-Thu, to 1pm Fri) Named after a renowned 1st century CE *tanna* (scholar-judge), the four Sephardi synagogues in this complex have very different histories and decoration. The two oldest date from the late 16th century and all four were in ruins before being restored between 1967 and 1972. With their associated study houses and charitable institutions, the synagogues were at the centre of the local Sephardi community's spiritual and cultural life until the late 19th century.

In accordance with a law of the time stating that synagogues could not be taller than neighbouring buildings, the grouping was sunk deep into the ground – a measure that certainly saved the buildings from destruction during the bombardment of the quarter in 1948. Instead, the synagogues were looted by the Jordanians and then used as sheep pens. Restored using the remains of Italian synagogues damaged during WWII, all four are physically linked and can be visited on one ticket.

The first synagogue in the grouping (closest to the ticket desk) is the Eliahu Hanavi Talmud Torah Congregation, the oldest of the four. Its arches and dome reference

Byzantine buildings. Two of the other synagogues are accessed from its northern side: the Qahal Qadosh Gadol (Great Congregation), built between the late 16th and early 17th centuries and featuring distinctive Spanish-Moorish windows, and the elongated Emtza'i (Middle) Synagogue, the smallest of the four. This was created when a roof was built over a courtyard between two of the synagogues in the mid-18th century, thus creating a 'middle' synagogue.

Doors in the Emtza'i lead to a small exhibit about the history of the synagogues, and to the Istanbuli Synagogue, which is the largest of the four and was the last to be built. It was constructed in the 1760s by immigrants from the Turkish city of the same name.

Burnt House
MUSEUM

(The House of Kathros; Map p46; ☑02-626 5921; Tiferet Israel St; adult/concession 35/17NIS; ⊙9am-5pm Sun-Thu, to 1pm Fri) Buried under rubble for centuries and only recently excavated, this house was destroyed in 70 CE when the Romans put the city to the torch. The archaeological remains on display include Roman-era coins, stone tablets, ovens, cooking pots and a spear that were found at the site, as well as a stone weight with the name 'Kathros' on it (Kathros was a priestly family living in the city at this time).

Piecing together the house's history, the museum has created a multimedia presentation shown in a number of languages, including English. Movies begin every 40 minutes, so be prepared to wait around for a bit until the next show.

Herodian Quarter Museum
ARCHAEOLOGICAL SITE

(Wohl Archaeological Museum; Map p46; ☑02-626 5922; 1 HaKara'im St; adult/concession 18/13NIS; ⊙9am-5pm Sun-Thu, to 1pm Fri) Descending from the ticket office to this archaeological site demonstrates how many layers have been added to the city over the centuries – the remains of the three palatial Herodian-era villas on display are 3m below the present-day street. Built on the slope of a hill facing Temple Mount (possibly for priests and their families), the villas were destroyed by the Romans in 70 CE. The site includes remnants of ritual baths, frescos, bathrooms, cisterns and coloured mosaic floors.

Hurva Square
SQUARE

(Map p46) Flanked by fast-food joints and upmarket jewellery stores, Hurva Sq is an attractive open space in the middle of the

Jewish Quarter that is inevitably full of local families, tourists and groups of young adults on free 'heritage trips' to Israel. The reconstructed **Hurva Synagogue** (Map p46; ☑ 02-626 5900; www.rova-yehudi.org.il; adult/student 25/15NIS; ☺ Hebrew tours 11am, English tours noon Sun-Fri) stands on the western side of the square and can be visited on a pre-booked tour.

⊙ Muslim Quarter

Strolling does not come easy in the Muslim Quarter – visiting the sights here is more a matter of dodging, weaving and ducking. You'll need agility as heavily laden carts trundle past, children zip by with reckless abandon, groups of pilgrims pause in front of Stations of the Cross and merchants attempt to lure you into their shops.

The quarter, which has a resident population of 22,000, runs from permanently congested Damascus Gate to Bab al-Silsila St near Temple Mount/Al-Haram ash-Sharif. About 100m in from the gate, the street forks; bearing to the left is Al-Wad St, lined with shops selling everything from brass pots to burquas. There are also a number of sweets shops here. This route crosses the Via Dolorosa and leads directly to the Western Wall.

Bearing to the right at the fork is Souq Khan al-Zeit St, which is even busier than Al-Wad St. Its name means 'Market of the Guesthouse of the Olive Oil' – in addition to its namesakes you'll find shops selling fruit, vegetables, sweets, clothing, spices and nuts.

For an interesting perspective on this part of town, try to visit around midday on Friday. Position yourself near Damascus Gate or around the bottom of Aqabat al-Takiya St and watch the streams of Muslim faithful flood through the quarter towards Al-Haram ash-Sharif on their way to prayers. The alleys are filled with stands selling freshly baked snacks including *man'aish* (flat bread topped with olive oil and a mix of dried thyme, salt, sesame seeds and sumac) that are popular with hungry mosque-goers.

Damascus Gate   GATE
(Map p46) The scene in front of Damascus Gate is a colorful one – vendors heave goods in and out of the Old City, Israeli border police tap their truncheons, elderly Palestinian women from the villages squat on the pavement selling herbs, parents shepherd their young children through the crowds and tourists take it all in, appearing in turn bewildered and enchanted.

The gate itself dates in its present form from the time of Süleyman the Magnificent, although there had been a gate here long before the arrival of the Turks. This was the main entrance to the city as early as the time of Agrippa, who ruled in the 1st century BCE. The gate was considerably enlarged during the reign of the Roman emperor Hadrian.

A long-disappeared column erected by Hadrian once stood in the square, which is why the gate is known in Arabic as Bab al-Amud (Gate of the Column). In Hebrew it is known as Sha'ar Shchem (Nablus Gate).

St Anne's Church   CHURCH
(Map p70; adult/student/child under 13yr 8/6/3NIS; ☺ 8am-noon & 2-6pm Apr-Sep, 8am-noon & 2-5pm Mon-Sat Oct-Mar) The finest example of Crusader architecture in Jerusalem, St Anne's was built in 1138 on a site thought to have been the home of Joachim and Anne, the parents of the Virgin Mary. The building is unusually asymmetrical, and has a particularly beautiful interior. One of the sunken pools accessed from the rear of the church compound is traditionally thought to be the biblical **Pool of Bethesda** (Map p46) where Jesus is said to have healed a sick man (John 5:1-18).

When Jerusalem fell to the armies of Saladin, St Anne's became a Muslim theological school – an inscription above the church's entrance testifies to this. Successive rulers allowed the church to fall into decay, so by the 18th century it was roof-deep in refuse. In 1856 the Ottoman Turks presented the church to France in gratitude for its support in the Crimean War against Russia, and it was reclaimed from the garbage heap. It is still French-owned.

St Stephen's Gate (Lions Gate)   GATE
(Map p70) This is the gate that gives access to the Mount of Olives and Gethsemane. It is also where, from their positions on that biblically famed hillside, Israeli paratroopers fought their way into the Old City on 7 June 1967.

Although originally called Bab al-Ghor (Jordan Valley Gate), it became known as St Stephen's Gate after the first Christian martyr, who was stoned to death at a spot nearby. The Hebrew name, Sh'ar Ha'Arayot (Lions Gate), is a reference to the two pairs of heraldic lions carved on the exterior side of the archway.

MAMLUK ARCHITECTURE

The Muslim Quarter possesses a wealth of buildings constructed during the golden age of Islamic architecture. Most of these are in a sadly dilapidated state these days but retain vestiges of their original grandeur.

This part of the Old City was developed during the era of the Mamluks (1250–1517), a military dynasty of former slaves ruling out of Egypt. Driving the Crusaders out of Palestine and Syria, they followed up with an equally impressive campaign of construction, consolidating Islam's presence in the Levant with masses of mosques, madrassas (religious schools), hostels, monasteries and mausoleums. Mamluk buildings are characterised by the banding of dark and light stone (a technique known as *ablaq*) and by elaborate carvings and patterning around windows and in recessed portals.

All of these features are exhibited in the **Palace of the Lady Tunshuq**, built in 1388 and found halfway down Aqabat al-Takiya – 150m east of the Hebron Youth Hostel. Though the facade is badly eroded, the uppermost of the three large doorways still has some beautiful inlaid marble work and the third door down is decorated with another Mamluk trademark, the stone 'stalactites' known as muqarnas. The palace complex now houses the Department Islamic Orphanage Secondary School. Opposite the palace is the 1398 **Tomb of the Lady Tunshuq** – look for the carved panel above the locked green door.

Down the hill, towards the junction with Al-Wad St, you will see on your right the last notable piece of Mamluk architecture built in Jerusalem, the 1540 **Ribat Bayram Jawish**, which has a facade featuring handsome *ablaq* and shallow muqarnas. Compare this with the buildings on Tariq Bab an-Nazir St, straight across Al-Wad St, which are Jerusalem's earliest Mamluk structures, built in the 1260s before the common use of *ablaq*. This street is named after the gate at the end, which leads through into Temple Mount/Al-Haram ash-Sharif (entry for Muslims only).

Some 100m south on Al-Wad St is Tariq Bab el-Hadid St; it looks uninviting, but if you wander down through the archway you will come to a street entirely composed of majestic Mamluk structures. Three of the four facades belong to madrassas, dating variously from 1358 to 1440, while the single-storey building is a ribat (hospice) dating from 1293.

Back on Al-Wad St, continuing south, the road passes the Souq al-Qattanin and then, on the same side, a sabil (public fountain) dating from Ottoman times, **Sabil Suleyman**. The road terminates in a police checkpoint at the mouth of the tunnel down to the Western Wall plaza. However, the stairs to the left lead up to the busy Bab al-Silsila St and the Bab al-Silsila Gate (which leads to the Temple Mount). Just before the gate is the tiny kiosklike 1352 **Tomb of Turkan Khatun**, with a facade adorned with uncommonly asymmetrical carved geometric designs.

Bab al-Silsila St has a number of other handsome Mamluk buildings with muqarnas and mashrabiyyas (projecting oriel windows featuring carved wood latticework). Uphill, close to Souq Khan al-Zeit St, is the **Khan al-Sultan**, a 14th-century caravanserai (travellers' inn and stables). Enter this and head up the staircase tucked into the left-hand corner to access the rooftop, which offers a good view.

Souq al-Qattanin   MARKET
(Bazaar of the Cotton Merchants; Map p46) Enjoying a glass of mint tea or a Turkish-style coffee at the Arab cafe near the end of this atmospheric shopping arcade is a pleasant diversion when exploring the Muslim Quarter. Originally a Crusader marketplace, the building was extended by the Mamluks in the mid-14th century. The part closest to Al-Wad St dates from the Crusader period. The souq is lined with shops and has a caravanserai (travellers' inn) on its southern side housing a department of Al-Quds University.

◉ Armenian Quarter

Sequestered behind high walls and enormous wooden doors, life in the Armenian Quarter plods along unnoticed, as it has for nearly two millennia.

Armenia was the first nation to officially embrace Christianity, after its king converted in 303 CE. Armenians established themselves in Jerusalem sometime in the following century and when the Kingdom of Armenia disappeared at the end of the 4th century, Jerusalem was adopted as its spiritual capital. Armenians have had an uninterrupted presence here ever since, at one stage numbering 25,000.

Originally, this presence was purely religious, but a large secular element arrived early last century to work on retiling the Dome of the Rock and to escape Ottoman Turkish persecution. The community today numbers about 1500 and is still very insular, having its own schools, library, seminary and residential quarters arranged within the gated Armenian compound (not open to visitors).

St James' (Jacques') Cathedral   CHURCH
(Map p46; Armenian Orthodox Patriarchate Rd; ⊙ morning prayers 6.30am, vespers 3pm, Mass 8.30am Sat & 9am Sun) Glowing lamps hang from the ceiling, glittering icons adorn every wall and richly patterned carpets are strewn across the floors, giving this 12th-century cathedral an aura of mystery lacking in many other Christian sites of Jerusalem. It's open only for services, the most impressive of which is held on Sunday when the Armenian Patriarch of Jerusalem presides. At other times, you can enter the courtyard to see the exterior, which is decorated with *khatchkars* (carved Armenian stone crosses).

It was actually the Georgians who, in the 11th century, first constructed a church here in honour of St James, believing the site to be the place where he was beheaded and became the first martyred disciple. In the 12th century, the Armenians, in favour with the ruling Crusaders, took possession of the church and undertook its restoration. The blue-and-white tiles in the interior date from the 18th century.

Modest dress is required to attend services; women should cover their heads.

St Mark's Chapel   CHURCH
(Map p46; ☏ 02-628 3304; ⊙ 9am-noon & 2-5pm Mon-Sat Apr-Sep, 7am-4pm Mon-Sat Oct-Mar, 11am-4pm Sun) FREE This medieval chapel is the home of the small Syrian Orthodox congregation in Jerusalem, who believe that it occupies the site of the home of St Mark's mother, Mary. Peter is said to have come here after he was released from prison by an angel (Acts 12:12). Inside, look for the

---

ARMENIAN CERAMICS

In Jerusalem, the importance of the Dome of the Rock is unquestionable. And this importance isn't only due to its religious and historical significance. In 1919, the restoration of this magnificent building prompted the establishment of the first Armenian ceramics workshop in the city, a crafts tradition that continues strongly to this day.

Armenian ceramic techniques reached their height in Turkey during the 17th and 18th centuries, when many Armenian families operated workshops in the important ceramic centres of Kütahya and İznik. After the events of 1915–18, when most of Turkey's Armenian population had their property confiscated and were forcibly deported, a number of Armenian potters and their families were brought to Jerusalem by David Ohannissian (1884–1953), an Armenian ceramics master who had worked in Kütahya and who had fled Turkey for Jerusalem in 1919. On arriving, he was able to establish a ceramics workshop on the Via Dolorosa with the assistance of the Pro Jerusalem society, set up in 1918 by Sir Ronald Storrs, the military governor of Jerusalem, and Charles Robert Ashbee, an architect and leading designer of the Arts and Crafts Movement. Ohannissian and his Armenian master craftsmen went on to produce new tiles to replace the worn originals on the Dome of the Rock.

Local artisans claim that Jerusalem is now the only place in the world where genuine Armenian pottery is still produced. Old, hand-painted techniques have changed little over the centuries and are used to produce richly coloured ceramics featuring floral, animal and geometric patterns.

To see wonderful examples of Armenian tiles head to St James' (Jacques') Cathedral (p64), with its profusion of blue-and-white tiles, and to St Andrew's Church (p77), which features tiles at the entrances to the church and its guesthouse. To purchase ceramics to take home, try the **Armenian Ceramic Centre** (Map p46; ☏ 02-626 3744; www.sandrouni.com; HaAhkim St; ⊙ 9.30am-7pm Mon-Sat) in the Christian Quarter, **Armenian Ceramics** (Map p70; ☏ 02-628 2826; www.armenianceramics.com; 14 Nablus Rd) in East Jerusalem or **Arman Darian** (Map p76; ☏ 054 470 2582; 12 Shlomzion HaMalka St; ☐ City Hall) in West Jerusalem.

painting on leather of the *Virgin and Child,* which is attributed to St Luke.

Mt Zion

Home to a room venerated by Christians as the place where Jesus and his disciples had their Last Supper, as well as to a small prayer room marking the place where many Jews believe King David is buried, this cluster of buildings is an important pilgrimage site for peoples of both faiths.

Although it once encompassed the entire ridge of the upper Old City (including the Citadel), Mt Zion is now defined as the hill south of the Old City beyond Zion Gate.

King David's Tomb RELIGIOUS SITE

(Map p70; ⊙ 8am-6pm Sun-Thu, to 2pm Fri) Erected by Crusaders two millennia after King David's death, this ground-floor tomb is of dubious authenticity but is nonetheless a Jewish holy place. The prayer hall is divided into sides for men and women, both leading to the velvet-draped tomb. Behind is an alcove believed to be a synagogue dating back to the 5th century CE.

For those wondering, most archaeologists and historians believe that it is likely that David is buried under the hill of the original Mt Zion, east of the City of David.

The tomb is off the courtyard in front of the Franciscan Monastery, which is accessed through a doorway on the left-hand side of the path into the main complex, past an arch and the stairway leading to the Room of the Last Supper.

Room of the Last Supper RELIGIOUS SITE

(Cenacle, Coenaculum; Map p70; ⊙8am-6pm) Considered to be one of the most holy places in the Christian world (up there with the Church of the Holy Sepulchre and the Church of the Nativity in Bethlehem), this austere and somewhat underwhelming space was part of the Holy Zion church built in 390 CE. Retained in the 14th century Crusader structure that replaced the original church, it was converted to a mosque during the Ottoman period and retains stained glass and a mihrab from that time.

Also known as the Coenaculum (Latin for dining hall) or Cenacle (derived from *cena,* Latin for supper), the room is highly unlikely to have hosted the Last Supper but may have been the place where the disciples are said to have received the Holy Spirit on the Pentecost and started speaking in 'foreign tongues' (Acts 2). The event culminated

with the baptism of 3000 followers of Jesus, marking the birth of Christianity.

The room is reached via a stairway that leads up to a reception atrium. To find this, walk towards the main complex and take the first staircase on the left after the carved arch. It can also be reached via another staircase leading from the courtyard in front of the Franciscan Monastery, near King David's Tomb.

Church & Monastery of the Dormition CHURCH

(Map p70; ☑02-565 5330; www.dormitio.net; ⊙9am-5.30pm Mon-Sat, 10am-5pm Sun) One of Jerusalem's most recognisable landmarks, this mosaic-laden church occupies the site traditionally thought to be where the Virgin Mary died (the word 'dormition' means a peaceful or painless death). Its Latin name is Dormitio Sanctae Mariae (Sleep of Holy Mary). The current church and its monastery, owned by the German Benedictine order, was consecrated in 1906. To visit, you'll need to be modestly attired.

The building suffered damage during the battles for the city in 1948 and 1967. During the latter, Israeli soldiers occupied its tower overlooking Jordanian army positions on the Old City ramparts below. The soldiers nicknamed the tower 'bobby' because it resembles the helmet worn by London policemen.

The church's interior features a golden mosaic of Mary with the baby Jesus in the upper part of the apse; below are the prophets of Israel. The chapels around the hall are each dedicated to a saint or saints: St Willibald, an English Benedictine who visited the Holy Land in 724; the Three Wise Men; St Joseph, whose chapel is covered with medallions that feature kings of Judah as Jesus's forefathers; and St John the Baptist. The floor is decorated with names of saints and prophets, as well as zodiac symbols.

The crypt features a stone effigy of Mary asleep on her deathbed with Jesus calling her to heaven. In the apse is the Chapel of the Holy Spirit, with the Holy Spirit shown coming down to the Apostles.

Drinks, snacks and free wi-fi are available at the cafe in the front courtyard.

Grave of Oskar Schindler MEMORIAL

(Map p70; ⊙8am-noon Mon-Sat) The grave of the Austrian industrialist who saved more than 1200 Jews from the gas chambers and whose story was told by filmmaker Steven Spielberg in the Oscar-winning *Schindler's List* is in the Christian cemetery on Mt Zion.

From Zion Gate walk directly ahead, downhill, to find the Christian cemetery. Once inside, head down to the third (lowest) level. Schindler's grave is easy to recognise as it is covered in small stones (a Jewish custom signifying respect).

Church of St Peter of Gallicantu   CHURCH
(Map p70; ☑ 02-673 1739; www.stpeter-gallicantu. org; admission 7NIS; ⊘ 8.30am-5pm Mon-Sat) Almost hidden by trees and the slope of the hill, this church occupies the site where Jesus is said to have been denied by his disciple Peter (Mark 14:66-72) – 'before the cock crow thou shalt deny me thrice' (Gallicantu means 'cock crow' in Latin). Built on the foundations of previous Byzantine and Crusader churches, the modern structure has a balcony with a magnificent view across to the City of David, the Palestinian village of Silwan and the three valleys that shape Jerusalem.

The church is reached by turning east as you descend the road leading from Mt Zion down and around to Sultan's Pool. Roman steps lead down from the church garden to the Gihon Spring in the Kidron Valley.

◉ Kidron Valley

Historically the oldest section of Jerusalem, the Kidron Valley and its western slopes are the location of archaeological remnants that date back more than 4000 years. It is the site of the legendary City of David, which was actually a city long before David slung any stones, and there are also a number of graves and tombs in the area, particularly in the Valley of Jehoshaphat. Steep topography has isolated the valley from the rest of the city (the best access is via Dung Gate or St Stephen's/Lions Gate), but it's definitely worth trekking down here for a morning of exploration.

★ City of David   ARCHAEOLOGICAL SITE
(Map p46; ☑ *6033; www.cityofdavid.org.il; adult/ child 29/15NIS, movie 13NIS, Enchanted Jerusalem tour adult/child 16-18yr 80/63NIS, Hebrew-language guided tour adult/child 60/45NIS; ⊘ 8am-5pm Sun-Thu, 8am-2pm Fri Oct-Mar, to 7pm Sun-Thu, to 4pm Fri Apr-Sep; ☐ 1, 2, 38) Excavations at this site started in the 1850s and are ongoing, proof of how rich an archaeological find it was. The oldest part of Jerusalem, it was a settlement during the Canaanite period and was captured by David, who is said to have brought the Ark of the Covenant here 3000 years ago. The main attraction is

Hezekiah's Tunnel, a 500m-long passage of waist-deep water, but there is plenty more to see – allow at least three hours for your visit.

From Dung Gate, head east (downhill) and take the road to the right; the entrance is then on the left. At the visitors centre you can buy water (in summer, you'll need it) and watch a 3D movie about the city. If you intend to walk through Hezekiah's Tunnel – and we suggest that you do – you can change into a swimming costume in the bathrooms and leave your gear in a locker (10NIS); alternatively, wear shorts. You will also need suitable footwear (flip-flops or waterproof shoes) and a torch (flashlight). Key-chain lights can be purchased from the ticket office for 4NIS.

Note that the entrance fee covers admission to the underground areas of the site (Warren's Shaft, Hezekiah's Tunnel, Pool of Siloam, Temple Road Ascent); admission should be free if you only explore aboveground areas.

Once you reach the bottom of the hill you can walk back up through the Temple Road Ascent or via the road that passes through the Arab village of Silwan.

It's inevitable that controversy surrounds any site that concerns Jerusalem's history and the City of David is no different. Key issues of contention include the treatment of Palestinian residents in the neighbourhood and complaints by archeologists that the official narrative presented is Jewish-centric and politicised.

➜ Royal Quarter (Area G)
Area G, also called the Royal Quarter, was first constructed in the 10th century BCE, most likely as a fortification wall for a palace on the ridge. During the First Temple period an aristocrat's home (Achiel's House) was built against the wall, but it was destroyed along with the Temple in 586 BCE. Judean and Babylonian arrowheads found at the site are vivid reminders of the bloody battle waged here. Archaeologists have also located 51 royal seals (in ancient Hebrew script), including one belonging to Gemaryahu Ben Shafan, the scribe of the prophet Jeremiah, who is mentioned in Jeremiah 36:10. The seals were all located in one chamber, indicating that the room once served as an office.

➜ Warren's Shaft
The long, sloping Warren's Shaft was named after Sir Charles Warren, the British engineer who rediscovered it in 1867. The tunnel, which runs underneath the City of David to

the Spring of Gihon, allowed the Canaanites to obtain water without exposing themselves to danger in times of siege. It's just inside their city's defence wall and is possibly the tunnel that David's soldiers used to enter and capture the city, as mentioned in II Samuel 5. Modern archaeologists, however, tend to doubt this theory, suggesting the invaders used a different tunnel. From Warren's Shaft, you can proceed down to Hezekiah's Tunnel at the bottom of the hill.

➡ Hezekiah's Tunnel

This 500m-long underground passage of waist-deep water ends at the Pool of Siloam, where it is said that a blind man was healed after Jesus told him to wash in it. The purpose of the tunnel was to channel water flowing from the Gihon Spring, a temperamental source that acts like a siphon, pouring out a large quantity of water for some 30 minutes before drying up for several hours.

Gihon means 'gushing', and the spring is the main reason the Canaanites settled in the valley rather than taking to the adjacent high ground. There is believed to be enough water to support a population of about 2500 people. The tunnel was constructed around 700 BCE by King Hezekiah to bring the water of the Gihon into the city and store it in the Pool of Siloam, so preventing invaders, in particular the Assyrians, from locating the city's water supply and cutting it off (an account of this is in II Chronicles 32:3).

Although the tunnel is narrow and low in parts, you can wade through it; the water is normally between 0.5m and 1m deep. The tunnel is as little as 60cm wide at some points.

About 20m into the tunnel, the cavern turns sharply to the left, where a chest-high wall blocks another channel that leads to Warren's Shaft. Towards the tunnel's end the roof rises. This is because the tunnellers worked from either end and one team slightly misjudged the other's level. They had to lower the floor so that the water would flow. A Hebrew inscription was found in the tunnel (a copy can be seen in the Israel Museum): carved by Hezekiah's engineers, it tells of the tunnel's construction.

The walk through Hezekiah's Tunnel takes about 20 minutes. If you don't want to get wet there is a second tunnel without water, which takes about 15 minutes to walk through. To find the entrance to the dry tunnel, go left just before the opening to Hezekiah's Tunnel. Children must be at least five years of age to walk through Hezekiah's Tunnel.

➡ Pool of Siloam

As you exit from Hezekiah's Tunnel there is a small pool with round stones. This is the Byzantine Pool of Siloam, which was built in the 5th century to commemorate the Christian tradition of the healing of the blind man (John 9). The Byzantines built the pool because they could not find the Shiloach Pool, which was buried under a thick layer of debris and garbage.

➡ Shiloach Pool

From the Pool of Siloam, head up the stairs and out to an open area with crumbling steps that lead down to a small pond. This is the Shiloach Pool. Discovered during excavations in 2005, the pool was built during the Second Temple period and was used for purification rituals. Archaeologists and historians have theorised that this is the pool where Jesus is said to have healed a blind man.

➡ Eastern Stepped Street

From the Shiloach Pool head up the flight of wooden steps to the Eastern Stepped Street, an ancient flight of stone steps. A drainage ditch is located under the steps and it was here that archaeologists found Roman-era coins and pottery, leading historians to believe that the ditch served as a hideout for Jews while the city was being sacked in 70 CE.

➡ Temple Road Ascent

This recently constructed 650m-long tunnel is a drainage ditch that channelled water out of the Temple Mount area. The bottom of the tunnel is near the Shiloach Pool; from here it's possible to walk uphill back to the Old City, exiting near Dung Gate. Note that the tunnel ceiling is low and the walls are narrow in spots, so if you are particularly tall or wide maybe give this one a miss.

Valley of Jehoshaphat　　　　RELIGIOUS SITE

The word Jehoshaphat (Yehoshafat in Hebrew) means 'God shall judge', and this narrow furrow of land located between the Temple Mount and the Mount of Olives is where it is said that the events of Judgment Day will take place. The Book of Joel describes how all nations will be gathered here and the 'heathens' (nonbelievers) will be judged. At the southern end is a series of tombs dating from the Second Temple period.

The northernmost tomb is that of **Jehoshaphat**. It's a 1st-century burial cave notable for the impressive frieze above its entrance. Just in front of it is **Absalom's**

Pillar, the legendary tomb of David's son (II Samuel 18:17). Just beyond Absalom's Pillar is the **Grotto of St James**, where St James is believed to have hidden when Jesus was arrested nearby. Next to the grotto, carved out of the rock, is the **Tomb of Zechariah**, where Jewish tradition believes the prophet Zechariah is buried (II Chronicles 24:25).

Despite their names, the tombs most likely belong to wealthy noblemen of the Second Temple period. The Grotto of St James is believed to be the burial place of the Bnei Hezirs, a family of Jewish priests.

◉ Mount of Olives

According to the Book of Zechariah, this is where God will start to redeem the dead when the Messiah returns on Judgment Day. In order to get a good place in the line, many Jews have chosen to be buried here, and to date some 150,000 people have been laid to rest on these slopes. Aside from being the world's oldest continually used cemetery, there are many churches and sites commemorating the events that led to Jesus's arrest and, as the faithful believe, his ascension to heaven.

For a panoramic view of the Old City, head up to the promenade near the Seven Arches Hotel; try to visit in the early morning, when you'll get the best light.

Church of the Ascension   CHURCH
(✆02-628 7704; www.evangelisch-in-jerusalem. org; admission 5NIS; ☉8am-1pm Mon-Sat; 🚍75) In 1898, the Ottomans granted Germany 8 hectares of land on the Mount of Olives. This was set aside for a church and hospice, and the complex was named after Augusta Victoria, wife of Kaiser Wilhelm II. Completed in 1910, the church is decorated with mosaics and frescos, and has a 60m-high bell tower that can be climbed by visitors (203 steps). Unfortunately, views from the bell tower are underwhelming and obscured by a safety grille.

The Turkish army occupied the hospice during WWI and the British later converted it into a military hospital – it's still a hospital today.

Russian Chapel of the Ascension   CHURCH
(Map p70; ✆02-628 4373; ☉10am-1pm Tue & Thu Apr-Sep, 9am-noon Tue & Thu Oct-Mar) Marked by a needle-point steeple – the tallest structure on the Mount of Olives – and built over the spot from which the Russian Orthodox Church claims Jesus made his ascent to heav-

en, this 19th-century chapel is part of a working monastery and can be a little bit hard to find; look for a narrow alleyway leading off from the main street, in among the shops.

Mosque of the Ascension
(Chapel of the Ascension)   RELIGIOUS SITE
(Map p70) It's easy to overlook this chapel, which is diminutive and decrepit. Thought to mark the site where Jesus ascended to heaven (Luke 24:50-51), it was built in the Byzantine era, reworked by the Crusaders and then converted to a mosque by Saladin in 1198. In its present form, it is a rotonda set inside an octagonal compound whose walls incorporate a squat stone minaret. Hours are irregular, but there's usually someone around in the morning to open it up.

Inside, the stone floor bears an imprint said to be the footstep of Jesus. Perhaps the reason for its unconvincing appearance today is that pilgrims in the Byzantine period were permitted to take bits of it away. Only the right footprint is now visible, as the left footprint was taken to Al-Aqsa Mosque during the Middle Ages.

Church of the Pater Noster   CHURCH
(Map p70; ✆02-626 4904; admission 8NIS; ☉8.30am-noon & 2.30-4.30pm Mon-Sat Apr-Sep, 8am-noon & 2.30-4.30pm Mon-Sat Oct-Mar) There has been a church on this site since the 4th century CE, when Queen Helena, mother of Emperor Constantine, organised for one to be built over a cave in which Jesus was thought to have spoken to his disciples. The Crusaders, who believed that the cave was in fact where Jesus taught the Lord's Prayer to the disciples, built a new church in 1152. The current building is a partial reconstruction of the Byzantine church with a 19th-century cloister.

The Byzantine church was known as the Church of the Eleona – from the Greek word *elaionas* (olive grove) – and the site still incorporates an olive grove. It also has an attached Carmelite convent. When visiting, look out for the tiled panels in the cloister, on which the Lord's Prayer is inscribed in over 160 languages.

The cave is located in an enclosed courtyard in front of the church, down a few stairs.

Tombs of the Prophets   RELIGIOUS SITE
(Map p70; ☉9am-3pm Mon-Thu) **FREE** Head into the section of cemetery below the panoramic viewpoint to find this set of ancient tombs. Jewish tradition tells us that they house the graves of the prophets Haggai,

ⓘ TOURING THE MOUNT OF OLIVES

Tackling the Mount of Olives on foot can be hard work, especially during summer. You can make things a little easier by starting at the top of the hill and working your way down. Take Arab bus 75 (5NIS) from the bus station opposite Herod's Gate on Sultan Suleiman St in East Jerusalem or hail it outside Damascus Gate and get off at the Church of the Ascension (you'll spot the sign outside the gate that reads: 'Augusta Victoria Hospital'); the trip takes around 15 minutes. From the church you can walk down the main road for 15 minutes to the Russian Chapel of the Ascension, the Mosque of the Ascension, the Church of the Pater Noster, the Tombs of the Prophets, and then downhill to the remaining sites at the bottom of the Mount of Olives. From the Tomb of the Virgin Mary it's a short uphill walk to St Stephen's (Lions) Gate and the Old City.

Most of the churches and gardens open in the morning, close for at least two hours from noon and reopen again midafternoon.

Zachariah and Malachi, who lived in the 5th century BCE, but modern archaeologists tend to dispute this. To find it, take the staircase downhill, just next to a TV satellite dish. The tomb is overseen by the Russian Orthodox Church.

Church of Mary Magdalene   CHURCH
(Map p70; ⊘10am-noon Tue & Thu) The seven golden onion-shaped domes of the Russian Church of Mary Magdalene form one of Jerusalem's most attractive and surprising landmarks. Built in 1888 by Alexander III in memory of his mother, the church is now a convent and has one of the city's best choirs.

Church of All Nations   CHURCH
(Basilica of Gethsemene; Map p70; ⊘8am-5.50pm Apr-Sep, to 4.50pm Oct-Mar) Glistening golden mosaics mark the facade of this neoclassical Franciscan church built on the site of the Garden of Gethsemene and dedicated in 1924. The mosaic depicts Jesus assuming the suffering of the world, hence one of the church's alternative names – the Sanctuary of the Agony of Jesus Christ. More gold mosaics glint in the dim interior.

Despite the name, not all of the world's nations are represented: the seals of the 12 countries that financed the project are located in the church ceiling, but no others. The church is the successor to two earlier sites of Christian worship; the first was a church erected in the 4th century but destroyed by an earthquake in the 740s, and the second was an oratory built over the ruins by the Crusaders but abandoned in 1345 for reasons unknown.

Garden of Gethsemane   GARDENS
(Map p70; ⊘8.30am-noon & 2.30-5pm, to 4pm Sun & Thu) Jesus is believed to have been arrested in this garden (Mark 14:26, 32-50), which is attached to the Church of All Nations. It has some of the world's oldest olive trees (in Hebrew *gat shmanim* means 'oil press'), three of which have been scientifically dated as being over 2000 years old, making them witnesses to whatever biblical events may have occurred here. Enter from the narrow alleyway leading up the Mount of Olives.

Tomb of the Virgin Mary   RELIGIOUS SITE
(Map p70; ⊘5am-noon & 2.30-5pm Apr-Sep, from 6am Oct-Mar) One of the holiest sites in Christianity, this dim space is hung with ancient brass lamps and infused with a millennium of must. On her death (sometime in the middle of the 1st century), Mary was supposedly interred here by the disciples. A monument was first constructed in the 5th century but was repeatedly destroyed. The facade of the current structure dates back to the Crusader period of the 12th century, but the crypt is Byzantine.

On the main road beside the stairs down to the tomb, the small cupola supported by columns is a memorial to Mujir ad-Din, a 15th-century Muslim judge and historian.

⊙ East Jerusalem

Predominantly Arab, East Jerusalem occupies the land that before 1967 was annexed by Jordan. The green line (1948–67 border) between the Israeli- and Jordanian-overseen sections of the city was Chel Handasa St, which is now part of the JLR route. East of Chel Handasa St, the major roads running north and south are Derekh Shchem (Nablus) Rd and Salah ad-Din St.

When exploring this area, consider stopping for a drink or meal at the historic American Colony Hotel, one of Jerusalem's top hotels. Legend has it that when the

Inner Jerusalem

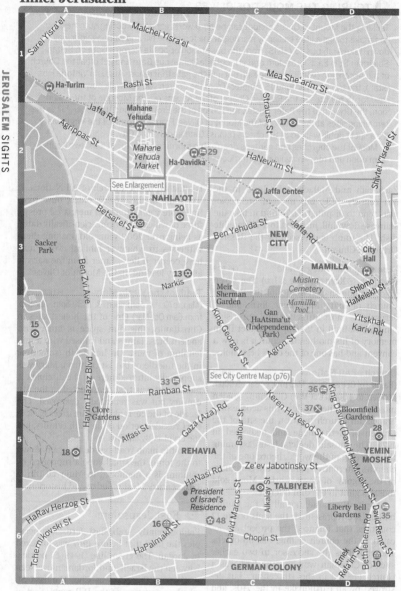

Ottomans surrendered the city to British rule, the Turkish governor of Jerusalem snatched a sheet from one of the beds (it was a hospital at the time) and used it as a flag to surrender. The 'flag' is now in the Imperial War Museum in London.

★ **Museum on the Seam** GALLERY
(Map p70; ☎02-628 1278; www.mots.org.il; 4 Chel Handasa St; adult/student/child under 14yr 30NIS/25NIS/free; ☉10am-5pm Sun-Mon & Wed-Thu, to 2pm Fri, 2-9pm Tue; ☐ Shivtei Israel) Located on the 'seam' (border) between

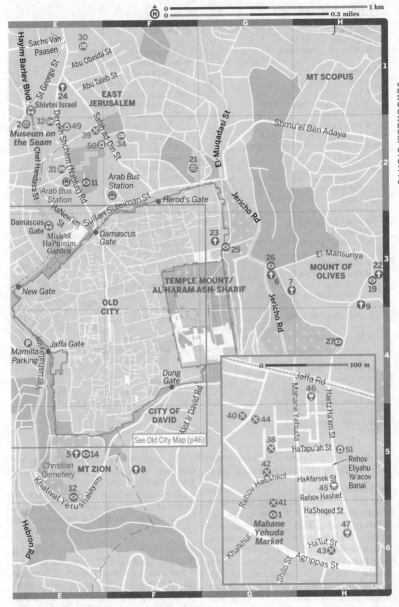

East and West Jerusalem, this gallery presents contemporary-art exhibitions that are challenging, controversial and satisfying in equal measure. The building itself served as a forward military position for the Israeli army from 1948 to 1967 and still bears the scars of war. Exhibitions change every six months, showcase work from regional artists and focus on issues of global conflict, prejudice, racism and human rights.

There is a pleasant rooftop cafe where you can enjoy a coffee, and a downstairs

Inner Jerusalem

gift shop. Note that some of the work shown here may not be suitable for small children.

Rockefeller Museum　　　　MUSEUM
(Map p70; ☑02-628 2251; Sultan Suleiman St; ◷10am-3pm Sun-Mon & Wed-Thu, to 2pm Sat; ⊞Damascus Gate) **FREE** Though overlooked by many visitors to the city, this archaeological museum is well worth a visit. Exhibits date from prehistoric times through to the Middle Ages and are presented chronologically. They include carved 12th-century lintels from the Church of the Holy Sepulchre, detailed 8th-century carvings and moldings recovered from Hisham's Palace near Jericho – don't miss the extraordinary stucco dome from the diwan (Muslim meeting place) – and an exquisite wooden model of the Church of the Holy Sepulchre inlaid with mother-of-pearl.

The distinctive castlelike building was designed by British architect Austen St Barbe Harrison and owes its existence to a gift of US$2 million from the Rockefeller family in 1927. In sore need of restoration, it has an internal courtyard with an ornamental pool and attractive mosaic decoration.

Garden Tomb　　　　GARDENS
(Map p70; ☑02-627 2745; www.gardentomb.org; ◷9am-noon & 2-5.30pm Mon-Sat; ⊞Damascus Gate) A tranquil patch of green in the middle of East Jerusalem's mayhem, this site is considered by its trustees to be both the garden and sepulchre of Joseph of Arimathea, and the place where Jesus was crucified, buried and resurrected. While enjoying little support for their claims, the trustees have provided a walled and attractively landscaped space that is more conducive to contemplation than the alternative site said to be that

of the crucifixion, the Church of the Holy Sepulchre.

Biblical significance was first attached to this location by General Charles Gordon (of Khartoum fame) in 1883. Gordon refused to believe that the Church of the Holy Sepulchre could occupy the site of Calvary, and on identifying a skull-shaped hill just north of Damascus Gate he began excavations. The ancient tombs he discovered under the mound further strengthened his conviction that this was the true site.

Archaeologists have since scotched the theory by dating the tombs as being from the 5th century BCE. Several cynics suggest that the continued championing of the Garden Tomb has more to do with the fact that it's the only holy site in Jerusalem that the Protestants, its owners, have any stake in.

To get there from Sultan Suleiman St head north along Derekh Shchem (Nablus) Rd and turn right at Schick St, opposite the bus station. The site is wheelchair accessible. Free guided tours are available in several languages, but reservations are required for any language other than English.

St George's Cathedral   CHURCH
(Map p70; www.j-diocese.org; Derekh Shchem (Nablus) Rd; ⊙ hours vary; ⌂ Shivtei Israel) Named after the patron saint of England, who is traditionally believed to have been martyred in Palestine early in the 4th century, St George's Cathedral was consecrated in 1910 and has a mixed Arabic- and English-speaking congregation. The church compound is a piece of the British Mandate frozen in time, featuring symbols of the British presence in Jerusalem including a font given by Queen Victoria, memorials to British servicemen and a tower built in memory of King Edward VII.

During WWI the Turks closed the church and used the bishop's house as their army headquarters. After the British took Jerusalem in 1917, the truce was signed here in the bishop's study.

⊙ City Centre

The city centre, or the New City as it's sometimes called, is the area northwest of the Old City. Its central axis is Jaffa Rd, running from Tzahal Sq to the Mahane Yehuda Market area. Between the square and the market is Zion Sq, a handy landmark and meeting point. Despite its status as Jerusalem's downtown, the area is pleasantly devoid of traffic and busy thoroughfares, making it easy to navigate on foot.

★ Mahane Yehuda Market   MARKET
(Map p70; www.machne.co.il; Jaffa Rd; ⊙ 8am-sunset Sun-Thu, 9am-2pm Fri; ⌂ Mahane Yehuda) All walks of local life converge at this bustling market, a fascinating spectacle for the first-time visitor and a bargain food fair for the city's Jewish residents. Crammed with fresh fruit, olives, nuts, vegetables and just about anything else grown or picked from the local soil, it's also a good place to purchase spices, teas, cheese, dried fruits, tahina, bread and pastries. At night, it reinvents itself as a restaurant and bar hub where local foodies, hipsters and tourists hang out.

The market has two major streets – Etz Chayim St (the covered market) and Mahane Yehuda St (the open-air market). Many of the names of the alleyways running between these relate to the products available; eg HaAfarsek means 'Peach St', HaTut means 'Berry St' and Ha'Egoz means 'Walnut St'.

The market is at its bustling best on Thursday and Friday during the pre-Shabbat scramble. As it closes on Friday a couple of Haredi men walk through the market blowing trumpets at the stall owners, warning them to close up shop, go home and prepare for Shabbat.

Russian Compound   CHURCH
(Map p76; ⊙ Church of the Holy Trinity 9am-1pm Mon-Sat Apr-Sep, 9am-1pm Mon-Fri & 9am-noon Sat Oct-Mar; ⌂ City Hall) Dominated by the green domes of its Church of the Holy Trinity, this compound was acquired by the Russian Orthodox Church in 1860 to strengthen the Russian imperial presence in the Holy Land. In the last years of the British Mandate, it and nearby streets were turned into a fortified administrative zone nicknamed 'Bevingrad' by Palestinian Jews after the reviled British foreign secretary Ernest Bevin. Today it is home to Jerusalem's central police station and law courts.

Mea She'arim   NEIGHBOURHOOD
(Map p70; ⌂ Jaffa Center) Walk north from Jaffa Rd along Strauss St and you'll soon enter a neighbourhood with squat, stone-fronted buildings, balconies adorned with drying laundry, bearded figures in black, and long-skirted mums trailed by a gaggle of formally dressed children. If you have the sense that you've stumbled upon an Eastern European shtetl (ghetto) of the 1880s then you are probably standing somewhere near Kikar Shabbat, the main intersection of Mea She'arim, Jerusalem's oldest ultra-Orthodox Jewish (Haredi) neighbourhood.

ULTRA-OTHODOX ATTIRE

Wearing 'modest' (nonrevealing) clothing is a central tenet of Haredi (ultra-Orthodox Jewish) life, so women wear long skirts or dresses (never trousers) and shirts or blouses with long sleeves. Men commonly wear black suits and white shirts with no tie. Married Haredi women cover their heads, usually with a wig, snood or scarf. All Haredi men wear some type of head covering, including the following:

Kippa (yarmulke in Yiddish, scullcap in English) Worn by all Jewish men in synagogues and at holy sites, and by most observant Jewish men all of the time, the kippa is a reminder that God is constantly above the wearer. Knitted or crocheted kippot are worn by modern Orthodox or religious Zionist men; Haredi men tend to wear black velvet or cloth kippot, often under a hat, though some groups, such as the Braslavers, prefer white. In general, the larger the kippa, the more Messianic the wearer is likely to be. In recent decades, women members of the Reform and Conservative movements have begun wearing kippot.

Shtreimel Said to be of Tartar origin, these large round fur hats are worn on Shabbat and holidays by married Hassidic and 'Yerushalmi' Jews (those belonging to the old-line Ashkenazi community of the city). Traditional fox- or martin-fur *shtreimels* can cost thousands of dollars, which is why their owners sometimes cover them in huge plastic shower caps when it rains.

Spodik Another fur hat worn by some Haredim on Shabbat or holidays, but these ones are taller and thinner than the *shtreimel*.

Fedoras Haredi men and boys wear black hats during the weekdays. These usually take the form of a wide-brimmed fedora made using rabbit fur, or a round, wide-brimmed hat.

Other regularly worn religious clothing includes the **tallit katan**, a four-cornered undershirt with knotted tassels called *tzitziot* (usually the only part you can see). The knots are tied according to a formula spelled out in the Talmud and some are coloured with a special blue dye called *t'chelet* (Numbers 15:38).

The sidecurls that many Hasidic and traditional Yemenite men and boys wear are called **payot** (*peyes* in Yiddish). These reflect an interpretation of the Biblical injunction against shaving the 'corners' (*payot*) of one's head (Leviticus 19:27), interpreted by the Mishnah as incumbent only on men.

A throwback to older times, Mea She'arim was developed by ultra-Orthodox Eastern European immigrants who modelled their Jerusalem home on the ones they remembered back in Poland, Germany and Hungary. Despite their transition to the Holy Land, residents have maintained the customs, habits and dress of 19th-century Eastern Europe. Fashions are conservative, including black suits and hats for men and floor-scraping dresses for women; even in the height of the Middle Eastern summer it's still customary among many Hassidic men to wear *shtreimels* (fur hats) on Shabbat and holidays.

Families are typically large and this fact has made Mea She'arim one of the fastest-growing neighbourhoods in Jerusalem, as well as contributing to the increasingly religious nature of the city. Yiddish is the preferred language on the street as the ultra-Orthodox believe Hebrew to be a holy language only fit for religious purposes. Days are often spent in prayer and business is a secondary pursuit – religious study is frequently financed by a combination of Israeli government subsidies and ultra-Orthodox communities abroad.

In the most conservative families, married women shave their heads and cover their bald scalp with a scarf, in the name of modesty. For some, though, this is not enough, and in 2011 extremist groups tried to segregate some of Mea She'arim's sidewalks – men on one side, women on the other. The campaign, opposed by many mainstream ultra-Orthodox Jews, was declared unconstitutional by Israel's Supreme Court.

As this is a religious neighbourhood, visitors are expected to dress and act in a conservative manner. Don't take pictures of the residents (they resent being treated as a touristic curiosity) or speak to children or members of the opposite sex. Do not walk arm in arm or even hand in hand with anyone; kissing is definitely taboo. Disobeying local customs will lead to verbal objections or even stone throwing. If a confrontation with the police seems to be brewing, steer clear.

Friday is perhaps the liveliest day to visit as you'll see families heading to and from market in their preparations for Shabbat. Neighbourhood bakeries are open all night on Thursday, baking challah (traditional braided soft bread eaten on Shabbat). On Friday nights the streets are awash with people taking a break from their Shabbat dinners.

Mea She'arim is a few minutes' walk from both Damascus Gate and the Jaffa Rd/King George V St junction.

Nahla'ot   NEIGHBOURHOOD
(Map p70; ⌂ Mahane Yehuda) Founded in the 1860s, this neighbourhood south of the Mahane Yehuda Market is a warren of narrow alleys where a number of old synagogues and yeshivot (Jewish religious seminaries) are hidden, many set in large stone-walled compounds. The most interesting street is HaGilboa, where you'll find a number of historic homes; each contains a plaque that describes the family that built the home. One street over, on HaCarmel, look for the attractive synagogue Hased veRahamim, with its unmistakable silver doors.

Among the dozens of synagogues, one of the better known is the **Ades Synagogue** (Map p70; cnr Be'ersheva & Shilo Sts), built by Jews from Aleppo (Haleb), Syria, in 1901. The synagogue was named for Ovadia and Yosef Ades, the Syrian-Jewish brothers who financed the project. It quickly became a centre for Syrian *hazzanut* (Jewish liturgical singing) and saw the training of many a Jerusalem cantor. Inside, you'll find a classically Middle Eastern–styled interior with a walnut ark that was carried here from Aleppo by donkey cart. Today it maintains the rare tradition of *bakashot*, a set cycle of Kabbalistic poetry sung in the early hours of Shabbat during the winter months. Unfortunately, the synagogue isn't open very often.

Museum of Italian Jewish Art   MUSEUM
(Map p76; ☎ 02-624 1610; http://ijamuseum. org/; 25 Hillel St; adult/child 20/15NIS; ⊙ 10am-5pm Sun, Tue & Wed, noon-9pm Thu, 10am-1pm Fri; ⌂ Jaffa Center) Incorporating the reconstructed interior and original fittings of an early-18th-century synagogue from Conegliano Veneto near Venice, this museum

collects, preserves and displays objects associated with Jewish life in Italy from the Renaissance period through to the present time. The synagogue was transported across the Mediterranean and rebuilt in the 1950s; it now serves the needs of Jerusalemites who follow the ancient liturgy and rites of Roman Jews. The collection includes textiles, metalwork, illuminated parchments, Torah arks and other Judaica.

Heichal Shlomo   RELIGIOUS SITE
(Map p76; ☎ 02-623 0628; www.hechalshlomo. org.il; 58 King George V St) The seat of the Chief Rabbinate of Israel, this vast complex was designed in the 1950s and styled along the lines of Solomon's Temple – Heichal Shlomo literally means 'Solomon's Mansion'. Check out the semicircular balcony, intended for the use of the Chief Rabbi as he addressed the throngs of believers. The small **museum** (Map p76; ☎ 02-588 9005; adult/student & child 20/15NIS; ⊙ 9am-3pm Sun-Thu) housed inside the massive building features exhibits about religious and traditional Jewish art and life. The **Great Synagogue** (1982), famous for its choir, is next door.

◉ King David (David HaMelekh) Street

The most coveted stretch of real estate outside the Old City lies along King David (David HaMelekh) St, on a hillside west of Jaffa Gate. Dominated by the **King David Hotel**, the area includes parks, gardens and upmarket restaurants. In adjoining **Mamilla**, rows of new luxury apartments – many owned by Jews who live overseas for most of the year – overlook the walls of the Old City. Important landmarks include the Reform Movement's **Hebrew Union College** (Beit Shmuel; Map p76; www.beitshmuel.co.il) complex, part of which was designed by Moshe Safdie (1986), and the 1933 **YMCA** building, designed by Arthur Loomis Harmon, architect of New York's Empire State Building.

Yemin Moshe   NEIGHBOURHOOD
(Map p70) Home to the landmark **Montefiore Windmill**, built in 1875 to provide the basis for a Jewish flour industry, this leafy neighbourhood was part of a scheme developed by English philanthropist Sir Moses Montefiore, who visited the Holy Land seven times in the mid-19th century. Hoping to aid the Jews living in Jerusalem and seeking to ease overcrowding within the city walls, Montefiore commissioned a block of 16

City Centre

Jaffa Center

Ticho St
8

HaRav Agan

HaRav Kook St

Sherut (Service Taxi) for Tel Aviv

Horkanos St

Albokher

Even Yisra'el

13

King George V St

Ya'Avetz St

Luntz

14

HaHavatzelet St

17
35
28
33

Ben Hillel St

27

Dorot Rishonim St

Zion Sq

Jaffa Rd

Ellyshar St

Heleni HaMalka St

24

9

32

10

Herbert Samuel St

23 41

12

39
42

44
26
30

Ben Yehuda St

HaHistadrut St

Shamai St

16

37

NAHALAT SHIV'A

25

Nakhalat Shiv'a

Joseph Rivlin St

Jerusalem Courtyard

Hassoreg St

Beit David

20

Darom

Angelo Bianchini

Hillel St

Beit HaKneset

Yoel Salomon St

40

Shim'on Ben Shatah St

18

5

Rivlin St

22
43

36

7

Hillel St

Shakham

Shakham

Hevo Ha-Matmid

King George V St

Eliezor Rivlin

Meir Sherman Garden

Muslim Cemetery

Mamilla Pool

Gan HaAtsma'ut (Independence Park)

Rabbi Akiva St

Ha-Ma'aravim

King George V St

Agron St

George Eliot

Zamenhof

MAKHNE YISRAEL

Hess

Elkharizi

2

3

4

George Washington

Lincoln

Ramban St

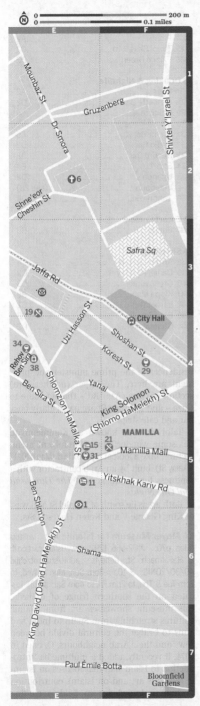

apartments that are today known as Mishkenot Sha'ananim (Tranquil Dwellings).

The flour mill was abandoned after only 18 years, made redundant by new steam-powered alternatives, and its upper portion was dismantled in the late 1940s. A new dome and blades identical to those of the original were added in 2012 (funded by Dutch Christians) and the mill's blades now turn for tourism and educational purposes.

St Andrew's Church CHURCH
(Map p70; 1 David Remez St; ☺ museum 9am-4pm Sun-Thu, to 1pm Fri) Also known as the Scottish Church, St Andrew's was built in 1927 to commemorate the capture of the city and the Holy Land by the British in WWI. The buildings are an intriguing mix of Western and Arabic influences; take note of the exquisite Armenian tiles outside the entrance to the guesthouse and church (these were designed in a workshop on the Via Dolorosa).

The church floor features an inscription to the memory of Robert the Bruce, who requested that his heart be buried in Jerusalem when he died. Sir James Douglas made an attempt at fulfilling Bruce's wish but en route he was killed in Spain, fighting the Moors. The heart was recovered and returned to Scotland, where it's now buried at Melrose.

◉ German Colony

Lounging in a cafe, sipping lattes and reading the *Ha'aretz* newspaper seem to be the main daily activities for residents of Jerusalem's German Colony. Built in the late 19th century by members of a German Protestant sect called the Templers (not to be confused with the Crusader-era Knights Templar), the German colony remains a pleasant, tree-lined neighbourhood of Templer and Arab villas. It has always carried an air of affluence and continues to attract a mix of moneyed locals and tourists. Evenings are a pleasant time to stroll here as there is a range of restaurants and cafes to spend time in.

Buses 4, 18 and 21 travel to Emek Refa'im St from King George V St in the city centre.

First Station HISTORIC BUILDING
(Map p70; ☏ 02-653 5239; www.firststation.co.il; 4 David Remez St; ☺ daily 7am-late) Inspired by European design models, this handsome railway station was built in 1892 as the Jerusalem terminus of the Jaffa–Jerusalem railway line. It was in almost continuous use until 1998, when the line from Tel Aviv

City Centre

⊙ Sights

1 Hebrew Union College	E5
2 Heichal Shlomo	B7
3 Heichal Shlomo Museum	B7
4 Moreshet Yisrael	B7
5 Museum of Italian Jewish Art	C3
6 Russian Compound	E2
7 Time Elevator	D4

⊜ Sleeping

8 7 Kook Boutique Hotel	C1
9 Arthur Hotel	B2
10 City Center Suites	A2
11 David Citadel Hotel	E5
12 Harmony Hotel	C3
13 Hotel Palatin	A1
14 Jerusalem Hostel & Guest House	C2
15 Mamilla Hotel	E5
16 Shamai Suites	B2

⊗ Eating

17 Darna	D2
18 Focaccio Bar	B3
19 Hamarakia	E3
20 Kadosh	D3
21 Mamilla Café & Brasserie	F5
22 Mantra Restaurant & Wine Bar	D3
23 Moshiko	B2
24 Pinati	A2
25 T'mol Shilshom	C2
26 Village Green	D2

⊙ Drinking & Nightlife

27 Bass	A2
28 Cassette Bar	D2
29 Hakatze	F4
30 Mike's Place	D2
31 Mirror Bar	E5
32 Radio Bar	D2
33 Record Bar	D2
34 Sira	E4
35 Uganda	D2
Videopub	(see 28)
36 Zabotinski	D4

⊛ Entertainment

37 Bimot	B3

⊜ Shopping

38 Arman Darian	E4
39 Daniel Azoulay	C2
40 Greenvurcel	C3
41 Kippa Man	B2
42 Lametayel	C2
43 Rina Zin	D3
44 Steimatzky	D2

to Jerusalem closed. Recently restored, it opened in 2013 as a shopping and entertainment complex.

As well as hosting popular restaurants and cafes including Adom and Fresh Kitchen, the station has a juice bar, a branch of the Vaniglia ice cream chain, the Up Stairs bar and a number of shops. It also has a busy entertainment program: daily one-hour yoga sessions are held at 7am from Sunday to Thursday and at 8am on Friday and Saturday (20NIS); there's a farmers market every Friday from 9am; and in summer the land on the northern side of the station is transformed into a sandy 'beach' complete with wave simulator (50NIS per hour).

Check the website for details of events held here. These include outdoor screenings for the Jerusalem Film Festival in July, and plenty of summer concerts.

⊙ Rehavia & Talbiyeh

These enclaves were built in the early 20th century and are among the city's more fashionable places to live – Talbiyeh was built by wealthy Christian Arabs and Rehavia by Jewish intellectuals. These days, the official

residences of the prime minister and president are here. The upper (northeastern) section of Gaza (Aza) Rd – the old route to Gaza – and Ramban St are particularly busy bar and cafe strips.

Talbiyeh, also known as Kommemiyut, has some wonderfully self-indulgent architecture; take a look at **Beit Jalad** (Map p70; 17 Alkalay St), built by an Arab contractor with a fondness for the imagery of *The Thousand and One Nights*.

Both areas lie south of Bezalel St and west of King George V and Keren HaYesod Sts.

LA Mayer Museum for Islamic Art MUSEUM (Map p70; ☏ 02-566 1291; www.islamicart.co.il; 2 HaPalmach St, Rehavia; adult/student/child 40/30/20NIS; ☺10am-3pm Sun, Mon & Wed, to 7pm Tue & Thu, to 2pm Fri, to 4pm Sat; ☐13) Located on the southern fringe of Rehavia, this museum showcases art from Islamic cultures stretching from Spain to India and aims to bridge the cultural divide between Jews and their Arab neighbours. Opened in 1974, it recently added a multimedia 'Introduction to Islam' hall that focuses on Islamic religious art and on Islam's contribution to human knowledge in fields including science, astronomy and medicine. Other exhibits include jewellery, carpets, silver, brassware, glasswork, paintings, clocks and watches.

The museum's world-renowned collection of clocks and watches includes many of the timepieces stolen in 1983 in Israel's most spectacular heist and recovered in France in 2008.

There are guided tours in English upon request (call ahead).

⊙ Talpiot

Haas Promenade
VIEWPOINT

The main reason to venture down to Talpiot is to walk along the garden-fringed Haas Promenade, which offers spectacular views over the Old City. To the east, atop the forested Hill of Evil Council, stand the UN's Jerusalem headquarters, until 1948 the seat of the British high commissioner of Palestine. Take bus 78 from the Central Bus Station and get off on the corner of Daniel Yanovski and HaAskan Sts. Circle Line 99 city bus tours also stop here.

⊙ Givat Ram & Museum Row

The political seat of the Israeli government and two important museums are located in the government and university neighbourhood of Givat Ram, south of the Central Bus Station.

★ Israel Museum
MUSEUM

(☑ 02-670 8811; www.imj.org.il; 11 Ruppin Blvd, Museum Row; adult/student/child 5-17yr 50/37/25NIS; ⊙ 10am-5pm Sun, Mon, Wed, Thu & Sat, 4-9pm Tue, 10am-2pm Fri; ☐ 7, 9, 14, 35, 66) One of Israel's most impressive cultural assets, this splendid museum gives an excellent grounding in the region's 5000 years of history in its huge archaeological wing and has another equally impressive wing concentrating on Jewish art and life. But that's not all – the fine arts wing has a significant collection of international and Israeli art, the museum's grounds feature an art garden, and there's a dedicated pavilion showcasing the museum's prize exhibit, the Dead Sea Scrolls.

Before starting your tour (dedicate at least half a day), be sure to pick up a complimentary audioguide from the visitor centre. If you decide to spend a full day – and many visitors do – the excellent Modern restaurant (p96) serves lunch. There are also two cafes on site.

➧ **Shrine of the Book**

The distinctive lid-shaped roof of this pavilion was designed to symbolise the pots in which the Dead Sea Scrolls were kept. The first of the scrolls, totalling 800 in all, were found in 1947 and date back to the time of the Bar Kochba Revolt (132–35 CE). Dealing with both secular and religious issues, they were thought to have been written by an ascetic group of Jews called the Essenes, who inhabited the area for about 300 years. The most important is the Great Isaiah Scroll, the largest and best preserved – it is reproduced in facsimile at the museum. The exhibit tells the story of the scrolls and the Essenes and displays some of the original documents.

➧ **Archaeology Wing**

There are so many significant pieces in this wing that is hard to single out any in particular. Forming the most extensive collection of biblical and Holy Land archaeology in the world, the exhibits are organised chronologically from prehistory to the Ottoman Empire. A group of 13th-century BCE human-shaped pottery coffins greets visitors in the first room, and other impressive displays include a 3rd-century mosaic floor from Nablus depicting events in the life of Achilles. Also notable is the 'House of David' Victory Stele, a fragmentary inscription from the First Temple period discovered at Tel Dan. This is the only contemporary, extra-biblical reference to the Davidic dynasty to have come to light thus far.

➧ **Jewish Art & Life Wing**

The prize exhibits here are four complete synagogues brought from various locations and reconstructed. One, the 18th-century Vittorio Veneto Synagogue, is adorned with gilt and plaster and was transported from Vittorio Veneto in Italy in 1965. The others are from Cochin in India, Paramaribo in Suriname and Horb am Main in Germany. Also worth seeking out is the painted Deller family sukkah (temporary wooden dwelling erected during the harvest festival of Sukkot), which dates from the 19th century and was smuggled out of Germany to Jerusalem in 1935. The rooms at the rear of the wing focus on Jewish costume and jewellery.

➧ **Fine Arts Wing**

The highlight here is the Impressionist and post-Impressionist Gallery, which showcases work by Renoir, Pissarro, Degas, Sisley, Monet and Cézanne among many others. The Modern Art Gallery has works by Schiele, Rothko, Motherwell, Pollock, Modigliani and Bacon, and Israeli art is well represented in the Israeli Art pavilion, with striking paintings by Reuven Rubin and Yosef Zaritsky.

➡ Art Garden

A paved promenade leads from the Shrine of the Book to this sprawling sculpture garden, which was designed by Japanese artist and landscape architect Isamu Noguchi and includes works by 19th-, 20th- and 21st-century artists including Moore, Kapoor, LeWitt, Oldenburg, Serra, Rodin and Picasso.

Bible Lands Museum MUSEUM
(☑ 02-561 1066; www.blmj.org; 25 Stefan Wise St, Museum Row; adult/student & child 40/20NIS; ☺ 9.30am-5.30pm Sun-Tue & Thu, to 9.30pm Wed, 10am-2pm Fri & Sat; ☐ 7, 9, 14, 35, 66) Exploring the people and civilisations who populate the Bible, this museum displays a wealth of artefacts showing how their different cultures were inter-related. The organisation of the exhibits can be a little confusing, so we recommend taking the free guided tour offered daily between Sunday and Friday at 10.30am (English) and 11am (Hebrew), on Wednesday at 5.30pm (English) and 6pm (Hebrew), and on Saturday at 11.30am (Hebrew only).

The museum was founded by Dr Elie Borowski, a Polish-born academic who fought the Nazis in Germany and later moved to Switzerland, where he became known as a leading dealer of antiquarian art. Borowski founded this museum so that biblical history and the history of the Ancient Near East could be studied, understood and appreciated by peoples of different faiths. The permanent exhibition, which was his private collection of ancient Near Eastern art, spans the period from earliest civilisation to the early Christian era.

Children under 18 are given free entrance on Saturday and Wednesday afternoons.

Knesset LANDMARK
(Map p70; ☑ 02-675 3333; www.knesset.gov. il; Ruppin Blvd, Kiryat Ben Gurion; ☐ 14, 35, 7, 7A) **FREE** Israel's 120 lawmakers convene at the Knesset, a 1966 building belonging to the unfortunate multistorey-car-park school of architecture. Visitors can take a free one-hour guided tour that visits the committee rooms, plenary chamber, Chagall Hall (featuring three tapestries and a mosaic by the great 20th-century Jewish artist) and a display of the Declaration of Independence.

These are conducted on Sunday and Thursday in Hebrew, Arabic, English, French, Spanish, German, Russian and Amharic; check the website for times.

Visitors must have a passport and be modestly dressed (no shorts, sleeveless shirts, T-shirts bearing political slogans, or flip-flops). It's also possible to observe Knesset plenary debates from the public gallery on Monday and Tuesday from 4pm and Wednesday from 11am.

Next to the bus stops opposite the Knesset is a giant bronze menorah, a gift from the British Labour Party in 1956. It's decorated with panels representing important figures and events in Jewish history.

Monastery of the Cross MONASTERY
(Map p70; ☑ 052-221 5144; Rehavia Valley; admission 15NIS; ☺ 10am-4pm Mon-Sat Oct-Mar, to 5pm Apr-Sep; ☐ 14) This fortresslike monastery in the valley below the Israel Museum was founded in the early 4th century CE by King Bagrat of Georgia to commemorate the tradition that Jesus's cross was constructed from a tree that grew here. Bagrat's monastery was destroyed by the Persians in 614, rebuilt in the Crusader era and sold to the Greek Orthodox Church in 1685. The interior features 17th-century frescos, a fragment of 6th-century mosaic floor in the chapel and a small museum.

The monastery can be reached by walking through Rehavia along Ramban St, crossing Hanasi Ben Zvi and following the path down the Valley of the Cross (Emeq HaMatzleva). From the city centre take bus 14 from the Central Bus Station and alight at the stop on Hayim Hazaz Blvd opposite the Rehavia Ben Gurion School, near the major intersection with HaRav Herzog St.

◉ Har Hazikaron

On the far western fringe of the city, between rows of housing blocks and the Jerusalem forest, is an area of wooded slopes and spectacular views known as Har Hazikaron (Mount of Remembrance). It is home to Mt Herzl, a military cemetery, and Yad Vashem, Israel's main memorial to victims of the Holocaust.

★ Yad Vashem MEMORIAL
(☑ 02-644 3802; www.yadvashem.org; Hazikaron St; ☺ 9am-5pm Sun-Wed, to 8pm Thu, to 2pm Fri; ☐ Mt Herzl) **FREE** If there is a more moving and powerful museum experience in the world, we've yet to encounter it. This

memorial to the six million Jews who died at the hands of the Nazis is sobering, of course, but it's also beautiful and uplifting. The museum's name was taken from Isaiah 56:5 and means 'A Memorial and a Name', and one of the highlights is the Hall of Names, where the names and personal details of millions of victims are recorded.

The centrepiece of the museum is the prismlike **Holocaust History Museum** on the lower level, with nine underground galleries telling the story of the Shoah from the Jewish perspective. The triangular design of the building represents the bottom half of a Star of David, because the population of Jews worldwide was almost cut in half as a result of the Holocaust. The galleries trace the story chronologically and thematically, and use artefacts, films, personal testimonies on video, photographs and art installations.

The **Hall of Names** is at one end of the museum and is organised around a hole in the floor that honours those victims whose names will never be known because they, their entire families, all their friends and everyone who had known them was killed, leaving no one to testify or say the Kaddish (Jewish memorial prayer).

Near the exit of the museum is a separate building where the **Museum of Holocaust Art** is located. Nearby there is an **Exhibitions Pavilion** housing temporary displays and a **Synagogue** that visitors can use for private prayer.

In the **Hall of Remembrance** on the ground level an eternal flame burns near a crypt containing ashes of victims brought from the death camps; the floor is inscribed with the names of 22 of the most infamous camps. Behind the hall are a number of other memorials, including the **Cattle Car Memorial**, one of the original train cars used to transport Jews from the ghettos to the camps. Also here is the **Garden of the Righteous Among the Nations**, established in honour of the thousands of non-Jews who risked their lives to rescue Jews during the Holocaust.

Closer to the visitors centre is the extraordinarily beautiful and moving **Children's Memorial**, dedicated to the 1.5 million Jewish children who died in the Holocaust. Dug into the bedrock, the sombre underground memorial contains a solitary flame reflected infinitely by hundreds of mirrors. Recorded voices read the names of children who perished. Be careful as you enter as it takes a while for eyes to adjust to the darkness.

You'll need at least three hours to walk around Yad Vashem, which is spread over 18 pine-scented hectares of the Mount of Remembrance. The JLR Mt Herzl stop is a short walk away; the journey from City Hall takes 15 minutes. When you alight from the tram, cross the road towards the forest and walk for 10 minutes up gently sloping Hazikaron St. Alternatively, wait at the bus stop for the free shuttle, which runs every 20 minutes. The Circle Line 99 city bus tour also stops here.

Note that on Thursday, many of the memorials close at 5pm (the Holocaust History Museum, Museum of Holocaust Art, Exhibitions Pavilion and Synagogue remain open until 8pm).

Herzl Museum   MUSEUM
(☑02-632 1515; www.herzl.org.il; Herzl Blvd; adult/student & child 25/20NIS; ⊙8.30am-5pm Sun-Wed, to 7pm Thu, to 12.15pm Fri; ☐Mt Herzl) The history of the Zionist dream is detailed in the Herzl Museum, a multimedia journey into the life of Theodor Herzl, the father of modern Zionism. A one-hour guided tour in various languages including English tells Herzl's story; advance bookings are essential.

Herzl's quest began in fin de siècle Paris, where the secular, Budapest-born journalist was working as a correspondent for a Vienna newspaper. After witnessing violent outbreaks of anti-Semitism in the wake of the 1894 Dreyfus treason trial, he dedicated himself to the creation of a Jewish state where Jews would not be subject to such hatred. Three years of campaigning culminated in the first World Zionist Congress, held in Basel, Switzerland, in 1897. Herzl continued campaigning over the next seven years, until his death in 1904. His grave, a simple black marker with his name etched upon it, is on a small knoll west of the museum. Nearby are the graves of several Israeli prime ministers and presidents, including Golda Meir, Yitzhak Rabin and Menachem Begin.

A short walk north leads to the military cemetery, or you can continue west down a path that leads to Yad Vashem.

◉ Ein Kerem

Hidden in a valley on Jerusalem's western outskirts is this pretty village of Arab-built stone houses surrounded by Lebanese cedars and native pine trees. The small community is home to several important churches related to John the Baptist, and

CHRISTOPHER CHAN / GETTY IMAGES ©

1. Church of the Holy Sepulchre (p54)
Christianity's holiest site is venerated as the site of
Jesus' crucifixion, burial and resurrection.

2. Mahane Yehuda Market (p73)
Fresh fruit and vegetable stalls abound at this bustling
and increasingly hip market.

3. Israel Museum (p79)
See Dead Sea Scrolls on display in Shrine of the Book
pavilion, designed after the scroll's earthenware pots.

4. Old City (p45)
Roads encircle the Old City walls, illuminating the
Citadel (Tower of David) at night.

3

SHRINE OF THE BOOK BUILDING AT THE ISRAEL MUSEUM, DESIGNED BY ARMAND PHILLIP BARTOS, FREDERICK JOHN KIESLER AND GEZER HELLER / PHOTO CREDIT: HANAN ISACHAR GETTY IMAGES ©

RELIGIOUS SERVICES IN JERUSALEM

Experience a slice of holiness in Jerusalem by attending Shabbat services, Friday prayers or a Sunday-morning church service. Dress modestly.

Shabbat services are typically held on Friday evening shortly after candle lighting (36 minutes before sunset) and on Saturday morning starting between 8.30am and 9.30am (Sephardic and especially Yemenite synagogues may begin earlier). Every Jewish neighbourhood has a variety of synagogues, the vast majority of them Orthodox or ultra-Orthodox. Nahla'ot is famous for the diversity of its scores of tiny houses of prayer, including one that follows the traditions of Aleppo (Syria).

Jerusalem synagogues that aren't traditionally Orthodox include:

Har El (Map p70; ☎ 02-625 3841, ext 201; www.kharel.org.il; 16 Shmuel HaNagid St, City Centre) Israel's first Reform synagogue, founded in 1958.

Kol HaNeshama (☎ 02-672 4878; www.kolhaneshama.org.il; 1 Asher St, Baka) Jerusalem's largest Reform congregation.

Moreshet Yisrael (Map p76; ☎ 02-625 3539; www.moreshetyisrael.com; 4 Agron St, Rechavia) Conservative/Masorti.

Shira Hadasha (☎ 054-817 3101; www.shirahadasha.org.il; 12 Emek Refa'im St, German Colony) Feminist Orthodox.

For details on **church services**, see the Christian information centre website (www.cicts.org) and click the 'Masses and Services' link.

Muslims can join Friday prayers in Al-Aqsa Mosque (p49), providing there are no security restrictions in place; check with the tourist office at Jaffa Gate.

---

the Chagall windows at Hadassah Medical Centre are not too far away. It's busiest on weekends, when Jerusalemites descend on the place for brunch.

The history of the town was rather ordinary until the middle of the 6th century, when Christian pilgrims identified it as the likely home of Elizabeth, mother of John the Baptist. Inevitably, shrines and churches were built over holy sites. The 1948 Arab–Israeli War caused the local Arab residents to flee the town; their homes were later taken over by immigrants from Morocco and Romania. A growing student population has breathed new life into the community.

To reach the village, take bus 28 from Central Bus Station or Mt Herzl.

Church of St John the Baptist　　CHURCH
(☎ 02-632 3000; ⊕ 9am-noon & 2.30-5.45pm Apr-Sep, to 4.45pm Oct-Mar) The blue-and-white interior of the Franciscan-owned Church of St John is reminiscent of European churches – not surprising, as it was funded and built by the Spanish monarchy in 1674. The paintings are by Spanish artists and there is a royal coat of arms above the entrance. Towards the front of the church is the grotto where it is believed John the Baptist came into the world (Luke 1:5-25, 57-80); a small marble circle under the altar marks the spot.

The church is located on the street to the right of the main road.

Church of the Visitation　　CHURCH
(⊕ 8-11.45am & 2.30-5pm Oct-Mar, to 6pm Apr-Sep) This modern church is built over what is said to have been the home of Zacharias and Elizabeth, and is named in remembrance of Mary's visit to Elizabeth (Luke 1:39-49). The prayer that Mary is said to have uttered ('My soul exalts the Lord'; Luke 1:46-56) is inscribed on the walls in 41 languages.

From the main intersection in Ein Kerem, walk along the narrow road that heads south and the church will appear on the left after about 10 minutes.

Chagall Windows　　SYNAGOGUE
(☎ 02-677 6271; www.hadassah-med.com; ⊕ 8am-3.30pm Sun-Thu) **FREE** The Hadassah Medical Centre, Ein Kerem (not to be confused with the Hadassah-Mt Scopus Medical Centre across town), is known internationally for its synagogue featuring stained-glass windows by Marc Chagall. Each of the 12 colourful abstract panels depicts one of the tribes of Israel, based on Genesis 49 and Deuteronomy 33.

To get here, take the tram from the Central Bus Station and get off at the last stop (Mt Herzl), where you can transfer to bus 27.

This will bring you to the hospital. You can also walk up here from Ein Kerem.

Courses

Ulpan Or   LANGUAGE COURSE
(☑02-561 1132; www.ulpanor.com; 2nd fl, 43a Emek Rafa'im St, German Colony) This ulpan (Hebrew-language school) claims that its students learn 'at the speed of light' through rapid immersion programs. Indeed, it says that after a 90-minute one-on-one 'Cup O'Hebrew' session (US$402), which is conducted over coffee, you will have acquired basic speaking-Hebrew skills. Based in the German Colony, it also offers one-week (US$1570) and two-week (US$2648) immersion programs.

Ulpan Beit Ha'Am   LANGUAGE COURSE
(☑02-624-0034, 02-545-6891, Hadassah 052-831 3949; Gerard Behar Center, 11 Bezalel St; 2/3/5 days a week per month 394/613/920NIS; ⊘8am-12.30pm Sun-Thu) Run by the Jerusalem municipality, this city-centre program offers rolling admission to its Hebrew classes.

Hebrew University Ulpan   LANGUAGE COURSE
(☑02-588 2600; https://overseas.huji.ac.il/heb programs; Boyar Bldg, Hebrew University of Jerusalem, Mt Scopus; 100/140/200 academic hours US$1270/1640/2250) Offers intensive Hebrew, spoken Palestinian Arabic and Modern Standard Arabic classes, especially over the summer (late June to late September). The approach is more academic than in non-university ulpans.

Ulpan Etzion   LANGUAGE COURSE
(☑02-636-7310, 02-636 7326; www.jewishagency. org/ulpan-etzion; 27 David Raziel St) Founded in 1949, Israel's first ulpan offers Hebrew study to university graduates aged 22 to 35. Five-month courses begin in January and July.

**Al-Quds Centre
for Jerusalem Studies**   LANGUAGE COURSE
(Map p46; ☑02-628 7517; www.jerusalem-studies. alquds.edu; Souq al-Qattanin, Muslim Quarter, Old City) Morning classes at this institute are held in the hugely atmospheric venue of the Al-Quds University in the Souq al-Qattanin. The centre offers 80-hour courses (4180NIS) in spoken Arabic and Modern Standard Arabic for those at beginner, intermediate and advanced levels.

☞ Tours

The municipality's website (www.itravel jerusalem.com) offers free maps and apps for 15 self-guided audio walking tours of the Old City. Four tours in the Jewish quarter are accessible for visitors in wheelchairs. To find the apps on the website go to Old City Jerusalem Essence/Old City Sites and Tours/Audio Walking Tours. The tours are in English, Russian and Hebrew and are available for download to both Apple and android devices.

Note that the tour guides offering their services outside the Jaffa Gate Tourist Office are usually unlicensed; if you need a guide, ask the tourist office to organise one for you. This will cost US$200 to US$300 per half day.

Jerusalem-based **Abraham Tours** (☑02-566 0045; www.abrahamtours.com; 67 HaNevi'im St), affiliated with the hostel of the same name, offers day tours into the West Bank; to Caesarea, Nazareth and Tiberias; and to the Dead Sea. It also runs trips to Petra and Wadi Rum in Jordan.

★**Sandemans
New Jerusalem Tours**   WALKING TOUR
(☑052-346 4479; www.newjerusalemtours.com; 67 Hanevi'im St) FREE Sandemans' free daily tours are an excellent introduction to the Old City and are warmly recommended (tips are appreciated – 50NIS per person is appropriate). Try to join one on your first day in the city so as to get your bearings; bookings aren't necessary. Tours start at Jaffa Gate at 9am, noon and 3pm daily. Look for the guides in red T-shirts.

The company also offers in-depth charged tours of the Old City and Mount of Olives – see the website for details.

Note that a slightly dodgy alternative outfit is also offering free tours from Jaffa Gate. Don't believe their shtick about free entry to monuments (none of the monuments they visit charge for entry). These guides wear orange T-shirts.

Free Saturday Tours   WALKING TOUR
(☑02-531 4600; www.itraveljerusalem.com; ⊘10am-1pm Sat) FREE Offered by the municipality, these three-hour tours start from Safra Sq (26 Jaffa St), near the palm trees. They are given by licensed guides and are usually conducted in English. Some tours visit the Mount of Olives, others tour areas including the Old City's Muslim Quarter and Mt Zion. See the website (explore/Israel tours) for details.

Green Olive Tours   WALKING TOUR
(☑03-721 9540; www.greenolivetours.com) This well-regarded company has Israeli and Arab owners and offers a daily walking

tour of the Old City (three hours, 130NIS), a twice-weekly walking and light-rail tour of West Jerusalem including Yad Vashem (three hours, 260NIS) and a twice-weekly walking tour of East Jerusalem (three hours, 140NIS). It also runs a number of tours into the West Bank.

City Bus Tour　　　　　　　BUS TOUR
(☎050-842 2473; www.citytourjerusalem.com; 2hr nonstop tour adult/child 60/48NIS, hop-on hop-off day tour 80/68NIS) This open-air coach service (aka Circle Line 99) cruises past many major sights, providing commentary in eight languages along the way. Stops include Herod's Gate (opposite the Rockefeller Museum), Dung Gate (City of David), Mt Zion, Jaffa Gate (the Citadel), Haas Promenade, the Zoo, Yad Vashem, the Israel Museum/ Bible Lands Museum and the Knesset.

There are four buses daily between Sunday and Thursday departing from the Central Bus Station at 9am, 11am, 1.30pm and 3.45pm. On Friday, buses depart at 9am, 11am and 1.30pm. Passengers can board the bus at any of the stops. See the website for a route map and schedule.

Festivals & Events

Israel Festival　　　　　　　CULTURAL
(http://israel-festival.org/) Music, dance and theatre performances by Israeli and inter-national artists over a three-week period stretching from late May to mid-June.

★ **Lights in Jerusalem**　　　　　ART
(www.lights-in-jerusalem.com) Features light shows, 3D light installations and huge video projections on streets and landmark buildings in the Old City and on the Old City walls; held throughout the month of July.

Jerusalem Film Festival　　　　FILM
(www.jff.org.il) One of the largest film festivals in the Middle East. Screenings are held in July in indoor and outdoor venues.

Jerusalem Beer Festival　　　　BEER
(www.jerusalembeer.com) Over 150 local and international beers are poured in Gan HaAtsma'ut (Independence Park) in Mamilla during August.

Jerusalem Wine Festival　　　　WINE
Held over four evenings in August, this festival in the garden of the Israel Museum is probably the most important Israeli wine event of the year.

Jerusalem Sacred Music Festival　　MUSIC
(www.jerusalemseason.com) Musical performances by pilgrims from around the world over four days in September. The festival includes an all-night performance in the Citadel.

JERUSALEM FOR CHILDREN

Spare your kids the agony of visiting another religious site and instead let them loose in the excellent **Zoological Gardens in Jerusalem** (Jerusalem Biblical Zoo; ☎02-675 0111; www.jerusalemzoo.org.il; 1 Derech Aharon Shulov; adult/child 50/40NIS; ⊙9am-6pm Sun-Thu, to 4.30pm Fri, 10am-6pm Sat), a 25-hectare park in the southwest of the city. The zoo focuses on animals from the land of Israel, with special emphasis on those species mentioned in the Bible. Another section displays endangered animals from other parts of the world. The best way to reach the zoo is to take the light rail to Mt Herzl, where you can pick up bus 33 to the zoo.

Kids also love the **Bloomfield Science Museum** (☎02-654 4888; www.mada.org.il; Hebrew University, Ruppin Blvd; admission 79NIS, under 5yr free; ⊙9am-6pm Sat-Wed, 4-8pm Thu, 10am-4pm Fri; ☐9, 14), a hands-on experience with loads of activities and introductory science exhibits. It's a 25- to 30-minute walk from the city centre and a 10-minute walk from the Israel Museum. Bus 9 travels here from the Central Bus Station.

Another possible diversion for children aged over five is the **Time Elevator** (Map p76; ☎02-624 8381; www.time-elevator-jerusalem.co.il; Beit Agron, 37 Hillel St; admission 54NIS, internet bookings 46NIS; ⊙10am-5pm Sun-Thu, to 2pm Fri, noon-6pm Sat; ☐Jaffa Center), an interactive cinema experience that involves motion-based seating, panoramic screens and special effects that are synchronised to the action of the film. It's best to book in advance.

The City of David (p66) is popular with older kids, as they enjoy wading through its spooky, water-filled Hezekiah's Tunnel. In the Old City, there is a good playground for small children a few steps north of Hurva Sq (tucked into a courtyard, behind the Broad Wall).

Jerusalem International Oud Festival
MUSIC

(www.confederationhouse.org) International and Israeli performers showcase the oud in this nine-day festival in early November. It's organised by the Confederation House Centre for Ethnic Music and Poetry and held in venues around town.

🛏 Sleeping

Most budget accommodation is located in the Old City's Muslim, Christian and Armenian Quarters or in the city centre. Decent midrange options are thin on the ground, but there are plenty of choices in the top-end category, including atmospheric Christian hospices in the Old City and boutique hotels in the city centre. There are no hotels or guesthouses of note in the Old City's Jewish Quarter.

If you want atmosphere, by all means stay in the Old City. But if you are after proximity to restaurants, bars, cafes and public transport, you are much better off staying in the city centre, Mamilla or Yemin Moshe. If you have a car you'll need to stay in the New City or pay 48NIS per 24 hours for a space at Mamilla Parking (p102) near Jaffa Gate.

Room rates can fluctuate wildly between seasons and in response to political disturbances. We have quoted high-season rates in our reviews; these apply from April to June and from September to October, as well as during Easter, Christmas and the New Year.

🛏 Old City

If you arrive in Jerusalem by taxi or sherut and are staying in the Old City, you'll need to alight at one of the city gates and walk to your hotel.

Note that the call to prayer can be a problem for light sleepers in the Muslim Quarter – bring earplugs.

Hashimi Hotel & Hostel
HOSTEL $

(Map p46; ☑02-628 4410; www.alhashimihotel-jerusalem.com; 73 Souq Khan al-Zeit St, Muslim Quarter; dm/s/d US$35/60/95; ✳@🛜) Slap bang in the middle of the souq, this Palestinian-owned hostel imposes a number of rules on its guests (no alcohol, no unmarried couples in the same room, no credit cards, no mixed dorms), but all is forgiven when the newly renovated rooms are inspected and the extraordinary view from the rooftop is admired.

Some of the rooms have views of the Dome of the Rock (request 313 or 311). Each of the two dorms has air-con, private bathroom and TV; the one on the 3rd floor has a view. Wi-fi is available in the lobby and on the 4th floor only.

Jaffa Gate Hostel
GUESTHOUSE $

(Map p46; ☑02-627 6402; www.jaffa-gate.hostel.com; Jaffa Gate; dm 100NIS, s/d 250/320NIS, with shared bathroom 200/280NIS; ✳@🛜) Arab-run, this small and friendly hostel has one dorm (sleeping four) and 23 small and very basic rooms. There's a lounge, a small roof terrace with wonderful views and a communal kitchen. Note that Muslim house rules prevent alcohol on the premises, breakfast isn't served and credit-card payments aren't possible.

Golden Gate Inn
GUESTHOUSE $

(Map p46; ☑02-628 4317; www.goldengate4.com; 10 Souq Khan al-Zeit St, Muslim Quarter; dm/d/tr 80/250/350NIS; ✳🛜) Set inside an atmospheric old home, this family-run guesthouse near Damascus Gate has single-sex dorms and clean rooms with en-suite bathroom, cable TV and air-con. The communal kitchen is spacious and well maintained, and there's a rooftop with views. Note that wi-fi only works in the lobby and alcohol is forbidden on the premises.

Citadel Youth Hostel
HOSTEL $

(Map p46; ☑02-628 5253; www.citadelyouthhostel.com; 20 St Mark's Rd, Armenian Quarter; mattresses on roof 55NIS, dm 70NIS, d 320NIS, s/d with shared bathroom 180/200NIS; @🛜) A perfect example of a hostel with unrealised potential, the Citadel is only worth considering if the Abraham, Hashimi and Jaffa Gate Hostels are full. A labyrinthine 500-year-old building with plenty of jerry-built additions, it offers thin foam mattresses on the rooftop in summer, old mattresses on the dorm beds, cramped and smelly shared bathrooms and overpriced private rooms.

Petra Hostel
HOSTEL $

(Map p46; ☑02-628 6618; www.newpetrahostel.com; Omar ibn al-Khattab Sq, Jaffa Gate; mattress on roof 50NIS, dm 70NIS, s/d 220/320NIS; 🛜) Built in the 1820s, this is the oldest hotel in Jerusalem. Some of its illustrious former patrons include Mark Twain and Herman Melville. Unfortunately, the antiquated charm counts for little when the hot, stuffy and grubby rooms and dorms are taken into account. Only worth considering if you're on a very tight budget and don't mind roughing it.

★**Austrian Hospice** GUESTHOUSE $$
(Map p46; ☑02-626 5800; www.austrianhospice.
com; 37 Via Dolorosa, Muslim Quarter; dm/s/d/tr
€26/76/118/165; @ 🤶) This castlelike guest-
house first opened in 1863 and has plenty
of heritage features. Rooms are simply furn-
ished but are large and have good beds;
three have a balcony and two have air-con
(€5 surcharge). Single-sex dorms are in the
basement, where there are also squeaky-
clean shared bathrooms. The cloistered
garden cafe is a popular retreat for guests.

The hospice is on the corner of Al-Wad
St and Via Dolorosa. Ring the intercom to
enter (reception is open 7am to 11pm).

★**Lutheran Guest House** GUESTHOUSE $$
(Map p46; ☑02-626 6888; www.luth-guest-
house-jerusalem.com; St Mark's Rd, Armenian
Quarter; s/d/tr €; ❄🤶) Beyond the heavy
steel door are a welcoming lobby, a variety
of rooms, a courtyard garden and rooftop
reading room and a lounge. Guest rooms
are simply furnished but comfortable, and
there's a generous buffet breakfast. From
Jaffa Gate, walk down David St, then take
the first right up a narrow staircase; the
guesthouse is 100m down on the left.

Ecce Homo Pilgrim House GUESTHOUSE $$
(Map p46; ☑02-627 7292; reservation@ecce
homoconvent.org; 41 Via Dolorosa, Muslim Quarter;
dm/s/tw US$35/63/106; 🤶) If staying a few
nights in a convent sounds intriguing, book
yourself into this 150-year-old pilgrim guest-
house on the Via Dolorosa. The stone walls
and dim corridors certainly evoke the feel-
ing of a time gone by, and the rooftop terrace
and comfortable reading lounge are lovely.
Rooms are simply furnished and can be hot
(no air-con). There's a curfew.

Hotel East New Imperial GUESTHOUSE $$
(Map p46; ☑02-628 2261; www.newimperial.com;
Jaffa Gate; s/d US$70/120; @ 🤶) Owner Abu
el-Walid Dajani provides a warm welcome
to his family's hotel (they've owned it since
1949) and can spin some nice stories about
its history. The labyrinthine layout can be
confusing and rooms are of varying quality;
ask for a newly renovated one overlooking
the side street, as the others aren't great. A
four-course dinner costs US$20.

Armenian Guesthouse B&B $$
(Map p46; ☑02-626 0880; armenianguesthouse@
hotmail.com; 36 Via Dolorosa, Muslim Quarter; dm
US$39, s US$97, d US$136; ❄🤶) Recent reno-
vations and reasonably priced rooms make
this guesthouse in the Armenian Catholic
Patriarchate worth considering. There's no
garden and no atmospheric common areas
(the things that make the guesthouses run by
other religious orders in the city so special),
but the very clean rooms are modern with
good bathrooms and comfortable beds.

★**Christ Church
Guesthouse** GUESTHOUSE $$$
(Map p46; ☑02-627 7727; www.cmj-israel.org;
Omar ibn al-Khattab Sq, Jaffa Gate; s US$128, d
US$194; ❄@🤶) This wonderfully main-
tained guesthouse gets high marks for its
period atmosphere, multilingual staff, prime
location and garden setting. The simply
furnished rooms have stone floors, domed
ceilings and comfortable beds, and there
are lounges where guests can relax over free
tea and coffee. Breakfast (included), lunch
(20NIS to 60NIS) and dinner (65NIS) are
served in the on-site cafe.

🛏 East Jerusalem

The area immediately east of the Old City's
Damascus Gate is predominantly Palestinian and has a pronounced Middle Eastern
vibe – street traders hawk their wares to
housewives wearing hijab, Arabic music
blares from cars, and shopfronts and streets
are decidedly less manicured than their
often-staid West Jerusalem equivalents.
There is a mix of Arab- and multinational-
owned hotels here, but few are worthy of
recommendation. The Damascus Gate, Shiv-
tel Israel and Shimon HaTzadik JLR stops
are close by.

★**American Colony Hotel** HISTORIC HOTEL $$$
(Map p70; ☑02-627 9777; www.americancolony.
com; 1 Louis Vincent St; s US$265, d US$310-640,
ste US$675-955; ❄@🤶🏊) This historic ho-
tel, built in 1902 and now Swiss-run, was a
popular lodging for wealthy Westerners in
the early 20th century and is still is a des-
tination of choice for many VIPs. There's a
variety of rooms spread across three wings;
all are elegant and comfortable, but those in
the original building are definitely the best.
The breakfast buffet is excellent.

The facilities here include a pool, a well-
equipped gym, a courtyard cafe, a lobby
lounge, a cellar bar and a garden.

Jerusalem Hotel BOUTIQUE HOTEL $$$
(Map p70; ☑02-628 8982, 02-628 3282; www.
jrshotel.com; Derekh Shchem (Nablus) Rd; s/d
US$160/240; ❄@🤶; 🚌 Shivtei Israel) With tile-

clad stone walls, high ceilings and antique furnishings, this small and friendly hotel in an 1890s building opposite one of the East Jerusalem bus stations can rightfully claim boutique status. The vine-covered courtyard restaurant is a lovely spot for dinner in warm weather.

St George's Guesthouse
GUESTHOUSE $$$
(Map p70; ☑02-628 3302; stgeorges.gh@j-dio cese.org; 20 Derekh Shchem (Nablus) Rd; standard s/d US$110/150, deluxe s/d US$150/180; ✳@ 🛜; 🛗Shivtei Israel) Located on the property of a 110-year-old Anglican church, this tranquil guesthouse has twin guest rooms set around a lovely courtyard garden. Amenities are good – each room has beds with crisp linen, satellite TV and a kettle; the deluxe versions with their stone walls, extra space and modernised bathrooms are worth the extra charge.

Legacy Hotel
HOTEL $$$
(Map p70; ☑02-627 0800; www.jerusalemlegacy. com; 29 Derekh Shchem (Nablus) Rd; royal s/d US$150/185, executive s/d US$175/195; ✳@ 🛜; 🛗Shivtei Israel) After changing its name and having a major facelift, the former YMCA hostel in East Jerusalem is looking pretty snazzy. There are two types of room (deluxe and standard), both of which have kettles and cable TV. It's worth paying extra for a deluxe version as these have larger bathrooms and balconies with views over the Mount of Olives.

Facilities include a 5th-floor restaurant with great views over the Old City, a lobby bar and a garden cafe. Guests are given free entry to the YMCA gym and indoor pool in the building next door.

National Hotel
HOTEL $$$
(Map p70; ☑02-627 8880; www.nationalhotel-jeru salem.com; As-Zahra St; s/d/tr US$170/200/270; ✳🛜; 🛗Shivtei Israel) It wouldn't win any awards for its design, but this modern hotel near Herod's Gate has a number of things working in its favour, including good service, free parking and an on-site restaurant with views over the Mount of Olives (no alcohol, though). Wi-fi is available in the lobby only.

🛏 City Centre

The commercial heart of predominantly Jewish West Jerusalem, this area is full of sleeping, eating and drinking options but almost totally closes down over Shabbat.

The JLR travels down the city centre's spine, Jaffa Rd, and both the Old City and the Central Bus Station are within walking distance.

★ Abraham Hostel
HOSTEL $
(Map p70; ☑02-650 2200; https://abrahamhos tels.com; 67 HaNevi'im St, Davidka Sq; dm 114NIS, s 300NIS, d 480NIS; ✳@ 🛜; 🛗Ha-Davidka) Put simply, the Abraham is an exemplar for hostels everywhere. The best backpacker option in the city (none of the others come close), it's conveniently located next to the Davidka tram stop, its en-suite rooms are basic but clean, the convivial lounge-bar has an attached communal kitchen and – best of all – there's a huge entertainment and tours program.

Try to be here on Shabbat, when the hostel holds a dinner for up to 40 people (40NIS). You should also take advantage of the free Hebrew and Arabic lessons, enjoy happy hour (6pm to 8pm) at the bar and sign up for at least one tour. The entrance is on HaNevi'im St, near the bus stop.

Jerusalem Hostel & Guest House
HOSTEL $
(Map p76; ☑02-623 6102; www.jerusalem -hostel.com; 44 Jaffa Rd, Zion Sq; dm 90NIS, s 220-340NIS, d 270-360NIS; ✳@ 🛜; 🛗Jaffa Center) A fine option for budget travellers keen to base themselves in the city centre, this hostel offers clean en-suite rooms, single-sex dorms, a communal kitchen and a rooftop. There's a healthy traveller vibe, with lots of info tacked onto the walls and plenty of other guests willing to lend free advice.

In addition to the main backpacker wing the hostel has a new section in a separate building with private rooms (300NIS).

City Center Suites
APARTMENT $$
(Map p76; ☑02-650 9494; www.citycenter vacation.com; 17 King George St (cnr HaHistadrut St); d US$130-150, ste US$165-190, economy studio s/d without breakfast US$110/130; @🛜; 🛗Jaffa Center) 'Plenty of character, but looking a bit worn' is a common descriptor for accommodation in this ancient city. And that's why the existence of this spick-and-span modern hotel should be wholeheartedly celebrated. Spread over two buildings in a conveniently located part of the New City, it offers 38 comfortable rooms with kitchenette; the economy studio is the least impressive.

The same owners operate the equally impressive Shamai Suites (Map p76; ☑02-579 7705; www.shamaisuites.com; 15 Ben Hillel St; studio r US$140-160, ste US$200-220; ✳🛜; 🛗Jaffa Center).

JERUSALEM SLEEPING

Hotel Palatin   HOTEL $$
(Map p76; ✆02-623 1141; www.palatinhotel.com;
4 Agrippas St; s US$110, d US$155; 🏵🐾; 🚇Jaffa
Center) Located near the hub of Jerusalem's
shopping and cafe district, the Palatin has
small but reasonably comfortable rooms
that are overpriced at the rack rates cited
above but can be found at much better
prices on booking sites. The friendly service
almost (but not quite) compensates for the
polyester sheets.

★**Arthur Hotel**   BOUTIQUE HOTEL $$$
(Map p76; ✆02-623 9999; www.atlas.co.il; 13 Dor-
ot Rishonim St; s/d US$275/325; 🏵@🐾; 🚇Jaffa
Center) There are plenty of small hotels in
Jerusalem, but few are as well run as this
classy place near Zion Sq. Rooms come in
many shapes and sizes, but the best are
those at the rear of the building (ask for one
with a balcony). The breakfast here is impressive, and the complimentary afternoon
aperitivo is a hit with guests.

7 Kook Boutique Hotel   BOUTIQUE HOTEL $$$
(Map p76; ✆02-580 8068; www.7kookhotel.com;
Ticho St; d US$240-380, s without breakfast US$216-
342; 🏵🐾; 🚇Jaffa Center) There aren't too
many boutique hotels in Jerusalem, so the
2014 opening of this well-located example
of the genre was a welcome occurrence. Part
of an upmarket apartment development, 7
Kook offers four stylish room types – studio,
deluxe, family and suite – all of which have
comfortable bed, excellent bathroom with
tub, espresso machine and kettle.

Harmony Hotel   HOTEL $$$
(Map p76; ✆02-621 9999; www.atlas.co.il; 6 Yo'el
Salomon St; s/d US$275/325; 🏵@🐾; 🚇Jaffa
Center) A spacious lounge with pool table,
books and a fireplace is the major draw at
this well-run hotel near Zion Sq, especially
during the free afternoon *aperitivo*. There
are 50 rooms in total; those on the 1st floor
are new and the others are being renovated
(opt for a corner one if possible). Free parking is available.

Notre Dame Guest House   GUESTHOUSE $$$
(Map p46; ✆02-627 9111; www.notredamecenter.
org; 3 Paratroopers Rd; d & tw US$240-290, tr
US$290, ste US$450-550; 🏵🐾; 🚇City Hall)
Most of the rooms at this splendidly located
Vatican-owned guesthouse have wonder-
ful views of the Old City and the Mount of
Olives. The building dates from 1904 and
its recently refurbished rooms are a great
choice, especially as the guesthouse also has

a Mediterranean restaurant with a garden
terrace downstairs, and a cheese and wine
restaurant (p94) on the rooftop.

🛏 Mamilla & Yemin Moshe

St Andrew's Scottish
Guesthouse   GUESTHOUSE $$
(Map p70; ✆02-673 2401; www.scotsguesthouse.
com; 1 David Remez St, Yemin Moshe; s US$135,
d US$180, tw US$200, ste US$240, apt US$380;
@🐾) St Andrew's feels like a bit of Scotland
transported to the Middle East. Set on a hill
overlooking the Old City, with leafy gardens
and an imposing stone facade, it has simple
rooms and one two-bedroom apartment
sleeping four. The more expensive rooms
include balconies with a view; those that
don't have access to a large sun deck. All
have kettles.

Mamilla Hotel   HOTEL $$$
(Map p76; ✆02-548 2222; www.mamillahotel.com;
11 King Solomon (Shloma HaMelekh) St, Mamilla; r
US$510-635, ste US$785; 🏵@🐾🏊; 🚇City Hall)
The best location in Jerusalem (near Jaffa
Gate, on the edge of the Old and New Cities)
is but one of many inducements on offer at
this luxury hip hotel. Rooms are large and
well equipped, and leisure facilities include
spa with steam room and hamam, gym, in-
door pool, two bars, cafe and rooftop Italian
restaurant.

David Citadel Hotel   HOTEL $$$
(Map p76; ✆02-621 1111; www.thedavidcitadel.
com; 7 King David (David HaMelekh) St, Mamilla;
r US$510-634, ste US$1000; 🚇City Hall) Like
airports, some large hotels are microcities,
populated with different people, housing,
businesses and leisure facilities. The 400-
room David Citadel fits this description,
providing a city within a city for its pam-
pered guests. Rooms are spacious and
beautifully appointed (the suites are knock-
outs), there are three restaurants, and facilities include executive lounge, outdoor pool,
children's play centre, spa and gym.

YMCA Three Arches Hotel   HOTEL $$$
(Map p70; ✆02-569 2692; www.ymca3arch.
co.il; 26 King David St, Yemin Moshe; s/tw/tr/ste
US$200/220/250/290; 🏵@🐾🏊) This 1933
building is an important local landmark
and a decent place to spend a few nights.
The hotel's 56 rooms are simply furnished
and could be cleaner; all have twin beds and
cable TV. There's an on-site restaurant, a
gym and a pool.

JERUSALEM, SHABBAT & YOU

Thirty-six minutes before sunset on Friday you can hear the drone of a siren bellowing over the Jerusalem hills. This signifies the start of Shabbat and with it comes a pronounced spiritual vibe that permeates the streets. All across the city you can see Jewish Jerusalemites dressed in their Shabbat best, drawn to the Western Wall or carrying backpacks full of food as they head to the home of a friend or relative for the customary Friday-night dinner.

Put on the best clothes you've got and follow the crowds down to the Western Wall to marvel at the singing, dancing and prayer that ignite this magical place. Alternatively, visit a synagogue for Friday-night Kabbalat Shabbat services.

If given the opportunity, be sure to join a local family for their Shabbat meal. If you're staying at the Abraham Hostel (p89) in the city centre, you can join its Shabbat dinner. Otherwise, you'll need to scope out a restaurant ahead of time as most restaurants in West Jerusalem close on Friday night. Those that stay open include Rossini's Restaurant (p92) and the Armenian Tavern (p93) in the Old City, Le Petit Levant (p93) in East Jerusalem, Adom (p95) in the German Colony, and Focaccio Bar (p94), Mantra Restaurant & Wine Bar (p95) and the Notre Dame Cheese & Wine Restaurant (p94) in the city centre. Later in the evening, much to the chagrin of ultra-Orthodox Jews, many of the bars in the city centre will be open for business.

While the city centre and the Jewish Quarter of the Old City are closed on Saturday, this is just another day for Jerusalem's Arab population, and most of the sights are open in the rest of the Old City, Mt Zion, the Mount of Olives and East Jerusalem.

On Saturday, you can join two free walking tours: the three-hour walking tour (p85) offered by the municipality and the Sandemans tour of the Old City (p85).

There are no services on Egged buses and the light rail system on Shabbat, but some taxis continue to operate. The Arab bus network and service taxis operate from the Damascus Gate area, and Shabbat is as good a time as any to visit a West Bank city such as Jericho or Bethlehem. Ein Gedi, Masada and the Dead Sea are other popular day-trip options – all-inclusive tours are offered by tour operators and hostels in the city.

German Colony & Rehavia

Little House in Rehavia
HOTEL $$$

(Map p70; ☑02-563 3344; www.jerusalem-hotel.co.il; 20 Ibn Ezra St, Rehavia; s 450NIS; d 600-690NIS; ❋⊛) There's a boutique feel to this hotel in a restored 1942 stone building. Located in one of Jerusalem's prettiest neighbourhoods (a 1.5km walk to the Old City), it has 28 rooms, a roof terrace, a garden and a strictly kosher dining room where a daily breakfast and Shabbat lunch and dinner are served.

Arcadia Ba'Moshava
HOTEL $$$

(☑02-542 3000; www.arcadiahotels.co.il; 13 Yehoshua bin Nun St; s/d midweek US$240/270, weekend US$270/300; ❋⊛⊛; ☒4, 18, 21) Opened in 2014 after a major restoration, this hotel occupies a gorgeous Arab-style villa dating from 1935. 'Ba'Moshava' means 'in the Colony' and its location in a residential street off the Emek Refa'im shopping and entertainment strip is excellent. Rooms are smallish, but that won't matter, as you'll spend most of your time in the elegant lounge or leafy garden.

The hotel provides bikes for the use of its guests.

Jerusalem Garden Home
B&B $$$

(☑050 524 0442; www.jerusalemgardenhome.com; 74 Derech Beit Lehem; s/d/tr US$140/185/210; ❋⊛; ☒43, 71-75) Run by a friendly couple, this B&B near the German Colony has a real home-away-from-home feel. It offers four rooms sleeping between two and four persons; each has a kitchenette and cable TV. The same owners operate a garden restaurant across the road, where breakfast is served.

Romema & Mekor Baruch

Allenby 2 B&B
B&B $

(☑052 396 3160; www.dahliaandnirbnb.com/ALLENBY-2; Allenby Sq 2, Romema; s 180NIS, d 330NIS, d with shared bathroom 250NIS; ❋⊛⊛; ☒Central Station) One of the most popular B&Bs in Jerusalem, Allenby 2 combines a warm and convivial atmosphere with excellent service. With 11 rooms spread over a few properties, it's also one of the larger B&Bs in the city. The shared kitchen and location close to the Central Bus Station and JLR line are definite draws. There's no reception, so call ahead.

Eating

✗ Old City

Most Old City restaurants stick to hummus, kebabs, shwarma and other Middle Eastern fare. The only exceptions are around Jaffa Gate, where there are a few Mediterranean-style places, and in Hurva Sq in the Jewish Quarter, where there are American-style fast-food joints. Finding a meal after dark can be challenging, as the Old City shuts down when the crowds go home.

Note that many places in the Muslim Quarter close during Ramadan.

★**Abu Shukri**   MIDDLE EASTERN $
(Map p46; ☑02-627 1538; 63 Al-Wad St, Muslim Quarter; hummus 20NIS; ☺9am-4pm; ✗) After the best hummus in the Old City? This local favourite gets our vote. The standard platter includes a bowl of fresh hummus with your choice of topping (chickpea, tahina, fuul or pine nuts), some pickles and a basket of pita bread. We recommend adding a side order of felafel (10NIS) and glass of freshly squeezed juice (10NIS).

Head inside to find a table – there are three dining areas.

★**Zalatimo**   SWEETS $
(Map p46; Souq Khan al-Zeit St, Muslim Quarter; mutabbaq 14NIS; ☺hours vary) The Old City is home to many treasures: churches, mosques, synagogues and this pastry shop. Hidden in an arched vault underneath the Ethiopian Monastery, it is famous for its *mutabbaq* (filo pastry stuffed with clarified butter, cinnamon and walnuts or with unsalted sheep's cheese, baked in the oven until crisp and then drizzled with sugar syrup and rose water).

There is no shop sign, so look for the grey metal door halfway up the stairs (behind the juice stand). The owners keep erratic hours, so you may need to try a few times before you find it open.

Lina Restaurant   MIDDLE EASTERN $
(Map p46; ☑02-627 7230; Aqabat al-Khanqah St, Muslim Quarter; hummus 18-23NIS; ☺9am-5pm) A

good place to recover after battling the crowds at the nearby Church of the Holy Sepulchre, Lina has two dining rooms on opposite sides of the street, both of which serve good hummus, jugs of fresh juice (29NIS) and glasses of sweet mint tea (7NIS). The branch closest to Souq Khan al-Zeit St is air-conditioned and has a squeaky-clean toilet.

Ja'far Sweets   SWEETS $
(Map p46; www.jafargroup.com; 40-42 Souq Khan al-Zeit St, Muslim Quarter; kunafeh per kilogram 56NIS; ☺8am-7pm Sat-Thu) The lurid orange colour of Ja'far's famous knafeh can be somewhat offputting (Ye gods! Do you really expect me to eat that?!). But this sweet made with shredded filo pastry, soft goat cheese and sugar syrup is hugely popular with Palestinians and can be highly addictive. Order it with a glass of tea to cut the sweetness.

Austrian Hospice Café   CAFE $
(Map p46; Austrian Hospice, 37 Via Dolorosa, Muslim Quarter; cakes 23NIS, toasted sandwiches 25NIS; ☺10am-10pm) A good cup of tea can be difficult to find in the Old City (the locals like Lipton), so the fact that this cafe uses tea from Julius Meinl in Vienna is a strength. The coffee beans come from the same source, so cappuccino drinkers will be satisfied, too. A slice of Sacher torte is the almost obligatory accompaniment.

To find the cafe, ring the bell at the gate on the corner of Al-Wad St and the Via Dolorosa and when you are given entry walk into the charming guesthouse foyer and turn left; the cafe is at the end of the corridor. There is indoor and outdoor seating.

Families Restaurant   MIDDLE EASTERN $
(Map p46; ☑02-628 3435; Souq Khan al-Zeit St, Muslim Quarter; shwarma 20NIS, quarter roast chicken 28NIS) This popular place in the Muslim Quarter's busiest shopping strip is appropriately named – it opened 40 years ago and has since been operated by three generations of the same family. The cavernous interior is a pleasant place to eat (try a shwarma). No alcohol or credit cards.

Rossini's Restaurant   INTERNATIONAL $$
(Map p46; ☑02-628 2964; http://karkaronline.com/rossinis.html; 42 Latin Patriarchate Rd, Christian Quarter; pasta 40-70NIS, burgers 35-45NIS, mains 45-130NIS; ☺noon-11pm Mon-Sat; ☺; ☒Jaffa Gate) The vibe is modern at this popular place near Jaffa Gate, an antidote to the otherwise staid eating scene in the Old City. The burgers, pastas and steaks on offer really hit the spot after an exhausting

day pounding the pavements. Appetisers are enormous (one is easily enough for two to share) and the glasses of house wine are generous, too.

Christ Church Guesthouse Cafe
EUROPEAN $$
(Map p46; ☑02-627 7727; Omar ibn al-Khattab Sq, Jaffa Gate; lunch 20-60NIS, dinner 65NIS; ☺noon-2pm & 6.30-8pm) Alumni of boarding schools and university colleges will no doubt feel at home in this guesthouse cafe, which welcomes visitors to its English-style buffet lunch (soup and bread 20NIS, soup and salad 35NIS, main and salad 50NIS, full meal 60NIS). Dinner isn't always offered – reserve by 1pm that day.

Armenian Tavern
ARMENIAN $$
(Map p46; ☑02-627 3854; 79 Armenian Orthodox Patriarchate Rd, Armenian Quarter; mains 55-80NIS; ☺11am-10.30pm Tue-Sun) First, the good news: housed in a Crusader-era building, this Jerusalem institution has an extremely atmospheric antique-laden interior. It's also noteworthy because it serves dinner and alcohol. The bad news? The food is almost inedible and service is perfunctory.

✗ East Jerusalem

Kan Zaman
INTERNATIONAL $$
(Map p70; ☑02-628 3282; Jerusalem Hotel, Dereikh Shchem (Nablus) Rd; sandwiches & burgers 30-45NIS, salads 30-48NIS, pastas 45-54NIS; ☺7.30-11pm; ☑; ☐Shivtei Israel) The Jerusalem Hotel's courtyard restaurant is set under a pergola heavy with grapevines. It's a pleasant spot for a drink, coffee or light meal if you are in East Jerusalem, but the food can be disappointing (order as simply as possible). On Monday and Friday evenings there's live Arabic music.

Le Petit Levant
MIDDLE EASTERN $$$
(Map p70; ☑02-627 7232; www.stgeorgehotel jerusalem.com; St George Landmark Hotel, 6 Amr ibn-Al A'as St; mezes US$4-14, mains US$22-40; ☺1-10.30pm Thu-Sat, 5-10.30pm Sun-Wed; ☎☑; ☐Damascus Gate) Head here to sample delectable dishes from Lebanon and Syria. The service can be shambolic (sometimes reminding us of *Fawlty Towers*), but the food is sensational – flavoursome mezes, succulent grills, tasty fatteh (toasted pita, chickpeas and tahini-yoghurt sauce) and salads constructed with crunchy vegetables and aromatic herbs. The outdoor terrace is a lovely spot to dine on warm evenings.

✗ City Centre

The city centre is jam-packed with restaurants and cafes. Most are kosher, which means they're closed on Shabbat and Jewish holidays.

★Pinati
MIDDLE EASTERN $
(Map p76; ☑02-625 4540; 13 King George V St; hummus 24-34NIS; ☺8am-7pm Sun-Thu, to 3pm Fri; ☑; ☐Jaffa Center) The photos of loyal customers that cover the walls are testament to the longevity of this simple hummus joint, which is so popular that it can be almost impossible to get inside during the lunchtime rush. The half-chickpea, half-fuul (fava-bean paste) hummus option is served with a powerful and delicious garlic and green-chilli paste. Other menu options include shakshuka (a rich egg-and-tomato breakfast dish served in a frying pan), soup and couscous.

Mousseline
ICE CREAM $
(Map p70; ☑02-500 3601; www.mousseline-jerusalem.com; 6 Rehov HaEskol; 1/2/3 scoops 12/18/23NIS; ☺9am-9pm Sun-Thu, to 2pm Fri; ☐Mahane Yehuda) Genius. That's the only way we can describe Mousseline's decision to set up shop on the edge of Mahane Yehuda Market. After dodging the oft-dangerous shopping trollies and their bargain-hungry owners, a stop at this gorgeous *gelateria* (Italian ice-cream shop) will help restore your equilibrium. Choose between interesting flavours (eg, black sesame or wasabi) or opt for a classic fruit sorbet.

Hamarakia
CAFE $
(Map p76; ☑02-625 7797; 4 Koresh St; soups 30NIS, salads 28NIS; ☺12.30pm-midnight Sun-Thu, from 9pm Sat; ☑; ☐City Hall) The name of the place (Soup Pot) pretty much sums up the vegan-friendly menu – choose from five soups, a few salads and dips. The long shared table, open kitchen and piano make for a very social atmosphere, so you may end up eating with new friends and listening to some impromptu live music (jazz jams and acoustic grunge).

Pasta Basta
ITALIAN $
(Map p70; http://pastabasta.co.il; 8 HaTut Alley, Mahane Yehuda Market; pastas 19-26NIS; ☺noon-midnight, closed Shabbat; ☐Mahane Yehuda) Choose your pasta (penne, fettucine, fusilli) and then a sauce (there are nine options) and the chefs at this pasta eatery will serve you a fast and inexpensive meal. Claim a stool, order at the counter and absorb the market buzz as you wait.

JERUSALEM EATING

Moshiko   FAST FOOD $

(Map p76; 10 Ben Yehuda St; felafel options 8-35NIS, shwarma 18-45NIS; ☐ Jaffa Center) Jerusalemites are fans of fast food, and are always happy to join 'best snack in the city' debates. When they do, this place in pedestrianised Ben Yehuda St usually scores a mention. It's been frying felafel and slicing shwarma since 1985, and patrons enjoy both with the fresh salad options on offer. There's limited street seating.

★ **Yudaleh**   ISRAELI $$

(Map p70; ☑ 02-533 3442; 11 Beit Yaakov St; starters 34-76NIS, mains 58-147NIS; ☺ 6.30pm-late Sun-Thu, from 9.45pm Sat; ☐ Mahane Yehuda) The precocious sibling of Machneyuda looks like a Hawaiian beach shack, serves the same exciting modern Israeli food as its big bro and is even more fun (and that's really saying something). Sitting at the bar, ordering a few starters and watching the chefs work their arak-fuelled magic is the best entertainment the city has to offer.

**Notre Dame Cheese &
Wine Restaurant**   FRENCH $$

(Map p46; ☑ 02-627 9177; www.notredamecenter.org; 4th fl, Notre Dame Centre, 3 Paratroopers Rd; ☺ 5pm-midnight Mon-Thu, from noon Fri-Sun; ☐ City Hall) Is this the best view in Jerusalem? Quite possibly. A fantastic place to watch the sun set over the Old City, this rooftop wine and cheese bar is the perfect location for an aparitif. The selection of local and inter-

---

OTTOLENGHI'S JERUSALEM

A darling of the international culinary world, Jerusalem-born chef, author and television presenter Yotam Ottolenghi is an unofficial but highly influential ambassador for the city's culinary heritage. His cookbook *Jerusalem*, written with Sami Tamimi, showcases culinary combinations that he describes as 'belonging to specific groups but also belonging to everybody else'. Proving this point is the fact that Ottolenghi, who is Jewish from West Jerusalem, and Tamimi, a Palestinian from East Jerusalem, grew up eating slightly different versions of the same dishes. A number of our favourite traditional restaurants and pastry shops are profiled in the book, including Zalatimo (p92), Abu Shukri (p92) and Azura.

---

national cheeses is the best in the city, and the wine list is wonderful. The other menu choices aren't as impressive.

Focaccio Bar   MEDITERRANEAN $$

(Map p76; ☑ 02-625 6428; 4 Rabbi Akiva St; focaccia & pizza 30-57NIS, pasta 45-65NIS, mains 57-109NIS; ☺ 10am-midnight Sun-Fri, from 10.30am Sat; ☑; ☐ Jaffa Center) The chef in charge of the *taboun* (clay oven) at this popular place must be one of the hardest-working people in the city, producing crispy and delicious focaccias and pizzas from morning to night. Order these or a pasta dish, as the mains lack finesse. The covered terrace is popular with groups, and the bar is great for solo diners.

Kadosh   CAFE $$

(Map p76; ☑ 02-625 4210; 6 Shlomzion HaMalka St; breakfast 39-58NIS, pastries 12-21NIS, sandwiches 35-44NIS; ☺ 7am-12.30am, closed Shabbat; ☎; ☐ City Hall) A Parisian-style cafe complete with French chansons on the sound system, Kadosh has coffee and pastries that could hold their head high in the French capital. Its sandwiches, salads and all-day breakfast combos have a loyal following. The premium seating is on the street.

Azura   TURKISH $$

(Map p70; ☑ 02-623 5204; Iraqi Market, off Rehov HaEshkol St; hummus 22-40NIS, mains 22-100NIS; ☺ 9.30am-4pm, closed Shabbat; ☑; ☐ Mahane Yehuda) One of the city's best-loved eateries, Azura has been cooking up its Turkish-influenced comfort food since 1952. Its version of hummus scored well in our 'find the best hummus in Jerusalem' quest, and the signature dish – eggplant stuffed with cinnamon-scented minced beef and pine nuts – is delicious. On Friday, local shopkeepers head here for the oxtail special.

T'mol Shilshom   CAFE $$

(Map p76; ☑ 02-623 2758; 5 Yo'el Salomon St; shakshukas 42-50NIS, mains 49-83NIS; ☺ 8.30am-11pm, closed Shabbat; ☎☑; ☐ Jaffa Center) Named after an SY Agnon novel, this old-school bohemian haunt has been attracting a literary-minded crowd for 20 years. The food's nothing to get excited about and the chairs are possibly the most uncomfortable you'll ever encounter, but it's a great place to visit when there's a concert or book reading (check the events calendar on the website).

It's a little tricky to find: go through the stone arch on Yo'el Salomon St (look for the arrowed sign), walk down the passageway, turn left and head to the end of the courtyard – the cafe is upstairs.

Village Green VEGETARIAN, VEGAN **$$**
(Map p76; ☑02-625 3065; www.village-green.
co.il; 33 Jaffa Rd; salad bar 44-59NIS, soups
28NIS, quiches & pies 36NIS; ☺9am-10pm Sun-
Thu, to 3pm Fri; ✍; ☒Jaffa Center) One of an
ever-increasing number of city restaurants
meeting the needs of vegans, this kosher
vegetarian restaurant has a DIY salad bar
and also serves soups (at least eight types),
wholewheat pizzas, quiches and pies. Ser-
vice is cafeteria-style, so it's a good option
for a quick meal. There's another **branch**
(☑02-566 0011; 19 Emek Refa'im St; ☺10am-10pm
Sun-Thu, 9am-3pm Fri) in the German Colony.

★**Machneyuda** ISRAELI **$$$**
(Map p70; ☑02-533 3442; www.machneyuda.
co.il; 10 Beit Ya'akov St; mains 77-162NIS, tasting
menu 265NIS; ☺12.30-4pm & 6.30-11pm Sun-Thu,
to 3pm Fri; ☒Mahane Yehuda) A trio of chefs
has turned the local dining scene on its
head at this fabulous restaurant near the
market. It's not kosher, it's not staid (quite
the opposite) and its menu travels the
globe. Strangely enough, the locals adore
it, so you'll need to book well in advance to
score a table. The menu changes daily and
through the seasons.

A couple of hints for those eating here:
firstly, don't expect to converse with your
dining companions, as the people on the
table next door are likely to be literally on
the table next door (ie, dancing on top of it);
secondly, if the polenta with parmesan and
truffle oil is on the menu, order it.

**Mantra Restaurant &
Wine Bar** INTERNATIONAL **$$$**
(Map p76; ☑02-624 4994; www.mantrajerusalem.
com; Jerusalem Courtyard, 31 Jaffa Rd; mains 62-
142NIS; ☺6.30pm-late Sun-Thu, 1pm-late Fri &
Sat) The world needs more restaurants like
Mantra. It doesn't have hipster credentials,
there's no celebrity chef in the kitchen and
the interior design is never going to make
it into the pages of a glossy magazine. What
it does have – in spades – is great food, a
thoughtful wine list and attentive service.

Access is through the Jerusalem Court-
yard (enter from Rivlin St, through the arch
next to the Gent Bar).

Darna MOROCCAN **$$$**
(Map p76; ☑02-624 5406; www.darna.co.il; 3 Hor-
kanos St; mains 90-155NIS, set menus 175-240NIS;
☺noon-5pm & 6-10pm Sun-Thu, after Shab-
bat-10pm Sat; ☒Jaffa Center) Aromatic and
delicious dishes from Morocco – including

plenty of tagine and couscous choices – are
served in atmospheric surrounds at this
longstanding kosher favourite. Be sure to
try the *pastilla fassia* (filo pastry stuffed
with poussin and almonds) and consider
the *mechoui* (slow-cooked lamb shoulder).
When booking, opt for the richly decorated indoor dining space rather than the
courtyard.

✖ Mamilla & Yemin Moshe

Mamilla Café & Brasserie INTERNATIONAL **$$$**
(Map p76; ☑02-548 2230; www.mamillahotel.
com; 14 Mamilla Mall; salads 48-60NIS, pasta
64-68NIS; ☺noon-11pm Sun-Thu, 10am-3pm Fri,
9.30pm-midnight Sat; ☒City Hall) Decent eating
options are thin on the ground in the Old
City, so this stylish cafe and brasserie a short
walk from Jaffa Gate is an option worth con-
sidering for lunch. The interior has a stylish
tile-covered interior, and there's also an out-
door terrace with wicker chairs under trees.
The menu features pasta, pizza, soups, sal-
ads and toasted sandwiches.

Angelica INTERNATIONAL **$$$**
(Map p70; ☑02-623 0056; www.angelicarest.com;
4 George Washington St; mains 78-148NIS; ☺12.30-
10.30pm Sun-Thu, 8.30-11pm Sat; ☎) Sleek and
sophisticated, this upmarket American-style
grill restaurant is a favourite with guests
at the nearby King David Hotel. It offers a
crowd-pleasing menu featuring steaks, a
few fish choices, a burger and the occasional
vegetarian option. The food is good rather
than great, but the surrounds are comfortable, there's an excellent wine list and service is attentive.

✖ German Colony

There are plenty of chain cafes and burger
joints along Emek Refa'im St, but no restaurants of note.

Adom MEDITERRANEAN **$$$**
(Map p70; ☑02-624 6242; First Station, 4 David
Remez St; salads 46-52NIS, mains 62-128NIS;
☺noon-midnight Sun-Fri, noon-4.30pm &
6pm-midnight Sat; ☒4, 18, 21) If you can over-
look the inadequecies of its service, this
bustling place in the Old Jerusalem Train
Station is a decent option for lunch or din-
ner. The outdoor terrace and indoor bar
and dining area are equally popular with its
cashed-up regulars, who tend to order the
burger or a salad. It's particularly busy on
Shabbat.

✖ Givat Ram & Museum Row

★ Modern
ISRAELI $$$

(📞 02-648 0862; www.modern.co.il; Israel Museum, Ruppin Rd, Givat Ram; tapas platter 95NIS, mains 62-120NIS; ⊙11.30am-5pm Sun-Thu, to 11pm Tue & Wed Aug; 📝; 🚊 7, 9, 14, 35, 66) Talented chef Avi Peretz devises delicious menus that feature traditional Israeli dishes with a modern twist. His Jerusalem tapas platter is a case in point, with seven tapas dishes concocted from vegetables that are in season and bursting with flavour. Served with bread straight from the oven, it's as good to look at as it is to eat.

There's an emphasis on vegetarian dishes here, but there are always fish and meat dishes on offer as well – sea bass on root vegetables from the Judean region perhaps, or even a classic entrecote steak with red wine sauce. The surrounds are lovely, and staff are both friendly and efficient.

🍷 Drinking & Nightlife

Jerusalem's city centre is well endowed with bars. The best are in the Mahane Yehuda Market area and in the vicinity of Zion Sq, on Rivlin, Ben Shatah, Helene HaMalka and Dorot Rishonim Sts. East Jerusalem bars tend to be inside hotels, while the Old City is almost as dry as the Negev.

🍷 Old City

Amigo Emil
BAR, CAFE

(Map p46; 📞 02-628 8090; Aqabat al-Khanqah St, Christian Quarter; ⊙11am-9.30pm Mon-Sat) We can't in good conscience recommend the food here, but the Palestinian owner Costandi is one of the nicest chaps you're ever likely to encounter. A former banker, he opted for a career move and decided to open a restaurant in this 400-year-old former workshop owned by his family. It's an atmospheric place to enjoy a beer or cappuccino.

Cafe Rimon Himo
CAFE

(Map p46; Damascus Gate, Muslim Quarter; ⊙7am-10pm) Sitting on this cafe's small terrace and watching the action around Damascus Gate is an enjoyable way to spend an hour or so. The owner doesn't seem to mind if you order a drink from him but grab a *man'aish* from a nearby baker to snack on (you'll pay for the privilege, though, as he charges in euros).

Versavee
BAR

(Map p46; www.versavee.com; Jaffa Gate; breakfast 36-38NIS, sandwiches 28-42NIS, salads 26-50NIS; ⊙9am-late; 🛜) Located in a courtyard next to the Hotel East New Imperial, this place is notable for its convenient location next to Jaffa Gate and for the fact that it serves alcohol. It's a decent option for breakfast, a light lunch or a drink. The *limonata* (18NIS) is delicious.

🍷 City Centre

★ Uganda
BAR

(Map p76; 📞 02-623 6087; http://ugandajlm.com/; 4 Aristobulos St; ⊙noon-late Sun-Fri, 2pm-late Sat; 🚇 Jaffa Center) DJ sets, live gigs, exhibitions by local artists and political discussions are but some of the elements that make this alternative bar special. Named after the country once suggested as a location for the Jewish state, it doubles as a comics and record store, serves Palestinian beer (Taybeh), has comfortable seating and is a great place to spend a night.

★ Sira
BAR, CLUB

(Map p76; 📞 050 486 489; 1 Ben Shatakh St; ⊙5pm-late; 🚇 City Hall) This tiny bar off Ben Sira St is smoky, dark, crowded and loud. There's a mini dance floor, the DJs have eclectic tastes, and the beer flows fast and well into the night. It also goes by its old name, Diwan.

★ Cassette Bar
BAR

(HaCasetta; Map p76; 1 Horkanos St; ⊙8pm-5am Sat-Thu, 2pm-6am Fri; 🚇 Jaffa Center) Accessed from the street (look for the metal door covered with old cassette tapes) or through the rear of the Record Bar next door, this pint-sized bar is a longstanding hipster haunt. The crowd drinks well into the night, serenaded by alternative tracks.

Upstairs is Videopub (Map p76; 1st fl, 1 Horkanus St; ⊙8pm-4am Mon-Thu & Sat-Sun, from 10pm Fri; 🚇 Jaffa Center), a popular gay bar. Members of the local LGBT community flock to this teensy space to drink and dance (Thursday and Saturday are particularly busy).

Record Bar
BAR

(HaTaklit; Map p76; 7 Helene Hamalka St; ⊙4.30pm-3am or later; 🚇 Jaffa Center) Here's the lowdown: Record Bar regulars start their night sitting at the outdoor tables, enjoying two drinks for the price of one (4.30pm to 9pm) and sizing up the other drinkers, working out who they're going to hit on when they kick on to the nearby Cassette Bar, Videopub or Radio Bar.

LGBT JERUSALEM

Owing to Jerusalem's religious nature, the city's lesbian, gay, bisexual and transgender scene is much more subdued than its Tel Aviv equivalent. Public displays of affection, especially between same-sex couples, will be unwelcome in Jewish Orthodox areas and East Jerusalem. Two places to flaunt it are Videopub, a spangleicious bar with a tiny dance floor, and **Hakatze** (The Edge; Map p76; http://hakatze.com; 4 Shoshan St; ⊙9pm-late; ⋒City Hall), a small bar on a quiet alley south of Safra Sq that has drag shows on Monday from 11pm, and parties on Thursday and Friday.

In late June, the LGBT community takes to the streets in the **Jerusalem Gay Pride Parade**, a serious political march rather than a festival-like celebration.

If you want more information on the LGBT community, visit the **Jerusalem Open House** (⌑02-625 0502; www.joh.org.il; 1st fl, 2 HaSoreg St; ⊙11am-3pm Mon-Thu; ⋒City Hall). New visitors are invited to come Sunday to Thursday from 10am to 5pm to learn about community events. It organises a variety of events, many of which are English-speaker friendly.

Radio Bar
BAR

(HaRadio; Map p76; 5 Helene HaMalka St; ⊙8pm-late; ⋒Jaffa Center) Home to the Voice of Free Jerusalem, an independent internet radio station, this dive bar is part of the Record/Cassette/Video bar operation and has a similarly loyal following. Patrons enjoy having a drink and a chat while listening to the station and watching the broadcasts.

Cafelix
CAFE

(Map p70; www.cafelix.de; 20 Haetz Ha'em St, Mahane Yehuda Market; ⊙7am-10pm Sun-Thu, to noon Fri; ⋒Mahane Yehuda) Jerusalem's only branch of the speciality coffee-roasting operation from Tel Aviv takes its craft seriously – there's cold drip and espresso versions on offer, and the baristas love nothing more than having a chat about the origin of the beans they're using. Perch at one of the benches while you sip and watch the market trade.

Casino de Paris
BAR

(Map p70; Mahane Yehuda Market; ⊙noon-2am Sun-Thu, from 9pm Sat; ⋒Mahane Yehuda) During the British Mandate this building was an officers club for British soldiers. Known as the Casino de Paris, it housed a bar downstairs and a brothel on the 2nd floor. It now houses an indoor-outdoor bar serving tapas, pizza and a large range of Israeli boutique beers (we like the wonderfully named Dancing Camel).

Mirror Bar
BAR

(Map p76; www.mamillahotel.com; mezzanine, Mamilla Hotel, 11 King Solomon (Shloma HaMelekh) St; ⊙8pm-2am Sun-Thu, from 9pm Sat; ⋒; ⋒City Hall) Mood lighting, comfortable seating and talented mixicologists behind the bar make

this a great choice for a nightcap. The long bar with its backlit alabaster is nearly as glam as the waitstaff (and that's really saying something). On Wednesday a DJ spins world music.

In summer the panoramic rooftop bar here is equally glamorous, but it can be hard to score a seat. Try around sunset, when the view over the Old City is lovely.

Bass
CLUB

(Map p76; ⌑054 460 4492; 1 HaHistadrut St; ⊙9am-6pm Wed-Sat; ⋒Jaffa Center) The name says it all. The foundations of this dance club shake with the dull throb of the electronica, trance and house tracks spun by the city's best DJs and the occasional foreign blow-in. There's a weekly roots reggae show, too. Check the Facebook feed for the program.

May 5th
BAR, CAFE

(Map p70; 56 Ha'etz Ha'em, Mahane Yehuda Market; ⊙11am-late, closed Shabbat; ⋒Mahane Yehuda) Run by a group of young friends who have designated 5 May as their own personal holiday, this micro bar on the market's main thoroughfare is a convivial place for a drink or coffee. To find it, look for the 'Danesi Caffè' sign above the entrance.

Zabotinski
PUB

(Map p76; 2 Shim'on Ben Shatah St; ⊙7pm-2am Sun-Fri, 1pm-late Sat; ⋒; ⋒City Hall) Named after the Russian-born Zionist Ze'ev Jabotinsky (1880–1940), this pub is one of a number of popular watering holes on Shim'on Ben Shatah St. The food is forgettable, but the beer is cold and there's plenty of streetside seating.

Mike's Place PUB
(Map p76; ☑054 799 1220; www.mikesplacebars. com; 33 Jaffa Rd; ⊘11am-late, closed Shabbat; 🚇 Jaffa Center) There's nothing secret about Mike's well-honed formula for success: Guinness, open-mic nights, live rock bands and sport on the big screen. At the top of the Rivlin St bar strip, it has an indoor area plus a few outdoor tables that offer excellent people-watching opportunities.

German Colony

Coffeemill CAFE
(☑02-566 1665; 23 Emek Refa'im St; ⊘7am-midnight Sun-Thu, to 3pm Fri; 🚌4, 18, 21) Decorated with covers of the *New Yorker* and with wooden drawers full of an exotic array of coffee beans, this bohemian-flavoured cafe is a good place for cake and a shot of caffeine.

☆ Entertainment

Theatre & Classical Music

Jerusalem has a rich tradition of theatre and music. You can check what's on at www. itraveljerusalem.com or in the Friday edition of the *Jerusalem Post*. Book advance tickets through **Bimot** (Map p76; ☑02-622 2333; 8 Shamai St; 🚇 Jaffa Center).

**Jerusalem Centre for
the Performing Arts** CONCERT VENUE, THEATRE
(Jerusalem Theatre; Map p70; ☑02-560 5755; www.jerusalem-theatre.co.il; 20 David Marcus St, Talbiyeh) This complex includes a concert hall, theatres and a cafe. Its Sherover Theatre has simultaneous English-language surtitles during certain performances. It's home to the Jerusalem Symphony Orchestra, and comedy, music, children's theatre and dance performances are also held here.

**International
Convention Center** CONCERT VENUE
(ICC; ☑02-655 8558; www.iccjer.co.il; 1 Shazar Blvd; 🚇 Central Station) The Jerusalem venue of the **Israel Philharmonic Orchestra** (www.ipo.co.il).

Live Music

Zappa in the Lab LIVE MUSIC
(☑*9080; www.zappa-club.co.il; 28 Hebron Rd) Crafted out of a disused railway warehouse, this small live-music venue stages jazz, folk, rock and pop. It's open most days of the week, but you need to check the website or call for upcoming events.

Yellow Submarine LIVE MUSIC
(☑02-679 4040; www.yellowsubmarine.org.il; 13 HaRechavim St, Talpiot) Aiming to promote music and foster musical talent, this venue has a crowded program of live performances. Check the website for details.

Sport

Teddy Kollek Stadium FOOTBALL
(Malha) The 22,000-seat Teddy Kollek Stadium is home to the Beitar Jerusalem, Hapoel Jerusalem and Hapoel Katamon Jerusalem football clubs. You can buy tickets on the day of the game. The stadium is close to the Jerusalem (Malha) Mall; take bus 6 from Central Bus Station.

Shopping

Jerusalem is the best place in the country to shop for Judaica (Tsfat also has a fine selection). In the Old City, browse the shops in the Cardo, which has some reliable outlets.

Some of the best Judaica and fine-art shops are right along Yo'el Salomon St in the city centre. If you are a serious shopper, avoid the Judaica shops on David St in the Old City as the products here do not necessarily conform to Jewish law (despite what the salespeople will tell you) and are generally of inferior quality.

Old City

★**Alan Baidun** ANTIQUES
(Map p46; ☑02-626 1469; www.baidun.com; 28 Via Dolorosa, Muslim Quarter; ⊘10am-7pm Sat-Thu) It would be an understatement to say that little of the merchandise sold in the Old City's souvenir and craft shops is of high quality. Thank goodness, then, for Alan Baidun's store, which sells absolutely exquisite antiquities and antiques. All come with export certificates and papers proving provenance. Before entering, make sure your credit card has lots of leverage.

★**Fair Trade
Women Cooperative** HANDICRAFTS
(Map p46; HaAhkim St, Christian Quarter; ⊘8am-7pm Mon-Sat; 🚇 Jaffa Gate) Operated by the **Arab Orthodox Society** (www.araborthodox society.com), a longstanding charitable organisation based in Jerusalem, this shop sells embroidered clothing, bags, purses and pillows made at the Melia Art and Training Center, an organisation of West Bank women working to preserve the Palestinian cultural tradition of cross-stitch embroidery

while providing income for themselves and their families.

Heifetz
JUDAICA, JEWELLERY

(Map p46; ☑02-628 0061; www.bennyheifetz.com; 22 Tiferet Israel Rd, Jewish Quarter; ◷10am-5pm Sun-Thu, to 2pm Fri) Jeweller Benny Heifetz creates both Judaica (mezuzot, candlesticks, challah boards etc) and jewellery with Jewish themes at his atelier and shop on Hurva Sq. The sleek contemporary designs make his mainly silver pieces stand out in a very crowded industry here in Jerusalem, so it's worth seeking them out.

Moriah
JEWELLERY

(Map p46; ☑02-627 4050; www.moriah-collection. com; 7 Beit-El St, Jewish Quarter; ◷10am-6pm Sun-Thu, to 2pm Fri) Situated in a lovely old house near the Hurva Synagogue, this upmarket shop sells jewellery made with gold, diamonds and fragments of stone excavated during local archaeological digs seeking physical traces of the Age of the Patriarchs.

🔒 East Jerusalem

Educational Bookshop & Cafe
BOOKS

(Map p70; ☑02-628 3704; www.educationalbookshop.com; 19 Salah ad-Din St, East Jerusalem; ◷8am-8pm) Journalists, aid workers, activists and other politically aware people make this bookshop cafe a regular stop on their East Jerusalem wanderings. It has an impressive range of books and DVDs pertaining to the Arab–Israeli conflict, as well as a good selection of magazines and Palestinian music CDs.

Sunbala
HANDICRAFTS

(☑02-672 1707; www.sunbula.org; 15 Derekh Shchem (Nablus) Rd, East Jerusalem; ◷1-6pm Sun-Thu; ◷Shimon Hatzadik) This not-for-profit outfit empowers Palestinian artisans by promoting and selling traditional handicrafts including embroidery, basketry, weaving, carving and olive-oil soap. It runs two shops in Jerusalem, one of which is inside the St Andrew's Guesthouse (p90) in the New City and the other here in East Jerusalem. All of the items for sale are handmade.

🔒 New City

Daniel Azoulay
JUDAICA

(Map p76; ☑02-623 3918; www.ketubahazoulay-art.com; 5 Yo'el Salomon St, City Centre; ◷10am-7.30pm Mon-Thu & Sat, to 3pm Fri; ◷Jaffa Center) Daniel Azouley is known across the globe

for his hand-painted porcelain and beautiful *ketubahs* (Jewish wedding contracts).

Greenvurcel
JUDAICA, JEWELLERY

(Map p76; ☑02-622 1620; www.greenvurcel.co.il; 27 Yo'el Salomon St; ◷10am-10pm Sun-Thu, to 2pm Fri, 1hr after Shabbat-11pm Sat; ◷Jaffa Center) Silversmith Yaakov Greenvurcel designs and makes Judaica and 'silver art' including jewellery.

Rina Zin
CLOTHING

(Map p76; ☑02-674 4488; www.rinazin.com; 13 Shimon Ben Shetach; ◷City Hall) Israeli fashion designer Rina Zin uses natural fabrics (linen, cotton, wool) in muted hues to craft her casual yet elegant pieces, which suit women of all ages. The knits and kaftanlike dresses are particularly lovely.

Steimatzky
BOOKS

(Map p76; 33 Jaffa Rd; ◷8.30am-8pm Mon-Thu, to 2pm Fri; ◷Jaffa Center) Chain bookshop with several branches around town, including this one in Jaffa Rd and another in the **German Colony** (43 Emek Refa'im St). It has a good range of English-language novels and guidebooks.

Lametayel
OUTDOOR EQUIPMENT

(Map p76; ☑077 333 4509; www.lametayel.co.il; 5 Yo'el Salomon St; ◷10am-8pm Sun-Thu, to 2pm Fri; ◷Jaffa Center) Sells maps and travel guidebooks (including Lonely Planet), as well as quality camping supplies and outdoor gear.

Halva Kingdom
FOOD & DRINK

(Map p70; ☑02-540 2071; 12 Haetz Ha'em St, Mahane Yehuda Market; ◷8am-sunset Sun-Thu, to 2pm Fri; ◷Mahane Yehuda) Watch the large round stone grinding sesame into a paste at the city's best-known tahina shop before buying a tub (25NIS) to take home.

Kippa Man
ACCESSORIES

(Map p76; ☑02-622 1255; 5 Ben Yehuda St,; ◷Jaffa Center) Avi Binyamin, Jerusalem's well-known Kippa Man, sells a huge range of kippot (yarmulkes; skullcaps) from his shop in pedestrianised Ben Yehuda St. He'll also make to order.

ⓘ Information

DANGERS & ANNOYANCES

Demonstrations and marches by both Jews and Arabs are pretty common in Jerusalem and while they are usually peaceful, it's still a good idea to remain vigilant in case things get rowdy (Damascus Gate and Temple Mount are regular

JERUSALEM HILLS GETAWAY

The Jerusalem Hills region is one of Israel's most fertile areas, a heavily forested stretch of the Judean Mountains with Jerusalem nestled at its centre. Pilgrims have travelled across the hills for millennia on their way to the Holy City, building and endowing monasteries, churches and shrines along the way.

These days, the pine-scented hills are the location of some of the country's best vineyards and wineries. Sadly, not many of these have cellar doors, but their vintages can be enjoyed at the **Cramin Resort** (☑08-638 7797; www. isrotel.com; Kiryat Anavim; r from US$360; ✳@🛜🏊), a super-swish spa hotel in Kiryat Anavim, a 15-minute drive from Jerusalem. In addition to its luxe rooms, pool terrace and sleek spa specialising in vino-therapy treatments (utilising wine and grape products), the resort also has a wine bar and restaurant where wines from major names including Yatir, Katlav, Flam, Ella Valley, Soreq and Tzora can be sampled.

flashpoints). The Mount of Olives has not always been the friendliest area to walk in and some female travellers strolling there alone have been hassled. If possible, visit the area in pairs. Ultra-Orthodox Jewish groups sometimes stone buses, burn trash bins and confront the police at Shabbat Sq in Mea She'arim, which even on quiet days can turn hostile when tourists (especially immodestly dressed ones) saunter in.

EMERGENCY
Ambulance (☑101)

Fire (☑102)

Police (☑100; 107 Jaffa Rd, Mahane Yehuda)

Tourist Police (Armenian Orthodox Patriarchate Rd)

MEDICAL SERVICES
Hadassah Medical Centre Ein Kerem (☑02-677 7201; www.hadassah.org.il) The Ein Kerem campus of this venerable, not-for-profic hospital has a 24-hour emergency department.

Hadassah Medical Centre Mount Scopus (☑02-584 4333; www.hadassah.org.il) The Mt Scopus campus of this nonprofit hospital has a 24-hour emergency department and a specialist pediatric emergency department that is also open 24 hours.

Orthodox Society (☑02-627 1958; Greek Orthodox Patriarchate Rd; ⏰9am-2pm Mon-Thu, to 2pm Fri, to 1pm Sat) In the Old City's Christian Quarter, the Orthodox Society operates a low-cost medical and dental clinic that welcomes travellers.

Super-Pharm (☑077 888 1450; 9 Mamilla Mall; ⏰8.30am-11pm, closed Shabbat) Pharmacy located between Jaffa Gate and the city centre.

Terem (☑1 599 520 520; www.terem.com; 80 Yirmiyahu St, Romema; ⏰24hr; 🚌 Central Station) Efficient multilingual walk-in medical clinic that handles everything from minor ailments to emergencies. It's a five-minute walk from Central Bus Station.

MONEY
The best deals for changing money are at the private, commission-free exchange offices in the New City (around Zion Sq), East Jerusalem (Salah ad-Din St) and in the Old City (Jaffa Gate). Note that many close early on Friday and remain closed all day Saturday.

Mizrahi and Leumi ATMs are found across the city, Including at Zion Sq in the city centre.

POST
Main Post Office (Map p76; ☑02-624 4745; 23 Jaffa Rd; ⏰8am-6pm Sun-Thu, to noon Fri)

TOURIST INFORMATION
Christian Information Centre (Map p46; ☑02-627 2692; www.cicts.org; Omar ibn al-Khattab Sq; ⏰8.30am-5.30pm Mon-Fri, to 12.30pm Sat) This office opposite the entrance to the Citadel is operated by the Franciscans and provides information on the city's Christian sites.

Jaffa Gate Tourist Office (Map p46; ☑02-627 1422; www.itraveljerusalem.com; Jaffa Gate; ⏰8.30am-5pm Sat-Thu, to 1.30pm Fri) This is the main tourist office for Jerusalem. It supplies free maps, organises guides and provides information and advice. It's the second office after Jaffa Gate – don't confuse it with the 'Jerusalem Tourist Information Center', a private tourist company next door that sports an information icon above the door.

Tourist Line (☑*3888) Call this number for immediate answers regarding tourist services as well as assistance from the Israel Police, Ministry of Interior Services and Airport Authority. Operates 24/7.

WEBSITES
www.gojerusalem.com Handy tourist website that includes events information.

www.itraveljerusalem.com Extremely useful website operated by the municipality.

www.jerusalem.com Overview of the city, its attractions and events; includes virtual tours of important sites.

❶ Getting There & Away

BUS

Buses to major cities and towns across Israel leave from the **Central Bus Station** (www.bus.co.il; Jaffa Rd; 🚌 Central Station). Services include Tel Aviv (bus 405, 19NIS, one hour, every 15 minutes), Haifa (bus 940, 947 or 960, 44NIS, two hours, every 15 minutes), Tiberias (bus 962, 44NIS, 2½ hours, hourly), Masada (bus 421, 444 or 486, 44NIS, 1¾ hours), Be'er Sheva (bus 446 or 470, 31.50NIS, 1¾ hours, twice hourly) and Eilat (bus 444, 82NIS, five hours, four daily). You'll need to book your ticket to Eilat in advance, as these services are often full.

To get to parts of East Jerusalem such as the Mount of Olives (bus 75, 5NIS), use the **Arab bus station** located on Sultan Suleiman St in East Jerusalem, near Herod's Gate. The buses that leave from here are blue-and-white.

If you are headed into northern areas of the West Bank such as Ramallah (bus 18, 7NIS), use the **Arab bus station** on Derekh Shchem (Nablus) Rd, the street straight in front of Damascus Gate. The buses that leave from here are green-and-white.

For Bethlehem, take bus 21 (8NIS) from the **Arab bus station** west of the Damascus Gate next to the tram stop. The buses that leave from here are blue-and-white. For Hebron, take bus 21, alight at Bab al-Zqaq and then take a Hebron bus (5NIS).

The general rule is that blue-and-white buses go to southern West Bank destinations and green-and-white buses go to northern West Bank destinations.

CAR

Most Jerusalem-based rental-car agencies forbid you to take their cars into the Palestinian Territories (Rte 1 to the Dead Sea and Rte 90 north to the Sea of Galilee or south to Eilat are not a problem). Two exceptions are East Jerusalem–based Dallah Rent a Car (p415), which has an office at the American Colony Hotel; and **Green Peace** (📞 02-585 9756; www.greenpeace.co.il; Shu'fat, East Jerusalem), also located in East Jerusalem.

Most of the major international and national agencies have offices on King David St.

SHERUT (SHARED TAXI)

Sheruts (shared taxis, *servees* in Arabic) are much faster than buses, depart more frequently and cost only a few shekels more; on Shabbat they're the only public transport to destinations in Israel. Sheruts for Tel Aviv (24NIS per person on weekdays, 34NIS on Shabbat) depart from the corner of HaRav Kook St and Jaffa Rd, near Zion Sq; in Tel Aviv, they stop just outside the Central Bus Station.

TAXI

Taxi prices to destinations around Israel are set by the government and include the following: Dead Sea Hotels (499NIS weekdays, 608NIS on Shabbat), Ben Gurion Airport (268/320NIS), Tel Aviv (319/383NIS), Nazareth (785/960NIS), Haifa (780/960NIS) and Eilat (1417/1756NIS).

❶ Getting Around

TO/FROM THE AIRPORT

Ben-Gurion airport is 52km west of Jerusalem, just off Rte 1 to Tel Aviv. Sheruts (running 24 hours) leave the rank outside the international arrivals hall when full and charge 41NIS per person for stops along a set route, including Paratrooper Rd near Jaffa Gate and the City Hall light rail stop. It costs 69NIS to be dropped at a specific address in the city centre. Seats cannot be reserved in advance.

The sherut service is operated by **Nesher service taxis** (📞 1 599 500 205, 02-625 7227), which also offers transport to the airport. These sheruts operate 24 hours, pick up passengers from their accommodation in Jerusalem (or near one of the city gates if you are staying in the Old City) and charge 69NIS per person. Book your seat 24 hours in advance.

JERUSALEM GETTING THERE & AWAY

---

❶ RAV-KAV CARDS

For easy travel around the city, purchase an 'anonymous' (*anonimi*) Rav-Kav Smart Card (5NIS) from the Egged public ticketing office at the Central Bus Station or from any bus driver and then load it with a certain number of rides (6.90NIS each, minimum two rides) or with a multiple-entry ticket. The latter costs 55.20NIS and allows 10 trips (a 20% discount on the usual cost).

Once purchased, your card can later be recharged at ticket machines at tram stops, on any bus or at the Egged desk near platform 22 at the Central Bus Station. It is valid on the light rail and all buses within the Greater Jerusalem area (but not East Jerusalem or on Egged tourist bus 99) and allows free transfers for a single, one-way journey within a 90-minute window. One child under five years of age can travel free with every paying customer (but note that strollers require a separate ticket between 7am and 9am).

For information, go to http://jet.gov.il.

A private taxi will cost 268NIS on weekdays, 320NIS on weekends.

BICYCLE

The hills of Jerusalem make biking tough going, but if you want to hire a bike or sign up for a bike tour the tourist information office at Jaffa Gate can supply you with a list of recommended bike-hire companies.

The Arcadia Ba'Moshava hotel in the German Colony offers bikes for the use of its guests, and the Abraham Hostel can organise bike hire.

BUS

Jerusalem is laced with a good network of city bus routes (6.90NIS per ride). To access information about routes and schedules and to download handy public transport maps, see www.jet.gov.il.

Rav-Kav cards can be used on all buses in the Greater Jerusalem area except those in East Jerusalem and Egged tourist bus 99.

CAR

The only street parking available to non-residents are those spaces marked by a blue-and-white kerb. You'll then need to purchase a parking ticket from a nearby machine (5.70NIS per hour) and display this on your dashboard. Alternatively, register with the **Pango+** (☑ *4500; http://en.pango.co.il/) cellular-phone parking system. Street parking is usually free in the evening and during Shabbat.

For convenient and secure parking near Jaffa Gate, head to **Mamilla Parking** (Map p70; ☑ 02-636 0027; 17 Kariv St; 1hr free, each subsequent hour 12NIS, full day 48NIS ; ⊙ 6am-2am).

LIGHT RAIL

Inaugurated in 2011, **Jerusalem Light Rail** (JLR; ☑ *3686; www.citypass.co.il) consists of a single line that runs from Mt Herzl in the west of the city to Heyl HaAvir in Pisgat Ze'ev, in the city's far northeast. There are 23 stops along a 13.9km route including the Central Bus Station, Mahane Yehuda Market and Damascus Gate. It runs every 10 minutes or so from 5.30am to midnight daily except on Shabbat; on Saturday services start one hour after Shabbat concludes. Tickets (6.90NIS) can be purchased from the machines at tram stops but must be validated on board the tram.

TAXI

Plan on spending between 25NIS and 50NIS for trips anywhere within the central part of town. Always ask to use the meter. To order a taxi, call **Hapalmach taxi** (☑ 02-679 2333).

Be aware that drivers at Jaffa Gate are notorious for refusing to use the meter and then over-charging – if you need a taxi from this location ask the nearby tourist information office to call one for you. Drivers waiting next to the Tomb of the Virgin Mary on the Mount of Olives also dislike using their meters.

Around Jerusalem

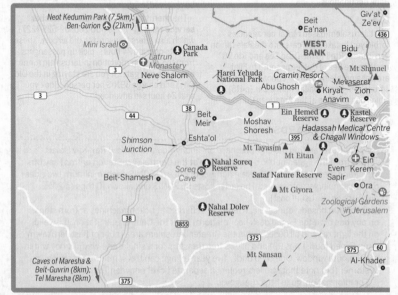

AROUND JERUSALEM

There are a number of sites near Jerusalem that you can visit on a half-day or full-day trip.

Abu Ghosh   אבו גוש   ابو غوش

☑ 02 / POP 6500

The hillside Arab town of Abu Ghosh, 13km west of Jerusalem off the main highway to Tel Aviv, makes for a pleasant half-day trip from Jerusalem. It's known in the Bible as Kiryat Ya'arim (Town of Forests), where the Ark of the Covenant was said to have been located for 20 years until David moved it to Jerusalem (I Chronicles 13:5-8). Nowadays it's equally known as a contender for the title of hummus capital of Israel.

There are two interesting churches here. The first, **Our Lady of the Ark of the Covenant** (Notre Dame de l'Arche d'Alliance; ⊘ 8.30-11.30am & 2.30-5.30pm), was built on the hill above the present-day town in 1924 and its statue of Mary carrying the baby Jesus is a local landmark. The church belongs to the French Sisters of St Joseph of the Apparition, and they believe that it stands on the site of Abinadab's house, where the Ark of the Covenant was kept (I Samuel 7:1). Built on the same site as a larger Byzantine church, it retains parts of the mosaic floor from its Byzantine predecessor.

The second, the **Church of the Resurrection** (☑ 02-534 2798; ⊘ 8.30-11.30am & 2.30-5.30pm Mon-Wed, Fri & Sat), is one of the country's best-preserved and most attractive Crusader churches. Built around 1140, it was later used as both a mosque and a stable. The building was rededicated as a church in 1907. It's located next door to the mosque, so look for the minaret in the valley.

✕ Eating

Abu Ghosh is known throughout Israel for its **hummus restaurants**. A number of them are called Abu Shukri (all claim to be the 'original'), but none bears any relation to the similarly named world-famous place in Jerusalem's Old City.

❶ Getting There & Away

Superbus 185 travels to Abu Ghosh from a stop on Shazar Blvd opposite the Jerusalem International Convention Center, close to the Central Bus Station (9.60NIS, 20 minutes, every 30 minutes).

Soreq Cave   מערת שורק   مغارة سوريك

One of Israel's most spectacular natural wonders, the **Soreq Cave** (☑ 02-991 1117; www.parks.org.il; adult/student/child 29/25/15NIS; ⊘ 8am-4pm Sat-Thu, to 3pm Fri Apr-Sep, to 3pm/2pm Oct-Mar) was only found by accident in 1967 when a local quarry crew blasted away some rock to reveal this underground cavern. Also known as Avshalom (Absalom's) Cave, it contains stalactites, stalagmites and rock pillars in every form and shape. The cave is located some 20km west of Jerusalem along the road from Ein Kerem and is only accessible by car.

Caves of Maresha & Beit-Guvrin

גן לאומי בית גוברין–מרשה

حديقة وطنية بيت جبرين

Added to Unesco's World Heritage list in 2014, the **Caves of Maresha and Beit-Guvrin** (☑ 08-681 2957; www.parks.org.il; adult/student/child 29/25/15NIS; ⊘ 8am-4pm Apr-Sep, to 3pm Oct-Mar) is an archaeological site, natural wonder and feat of human ingenuity all rolled into one. The site contains approximately 3500 underground chambers carved into the soft chalk of Lower Judea under the former towns of Maresha and Beit Guvrin.

Some of the caves are natural, the result of water eroding the soft limestone surface. Others, however, are thought to be the result of quarrying by the Phoenicians, builders of Ashkelon's port between the 7th and 4th centuries BCE. During the Byzantine period the caves were used by monks and hermits and some of the walls are still discernibly marked with crosses. St John the Baptist is said to have been one of the pious graffitists.

Excavations at Maresha have uncovered remains from a 3rd-century synagogue and various Greek and Crusader artefacts, all of which are now on display at Jerusalem's Rockefeller Museum. Some Byzantine mosaics also found here are now in the Israel Museum in Jerusalem. Among the finds that haven't been transported elsewhere are the ruins of the 12th-century Crusader Church of St Anna (or Sandhanna).

The easiest caves to explore are those west of Maresha – you can see tracks leading from the road. Some of the caves have elaborate staircases with banisters leading down below ground level. The rows of hundreds of niches suggest that they were created for raising small domesticated doves to be used in the worship of Aphrodite by the Sidonian colony between the 3rd and 1st centuries BCE.

The park is fairly large and the sights are spread out. The only practical way to visit is by private car. To get here, take Rte 38 south until it hits Rte 35, then take Rte 35 west for 2km until you see the entrance to the park.

Latrun   לטרון   اللطرون

This area located halfway between Tel Aviv and Jerusalem is home to the **Latrun**

Monastery (www.holy-wine.com; 7.30-11.30am & 2.30-4.30pm Mon-Sat), a picturesque settle-ment surrounded by olive trees, cypress-es and vineyards. Founded in 1890 by the French Trappist Order of monks (locals call it the Monastery of the Silent Monks), the monastery is known for its olive oil and wine (merlot, pinot noir, cabernet sauvignon, chardonnay and sémillon) and there is a shop near the monastery gate where these are sold. Visitors are welcome to walk through the monastery gardens.

After visiting, those travelling with children should consider visiting **Mini Israel** (1 700 559 569; www.minisrael.co.il; adult/concession 69/59NIS; 10am-5pm Sun-Thu & Sat, to 2pm Fri Apr-Jun & Nov-Mar, hours vary Jul-Oct, closed Dec-Feb), a theme park that shrinks 385 of Israel's famed attractions down to scale-model size. Check the website for opening hours, as they shift during the year.

Buses 404, 433, 434 and 435 travel from Jerusalem's Central Bus Station to/from Latrun (19NIS, 30 minutes, frequent).

Around Latrun

Neot Kedumim Park   PARK
(Biblical Landscape Reserve; 08-977 0777; www.neot-kedumim.org.il; adult/child 25/20NIS; 8.30am-4pm Sun-Thu, to 1pm Fri) This 2.5-sq-km reserve 9km southeast of Ben-Gurion airport is the best place in Israel to get a sense of what the natural and agricultural landscapes of the Holy Land looked like back in biblical times. Self-guided tours take visitors along four nature trails to places such as the Dale of the Song of Songs.

Tel Aviv-Jaffa (Yafo)

תל אביב-יפו   تل ابيب-يافا

03 / POP 414,600

Best Places to Eat

➡ Miznon (p128)

➡ Orna and Ella (p129)

➡ Catit (p131)

➡ Bindella Osteria & Bar (p131)

➡ Ali Caravan (p135)

Best Places to Stay

➡ Shenkin Hotel (p125)

➡ Hotel Montefiore (p125)

➡ Mendeli Street Hotel (p127)

➡ Old Jaffa Khan (p127)

➡ Beachfront Hotel (p127)

Why Go?

Israel's second-largest city – modern, vibrant and cosmopolitan – is one of the country's greatest assets, a sun-bronzed strip of coastline where coffee and culinary innovation are the local obsessions, where residents speak every language under the sun, and where life is lived outdoors and to the fullest.

The Unesco-listed Bauhaus-era buildings that give the place its popular title of 'White City' are a major draw, as is the historic port of Jaffa (Yafo), which has a fascinating Arab heritage. But the city's real attraction is the local lifestyle. Visitors tend to get into the Tel Avivi swing of things straight away, flitting between contemporary art galleries and chic cafes one day, artisan boutiques and blissfully balmy beaches the next. A few days here is fun, but a week can be a revelation – don't miss it.

When to Go
Tel Aviv

Mar–May Hot-pink bougainvillea flowers, and locals reclaim the outdoor tables at cafes.

Jun–mid-Sep Visitors party during Tel Aviv Pride (June) and recover at the beach.

Dec–early Mar Though cold and occasionally wet, the city is blessed with winter sun.

Tel Aviv Highlights

1 Joining swimmers, sun-lovers and scenesters on the golden sands of Tel Aviv's world-famous **beaches** (p121).

2 Investigating the bohemian bars and boutiques in Jaffa's historic **Flea Market** (p118).

3 Contemplating impressionist masterpieces and contemporary artworks at the **Tel Aviv Museum of Art** (p110).

4 Checking out stylish cafes and Unesco-listed Bauhaus buildings on and around **Rothschild Boulevard** (p108).

5 Bar-hopping in the hipster hang-out of **Florentin** (p136).

6 Enjoying exciting modern Israeli cuisine at a restaurant run by a local **celebrity chef** (p131).

7 Walking, jogging or cycling through the green expanse of **Park HaYarkon** (p121).

History

Ancient Jaffa

According to archaeologists, Jaffa was a fortified port at least as far back as the 18th century BCE. An Egyptian document from around 1470 BCE mentions the city's conquest by Pharaoh Thutmose III.

Over the centuries, Jaffa was conquered by, among others, the Assyrians (701 BCE), the Babylonians (586 BCE), Alexander the Great (332 BCE), the Egyptians (301 BCE) and the Maccabees (mid-1st century BCE) but was neglected by the Romans, who had their own port up the coast at Caesarea. Some say that Greek mythology's Andromeda was chained to a rock just off the coast of Jaffa.

Byzantine Jaffa fell to Arabs in 636 CE. In 1100 the Crusaders captured Jaffa and then held it for most of the period until 1268, when the Egyptian Mamluks arrived (the exception was between 1187 and 1191, when Salah ad-Din took the city and then lost it to Richard I 'The Lionheart' of England). Four centuries of Ottoman rule (1515–1917) were briefly interrupted by Napoleon, who in 1799 conquered the city and then massacred 2440 Ottoman prisoners on the seashore.

In the very early 1800s Jaffa was hardly more than a village, but reconstruction began in 1807 under Muhammad abu Nabbut; it was at this time that the main Mahmoudiya Mosque was built. Jews returned in the 1820s, and by the end of the century Jaffa had become a major gateway for boatloads of Jewish pilgrims and immigrants.

During the latter half of the 1800s, several new neighbourhoods were established northeast of Jaffa's walled city. In 1866 a group of American Christians from Maine founded the American Colony; when the group disbanded a few years later, the Templers, members of a messianic Protestant sect from Germany, moved in. And in the late 1800s, groups of Jews tired of the cramped and sometimes insalubrious conditions in Jaffa's old city established two new neighbourhoods on the sand dunes, Neve Tzedek (1887) and Neve Shalom (1890).

The New City of Tel Aviv

In 1906, 60 Jewish families – led by the dynamic Meir Dizengoff (1861–1936), a Zionist pioneer (of the non-Socialist variety) – from Kishinev and Odessa met in Jaffa to lay out plans to establish an entirely new Jewish city. They purchased 12.8 hectares of empty sand dunes north of the city, divided much of it into 60 lots and in 1909 held a lottery –

using seashells – to divvy up the land around what is now the intersection of Herzl St and Rothschild Blvd. They took as a model the English 'garden city' (a planned, self-contained community with plenty of public parks and open spaces). By the time WWI broke out in 1914, 140 homes had been built.

The name of the new city, Tel Aviv (Hill of Spring), comes from the title of the Hebrew translation of Theodor Herzl's utopian novel *Altneuland;* it's also mentioned in Ezekiel 3:15.

From Eclectic to Bauhaus

Tel Aviv's development ground to a halt during WWI, and in the spring of 1917 the Ottoman administration expelled the entire Jewish population from both Tel Aviv and Jaffa. But after WWI the British Mandate in Palestine made it possible for the city to resume its exponential growth. Arab riots in Jaffa in 1921 sent many Jews fleeing north to Tel Aviv, helping to bring the new city's population to around 34,000 by 1925.

In the 1920s Tel Aviv added some 800 structures in the aptly named Eclectic Style, which – in a self-conscious fusion of East and West – mixed Greek columns, Romanesque arches, Oriental domes, colourful ceramic tiles and plenty of ornamentation.

The 1930s saw waves of new arrivals, many fleeing Nazi Germany, and in the mid-1930s anti-Zionist strikes and rioting caused the rest of Jaffa's Jewish population to flee north; many refugees settled in shacks along the seashore. A boycott of Jewish passengers and cargo by Jaffa's Arab port workers, beginning in 1936, led Tel Aviv to build its very own port. By 1939 Tel Aviv's population had reached 160,000, one-third of the country's total Jewish population. Meanwhile, a few kilometres to the northeast in the Templer settlement of Sarona, the patriotically German residents were flying the Nazi flag.

To accommodate well-off refugees from places such as Berlin – in the early years of Nazi rule, Jews were allowed to take some of their assets with them – Jewish architects who had themselves fled Nazi Germany set about designing apartment houses in the clean-lined, ultramodernist Bauhaus (International) style that would soon become the city's hallmark.

With the outbreak of WWII in 1939, many local Jews volunteered for the British army and Tel Aviv played host to Allied troops while simultaneously serving as a centre of Zionist opposition to Britain's

TEL AVIV'S BAUHAUS HERITAGE

Central Tel Aviv has more 1930s Bauhaus (International)–style buildings than any other city in the world, which is why the area known as the 'White City' (roughly the streets of the city centre and south city centre northwest and west of Jaffa/Begin Rd) was declared a Unesco World Heritage site in 2003.

Tel Aviv's White City heritage is easy to spot, even through the modifications and dilapidation of the past 70 years. Look for structures characterised by horizontal lines, flat roofs, white walls, vertical 'thermometer' stairwells and an almost complete absence of ornamentation.

Founded by the architect Walter Gropius and later led by Ludwig Mies van der Rohe, the Bauhaus was an enormously influential art and design school active in the German cities of Weimar, Dessau and Berlin from 1919 to 1933. The Nazis detested the Bauhaus style, considering it 'cosmopolitan' and 'degenerate' and forced the school to close when they came to power.

The modernist ideas and ideals of Bauhaus were brought to Palestine by German-Jewish architects fleeing Nazi persecution; 19 of these had studied at the Bauhaus, two had worked with Erich Mendelsohn (a pioneer of the Streamline Moderne style) and at least two others had worked with the great modernist Le Corbusier. As Tel Aviv developed in the 1930s (following a street plan drawn up in the late 1920s by the Scottish urban planner Sir Patrick Geddes), some 4000 white-painted Bauhaus buildings – the quintessence of mid-20th-century moderism – were built. Approximately 1000 of these are identified in the Unesco listing.

Today, many of these buildings are in a dreadful state of disrepair (the climate is particularly tough on the rebar in concrete, the Bauhaus building material of choice), but several hundred have been renovated and each year more are being restored to their former glory. Superb examples of the Bauhaus style can be found along the length of Rothschild Blvd and on the streets running across it (eg, Mazeh and Nahmani Sts), on Bialik St near Gan Meir Park, and around Dizengoff Sq.

The **Bauhaus Centre** (Map p116; ☎ 03-522 0249; www.bauhaus-center.com; 99 Dizengoff St; ⊙ 10am-7.30pm Sun-Thu, to 2.30pm Fri) sells a variety of architecture-related books and plans of the city, including a 1:6000 preservation map and guide to Tel Aviv-Yafo. It also has two Bauhaus walking-tour offerings: hire of an MP3 player with headset outlining a self-guided Bauhaus walk in the streets around the centre; and a two-hour guided walking tour of the same streets starting every Friday at 10am. Each option costs 60NIS per person. A much better alternative is the free English-language guided **Bauhaus tour** run by the Tel Aviv Tourist Office. This departs from 46 Rothschild Blvd (corner Shadal St) every Saturday at 11am.

anti-immigration policies. The city was bombed by Mussolini's air force in 1940.

In late 1947 and into 1948, as the British prepared to pull out of Palestine, Jewish–Arab tensions rose, with Arab snipers firing at Jewish neighbourhoods from the minaret of beachfront Hassan Bek Mosque. The Haganah and the Irgun (Jewish underground forces) responded by laying siege to Jaffa, a major centre of the Palestinian national movement. In April 1948 Jaffa was captured by Jewish forces and the vast majority of the 70,000 Arab residents were expelled or fled, most for Gaza or Beirut.

From City to Metropolis

In April 1949 Tel Aviv and Jaffa were joined to create a single municipality. The previous Arab residents were not allowed to return to their homes under the 'Absentees Property Law' and many of the vacant properties in Jaffa were taken over by Jewish immigrants. Among them were thousands of Jews from Bulgaria, which is why the city came to be known as 'Little Sofia'.

The decades after the establishment of the state of Israel saw metropolitan Tel Aviv expanding in every direction, turning neighbouring towns such as Ramat Gan and Givatayim to the east and, to the south, Bat Yam and Holon into bustling inner suburbs. The city flourished as Israel's main centre of newspaper publishing, Hebrew literature, theatre and the arts. Early restrictions on the height of buildings had to be modified when authorities realised that the only place to go was up – and that that if Tel Aviv didn't get the skyscrapers (and the municipal taxes they generate), neighbouring Ramat Gan would.

During the First Gulf War (1991), greater Tel Aviv was hit by about three dozen Iraqi Scud missiles, damaging thousands of apartments. On 4 November 1995, Prime Minister Yitzhak Rabin was assassinated by a right-wing Orthodox Jew during a peace rally at what is now Rabin Sq. The following year the city centre was hit by a wave of Palestinian suicide bomb attacks. The confident optimism of the Oslo Peace Process years was over, especially after the implosion of the dot-com bubble at the end of the 1990s.

Into the 21st Century

The new millennium brought more hard times, with more than a dozen suicide bombings in downtown Tel Aviv during the Second Intifada. But the early 21st century also saw a rejuvenated economy based largely on high-tech innovation. Young Israelis started to move back to TLV, and older neighbourhoods such as Neve Tzedek and parts of Jaffa underwent gentrification.

In recent years Tel Aviv has gained in both confidence and sophistication. In 2003 the city accepted Unesco World Heritage status for its 'White City' Bauhaus buildings; restoration of these is proceeding, albeit slowly. And it's also gaining additions to its infrastructure, including a light-rail line from Petach Tikva to Bat Yam (the first in what is hoped to be a series of new lines) and affordable housing.

◉ Sights

This is a city that is best explored by foot or bicycle. There aren't many top-drawer sights, so you should spend most of your time wandering through the colourful and diverse neighbourhoods in and around the city centre (aka *merkaz ha-Ir*) and relaxing on the wonderful beaches on the city's western edge. In summer there's a simple rule: spend your days at the beach and your nights investigating one of the Middle East's best eating and drinking scenes. In winter, there are enough museums and shopping opportunities to keep you busy during the day, and the night-time eating and drinking scene is just as vibrant as its warm-weather equivalent.

The ancient port of Jaffa (Yafo) is a 30-minute walk from the city centre along the beachside promenade or through the atmospheric neighbourhood of Neve Tzedek. To get to Ramat Aviv (north of the Yarkon River) and the satellite suburb of Holon, south of the city, you'll need to take a bus or taxi.

◉ City Centre

The area running from Arlozorov St south to Sheinken St is generally referred to as the city centre (*merkaz ha-Ir* or *lev ha-Ir*). It includes the cultural precinct around Ha-Bima (Stage) Sq; the upper stretch of the city's favourite promenade, Rothschild Blvd; the shopping hubs of the Dizengoff Centre and Carmel Market; and the popular retail and cafe strips along Dizengoff, Allenby and King George Sts.

TEL AVIV-JAFFA (YAFO) SIGHTS

TEL AVIV IN...

Two Days

With only two days at your disposal and lots to experience, you'll need to get cracking! Have breakfast at one of the **cafes** around Rothschild Blvd and then wander around this area admiring its **Bauhaus building stock**. Next, browse the boutiques in the historic **Neve Tzedek** district before heading to even-more-historic Jaffa, where you can have lunch in the **flea market** (p118) before wandering around **Old Jaffa**. In the evening, sample some new Israeli cuisine at **Catit** (p131), **Mizlala** (p134) or **North Abraxas** (p130).

On day two, brunch on the beach at **Manta Ray** (p135), walk along the beachside promenade and then head up through the **Carmel Market** (p110) to the city centre before making your way to the wonderful **Tel Aviv Museum of Art** (p110). At night, eat French at **Brasserie M&R** (p129) or Italian at **Bindella Osteria & Bar** (p131).

Four Days

An extra couple of days will allow you to spend more time at the beach and at your choice of the city's many **museums**. You should also take a walking tour or two, and make the most of the city's fantastic **cafe and bar culture**.

Carmel Market
MARKET

(Shuk HaCarmel; Map p112; ⊙8am-late afternoon Sun-Thu, to mid-afternoon Fri) Squeezed between the dishevelled streets of the Yemenite Quarter and the pedestrianised section of Nahalat Binyamin St, Tel Aviv's busiest street market is, in many ways, the heart of the city. The total opposite of the characterless air-conditioned shopping malls and supermarkets found elsewhere in the city, it's a crowded and noisy place where vendors hawk everything from cut-price beachwear to knock-off designer accessories, and where locals come to buy olives, pickles, nuts, fruit, vegetables, cheese and freshly baked bread.

Rubin Museum
GALLERY

(Map p112; ☑03-525 5961; www.rubinmuseum. org.il; 14 Bialik St; adult/child 20NIS/free; ⊙10am-3pm Mon, Wed, Thu & Fri, to 8pm Tue, 11am-2pm Sat) Sometimes referred to as the Gauguin of Palestine but to our mind more reminiscent of Matisse, Romanian-born Reuven Rubin (1893–1974) immigrated to Palestine in 1923 and painted wonderful landscapes and scenes of local life in his adopted country, many of which are on display at this gallery in his former home. There are a number of scenes of Jaffa and plenty of portraits, providing a fascinating account of Jewish immigration and the early years of Israel.

Bialik Museum
MUSEUM

(Map p112; ☑03-525 4530; 22 Bialik St; adult/student & child 20/10NIS, combined Beit Ha'ir & Bialik Museum ticket adult 30NIS; ⊙11am-5pm Mon-Thu, 10am-2pm Fri & Sat) Israel's national poet Chaim Nachman Bialik lived in this 1920s villa, which is designed in the style of the Arts and Crafts movement. Its richly decorated downstairs interiors include custom-made furniture, a vivid colour scheme and ceramic tiles representing the Twelve Tribes of Israel, the Star of David and the signs of the zodiac. Bialik's private library, study and bedroom are preserved upstairs, and there's an archive of his papers in the basement.

Beit Ha'ir
CULTURAL CENTRE

(Town House; Map p112; ☑03-724 0311; http:// beithair.org; 27 Bialik St; adult/student & child 20/10NIS, combined Bialik Museum & Beit Ha'ir ticket adult 30NIS; ⊙9am-5pm Mon-Thu, 10am-2pm Fri & Sat) Located in a cul de sac at the end of Bialik St, which is full of significant Bauhaus-style buildings, this cultural centre comprises two galleries where temporary exhibitions are held, as well as a permanent exhibition of historical photographs and documents about the city. The building, which dates from 1925, was used as Tel Aviv's city hall from 1925 to 1965 and visitors can see a reconstruction of the office once used by Meir Dizengoff.

Helena Rubenstein Pavilion
GALLERY

(Map p112; ☑03-528 7196; www.tamuseum.com; 6 Tarsat Blvd; admission 10NIS; ⊙10am-6pm Mon, Wed & Sat, to 9pm Tue & Thu, to 2pm Fri) FREE Endowed by the cosmetics entrepreneur of the same name, this contemporary art space is an annexe of the Tel Aviv Museum of Art. There's a permanent collection of decorative arts on the top floor, but the main draw is the temporary exhibition space downstairs, which showcases work by both Israeli and international artists. The Bauhaus-style building, which opened in 1959, is just off HaBima Sq, home to Israel's national theatre and to the Charles Bronfman Auditorium.

★ Tel Aviv Museum of Art
GALLERY

(Map p112; ☑03-607 7020; www.tamuseum.com; 27 Shaul HaMelech Blvd; adult/student under 15yr 50/40NIS, under 15yr free; ⊙10am-6pm Mon-Wed & Sat, to 9pm Tue & Thu, to 2pm Fri; ☐7, 9, 18, 38, 42, 70, 82) The ultramodern 'envelope' building by American architect Preston Scott Cohen is one of many reasons to visit this impressive gallery located on the eastern edge of the city centre. There's a huge amount to see here (including loads for kids), but the undoubted highlight is the superb collection of impressionist and postimpressionist art on the 1st floor of the main building, which includes works by Renoir, Gauguin, Degas, Pissarro, Monet, Picasso, Cézanne, Van Gogh, Vuillard, Matisse, Soutine and Chagall.

Also worth investigating are the temporary exhibitions (there are always a number to choose from), the architecture and design wing, and the galleries showcasing 20th-century Israeli art. The museum's Pastel Brasserie & Bar has indoor and outdoor seating and is a convenient lunch choice.

⊙ South City Centre

Tel Aviv is a vibrant and cultured city where art galleries, cafes, bars and boutiques seem to be around every corner. But it's here, on the southern fringe of the city centre, where the culture is most pronounced and where the city's avant-garde and hipster communities congregate.

The wedge between Sheinken and Allenby Sts is littered with upmarket restaurants, stylish cafes and boutique hotels and

MILITARY MUSEUMS

Military history buffs and those with an interest in modern Israeli history told from a patriotic perspective can visit a number of museums in Tel Aviv catering to this area of interest.

Thirteen pavilions and sheds in the old Jaffa railway station house the **IDF History Museum** (Map p112; ☑ 03-516 1346; Prof Yehezkel Kaufmann St, Tel Aviv Promenade; adult/child & student 15/10NIS; ☺ 8.30am-4pm Sun-Thu) `FREE`, a repository of tanks, armoured fighting vehicles, antiaircraft guns, rifles and machine guns used by the Israel Defense Forces (IDF) since its establishment in 1948. Most kids seem to love clambering over the vehicles, but the lack of signage or interpretative panels in languages other than Hebrew is a problem for adult visitors who aren't military equipment enthusiasts. Enter through the car park next to the HaTachana centre.

Splendidly located on Rothschild Blvd, the **Haganah Museum** (Map p112; ☑ 03-560 8624; 23 Rothschild Blvd; adult/student & child 15/10NIS; ☺ 8am-4pm Sun-Thu) chronicles the formation and activities of the paramilitary organisation that was the forerunner of today's Israel Defense Forces (IDF). A civilian guerrilla force protecting Jewish farms and kibbutzim from attack in the 1920s and '30s, the Haganah went on to assist in the illegal entry of over 100,000 Jews into Palestine after the British Government's 1939 white paper restricting immigration.

The story of the Palmach, an elite Haganah strike force that was established in 1941, is told at the multimedia-rich **Palmach Museum** (☑ 03-643 6393; www.palmach.org.il; 10 Haim Levanon St, Ramat Aviv; adult/child 30/20NIS; ☺ by appointment only Sun-Fri) in Ramat Aviv. Starting in a memorial hall for members who died fighting for establishment of the state of Israel, a Hebrew-speaking guide takes visitors on a tour that focuses on the stories of individual soldiers. Headphones provide translations into other languages.

A small museum on the 1st floor of the **Jabotinsky Institute** (Map p112; ☑ 03-528 6523; www.jabotinsky.org; 38 King George St; ☺ 8am-4pm Sun-Thu) `FREE` documents the history and activities of the Etzel (Irgun), an underground militia founded by Ze'ev Jabotinsky in 1931. Exhibits concentrate on Jabotinsky's political, literary and journalistic activities, and also document the creation of the Jewish Legion (five battalions of Jewish volunteers who served in the British army during WWI).

You'll need to show your passport to gain entry to all of these museums. Note that a combined entry pass to five IDF-operated museums including the IDF History Museum and Haganah museum costs 20NIS.

is edged to the east by the lower stretch of Rothschild Blvd, which is rich in Bauhaus building stock – on weekends, Tel Avivians flock here to meet friends and enjoy the highly social street scene.

The bohemian enclave of Neve Tzedek, a gentle slope running downhill to Tel Aviv Promenade, was founded in 1887 and is the oldest quarter in the new city. A hugely atmospheric tangle of narrow streets lined with bars, cafes and edgy artisan boutiques, it rewards exploration. Nearby, the gritty neighbourhoods of Florentin and Neve Sha'anan are where hipsters, foreign workers, asylum seekers and the occasional intrepid tourist can be found.

Maine Friendship House MUSEUM
(☑ 03-681 9225; www.jaffacolony.com; 10 Auerbach St; ☺ noon-3pm Fri, 2-4pm Sat, call to visit

other times) The first neighbourhood outside Jaffa's city walls, the American Colony was established by a group of American Christians in the 1860s. The story of their star-crossed (some would say hare-brained) settlement scheme is told at the engaging Maine Friendship House museum. The colony area, run-down but charming, is centred on the corner of Auerbach and Be'er Hoffman Sts, 1km northeast of Jaffa's old city.

In 1866 157 men, women and children, led by an eccentric and charismatic preacher (and excommunicated Mormon) named George J Adams, set sail from Jonesboro, Maine, on the three-masted clipper *Nellie Chapin*. In the hold were 22 prefabricated wooden houses and the latest in agricultural implements. Their destination: the Holy Land, where they hoped to make preparations for the return of the Jews. The entire

TEL AVIV-JAFFA (YAFO) SIGHTS

South City Centre

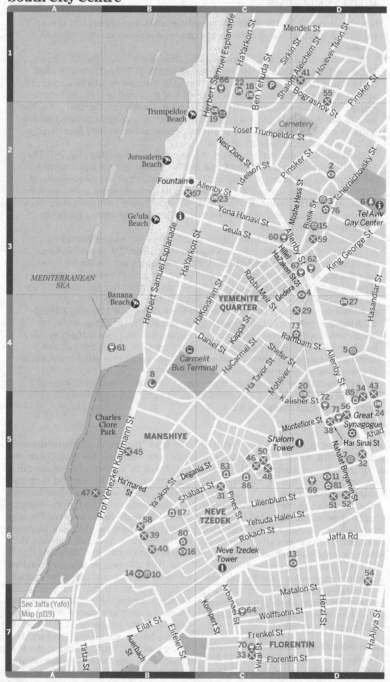

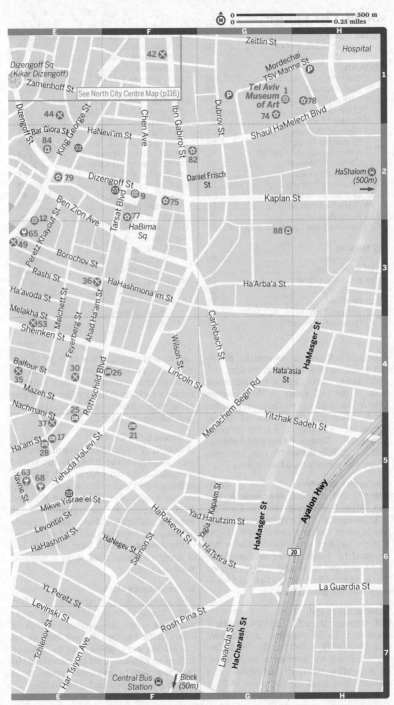

N

0   500 m
0   0.25 miles

E **F** **G** **H**

Zeitlin St

Hospital

Dizengoff Sq
(Kikar Dizengoff)

Zamenhoff St

Mordechai
TSV Manne St

Tel Aviv
Museum
of Art

See North City Centre Map (p116)

Dubrov St

Shaul HaMelech Blvd

44

Dizengoff St

Bar Giora St

King George St

HaNevi'im St

Chen Ave

Ibn Gabirol St

82

84

79

Dizengoff St

Daniel Frisch
St

HaShalom
(500m)

Ben Zion Ave

Tarsat Blvd

9

75

Kaplan St

12

Peretz Khayout St

77

HaBima
Sq

65

49

Borochov St

88

Rashi St

36

HaHashmona'im St

Ha'Arba'a St

Ha'avoda St

Melchett St

Melakha St

Sheinken St

Feyerberg St

Ahad Ha'am St

Carlebach St

53

Balfour St

35

Rothschild Blvd

30

26

Lincoln St

Wilson St

Hata'asia
St

HaMasger St

Mazeh St

Nachmani St

25

37

21

Menachem Begin Rd

Yitzhak Sadeh St

Ha'am St

17

28

63

68

Yehuda HaLevi St

Yavne St

Mikve Yisrae'el St

HaRakevet St

Yad Harutzim St

Yagia Kapaim St

HaTsfira St

HaMasger St

Ayalon Hwy

Levontin St

HaHashmal St

HaNegev St

Salmon St

20

La Guardia St

YL Peretz St

Levinski St

Tchlenov St

Har Tsiyon Ave

Rosh Pina St

Lavanda St

HaCharash St

Central Bus
Station

Block
(50m)

South City Centre

◎ Top Sights

1 Tel Aviv Museum of Art G1

◎ Sights

2 Beit Ha'ir D2
3 Bialik Museum...................................... D3
4 Carmel Market D3
5 Chelouche Gallery................................ D4
6 Gan Meir Park...................................... D3
7 Haganah Museum................................. D5
8 Hassan Bek Mosque.............................. B4
9 Helena Rubenstein Pavilion.................... F2
10 IDF History Museum.............................. B6
11 Independence Hall................................ D5
12 Jabotinsky Institute...............................E2
13 Levinsky Spice Market.......................... D6
14 Old Railway Station B6
15 Rubin Museum D3
16 Suzanne Dellal Centre........................... B6

◎ Sleeping

17 Alma Hotel E5
18 Art Plus Hotel C1
19 Beachfront Hotel C2
20 Brown TLV D5
21 Diaghilev..F5
22 Embassy Hotel C1
23 Hayarkon 48 Hostel............................... C2

24 Hotel Montefiore D5
25 Rothschild 71..E5
26 Rothschild Hotel F4
27 Shenkin Hotel....................................... D4
28 Townhouse Tel Aviv E5

◎ Eating

29 Agadir D4
30 Ahathaan E4
31 Anita C5
32 Benedict... D5
33 Bet Lehem Hummus C7
34 Bindella Osteria & Bar D5
35 Cafe Lucia...E4
36 Cafe Noah E3
37 Café Noir...E5
    Casbah Cafe ....(see 33)
38 Catit D5
39 Dallal B6
40 Dallal Bakery B6
41 Felafel Gabai... D1
    Gala Gelateria ....(see 49)
42 Gelateria Siciliana..................................F1
43 Giraffe D5
44 HaKosem E1
45 Herbert Samuel B5
    Hotel Montefiore ....(see 24)
46 Lulu.. C5

---

enterprise collapsed in short order, the result of disease, dissension and drinking (Adams'), and by 1868 only 20 settlers remained; most of the real estate in the American Colony was sold to the German Templers the following year. Today, some of the old houses are still standing, as is the Templers' **Immanuel Church** (www.immanuelchurch -jaffa.com; 15 Be'er Hofman St), now Lutheran, whose fine organ is used for concerts.

Chelouche Gallery
GALLERY
(Map p112; ☑ 03-620 0068; www.chelouchegallery. com; 7 Mazeh St; ⊙ 11am-7pm Mon-Thu, 10am-2pm Fri & 11am-2pm Sat) This contemporary art gallery is set in the neoclassical 'Twin House', a 1920s building with two identical wings designed by Joseph Berlin as a residence for himself and his brother. The welcoming Tola'at Sfarim (Book Worm) Cafe and Bookshop is on the ground floor.

Independence Hall
HISTORIC SITE
(Beit Haatzmaut; Map p112; ☑ 03-510 6426; http:// eng.ihi.org.il; 16 Rothschild Blvd; adult/student/ child 24/18/16NIS; ⊙ 9am-5pm Sun-Thu, to 2pm Fri) Scheduled to be given a sorely needed renovation when we last visited, this building was originally the home of Meir Dizengoff, one of the city's founding fathers

and its first mayor. It was here, on 14 May 1948, that David Ben-Gurion declared the establishment of the state of Israel. Entry includes a short introductory film and a tour of the room where Israel's Declaration of Independence was signed.

Suzanne Dellal Centre
ARTS CENTRE
(Map p112; ☑ 03-510 5656; www.suzannedellal. org.il; 5 Yechiely St, Neve Tzedek) The first school built outside the city walls of Jaffa, this 1892 building set in leafy surrounds was converted into a cultural centre between 1984 and 1989, triggering the gentrification of the formerly dishevelled Neve Tzedek neighbourhood. A popular venue for festivals and cultural events, it has a focus on dance and is home to the internationally recognised Batsheva troupe.

Levinsky Spice Market
MARKET
(Shuk Levinsky; Map p112; www.shuktlv.co.il; Florentin) Equally beloved by celebrity chefs and local cooks, this aromatic stretch of stores along Levinsky St near the Central Bus Station was established in the 1920s by Balkan immigrants. This is where locals in the know come to source fresh spices, dried fruit, olive oil, cheese and other goodies.

TEL AVIV-JAFFA (YAFO) SIGHTS

◉ Tel Aviv Beach & Port

Ask any local to nominate the thing that they most love about their home town, and their answer will almost inevitably be the same: 'The beaches, of course!' When the sun is out – and especially during the summer months – the string of sandy beaches between Tel Aviv Port and Jaffa has an all-pervading pull, and city residents head here to laze on the sand, play *matkot* (paddle ball), frolic in the surf or relax in green spaces including Charles Clore Park near Neve Tzedek. A beachside promenade is divided into lanes for walkers and cyclists and is particularly busy in the early morning, around sunset and on the weekend.

Old Port   PORT

(Namal; www.namal.co.il) Originally opened in 1936, Tel Aviv's port went into decline with the construction of a better, deeper harbour at Ashdod in the 1960s. In the early 2000s the Tel Aviv municipality finally overhauled the area, creating a wide wooden boardwalk, including playgrounds and bike paths, and transforming the derelict warehouses into a commercial centre with big-name stores (Castro, Levi's, Steve Madden etc) to draw local shoppers.

On weekends, the port is buzzing with families wandering around its waterfront shops, restaurants and cafes while planes swoop in low overhead to land at nearby Sde Dov airport. An organic farmers market attracts locals on Friday between 9am and 3pm, and after dark and on weekends hordes of young clubbers descend on the strip of bars and nightclubs after midnight.

Ben-Gurion Museum   MUSEUM

(Map p116; ☎03-522 1010; www.bg-house.org; 17 Ben-Gurion Ave; ⊕8am-3pm Sun & Tue-Thu, to 5pm Mon, to 1pm Fri, 11am-2pm Sat) **FREE** Built between 1930 and 1931, this modest house near the marina was the Tel Aviv home of David Ben-Gurion, Israel's first prime minister. Built in a workers' neighborhood established on Keren Kayemet Le'Israel (Jewish National Fund) land, it is maintained more or less as it was left on the great man's death. An audiovisual presentation gives background on Ben-Gurion's life and on the foundation of the state of Israel.

Old Railway Station   HISTORIC SITE

(HaTachana; Map p112; www.hatachana.co.il; Neve Tzedek; ⊕10am-10pm; ☒18, 10, 100) Once the terminus of the Jerusalem–Jaffa train line, this station near the southern end of the

North City Centre

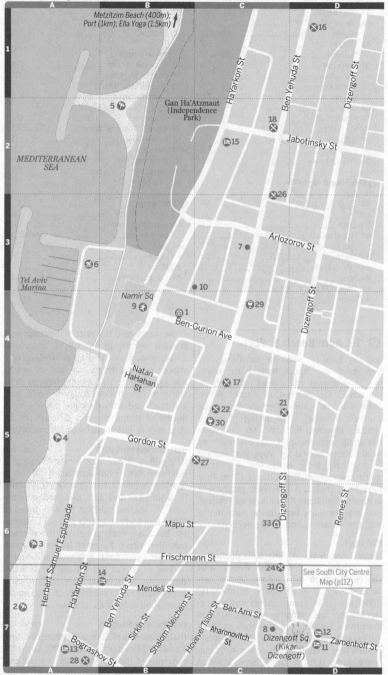

Metzitzim Beach (400m);
Port (1km); Ella Yoga (1.5km)

16

HaYarkon St

Ben Yehuda St

Dizengoff St

MEDITERRANEAN
SEA

Gan Ha'Atzmaut
(Independence
Park)

5

18

15

Jabotinsky St

26

Arlozorov St

7

Tel Aviv
Marina

6

10

Namir Sq

9

1

Ben-Gurion Ave

29

Dizengoff St

Natan
HaHahan
St

17

22

21

30

4

Gordon St

27

Mapu St

33

Dizengoff St

Reines St

3

Herbert Samuel Esplanade

Frischmann St

24

See South City Centre
Map (p112)

14

HaYarkon St

Ben Yehuda St

Mendeli St

31

2

Sirkin St

Shalom Aleichem St

Hovevei Tsion St

Ben Ami St

Aharonovitch
St

8

Dizengoff Sq
(Kikar
Dizengoff)

12

11

Zamenhoff St

Bograshov St

13

28

North City Centre

⊙ Sights

⊙ Activities, Courses & Tours

⊝ Sleeping

⊗ Eating

⊝ Drinking & Nightlife

⊝ Shopping

beachfront promenade operated between 1892 and 1948 and was subsequently used by the Israel Defense Forces (IDF) as a storage facility before being converted into a retail and entertainment complex between 2005 and 2010. Now home to shops, cafes, bars and a branch of the popular ice-cream chain Vaniglia, it's known locally as HaTachana (The Station). On Friday, a vegan market is held here.

Note that cafes and restaurants open on Friday evening, but the shops in the complex close at 5pm.

Hassan Bek Mosque   MOSQUE

(Hasan Bey Mosque; Map p112) Built in 1916 by Jaffa's Ottoman governor of the same name, this white limestone mosque built on the border of Tel Aviv and Jaffa has always had symbolic significance for Jaffa's Arab population.

◉ Jaffa (Yafo) & Ajami

Jaffa is the oldest part of Tel Aviv, and the quarter with the most pronounced Arab atmosphere. Its three major draws are a flea market near Jaffa's landmark 1903 clock tower, the hilltop Old City enclave and the shopping and entertainment centre at the old port.

South of the Old City and port is the Ajami district, where Ottoman-era homes still exist side-by-side with tiny, ramshackle fisherfolk's shacks. Once notorious for crime and drugs (as featured in Scandar Copti and Yaron Shani's 2009 film *Ajami*), its seafront opens out into a large green park and a boardwalk that connects Old Jaffa to Bat Yam.

Most buses from the city centre stop on Sderot Yerushalayim, the southern extension of Herbert Samuel Esplanade/Kaufmann St. Alight at the stop near Shalma (Salameh) Rd, or at the one near Olei Zion St.

★ Flea Market   MARKET

(⊙ stalls 10am-3pm Sun-Fri; ☐ Dan 10, 18, 25, 41) In recent years, lots of energy has gone into giving Jaffa's Old City a tourism-triggered makeover, and the results are undeniably attractive. However, the real draw in this part of the city is considerably more dishevelled. Spread over a grid of streets south of the clock tower, Jaffa's much-loved *pishpeshuk* or *shuk ha-pishpeshim* (flea market) is full of boutiques, laid-back cafes, pop-up bars and colourful street stalls selling vintage clothes and furniture, curios and the occasional antique.

Note that stalls and shops are closed on Saturday, but cafes, bars and restaurants are open. On summer nights, outdoor entertainment is sometimes staged in the main stall area.

★ Old City   HISTORIC SITE

(☐ Dan 10, 18, 25, 41) Centred on **Kikar Kedumim** (Kedumim Sq), a paved space edged by touristy shops and cafes, this hilltop area overlooks the Mediterranean Sea and is visually dominated by the Franciscan **St Peter's Church** (⊙ 8-11.45am & 3-5pm Oct-Feb, to 6pm Mar-Sep). The surrounding laneways are home to boutique tourist accommodation, galleries and the occasional artisan's atelier.

To the east of the square, perched on Jaffa's highest point, **HaPisgah Gardens** offers nice views north up the coast to Tel Aviv.

Jaffa Port   PORT

(www.namalyafo.co.il; ⊙ 10am-10pm Mon-Wed, to 11pm Thu, 9am-11pm Fri & Sat; ☐ Dan 10, 18, 25, 41) One of the oldest known harbours in the world, the port of Jaffa was mentioned in the Bible and was once the disembarkation point for pilgrims to the Holy Land. These days it's predominantly an entertainment facility incorporating a boardwalk and warehouses hosting bars, restaurants, shops and the not-for-profit Nalaga'at Centre, home to a deaf-blind theatre company, a cafe employing deaf waiters and a 'black out' restaurant with a staff of blind waiters.

The port is busiest on summer evenings, when free entertainment is sometimes staged and the boardwalk restaurants are packed with local diners.

Ilana Goor Museum   GALLERY

(☑ 03-683 7676; www.ilanagoormuseum.org; 4 Mazal Dagim St; adult/student/child 30/25/20NIS; ⊙ 10am-4pm Sun-Fri, to 6pm Sat; ☐ Dan 10, 18, 25, 41) Built in the 18th century, this imposing stone building just south of Kikar Kedumim originally served as a hostel for Jewish pilgrims arriving at Jaffa and later was converted into a soap and perfume factory. Now the residence of local artist Ilana Goor, it is open to the public as a gallery. The collection here won't be to all tastes, being dominated by tribal art and works by Goor, but the interior spaces and panoramic terrace are extremely attractive.

◉ HaYarkon Park & Ramat Aviv

North of the city centre, across the Nakhal Yarkon (Yarkon River), are the huge green space of HaYarkon Park and the upmarket residential suburb of Ramat Aviv, location of Tel Aviv University and a number of museums and cultural institutions.

Beit Hatfutsot   MUSEUM

(Museum of the Jewish People; ☑ 03-745 7800; www.bh.org.il; Gate 2, Tel Aviv University, 2 Klausner St, Ramat Aviv; adult/student & child 42/32NIS; ⊙ 10am-4pm Sun-Tue, to 7pm Wed & Thu, 9am-1pm Fri; ☐ Dan 7, 13, 25, 45) Beit Hatfutsot recounts the epic story of Jewish exile and the global Jewish Diaspora using objects,

Jaffa (Yafo)

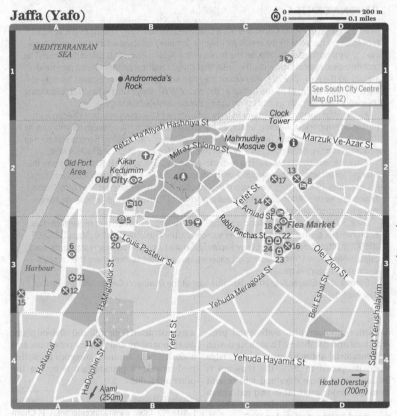

MEDITERRANEAN SEA

Andromeda's Rock

Old Port Area

Kikar Kedumim

Old City

Retzit Ha'Aliyah Hashniya St

Mifraz Shlomo St

Mahmudiya Mosque

Clock Tower

Marzuk Ve-Azar St

Yefet St

Amiad St

Rabbi Pinchas St

Flea Market

Louis Pasteur St

HaMigdalor St

Harbour

Yeret St

Yehuda Meragoza St

Bet Eshat St

Olei Zion St

Sderot Yerushalayim

HaNamal

HaDolphin St

Ajami (250m)

Yehuda Hayamit St

Hostel Overstay (700m)

See South City Centre Map (p112)

TEL AVIV-JAFFA (YAFO)

200 m
0.1 miles

Jaffa (Yafo)

SARONA CENTRE

In 1871 a group of Pietist Christians from southwestern Germany known as the Templers (not to be confused with the medieval Knights Templar) established a small agricultural colony 4km northeast of Jaffa, on the banks of the Ayalon River, and called it Sarona. The technologies, agricultural and otherwise, that they brought with them had a profound impact on the early Zionists, with whom they had correct and in some cases friendly relations. Exiled to Egypt by the British at the end of WWI, they returned in 1921, expanding their agricultural holdings and constructing Bauhaus-style buildings.

As the Nazi party rose to power in Germany, some of Sarona's residents became enthusiastic supporters, leading, unsurprisingly, to friction with their Jewish neighbours. At the outbreak of WWII, the Templers were declared 'enemy aliens' and Sarona was turned into an internment camp; in 1943 most of the Templers were deported to Australia.

After the war, the fortified camp became a military base for the British forces and thus a target for attacks by the various Jewish undergrounds — the Haganah, Etzel and Lehi. In December 1947, as they were about to leave, the British turned over the camp to the Jewish leadership. After 1948, the Israeli government turned the old Templer buildings into government offices.

Over 30 of the colony's historic buildings were recently restored and redeveloped as a commercial centre. Set in lush green surrounds, the **Sarona Centre** (Map p112; ☑ 03-609 9028; http://saronatlv.co.il; Eliezar Kaplan St, Sarona) includes offices, restaurants, bars, cafes, fashion and lifestyle stores, art galleries, and a visitor centre where the colony's fascinating history is told.

Sarona is on Eliezer Kaplan St, 1km due east of the Dizengoff Center and just east of Habima Sq.

dioramas, photographs, audiovisual presentations and databases. Though its design and curatorial approach were cutting edge when it opened in 1978, the museum is looking dated these days and will benefit from the major renovation and redevelopment that is currently under way. This is scheduled to be completed in 2017.

The museum includes the Feher Jewish Music Centre, the Douglas E Goldman Jewish Genealogy Centre (where visitors can register their family tree) and a Visual Documentation Centre, the largest database of Jewish life in the world. There's also a temporary exhibition gallery on the ground floor.

Eretz Israel Museum　　　　　MUSEUM
(Land of Israel Museum; ☑ 03-641 5244; www.eretzmuseum.org.il; 2 Chaim Levanon St, Ramat Aviv; adult/student 48/32NIS, child under 18yr free, incl planetarium adult/child 80/32NIS; ☺ 10am-4pm Sun-Wed, to 8pm Thu, to 2pm Fri, to 3pm Sat, planatarium shows 11.30am & 1.30pm Sun-Thu, 11am & noon Sat; ⊞ Dan 7, 13, 24, 25, 45, 127) Incorporating the archeological excavations of Tel Qasile, an ancient port city dating from the 12th century BCE, this museum sports a huge and varied range of exhibits and deserves at least half a day of your time. Sights include pavilions filled with glass and coins,

a reconstructed flour mill and olive-oil plant, an ethnography and folklore collection, and a garden built around a gorgeous Byzantine bird mosaic. A planatarium is among the other attractions.

Yitzhak Rabin Centre　　　　　MUSEUM
(☑ 03-745 3358; www.rabincenter.org.il; 14 Chaim Levanon St; self-guided tour adult/student & child 50/25NIS, guided tours adult/student & child 60/35NIS; ☺ 9am-5pm Sun, Mon & Wed, to 7pm Tue & Thu, to 2pm Fri; ⊞ Dan 7, 85, 29) Established in 1997 to promote democratic values, narrow socio-economic gaps and address social divisiveness, this centre is also home to the Israeli Museum, which includes 150 films and 1500 photographs telling the story of modern Israel's struggle for peace with its neighbours. Visitors can take a self-guided tour using a multilanguage audio device or book in advance to join a guided tour in Hebrew or English.

The musem's central narrative is interwoven with the story of former Prime Minister Yitzhak Rabin (1922–95), assassinated by a radical right-wing Orthodox Jew due to his work devising and implementing the Oslo Accords, which created the Palestinian National Authority and granted it partial control over parts of the Gaza Strip and West Bank.

🏖 Beaches

In hot weather, Tel Avivim (residents of Tel Aviv) flock to the city beach, a 14km-long stretch of golden sand divided into individual sections, each with its own character. You'll find young and old soaking up the Mediterranean rays, swimming and playing fierce games of *matkot*.

The water here is clean, and there are changing rooms and freshwater showers scattered along its length. Swimmers, however, must heed lifeguard warnings when conditions become rough; a black flag means that swimming is forbidden, a red flag means that swimming is dangerous and a white flag means that the area is safe. Beaches are patrolled between May and October.

The beaches are packed in summer, especially on Saturday, when crowds descend early to nab a prime spot. The prices of beach-furniture hire are regulated by the municipality: beach chairs cost 6NIS, an umbrella 6NIS and a lounge bed 12NIS. The municipality provides free wi-fi for beach-goers, as well as a mobile beach library at Metzitzim Beach that offers books in a number of languages.

Metzitzim Beach   BEACH
Named after a 1972 comedy film, Hof Metzitzim (Peeping Tom Beach) is a family-friendly bay with a small play area for children. It also hosts Friday-afternoon beach parties during summer.

Nordau Beach   BEACH
This is the city's religious beach, where men and women are segregated. Women can use the beach on Sunday, Tuesday and Thursday; it's the men's turn on Monday, Wednesday and Friday. It's open to everyone on Saturday, when observant Jews don't go to the beach.

Hilton Beach   BEACH
(Map p116) Named after the nearby hotel, Hilton Beach is divided into three parts: the city's unofficial gay beach is in the middle, the dog-walkers' beach is to the north (it's the only beach where dogs are officially allowed) and surfers hang 10 near the breakwater in the south.

Gordon Beach   BEACH
(Map p116) South from Hilton, this along with its neighbours to the south, **Frischmann Beach** (Map p116) and **Bograshov Beach** (Map p116), is party central. Well equipped with sun lounges, beach bars, an outdoor gym and restaurants, they're popular with young Tel Avivim, tourists and *matkot* players. The Gordon Swimming Pool is at the nearby marina.

Alma Beach   BEACH
(Charles Clore Beach) This is probably the most attractive beach in the city, with spectacular views across the water to Jaffa. It's home to the hugely popular Manta Ray (p135) restaurant.

🏃 Activities

Tel Avivim are an active lot and can often be found running towards the nearest park, cycling to the beach or heading off to the gym.

⭐ **Park HaYarkon**   OUTDOORS
(Ganei Yehoshua; www.park.co.il; Rokach Blvd) Joggers, cyclists, in-line skaters, footballers

---

BICYCLE BOOM

Being a compact city, there is no better way to see Tel Aviv than on two wheels. The city now has about 120km of dedicated bike paths running along many of the major thoroughfares, through Park HaYarkon and along the coastline from just north of Sde Dov airport southward, via Jaffa, to the suburb of Bat Yam. A free map of the bike-path network can be picked up at tourist information offices.

In 2011, the municipality introduced **Tel-O-Fun** (📞6070; www.tel-o-fun.co.il), a citywide bike-rental scheme similar to Paris' Vélib'. Intended for commuters, it lets riders pick up and drop off the green bicycles at over 75 docking stations. A daily access card costs 17NIS (23NIS between 2pm Friday and 7pm Saturday) and a weekly card costs 70NIS.

The first 30 minutes of usage are free; after that – to encourage quick turnover – there are fees that get progressive higher, starting at NIS5 per 30 minutes and quickly rising to 20NIS, 40NIS, 80NIS and then 100NIS an hour. To avoid fees, simply return your bike and, after waiting at least 10 minutes, take another one. Pay with your credit card at any Tel-O-Fun station, but be aware that instructions are in Hebrew only – you'll need to ask a local to translate.

and frisbee-throwers should head for this 3.5-sq-km stretch of grassy parkland along the Yarkon River, which makes up Tel Aviv's largest green space – its Central Park, if you will. The **Sportek Centre**, located here, has a climbing wall, basketball courts, a skate park and trampolines.

Gordon Swimming Pool
SWIMMING

(Map p116; ☑03-762 3300; www.gordon-pool. co.il; Tel Aviv Marina; adult/student & child Sun-Fri 67/57NIS, Sat 77/67NIS; ☺6am-9pm Mon-Thu, to 7pm Fri, 7am-6pm Sat, 1.30-9pm Sun) Originally opened in 1956, the outdoor Gordon Swimming Pool was rebuilt in 2009. Next to the marina and surrounded by palm trees, it has a 50m saltwater pool whose water is frequently changed, plus dedicated pools for children and toddlers. Pay extra and you can also use the sauna, hot tub or gym.

Surf House
WATER SPORTS

(Map p116; ☑09-9574522, 03-527 5927; www. surfhouse.co.il; 169 HaYarkon St; lessons from 250NIS) Conveniently located near Gordon Beach, this school offers kitesurfing, windsurfing, paddleboard and surfing lessons for beginners.

Ella Yoga
YOGA

(☑03-544 4881; www.ellayoga.co.il; Hangar 4, Old Port; 3 classes 225NIS) A great place to salute the sun or arrange your asanas, Ella Yoga at the Old Port offers a range of classes from ashtanga to kundalini. Call to register and inquire about drop-ins.

Courses

Tel Aviv University Ulpan
LANGUAGE COURSE

(☑03-640 8639; www.international.tau.ac.il; Ramat Aviv) The city's most prestigious university has an *ulpan* (Hebrew-langauge school) offering students the opportunity to develop their Hebrew skills. Courses include a seven-week intensive Hebrew program (US$1700) and a four-week intensive program (US$1450). On-campus accomodation is available.

Ulpan Gordon
LANGUAGE COURSE

(Map p116; ☑03-522 3181; www.ulpangordon.co.il; 7 LaSalle St) The most popular *ulpan* in Tel Aviv charges around 700NIS per month for tourists; classes meet 2½ to 4½ hours a day two or three times a week.

Kabbalah Centre
COURSE

(Map p116; ☑03-526 6800; www.kabbalah.com; 14 Ben Ami St) The Kabbalah Center has its own California-inflected take on Jewish mysticism. If you want to know more, stop by the centre just off Dizengoff Sq.

Tours

Free City Walks
WALKING TOUR

(www.visit-tel-aviv.com) Three free walking tours and one based on tips are offered by the municipality's tourism office. One focuses on art and architecture at Tel Aviv University; a second investigates the city's vibrant nightlife; a third concentrates on the city's Bauhaus heritage; and a fourth (requiring a tip) tours Old Jaffa. Bookings aren't necessary – see the website for details.

Delicious Israel
WALKING TOUR

(☑052 569 9499; www.deliciousisrael.com; tours per person from US$110) American-born Inbal Baum immigrated to Israel in 2009 and soon established a successful business conducting culinary tours around the country. Her Tel Aviv offerings include a 4½-hour walking tour through Jaffa and the city centre, a 2½-hour walking tour around the Levinsky Market, a shorter Carmel Market tour, a hummus crawl and a street-food hop.

Sandemans Tours
WALKING TOUR

(www.newtelavivtours.com) Two tours – one of Old Jaffa at 11am daily and a second of Jaffa and the new city at 2pm on Monday, Wednesday and Saturday – are conducted by freelance tour guides working with this well-regarded company. The first relies on tips (50NIS per person is standard); the second costs €18 per person. Check the website for details.

Mekomy Offbeat Guides
TOUR

(www.mekomy.com) Tailored to individual interests, these tours connect travellers with local experts based on mutual passions including food, art, history, fashion, architecture and photography.

Israeli Center for Bicycle Tourism
BICYCLE TOUR

(Map p116; ☑077-481 4326; www.icbiketour.com; 135 Ben Yehuda St; tours 160NIS) This outfit runs a number of tours on two wheels, including a daily 3½-hour tour covering all the city's major sights, a tour around Park HaYarkon and a tour along the promenade from the Old Port to Jaffa Port.

THE REVIVAL OF HEBREW

Many Israelis feel that one of the supreme cultural achievements of the Zionist movement was the resurrection of the Hebrew language, which had not been used for everyday living for a couple of thousand years.

During the Diaspora, Jews adapted to local cultures and picked up the local lingo wherever they settled, combining it with Hebrew to create uniquely Jewish languages such as Yiddish (based on medieval German) and Ladino (Judeo-Espanyol, based on medieval Spanish). Classical Hebrew was preserved in sacred texts and synagogue prayers but was rarely heard on the street.

The turning point came when early Zionists began publishing secular literature in Hebrew in the mid-1800s and, in the latter decades of the 19th century, settling in Palestine. Among them was Eliezer Ben Yehuda, born in Lithuania in 1858. Like most Jewish children of his era, he was introduced to biblical Hebrew as part of his religious upbringing. When he arrived in Palestine in 1881, he was determined to turn Hebrew, the archaic language of study and prayer, into a secular tool of everyday communication, thus enabling Jews from all over the world to communicate with each other. (Herzl, the founder of modern Zionism, never spelled out what language he thought would be spoken in the Jewish state, but it appears that he assumed it would be German.)

When Ben Yehuda began living a Hebrew-speaking life, he found himself at a loss when trying to describe modern inventions such as trains and incandescent light bulbs. He began updating the language while simultaneously spreading it, as a spoken language, among his peers. His oldest son was the first all-Hebrew-speaking child in modern history.

Ben Yehuda's persistence and proselytising – and the work of generations of Hebrew-language *ulpanim* (language schools) for new immigrants – paid off, and today there are some nine million Hebrew speakers worldwide, including quite a few Palestinian Arabs. (By contrast, on the eve of WWII there were 11 million to 13 million speakers of Yiddish, while today there are fewer than one million.) People working to preserve shrinking minority languages such as Irish and Corsican often look to Hebrew – the only case of a 'retired' language having been completely resurrected – for inspiration and methods of propagation.

As in ancient times, when all sorts of Greek, Aramaic, Persian and Egyptian words crept into Hebrew, latter-day globalisation has resulted in an influx of words and concepts from languages such as English, German, French, Russian and Arabic. A classic case of word adoption is the @ symbol, which Israelis call a *shtrudel* because it looks like the Austrian pastry.

On the streets of Tel Aviv – which once proudly billed itself as 'the first Hebrew city' – you may hear some 'Hebrish', as Israelis tend to drop English (including obscenities) into the middle of Hebrew sentences. Much Israeli slang comes from Arabic – for instance, you'll often hear the words 'sababa' (cool, OK) and 'achla' ('excellent' or 'sweet'). A classic Arabic-English-Hebrew hybrid phrase, used when hip young people are saying goodbye to each other, is '*Tov, yallah,* bye' (OK, let's go, bye).

🎊 Festivals & Events

Tel Aviv Marathon   SPORTS
(www.tlvmarathon.co.il) Up to 35,000 runners pound the pavements in the new city and Jaffa during this event in late February.

Open House Tel Aviv   CULTURAL
(Batim Mibifnim; www.batim-il.org) Held in late May, this three-day event sees approximately 150 architecturally distinctive homes, apartments and public buildings open to visitors. There are also free architectural tours through the city.

Tel Aviv Pride   GAY & LESBIAN
(www.visit-tel-aviv.com) Held in the second week of June, this celebration of Israel's LGBT community draws a huge number of international visitors and is the country's biggest festival. Its centrepiece is the Pride Parade, but other events include parties at Hilton Beach and the **LGBT International Film Festival** (www.tlvfest.com).

White Night   CULTURAL
(Laila Lavan; www.visit-tel-aviv.com) Each June, the city has one sleepless night when the

> ### DON'T MISS
>
> ### DRUMMING INTO SHABBAT
> ....
>
> Every Friday as the sun goes down, Dolphinarium Beach near Charles Clore Park comes alive with hypnotic tribal rhythms and freestyle dancers. Situated next to the derelict but soon to be redeveloped Dolphinarium nightclub, this fabulous jam session provides an atmospheric and unique lead-up to Shabbat.

city's cultural venues stay open and free events are staged in venues including the HaTachana, Sarona Colony, Jaffa Port, beaches, HaBima Sq and Hatikya Market.

Cycling Tel Aviv   SPORTS
(www.sovevtlv.org.il) Held in mid-October, this three-day cycling festival is devoted to healthy living, an active lifestyle and green transportation. The main event is a 42km race open to professionals, cycling enthusiasts and families.

🛏 Sleeping

There are accommodation choices to meet every budget and style requirement in Tel Aviv, but the city's ever-expanding range of boutique hotels includes the most alluring options. The best location for visitors is the wedge of the south city centre bounded by Rothschild Blvd, Sheinkin St and Allenby St, which is richly endowed with cafes and restaurants. It's also within walking distance of most sights. Further away, Jaffa offers some stylish boutique options and a vibrant Arab-influenced street life.

The major hotel chains tend to locate their monoliths on HaYarkon St overlooking the beaches, which is fine in summer but not particularly pleasant in the colder months.

On-site parking is rare; instead, most hotels have deals with nearby car parks for around 65NIS per day. In Jaffa, there's free street parking at the Old City during the day and overnight parking there for 10NIS.

You'll need to book ahead at weekends and at most times of the year, particularly during July, August and festival periods such as Sukkot, Rosh Hashana, Hanukkah and Passover. During Tel Aviv Pride Week every hotel in the city is full – make your booking as far ahead as possible.

Note that we have cited high-season prices in our reviews – low-season prices can drop by up to 50%.

🛏 City Centre

Brown TLV   BOUTIQUE HOTEL $$$
(Map p112; ☑03-717 0200; www.browntlv.com; 25 Kalisher St; budget s US$135, d US$250-350; ❄@🛜) Attention all party animals: this 'urban hotel' is after your business. It may not be in the best part of town, but scenesters love the rooftop bar with its sundeck and hot tub, can't wait for Tuesday's art event in the downstairs cocktail lounge and adore the weekend yoga sessions. Rooms are compact but stylish; some have hot tubs.

Other enticements include free bike hire, on-site parking (35NIS per day) and vouchers for a complimentary breakfast in a range of chic Neve Tzedek cafes.

Center Chic Hotel   HOTEL $$$
(Map p116; ☑03-526 6100; www.atlas.co.il; 2 Zamenhoff St; s US$189, d US$210; ❄🛜) The name is cringe-worthy, but this 50-room hotel in a Bauhaus-style building is worth considering for its central location, its well-equipped and attractively decorated rooms and its pleasant roof terrace. Breakfast (US$21) is served in the next-door Hotel Cinema, which is operated by the same company, and guests can also enjoy a complimentary early-evening aperitif there.

Hotel Cinema   HOTEL $$$
(Map p116; ☑03-520 7100; www.atlas.co.il; 1 Zamenhoff St; r US$240, ste US$300; ❄@🛜) Fans of the silver screen will appreciate the decor of this converted Bauhaus-era cinema. Public spaces feature old projectors and cinema memorabilia, and the 83 rooms have movie posters and lights made from tripods. The feel is functional rather than glamorous, though the complimentary early-evening aperitif on the roof terrace strikes a Hollywood note. There's free parking and bike hire.

Lusky Hotel   HOTEL $$$
(Map p116; ☑03-516 3030; www.luskysuites-htl. co.il; 84 HaYarkon St; s/d/ste US$140/200/315; ❄🛜) This family-run choice offers well-appointed rooms featuring large windows letting in lots of light. Most of these have kitchenettes, and a number have balconies with sea view – the pick of the bunch is undoubtedly the one-bedroom penthouse, which has a huge balcony overlooking the beach. Drivers will appreciate the free underground parking.

🛏 South City Centre

★ Florentine Hostel
HOSTEL $

(📞 03-518 7551; www.florentinehostel.com; 10 Elifelet St, Florentin; dm 88NIS, d 280/300NIS, s/d without bathroom 240/260NIS; ✱◉⊛) On first view, the less-than-picturesque district in which this hostel is located can be off-putting. However, it doesn't take backpackers long to appreciate the location, which is close to Neve Tzedek, Florentin, Jaffa and the beach. Eight six-bed dorms and nine private rooms are on offer (all small), as is a rooftop bar and busy entertainment program.

Hostel Overstay
HOSTEL $

(📞 057-421 0200; http://overstaytlv.com; 47 Derech Ben Tsvi St; mattresses on roof 50NIS, dm 80NIS, d 260NIS; ✱◉⊛; 🚍Dan 41) Friendly owner-manager Omer knows exactly what backpackers want from a hostel: cheap prices, secure and clean rooms, a communal kitchen, bathrooms with plenty of hot water, a laid-back lounge area (there's a great one on the roof here) and a busy entertainment program. The location on a busy road in an industrial area southeast of Jaffa is the major drawback.

Beit Immanuel
HOSTEL $$

(📞 03-682 1459; www.beitimmanuel.org; 8 Auerbach St, American Colony; s/d 200/390NIS; ⊛) This convent-style hostel is located in an 1884 building opposite a pretty Lutheran church. Operated by an evangelical congregation known as CMJ, who aim to convince Jews that Jesus is the Messiah, its rooms are clean and comfortable and it has a private garden and a free car park. Unfortunately, the atmosphere isn't particularly welcoming.

The building once housed a fashionable hotel – German Kaiser Wilhelm II stayed here in 1898 – owned by Baron Plato von Ustinov, grandfather of the actor Peter Ustinov. It's located on a quiet street just off Eilat St (the continuation of Jaffa Rd).

★ Hotel Montefiore
BOUTIQUE HOTEL $$$

(Map p112; 📞 03-564 6100; www.hotelmontefiore. co.il; 36 Montefiore St; s/d 1420/1560NIS; ⊛⊛) A truly classy choice, the Montefiore occupies a heritage-listed 1920s villa in a tree-lined street running between Rothschild Blvd and Allenby St. The 12 elegant rooms have high ceilings, wooden floors, an armchair, a generously endowed bookshelf, double-glazed windows and a spacious bathroom. As is the case in the fashionable downstairs bar and restaurant, contemporary Israeli art adorns the walls.

★ Shenkin Hotel
BOUTIQUE HOTEL $$$

(Map p112; 📞 03-600 9401; www.shenkinhotel. com; 21 Brener St; s US$240-350, d US$300-380; ✱◉⊛) Its mantra is 'Locals Know Best', and the excellent recommendations

TEL AVIV-JAFFA (YAFO) SLEEPING

TEL AVIV-JAFFA (YAFO) SLEEPING

DESIGN MUSEUM HOLON

Ron Arad's elongated and extremely elegant swirl of red concrete and steel is one of Greater Tel Aviv's most striking examples of contemporary architecture. Inside, the **museum** (☏073-215 1515; www.dmh.org.il; 8 Pinhas Eilon St; adult/child 11-17yr/child 5-10yr 35/30/20NIS; ☉10am-4pm Mon & Wed, to 6pm Tue, Thu & Sat, to 2pm Fri) includes two spaces that house regularly refreshed temporary exhibitions showcasing fashion, furniture and other design. There's also a cafe and design store.

Although Holon is a rather dreary, working-class suburb of Tel Aviv, the museum represents the city's goal to transform itself into a centre of culture and education. It's in the east of town near the library, Mediateque and the Holon Institute of Technology. Holon is just 6km south of Tel Aviv and the museum can be reached by Dan bus 3 from Allenby St, Dan bus 41 or 89 from Levinsky St or Egged bus 71 from the Arlozorov Terminal. Get off at Weizman St, near Hoofien St, and it's a short walk to the museum, behind the mediateque. Alternatively, it's a 15-minute taxi ride from the centre.

supplied by the Shenkin's friendly staff certainly prove the point. A small and stylish place in a great location behind Sheinkin St, it offers four attractive room types, common areas showcasing local contemporary art, a roof terrace and a lovely rear terrace where complimentary tea, coffee and biscuits are available.

Rothschild 71 BOUTIQUE HOTEL $$$
(Map p112; ☏03-629 0555; www.the-rothschild. com; 71 Rothschild Blvd; r US$300, ste US$350-750; ❄❅) Housed in a 1934 Bauhaus-style apartment block, this luxe hotel offers 32 sleek and stylish studios and suites with good amenities (Nespresso machine, iPod dock, work desk). Located in the centre of the inner-city action, it's a great choice for couples as it doesn't accept guests under 16, has an attached cafe and offers unobtrusive yet efficient service.

Guests have free access to bicycles and a nearby gym. Breakfast isn't included in the room charge, but croissants, biscuits, tea and coffee are available in the small lobby lounge.

Diaghilev BOUTIQUE HOTEL $$$
(Map p112; ☏03-545 3131; www.diaghilev.co.il; 56 Mazeh St; d US$190-280; ❄❆❅) Paintings, prints and sculptures decorate every wall and common area in this 'Live Art Hotel', which occupies a handsome Bauhaus-style building off Rothschild Blvd. The spacious rooms have sitting area, kitchenette and separate bedroom. Top marks go to the quiet location, on-site parking (US$15) and helpful front-desk staff. Breakfast isn't included in the room rate.

Rothschild Hotel BOUTIQUE HOTEL $$$
(Map p112; ☏03-957 8888; www.rothschild-hotel.co. il; Rothschild Blvd; s 1070-1350NIS, d 1100-1400NIS, ste 1700-2800NIS; ❄❅) Ofra Zimbalista's sculpture of choral singers on the exterior is but one of many whimsical features at this exemplary boutique hotel. Predating Tel Aviv's recent boutique-hotel boom, the Rothschild's decor has worn extremely well and the place still leads the pack when it comes to service. The in-house restaurant serves what it describes as 'Zionist cuisine with a French accent'.

Alma Hotel BOUTIQUE HOTEL $$$
(Map p112; ☏03-630 8777; www.almahotel.co.il; 23 Yavne St; s/d deluxe US4420/470, executive US4440/490) The lovely 1920s building, theatrical decor and on-site restaurant and tapas bar are the main draws at this recently opened boutique choice just off Rothschild Blvd, but the rooftop bar and pretty rear courtyard garden provide additional inducement. Both room types offer plenty of space, a huge bed, an espresso machine and a lovely bathroom with luxe Sabon toiletries.

Townhouse Tel Aviv BOUTIQUE HOTEL $$$
(Map p112; ☏03-944 4300; www.townhousetelaviv. com; 32 Yavne St; s/d US$200/240, ste US$350; ❄❅) Reasonable prices and a good location mean that this 19-room place deserves consideration. Though not as stylish as many other boutique hotels in this area, it offers comfortable rooms with large beds, airy white bathrooms and espresso machines, and has a small downstairs lounge where breakfast and all-day tea and coffee are served.

🛏 Tel Aviv Beach & Port

★ Beachfront Hotel   HOSTEL $
(Map p112; ☑ 03-726 5230, 03-744 0347; www.tel
avivbeachfront.co.il; 78 Herbert Samuel Esplanade;
dm US$30, s US$80, d US$99, without bathroom
US$79; ❄ @ 🛜) The beach-party vibe is one
of many reasons to stay at this hostel opposite Trumpeldor Beach. An array of clean,
well-maintained dorms and rooms – some
with views and private terraces – awaits,
as does a rooftop bar serving free sangria
nightly. Free wi-fi and beach towels are provided for guest use, but internet costs 60NIS
per hour. No breakfast.

Hayarkon 48 Hostel   HOSTEL $
(Map p112; ☑ 03-516 8989; www.hayarkon48.com;
48 HaYarkon St; dm 113NIS, r 385NIS, without bathroom 330NIS; ❄ @ 🛜) Just two blocks from
the beach, this hostel has decent facilities including communal kitchen, rooftop terrace
and lounge with pool table and TV/DVD.
Dorms are mixed and female-only, and the
simple private rooms have double bed and
cable TV. All dorms and half of the private
rooms have air-con.

Embassy Hotel   BOUTIQUE HOTEL $$
(Map p112; ☑ 03-679 9999; www.embassy-hotel-
telaviv.co.il; 76 Hayarkon St; s US$150-160, d
US$160-170, ste US$180; ❄ 🛜) A decor reminiscent of *Mad Men* (series one) and a location
directly opposite Trumpeldor Beach mean
that this small hotel will please summer
style-meisters whose budgets can't quite
stretch to the prices charged by boutique
hotels in the Rothschild enclave. Opt for a
suite if possible, as these are larger than the
slightly cramped standards and come with
a kitchenette.

Port Hotel   BOUTIQUE HOTEL $$
(☑ 03-544 5544; www.porthoteltelaviv.com; 4
Yirmiyahu St; s/d US$150/160; ❄ 🛜) This self-
titled 'mini hotel' near the Old Port offers
something that is very rare in Tel Aviv – stylish accommodation for those on a budget.
Though small and without views, rooms are
clean and comfortable. The roof terrace and
proximity to the beach are major assets.

★ Mendeli Street Hotel   BOUTIQUE HOTEL $$$
(Map p116; ☑ 03-520 2700; www.mendelistreet
hotel.com; 5 Mendeli St; ❄ @ 🛜) In summer,
the living is both easy and glamorous at this
hotel close to Bograshov and Frischmann
Beaches. The hotel lobby and restaurant are
design-magazine chic, and the rooms are

similarly stylish, with contemporary fittings
and good amenities. The standard room is
compact, so consider opting for a deluxe or
superior version. Staff are young, charming
and extremely helpful.

Shalom Hotel & Relax   BOUTIQUE HOTEL $$$
(Map p116; ☑ 03-542 5555; www.atlas.co.il; 216
Hayarkon St; standard/superior r US$263/303;
❄ @ 🛜) Styled as a beach house – albeit one
with 51 rooms – this spa hotel offers a free
15-minute massage to every guest at its rooftop treatment room. Rooms are attractive
but small, so you should opt for a superior
one if possible. Common areas include a
rooftop sundeck and a welcoming lobby
lounge where a delicious breakfast is served.

Art Plus Hotel   BOUTIQUE HOTEL $$$
(Map p112; ☑ 03-797 1700; www.atlas.co.il; 35 Ben
Yehuda St; s/d/ste US$265/280/310; ❄ @ 🛜)
The interiors at this five-year-old art-
themed hotel haven't aged particularly well
and are definitely in need of refurbishment.
Fortunately, a new gym and spa provide
compensation, as does the free parking and
complimentary afternoon aperitif. There's a
roof terrace with sun lounges, though most
guests prefer lazing on the nearby beach.

🛏 Jaffa (Yafo)

Old Jaffa Hostel   HOSTEL $
(☑ 03-682 2370; www.telaviv-hostel.com; 13 Amiad
St; dm US$25, s US$70-98, d US$80-105; ❄ @ 🛜;
🚌 Dan 10, 18, 25, 41) Occupying an Ottoman-
era house in the flea market, this hostel is
definitely the most atmospheric option in
its price range in Tel Aviv, but it's not the
most comfortable. Dorm beds are reasonably priced and there is a generous number
of communal bathrooms, but the private
rooms are overpriced. There's a communal
kichen and a roof terrace with sea glimpses.

In summer, guests can sleep on the rooftop for US$21.

★ Old Jaffa Khan   APARTMENT $$$
(☑ 052 866 6232; info@oldjaffakhan.com; 5 Mazar
Taleh St, Old Jaffa; d US$350; ❄ 🛜; 🚌 Dan 10, 14,
25, 41) Hidden in an quiet enclave of artists'
studios in Old Jaffa, these studio apartments
are perfect for a romantic getaway. Two have
a sea view and two have private gardens –
all are gorgeous. Amenities include hot tub,
cable TV, music system, and kitchenette
with kettle and espresso machine. Breakfast
is served at a nearby cafe.

TEL AVIV & SHABBAT

If you've already experienced the hush that descends on Jerusalem as Shabbat is welcomed in – and wondered what on earth you're going to do without public transport, ATMs, restaurants and shops for a full 24 hours or so – don't despair: simply go to Tel Aviv and spend Shabbat the secular way.

Here, most shops close on Friday afternoon and don't open again until Saturday evening or Sunday morning, but that seems to be the extent of the city's nod to the holy day of rest. On Friday evening, bars, restaurants and clubs are packed to the rafters until dawn. Saturday sees locals thronging to the beach, lazing at cafes, dining at restaurants and generally being active throughout the day. And although municipal laws make it illegal to operate retail stores on Shabbat, there are also plenty of AM:PM, Tiv Ta'am, Super Yuda, Drugstore Food and Dor Alon minisupermarkets that remain open 24/7. This fact infuriates both the big supermarket chains and Orthodox Jews, and led to 21 minisupermarkets being taken to Tel Aviv's Municipal Court in 2014, charged with being repeat and unrepentant Shabbat violators. The court ruled that the stores could remain open.

You will notice less noise on the streets as there are no buses, but there are sheruts and taxis if you need to get around.

Market House Hotel
BOUTIQUE HOTEL **$$$**

(☏ 03-542 5555; www.atlashotels.co.il; 5 Beit Eshel St, Jaffa; s US$285, d US$300; ⊛🛜; 🚍 Dan 10, 18, 25, 41) There aren't many opportunities in life to stay in a building incorporating remnants of a 8th-century Byzantine chapel, but that's what's on offer at this recently opened hotel in the middle of the flea market. Rooms are stylish, soundproofed and equipped with kettle and fridge; the standards are a bit cramped, so opt for a superior or penthouse if possible.

Breakfast is enjoyed in the downstairs lobby and there's a complimentary aperitivo session in the upstairs lounge in the early evening.

Eating

Tel Aviv's eating scene is both varied and exciting. Coinciding with the boutique makeover that the city is undergoing, there is a rising crop of 'chef restaurants' (i.e. those run by celebrity chefs), as well as an ever-growing number of swanky brasseries. But don't worry if you're on a budget – there are still plenty of cheap street-food eateries and kiosks to choose from.

If you're self-catering, the best fresh fruit and vegetables in town are sold at the Carmel Market. Convenience supermarkets offering a good selection of products, reasonable prices and late-night hours are found all over the city.

Between Sunday and Friday, many restaurants offer 'business lunch' deals whereby diners get a free starter, or sometimes even a starter and a glass of wine, with every main course ordered.

✖ City Centre

★ Miznon
ISRAELI **$**

(Map p112; 30 King George St; pittas 23-44NIS; ⊙ noon-1am Sun-Thu, to 3pm Fri, from 7pm Sat; ✍) The vibe here is bustling, the prices are (very) reasonable and the staff are young, friendly and full of energy. And let's not forget the most important thing – the food is exceptionally delicious. Huge pittas stuffed with your choice of veggies, chicken, offal or meat await, as do fish and chips or roasted spiced yam and cauliflower (yum!).

You'll need to line up to order and give your name. Then make your choice from the tahina, labneh, green chilli sauce and pickle spread, claim a seat and wait for your order to be announced. Drinks include lemonade, beer and arak.

Felafel Gabai
MIDDLE EASTERN **$**

(Map p112; 25 Bograshov St; felafel 16NIS; ⊙ 10.30am-10.30pm Sun-Thu; ✍) In a city where every felafel stall claims to be the best, Gabai is a strong contender for the title. Like most stalls, its crispy balls of felafel come with as much salad, pickles and tahina sauce as you can squeeze in a pita bread. It also serves a fine shakshuka and schnitzel.

Sabich Frishman
MIDDLE EASTERN **$**

(Map p116; 42 Frishman St; sabich 18NIS; ⊙ 9am-11.30pm Sun-Thu, Fri before Shabbat, Sat after Shabbat; ✍) This tiny stall specialises in sabich, an Iraqi-derived snack consisting of fried aubergine, boiled egg, cabbage, salad, potato, hummus and spicy amba (mango) sauce, all stuffed into a pita. It's on the corner of Dizengoff and Frishman Sts – just look for the long lines and the felafel stall next door.

HaKosem
MIDDLE EASTERN $

(Map p112; 1 Shlomo HaMelech St; felafel from 18NIS; ⊙10.30am-11.30pm Sun-Thu, to 3pm Fri; ✐) One of the friendliest felafel stalls in town, HaKosem (the Magician) is a popular snack stop on the corner of King George St. Aside from its trademark green, fried chickpea balls in pita, it also offers sabich, schnitzel and shwarma (meat sliced off a spit and stuffed in a pocket of pita-type bread with chopped tomatoes and garnish).

If you're lucky, you'll get a free felafel ball straight from the pan while you queue: magic.

Gala Gelateria
ICE CREAM $

(Map p112; 30 King George St; 1/2/3 scoops 14/19/23NIS; ⊙10am-1am) Special choices for vegans (including a chocolate concoction) plus plenty of yoghurt and fruit options make this hole-in-the-wall gelateria opposite Gan Meir Park stand out from the Tel Aviv pack. We recommend anything with pistachio, tahina or mango in it.

★Orna and Ella
ISRAELI $$

(Map p112; ☑03-525 2085; www.ornaandella.com; 33 Sheinken St; breakfast 36-58NIS, mains 42-92NIS; ⊙8.30am-midnight Sun-Thu, from 10am Fri & Sat; ✆✐) Effortlessly melding its serious gastronomic focus with a casual-chic decor and a neighbourhood vibe, this restaurant-cafe is beloved of locals for good reason. Seasonal, often organic, ingredients are used to excellent effect in hearty breakfasts and refined lunches and dinners. Vegans, vegetarians and anyone who appreciates good food will be very happy here. Dine inside, or in a rear courtyard.

Brasserie M&R
FRENCH $$

(Map p116; ☑03-696 7111; www.brasserie.co.il; 70 Ibn Gabirol St; breakfast 22-49NIS, mains 62-110NIS; ⊙24hr) Somewhat officious maîtres d' orchestrate the service at this hugely popular cafe-brasserie opposite Rabin Sq. The art-deco-inspired interior is *très* Parisian, as is the menu, which includes choices such as oysters, salads, steaks and a *plat du jour*. There are plenty of French wines to choose from, but many diners opt for an expertly made cocktail instead.

Cafe Noah
CAFE $$

(Cafe Noach; Map p112; 93 Ahad Ha'am St; breakfast 36NIS, sandwiches 35NIS; ⊙8am-11pm Sun-Thu, to 5pm Fri; ✆✐) Popular with writers, poets, pundits and other folk desperately attempting to avoid a nine-to-five job, Noah has big windows, a small library and a palm-tree-shaded terrace. The menu offers salads, sandwiches and all-day breakfasts.

Agadir
BURGERS $$

(Map p112; www.agadir.co.il; 2 Nahalat Binyamin St; burgers from 49NIS; ⊙noon-4am Sun-Thu, to 5am Fri, to 3am Sat; ✆) Locals swear by the burgers here, which feature beef or vegetarian patties of varying sizes sizzled up with choose-your-own toppings. The perfect place to indulge a beer-and-burger craving, it's on Nahalat Binyamin St and is always busy. An Israel-wide chain, it also has another **city-centre branch** (Map p116; ☑03-522 7080; www.agadir.co.il; 120 Ben Yehuda St) and one in the Old Port (Hangar 3).

Fresh Kitchen
HEALTH FOOD $$

(Map p116; ☑03-529 2687; www.freshkitchen.co.il; 37 Basel St; salads from 36NIS; ⊙11.30am-midnight Sat-Thu, noon-5pm Fri; ✆✐) With over a dozen types of salad on the menu, this is the place to get your daily five portions of greens and then some. The menu also has a multitude of muesli, sandwiches and refreshing shakes – and it even lists the calories. There are a few branches dotted around town, including another in the **city centre** (Map p116; 149 Dizengoff St).

Tchernihovsky 6
PORTUGUESE $$$

(Map p112; ☑03-620 8729; 5 Tchernichovsky St; mains 68-110NIS; ⊙noon-11.45pm Mon-Thu, 10am-noon Fri, 10.30am-5pm Sat, 11.45am-6pm Sun; ✆) A little taste of Lisbon here in the Middle East, Tchernihovsky 6 is owned and operated by a Portuguese-Israeli chef and is known for dishes featuring octopus, pulses, meats and other Iberian favourites. There's a streetside terrace that's invariably packed on warm evenings. The same crew operates the Porto wine bar opposite.

✕ South City Centre

Anita
ICE CREAM $

(Map p112; cnr Shabazi & Pines Sts, Neve Tzedek; 1/2/3 scoops 15/20/24NIS; ⊙8am-midnight) Neve Tzedek's 'Mama of Gelato' has a loyal local following, a fact that will immediately become apparent if you head here on a summer evening (expect a queue). Flavours are many and varied, and come in both sorbet and ice-cream styles. There's a second branch opposite, and a third down the street that sells frozen yoghurt.

Bet Lehem Hummus
MIDDLE EASTERN $

(Map p112; 5 Florentin St, Florentin; hummus 17NIS; ⊘10am-9pm) The free self-service *tshai nana* (mint tea) is a nice touch, but regulars are drawn here solely on the strength of the hummus. Choose from ful (with mashed and spiced fava beans) or masabacha (with chickpeas and warm tahina) versions, and consider ordering an egg topping (2NIS).

★ Port Sa'id
MIDDLE EASTERN $$

(Map p112; Har Sinai St 5; small plates 22-52NIS, mains 34-180NIS; ⊘noon-late) The mothership for innercity hipsters, this restaurant-bar next to the Great Synangogue is decorated with a library of vinyl records on wooden shelves and has a coterie of heavily tattooed regulars (really, do these guys live here?). There's good Middle Eastern–accented food on offer (no English menu, so you'll need to consult with the waiters) and lots of drink choices.

Get here early to score a table, and don't expect much in terms of service.

North Abraxas
ISRAELI $$

(Map p112; ☑03-516 6660; 40 Lilienblum St; small plates 22-52NIS, mains 34-120NIS, pizza 54NIS; ⊘noon-midnight Sun-Thu, 1pm-midnight Fri & Sat) The food at this flamboyant place is relegated to secondary importance – here, it's all about the vibe. Sitting at the bar and watching the chefs and waiters chop, flambée, plate, sing and down arak shots with customers is fabulous fun, and the modern Israeli menu with its pizzas, colourful vegetable dishes and flavorful slow-cooked meats will please most diners.

Nachmani
ITALIAN $$

(Map p112; ☑03-566 3331; http://noirgroup.co.il; 26 Nachmani St; pastries 12-16NIS, pizzas 46-58NIS, mains 58-134NIS; ⊘8am-midnight Sun-Fri, from 9am Sat) A perfect example of the casual yet stylish eatery trending in Tel Aviv, this cafe-restaurant serves generous antipasto platters, piping-hot pizzas from its brick oven, handmade pasta dishes and an array of sandwiches and salads. The outdoor tables are popular between 4.30pm and 7pm on weekdays, when every alcoholic drink comes with a free focaccia or bruschetta.

Ouzeria
GREEK $$

(Map p112; 44 Matalon St, Florentin; mezes 35-60NIS; ⊘noon-midnight; ☑) Popular with locals of every age and style, this exuberant corner restaurant in the Levinsky Spice Market precinct is busy every night but is absolutely hopping on Friday after the market closes. It doesn't accept bookings, so you may need to queue. Greek mezes showcase vegetables and seafood and are both tasty and well priced.

Ahathaan
CAFE $$

(Map p112; ☑03-560 8070; crn Ahad Ha'am & Balfour Sts; breakfast 36-59NIS; ⊘8am-midnight Sun-Thu, to 5.30pm Fri, 9am-midnight Sat; ☜) Shaded by an awning, lit by multicoloured lights at night and inevitably full of locals, the streetside terrace at this thrift shop–chic cafe is a popular meeting point at any time of the day but is particularly busy in the morning. Inside, there are plenty of laptop-friendly tables catering to the telecommuting crowd.

Cafe Lucia
CAFE $$

(Map p112; ☑03-744 8088; 18 Balfour St; breakfast 10-46NIS, sandwiches 36-42NIS, mains 32-48NIS; ⊘7am-midnight Sun-Thu, to Shabbat Fri, 7pm-midnight Sat) Every neighbourhood should have its own Cafe Lucia. Known for its breads and pastries (the owners also operate the Lachmanina Bakery), its shady streetside terrace is inevitably full of locals catching up over coffee and ordering from the well-priced menu, which is strong on comfort foods including sandwiches (fresh and toasted), schnitzels, pastas, meatballs and fish and chips.

Lulu
CAFE, BAR $$

(Map p112; ☑03-516 8793; www.lulucafe.co.il; 55 Shabazi St, Neve Tzedek; breakfast 38-58NIS, sandwiches 44-48NIS, mains 64-96NIS; ⊘7.30am-11.30pm; ☜) A perfect example of Neve Tzedek's laid-back but carefully curated style, this cafe-bar-restaurant has a vaguely arty ambience, Mediterranean menu and fashionable clientele. The food is a notch or two up the quality scale from standard cafe fare, and the indoor-outdoor seating arrangement suits all weather.

Meshek Barzilay
CAFE $$

(Map p112; ☑03-516 6329; www.meshekbarzilay.co.il; 6 Ahad Ha'am St, Neve Tzedek; breakfast 38-64NIS, mains 46-68NIS; ⊘7am-4pm Sun, to midnight Mon-Fri, from 9am Sat; ☑) Vegetarians and vegans are well catered for in Tel Aviv, but this place goes that extra mile when it comes to making them happy. One of only

CELEBRITY CHEFS

As is so often the case in this era of *Master Chef*, Tel Aviv has a number of popular restaurants owned and operated by local celebrity chefs. The best known of these culinary celebrities are Eyal Shani, Yonatan Roshfeld and Meir Adoni, who together are cementing the city's reputation as host to one of the world's most exciting food scenes.

Like many locals, we're unrepentent members of the Eyal Shani fan club. A devotee of simple, seasonal cuisine, he seems to have the magic touch when it comes to putting together casually chic eateries – Miznon (p128), Port Sa'id and North Abraxas – where having fun is as much of a priority as enjoying the food. Foodies will know of him courtesy of his appearance on Yotam Ottolenghi's *Mediterranean Feasts* TV show.

Yonatan Roshfeld and Meir Adoni have a more refined take on Israeli cuisine, and operate two outstanding fine-dining destinations: Herbert Samuel (p135) and Catit. The prices and surrounds at these places won't suit everyone, as they're more haute than hip, but both chefs have less formal spin-off venues that might (Adoni's Mizlala (p134) and Yoshfeld's Tapas 1 at the Alma Hotel).

two restaurants we found serving organic free-range eggs (bravo!), it has plenty of interesting Indian- and Asian-influenced dishes on its menu and some great breakfast choices. Regulars swear by the vegan farm breakfast.

Giraffe
ASIAN $$
(Map p112; ☎ 03-685 1155; cnr Montefiore & Yavne Sts; mains 51-98NIS; ☺ noon-midnight; 🛜) Robustly flavoured pan-Asian dishes including dumplings, noodles and sushi rolls are served at this bustling branch of the popular local chain. The food lacks finesse, but it's fresh and tasty. Despite being ever-busy, the friendly waiters and bar staff are always happy to have a chat.

Suzanna
MIDDLE EASTERN $$
(Map p112; ☎ 03-944 3060; www.suzana.rest-e.co.il; 9 Shabazi St, Neve Tzedek; breakfast 49NIS, meals 55-86NIS; ☺ 10am-2am) A longstanding Neve Tzedek favourite, Suzanna offers a Middle Eastern mix of dishes. Some of these are more successful than others, so the 'I'll have what they're having' approach pays off here. Enjoy your meal during summer months on the large open courtyard in the shade of an enormous ficus tree.

Nanuchka
VEGAN $$
(Map p112; ☎ 03-516 2254; http://nanuchka-tlv.com/; 30 Lilienblum St; mains 49-68NIS; ☺ noon-late) A vegan Georgian restaurant? Surely not. But that is indeed what Nanuchka – once a traditional Georgian eatery – has transformed itself into. We're puzzled as to the place's popularity, as our meals have been bland and uninteresting, but there's a bohemian buzz about the place

that may provide an explanation. The starter of seven salads (58NIS) is a safe bet.

Thai House
THAI $$
(Map p116; ☎ 03-517 8568; www.thai-house.co.il; 8 Bograshov St; mains 42-128NIS; ☺ noon-11pm; 🍴) Dedicated restaurants serving Thai food are few and far between in Tel Aviv. So if you're craving green, yellow or red curry, try a dinner at Thai House (Beit Thailandi), a bamboo-laden restaurant on the corner of Ben Yehuda and Bograshov Sts.

★ Catit
ISRAELI $$$
(Map p112; ☎ 03-510 7001; www.catit.co.il; 57 Nahalat Binyamin St; 3/4/5 courses 349/399/479NIS; ☺ 6.30-11pm Sun-Fri; 🍴) Meir Adoni is generally acknowledged to be Tel Aviv's most exciting and accomplished chef, and this intimate restaurant is his flagship restaurant (he also operates the attached Mizlala bistro and two venues at the Carleton Hotel). The food here is spectacular – ultrarefined dishes that are wonderful to look at and even better to eat. Service is impressive, too.

Vegetarians and vegans should mention their requirements when booking.

★ Bindella Osteria & Bar
ITALIAN $$$
(Map p112; ☎ 03-650 0071; www.bindella.co.il; 27 Montefiore St; pasta 49-99NIS; mains 68-128NIS; ☺ 12.30pm-late) Bindella is the epitome of a modern Tuscan *ristorante* – elegant, with an uncompromising focus on quality food, wine and service. Our meals here have been exemplary, featuring al dente pasta, meat and fish cooked simply so as to showcase its quality, and delectable desserts. The wine list is similarly impressive, being full of premium Israeli and Italian drops.

1

1. Beaches (p121)

Tel Avivim flock to the city's beaches for sports and sunbathing by the sparkling Mediterranean Sea.

2. Juice stands

Beat the heat with a glass of freshly squeezed orange or pomegranate juice at a hole-in-the-wall juice stand.

3. Tel Aviv Museum of Art (p110)

This museum is impressive both inside and out, with its superb collections and ultra-modern architecture.

4. Old City (p118), Jaffa

Stroll the cobbled streets of Jaffa's Old City, the oldest part of Tel Aviv.

Mizlala

ISRAELI $$$

(Map p112; ☎03-566 5505; http://mizlala.
co.il; 57 Nahalat Binyamin St; mains 89-169NIS;
⊙noon-midnight; ⊘) Catit's younger sibling
has cheaper prices, a simpler menu and way
more va-va-voom than her big sis but still
showcases Meir Adoni's refined approach
to cooking. The stylish dining space with its
long bar is most definitely one of the city's
places to be seen, and the menu's Mediterra-
nean slant is particularly pleasing. Whatever
you do, don't contemplate skipping dessert.

Café Noir

FRENCH $$$

(Map p112; ☎03-566 3018; http://noirgroup.
co.il; 43 Ahad Ha'am St; brunch 34-64NIS, mains
66-128NIS; ⊙noon-midnight Sun-Wed, to 1am
Thu, 8am-1am Fri, 9am-midnight Sat; 🕾) This
bustling French-style brasserie is known
locally for two things: weekend brunches
and its signature schnitzels. We're big fans
of the first but prefer to order one of the
consistently excellent salads or pastas rather than the second. It's worth paying extra
for a bread basket.

Hotel Montefiore

FUSION $$$

(Map p112; ☎03-564 6100; www.hotelmontefiore.
co.il; 36 Montefiore St; burgers & sandwiches
42-46NIS, mains 62-160NIS; ⊙7am-midnight;
🕾) For a special night out, you need look
no further than the Montefiore's French-
flavoured restaurant. Though not quiet
(the place is far too fashionable for that),
it's a favourite with glam things out
on dates and with businesspeople sealing
deals. The menu travels across Asia and
Europe, the wine list is impressive and the
bar is perfect for solo diners.

Nana Bar

INTERNATIONAL $$$

(Map p112; ☎03-516 1915; www.nanabar.co.il; 1
Ahad Ha'am St, Neve Tzedek; mains 60-120NIS;
⊙noon-1am Sun-Thu & Sat, from 5.30pm Fri; 🕾⊘)
Nana's long bar is propped up at weekends,
while its twinkling courtyard garden is
packed on balmy evenings. The clientele of
Tel Aviv's wealthier young 30-somethings
comes on Friday evening to drink and snack
on everything from New Orleans–style BBQ
wings to house-chopped liver; at quieter
times they enjoy meals of paellas, curries
and perfectly grilled steaks.

Dallal

FRENCH, BREAKFAST $$$

(Map p112; ☎03-510 9292; www.dallal.info; 10
Shabazi St, Neve Tzedek; breakfast 32-62NIS, mains
76-170NIS; ⊙9am-11.30pm Sun-Fri, noon-11pm
Sat) For one of Tel Aviv's best brunches, head
here on Saturday between noon and 6pm,
when the garden tables are full of locals
noshing on organic egg dishes such as the
roasted eggplant shakshuka with spinach,
tomato coulis and goat yoghurt. Dinner
in the slightly twee dining room is a more
formal affair, featuring conservative French-
influenced meat and fish dishes.

The nearby **Dallal Bakery** (Map p112; 7 Kol
Israel Haverim St, Neve Tzedek; ⊙7am-10pm Sun-
Thu, to 5pm Fri) is a great spot for a simple
lunch, but seating is extremely limited. If it's
full, consider ordering to go and heading to
nearby Alma Beach for a picnic.

Adora

MEDITERRANEAN $$$

(Map p116; ☎03-605 0896; 226 Ben Yehuda St;
brunch 99NIS, 2-course business lunch 69NIS, mains
79-96NIS; ⊙noon-midnight Mon-Thu, 9am-mid-
night Fri & Sat; ⊘) One of the original foodie
destinations in town, Adora is looking a little
bit worn these days but still attracts attention for the quality of its Mediterranean
cuisine. Meat and fish dishes jostle for attention on the menu: vegetarians may feel hard
done by. The business lunch is a great deal.

✗ Tel Aviv Beach & Port

Gelateria Siciliana

ICE CREAM $

(Map p116; http://glideria.co.il; 110 Ben Yehuda
St; 1/2/3 scoops 15/20/25NIS; ⊙noon-midnight
Sun-Thu, 11am-late Fri & Sat; 🕾) Most Italians
will agree that the test of a good *gelateria* is
always its pistachio gelato, which should be
a soft green colour and have a sweet yet nut-
ty taste. Happily, Tel Aviv's Gelateria Siciliana passes this and other gelato-associated
tests with flying colours. There's a second
branch **near Rabin Sq** (Map p112; 63 Ibn Gabirol St), and one in Herzliya.

Tamara

FROZEN YOGHURT $

(Map p116; 96 Ben Yehuda St; small/medium/large
cup 22/27/32NIS; ⊙9.30am-12.30am Sun-Fri,
from 10.30am Sat; ⊘) We're going to break
some bad news here: despite the spin, we
suspect that frozen yoghurt isn't particularly healthy. It's undoubtedly delicious,
though, so we're all for damning the cons-
equences and following the world-wide
frozen-yoghurt wave to this excellent place
near Gordon Beach. Enjoy your cup plain or
choose from a range of indulgent toppings.

Pinati

MIDDLE EASTERN $

(Map p112; http://pinati.co.il/; 43 Bograshov St; hummus 20-33NIS; ⊙10am-10pm Sun-Thu, to 4pm Fri)
Close enough to the beach that the picnic potential is obvious, this branch of Jerusalem's

favourite hummus joint sells hummus, chicken schnitzels and other fast-food favourites.

Benedict   BREAKFAST $$
(Map p116; www.benedict.co.il; 171 Ben Yehuda St; breakfasts 38-98NIS; ☉24hr; 🐾🖋) Those craving blueberry pancakes, bacon and eggs, shakshuka or eggs benedict at five in the afternoon – or, for that matter, in the morning – need go no further than this constantly crowded all-night breakfast place. Bring a big appetite: servings are huge, and come with bread. There's another branch in **Tel Aviv** (Map p112; 29 Rothschild Blvd) and one in Herzliya.

Shila   SEAFOOD $$$
(Map p116; ☎03-522 1224; www.shila-rest.co.il; 182 Ben Yehuda St; tapas 46-59NIS, raciones 48-79NIS, mains 74-148NIS; ☉noon-1am Sun-Thu & Sat) Only a castanet click or two away from the beach, Sharo Cohen's Spanish-inspired seafood restaurant offers an array of vividly coloured and robustly flavored tapas, *raciones* (small plates) and grilled main courses – those in the know tend to start with a few carpaccio and tartar tapas and then graze on the vegetable, fish and seafood *raciones* on offer.

Manta Ray   BREAKFAST, SEAFOOD $$$
(Map p112; ☎03-517 4773; www.mantaray.co.il; southern Tel Aviv Promenade; breakfast 39-45NIS, mains 75-175NIS; ☉9am-11pm) It's stylish, casual and at the beach – the perfect Tel Avivian triumvirate. On the slope directly above Alma Beach, this is the summer breakfast and lunch venue of choice for locals and tourists alike, so be sure to book (specify an outside table with a view). Try an omelette at breakfast and fish at other times of the day.

Herbert Samuel   MEDITERRANEAN $$$
(Map p112; ☎03-516 6516; www.herbertsamuel.co.il; 6 Kaufmann St, Neve Tzedek; business lunch 88NIS, pasta 88-98NIS, mains 112-168NIS; ☉12.30-11.30pm; 🖋) Home turf for *Master Chef Israel* judge Yonatan Roshfeld, this upmarket choice offers refined Mediterranean dishes from a menu that changes daily. Surrounds are elegant, with sea views. Come for the two-course business lunch, which is available every day except Saturday and represents good value.

🍴 Jaffa (Yafo)

★ Ali Caravan   MIDDLE EASTERN $
(1 HaDolphin St; hummus portions 18NIS; ☉8am-3pm Sun-Fri; 🖋; 🚍Dan 10, 18, 25, 41) If hum-

TEL AVIV-JAFFA (YAFO) EATING

CAFE CULTURE
....

Tel Aviv has developed a global reputation as a hub of the creative industries, particularly in the fields of software and game design, architecture, advertising and graphic design. The fact that many members of this creative class are involved in start-up or speculative projects means that many are idea-rich but cash-poor, and so can't afford to pay the extremely high office rents that apply in the city centre.

Their solution is suitably creative – taking advantage of the tables, caffeine fixes and free wi-fi offered in cafes. This has led to the local cafe scene booming and to every local having one or more favourites. Ours include Cafe Noah (p129), Ahathaan (p130), Rothschild 12 (p137), Puaa (p136) and Shafa Bar, but there are hundreds more to choose from. Many serve great food, and most morph into bars after the sun goes down.

---

mus is a religion, then this could well be its Mecca. This tiny restaurant near Jaffa Port offers a limited menu of three hummus choices: plain, ful (with mashed and spiced fava beans) or masabacha (with chickpeas and warm tahina). It's always busy, so you'll probably need to queue.

Shafa Bar   CAFE $
(2 Rabbi Nachman St, Jaffa; sandwiches 32NIS, mains 28-52NIS; ☉9am-late; 🐾; 🚍Dan 10, 18, 25, 41) Another hipster hangout (Jaffa is full of them), Shafa is our favourite of the flea-market cafe-bar hybrids, a place where the coffee machine and cocktail shaker get an equal workout, and where it's possible to order everything from a simple sandwich to a crunchy Thai salad or a dude-food choice such as Irish sausages and fries.

Said Abu Elafia & Sons   BAKERY $
(Aboulafia Bakery; 7 Yefet St, Jaffa; pastries from 3NIS; ☉24hr) Jaffa's first bakery was established in 1880, and four generations down the line the Abu Elafia family is busier than ever. The main attractions are its giant *sambusas* (filled pastries), *bourekas* (stuffed breads with sheep's cheese) and a unique Arab oven-baked pizzalike concoction filled with eggs, tomato, cheese and olives. Takeout only.

SHAKSHUKA

Many cultures claim this dish as their own (Tunisia being the main contender), but only in Israel has it attained the status of national treasure. Eggs baked in a rich sauce of tomatoes, onions and spices (usually paprika, cumin and chilli powder), it is sometimes customised with peppers, sausage, cheese, spinach or other ingredients.

Baked and served in a flat cast-iron, copper or terracotta pan and accompanied by crusty white bread, it's delicious at all times of the day but is most popular at breakfast and brunch. The most famous version in the city is served at Dr Shakshuka in Jaffa, but we prefer those at Orna and Ella (p129), Manta Ray (p135) and Dallal (p134).

Members of the family run branches near **Rabin Sq** (Map p116; 73 Ibn Gabirol St) and on the **esplanade** (Map p112; cnr Herbert Samuel Esplanade & Yonah HaNavi St).

Dr Shakshuka   MIDDLE EASTERN $$
(http://shakshuka.rest.co.il; 3 Beit Eshal St, Jaffa; shakshuka 36-42NIS, couscous 42-58NIS, shwarma 48-58NIS; ⊗8am-midnight Sun-Fri; 🅿) Set in an atmospheric Ottoman-era building in the flea market, the doctor has been working his shakshuka magic since 1991 and shows no sign of giving up. The eponymous egg dish is great, of course (his secret is loads of spice, particularly paprika), but locals tend to prefer the shwarma and couscous. Dine inside or in the shaded courtyard.

Puaa   CAFE $$
(📞03-682 3821; www.puaa.co.il; 8 Rabbi Yohanan St; breakfast 38-48NIS, sandwiches 38NIS, mains 42-58NIS; ⊗9am-1am Sun-Fri, from 10am Sat; 🤳; 🚊Dan 10, 18, 25, 41) The thrift-shop-chic decor is truly authentic here – every piece of furniture and decorative knicknack is for sale. In the midst of the flea-market action, laid-back Puaa serves an all-day breakfast and is particularly busy on weekends, when the shakshuka, sabich and *bundash* (fried challah served with jam and halva or with sour cream and cucumber) are must-order treats.

El Jamila   MIDDLE EASTERN $$$
(📞03-550 0042; 4 Olei Zion St, Jaffa; mains 60-120NIS; ⊗noon-midnight; 🚊Dan 10,14, 25, 41) Traditional fish dishes from the Ajami district are on offer at this Arab-run restaurant in the flea market. The stone-walled dining space has a high ceiling and attractive tiled floor, and is a lovely place to park your shopping bags after a busy morning in the souq. Try the *ta'ashima* (fish fillets baked in dough and served with almond tahina).

Container   FUSION $$$
(📞03-683 6321; www.container.org.il; Warehouse 2, Jaffa Port; pasta & risotto 68-118NIS, seafood mains 68-118NIS; ⊗noon-late Sun-Thu, from 10am Fri & Sat; 🚊Dan 10, 14, 25, 41) Equal parts restaurant, late-night bar, club and art space, the port's most popular venue serves a mix of mezes, seafood, pasta and Israeli-style brunches. Like the food, the music is fusion, with well-known local DJs spinning world, dub and dance. There are live sets on Tuesday, Thursday and Saturday after 10pm.

Kalimera Bar & Restaurant   SEAFOOD $$$
(📞03-682 3232; www.kalimera.co; Jaffa Port; mains 68-118NIS; ⊗5pm-late Sun-Wed, noon-late Thu-Sat; 🅿; 🚊Dan 10, 14, 25, 41) With its Greek-island–style decor and menu, Kalimera is the perfect choice for a laid-back summer meal. Order an array of vegetable and seafood meze dishes to share, set the kids up with something from the children's menu and prepare to enjoy yourselves.

🍷 Drinking & Nightlife

The city has a fantastic bar scene – there are drinking dens to suit every taste and budget. Some are hipster hot spots, others are neighbourhood joints that are so chilled they're almost comatose. When it comes to clubbing, dance bars and bars hosting live gigs dominate the scene – there aren't too many mega-clubs here. Dress codes are relaxed, so you can forget about dressing up.

If you order a beer you can usually order a shot of spirits as a chaser – this is cheaper than ordering a single shot. Beers are sold in one third (*shlish*) and one half (*hetsi*) of a litre. These usually cost around the same, so it makes sense to order a *hetsi*.

City Centre

Deli   CLUB
(Map p112; 47 Allenby St; ⊗from 9pm) Hidden at the back of a sandwich bar (hence the name), this place is ruled by a talented array of local DJs spinning techno, house, '80s and '90s indie and electro. Check its Facebook feed for details.

Meira
BAR

(Map p112; 32 King George St; ⊙ 8pm-late Sun-Thu, 9am-late Fri & Sat; �) Meira's garden deck is particularly popular on summer evenings, when drinkers enjoy watching the passing parade along King George St. Inside, the decor is rough-and-ready, but bar staff are always happy to have a natter.

Minzar
PUB

(Map p112; 60 Allenby St, cnr Gedera St; ⊙ 24hr; wifi) A few metres back from the main street and a few hundred miles from the mainstream, the Minzar is that rare thing: a pub without a closing time. A now legendary drinking hole, it has indoor and outdoor seating and is popular with Israelis, expats and drifters.

🍸 South City Centre

★ Rothschild 12
BAR, CAFE

(Map p112; www.rothschild12.co.il; 12 Rothschild Blvd; ⊙ 7am-late Sun-Thu, from 8am Fri & Sat) Be warned: it's all but impossible to restrict oneself to a single visit here. One of our favourite breakfast stops (pastries and bread are French-style and delicious), it's equally good for lunch (burgers, sabich, toasted sandwiches), afternoon coffee, aperitifs or late-night drinks. The soundtrack comes courtesy of jazz discs during the day and live bands and DJs at night.

★ Radio EPGB
CLUB

(Map p112; 7 Shadal St; ⊙ from 9pm) Dubbing itself the 'Home of Underground Rock & Indietronica in Tel Aviv', this basement venue spins alt rock, electronica and dubstep and also has the occasional live gig. Check its Twitter feed for what's on.

★ Block
CLUB

(www.block-club.com; 157 Shalma (Salame) Rd, Neve Sha'anan; early arrivals 50-70NIS, late arrivals 70-90NIS; ⊙ 11pm-late Thu-Sat) In the Central Bus Station building, Block is known as Tel Aviv's best club for good reason, hosting big-name international DJs playing anything from funk, hip-hop and Afrobeat to drum 'n' bass, house and trance. There's an impressive sound system and a smoker's lounge.

Satchmo
BAR

(Map p112; 2 Vital St, Florentin; ⊙ daily till late) The longest-running and possibly best-loved bar in Florentin, Satchmo has an old-school neighbourhood vibe and a fantastic selec-

tion of over 70 whiskeys. A DJ spins classic and alternative rock every night. We particularly like its mantra 'Bad decisions make great stories' – so true.

Jackson Bar
BAR, CLUB

(Map p112; 6 Vital St, Florentin; ⊙ daily till late) On Wednesday night, there's only one truly hip (hop) place to be, and that's here. Owned by the well-known Tel Aviv rapper Axum (aka Mr Jackson), this street-art-decorated bar has DJ sets every night but really goes off midweek.

Hoodna Bar
BAR

(Map p112; 13 Arbarbanel St, Florentin; ⊙ 6pm-late Sun-Thu, from 1pm Fri & Sat) Hoodna ('truce' in Arabic) is a carpenter's workshop zone by day but transforms itself at night, when tables and sofas are dragged into the street to create a chilled-out drinking space. Inside there are almost daily live sets. In the last week of February, the owners, who play in an afro-beat band, host the 'Southern Wind' indie rock festival.

The owners also run the nearby Casbah Cafe (Map p112; 3 Florentin St), one of the neighbourhood's most popular cheap eateries (try the sweet-potato fries).

Comfort 13
CLUB

(13 Kompert St, Florentin; admission 60NIS; ⊙ 11pm-late) Down an alleyway in the grungy enclave of Florentin, Comfort 13 is one of the city's biggest and best clubs; nights span from trashy pop to trance to electronica, as well as occasional live rock bands. Check its Facebook page for updates.

Shisko
BAR

(Map p112; 2 Har Sinai St; ⊙ 5pm-midnight Sun-Thu, noon-6pm Fri, from 7pm Sat) Shisko ('fat man' in Bulgarian) is in one of the city's favourite drinking hot spots. Located in the square behind the Great Synagogue on Allenby St, it offers a mad mix of Bulgarian tapas, rakia (plum brandy) and klezmer music, making for a merry start to any night out.

🍸 Tel Aviv Beach & Port

Heder 140
BAR

(Room 140; Map p116; 140 Ben Yehuda St; ⊙ 8pm-8am Sat-Thu, from 9pm Fri) These days, hipster bars are opening in Tel Aviv's inner city as often as shakshuka is spotted on cafe menus (and that's a lot). This underground joint is one of the better examples, with outdoor

LGBT TEL AVIV

Tel Aviv is rapidly developing a reputation as one of the world's great destinations for LGBT travellers. In June it plays host to the week-long **Tel Aviv Pride**, the region's biggest and most flamboyant gay and lesbian festival.

The city's hotels are almost all LGBT-friendly, as are its cafes, bars and restaurants. LGBT-focused venues include the much-loved **Evita** (Map p112; ☑03-566 9559; www.evita. co.il; 31 Yavne St; ⊗noon-late), a cafe that turns into a gay lounge bar by night; the hip gay bar **Shpagat** (Map p112; 43 Nahalat Binyamin St; ⊗9pm-late); and the male-only hook-up bar-club **Apolo** (Map p112; ☑03-774 1106; www.apolo.co.il; 46 Allenby St; ⊗10pm-4am). Every Saturday night, the **Cabina Club** under the Crowne Plaza Hotel on the Herbery Samuel Esplanade hosts the Boyling gay night. To keep abreast of what's on, check the **Atraf** (www.atraf.com), **TLV Scene** (www.tlvscene.com) and **Tel Aviv Gay Vibe** (http:// telavivgayvibe.atraf.com/) websites; the latter has a Tel Aviv gay map and iPhone app.

Beachgoers might also want to visit Hilton Beach (p121), Tel Aviv's unofficial gay beach. For assistance when planning your trip, check **GaywayTLV** (www.gaywaytlv.com), a gay-focused travel agent.

The **Tel Aviv Gay Center** (Map p112; ☑03-525 2896; www.gaycenter.org.il; Gan Meir Park) off King George St hosts gay- and lesbian-themed events, lectures, sports groups and pot-luck picnics.

---

seating and DJs and bartenders who are good at their jobs.

Wineberg
WINE BAR

(Map p116; ☑03-522 3939; 106 Ben Yehuda St; tapas 16-47NIS; ⊗5.30pm-1am Sun-Thu, 11.30am-late Fri & Sat) This old-fashioned neighbourhood bar close to Gordon Beach wouldn't win any awards for the quality of its food or the depth of its wine list, but it has a loyal following due to its reasonable prices and unpretentious vibe. Choose from indoor or outdoor seating.

Clara Beach Bar
CLUB

(Map p112; http://clara.co.il; 1 Koifman St, Dolphinarium Beach; ⊗summer only) Clara is a popular gal – loud, slightly brassy, ultrafriendly and full of fun. Located right on the beach, it has wooden decking, hammocks and a lawn area. Music is electro and house, and crowds are a given on balmy summer nights. Spray tans and skimpy shorts or swimsuits are *de rigueur*.

Mike's Place
PUB

(Map p112; www.mikesplacebars.com; 86 Herbert Samuel Esplanade; ⊗11am-late; ☎) On the beach next to the US Embassy, the original branch of this country-wide operation offers frothy pints, sport on the big screen, open-mic nights, jam sessions and live gigs (mainly rock and acoustic). The sizeable menu has grill-style meals, cocktails and beer.

 Jaffa (Yafo)

★ Anna Loulou Bar
BAR, CLUB

(www.annaloulobar.com; 1 HaPninim St, Old Jaffa; ⊗9pm-3am Mon-Sat; ☐Dan 10, 18, 25, 41) Describing itself as a cross between underground bar and cultural center, this gay- and smoker-friendly hipster bar is perhaps the only joint in town where Arab and Jewish locals party together. The music is predominantly electro-Arab, African or Middle Eastern, although there's the occasional wild-card event (country, hip-hop, drag shows). Wednesday is the night to party.

☆ Entertainment

Theatre & Dance

Cameri Theatre
THEATRE

(Map p112; ☑03-606 0960; www.cameri.co.il; 30 Leonardo da Vinci St) Hosts first-rate theatre performances in Hebrew, on some nights with simultaneous English translation or English-language surtitles.

Habima National Theatre
THEATRE

(Map p112; ☑03-629 5555; www.habima.co.il; 2 Tarsat Blvd, HaBima Sq) Home to Israel's national theatre company, Habima stages weekly performances. Most have simultaneous subtitles in English.

Suzanne Dellal Centre
DANCE

(Map p112; ☑03-510 5656; www.suzannedellal.org. il; 5 Yechieli St) Stages a variety of performing arts including dance, music and ballet, and is home to the world-famous Bat Sheva dance company.

Tzavta THEATRE
(Map p112; ☑03-695 0157, 03-695 0156; www.tzavta.co.il; 30 Ibn Gabirol St) This 'progressive' club-theatre, founded by the far-left HaShomer HaTzair youth movement, has pop and folk Israeli music, as well as Hebrew-language theatre and comedy.

Live Music

Live bands can also be found in bars and cafes and on Rothschild Blvd in summer. In recent years, big stars such as Madonna, Bob Dylan and Paul McCartney (to name a few) have all added Tel Aviv to their tours. The biggest open-air venue is the amphitheatre at the heart of Park HaYarkon, which also hosts a free concert by the Israeli Opera every July.

Tickets to many major events can be pre-purchased online at **Mr Ticket** (http://misterticket.co.il/en).

Beit HaAmudim JAZZ
(Map p112; ☑03-510 9228; 14 Rambam St; ☺6.30pm-2am Wed, Thu & Sat-Mon, from 11am Tue, 9am-4pm Fri) As the great Herbie Hancock said: 'It's not exclusive, but inclusive, which is the whole spirit of jazz'. Tel Aviv's major live jazz venue shares his sentiment and welcomes a disparate crowd to its almost nightly gigs, which kick-off at 9.30pm. Close to Carmel Market, it functions as a cafe during the day. Check its Facebook page for details.

Tsuzamen LIVE MUSIC
(Map p112; 25 Lilienblum St; occasional cover; ☺from 9pm) Local bands, many up-and-coming, have been playing this teensy venue for years. Check its Twitter feed for details.

**Charles Bronfman
Auditorium** CLASSICAL MUSIC
(Map p112; ☑03-621 1777; www.ipo.co.il; HaBima Sq) Home to the Israel Philharmonic Orchestra, the Charles Bronfman Auditorium hosts performances several times a week.

Barby LIVE MUSIC
(☑03-518 8123; www.barby.co.il; 52 Kibbutz Galuyot St) This Tel Aviv institution at the southernmost point of the city is a favourite venue for reggae, rock and random alternative bands.

Goldstar Zappa Club LIVE MUSIC
(☑03-762 6666; www.zappa-club.co.il; 24 Raoul Wallenberg St, Ramat HaChayal) Local and inter-

national music luminaries play at this intimate club, situated 8km northeast of central Tel Aviv, so it's best accessed by car or taxi. Call or look out for listings to find out who's on while you're here.

**Felicja Blumental
Music Centre** CLASSICAL MUSIC
(Map p112; ☑03-620 1185; www.fbmc.co.il; 26 Bialik St) Named in honour of Polish-born Brazilian pianist Felicja Blumental, this regal but intimate 115-seat auditorium hosts classical, jazz and chamber music concerts.

Israeli Opera OPERA
(Map p112; ☑03-692 7777; www.israel-opera.co.il; 19 Shaul HaMelech St) The city's major opera house is also home to the Israel Ballet.

Ozen Bar LIVE MUSIC
(Map p112; ☑03-621 5210; www.ozenbar.com; 48 King George St) Known for its Third Ear music store downstairs; at night it hosts live gigs.

Sport

Ramat Gan National Stadium FOOTBALL
(229 Aba Hillel Silver Rd, Ramat Gan) Home to Israel's national soccer team and the UEFA Champions League games of Maccabi Tel Aviv and Haifa, this is the biggest stadium in the country, reached from downtown by bus 42 or 67.

🔒 Shopping

There are plenty of shopping areas, markets and malls in the city. The most interesting boutiques are found in the Jaffa Flea Market, Shabazi St in Neve Tzedek and Sheinkin St in the city centre.

🔒 City Centre

Steimatzky BOOKS
(Map p116; ☑03-522 1513; www.steimatzky.co.il; 109 Dizengoff St; ☺9am-8pm Sun-Thu, to 4pm Fri) This branch of the chain bookstore has helpful staff and a decent array of English-language titles.

Lametayel OUTDOOR EQUIPMENT
(Map p112; ☑077-333 4501; www.lametayel.co.il; top fl, 50 Dizengoff St, Dizengoff Center; ☺10am-9pm Sun-Thu, to 2.30pm Fri) Israel's largest camping and travel equipment shop carries a full range of Lonely Planet guides and is a prime source of information for Israeli backpackers. A worthwhile stop – for kit or tips – if you'll be doing any camping, eg along

MARKETS & MALLS

Locals like to shop, and the city has more than its fair share of street markets and shopping malls. You should head to the Carmel Market (p110) for fresh produce and cheap clothing, to Jaffa's Flea Market (p118) for avant-garde and vintage fashion, to the Old Port (p115) for big-brand stores and to the Sarona Centre (p120) for international upmarket brands. Then if you have any energy and credit left, you could consider the following:

Gan Ha'ir Mall (Map p116) In a central location just north of Rabin Sq, this small mall has some international brand-name boutiques and an organic market.

Ramat Aviv Mall (www.ramat-aviv-mall.co.il; Ramat Aviv) The city's biggest and swankiest mall, with pretty much everything you're likely to be seeking. Take bus 42 from the Central Bus Station, bus 25 from Rabin Sq or a taxi from the city centre for around 50NIS (15 minutes).

Kikar HaMedina (HaMedina Sq) This wide circular plaza is the place to fulfil all your Gucci, Tag Heuer and Versace needs.

Dizengoff Centre (Map p112; ☑03-621 2400; cnr Dizengoff & King George Sts; ⊘9am-midnight Sun-Thu, to 4pm Fri, 8pm-midnight Sat) Israel's first mall is filled with cafes, fast-food joints, telephone-company stands and high-street retail stores. A popular Israeli cooked-food market is held every Friday before Shabbat from 9am.

Nahalat Binyamin Crafts Market (www.nachlat-binyamin.com; ⊘10am-5pm Tue, to 6pm or 7pm summer, 10am to 4.30pm Fri) On Tuesday and Friday, arts-and-crafts street stalls are set up in this pedestrianised street next to Carmel Market. The goods won't be to all tastes, but an occasional treasure can be unearthed.

the Jesus Trail, around the Sea of Galilee or in the Dead Sea area.

🏠 South City Centre

Orit Ivshin　　　　　JEWELLERY
(Map p112; ☑03-516 0811; www.oritivshin.com; 54 Shabazi St, Neve Tzedek; ⊘10am-7pm Sun-Thu, to 3pm Fri) Jeweller Orit Ivshin makes delicate handmade pieces in 19-carat gold at his Neve Tzedek atelier, many of which he encrusts with diamonds. Gorgeous.

Ronit　　　　　JEWELLERY
(Map p112; ☑03-516 2721; http://ronitjewelry.com/; 20 Shabazi St, Neve Tzedek; ⊘10am-7pm Sun-Thu, to 3pm Fri) Necklaces featuring leaf and boat motifs are some of the many hand-crafted pieces on offer at Ronit Cohen's atelier. Most are plated with 24-carat gold rather than being solid, meaning that they fall within most budgets.

Agas & Tamar　　　　　JEWELLERY
(Map p112; ☑03-516 8421; www.agasandtamar design.com; 43 Shabazi St, Neve Tzedek) Pass through an old metal door to discover the workshop and retail space of Einat Agassi and Tamar Harel-Klein, who use gold and silver to create 'storytelling jewellery'

inspired by a theme or historical artefact (coin, nail, seal etc).

Notbook　　　　　CRAFTS
(Map p112; ☑03-566 4356; www.notbook.co.il; 25 Montefiore St; ⊘10.30am-7pm Sun-Thu, to 3.30pm Fri) Hand-bound notebooks featuring recycled paper and colourful covers, gift cards and other stationery items are made and sold at this 'paper fashion' atelier off Allenby St.

🏠 Jaffa Yafo)

Zielinski & Rozen　　　　　BEAUTY
(☑054 774 0566; 10 Rabbi Pinchas St; ⊘10.30am-7pm Sun-Thu, 9.30am-4pm Fri; ☐Dan 10, 18, 25, 41) Planters filled with sweetly scented jasmine adorn the front of this chic perfumerie, which has the appearance and feel of an old-fashioned apothecary's shop. Bottles of perfume, hand wash, room scent and body wash are ready to buy, but it's also possible to book a consultation to have a personalised perfume created.

Una Una　　　　　SHOES
(☑03-518 4782; www.una-una.com; 8 Rabbi Yohanan St, Jaffa; ⊘10am-7.30pm Sun-Thu, to 4pm Fri; ☐Dan 10, 18, 25, 41) Inspired by an eclectic and somewhat eccentric range of everyday objects (sailboats, Transformer toys, Lam-

borghini cars, dominoes, helicopters, even the Rubik's Cube), the handmade shoes and sandals sold from this atmospheric atelier in Jaffa's flea market are made using soft leather and are true works of art.

Shelley Dahari FASHION
(☐03-620 8004; www.shelleydahari.com; 14 Rabbi Yohanan St, Jaffa; ☺9.30am-8pm Sun-Thu, to 4pm Fri) Beach-loving fashionistas should head to this boutique in Jaffa's flea market to source a designer swimsuit by the Israeli label Ugly Duckling and a stylish *galabiya* (loose, full-length kaftan) by Karen Shavit to wear over it.

ℹ Information

The English-language *Tel Aviv-Jaffa Tourist* map (5NIS) is an excellent resource and is available from the tourist information offices. Most hotels supply free tourist maps of the city.

DANGERS & ANNOYANCES

Despite the spectre of suicide attacks (the most recent of which occurred in 2006), Tel Aviv is a remarkably safe city. The streets are safe to walk at all times of the day, and theft from public areas is relatively rare – the only exceptions are the beaches, where it's wise not to leave valuables unattended (you can usually find a congenial local to keep an eye on your belongings while you're taking a dip). Bicycles should be locked with a heavy-duty chain, too.

EMERGENCY
Ambulance (☐101)
Fire Department (☐102)
Home Command (☐104)
Police (☐03-545 4444; 221 Dizengoff St)

MEDICAL SERVICES

Tel Aviv has top-quality medical services and hotels can contact a doctor or hospital in case of emergency.

Ichilov Hospital (Tel Aviv Sourasky Medical Centre; ☐03-697 4444; www.tasmc.org.il; 6 Weizmann St) Near the city centre, Ichilov is the city's big central hospital, with 24-hour emergency room and a travellers' clinic (the Malram Clinic) for immunisations.

Superpharm (62 Sheinken St) This pharmacy chain has a number of branches in town, including at 131 Dizengoff St (open on Shabbat) and 4 Shaul HaMelech Ave.

Tel Aviv Doctor (☐054 941 4243; toll-free 1-800-201 999; www.telaviv-doctor.com; Room 106, 35 Basel St, Basel Heights Medical Centre; ☺daily) A medical clinic aimed at travellers and English speakers. For minor problems it's

less expensive than Ichilov Hospital's emergency room.

MONEY

If you're seeking exchange bureaux, you'll find no shortage on Allenby and Dizengoff Sts. Most are open from 9am to 9pm Sunday to Thursday, and until 2pm on Friday.

You'll have no problem finding ATMs, but as they aren't refilled on Friday night or on Saturday, they sometimes run out of cash at those times.

POST

Post Office (www.israelpost.co.il; ☺8am-6pm Sun-Thu, to noon Fri); North City Centre (☐03-604 1109; 170 Ibn Gabirol St); City Centre (61 HaYarkon St); South City Centre. (Map p112; ☐03-564 3650; cnr Mikve Yisrae'el & Levontin Sts)

TOURIST INFORMATION

Jaffa Tourist Information Office (☐03-681 4466; www.visit-tel-aviv.com; 2 Marzuk Ve-Azar St, Jaffa; ☺9.30am-5.30pm Sun-Thu, to 1pm Fri, 10am-4pm Sat Apr-Oct, 9.30am-5.30pm Sun-Thu, 9am-2pm Fri Nov-Mar) The friendly and helpful staff at this office near the clock tower can provide recommendations and a free Jaffa map.

Tourist Information Office (Map p112; ☐03-516 6188; www.visit-tlv.com; 46 Herbert Samuel Esplanade; ☺9.30am-5.30pm Sun-Thu, to 1pm Fri Nov-Mar, to 6.30pm Sun-Thu & 2pm Fri Apr-Oct) Tel Aviv's main tourist-information office has superhelpful staff and can provide maps, brochures and plenty of advice.

USEFUL WEBSITES

DIY Tel Aviv (www.diytelavivguide.com/blog/) Alternative guide to food, drink, nightlife, shopping and culture.

Midnight East (www.midnighteast.com/mag/) Interesting arts- and culture-focused blog.

Secret Tel Aviv (www.secrettelaviv.com) Listings and advice from locals.

Tel Aviv City (www.telavivcity.com/eng) Local guide to Tel Aviv.

Tel Aviv Guide (www.telavivguide.net) Entertainment, hotel and restaurant reviews.

Time Out Israel (http://timeout.co.il/en) Plenty of Tel Aviv listings and features.

Visit TLV (www.visit-tlv.com) The municipality's excellent website.

ℹ Getting There & Away

AIR

Most airlines fly into and out of Ben-Gurion Airport, 22km southwest of the city centre, but some domestic flights use the smaller Sde Dov airport, on the coast a few kilometres north of the city centre. See the **Israel Airports Authority website** (www.iaa.gov.il) for details.

BUS

Most intercity buses depart from the 6th floor of Tel Aviv's enormous, confusing and filthy **Central Bus Station** (Map p112; ☑ 03-638 3945), where there's also an information desk. Suburban and city buses use the 4th and 7th floors. Tickets can be bought from the driver or from ticket booths. Note that during Shabbat you'll have to resort to sheruts (shared taxis).

Egged (☑ 03-694 8888; www.egged.co.il) buses leave for Jerusalem (405, 19NIS, one hour, every 15 minutes); Haifa (921, 25NIS, 1½ hours, frequent); Tiberias (836, 44NIS, 2½ hours, every 30 minutes); Nazereth (826, 39.50NIS, 2¾ hours, every 45 minutes); and Eilat (393, 394 and 790, 82NIS, 5½ hours, hourly). You'll need to book tickets to Eilat in advance (call ☑ *2800 or go to www.egged.co.il), as these services are usually full. Metropoline buses travel to/from Be'er Sheva (353, 369 and 370, 17.80NIS, 1½ hours) every 30 minutes.

Tel Aviv's second bus station, the open-air **Arlozorov Bus Terminal**, adjoins the Tel Aviv Savidor Merkaz train station northeast of the city centre. To get there, take bus 61 (6.90NIS), which goes along Allenby, King George, Dizengoff and Arlozorov Sts, or bus 10 (6.90NIS), which goes along Ben Yehuda St. If staying in the centre or the north, Egged bus 480 (19NIS, one hour, every 10 minutes) is the most convenient service to Jerusalem.

CAR

Finding street parking in downtown Tel Aviv can be very difficult. Cars are only allowed to park in spaces with blue-and-white kerbs. Many of the latter require payment during the day (6.20NIS per hour) and are reserved for residents from 5pm to 9am. Among the complicating factors: the yellow signs that explain the rules that apply to the side of the street they're on may not be in English; and the only practical way to pay for parking is through your mobile phone using Cellopark (www.cellopark.com/eng) – call ☑ *9070 to register and give your credit-card number, then call each time you park and leave. Parking next to a red-and-white kerb is illegal – if you park in one of these spaces your car *will* be towed.

Privately owned parking lots and garages (often signposted with electronic information on whether they're full) charge upwards of 60NIS per 24 hours of parking. Public car parks charge considerably less (usually a flat rate of 20NIS from 7am to 7pm, or 8NIS to 10NIS per hour). There is a conveniently located large public car park in front of the Old Railway Station (Ha-Tachana) on the Herbert Samuel Promenade.

Most of the main car-rental agencies have offices on HaYarkon St.

SHERUT (SHARED TAXI)

Sheruts (shared taxis, in most cases yellow minibuses) depart from Tsemach David St outside the Central Bus Station and head to Jerusalem (24NIS, on Shabbat 34NIS) and Haifa (30NIS, on Shabbat 45NIS).

From Ben-Gurion Airport there are sheruts to Jerusalem (41NIS or 69NIS to a specific address), Haifa (77NIS or 119NIS to a specific address) and Akko (90NIS or 140NIS to a specific address). The ticket price is the same on weekdays and Shabbat and includes up to two suitcases.

TRAIN

Tel Aviv has four train stations: Savidor, Ha-Hagana, HaShalom and University.

From Savidor, you can travel by train to Haifa (30.50NIS, one hour) via Netanya (15.50NIS, 25 minutes) every 20 minutes from 6am to 8pm Sunday to Friday, and on to Akko (39NIS, 1½ hours) and Nahariya (44.50NIS, 1¾ hours). Heading south, you can travel down the coast to Ashkelon (25.50NIS, one hour) and as far as Be'er Sheva (30NIS, 1¼ hours), both departing hourly. To reach Savidor from the city centre, take bus 61 north from Dizengoff St to the Arlozorov Bus Terminal, which is a two-minute walk from the station.

Savidor Train Station Situated 2.7km east of the beach and 1.5km east of Ibn Gabirol St, at the eastern end of Arlozorov St. The station is sometimes also called Tel Aviv Merkaz (Central Tel Aviv), Tel Aviv Tzafon (North Tel Aviv) and Arlozorov.

HaShalom Train Station Near the Azrieli Centre east of the centre.

HaHagana Train Station A five-minute walk from the Central Bus Station.

University Train Station Near Tel Aviv University and HaYarkon Park.

ⓘ Getting Around

TO/FROM THE AIRPORT

The most straightforward method of getting from Ben-Gurion Airport into Tel Aviv is by train – the station entrance is outside the international terminal building, to the left. Except on Shabbat and Jewish holidays, trains run every 30 minutes between 5.35am and 11.47pm, stopping at all four Tel Aviv stations, with extra services at 1.02am, 2.02am, 3.02am, 4.02am and 5.02am to Savidor station only. The fare is 16NIS.

Prices for taxis are controlled, and either meters or preset official prices are used; there's an orderly taxi rank just outside the international terminal building. Depending on traffic, the ride into central Tel Aviv takes about 20 minutes and should cost 150NIS (day rate) and 200NIS (9pm to 5.30am). There's usually an extra charge of 4.40NIS per suitcase.

RISHON LEZION

ريشون لتسيون   ראשון לציון

Rishon LeZion (First to Zion), just 20km south of Tel Aviv, makes for a pleasant half-day trip. Founded in 1882 by European Jewish immigrants, its Old City is based on Rothschild St and includes the **Great Synagogue**, built in 1885 and registered as a warehouse because the Turkish authorities wouldn't allow the Jews a place of worship. Across the street from the synagogue, the quaint **History Museum** (☑ 03-959 8860, 03-959 8862; 2 Ahad Ha'am St; admission 10NIS; ☺ 9am-noon & 4-7pm Mon, 9am-2pm Sun, Tue, Wed & Thu) is housed in a collection of period buildings that lend insight into the pioneer spirit that drove the early Zionist settlers and the obstacles they faced. Nearby you can stroll around the **Village Park**, passing the large **water tower** (built in 1898) and **village well**.

Dan buses run a service (129, 6.90NIS) from Tel Aviv's Dizengoff St to Rishon or you can take an Egged bus (201 or 301, 6.90NIS) from the Central Bus Station. Trains (15NIS, 30 minutes) from any of the four Tel Aviv stations also come to Rishon, departing every 20 minutes.

A taxi between Sde Dov airport and the city centre should cost less than 50NIS.

BICYCLE

The quickest and easiest way to travel around Tel Aviv is on a bicycle, thanks in part to 120km of dedicated bike paths along thoroughfares such as Rothschild Blvd, Chen Ave, Ben-Gurion Ave and Ibn Gabirol St. For epic rides, go to Park HaYarkon and head east, or pedal along the 10km coastal promenade.

Bike theft is common, so whenever you park your wheels (especially at night), use a massive chain lock.

For rentals, try **O-Fun** (☑ 03-544 2292; www.rentabikeisrael.com; 197 Ben Yehuda St; per hr/24hr/weekend 25/75/130NIS; ☺ 9.30am-7pm Sun-Thu, to 2pm Fri), **Wheel Bee** (☑ 03-683 8080; www.wheelbeetlv.com; 7 Hahalfanim St, Jaffa; bike/electric bike per 3hr 40/75NIS, per day 75/160NIS) or **Funoa** (☑ 03-527 7784; 9 Ben Yehuda St; electric bike per 2/8/24hr 69/150/200NIS; ☺ 10am-7pm Sun-Thu, to 1pm Fri).

BUS

Tel Aviv city buses are operated by the **Dan cooperative** (☑ 03-639 4444; www.dan.co.il; single fare 6.60NIS) and follow an efficient network of routes, from 5.30am to midnight, except Shabbat.

A ticket for a single ride costs 6.90NIS and a one-day pass *(hofshi yomi)* allowing unlimited bus travel around Tel Aviv and its suburbs costs 15NIS. To buy a one-day pass, you'll need a personal Rav Kav travel card. These can be obtained at no charge from a Dan information counter at the Central Bus Station or the Arlozorov Bus Terminal from 8am to 6pm Sunday to Thursday or until 1pm on Friday, but you'll need to download and fill out an application form and bring it, a passport photograph and your passport with you. It's easier to purchase an anonymous Rav Kav card from any bus driver (5NIS, no photo-

graph or ID needed), which entitles you to a 20% discount when loading the card with a single or multitrip pass.

There are three major local bus terminals: the Central Bus Station, 3km south of Dizengoff Center; the Arlozorov (Masof 2000) Terminal, at the eastern end of Arlozorov St near the Savidor (Merkaz/Tzafon/Arlozorov) train station; and Reading Terminal, just across the Yarkon River from the Old Port. At the Central Bus Station, local buses leave from the 4th and 7th floors, and also from Levinsky St, outside.

Currently, these are the major Tel Aviv bus routes:

Bus 4 Central Bus Station via Allenby St and Ben Yehuda St to the Reading Terminal, north of the Yarkon River. From the 4th floor.

Bus 5 Central Bus Station, along Allenby St, up Rothschild Blvd, along Dizengoff St, Nordau Ave, Ibn Gabirol St, Pinkas St, Weizmann St and HaMaccabi St and then back. Useful for the HI Hostel, the Egyptian Embassy, HaBima Sq and Dizengoff Sq.

Bus 10 Savidor train station via Arlozorov St, Ben Yehuda St, Allenby St, Herbert Samuel Esplanade, Yerushalayim Ave (Jaffa) and on to Bat Yam.

Bus 18 Savidor train station to Alozorov Bus Terminal, Shaul HaMelech Ave to Rabin Sq, King George St, Allenby St, Yerushalayim Ave (Jaffa) and on to Bat Yam.

Bus 25 Tel Aviv University to Reading Terminal then Rabin Sq, King George St, Allenby St and Carmel Market, then on to Jaffa and Bat Yam.

Bus 61 From Carmelit Bus Terminal along Allenby St, King George St, Dizengoff St, Arlozorov St and Jabotinksy St to Ramat Gan.

Bus 129 From Reading Terminal along Dizengoff St, King George St, Carmel Market, then down Allenby St and south to Holon and Rishon LeZion.

WORTH A TRIP

WEIZMANN INSTITUTE OF SCIENCE

The world-renowned **Weizmann Institute of Science** (www.weizmann.ac.il; 234 Herzl St, Rehovot; 🚇 Egged 434, 435) was named after the first president of Israel, Chaim Weizmann, a leading research chemist and statesman. During WWI, Weizmann's scientific research proved invaluable to the Allied war effort, and the goodwill he generated may have influenced Britain's granting of the Balfour Declaration in 1917. Established in 1934 on *moshav* (cooperative settlement) land, the institute now provides facilities for cutting-edge research in fields such as biology, chemistry, biochemistry, physics and computer science.

The institute's **Levinson Visitors Centre** (📞08-934 4499; visitors.center@weizmann. ac.il; Lopatie Conference Centre, Weizmann Institute of Science; ⊙9am-4pm Sun-Thu) has an multimedia introductory exhibition about the institute's work, and can organise free guided walking tours around the campus in English or Hebrew. A highlight is the **Clore Garden of Science** (www.weizmann.ac.il/garden; adult/child 30/20NIS; ⊙10am-4pm Mon-Thu, to 1pm Fri), an outdoor science museum with a glass ecosphere. Its hands-on exhibits explore solar energy, water power and other natural phenomena.

Also on the institute's grounds, next to the tombs of Dr Chaim Weizmann and his wife, Vera, is **Weizmann House** (adult/child 20/15NIS). Designed by German architect Erich Mendelsohn, a refugee from Nazism, the house was built in 1936–37. There is a museum inside displaying his personal collection of photos, books and memorabilia, notably his passport (the first in Israel). Parked outside is the Lincoln limousine given to Weizmann by Henry Ford Jr, one of only two ever made (the other was given to US President Truman).

It's best to call in advance if you want to visit any of the institute's attractions.

The campus is in Rehovot, 25km south of Tel Aviv. You can get there by train (16NIS, 25 minutes) from any Tel Aviv station. From the train station it's a 10-minute walk to the institute. You can also catch an Egged bus (201 or 301, 12.40NIS, 45 minutes, frequent) from the Central Bus Station.

Sherut 4 Same route as bus 4; operates on Shabbat.

Sherut 5 Same route as bus 5; also operates on Shabbat.

City Tour (Bus 100) Dan also runs a special tourist service in a panoramic open-top bus. It starts at the Old Port and includes stops at all the major museums and Old Jaffa. A daily pass that allows you to hop on and off at every station costs 65/56NIS adult/child.

TAXI

By law, all taxis must use their meter. Plan on 30NIS to 40NIS for most trips within the central city. Taxis operate according to two tariffs: the lower tariff between 5.30am and 9pm and the 25% higher night tariff between 9pm and 5.30am and on Shabbat and Jewish holidays.

AROUND TEL AVIV

The greater Tel Aviv area, known as the Gush Dan region, comprises a web of affluent suburbs (mainly to the east and north) and not-so-affluent suburbs (mainly to the south and southeast). The highlight of the region is the long stretch of golden beaches between Tel Aviv and Netanya, which is particularly alluring around the upscale Herzliya Pituach. Unfortunately, you won't be alone; Israelis flock to the coast, especially on weekends.

Herzliya ﺍﻟﻬﺮﺗﺴﻠﻴﺎ הרצליה

📞09 / POP 89,230

Just 12km north of central Tel Aviv, Herzliya is popular due to its fine, clean beaches, marina mall and string of seafront cafes. Named after Theodor Herzl, the founder of modern Zionism, Herzliya started as a small farming community in 1924 and now consists of two main areas separated by Hwy 2. Middle-class, suburban central Herzliya, east of the highway, is mainly residential and commercial, while **Herzliya Pituach** (west of the highway) – a neighbourhood of huge villas that's home to some of Israel's wealthiest residents – is where the beaches are. Herzliya Pituach is also home to Israel's blossoming high-tech industry; as a result, modern office blocks are rising up all over the area. *Pituach*, by the way, means 'development'.

◎ Sights

Apollonia National Park
PARK

(☑ 03-903 3130; adult/student/child 22/19/10NIS; ☺ 8am-5pm Apr-Sep, to 4pm Oct-Mar, closes 1hr earlier Fri & holiday evenings) This picturesque coastal park contains the ruins of a Crusader castle that becomes the venue for open-air concerts during summer weekends. There are some stunning views out over the Mediterranean and nearby you can see the remains of a Roman villa and the well-kept 13th-century Sidni Ali Mosque. The park can be reached by a fairly long walk up Wingate St or easily by car from the highway.

It is about 3km north of Herzliya Pituach's main beach, just beyond the small town of Nof Yam.

Herzliya Museum of Modern Art
GALLERY

(☑ 09-950 0762; www.herzliyamuseum.co.il; 4 HaBanim St; admission 10NIS; ☺ 10am-2pm Mon, Wed, Fri & Sat, 4-8pm Tue & Thu) Dedicated to Israeli and international contemporary art with an emphasis on political subject matter, this gallery aims to engage as well as entertain.

✕ Eating

As you would expect from such an affluent area, Herzliya accommodation consists of luxury spa hotels, but there are many restaurants for all budgets around the marina and on the beach.

Gelateria Siciliana
ICE CREAM $

(http://glideria.co.il; 14 Shenkar St; 1/2/3 scoops 15/20/25NIS; ☺ noon-midnight Sun-Thu, 11am-late Fri & Sat) When at the beach, it's almost obligatory to enjoy an ice cream. And in Herzliya, the best place to do this is at the local branch of the Tel Aviv gelateria.

Derby Bar
SEAFOOD $$

(☑ 09-951 1818; http://derbybar.co.il; Arena Mall; pastas 69-89NIS; mains 99-135NIS; ☺ noon-midnight) Attached to the Arena shopping mall next to the marina, this well-known restaurant has an expansive waterside terrace where it serves seafood, fish and pasta dishes. Beer is the usual accompaniment – there are six brands on tap.

Benedict
BREAKFAST $$

(☑ 09-958 0701; www.benedict.co.il; 1 Haetzel St; breakfast 39-98NIS; ☺ 24hr) The Herzliya branch of the popular Tel Aviv all-day breakfast joint is as popular as its inner-city equivalents. Diners can fill up on eggs Benedict, shakshuka or their choice from an enormous menu.

Agadir
BURGERS $$

(☑ 09-951 6551; www.agadir.co.il; 9 Hamanofim St; burgers 44-69NIS; ☺ noon-3am Sun-Thu, to 4am Fri, to 3am Sat) A 20-minute walk from the Arena Mall, Agadir sticks with what it does best: tasty meat or veggie burgers with your choice of toppings and sides.

ⓘ Getting There & Away

Egged buses 501, 502, 524, 525 and 531 run every 20 minutes to and from Tel Aviv (10.90NIS, 30 minutes). Trains run every 20 minutes (10NIS, 10 minutes). The station is quite a way from the beach, so take a taxi or bus 29 (6.60NIS) to the marina.

Netanya
נתניה نتانيا

☑ 09 / POP 192,160

The self-titled 'Israeli Riviera' offers 12km of the finest beaches in Israel and the Palestinian Territories, while the town itself exudes a strange, time-warp feeling, almost like an out-of-season French seaside resort. It's popular with families, who flock to the spacious promenade with its parks, flower beds and water features. As at Herzliya, the beaches

Around Tel Aviv

Map: Around Tel Aviv. Features include Mediterranean Sea, Netanya, Tulkarem, Separation Wall Section (November 2014), 1967 Green Line, Apollonia National Park, Rishpon, Ra'anana, Kfar Sava, Qalqilya, Herzliya Pituach, Herzliya, Ramat HaSharon, Tel Aviv University, Kafr Qasim, Tel Aviv, B'nai Brak, Petah Tikva, Jaffa, Ramat Gan, Bat Yam, Holon, Ben-Gurion Airport, WEST BANK, Rishon LeZion, Lod, Ramla, Rehovot. Scale: 5 km / 2.5 miles.

are a favourite with visiting European (especially French and Russian) tourists but are far less crowded than those of Tel Aviv. In August or September, the town has the dubious distinction of hosting the annual two-day Netanya International Clown Festival.

Activities

Israelis come from all over to enjoy Netanya's expansive golden **beaches**. There are lifeguards on duty, plus changing rooms, showers, lounge chairs and umbrellas. HaRishonim Promenade, the cliff above the beach, is great for strolling and sea views. From here you can even take an **elevator** down to the beach.

Eating

Shtampfer   CAFE $$
(6 Shtampfer St; dishes 45-70NIS; ☺9am-2am; 🛜)
Named after one of the founders of the city of Petah Tikva, Shtampfer is located in the centre of town and attracts a lively multinational crowd, who can be found chatting on the large patio or in the upstairs dining area. The menu runs from fruit shakes and salads to pastas and stir-fries. In the evening it morphs into a bar.

Marrakesh   MOROCCAN $$$
(📞09-833 4797; 5 David Hamelech St; mains 60-125NIS; ☺noon-midnight Sun-Thu, noon-3.30pm Fri, 8pm-midnight Sat) Tuck into tasty tagines, couscous and meat dishes in this kosher Moroccan restaurant near the seafront. The building is a cross between a giant tagine pot and a Bedouin tent; inside it is decorated with exotic lanterns and comfy cushions.

ℹ Information

Tourist Office (📞09-882 7286; www.go netanya.com; Ha'Atzmaut Sq 12; ☺8.30am-4pm Sun-Thu, 9am-noon Fri) This office is housed in a kiosk at the southwestern corner of Ha'Atzmaut Sq. The square itself has recently had an interactive makeover, and its central fountain now includes a huge metal ball with a hidden water screen and lights that are synchronised with music – all very disco-swish.

In the square, visitors can use information corners that include touch screens imparting information about places to visit and activities taking place around the city.

ℹ Getting There & Away

Nateev Express buses (600, 601 and 605, 10.50NIS, 30 minutes) run roughly every 15 minutes to and from Tel Aviv's Central Bus

Station and the Arlozorov Bus Station. Trains to/from Tel Aviv run twice an hour (16NIS, 25 minutes) but stop 2.5km west of the city centre, on the western side of Hwy 2.

Ramla   الرملة   רמלה
📍03 / POP 68,000

It's not quite as old as nearby Jaffa – history here stretches back 'only' 1300 years – but Ramla's bustling market, underground pools and crumbling Islamic architecture make it an interesting half-day trip from Tel Aviv. Try to visit on a Wednesday, when the market is at its busiest and most colourful.

Established in 716 CE by the Umayyid caliph Suleiman, Ramla (spot of sand) was a stopover on the road from Egypt to Damascus. Prior to the arrival of the Crusaders in the 11th century, it was Palestine's capital and it maintained its importance in the Middle Ages as the first stop for the Jerusalem-bound pilgrims who came ashore at Jaffa. Following the 1948 Arab–Israeli War the majority of the Arab population were expelled or fled and was replaced by poor Jewish immigrants, mainly from Asia (eg India) and North Africa. It's now a friendly mix of Arabs (20%) and Jews (80%).

◉ Sights

A joint ticket for the Ramla Museum, White Tower and Pool of Al-Anazia costs 22/25NIS adult/concession and can be purchased at the museum. The museum acts as the town's de facto tourist information centre. For information, see the municipality's **Goramla** (http://en.goramla.com) website.

★ **Pool of Al-Anazia**   HISTORIC SITE
(Breichat Hakeshatot; HaHaganah St; adult/concession 14/12NIS; ☺8am-4pm Sat-Thu, to 2pm Fri, to 6pm Wed & Thu Jun-Aug) The name means 'Pool of Arches', a reference to the majestic stone structures in this underground 8th-century reservoir. The most significant structure left from the Abbasid period, it is sometimes called the Pool of St Helena in reference to a Christian idea that the Empress Helena, mother of Constantine I, ordered its construction. Visitors explore the structure by rowboat.

Ramla Museum   MUSEUM
(📞08-929 2650; 112 Herzl Ave; adult/concession 12/10NIS; ☺10am-4pm Sun-Thu, to 1pm Fri) Housed in a building dating from the British Mandate, this small museum provides

Ramla

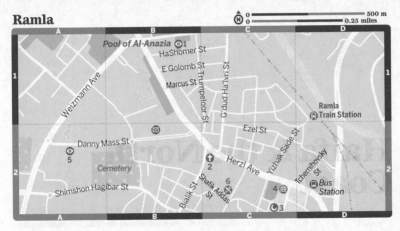

Ramla

an overview of the town's history. Exhibits include locally excavated gold coins from the 8th to 15th century CE, a collection of traditional products of Arab soap manufacture from the beginning of the 20th century and a display on the 1948 Arab–Israeli War in and around Ramla.

White Tower   HISTORIC SITE
(Danny Mass St; adult/concession 10/9NIS; ⊙8am-4pm Sat-Thu, to 2pm Fri) Experts can't agree whether this 14th-century tower was built as a minaret or a watch tower. One indisputable fact is that the 30m-high structure was built as an addition to the 8th-century White Mosque (Jamaa al-Abiad), of which only traces remain. The site includes three now-dry cisterns and the shrine of Nabi Salih, an ancient prophet mentioned in the Quran.

Great Mosque   MOSQUE
(Al-Umari Mosque; ☑08-922 5081; admission 7NIS) Though it doesn't look particularly impressive from the outside, this is one of the few Crusader buildings in Israel and the Palestinian Territories to have survived almost completely intact. Erected in the 12th century as a Christian church, it was converted into a mosque in the 13th century and the minaret and mihrab (prayer niche facing Mecca) were added at this time. Visits are by appointment only.

**Church of St Nicodemus &
St Joseph of Arimathea**   CHURCH
(☑08-912 7200; cnr Bialik St & Herzl Ave; ⊙9am-noon Mon-Fri) FREE Constructed in the 19th century on a site that Christians believe to be the site of biblical Arimathea, the hometown of Joseph, this Franciscan church has a distinctive square bell tower and a painting above the altar that is attributed to Titian (The Deposition from the Cross). To visit, you'll need to call ahead.

✖ Eating

Samir Restaurant   KEBAB $$
(☑08-922 0195; 7 Kehlat Detroit St; mains 40-90NIS; ⊙8am-7pm Mon-Thu & Sat, to 6pm Fri) The clock turns back several centuries in historic Samir, an old Arab family-run restaurant hidden in a dusty backstreet behind the market and set in a refurbished Turkish house. It has an English menu and serves various meat kebabs, dips (try the excellent hummus), felafel and salads.

❶ Getting There & Away

There are trains to Ramla (13NIS, 25 minutes) from Tel Aviv departing every 20 minutes throughout the day. Buses 450 and 451 depart from Tel Aviv's Central Bus Station every 20 minutes (14.90NIS, 40 minutes).

Haifa & the North Coast

Why Go?

Israel's north coast is a tranquil stretch of the Mediterranean punctuated with old farms, quaint seaside towns and historic sites. The principal settlement is Haifa, a mixed Jewish-Arab city that often surprises visitors with its openness and tolerance. Sprawling across Mt Carmel, Haifa has stunning views, a wealth of museums and the magnificent Baha'i Gardens. Redevelopment has created a thriving nightlife and arts scene.

Haifa is the starting point for a journey north to the historic port of Akko (Acre) and the luminous sea grottoes of Rosh HaNikra. In the other direction, Herod's port at Caesarea and the ancient civilisations of Megiddo should be on the radar of any history buff. Ein Hod and Zichron Ya'acov – home to Israel's oldest winery – are both fine destinations for anyone with a taste for art, wine and homemade beer. After your travels, take some time to chill out on the beaches around Nahariya and Akhziv.

Best Places to Eat

➡ Faces (p160)

➡ Ma'ayan HaBira (p161)

➡ HaMis'ada shel Ima (p162)

➡ Port Cafe (p174)

➡ Uri Buri (p180)

Best Places to Stay

➡ Port Inn (p158)

➡ Juha's Guesthouse (p171)

➡ Effendi Hotel (p179)

➡ Akkotel (p179)

When to Go
Haifa

°C/°F Temp
40/104 —
30/86 —
20/68 —
10/50 —
0/32 —

Rainfall inches/mm
8/200
6/150
4/100
2/50
0

J F M A M J J A S O N D

Apr & May Temperatures are pleasant and the Baha'i Gardens are in full bloom.

Jul & Aug Take refuge from the summer heat in the parks and cafes of Haifa's Carmel Centre.

Dec Every weekend, a Wadi Nisnas carnival celebrates the season's Jewish, Christian and Muslim holidays.

Haifa

חיפה Haifa

🎵 04 / POP 272,000

Haifa is one of the Middle East's most picturesque cities. The views from the top of majestic Mt Carmel (546m) are breathtaking, especially from the Baha'i Gardens, but almost everywhere you look in the city there are interesting, if not always beautiful, urban landscapes, many from the late Ottoman and Mandate (Bauhaus) periods.

Haifa was intended by British planners to serve as the Levant's main port and transport hub, linked – thanks to rail lines and an oil pipeline – to a hinterland that encompassed Transjordan and Iraq. That vision

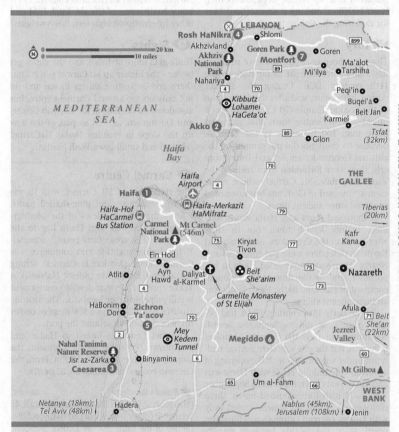

Haifa & the North Coast Highlights

❶ Admiring the sea views, fountains and flower beds of the sublime **Baha'i Gardens** (p150).

❷ Exploring the vaulted halls and hidden tunnels left by the Crusaders in the walled seaside city of **Akko** (p175).

❸ Strolling from the Crusader ramparts to the Roman amphitheatre at **Caesarea** (p171), Herod's grandiose port city.

❹ Feeling the immense power of the sea in the shimmering turquoise grottoes of **Rosh HaNikra** (p182).

❺ Sampling wine and dining well in **Zichron Ya'acov** (p169), a 19th-century village on the flanks of Mt Carmel.

❻ Preparing for Armageddon at **Megiddo** (p174), a biblical site where some believe the end of the world will begin.

❼ Stretching your legs on the hike to **Montfort** (p181), a Crusader castle accessible only on foot.

came to an abrupt end in 1948, when much of the city's Arab population were expelled or fled. Today, Haifa's Jews, Christians and Muslims live side by side, largely in harmony and the city is proud to serve as a model for Jewish-Arab coexistence.

Haifa – Israel's third-largest city – is about equidistant (a bit over 40km) from Caesarea, Nazareth and, up on the Lebanese border, Rosh HaNikra, making it an excellent base for exploring the Galilee by car.

History

There has been port on the site of modern-day Haifa since at least as far back as the 14th century BCE. During the Roman period, both before and after the destruction of the Second Temple (70 CE), Haifa was a mixed Jewish-Gentile town that garnered more than 100 mentions in the Talmud; because its residents did not pronounce the guttural Hebrew letters *het* and *'ayin* properly, they were forbidden from reciting the Torah in public. Mt Carmel, whose name means 'vineyard of God', has been regarded as sacred since ancient times.

A thousand years ago, Haifa was a fortified, mainly Jewish town, but in 1100, after it fell to the Crusaders, its Jewish and Egyptian defenders were put to the sword. Nearby Akko soon superseded Haifa in importance, and by the time of the Ottoman conquest of Palestine in the 1500s Haifa was an insignificant village.

By the early 19th century, Haifa had begun to grow, as did its Sephardic Jewish community. In 1868 the German Templers moved in, but the city's modern revival really got under way in 1905 with the opening of a railway line linking Haifa with Damascus and, three years later, Medina. In September 1918, as British forces pushed north, three platoons of Indian horsemen, armed only with lances, overran Ottoman machine-gun positions in the world's last-ever cavalry charge.

During the British Mandate, Haifa rapidly became Palestine's main port, naval centre, rail-transport hub and oil terminal. The Technion-Israel Institute of Technology, whose graduates and professors would go on to win four Nobel Prizes in chemistry, opened its doors in 1924. In April 1948, shortly before the British withdrawal, Haifa fell to Jewish forces and some 65,000 of the city's Arab residents fled.

From the 1920s to the 1950s, Haifa was the first sight of the Promised Land for many ship-borne Jewish refugees. Today, the mostly secular Jewish community enjoys a generally good relationship with the city's Arab population (10% of the total), which is mainly Christian.

In recent years Haifa has shifted its economic centre from heavy industry (oil refining and chemicals) to high-tech. An IT park near Haifa-Hof HaCarmel bus station is home to divisions of Google, Intel, IBM and other international high-tech heavyweights.

◉ Sights

Haifa gets more stylish – and the views get better – the higher up Mt Carmel you go, but there are interesting things to see and do not only up top around Carmel Centre, but also down on the flats in the German Colony and Downtown, as well as part of the way up the slope in bustling Hadar HaCarmel (Hadar) and small-town Wadi Nisnas.

◉ Carmel Centre

The ridge line of Mt Carmel, with its exclusive residences and pine-shaded parks, affords magnificent views of the Mediterranean to the west and Haifa Bay to the northeast. The area's focal point – especially for dining, nightlife and commerce – is Carmel Centre (Merkaz HaCarmel), strung out along HaNassi Ave (Sderot HaNassi). A Yekke (prewar German-Jewish) component is still palpable in the local vibe. The altitude ensures that it's always a few degrees cooler up here than down around the port.

Carmel Centre is linked to Hadar and Downtown (Paris Sq) by the Carmelit; the stop up here is called Gan HaEm. From the German colony, take buses 28, 37 or 37א.

★ **Baha'i Gardens** GARDENS
(Map p152; ☑ 04-831 3131; www.ganbahai.org.il; 45 Yefe Nof St (Upper Terrace Tour), 80 HaTziyonut Blvd (Shrine of the Bab); ⊙ lower gardens 9am-5pm, Shrine of the Bab 9am-noon, closed Baha'i holidays & Yom Kippur) **FREE** The best way to see these world-famous gardens is to take a free, 45-minute **Upper Terrace Tour** from the top of the gardens. Except on Wednesday, an English-language tour starts at noon, with additional tours in Hebrew or Russian on most days at 11am and 2pm (see the website for the monthly schedule). It's first come, first served, so get there a half-hour ahead. Both men and women must wear clothing that covers their shoulders (a shawl is OK) and knees.

Haifa

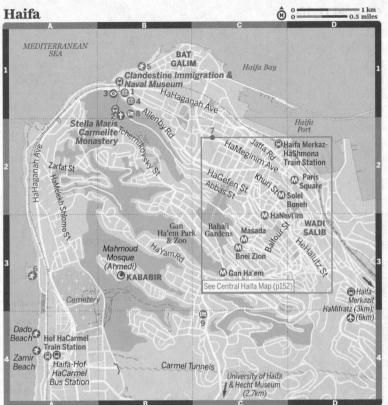

Haifa

Top Sights

Sights

Activities, Courses & Tours

Sleeping

Laid out on the slopes of Mt Carmel between 1987 and 2001, the Baha'i Gardens have 19 terraces with a distinctly classical feel – wrought-iron gates lead to flower beds, soothing pools, fountains, stone balustrades, sculptures and impossibly steep lawns, all with panoramas of Haifa Bay that defy superlatives. One hundred full-time gardeners are on hand to maintain the site. Along with Akko's Shrine of Baha'ullah, the gardens were given Unesco World Heritage status in 2008.

The golden-domed **Shrine of the Bab** (Map p152; 80 HaTziyonut Blvd), completed in 1953, is the final resting place of the Bab, Baha'ullah's spiritual predecessor, who was executed in Persia in 1850; his remains were brought to Haifa in 1909. Combining the style and proportions of European architecture with motifs inspired by Eastern traditions, it was designed by a Canadian architect, built with Italian stone and decorated with Dutch tiles.

Buildings (closed to the public) around the gardens include the **Universal House of Justice** (Map p152), a domed neoclassical

Central Haifa

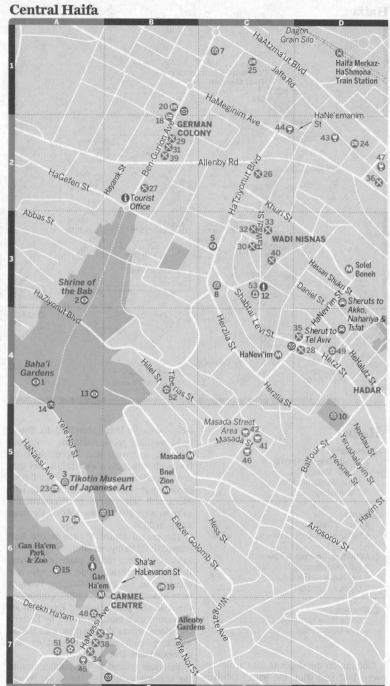

structure with Corinthian columns from which the Baha'is' spiritual and administrative affairs are governed; and the **Archives**, in a green-roofed structure that looks like the Parthenon.

About 100m up the hill from the tour entrance, extraordinary views can be had from the **Viewing Balcony** (Map p152; 61 Yefe Nof St; ◷9am-5pm daily).

Note that the line for the Upper Terrace Tour can be long when there's a cruise liner or US Navy ship in port. Admission is limited to 60 people (120 if there are two guides available). Eating, smoking and chewing gum are forbidden in the gardens.

To get to the start of the Upper Terrace Tour from Carmel Centre (the Carmelit's Gan HaEm stop), walk 1km north along **Yefe Nof St**, which affords the city's finest bay views. The tour ends down on HaTziyonut Blvd – to get back up to Carmel Centre, take bus 136 (6.90NIS, every 15 minutes) or a sherut (line 136, 7NIS); count on paying about 30NIS for a taxi. Bus 115 links the gardens' lower entrance on HaTziyonut Blvd with both the Haifa-Merkazit HaMifratz and Haifa-Hof HaCarmel bus stations.

Mané-Katz Museum
MUSEUM

(Map p152; www.mkm.org.il; 89 Yefe Nof St; adult/child 30/20NIS; ◷10am-4pm Sun-Wed, to 7pm Thu, to 1pm Fri, to 3pm Sat) Emmanuel Mané-Katz (1894–1962), known – like Chagall – for his colourful depictions of the shtetls of Eastern Europe, was an influential member of a group of early-20th-century artists known as the Jewish School of Paris. In the late 1950s he was given this home by the Haifa city authorities in return for the bequest of his works.

★ Tikotin Museum of Japanese Art
MUSEUM

(Map p152; www.tmja.org.il; 89 HaNassi Ave; adult/child 30/20NIS; ◷10am-4pm Sun-Wed, to 7pm Thu, to 1pm Fri, to 3pm Sat) Founded by Felix Tikotin in 1957, this museum – unique in the Middle East – puts on superb exhibits of Japanese art.

Gan Ha'Em
PARK

(Map p152; HaNassi Ave; ◷6am-9pm, all night Thu & Fri) On the crest of Mt Carmel, across from the upper terminus of the Carmelit metro line, this shady, kid-friendly public garden – whose name means 'Mother's Park' – has a zoo, a playground and an amphitheatre that hosts concerts on summer evenings.

Central Haifa

Zoo
ZOO

(Haifa Educational Zoo; Map p152; www.haifazoo.co.il; HaNassi Ave; adult/child 38/25NIS; ⊙9am-5pm Sat-Thu, to 3pm Sat, last entry 1hr before closing, longer hours Jun-Aug) The shaded slopes below Gan HaEm are home to a compact but attractive zoo with an aviary, a reptile house and habitats for bears, lions, monkeys, Bengal tigers, ibexes, deer and all sorts of other creatures, quite a few of them native to Israel. Kids will love the free-range peacocks who strut their stuff among the visitors.

◉ German Colony

Situated directly below – and in alignment with – the Baha'i Gardens, Ben-Gurion Ave is lined with handsome 19th-century houses with steep, red-shingled roofs and quotes from the Bible – in German – over the doors. This is the German Colony, established in 1868 by the Templers (not to be confused with the Crusader-era Knights Templar), a Pietist Protestant sect from southwestern Germany that sought to hasten the Second Coming by settling in the Holy Land. In the latter decades of the 1800s, the Templers built seven colonies in Palestine and are credited with introducing improved methods of transport, technology and agriculture.

The German Colony (Moshava Germanit in Hebrew) impressed Baha'ullah, the founder of the Baha'i faith, and was visited by Germany's Kaiser Wilhelm II in 1898. The Templers continued to live in the colony until 1939, when the British interned them as enemy aliens (many had joined the Nazi Party in the 1930s); most were later deported to Australia.

Today, the German Colony is one of Haifa's premier dining areas. Look up the hill and you'll see the Baha'i Gardens, down the hill and you can often see cargo ships docked in the port. Metronit lines 1 and 2 stop right nearby.

Haifa City Museum
MUSEUM

(Map p152; ☑04-911 5888; 11 Ben-Gurion Ave; adult/child 20/10NIS; ☻10am-4pm Sun-Thu, to 1pm Fri, to 3pm Sat) Near the bottom of Ben-Gurion Ave, a Templer-era structure houses exhibits that focus on 'history, urbanism, identity, multi-nationalism and multi-culturalism', as befits a city with as rich a cultural tapestry as Haifa.

◉ Wadi Nisnas

This villagelike, mainly Christian Arab neighbourhood, in a little valley midway between Hadar and the German Colony, retains the feel of the old Middle East, with narrow lanes, stone buildings and a bustling food market.

Beit HaGefen Arab-Jewish Cultural Centre
CULTURAL CENTRE

(Map p152; ☑04-852 5252; www.beit-hagefen. com; 2 HaGefen St; ☻gallery 10am-4pm, to 2pm Fri & Sat) FREE In an old stone building across the street from the modern Beit HaGefen Arab-Jewish Centre theatre, this cultural centre sponsors joint Arab-Jewish social and cultural activities; see the website for details. The upstairs **gallery** puts on exhibitions related to intercultural coexistence and shared spaces and values. Two-hour **tours** of multicultural and interreligious Haifa (40NIS per person; call ahead to reserve) are also available.

Museum Without Walls
PUBLIC ART

(Map p152; www.mwwart.com) FREE More than 100 pieces of art – both sculptures and installations – grace the streets and alleys of Wadi Nisnas (eg along HaWadi St). Some are large and eye-catching, others so small you could walk right past them. The Beit HaGefen Arab-Jewish Cultural Centre can supply you with a brochure.

Haifa Museum of Art
MUSEUM

(Map p152; ☑04-911 5997; www.hms.org.il; 26 Shabtai Levi St, Wadi Nisnas; adult/child 30/20NIS; ☻10am-4pm Sun-Wed, to 7pm Thu, to 1pm Fri, to 3pm Sat) Exhibits contemporary Israeli and international painting, sculpture and video art.

◉ Hadar

Established as a 'garden city' in 1920, Hadar HaCarmel (Hadar for short) became Haifa's bustling commercial heart in the 1930s, when some superb Bauhaus buildings were constructed. Among the area's architectural gems is **Beit HaKranot**, on the northwest-

ern corner of the intersection of Balfour and Herzl Sts – this is where Haifa's first traffic light was installed in 1949. Nearby shops sell inexpensive and midrange clothing, accessories and shoes – and books in Russian.

Hadar is one of this diverse city's most diverse neighbourhoods. Over a third of the residents are immigrants from the former Soviet Union (especially Ukraine) and a quarter are Arabs, and Hadar has small ultra-Orthodox and Filipino communities.

The district occupies the lower slopes of Mt Carmel – Herzl St, the main drag, is about 1km south of Paris Sq and 1.6km northeast of Carmel Centre. The Carmelit's Nevi'im stop is at the northwestern end of Herzl St, which – along with parallel HeHalutz St – is linked to both central bus stations by bus 115 and to Haifa-Hof HaCarmel by bus 112.

MadaTech
MUSEUM

(National Museum of Science; Map p152; ☑04-861 4444, ext 1; www.madatech.org.il; 25 Shemaryahu Levin St; adult/child 75/65NIS; ☻10am-3pm Sun-Wed, to 5pm Thu & Sat, to 1pm Fri) Fascinating interactive science exhibits fill the impressive first home of the Technion-Israel Institute of Technology, built in 1913. (Classes didn't begin until 1924 because of a disagreement over whether the language of instruction should be German or Hebrew.) When Albert Einstein visited in 1923, he planted a palm tree that still stands out front.

◉ Downtown & Port Area

After decades of neglect, Haifa's Downtown (Ir Tachtit) and Port Area (Ezor HaNamal) are experiencing a gradual renaissance, with hostels, restaurants and nightlife moving into run-down storefronts and derelict warehouses. The best time to visit is on Friday during the Turkish Market, when crafts stalls come to Paris Sq.

HAIFA MUSEUM TICKET

Museum aficionados can save some major money with a **combo ticket** (single/family 50/120NIS) valid for six Haifa exhibition spaces: the Mané-Katz Museum, the Tikotin Museum of Japanese Art, the Haifa Museum of Art, the Haifa City Museum, the Hermann Struck Museum and the National Maritime Museum. A family pass covers two adults and two children. The pass is sold at each of the six museums.

THE BAHA'I

Founded in the middle of the 19th century, the Baha'i faith (www.bahai.org) believes that many prophets have appeared throughout history, including Abraham, Moses, Buddha, Krishna, Zoroaster, Jesus and Mohammed. Its central beliefs include the existence of one God, the unity of all religions, and the equality and unity of all human beings, including men and women (a truly revolutionary idea in Iran in the mid-1800s).

The origins of the Baha'i faith go back to Ali Muhammad (1819–50), a native of Shiraz, Iran. In 1844 he declared that he was 'the Bab' (Gate) through which prophecies would be revealed. The charismatic Ali was soon surrounded by followers, called Babis, but was eventually arrested for heresy against Islam and executed by firing squad in Tabriz, Iran.

One of the Bab's prophecies concerned the coming of 'one whom God would make manifest'. In 1866, a Babi named Mirza Hussein Ali (1817–92) proclaimed that he was this prophetic figure and assumed the title of Baha'ullah, having received divine inspiration while imprisoned in Tehran's infamous Black Pit.

As with the Bab, Baha'ullah's declarations were unwelcome in Persia and he was expelled first to Baghdad, and then to Constantinople, Adrianople and finally the Ottoman penal colony of Akko. Sitting in his cell in Akko, he dedicated himself to laying down the tenets of a new faith, the Baha'i, whose name is derived from the Arabic word baha (glory).

Among his writings, Baha'ullah stated that one could not be born into the Baha'i faith; at the age of 15, a person chooses whether or not they want to take on the obligations of being Baha'i. He also spoke of gender equality, the oneness of humankind, world peace, the need for universal compulsory education, and harmony between religion and the sciences.

The Baha'i World Centre (the religion's global headquarters), famed for its gardens, is on Haifa's Mt Carmel, while the holiest Baha'i site, the Shrine of Baha'ullah, is near Akko; both are staffed by volunteers from around the world. Part because of Jewish and Muslim sensibilities, the Baha'is do not seek converts in Israel and Israeli citizens are not permitted to join the faith. There is no Baha'i community in Israel.

The Baha'i faith now has an estimated five to six million followers worldwide. Tradition prescribes that a Baha'i who is able should make a pilgrimage (https://bahai.bwc.org/pilgrimage) to Akko and Haifa.

Al-Jarina Mosque
MOSQUE

(Map p152) A few hundred metres east of Paris Sq is Al-Jarina Mosque, aka Al-Masjid al-Kabir (Great Mosque), marked by an early-20th-century minaret that looks more than a little like a provincial English clock tower.

Istiqlal Mosque
MOSQUE

(Independence Mosque; Map p152) Built in 1926, this mosque is still used for worship.

⊙ University of Haifa

Perched high atop Mt Carmel, its 27-storey tower visible for miles around, the University of Haifa is 6.5km southeast of Carmel Centre along the Mt Carmel Ridge. Arabs make up more than 30% of the student body, far more than at any other Israeli university.

From Sunday to Thursday when the university is in session, on-campus parking is limited to permit holders, but there's an arrangement for Hecht Museum visitors – just tell the guard where you're going and leave

ID; you'll get it back when you produce a 10NIS parking receipt from the museum.

To get to the university, take buses 37 or 37א from Hadar or Carmel Centre, buses 46 or 146 from Haifa-Hof HaCarmel, or buses 141, 146 or 171 from Haifa-Merkazit HaMifratz.

★ Hecht Museum
MUSEUM

(http://mushecht.haifa.ac.il; 199 Abba Hushi Blvd; ⊙10am-4pm Sun, Mon, Wed & Thu, to 7pm Tue, to 1pm Fri, to 2pm Sat) FREE One of Israel's most engaging museums, the Hecht's standout highlight is the extraordinary Ma'agan Mikhael Shipwreck, the remarkably well-preserved remains of a 13.5m-long merchant ship from 400 BCE – that's four centuries older than the Ancient Galilee Ship on display at the Sea of Galilee! The archaeology section also features a whole room on the Phoenicians; Israelite, Moabite and Phoenician seals from the First Temple period; and an important collection of ancient coins, including some issued by revolt leader Bar Kochba.

The art section has works by such luminaries as Corot, Soutine, Manet, Monet, Modigliani (one fascinating canvas has two portraits, one on each side), Pissarro and Van Gogh; a collection of works by Jewish artists, most from Germany and Eastern Europe; and the Oscar Ghez Collection, which showcases the works of 18 Paris-based artists who perished in the Holocaust.

Don't confuse the Hecht Museum, under the Eshkol Tower, with the nearby Dr Hecht Art Centre.

Eshkol Tower TOWER
(www.haifa.ac.il; 199 Abba Hushi Blvd; ⊙ work-day hours Sun-Thu, to 1pm Fri) FREE A case can be made that building a 30-storey skyscraper on top of a mountain was an act of monumental folly, but renowned Brazilian architect Oscar Niemeyer didn't think so – he's the one who designed the Eshkol Tower, opened in 1978. To get to the observation deck and its panoramic views, take the lift to the 29th floor and walk up one flight of stairs.

◎ Stella Maris

Situated at the northern tip of the Mt Carmel massif, Stella Maris is accessible by aerial cable car (☎ 04-833 5970; one way/return 21/29NIS; ⊙ 10am-8pm, to 6pm winter) from Bat Galim's seafront promenade; by bus 115 from Hadar and Haifa-Hof HaCarmel; by buses 30 and 31 from Carmel Centre; and on foot from near Elijah's Cave. The path from Stella Maris to the cave begins from the parking lot across the street from the church, along the fence of the Israeli navy base.

★ Stella Maris
Carmelite Monastery CHURCH
(Map p151; www.ocarm.org; ⊙ 6.30am-12.30pm & 3-6pm) The Carmelite Order was established in the late 12th century when Crusader-era pilgrims, inspired by the prophet Elijah, opted for a hermitic life on the slopes of Mt Carmel. Today, the order lives on around the world and in the 'Star of the Sea' monastery, whose current building was constructed in 1836 at the northern tip of Mt Carmel. The sea views are spectacular. Wear clothing that covers your knees and shoulders; men should remove hats.

Inside the church, the beautifully painted ceiling and dome portray Elijah and the chariot of fire in which he is said to have ascended to heaven; King David with his harp; the saints of the order; the prophets Isaiah, Ezekiel and David; and the Holy Family with the four evangelists below.

On the path leading to the church entrance, a pyramid with a wrought-iron cross on top serves as a memorial for 200 sick and wounded French troops, hospitalised here, who were slaughtered by the Ottomans after Napoleon returned to Paris in 1799.

◎ Maritime Museums & Elijah's Cave

Awkwardly situated across the train tracks and the highway from the lower station of the Stella Maris cable car, this area is 2km northwest of the German Colony. It is served by buses 111 and 112 from the German Colony, Wadi Nisnas and Hadar; bus 111 also goes to Haifa-Hof HaCarmel.

★ Clandestine Immigration &
Naval Museum MUSEUM
(Map p151; www.amutayam.org.il; 204 Allenby Rd; adult/child incl National Maritime Museum 15/10NIS; ⊙ 10am-4pm Sun-Thu) A lot more evocative and dramatic than you might expect, this museum showcases the Zionist Movement's determined efforts to infiltrate Jewish refugees from Europe into British-blockaded Palestine from 1934 to 1948. The centrepiece is a WWII landing craft rechristened the *Af-Al-Pi-Chen* ('nevertheless' in Hebrew) that carried 434 refugees to Palestine in 1947; intercepted by the British, they were sent to internment camps on Cyprus. The museum is run by the Ministry of Defense, so you'll need your passport to get in.

Other exhibits tell of the famed *Exodus,* a vastly overloaded ship that carried over 4500 Holocaust survivors to Palestine in 1947 but was forced by the British to return to Germany (of all places).

National Maritime Museum MUSEUM
(Map p151; ☎ 04-853 6622; www.nmm.org.il; 198 Allenby Rd; adult/child 30/20NIS; ⊙ 10am-4pm Sun-Thu, to 1pm Fri, to 3pm Sat) Undersea archaeological finds, models of ancient ships, coins with maritime themes, Hellenistic figurines and pre-modern navigation technology illustrate 5000 years of shipping in the Mediterranean basin.

Elijah's Cave RELIGIOUS SITE
(Map p151; Allenby Rd; ⊙ 8am-6pm, to 5pm winter Sun-Thu, to 1pm Fri, closed Sat & Jewish holidays) FREE Holy to Jews, Christians, Muslims and

Druze, this cave is where the prophet Elijah is believed to have prayed before challenging the priests of Ba'al on Mt Carmel (1 Kings 18) and where he is said to have hidden from the wrath of Queen Jezebel afterwards (1 Kings 19:1-3). These days there's not much to see unless you're interested in Jewish pilgrimage sites. Dress modestly; there are separate sections for men (to the right) and women (to the left).

According to a Christian tradition, Mary, Joseph and Jesus sheltered here on their return from Egypt. Muslims associate the site with Al-Khidr (the Green Prophet), sometimes seen as an Islamic version of Elijah, or as his companion. Prior to 1948, the cave was controlled by a Muslim waqf (religious endowment).

To get to Elijah's Cave from the National Maritime Museum, head up the slope, cross the street and take the staircase (marked by a Hebrew sign) up the 6m-high stone retaining wall; an asphalt path then leads 200m around the limestone bluff, under the wires of the Stella Maris cable car. A steep path links the cave with the Stella Maris Carmelite Monastery.

🏃 Activities

Bat Galim Beach BEACH
(Map p151; www.batgalim.org.il; Aharon Rosenfeld St) This ain't Hawaii, but surfers do come here to catch waves. Situated in the lower-middle-class Bat Galim neighbourhood about 1km northwest of Rambam hospital (the terminus of Metronit line 2) and a few blocks northeast of the lower cable-car station.

★ Hof HaCarmel Beach BEACH
(Map p151) Haifa's best beaches, with an inviting promenade and a number of restaurants and cafes, stretch along the north–south-oriented coastline to the west of Mt Carmel. To get there, take Metronit line 1 to Haifa-Hof HaCarmel or a train to Hof HaCarmel train station (6NIS, every 20 minutes from Haifa Merkaz-HaShmona). Nearby Zamir and Dado beaches are also decent.

🍵 Courses

University of Haifa Ulpan LANGUAGE COURSE
(📞 04-824 0766; http://overseas.haifa.ac.il; University of Haifa) Offers some of Israel's most highly regarded and flexible university language programs. Intensive Hebrew and Arabic classes meet five or six hours a day Sunday to Thursday, both during the academic year (US$900 per semester) and in

July and August (US$1280/1850 for four/eight weeks, plus US$320/460 for dorm accommodation).

Ulpan Aba Hushi LANGUAGE COURSE
(Map p151; 📞 04-605 5149; www.ulpanhaifa.com; 131 HaMeginim Ave) Intensive five-month, five-day-a-week Hebrew courses.

✨ Festivals

Holiday of the Holidays CARNIVAL
(www.haifahag.com) On every weekend in December, Wadi Nisnas hosts an outdoor carnival and concerts celebrating the season's Jewish, Christian and Muslim holidays. The event is known as Chag HaChagim in Hebrew and 'Id al-A'yad in Arabic.

🛏 Sleeping

Haifa gets lots of Baha'i pilgrims, so it's a good idea to reserve ahead, especially in July and August.

🛏 Port Area & Downtown

This up-and-coming area started with one hostel back in 1999 and now has several. Located a few blocks north of the German Colony, it's very near the Haifa Merkaz-HaShmona train station and is on Metronit lines 1 and 2.

★ Port Inn GUESTHOUSE $
(Map p152; 📞 04-852 4401; www.portinn.co.il; 34 Jaffa Rd, Port Area; dm/s/d/tr/q 130/290/340/450/550NIS, dm without breakfast 90NIS; ❄ @ 🛜) A magnet for budget travellers, this friendly guesthouse has helpful staff, a lovely back garden, a small kitchen and washing machines; the lounge and dining room are great for meeting other guests. The 16 rooms are spotless and colourfully, if simply, furnished; dorm rooms have four, five and nine beds. Apartments across the street cost 400/500/600NIS for three/four/five people (breakfast not included).

St Charles Hospice GUESTHOUSE $
(Map p152; 📞 04-855 3705; www.pat-rosary.com; 105 Jaffa Rd, Port Area; s/d/q 180/300/390NIS; ❄ @ 🛜) Operated by the Catholic Rosary Sisters, this guesthouse occupies a beautiful building (built 1880) with a lovely garden out back. Rooms are simple but comfortably furnished and come with private showers. The gate is often locked – just ring the bell. Curfew is generally 11pm. Payment must be made in cash.

WHAT TO DO ON SHABBAT IN HAIFA

Thanks to Haifa's multireligious population, there's plenty to do here on Friday night and Saturday. (Note that Christian areas, such as Wadi Nisnas, close down on Sunday.)

Public transport operated seven days a week during the British Mandate and it continues to do so today, at least to a certain extent. Metronit line 1 runs at least twice an hour, 24 hours a day, seven days a week, linking everything along the coast between the Haifa-Hof HaCarmel and Haifa-Merkazit HaMifratz bus terminals, including Downtown (the Port Area), the German Colony and Hof HaCarmel Beach. Various local bus lines also operate on Shabbat, as do buses from Haifa-Merkazit HaMifratz to Nazareth (one hour, hourly), where Saturday is pretty much a weekday (Sunday, however, is almost like Shabbat in Jerusalem). Sheruts (shared taxis) link Hadar with Akko, whose Old City is completely open on Shabbat, and Nahariya.

All museums, except the two maritime museums, are open on Saturday, though they tend to close an hour or two earlier than on weekdays. Also open are the Baha'i Gardens, the Shrine of the Bab and the zoo. The souq (market) and shops in Wadi Nisnas stay open, as do almost all the eateries there and in the German Colony, Hadar and Carmel Centre. Also open for business: the flea market in Wadi Salib. The Druze village of Daliyat al-Karmel is at its liveliest and most crowded on Saturday.

🛏 German Colony

Haddad Guest House   HOTEL $
(Map p152; ☑077-201 0618; www.haddadguest house.com; 26 Ben-Gurion Ave, German Colony; s 280-320NIS, d 330-380NIS, tr 400-450NIS; ❋🕾) In the middle of the German Colony, ensconced in a completely remodelled 19th-century house, this family-run hotel has four clean, comfortable rooms on the ground floor and seven more – with kitchenettes – on the 2nd floor (in between are several lawyers' offices). Some of the bathrooms are showing signs of age. There's free parking around back.

Colony Hotel Haifa   BOUTIQUE HOTEL $$$
(Map p152; ☑04-851 3344; www.colony-hotel. co.il; 28 Ben-Gurion Ave, German Colony; s/d/tr/q 666/740/1050/1260NIS; ❋@🕾) Built in 1905 by the Appinger family, this Templer building and its old-time tile floors have been tastefully updated. The 40 attractive rooms have large windows, high ceilings and all-marble bathrooms, and some come with hot tub. Wheelchair accessible.

🛏 Carmel Centre

Not only is it cooler up on top of Mt Carmel, but the places we list are all within easy walking distance of heaps of restaurants and cafes.

Molada Guest House   GUESTHOUSE $
(Map p152; ☑04-838 7958, ext 102 or 103 after 3pm); www.rutenberg.org.il; 82 HaNassi Ave, Carmel Centre; s/d/tr 250/350/520NIS; ❋🕾) This spartan, college-dorm-style guesthouse has 16 large rooms with single beds and desks. Reception is down the street at the Ruthenberg Institute for Youth Education (77 HaNassi Ave; staffed 8.30am to 3pm Sunday to Thursday). Reserve ahead by phone or through the website and they'll explain how to pick up the key when reception is closed.

Situated down a driveway across the street from the Dan Carmel Hotel.

Beth Shalom Hotel   HOTEL $$
(Map p152; ☑04-837 7481; www.beth-shalom. co.il; 110 HaNassi Ave, Carmel Centre; s/d/tr NIS380/500/630; ❋🕾) Run by a Lutheran group based in Zurich, this spotless guesthouse feels a bit institutional in a very Swiss sort of way. The 30 rooms are compact, with practical furnishings, fake parquet floors and tile bathrooms. Amenities include a small play area for kids, a small library and a comfortable lounge with complimentary hot drinks.

Villa Carmel   BOUTIQUE HOTEL $$$
(Map p151; ☑04-837 5777; www.villacarmel.co.il; 30 Heinrich Heine St, Carmel Centre; r US$210-285, US$25 extra Fri; ❋@🕾) Set amid pine and cypress trees, this boutique hotel has a sophisticated, European feel. All 15 rooms are very comfortable, but deluxe rooms come with balconies. Amenities include a rooftop sundeck with hot tub and sauna, and massage treatments. Situated 800m southwest of Carmel Centre.

Crowne Plaza HOTEL $$$
(Map p152; ☎1 700 700 884; www.crowneplaza.
com; 111 Yefe Nof St, Carmel Centre; d US$153-261;
❋@☎❋) One of Carmel Centre's nicest
hotels, with ravishing views, a spa and 100
rooms.

🛏 Stella Maris Area

Stella Maris Hospice GUESTHOUSE $$
(Map p151; ☎04-833 2084; stelama@netvision.
net.il; Stella Maris Rd; s/d/tr US$75/110/135;
❋@☎) It's not the most central place to
stay in Haifa, but this Catholic guesthouse,
run by Carmelite nuns and geared towards
pilgrims, offers plenty of old-world charm
(the building dates from about 1840). The
45 crucifix-adorned rooms are simple but
spacious, and some offer sea views. Curfew
is 10.30pm or 11pm; check in by 8pm. Situated through the green gates to the left as
you face Stella Maris Carmelite Monastery;
ring the bell to get in.

Bus 115 links the guesthouse with Hadar
and both central bus stations.

🛏 Hadar

Loui Hotels HOTEL $
(Map p152; ☎04-432 0149; www.louihotels.com;
35 HeHalutz St, Hadar; without breakfast d US$70-
90, q US$125-105; ❋☎) This apartment hotel
has friendly staff, six proper apartments
and 35 simple, practical rooms – all with
kitchenettes, many with atrocious chandel-
iers and exposed hot-water heaters, some
with balconies. The rooftop lounge sports
port views, tables, chairs and fake grass.
Guests get free cellphones with unlimited
calling within Israel.

Art Gallery Hotel HOTEL $$
(Map p152; ☎04-861 6161; www.hotelgallery.co.il;
61 Herzl St, Hadar; s/d 450/500NIS; ❋@☎)
Original works by local artists adorn both
the public spaces and the 40 rooms, which
are smallish but otherwise pleasant and
nicely outfitted. Opened as a small hotel in
1938, this creative hostelry has a small fitness rooms, massage and a 5th-floor deck
with port views and picnic tables. Situated
near the Metronit's Talpiyot Market stop.

Hotel Theodor HOTEL $$
(Map p152; ☎04-867 7111; www.theodorhotel.
co.il; 63 Herzl St, Hadar; s/d/tr US$110/120/155;
❋@☎) Occupying floors six through 17 of a
Hadar tower, the 97 tourist-class rooms here
are modern and midsized and come with

minibars, all-tile bathrooms and great views
from every angle. Reception is through the
black-and-white-tiled shopping arcade and
up one floor. Situated near the Metronit's
Talpiyot Market stop.

🍴 Eating

Many of the cafes in the Masada St area (see
Drinking & Nightlife, p162), 500m up the
hill from Hadar, serve light meals.

🍴 German Colony

More than a dozen excellent restaurants,
some owned by Arab celebrity chefs, line
elegant Ben-Gurion Ave in the German Colony. Almost all are open seven days a week.

★Faces MEDITERRANEAN $$
(Map p152; ☎04-855 2444; www.faces.rest-e.co.
il; 37 Ben-Gurion Ave, German Colony; mains 85-
135NIS; ☺9am-midnight or later; ☎🅿) Nazareth-
born chef Manhal abu Muwara plucks
culinary ideas from the Mediterranean to
create dishes such as breaded mushrooms
with goat cheese and feta filling, and Cor-
don Bleu–style chicken medallions stuffed
with ground duck breast and mozzarella.
Other excellent options include giant salads
and handmade pasta with cream or tomato
sauce. Breakfast (45NIS to 52NIS) is served
all day. Wheelchair accessible.

Shahrazad MIDDLE EASTERN $$
(Map p152; ☎077-434 1907; 37 Ben-Gurion Ave,
German Colony; mains 42-120NIS; ☺11am-2am
or 3am; ☎🅿) Serves beautifully presented
Arab dishes with a (sometimes shocking)
twist – for instance, mansaf (rice with
ground lamb, tangy goat yoghurt, pine nuts,
saffron and nutmeg), a formal holiday dish,
is accompanied by workaday felafel balls.
The tamarind juice is superb. The Middle
Eastern desserts here are less overwhelm-
ingly sweet than usual.

A nargileh (water pipe) costs 35NIS to
45NIS; the balcony is nonsmoking.

Al-Diyar MIDDLE EASTERN $$
(Map p152; ☎04-852 8939; 55 Ben-Gurion Ave;
mains 55-98NIS; ☺noon-midnight; 🅿) When
members of Haifa's Arab community are in
the mood for a hearty meal of grilled meat –
kebab with pine nuts, for instance – they
often head to Al-Diyar, which also serves
fish, seafood and pasta. A selection of 15
salads – a veritable vegetarian feast – costs
35NIS (30NIS if you order a main dish).

Douzan
LEBANESE $$$

(Map p152; ☑04-852 5444; 35 Ben-Gurion Ave, German Colony; mains 70-110NIS; ☺9am-1am or later; ☑) Dishes of Lebanese, French and Italian inspiration make this atmospheric restaurant one of the German Colony's most beloved dining spots. Specialities include *sfeeha* (pastries topped with minced beef, onions and pine nuts), kebab grilled on cinnamon skewers, and veal rolls filled with goat cheese, pesto and garlic sauce. For vegetarians, there's tabouleh (38NIS) and *rolettini* (cheese rolled in fried eggplant slices).

✕ Carmel Centre

Carmel Centre has a nice mix of upscale restaurants, sleek cafes and takeaway joints.

Gal's Bakery
BAKERY $

(HaKonditoria shel Gal; Map p152; www.galsbakery.co.il; 131 HaNassi Ave, Carmel Centre; mains 25-45NIS; ☺7am-10pm Sun-Thu, to 3pm Fri; 🛜☑) Serves scrumptious pastries – the best in the city – plus pies, cookies, homemade muesli (35NIS), bourekas (savoury, flaky Balkan pastries), quiche, lasagna, sandwiches and, in winter, soups. Take-out or sit-down. Kosher (dairy).

Meat
STEAK $$

(Map p152; ☑04-837 3222; http://meat.rest.co.il; 129 אHaNassi Ave, Carmel Centre; mains 59-149NIS; ☺noon-11pm; 🛜) A carnivore's dream, this rustic courtyard grill house serves up hearty steaks and burgers and some tasty appetisers, including sirloin carpaccio (52NIS) and chorizo sausages. The top-quality beef comes from the Golan and Argentina. Vegetarians can choose from salads, soups and pasta. Kids' meals cost 45NIS.

Mandarin
CAFE $$

(Map p152; ☑04-836 3554; 129 HaNassi Ave, Carmel Centre; mains 39-74NIS; ☺8am-1am, to 2am or 3am Fri; 🛜) There's nothing Chinese about this cosy cafe-bistro, whose wooden deck – along a garden path from busy HaNassi Ave – is a relaxing spot for salads, sandwiches and pasta, or breakfast (36NIS to 58NIS). The soundtrack ranges from jazz and blues to French chansons.

✕ Downtown & Port Area

A few culinary gems shine brightly amid the derelict warehouses of this long-neglected area.

★ Ma'ayan HaBira
JEWISH $$

(Map p152; ☑04-862 3193; 4 Nathanson St; mains 30-120NIS; ☺10am-5pm Sun-Fri, to 11pm Tue, to 10pm Thu) Founded in 1950 as a butcher's shop and sausage factory, this old-timer is famous for serving beer (thus the name) and Eastern European Jewish 'soul food', including jellied calf's foot, gefilte fish, chopped liver and *kreplach,* a meat-stuffed dumpling known affectionately as a 'Jewish wonton'. Serves goulash in summer and cholent (a stew of meat, beans, barley and potatoes) in winter.

Don't miss the street party held here every Tuesday, when dinner (7.30pm or 8pm) is accompanied by live music (rock, blues or country); reservations are a must. There's live guitar music, with lyrics in Spanish, on Thursday from 8pm.

✕ Wadi Nisnas

Rival felafel joints face each other across Ha-Wadi St. Three blocks north, the shwarma shops around the intersection of Allenby Rd and HaZiyonut Blvd include **Shwarma Emil** (33 Allenby Rd).

Almost everything here is closed on Sunday.

Felafel HaZkenim
FELAFEL $

(Map p152; 18 HaWadi St, Wadi Nisnas; felafel 15NIS; ☺8am-7.30pm, closed Sun; ☑) Bring your appetite to Felafel HaZkenim (opened 1950). Owner Afif Sbait greets every customer with a smile and a felafel ball dipped in hummus.

Felafel Michel
FELAFEL $

(Map p152; 21 HaWadi St, Wadi Nisnas; felafel 16NIS; ☺8am-7.30pm, closed Sun; ☑) For the best felafel you've ever tasted, come hungry to Felafel Michel (opened 1972). A meat-filled kibbeh ball costs 6NIS.

Abd al-Hadi
PASTICCERIA $

(Map p152; 3 Sh'hadah Shalach St, Wadi Nisnas; ☺9am-11pm daily) Delicious Arab pastries, including *kunafeh* (flat, warm cheese cake) and a dozen kinds of baklava.

Souq
MARKET $

(Map p152; Yochanan HaKadosh St, Wadi Nisnas; ☺6.30am-5pm, closed Sun) The best place in Haifa for fresh fruit and veggies; also has other picnic fixin's.

Ein El-Wadi
MIDDLE EASTERN $$

(Map p152; ☑04-855 3353; 26 HaWadi St, Wadi Nisnas; mains 55-80NIS; ☺10am-8pm Mon-Sat) Opened 2013, this restaurant serves – under ancient stone arches – Lebanese and Palestinian dishes such as *shishbarak* (meat dumplings in yoghurt sauce; 80NIS), *musakhan* (sumac chicken; 5NIS), *makloubeh* (layers of stewed chicken, rice and vegetables; 55NIS) and *fatayer* (spinach-stuffed pastry; 35NIS). For dessert, try *hariseh* (semolina cake made with rose syrup).

Hadar

There are falafel, shwarma and other cheap eats along the northwestern part of Herzl St.

★ HaMis'ada shel Ima
ETHIOPIAN **$**

(Mother's Restaurant; Map p152; 20 HaNevi'im St, Hadar; mains 35-40NIS; ⏱11am-11pm Sun-Fri, sundown-10pm or 11pm Sat night; 🖉) Stepping into this utterly unpretentious eatery is like a quick trip to Addis Ababa. The spicy and lip-smackingly satisfying Ethiopian dishes are served – and eaten – with *injera* (spongy Ethiopian flatbread made with teff flour) and can be washed down with two kinds of Ethiopian beer (13NIS). It's hidden away in the courtyard of the Amisragas building.

Mains include *doro* (chicken prepared with butter, garlic and ginger), *kitfo* (raw or lightly cooked marinated beef) and, for vegetarians and vegans, *beyaynetu* (a combination platter with dollops of lentils, potatoes, carrots and spinach).

Café Nitsa
CAFE **$**

(Map p152; 19 HaNevi'im St, Hadar; cake 12NIS; ⏱6am-4pm; 🕾) Founded in 1947 and hardly changed since, this tiny coffee shop serves Central European cakes, croissants, light sandwiches and fresh-squeezed orange and grapefruit juice (12NIS).

🍷 Drinking & Nightlife

For an evening out, locals often head to the German Colony, where many restaurants double as cafes and bars; to the hip, lefty cafes of the Masada St area; or to the grimy Port Area (Downtown), where there are a number of bars along HaBankim St. Carmel Centre has plenty of coffeehouses and a few pubs.

🍷 Carmel Centre

Pundak HaDov
PUB

(Bear Inn; Map p152; www.pundakhadov.rest-e.co.il; 135 HaNassi Ave, Carmel Centre; ⏱5pm-1am or later, from noon Fri) One of the city's main expat hang-outs, this popular Irish-style pub-restaurant pours 12 draught beers, among them Murphy's and the Israeli microbrew

Alexander. Main dishes (56NIS to 125NIS) include salads, sandwiches, chicken, steak and seafood. Screens major sports matches (rugby, footy).

🍷 Downtown

Li Bira
BAR

(Map p152; 📱052-228 4840; www.libira.co.il; 21 HaNe'emanim St, Downtown; ⏱7pm-1am or later) This laid-back basement beer hall has long been a Downtown favourite. Owner Leonid Lipkin uses his own recipes to make non-filtered, nonpasteurised brews (28NIS a pint): weiss bitter, double pils, smoked stout and strong Belgian ale (seasonal). A 'beer tasting' gets you 100mL of each for 22NIS. Snacks include carpaccio (29NIS), smoked goose breast (88NIS) and rösti (Swiss hash browns; 44NIS).

Syncopa
BAR

(Map p152; 5 Khayat St, Downtown; ⏱8.30pm-2am or later) A double-decker night spot with a softly lit, burgundy-coloured bar downstairs and a performance space upstairs. There's live music on Monday, Wednesday and Saturday from 10pm, and DJs do their thing on Tuesday from 10.30pm. Some concerts are free, others are not.

Eli's Pub
BAR

(Map p152; 35 Jaffa Rd, Downtown; ⏱8pm-3am or later) Owner Eli likes travellers, so introduce yourself and he'll find you a nice spot at the bar, where you can choose from among 11 beers on tap (from 24NIS). A hammam in Ottoman times, this place really rocks from 10.30pm or 11pm on Monday (jam sessions), Tuesday (open mic), Wednesday (live jazz) and Saturday (local bands).

🍷 Masada Street Area

In recent years, Masada St and its environs have turned into a Bohemian, multicultural enclave that, denizens say, feels a bit like a kibbutz. Thanks to cheap rents, it's home to a growing number of funky shops and little cafes that serve breakfast, salads and sandwiches along with generous portions of left-wing politics. To get there from Herzl St in Hadar, walk about 500m up the hill (southwest), or take the Carmelit to the Masada stop and walk east.

Cafe Masada
CAFE

(Map p152; 16 Masada St; ⏱7am-2am or later, from 9am Sat; 🕾) Like talking politics over your java? At this politically charged cafe everyone seems to be in the far-left pro-peace camp and no one is shy about expressing opinions. It's a great place to mingle with locals and chat with the friendly owner, Eran Prager. Edibles include shakshuka (28NIS) and toasted sandwiches (16NIS to 28NIS); breakfast costs 45NIS.

Puzzle Café CAFE
(Map p152; 21 Masada St; ⊘10am-midnight or later; 🐦) The name of this small, friendly place reflects the clientele: an odd collection of pieces that, when put together, form a whole that's full of surprises. Popular with scenesters, students and young artists. Feeling peckish? Options include brunch (49NIS), sandwiches (38NIS to 44NIS), quiche (44NIS) and home-made cakes (32NIS to 36NIS), served to the accompaniment of classic rock.

Elika CAFE
(Map p152; 24 Masada St; ⊘7am-3am) For a Palestinian nationalist vibe, head over to Elika, a favourite hang-out of Haifa's Arab cultural elite. The walls are plastered with old posters for Arab music concerts. Edibles include salads (36NIS to 44NIS), mezze and sandwiches (17NIS to 27NIS); breakfast (26NIS to 45NIS) is served until 3pm.

☆ Entertainment

For details on cultural events, see www.ethos.co.il, run by the Haifa municipality; tickets can be ordered by calling 📞04-833 8888.

Beat LIVE MUSIC
(Map p152; 📞04-810 7107; www.ethos.co.il; 124 HaNassi Ave, Carmel Centre; admission 50-100NIS) Both a music school, run by the city, and one of Haifa's top performance venues, with live music by Israeli and overseas bands. Call to find out what's on.

Haifa Cinematheque CINEMA
(Map p152; 📞04-833 8888; www.ethos.co.il; 142 HaNassi Ave, Carmel Centre; ticket 33NIS) Screens avant-garde, off-beat and art films in two halls. Out front, bronze stars in the pavement honour major figure in Israeli cinema.

Haifa Auditorium CONCERT VENUE
(Map p152; 📞04-833 8888; www.ethos.co.il; 140 HaNassi Ave, Carmel Centre) One of Haifa's principal venues for ballet, modern dance and music, with over 1100 seats.

Capoeira Angola Israel LIVE MUSIC, DANCE
(Map p152; 📞054-436 5375; www.capoeira-angola.co.il; 8 Amos St, Hadar; ⊘7-9pm Sat) The Saturday-evening *roda* (music and dance

circle), open to the public, is an excellent way to get acquainted with capoeira (an Afro-Brazilian martial art).

Matnas Tverya 15 LIVE MUSIC
(Gould-Shenfeld Community Center; Map p152; 📞04-850 7785; tveria15@gmail.com; 15 Tiberias St) A community centre with frequent amateur concerts, performances and classes (eg Feldenkrais, yoga and tango). Lots of interesting people hang out here, making it a great place to meet locals. In July and August there's live ethnic music on the roof from 8pm on Saturday. Served by buses 115 and 133, or you can take the Carmelit to Masada.

The last Friday of the month is Shishi Nashi (Feminine Friday; 10am to 1pm) – women travellers are welcome to attend this pot-luck breakfast, bartering market and discussion forum. Tuesday afternoon there's acupuncture for 50NIS (reserve by calling Naomi on 📞054-772 2024).

🛍 Shopping

ElWadi MUSIC
(Map p152; 📞052-269 2412; 36 HaWadi St, Wadi Nisnas; ⊘9.30am-7pm Tue-Sat, 2.30-7pm Mon) Run by oud player Bishara Deeb, this boutique of Middle Eastern music sells ouds (1000NIS to 6500NIS) from Nazareth, Egypt, Syria and Iraq, darbouka drums (160NIS to 1600NIS) with beautiful mother-of-pearl inlay, qanuns, bouzoukis, guitars and tambourines.

Turkish Market MARKET
(HaShuk HaTurki; Map p152; Paris Sq, Downtown; ⊘10am-4pm Fri) A crafts market that draws artists and artisans from around the region.

Flea Market MARKET
(Shuk Pishpeshim; Map p152; Kibbutz Galuyot St, Wadi Salib; ⊘Sat & Sun) Stores and sidewalks display a range of (worthless) junk and (valuable) junque. Situated 700m southeast of Paris Sq.

ℹ Orientation

The higher up the slopes of Mt Carmel you go, the wealthier the neighbourhoods are.

The gritty **Downtown** (Ir Tachtit) and adjacent **Port Area**, built during the late Ottoman period and the British Mandate, are on the flats adjacent to Haifa Port and the railway tracks. Landmarks include the Haifa Merkaz-HaShmona train station, which affords easy access to Ben-Gurion airport, Tel Aviv, Akko and Nahariya; and **Paris Square** (Kikar Pariz), the lower terminus of the

Carmelit funicular railway (a steep, six-station metro). About 1km west of there, directly below the Baha'i Gardens, is Ben-Gurion Ave, the elegant main thoroughfare of the **German Colony**. The mostly Arab neighbourhood of **Wadi Nisnas** is in a little valley midway between Paris Sq and the German Colony. To the northwest, across the train tracks, is **Bat Galim**, home of Rambam hospital and a beach.

About 1km south (up the slope) from Paris Sq is Herzl St, the heart of Hadar HaCarmel, universally known as **Hadar**. The city's mid-20th-century commercial centre, its bustling streets are lined with eateries and inexpensive shops. The HaNevi'im stop on the Carmelit is 350m northwest of the corner of Herzl and Balfour Sts, the heart of Hadar, and 350m southeast of Wadi Nisnas' main drag, HaWadi St.

Around the Carmelit upper terminus, Gan HaEm, is **Carmel Centre** (Merkaz HaCarmel), the commercial heart of the affluent neighbourhoods that are strung out along the ridge of Mt Carmel. The area's finest views are from **Yefe Nof Street**, which roughly parallels HaNassi Ave and leads to the Baha'i Gardens' visitors entrance.

Free street maps are available at most hotels and the Haifa tourist office.

ⓘ Information

There are plenty of banks in Hadar, and more up around Carmel Centre.

Exchange Bureau (47 Herzl St, Hadar)

Police Station (☑04-864 8811, 100; 1 Natan Elbaz St, Wadi Salib) Situated 2km southeast of Paris Sq.

Post Office (Map p152; 63 Herzl St, Hadar) There are other branches in the German Colony (Map p152; 27 Ben-Gurion Ave) and Carmel Centre (Map p152; 9 Wedgewood Ave). All three change foreign currency and American Express travellers cheques.

Rambam Medical Centre (Rambam Health Care Campus; ☑1-700 505 150, emergency room 04-777 1300; www.rambam.org.il; 8 HaAliya HaShniya St, Bat Galim; ☺24hr) One of Israel's largest and most respected hospitals.

Tourist Office (Haifa Tourist Board; Map p152; ☑1-800 305 090, 04-853 5606; www.tour-haifa.co.il; 48 Ben-Gurion Ave, German Colony; ☺8.30am-6pm Sun-Thu, to 1pm Fri) Has useful publications, including *A Guide to Haifa Tourism* and a city map (4NIS) outlining four themed walking tours. Situated near the top of Ben-Gurion Ave.

ⓘ Getting There & Away

Arkia (www.arkia.com) flies to Eilat (one way US$52 to US$113, 70 minutes, four per week)

from **Haifa Airport** (HFA; www.iaa.gov.il), which is 7.5km southeast of Paris Sq.

Haifa has two central bus stations. **Haifa-Hof HaCarmel** (Map p151), used by buses heading south along the coast (i.e. towards Tel Aviv), is on the Mediterranean (western) side of Mt Carmel. It's 8km around the base of Mt Carmel from the German Colony, near the Haifa-Hof HaCarmel train station. The quickest way to get to Tel Aviv and other coastal cities is by train. Other destinations:

Atlit 'Illegal' Immigrant Detention Camp (bus 221; 25 minutes, every 30 minutes)

Jerusalem (Egged bus 940, 44NIS, two hours, every 30 to 90 minutes except Friday evening to sundown Saturday)

Zichron Ya'akov (Egged bus 202, 16.80NIS, one hour, every 90 minutes except Friday afternoon to Saturday night)

Haifa-Merkazit HaMifratz, on the Haifa Bay side of Mt Carmel, is used by most buses to destinations north and east of Haifa. It is 8km southeast of the German Colony, a few hundred metres – through the giant Lev HaMifratz shopping mall – from the Lev HaMifratz train station. Train is the fastest way to Akko and Nahariya. Destinations:

Afula (Nateev Express bus 301, 40 minutes, every 15 minutes except Friday afternoon to sundown Saturday) Frequent buses link Afula with Beit She'an.

Akko (Nateev Express buses 271 and 361, 16NIS, 35 to 45 minutes, every 10 minutes) Bus 271 continues north to the Baha'i Gardens, Kibbutz Lohamei HaGeta'ot and Nahariya.

Beit She'arim (HaShomrim Junction; Nateev Express bus 301, 13.50NIS, 15 minutes, three times a hour)

Jerusalem (Egged bus 960, 45.30NIS, 1¾ hours, one or two times an hour except Friday afternoon to sundown Saturday)

Kiryat Shmona (Egged bus 500, 44NIS, two hours, twice an hour except Friday afternoon to sundown Saturday)

Nazareth (buses 331 and 339, shared by Nazareth Tourism & Transport and GB Tours; 19NIS, one hour, twice an hour Sunday to Friday, hourly all day Saturday) Some buses on this line also stop in the Port Area (Downtown) at Sha'ar Palmer St (every hour or two).

Tiberias (Egged bus 430, 25NIS, 1¼ hours, twice an hour except Friday afternoon to sundown Saturday)

Tsfat (Nateev Express bus 361, 1¾ hours, twice an hour) Via Akko (45 minutes).

Linking the two central bus stations is Metronit line 1 (30 minutes), which loops around via the German Colony and the Port Area; and bus 101

BEIT SHE'ARIM

بيت شعاريم בית שערים

An ancient Jewish town and later a necropolis, Beit She'arim (www.parks.org.il; adult/child 22/10NIS; ⊙8am-5pm daylight-saving time, to 4pm winter time, closes 1hr earlier Fri, last entry 1hr before closing) is now a shady park and a prime destination for visitors interested in the early years of rabbinic (post-Temple) Judaism.

For part of the late 2nd century CE, Beit She'arim was the meeting place of the Sanhedrin (the era's supreme council of rabbis), headed by Rabbi Yehuda HaNassi, who took on responsibilities both secular and religious and handled political affairs between Jews and their Roman overlords. He assembled Jewish scholars and compiled the Mishnah (the earliest codification of Jewish law) at Tzipori but asked to be buried here, inspiring others to do the same.

During the 4th century the town was destroyed by the Romans, presumably in the process of suppressing a Jewish uprising. During the following 600 years the many tombs were looted and covered by rock falls. Archaeologists stumbled upon the remains of Beit She'arim in 1936.

As you drive towards the entrance of the park, the ruins of a 2nd-century synagogue are off to the left. At the park itself there are 31 catacombs and a small museum in an ancient rock-cut reservoir. The largest catacomb contains 24 separate chambers with more than 200 sarcophagi. Note the variety of symbols and inscriptions carved onto the coffins, including epithets written in Hebrew, Aramaic, Palmyran and Greek. Some of the people buried here, it is believed, came from as far away as Persia and Yemen.

Beit She'arim is about 23km southeast of Haifa, mostly along Rte 75. By bus you can take Nateev Express bus 301 from Haifa-Merkazit HaMifratz (13.50NIS, 15 minutes, three times a hour); tell the driver you want to go to Beit She'arim and they will let you off at HaShomrim Junction, which is 700m north of the park along Rte 722.

(15 minutes), which goes through the Carmel Tunnels, a toll-road tunnel under Mt Carmel.

All intercity bus tickets to Haifa include transport from one of the central bus stations into the city – provided you ask for a *kartis hemshech* (transfer ticket) when you buy your ticket (eg from the driver). The only catch is that you have to have a rechargeable Rav-Kav smartcard (sold by the driver).

CAR
Northern Israel is compact, so having a car lets you cover a lot of territory. Akko is just 25 minutes away (via new Rte 22, known as Okef Krayot), with Rosh HaNikra 30 minutes further north; Caesarea and Zichron Ya'akov are 35 or 40 minutes south; and Nazareth and Beit She'an are one hour southeast. Of course, having wheels makes getting to places without convenient bus links such as Ein Hod, Megiddo and Montfort a breeze.

In Haifa, all of the major car-rental companies have agencies on side streets near Haifa-Merkazit HaMifratz bus terminal.

SHERUT
Seven-day-a-week sheruts (service or shared taxis) to **Akko, Nahariya and Tsfat** (Map p152; ☑04-862 2115) and **Tel Aviv** (Map p152; ☑04-862 2115) depart from Hadar, from various places around the intersection of Herzl and HaNevi'im Sts (weekday/Shabbat 30/45NIS).

Book a day in advance for a sherut to the airport (77NIS from the sherut station, 119NIS from your hotel); call ☑04-866 2324.

TRAIN
Haifa has four train stations:
Haifa-Hof HaCarmel – 8km from the German Colony, west and then south around the base of Mt Carmel; near the Haifa-Hof HaCarmel bus station.

Haifa Merkaz-HaShmona (Haifa Center-HaShmona) – in the city's Downtown (Port Area), 700m northwest of Paris Sq and 700m east of the German Colony.

Haifa-Bat Galim – in the seaside Bat Galim neighbourhood, near Rambam hospital and 1km southeast of the Stella Maris cable car.

Lev HaMifratz – 8km southeast of the German Colony and a few hundred metres – through the giant Lev HaMifratz shopping mall – from the Merkazit HaMifratz bus station.

Travel by train within Haifa, between any of these stations (every 10 to 20 minutes), costs 6NIS. Other rail destinations:
Akko (16NIS, 30 minutes, three times an hour)
Ben-Gurion airport (41.50NIS, 1¾ hours, twice an hour)
Nahariya (20.50NIS, twice an hour, 35 minutes)

➡ **Tel Aviv** (32NIS, one hour, two or three times an hour)

Trains do not run from Friday afternoon until sundown Saturday.

❶ Getting Around

BUS

The Carmelit metro is great for getting up and down the mountain, but for travel along Mt Carmel's flanks you'll need buses (run by Egged, Nateev Express and Omni Express) and the **Metronit**, a three-line bus service, inaugurated in 2013, that's as fast as light rail thanks to its dedicated lanes (with a red stripe running down the middle) and synchronised traffic lights.

Metronit line 1 links the two central bus stations, Haifa-Merkazit HaMifratz and Haifa-Hof HaCarmel, via the Port Area and the German Colony at least twice an hour (every six minutes at peak times) 24 hours a day, seven days a week (yes, including Shabbat!). Line 2 links Bat Galim (Rambam hospital) with Haifa-Merkazit Ha-Mifratz, also via the German Colony and the Port Area. Tickets (6.90NIS, the same price as for the bus), valid for 90 minutes, are sold by machines at each stop.

METRO

The six-station **Carmelit** (☏ 04-837 6861; www.carmelithaifa.co.il; single trip 6.90NIS, daily pass 15NIS; ⊗ 6am-midnight Sun-Thu, to 3pm Fri, sundown-midnight Sat), Israel's only metro (technically, it's a funicular railway), connects Paris Sq (Kikar Pariz) in the Downtown (Port Area) with Hadar (HaNevi'im stop) and Carmel Centre (Gan HaEm stop). About 2km long, it whisks you up 268 vertical metres at a gradient of up to 17.5 degrees. Bicycles are allowed on board.

Daliyat al-Karmel

دالية الكرمل   דאליית אל-כרמל

☏ 04 / POP 16,000

The largest Druze settlement in Israel, Daliyat al-Karmel is a sprawling town on top of Mt Carmel, about 16km south of Haifa (11km south of Haifa University). Years of growth have sent Daliya washing over the neighbouring hills and have nearly fused it with the smaller Druze village of Isfiya (Usfiyeh), just to the north.

Daliya's 'downtown' is a 200m stretch of the main street through town, Rte 672. In and among the restaurants, shops sell locally made Druze textiles, brightly coloured shawls and trousers, tabla drums, pottery and souvenirs – bargains for one and all! The town is at its busiest on Shabbat and Jewish holidays.

◉ Sights

Shrine of Abu Ibrahim   RELIGIOUS SITE

This square little building, fronted with Jerusalem stone and topped with a small red dome, is the Shrine of Abu Ibrahim, in whom the Druze believe the soul of Elijah was reincarnated. Both men and women must be modestly dressed, including long sleeves, and must remove their shoes.

From the T-junction just beyond the shops (Rte 672 does a 90-degree turn to the left, i.e. southeast, here), turn right (west) – the shrine is about 600m along; to get there, follow the signs to 'Holy Place'.

Beit Oliphant   HISTORIC SITE

(⊗ 8am-8pm daily) **FREE** At the end of Twenty-Two St is Beit Oliphant (signposted as Beit Druze), home of the Christian Zionist Sir Lawrence Oliphant and his wife, Alice, between 1882 and 1887. The Oliphants were among the few non-Druze to have a close relationship with the sect and did much to help the community. Oliphant's assistant at the time was Naphtali Herz Imber, author of the words to Israel's national anthem, 'Ha-Tikva', first published in 1886.

The ancient Roman column out front is a memorial to Alice, who died at age 36 – and with whom Imber was said to have been madly in love. The house now serves as the **Druze Memorial Center**, which commemorates the 398 Druze who have died while serving in the Israel Defense Forces (IDF) since 1948.

✖ Eating

Daliya's main street has a number of felafel places.

Abu Anter   MIDDLE EASTERN $$

(☏ 04-839 3537; Rte 672; mains 45-140NIS; ⊗ 7am-7pm) Opened by owner Anter's father in 1954, this spotless, welcoming restaurant specialises in local favourites such as grilled meat and fish, stuffed grape leaves, *mansaf* (lamb cooked in sour yoghurt and served atop rice) and *siniya* (ground meat with tahina).

Andarin   MIDDLE EASTERN $$

(Rte 672; mains 35-120NIS; ⊗ 9am-11pm; ☏) Serves tasty grilled meats, seafood, fish and a good selection of lighter meals. Main dishes come with a clutch of side salads.

❶ Getting There & Away

Bus 37א links Daliyat al-Karmel and Isfiya with Haifa university, the German Colony, Wadi Nisnas and Carmel Centre's HaNassi Ave (6.80NIS, one hour, two or three an hour except from Friday afternoon to sundown Saturday).

Carmelite Monastery of St Elijah دير المحرقة מנזר המוחרקה

Carmelite Monastery of St Elijah MONASTERY
(Muhraqa; www.muhraqa.org; admission 4NIS; ⊙9am-5pm, last entry 4.30pm) 🖉 For some spectacular views, head to the Carmelite Monastery of St Elijah, known to Arab and Jewish Israelis as the Muhraqa. Built to commemorate Elijah's showdown with the 450 prophets of Ba'al (recounted in I Kings 18), the Catholic complex includes a chapel (built 1883; men are asked to remove their hats) and serves as a home for two monks from the Discalced Carmelite Order ('discalced' is a fancy way of saying 'barefoot').

From the roof (access is via the shop), you can see the Mediterranean, Mt Hermon (when it's clear) and everything in between. Out front is a peaceful little garden with a statue of Elijah.

The Muhraqa is 5km south of the centre of Daliyat al-Karmel; bear left at the signposted Y-junction.

Atlit עתלית عتليت
🎵 04

◉ Sights

Atlit 'Illegal' Immigrant Detention Camp HISTORIC SITE
(🎵04-984 1980; adult/child 32/27NIS; ⊙9am-5pm Sun-Thu, to 1pm or 2pm Fri, last tour departs 3pm or 4pm Sun-Thu, noon Fri) In 1939, as the situation of the Jews of Europe became increasingly dire, the British government issued a white paper limiting Jewish immigration to Palestine to 10,000 to 15,000 'certificates' a year. If Jewish refugees could not come to Palestine legally, the leaders of the Zionist Movement decided, they would do so illegally. Thousands of Jews fleeing Nazism made it past the British blockade, but many more were captured and interned at the Atlit 'Illegal' Immigrant Detention Camp.

On 10 October 1945, the Palmach (the Special Forces unit of the Haganah) broke into the camp and released 200 prisoners. The daring infiltration, led by a young Yitzhak Rabin, caused the British to close the camp. After that, Holocaust survivors and other Jews arrested for illegally entering Palestine were sent to camps on Cyprus.

You can walk around the site on your own, but the best way to see the camp is on a 1½-hour guided tour – call to find out when an English tour is scheduled. Guides present the barracks (reconstructed); a dreadful wash house (largely original) where new arrivals were stripped of their clothing and disinfected with DDT; and a 34m-long ship very much like the ones used to ferry *ma'apilim* (clandestine immigrants) to pre-state Israel (the vessel here is actually the *Galina*, built in Latvia in the 1970s). A ship this size would have been packed with 600 to 800 refugees.

The Atlit camp is 16km south of Haifa and 20km north of Zichron Ya'akov. Bus 221 (every 30 minutes) links the camp with the Atlit train station (10 minutes), 3km to the south, and Haifa's Hof HaCarmel bus station (25 minutes).

Crusader Castle CASTLE
An impressive Crusader castle, known in Latin as Castrum Pergrinorum and in French as Château Pèlerin (Pilgrims' Castle), sits on a promontory about 1.5km southwest of Atlit detention camp. It's inside a military base used for training by Israel's marine commandos and so can't be visited, but you can see it from **Atlit Beach Nature Reserve** (Shmurat Hof Atlit).

✗ Eating

For a bite to eat, head to the **Paz or Sonol petrol stations** a few hundred metres south of the detention-camp gates – both have restaurants.

Ein Hod & Ayn Hawd עין הוד עין חוד עين هود عين حوض
🎵 04

Dadaist painter Marcel Janco happened upon Ein Hod in 1950 – just two years after its Arab residents had been expelled or fled – and fell in love with the place. A good part of Israel's artistic elite followed and today the village is home to around 60 artists and their families. It is busiest on Saturday but relatively quiet on Friday, especially after 2pm.

About 700 to 900 Arab residents left Ein Hod during the 1948 fighting. Most ended up in the Jenin area, but one sheikh didn't go far. The Abu al-Hija family settled just a few kilometres away and in the 1960s

DON'T MISS

NORTH COAST BEACHES

A string of fine sand beaches stretches along Israel's northern Mediterranean coast. Among the nicest (from south to north):

Beit Yanai – bordered by **Nahal Alexander**, Israel's cleanest coastal stream, to the north and natural sand dunes to the east. Parking costs 24NIS; has a restaurant. Situated 14km south of Caesarea.

Aqueduct – right next to a section of Caesarea's Roman aqueduct. No admission fee. Situated 2.5km by road north of ancient Caesarea.

Dor – sand, tidal pools and the ruins of Dor, an important port city – successively Canaanite, Israelite, Assyrian, Persian and Hellenistic – mentioned repeatedly in the Old Testament. Situated 10km northwest of Zichron Ya'akov.

Atlit – part of Atlit Beach Nature Reserve and just north of a Crusader castle (p167) (closed to the public). Situated 1.5km southwest of the Atlit 'Illegal' Immigrant Detention Camp (p167).

Bat Galim (p158) – in Haifa's Bat Galim neighbourhood, about 1km northwest of Rambam hospital, terminus of Metronit line 2.

Hof HaCarmel (p158) – Haifa's best beach. Situated along the coast near the Hof HaCarmel train station and the Haifa-Hof HaCarmel bus station.

Argaman (p177) – Akko's municipal beach is 1.5km southeast of the old city.

Akhziv – part of Akhziv National Park (p182), about 4km north of Nahariya.

---

founded **Ayn Hawd**, recognised by the Israeli government in 1992 and now a prosperous hamlet 4km past Ein Hod (up the hill from the Modern Orthodox community of Moshav Nir Etzyion). These days there are friendly relations between the two villages.

From Ein Hod and Ayn Hawd, a back road goes up the slope to Daliyat al-Karmel.

◉ Sights

Several dozen artists live and work in Ein Hod. Most of their studios are closed to casual visitors, but you can visit various **galleries** and **exhibitions** and, with advance reservations, attend **workshops** and **courses** in fields such as ceramics, watercolour and oil painting, lithography and photography. For details, check out Ein Hod's official website, www.ein-hod.org, or the privately run www.ein-hod.info.

You can pick up a free map of Ein Hod from the rack in front of the Makolet (grocery).

Janco-Dada Museum MUSEUM
(☑ 04-984 2350; www.jancodada.co.il; adult/child 20/10NIS; ☉ 9.30am-3.30pm Sun-Thu, to 2pm Fri, 10am-4pm Sat) Exhibits collages, drawings and paintings by Marcel Janco and puts on temporary exhibits by contemporary Israeli and European artists. The top-floor porch affords the kinds of views that inspired Janco to settle here. Downstairs, **Dadolab**

(11am to 2pm Saturday and during the Passover, Sukkot and Hanukkah holidays) has activities for kids.

Ein Hod Gallery GALLERY
(10am-4pm Sun & Tue-Thu, 10am-2pm Fri, 11am-4pm Sat) Shows works by all the colony's plastic artists. If you see something interesting, it might be possible to visit the artist's studio. Situated opposite the Janco-Dada Museum.

Studio Magal GALLERY
(☑ 04-984 2313; ☉ 10am-5pm daily) Ceramics (including Judaica), mosaics and expressionist paintings (oil and watercolour), the latter by Ben-Tzion Magal (1908–99).

Yad Gertrude Kraus GALLERY
(☉ 11am-3pm Sat) FREE The house of the Vienna-born dancer and artist Gertrude Kraus (1901–77) displays works by all the founders of Ein Hod. Hosts concerts, lectures and other cultural events.

Nisco Museum MUSEUM
(☑ 052-475 5313; adult/child 30/20NIS; ☉ 10am-4pm daily, tours begin on the hour) This offbeat collection of mechanical music instruments was assembled by New York–born Nisan Cohen, who's happy to play records from his Yiddish music archive on a vintage Victrola. Situated a few hundred metres down the hill (towards Rte 4) from the gate to Ein Hod.

☞ Tours

Walking Tours   WALKING TOUR
(☎052-645 6072; shuliyarkony@gmail.com; per person 500NIS) Shuli Yarkony's walking tours visit artists' studios that are usually inaccessible. Reserve ahead.

🛏 Sleeping & Eating

For details on Ein Hod's many lovely B&Bs, see www.ein-hod.org (click 'Accommodations' under 'Visitor Information').

Makolet   SUPERMARKET $
(⊘to 5pm or later daily) Sells picnic supplies and superb homemade ice cream.

★HaBayit   MIDDLE EASTERN $
(Al-Beyt; ☎04-839 7350; Ayn Hawd; set meal adult/child 4-12yr 110/45NIS, vegetarian 80NIS; ⊘noon-8pm daily, open during Ramadan; ☑) Situated 4km up the hill from Ein Hod in Ayn Hawd, this family-run restaurant serves outstanding, authentic Arab cuisine. Set meals include salads, soup (often lentil) and a delicious main dish (in winter, made with herbs plucked from the slops of Mt Carmel). Reserve on Friday and Saturday.

Doña Rosa   STEAK $$
(☑04-954 3777; www.doniarosa.rest.co.il; steaks 94-120NIS, other mains 56-88NIS; ⊘noon-10.30pm Mon-Sat) At this Argentine steakhouse, everything is imported from the motherland – the meat, the wine, even the charcoal. Diners can sit on the balcony or in the rustic interior, with its gaucho-inspired decor. Reserve on Thursday night, Friday and Saturday.

Zichron Ya'acov

زخرون يعقوب   זכרון יעקב

☑04 / POP 21,000

With historic stone buildings, fine food, great wine, country air and throngs of holidaymakers, Zichron Ya'acov feels like a slice of Bordeaux transported to the Middle East.

In its early years, Zichron (as Israelis often call it) was supported by Baron Edmond de Rothschild of the French banking family, who named it after his father James, aka Jacob (Ya'akov). Baron Edmond is buried 5km southwest of the centre of town in the lovely **Ramat HaNadiv Gardens** (www.ramat-hanadiv.org.il).

◉ Sights

Established in 1882 by Jews from Romania, Zichron Ya'acov – near the southern end of the Mt Carmel massif – is best known for its pioneering role in Israel's wine industry and, more recently, for its attractive old town and upper-middle-class neighbourhoods.

HaMeyasdim Street   AREA
(⊘shops 10am-8pm Sun-Thu, to 3pm Fri, close 1hr earlier winter, some also open Sat) Zichron Ya'akov's late-19th-century main street, now pedestrianised, is lined with restored stone houses, many of them – along with nearby courtyards – converted into boutiques, jewellery shops and cafes. Great for a stroll. The area is at its most bustling on Shabbat.

Aaronsohn House NILI Museum   MUSEUM
(www.nili-museum.org.il; 40 HaMeyasdim St; adult/child 20/15NIS; ⊘tours 9am-2pm or 3pm Sun-Thu, 9-10am or 11am Fri) At the upper end of the *midrahov* (pedestrian mall), this museum and its period rooms showcase the fruitful life and turbulent times of Aaron Aaronsohn (1876–1919), a noted agronomist and botanist who, along with his family, led a pro-British WWI spy ring known as NILI. The entrance is around the side.

First Aliya Museum   MUSEUM
(2 HaNadiv St; adult/child 15/12NIS; ⊘9am-4pm Sun-Thu, to 2pm Fri) Commemorates the early Zionist pioneers who established Zichron Ya'akov and other agricultural villages between 1882 and 1904; multimedia presentations outline the trials and tribulations of those heady days. Situated two long blocks west of the bottom of the pedestrian zone on HaMeyasdim St. There's a children's **playground** across the street.

Carmel Winery   WINERY
(☑04-629 1788; www.carmelwines.co.il; 2 Derech HaYekev; tour incl tasting 30NIS; ⊘wine shop 9am-5pm Mon-Thu, to 2pm Fri, closed Sat & Sun) One-hour tours (available in English) include a stop in 120-year-old cellars; call for times and reservations (tours often begin in the early afternoon). Meet your guide at the wine shop in the **Center for Wine Culture** (Merkaz Tarbut ha-Yayin), inside a building from 1892. To get there from the northern end of HaMeyasdim St, go down the hill (east) for 350m and turn right for 50m.

Tishbi Winery   WINERY
(☑04-628 8195; www.tishbi.com; tour 15NIS, incl Valrhona chocolate 40NIS; ⊘shop 8am-5pm

Sun-Thu, to 3pm Fri, tours 10am, noon & 2pm Sun-Thu) Tours of this family-run winery include a chance to taste its excellent vintages. The wonderfully rustic **restaurant** is open from 8am to 3pm Sunday to Thursday and to 2pm on Friday. Situated 3km south of the centre of Zichron Ya'acov on the road to Binyamina (Rte 652).

🛏 Sleeping & Eating

You'll find lots of places to eat – most open on Shabbat – along HaMeyasdim St and HaNadiv St, especially where they intersect. Cheaper places are clustered along the non-pedestrianised part of HaMeyasdim St (i.e. north of the pedestrian zone).

Bet Maimon Hotel HOTEL $$
(☑04-629 0999, 04-639 0212; www.maimon.com; 4 Tzahal (Zahal) St; s/d 458/558NIS, Thu & Fri 658/758NIS, additional child 160NIS; ☸restaurant 8-10am & 1-9pm; ✳🏠🐾) This old-time, family-run hotel has 25 spacious rooms with pleasing modern decor. For a hot tub and views of the coast, spring for a romantic 'superior seaview' room (200NIS extra). The lobby restaurant, Casa Barone, serves Mediterranean dishes (mains 59NIS to 119NIS, breakfast 65NIS). Not wheelchair accessible. Situated in a residential area 1.2km due west of HaMeyasdim St.

Ayelet & Gili ISRAELI $$
(☑052-256 2329, 077-403 0455; www.ayeletgili.co.il; 27 HaNadiv St; mains 55-75NIS; ☸10am-11pm Sun-Thu, to 2hr before Shabbat Fri; 🐾) Stables that once belonged to one of Baron Rothschild's clerks now house this upbeat restaurant, known for its excellent Iraqi kibbeh, Yemenite meat soup and *siniyya* (Lebanese-style ground beef with pine nuts). Everything is healthy, natural and home-made, and there's plenty for vegetarians. Situated 100m down the hill, towards the winery, from the bottom of HaMeyasdim St's pedestrian zone.

❶ Getting There & Away

Zichron Ya'acov is 65km north of Tel Aviv, 15km northeast of Caesarea and 35km south of Haifa.

Buses stop on HaNadiv St between the First Aliya Museum and the HaMeyasdim St pedestrian zone. Destinations include:
➡ **Haifa-Hof HaCarmel** (Egged bus 202, 16.80NIS, one hour, every 90 minutes except Friday afternoon to Saturday night)
➡ **Tel Aviv** (Egged bus 872, 25NIS, 2¼ hours, seven to nine daily Sunday to Thursday, five to seven Friday, three or four Saturday night) In

Tel Aviv, stops at the Central Bus Station and Arlozorov Bus Terminal.

Mey Kedem   مي كيدم   מֵי קֶדֶם

Mey Kedem Tunnel ARCHAEOLOGICAL SITE
(☑04-638 8622; www.meykedem.com; adult/child 24/18NIS; ☸9am-5pm Sat-Thu, to 2pm Fri Mar-Nov) To supply water to Caesarea, the Romans built an extraordinary 23km-long system of canals, pipes and aqueducts – and a 6km-long tunnel. A 300m section of the tunnel is now open to exploration, provided you don't mind wading through knee-deep H^2O. Bring a torch (flashlight), a change of clothes and suitable footwear for walking in water. Admission includes a one-hour guided tour. This is a great activity if you've got kids, especially on a hot summer's day.

By road, Mey Kedem, near the religious community of Moshav Amikam and part of the larger Alona Park, is 18km from Zichron Ya'akov – drive south on Rte 652, east on Rte 653 and then north on Rte 654 and Rte 6533.

Jisr az-Zarka

جسر الزرقاء   גִ'סֶר אַזְרָקָא
POP 13,500
Sandwiched between Rte 2 (the Tel Aviv–Haifa expressway) and the Mediterranean, Jisr az-Zarka is Israel's only remaining seaside Arab village. It is named for a stone bridge over adjacent Al-Wadi Az-Zarka (the Blue River), constructed for the visit of Kaiser Wilhelm II in 1898.

Jisr az-Zarka was founded in the 1830s by families from Egypt who came to Palestine along with the forces of Egyptian ruler Muhammad Ali (1769–1849). Thanks to a history of good relations with nearby Jewish villages, it emerged unharmed from the 1948 war. Today, the town has some of the worst socioeconomic statistics of any Israeli town; to improve things, locals are working to encourage tourism by both overseas travellers and Jewish Israelis.

Jisr makes a convenient and affordable base for exploring the Mt Carmel area.

🏃 Activities

To become familiar with the town, follow the **Jisr Trail**, marked by signs in Arabic, Hebrew and English, and walk out to the **fisher's hamlet** on the beach (10 minutes). About 300m south of there is a **beach** with changing rooms, shade gazebos and lifeguards.

Situated on the **Israel National Trail**, Jisr az-Zarka is a 45-minute walk along the coast from Caesarea.

Ask at Juha's Guesthouse for details on **Palestinian cooking workshops** (per person 70NIS to 100NIS).

Sleeping & Eating

The centre of town (the area south of the main mosque) has several felafel joints. Ask at Juha's Guesthouse about **dining with a local family** (50NIS to 100NIS) – the home-style Arab cuisine is delicious!

Every year during Ramadan, Jisr families host Jewish Israelis for *iftar* (the break-the-fast meal) on Thursday, Friday and Saturday.

Juha's Guesthouse   HOSTEL **$**
(www.zarqabay.com; Markaz al-Qarya, Rte 6531; dm/d without breakfast 75/200NIS; ※) Opened in 2014, this super-welcoming guesthouse is run by Juha, a local guy, and Neta, a Jewish Israeli woman. Right in the centre of town, it has two doubles, an eight-bed dorm room and a chill-out lounge. Breakfast costs 10NIS. Guided tours of town are free. Accepts volunteers who are able to teach English, perhaps in exchange for Arabic lessons.

ⓘ Getting There & Away

The road to Jisr az-Zarka, Rte 6531, is accessible from Rte 4 (the old Tel Aviv–Haifa Hwy) but not from Rte 2 (the new Tel Aviv–Haifa Hwy). The town is 4km north of Caesarea as the crow flies but 10km by road (via Rte 4).

Infrequent Kavim bus 69 links Jisr az-Zarka with Binyamina's train station (12 minutes, four or five daily Sunday to Thursday, two Friday). Kavim bus 68 goes to Hadera's central bus station (30 minutes, hourly except Friday afternoon and Saturday), from where Egged bus 921 (two or three an hour) goes to both Haifa-Hof HaCarmel (45 minutes) and Tel Aviv's Central Bus Station (1¼ hours).

Caesarea   קיסריה   قيسارية
♪ 04 / POP 4500

Caesarea (Qeysarya; pronounced 'kay-*sar*-ee-ya' in Hebrew), gorgeously situated on the shores of the sparkling, turquoise Mediterranean, was one of the great ports of antiquity, rivalling storied harbours such as Alexandria and Carthage. Despite efforts by various conquerors to keep the port in service and the city alive, time and warfare eventually had their way, and by the 14th century most of Caesarea had disappeared

under the shifting dunes. Thanks to archaeological excavations – on land and under the sea – since the 1950s, Caesarea is now one of the Levant's most impressive Roman sites (rivalled, in Israel, only by Beit She'an). Cafes and restaurants add to the scene – you can dine al fresco by the sea until late at night.

Northeast of the ancient city, modern Caesarea – home to Israel's only golf course – is one of the country's most exclusive towns.

History

In 22 BCE Herod the Great (73 to 4 BCE) set about building the most grandiose port city imaginable, dedicating it to his patron, the Roman emperor Augustus Caesar, and for years, hundreds of builders and divers worked around the clock. To create the harbour's two breakwaters, stretching for 540m on the southern side and 270m on the north, vast quantities of stone were lowered into the open sea.

As he pursued his massive construction project, Herod became increasingly tyrannical, and those who questioned his orders, let alone disobeyed them, were often executed. Following Herod's death (to sighs of relief all round, no doubt), Caesarea Maritima – which at its height had 50,000 residents – became the capital of the Roman province of Judea (Iudaea).

Pontius Pilate resided here as prefect from 26 to 36 CE. His name appears on an inscription, found in the ruins of the theatre, that constitutes the only archaeological evidence that the man whom the Bible says ordered Jesus's crucifixion actually existed (the original is on display at the Israel Museum in Jerusalem). According to the New Testament (Acts 10), a Roman centurion named Cornelius, a member of the garrison here, was the first Gentile to be converted to Christianity, baptised by Peter himself.

Following the Great Jewish Revolt (66 to 70 CE), in which the Jews rose up against – and were crushed by – the Romans (and expelled from Jerusalem), thousands of captives were executed in Caesarea's amphitheatre. Some 65 years later, after the Romans put down the Bar Kochba Revolt, the amphitheatre again became an arena of cruelty as 10 Jewish sages, including Rabbi Akiva, were publicly tortured and executed.

The city was conquered by the Arabs in 638 CE and subsequently fell into disrepair. In 1101 the Crusaders under Baldwin I took Caesarea from the Muslims and discovered in the city a hexagonal, green-glass bowl that

Ancient Caesarea

Ancient Caesarea

they believed to be the Holy Grail (the vessel from which Jesus drank at the Last Supper). It is now kept at the Cathedral of St Lorenzo in Genoa. The Crusaders favoured Akko and Jaffa as their principal ports, so only part of Herodian Caesarea was rehabilitated.

The city changed hands between the Crusaders and the Muslims four times until King Louis IX of France captured it in 1251. That same year he added most of the fortifications visible today, but they proved

totally inadequate against the onslaught of the Mamluk sultan Beybars, who in 1261 broke through the Crusader defences and devastated the city.

The ruins remained deserted and over time were swallowed by shifting, wind-blown sands. In 1878 Muslim refugees from Bosnia, fleeing the Austrian conquest of their homeland, were settled here by the Turks – the mosque and minaret by the harbour date from this period. Their descendents fled or were forced to leave during the 1948 war.

It was only with the establishment of Kibbutz Sdot Yam in 1940 that ancient Caesarea began to re-emerge. While tilling the land, farmers found bits and pieces of the old city and archaeologists soon followed.

◉ Sights

Caesarea National Park (www.parks.org.il; adult/child 40/24NIS, harbour only 14NIS; ⏰8am-6pm Sat-Thu, to 4pm Fri Apr-Sep, 8am-4pm Sat-Thu, to 3pm Fri Oct-Mar, last entry 1hr before closing) has two entrances: the northern (Crusader gate) entrance, which takes you through the Crusader ramparts to the harbour and its restaurants; and, 600m to the south, the southern (Roman Theatre) entrance. Coach tours often drop visitors off at one and pick them up at the other, but if you'd like to circle back to your car, the northern entrance is a better bet.

A full-price ticket gets you into the Roman ruins (situated between the two entrances) and three multimedia presentations. A harbour-only ticket, available at the northern entrance, gets you access to the harbour area, including its restaurants, and the Crusader city but not the Roman city. After the park's closing time, entry to the harbour – whose restaurants and bars stay open until late at night – is free.

Crusader City ARCHAEOLOGICAL SITE
The ramparts, 900m long and 13m high, and the dry moat that surround the Crusader city were constructed by King Louis IX of France (St Louis), better known for building Ste-Chapelle in Paris. To get an overview of the site, head up the slope from the minaret by the harbour; a path leads to the remains (three rounded apses) of a 13th-century **Crusader church**, built over the site of Caesar's temple and destroyed by the Muslims in 1291.

The Crusader city, situated between the park's northern entrance and the harbour, is accessible whenever the site is open.

Caesarea Experience
VISITOR CENTRE

The park's visitor centre, aka the Caesarea Experience, is on the harbour's jetty. Inside, a 10-minute film (available in seven languages) presents an excellent historical overview of Caesarea's eventful history; it's shown in English twice an hour (hourly on the hour on Saturday). A second room contains computer-animated holograms of 13 historical personalities who 'answer' visitors' questions in six languages. The film can also be seen near the park's southern entrance, in the white, tentlike building.

Time Tower
FILM

Out on the harbour's the jetty, on the top floor of the Citadel (above Limani Bistro), is the Time Tower, whose computer-generated graphics present the city at different periods in its existence. Look out over the Roman harbour: the dark blotches 100m to 200m out to sea, hard to see unless the water is calm, are the remains of Herod's enormous breakwater. Not wheelchair accessible.

Herodian Amphitheatre & Bathhouse
HISTORIC SITE

Chariot races and bloody gladiatorial contests in which prisoners and slaves battled lions and crocodiles were held in the 10,000-seat amphitheatre (aka the hippodrome and the circus), the 250m-long dirt plaza between the harbour and the Promontory Palace. Because the chariots tended to crash when going around the turns, seats at each end of the amphitheatre were most prized. Next to the amphitheatre are the remains of a **bathhouse**; well-preserved geometrical mosaics are protected from the elements by a roof.

Promontory Palace
HISTORIC SITE

Jutting into the sea next to the southern end of the amphitheatre, the Roman-era Promontory Palace includes a pool believed to have been used as a fish market. To the south, you can see the smokestacks of Israel's largest power station, named in honour of assassinated Prime Minister Yitzhak Rabin.

Roman Theatre
HISTORIC SITE

Used these days for open-air concerts by top-tier international and Israeli talent, Herod's impressive theatre (often incorrectly referred to as 'the amphitheatre') could seat 4000 people. The semicircular platform behind the stage dates from the 3rd century, while the great wall with the two towers is part of a 6th-century Byzantine fortress built over the ruins.

Cardo
HISTORIC SITE

Outside the Crusader walls, a few hundred metres east (away from the sea) from the park's northern entrance, is the fenced-in, excavated Cardo (Byzantine street). The red porphyry statue – one of two large figures from the 2nd or 3rd centuries CE – may portray Emperor Hadrian holding an orb and sceptre. An inscription in the mosaic floor credits Flavius Strategius, a 6th-century mayor, with making improvements to the Cardo.

Kibbutz Sdot Yam Antiquities Museum
MUSEUM

(admission 10NIS; ⊙10am-4pm Sun-Thu, to 1pm Fri) Relics of ancient Caesarea, including some discovered offshore, are displayed in this three-room archaeological museum. It's inside Kibbutz Sdot Yam, whose main entrance is a few hundred metres east of the park's southern entrance.

🏃 Activities

Beach Bar
BEACH

(☑04-636 3989; www.beach-bar.co.il; mains 48-99NIS, breakfast 39-49NIS, beer 28-32NIS; ⊙9am-3am or 4am daily Mar-Oct, closes earlier in winter) FREE Admission to the beach – a protected little bay that's ideal for young children (though there's no lifeguard) – is free; order a drink or something to eat (salad, schnitzel with chips, pizza, a burger) and you can use the lounge chairs, umbrellas and changing rooms. Hosts live music, and has activities for children on Friday at 4pm.

Enjoy Greek music on Thursday from 9pm, jazz on Friday from 7pm and Brazilian music on Saturday from 9pm.

Old Caesarea Diving Centre
DIVING

(☑04-626 5898; www.caesarea-diving.com; ⊙9am-5pm Sun-Thu, 7am-5pm Fri & Sat Apr-Nov, 10am-4pm Sun-Thu, 7am-4pm Fri & Sat Dec-Mar) This fully certified diving centre offers half-hour introductory dives to a depth of up to 6m (no certification required; 240NIS) and guided group dives in Caesarea's underwater archaeological park (165/245NIS per person for one/two dives). Offers beginners' and advanced PADI diving courses so you can earn or renew your certification here before heading to Eilat.

A five-day course for open-water (one-star) certification costs 1460NIS. Scuba-gear rental is 150NIS a day. For details, see the excellent website.

🛏 Sleeping

Grushka B&B   B&B $$

(☎04-638 9810; www.6389810.com; 28 Ha-Meyasdim St, Binyamina; d 1/2 nights without breakfast 385/615NIS, weekend 485/775NIS, additional child 90NIS; ✹@🛜) This friendly Dutch- and Israeli-run B&B offers several comfortable rooms as well as a quiet cottage and a fully equipped villa for families. It's just a seven-minute walk from the Binyamina train station – or you can call ahead for a ride. Makes a good base for exploring Caesarea and Zichron Ya'acov.

Dan Caesarea   HOTEL $$$

(☎04-626 9111; www.danhotels.com; d US$600-730; ✹@✹) Relax on the spacious lawns around the pool, play golf at the adjacent 18-hole course, brush up on your tennis or pamper yourself in the spa – the Dan Caesarea was designed for luxury. Half of the 114 rooms have sea views, and the other half overlook the pool. Use of bicycles is free. Significant discounts are usually available online.

🍴 Eating & Drinking

The harbour, home to half a dozen midrange restaurants, is a gorgeous spot for a seaside meal – worth a trip even if you're not in the mood for antiquities. As you would expect, most places specialise in fish and seafood; one, Aresto, is kosher (dairy).

Port Cafe   EUROPEAN $$

(☎04-610 0221; www.portcafe.co.il; mains 48-75NIS; ⊗8am- about midnight daily) Offers a range of burgers, ravioli, fish, seafood, sandwiches, salads and kids' dishes (30NIS to 45NIS). Also serves breakfast.

ℹ Getting There & Away

Caesarea National Park is 40km south of Haifa, 14km southwest of Zichron Ya'akov, 10km (via

---

MEGIDDO (ARMAGEDDON)   مجيدو   מגידו

Prepare for Armageddon! If you're driving northeast along Rte 65, it will be on your left just off Rte 66. Known in Hebrew as Tel Megiddo, this is where it's said that St John predicted the last great battle on earth would take place (Revelation 16:14 and 16:16). It is now part of **Megiddo National Park** (☎04-659 0316; www.parks.org.il; Rte 66; adult/child 27/14NIS; ⊗8am-5pm daylight-saving time, to 4pm winter time, closes 1hr earlier Fri).

Although nothing too apocalyptic has happened yet, Megiddo has been the scene of many battles throughout the ages. Hieroglyphics on the wall of Karnak Temple in Luxor describe a battle that Thutmose III fought here in 1468 BCE. Megiddo remained a prosperous Egyptian stronghold for at least 100 years and later on held out against the Israelites (Judges 1:27), probably only falling to David. Under his son Solomon, Megiddo was transformed into one of the jewels of the Israelite kingdom and became known as the Chariot City – excavations have revealed traces of stables extensive enough to have held thousands of horses.

For a while Megiddo was a strategic stronghold on the important trade route between Egypt and Assyria, but by the 4th century BCE the town had inexplicably become uninhabited. However, its strategic importance remained, and among the armies that fought here were the British in WWI. On being awarded his peerage, General Edmund Allenby took the title Lord Allenby of Megiddo. Jewish and Arab forces clashed here during the 1948 war.

Excavations of Tel Megiddo have unearthed the remains of 26 or 27 distinct historical periods, from 4000 BCE to 400 BCE, but it takes some stretching of the imagination to see in the modern-day site any traces of its former grandeur. Help is given by an introductory **film**, some excellent models in the **visitor centre**, and signs that explain the importance of various earthen hummocks and depressions.

The most tangible aspect of the excavations is the 9th-century-BCE water system, which consists of a shaft sunk 30m through solid rock down to a 70m tunnel. This hid the city's water source from invading forces, rather like **Hezekiah's Tunnel in Jerusalem** (Map p46). There is no water to slosh through here, though. Save the tunnel until last, as it leads you out of the site, depositing you on a side road some distance away from the visitor centre.

Megiddo is 37km southeast of Haifa (along Rtes 75, 70 and 66), 38km northwest of Caesarea (via Rte 65) and 13km southwest of Afula (in the Jezreel Valley).

Rte 4) south of Jisr az-Zarka, and 57km north of Tel Aviv.

Kavim bus 77 links both park entrances and Kibbutz Sdot Yam with the Caesarea-Pardes Hanna train station (30 minutes); from there, trains go at least hourly to Tel Aviv and, via Binyamina, to Haifa. This is a commuter line, so buses run either early in the morning or in the late afternoon. Kavim bus 76, which also operates in the middle of the day, goes to the Hadera train station (one hour, every two to three hours except Friday afternoon and Saturday).

A taxi to/from Binyamina train station, which sends four trains an hour to Tel Aviv, or the Caesarea-Pardes Hanna train station costs about 50NIS.

Akko (Acre)   עכו עכא

☑ 04 / POP 47,000

Marco Polo passed through Akko (Acre; Akka in Arabic) around 750 years ago and, quite frankly, much of the place hasn't changed a lot since then. Today, old Akko – on a peninsula that pokes out into the Mediterranean – seduces visitors with towering ramparts, deep moats, green domes, slender minarets, church towers, secret passageways and subterranean vaults. It was awarded Unesco World Heritage status in 2001.

The city was mentioned in Egyptian sacred texts of the 19th century BCE, and in Greek mythology it is reputedly the place where Hercules found a medicinal plant to heal his wounds.

Akko can easily be visited on a day trip from Haifa, but there are a few places to spend the night if you'd like to soak up the atmosphere by moonlight.

History

In 333 BCE Alexander the Great granted the city the right to mint coins, something it continued to do for six centuries. After Alexander's death, Akko was taken by the Egyptian Ptolemites. In 200 BCE they lost it to the Syrian Seleucids, who struggled to keep it until the Romans, led by Pompey, began two centuries of rule.

The Arabs conquered Akko in 638 CE. The city enjoyed fairly untroubled times until the arrival of the Crusaders, who seized the city in 1104 and established it as their principal port (and lifeline to Europe), with separate quarters for merchants from the rival Italian maritime cities of Genoa, Pisa and Venice. The city fell to Salah ad-Din (Saladin) in 1187, but four years later it was retaken during the Third Crusade by armies under the command of Richard I of England (Richard the Lionheart) and Philip II of France.

Under the Crusaders, Akko – a city of some 60,000 – was home to one of the most important Jewish communties in Palestine. The Spanish philosopher, scholar and physician Maimonides spent five months here in 1165, and the Catalan philosopher, kabbalist and biblical commentator Nahmanides passed through Akko in 1267 on his way to Jerusalem.

In 1291 the Mamluks appeared with an army that outnumbered the defenders 10 to one. After a two-month siege, during which most of the city's inhabitants escaped to Cyprus, the city fell. To prevent Akko from being retaken by the forces of Christendom, the Mamluks reduced the city to rubble; it remained in ruins for the next 450 years.

The rebirth of Akko was the work of an Albanian mercenary, Ahmed Pasha, better known as Al-Jazzar (The Butcher) because of his ruthlessness in suppressing revolts. Taking advantage of the weak and corrupt Ottoman administration, Al-Jazzar established a virtually independent fiefdom and bullied the port back into working order. By 1799 the city had become important enough for the 30-year-old Napoleon to attempt its capture, but he was repelled by Al-Jazzar with some help from the English fleet; the defenders' resolve, it is said, was stiffened by reports of Napoleon's slaughter of Ottoman POWs after the fall of Jaffa. Among the more unlikely witnesses to Napoleon's efforts to capture the city was the Hasidic mystic and visionary Rabbi Nachman of Breslov (1772–1811), who at the end of a pilgrimage to the Holy Land spent a chaotic Shabbat here on his way back to Ukraine.

Akko remained in Ottoman hands until the British captured northern Palestine in September 1918. After they built modern port facilities in Haifa, Akko's importance declined, although its citadel was maintained as Palestine's main prison. During the 1930s, Akko was a hotbed of Arab hostility towards Jewish immigration, but Jewish forces captured the town fairly easily in 1948; three-quarters of the Arab population of some 17,000 were expelled or fled.

Today Akko, like Haifa, is a mixed city – about 70% of the residents are Jews and 30% Arabs; the population of the old city is about 95% Arab. In recent years, Arab families from villages around the Galilee have been moving into the city's historically Jewish neighbourhoods.

◉ Sights

City Walls
HISTORIC SITE

Old Akko is encircled by a **sea wall** to the west, south and southeast, and by **ramparts** (that you can walk on top of) and a **dry moat** – built mainly between 1750 and 1840 – to the north and northeast.

In the old city's northeastern corner stands **Burj al-Kommander**, a bastion that affords great views over the skyline of Akko and across the bay to Haifa. From there, the **Land Wall Promenade** – accessible by stairways from the interior of the old city – heads south for 200m to the 12th-century **Land Gate**, once the city's only terrestrial entrance. Until 1910, the only other way in or out was via the **Sea Gate**, which these days faces the **marina** and its colourful fishing boats.

The old city's northwestern corner is anchored by **Burj al-Karim**, also known as the **English Fort**. From here, the 12th-century **sea wall** (refaced in the 18th century by Al-Jazzar with stones scavenged from the Crusader castle at Atlit) runs due south (paralleled by HaHagana St) to the black-and-white-striped **lighthouse**, and then east – with the strollable **Sea Wall Promenade** on top – to the marina.

Visitor Centre
VISITOR CENTRE

(☑04-995 6706; www.akko.org.il; all sites adult/child 46/39NIS; ⊙visitor centre & sites 8.30am-6.30pm daylight-saving time, to 4.30pm winter time, closes 2hr earlier Fri; ☜) Facing a shady park, the Visitor Centre is the best place to begin a visit to Akko's Crusader sites. Staff can help you plan your tour of the city, sell you an indispensable map (3NIS), show you a **scale model** of the city and screen an eight-minute introductory **film** (available in nine languages). Tickets are sold at a kiosk out front (and at both entrances to the Templars' Tunnel); pick up your audioguide at a second kiosk (ID deposit required).

Some really great deals are available on combo tickets that include Rosh HaNikra and/or the Holocaust museum at Kibbutz Lohamei HaGeta'ot.

Seeing all five Crusader sites takes two hours at the very least. Coupons are valid for a year, so there's no need to cram everything into one day.

★ Knights Halls
HISTORIC SITE

(adult/child 25/22NIS) Step into the towering, stone-vaulted Knight's Halls, built 800 years ago by the Hospitallers (a monastic military order), and it's not hard to envision the medieval knights who once lived here. Marco Polo, on his way to meet Kublai Khan, may have dined in the **refectory**; in each of the two corners to the left as you enter, you can see a fleur-de-lis, emblem of the kings of France.

Right outside, a **tunnel** – just wide enough for one person and almost high enough to stand up in – leads out to the **Turkish Bazaar** via a souvenir shop that was here long before the tunnel was opened to the public.

Hammam al-Pasha
MUSEUM

(Turkish Bathhouse; adult/child 25/21NIS) Built in 1780 by Al-Jazzar and in use until the 1940s, the richly ornamented marble and tile chambers now play host to a 30-minute **multimedia show** entitled 'The Story of the Last Bath Attendant' (available in eight languages).

Templars' Tunnel
TUNNEL

(adult/child 15/12NIS) This extraordinary underground passageway, 350m long, was built by the Knights Templar (a Christian military order) to connect their main fortress, just north of the black-and-white-striped lighthouse at Old Akko's southwestern tip, with the marina (Khan al-Umdan). It was discovered by accident in 1994. You can enter at either end; tickets to all the Crusaders sites are sold at both access points. Inside, buttons let you start films in either Hebrew or English.

Treasures in the Wall Museum
MUSEUM

(Burj al-Kommander; adult/child 15/12NIS) Wedged into the upper ramparts in the far northeastern corner of the old city, this museum is laid out like a Galilee town souq (market) of the late Ottoman period, with blacksmith, tinsmith, potter, primus repair shop, pharmacy, hat maker and woodworking shop, all outfitted with period tools, equipment and furnishings (eg gorgeous inlaid furniture from Damascus). The entrance is up on the Land Wall Promenade, accessible from street level via a number of staircases.

Al-Jazzar Mosque
MOSQUE

(admission 10NIS; ⊙approximately 8-11am, 11.45am-3pm & 3.30-6pm winter, 8am-noon, 12.45-4pm & 4.45-7.30pm summer, longer prayer breaks Fri) Topped by a large green dome and accented by a slender pencil minaret, Al-Jazzar Mosque was built in 1781 in typical Ottoman

Turkish style – with some local improvisation: the columns in the courtyard, for example, were 'adopted' from Roman Caesarea. Around by the base of the minaret, the small twin-domed building contains the sarcophagi of Al-Jazzar and his adopted son and successor, Süleyman.

This mosque is the third most important mosque in Israel and the Palestinian Territories, after Al-Aqsa in Jerusalem and the Ibrahimi Mosque (Tomb of the Patriarchs) in Hebron. It stands on the site of a former Crusader cathedral, the cellars of which were put into use by the Turks as cisterns.

Acre Underground Prisoners Museum
MUSEUM

(adult/child 15/10NIS; ⊗8.30am-4.30pm Sun-Thu) Dedicated to Jewish armed resistance during the British Mandate, this museum occupies a massive structure built by the Turks in the late 18th century on 13th-century Crusader foundations and used as a prison by both the Ottomans and the British. People jailed here included Revisionist Zionist leader Ze'ev Jabotinsky (from 1920 to 1921) and eight Jewish underground fighters who were executed by hanging, most of them in 1947 (the gallows room is open to the public).

A film features the Etzel's (Irgun's) daring mass breakout of 1947 (that scene in the movie version of *Exodus* was filmed here).

Baha'ullah, founder of the Baha'i faith, was imprisoned here by the Ottomans in the late 19th century. His cell, a holy place for the Baha'i, is open only to Baha'i pilgrims.

The museum is run by Israel's Ministry of Defense, so you'll have to show your passport to get in.

Okashi Art Museum
MUSEUM

(adult/child 10/7NIS; ⊗9.30am-7pm, to 5pm winter, closes 1hr or 2hr earlier Fri) Devoted to the works of Avshalom Okashi (1916–80), an influential Israeli painter who lived in Akko for the last half of his life. Also puts on exhibitions of contemporary art.

Souq
MARKET

(⊗to late afternoon daily) Fresh hummus is boiled in giant vats, while nearby fresh-caught fish flop off the tables. As carts trundle past, children shuck corn and vendors hawk fresh fruit, all to a soundtrack of Arabic music. At the lower end of the souq, visit **Kurdi & Berit** (⊗9.30am-6pm), a tourist-friendly shop that ships herbs and spices worldwide.

Khan al-Umdan
HISTORIC BUILDING

Old Akko has four large **khans** (caravanserais) whose courtyards – surrounded by colonnaded storerooms and, upstairs, sleeping quarters – once served camel caravans bringing grain from, and imported goods to, the hinterland. The grandest is the 18th-century **Khan al-Umdan**, easily recognisable thanks to its square Ottoman clock tower, which is next to the **marina**. The pillars that give the khan its name were appropriated from Caesarea.

Plans to convert the complex into a hotel are stalled, so the site is in limbo, but visits may be possible from the nearby entrance to the Templars' Tunnel.

The other khans are easier to visit. **Khan ash-Shawarda**, just south of Salah ad-Din St, was recently spruced up and now shelters a number of restaurants. The courtyards of **Khan al-Faranj**, a few blocks southwest, and **Khan ash-Shune**, a few steps west of the eastern entrance to the Templars' Tunnel, are accessible through open archways.

Activities

Sailing Around the Walls
CRUISE

(☑050-555 1136, 04-991 3890; Marina; per person 20-25NIS) From the marina, passenger boats offer 30- or 40-minute cruises around the city. Call for sailing times.

Ghattas Turkish Baths
SPA

(☑04-689 7462; www.ghattasbath.com; 11 Ha-Hagana St; 2hr per person 300NIS, minimum/maximum 2/20 people; ⊗10am-8pm daily) When Emile Ghattas returned to Akko after a 25-year career with Intel, he decided to fulfil a lifelong dream: to open a hammam. (As a boy, he used to go to Hammam al-Pasha with his father.) The luxury bathhouse he built – using marble from Turkey, India and Guatemala – includes a hammam, dry sauna, hot tub and massage treatments.

By reservation only – call a few days ahead for weekdays, two weeks ahead for Friday and Saturday. Situated right behind Uri Buri restaurant.

Argaman Beach
BEACH

(admission 10NIS; ⊗May-Oct) A broad, sandy municipal beach with lifeguards. Situated about 1.5km southeast of the old city.

Sleeping

Akko Gate Hostel
HOSTEL $

(☑04-991 0410; www.akkogate.com; 13/14 Salah ad-Din St; without breakfast dm/s/d/tr/5-bed

Akko (Acre)

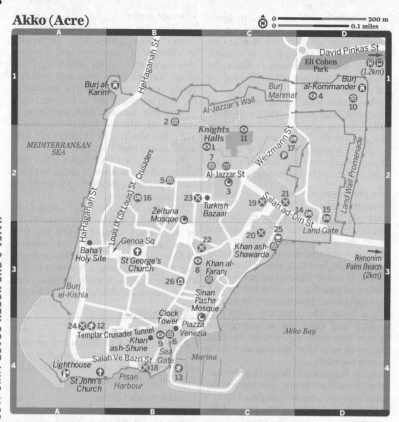

Akko (Acre)

◎ Top Sights
1 Knights Halls	C2

◎ Sights
2 Acre Underground Prisoners Museum	B1
3 Al-Jazzar Mosque	C2
4 City Walls	D1
5 Hammam al-Pasha	B2
6 Khan al-Umdan	B4
7 Okashi Art Museum	C2
8 Souq	B3
9 Templars' Tunnel	B4
10 Treasures in the Wall Museum	D1
11 Visitor Centre	C2

◎ Activities, Courses & Tours
12 Ghattas Turkish Baths	A4
13 Sailing Around the Walls	B4

◎ Sleeping
14 Akko Gate Hostel	D2
15 Akkotel	D2
16 Effendi Hotel	B2
17 HI – Knights Hostel & Guest House	C2

◎ Eating
18 Doniana	B4
19 Elias Dieb & Sons	C2
20 El-Khan	C3
21 Hummus Abu Suheil	C2
22 Hummus Said	C3
23 Kukushka	B2
24 Uri Buri	A4

◎ Drinking & Nightlife
25 Leale al-Sultan	C3

◎ Shopping
26 Kurdi & Berit	B3

r US$25/60/85/120/160; ❄@🛜) Run by the friendly Walid, this long-running hostel is just inside the old city, steps from the cheap eats of Salah ad-Din St. In an Ottoman-era building, the 12 rooms (12 more are planned) are simply furnished and a little dated but are clean and come with mini fridges. The basic kitchen is out on a balcony. Breakfast costs 25NIS.

HI – Knights Hostel &
Guest House
HOSTEL $$

(📞direct 02-594 5711, reservations 1 599 510 511; www.iyha.org.il; 2 Weizmann St; dm US$35, d 450NIS, additional adult/child 130/100NIS; @🛜) This modern hostel, opened in 2011, has 76 rooms spread over three floors. Like other IYHA places, it's very clean and institutional but has some unique features, including an ancient aqueduct running through it and in situ ruins in the courtyard. Guests get 50% off parking in nearby lots.

★ Effendi Hotel
HISTORIC HOTEL $$$

(📞074-729 9799; www.efendi-hotel.com; Louis IX St; d US$320-730) For the ultimate in Ottoman luxury, head to the Effendi, located in two meticulously restored Ottoman-era town houses. The 12 huge, 5m-high rooms and atmospheric public areas have the sumptuously painted ceilings, marble floors and old-fashioned bathtubs you'd expect in a pasha's palace.

Amenities include a Turkish hammam, a rooftop patio with sea views and a basement – now a wine bar – from the Crusader period.

Akkotel
HOTEL $$$

(📞04-987 7100; www.akkotel.com; Salah ad-Din St; s/d/q US$160/190/285; ❄@🛜) Embedded in the old city ramparts, this family-run hotel has 16 rooms (including five for families) with vaulted ceilings, stone windowsills and walls 1m or or even 2m thick. The rooftop terrace affords fantastic views of the city and Haifa Bay. Wheelchair accessible. Has seven reserved parking places.

Rimonim Palm Beach
HOTEL $$$

(📞04-987 7777, reservations *6333; www.palmbeach.co.il; s/d/tr US$136/172/268; 🛜❄) Located 2km southeast of the old city, around the bay, this tourist-class hotel has 125 rooms spread over eight floors. Amenities include indoor and outdoor pools, a sauna, a health spa and direct beach access. Offers lots of activities for kids, especially in summer.

✗ Eating

Old Akko has some excellent dining options, particularly if you're in the mood for fish or seafood. A number of restaurants and cafes shelter under the Turkish arches of the newly refurbished Khan ash-Shawarda. During Ramadan, most restaurants stay open throughout the day.

For cheap eats, there are quite a few places selling hummus, felafel and/or shwarma along Salah ad-Din St. Hummus joints are generally open from 6am or 7am until 3pm or 4pm.

For self-catering supplies, head to the old city's **souq** (market), which runs from just west of Khan ash-Shawarda southwest to the clock tower, or to **Elias Dieb & Sons** (Salah ad-Din St), a little cavelike supermarket opposite Souq al-Abiad (there's no English sign).

Hummus Abu Suheil
MIDDLE EASTERN $

(Hummus Suheila; 14/21 Salah ad-Din St; hummus 20NIS; ⊙7.30am or 8am-5pm Wed-Mon) A tiny and utterly unpretentious hummus joint acclaimed as one of the best in the city. To find it, look for a black sign with Hebrew lettering.

Hummus Said
MIDDLE EASTERN $

(hummus 15NIS; ⊙6am-2.30pm Sun-Fri; 🖋) Deep inside the souq, this place is something of an institution, doling out plates of soft, creamy hummus to connoisseurs from around the country. For 17NIS you get salads, pickles, pita and hummus with fuul (fava-bean paste) or garlic.

Kukushka
FAST FOOD $

(📞04-901 9758; Turkish Bazaar; ⊙11am-6pm or later daily) A hole-in-the-wall shop with amazing hot dogs made from veal or lamb; also has calamari and shrimp.

Doniana
SEAFOOD $$

(📞04-991 0001; Pisan Harbour; mains 48-115NIS; ⊙noon-midnight; 🖋) Excellent grilled fish and seafood and stunning Mediterranean views make this restaurant a great option for a romantic meal. (Its name, pronounced '*dun*-ya-na' in Arabic, means 'our world'.) Meat lovers can order a tender steak, perhaps complemented by a red wine from the Golan. Dishes come with all-you-can-eat sides and salads (45NIS if you order them as a meal).

Situated up the stairs from the eastern end of the Pisan Port.

★ **Uri Buri** SEAFOOD $$$
(04-955 2212; HaHaganah St; mains 65-114NIS, half portions 51-63NIS; ☉noon-midnight; ♪) Uri Buri is a man of many talents who's done everything from spear fishing to diffusing bombs to founding the luxurious Effendi Hotel. But he's best known for making award-winning fish and seafood dishes – recommended options include fish soup, crab with seaweed, creamy trout fast-cooked in a hot casserole, and sashimi served with wasabi-flavoured sorbet.

Staff are happy to prepare dishes that are vegan, gluten-free, lactose-free or non-allergenic. It's a good idea to call ahead, especially on Friday and Saturday.

El-Khan MIDDLE EASTERN, MEDITERRANEAN $$$
(04-901 9378; Khan al-Shawarda courtyard; mains 75-110NIS; ☉noon-midnight) Opened in 2013, this restaurant quickly aquired a reputation – first and foremost among locals – for its Arab and Mediterranean cuisine. You can dine on grilled meats or seafood (eg mussels and calamari) either indoors, in a gorgeous stone-vaulted dining room or, when it's warm, in the courtyard of an Ottoman-era caravanserai.

Drinking

Leale al-Sultan COFFEEHOUSE
(Khan ash-Shawarda; snacks 22-28NIS; ☉24hr) Nargileh (water pipe) dens have a seedy reputation, but this old-time coffeehouse, sporting woven cushions, colourful wall paintings and backgammon tables, is popular with perfectly respectable folk – locals and tourists alike. Turkish coffee costs 5NIS, freshly squeezed fruit juices and shakes are 15NIS to 20NIS, and a nargileh is 20NIS to 25NIS. Has a nonsmoking corner.

Breakfast (35NIS to 40NIS) is served from 9am to 2pm.

Information

The old city (eg around Al-Jazzar St) has several licensed exchange bureaux. Banks with ATMs can be found in the new city. There's a **post office** (13 Al-Jazzar St) – which can change currency and travellers cheques – and a **police station** (04-987 6736; 1 Weizmann St) in the old city.

DANGERS & ANNOYANCES
Old Akko shuts down after dark, and while most people feel comfortable strolling around after nightfall, women walking alone have been subject to unwanted attention and occasional sexual harassment.

Getting There & Away

Akko's train and bus stations are about 1.5km northeast of the main entrance to the old city.

Train is the fastest and most scenic way to travel to/from Nahariya (8.50NIS, seven minutes, twice an hour), Haifa Merkaz-HaShmona (16NIS, 30 minutes, three times an hour), Tel Aviv (41.50NIS, 1¾ hours, hourly) and Ben-Gurion airport (51.50NIS, two hours, hourly).

Nateev Express buses 271 and 361 link Akko with Haifa-Merkazit HaMifratz (16NIS, 35 to 45 minutes, every 10 minutes); bus 271 continues north to Nahariya (8.50NIS, 35 minutes, every 10 to 15 minutes) via the Baha'i Gardens and Kibbutz Lohamei HaGeta'ot, while bus 361 goes goes east to Tsfat (one hour, twice an hour).

Sheruts (shared taxis) wait outside the Akko bus station and depart when full to Haifa (Hadar) and Nahariya.

Getting Around

To get from the train and bus stations to old Akko, it's a 20-minute (1.5km) walk to the southwest, or you can take a taxi for 15NIS to 25NIS; **Moniot Karmel** (04-955 1118) has a taxi stand next to the train station.

Traffic in old Akko is often gridlocked, so trying to get around by car is usually a losing proposition. Parking costs 20NIS a day.

Around Akko

Baha'i Gardens & Shrine of Baha'ullah

The holiest site in the Baha'i faith is not in Haifa but near Akko, for it is here that Baha'ullah, founder of the faith, lived after his release from an Akko prison and where he died in 1892. The lovely formal gardens, with their meticulously tended flower beds and fountains, are similar in style to those in Haifa (p150). At the far end of the gardens is the **Shrine of Baha'ullah** (www.baha-ullah.com; ☉9am-noon Fri-Mon) FREE, his final resting place. **Bahji House**, where he lived from 1879 to 1892, is open only to Baha'i pilgrims. For both men and women, knees and shoulders need to be covered.

Akko's main Baha'i sites are 4.5km northeast of Akko's old city; the turn-off from Rte 8510 is opposite the entrance to the religious community of Moshav Bustan HaGalil. Buses that pass by this way include Nateev Express bus 271 (every 10 to 15 minutes Sunday to Friday afternoon, every 45 to 60 minutes Saturday evening), which serves Nahariya (one hour), Akko (25 minutes) and Haifa-Merkazit HaMifratz (50 minutes).

Kibbutz Lohamei HaGeta'ot

Kibbutz Lohamei HaGeta'ot (the name means Ghetto Fighters' Kibbutz) was established in 1949 by Jews who spent WWII fighting the Nazis in the Warsaw Ghetto and the forests of Poland and Lithuania. Founded the same year as the kibbutz, **Beit Lohamei HaGeta'ot** (Ghetto Fighters' House Museum; www.gfh.org.il; adult/child incl Yad Layeled 30/20NIS; ⊙9am-4pm Sun-Thu) – the first museum in the world dedicated to the Holocaust – focuses on Jewish resistance, including the uprisings in the ghettos and camps and the bravery of the partisans.

The adjacent **Yad Layeled Children's Memorial Museum** (adult/child incl Beit Lohamei HaGeta'ot 30/20NIS; ⊙9am-4pm Sun-Thu), appropriate for children 10 and over, is a moving memorial to the 1.5 million Jewish children who perished in the Holocaust. The hands-on exhibit include films, period artefacts and the stories and testimonies of children who lived during those terrible times.

Just south of the kibbutz, on the eastern side of Rte 4, you can see an **Ottoman aqueduct**, built by Al-Jazzar around 1780 to supply Akko with water from the Galilee uplands.

The kibbutz is on Rte 4 about midway between Akko and Nahariya. The many buses that pass by this way, linking the two cities, include Nateev Express 271 (every 10 to 15 minutes Sunday to Friday afternoon, every 45 to 60 minutes Saturday evening).

Nahariya נהריה نهريا

📞 04 / POP 53,000

Founded by German-Jewish refugees in 1935, Nahariya still feels a bit like a Central European beach resort of the interwar era. The town's focal point is 1km-long HaGa'aton Blvd, lined with cafes, ice-cream joints, flower shops and places to eat, which runs along both banks of the eucalyptus-shaded Ga'aton River (actually a concrete canal). This slightly shabby boulevard links the bus and train stations with the beachfront promenade, where folk dancing, concerts and other entertainments are often held, especially in summer. Nahariya makes a good base for exploring the area between Haifa and the Lebanese border.

🛏 Sleeping & Eating

Hotel Frank HOTEL $$
(📞04-992 0278; www.hotel-frank.co.il; 4 Ha'Alia St; s/d US$100/135; ❄@🔊) This meticulously maintained tourist-class hotel has friendly staff and 49 spacious, spotless rooms with a bit of a retro vibe – not surprising since the building dates from the year of the Beatles' first world tour (1964). Situated 1½ blocks north of HaGa'aton Blvd and 1½ blocks inland from the beachfront.

Carlton Hotel HOTEL $$$
(📞04-900 5555; www.carlton-hotel.co.il; 23 HaGa'aton Blvd; d/q 800/1200NIS, additional adult/child 250/200NIS; ❄🔊🏊) The smartest hotel in town has 200 rooms with a 1990s feel and sparkling bathrooms, a 25m outdoor pool and a top-floor spa. Wheelchair accessible. Situated halfway between the bus station and the beach.

🛈 Getting There & Away

Nahariya is 36km northeast of Haifa, 11km north of Akko and 10km south of Rosh HaNikra.

The best way to get here is by train. Two trains per hour head south to Akko (8.50NIS, seven minutes) and Haifa Merkaz-HaShmona (20.50NIS, 35 minutes); hourly trains go to Tel Aviv (46.50NIS, 1¾ hours) and Ben-Gurion airport (56.50NIS, two hours).

North of Nahariya

Montfort מונפורט مونفورت

Built by the noble De Milly family, Montfort is not the most impressive of Israel's Crusader castles (Nimrod's Castle is much more stirring), but it's interesting enough and a visit here involves a pleasant hike. The castle's name was changed from Montfort ('strong mountain' in French) to Starkenberg ('strong mountain' in German) when the De Millys sold it to the Teutonic knights. In 1271 the Muslims, led by the Mamluk sultan Beybars, took the castle after a previous attempt, five years earlier, had failed. The Crusaders surrendered and retreated to Akko.

Little except the view can be seen today. To the right of the entrance is the governor's residence, with the tower straight ahead. The two vaulted chambers to the right are the basement of the knights' hall; next to them is the chapel.

WORTH A TRIP

ROSH HANIKRA GROTTOES

The volatile border between Israel and Lebanon comes to an appropriately rugged and dramatic head at Rosh HaNikra, a frontier-straddling bluff where jagged white cliffs of limestone and chalk plunge into the deep blue sea. Turn on a radio here and many of the stations will be from Cyprus, a corner of the European Union just 250km to the northeast.

The 10km road from Nahariya ends at the **Rosh HaNikra Grottoes** (📞073-271 0100; www.rosh-hanikra.com), from where a **cable car** (adult/child 45/35NIS; ⊗9am-4pm Sun-Fri, to 6pm Sat Sep-Mar, 9am-6pm Sat-Thu, to 4pm Fri Apr-Jun) – made by an Austrian ski-lift company – descends steeply to the bottom of the flint-speckled cliffs. Inside the grottoes, lit by the luminescent blue of the Mediterranean, waves crash with awesome power against the bone-white walls. The site is at its most dramatic during stormy weather. The cable car is wheelchair accessible, but the caves are not. It's a good idea to wear sensible shoes with grippy soles.

Behind the lower cable-car station, inside a naturally cool rail tunnel, you can watch a **film** on the area's geography and the history of the Haifa–Beirut railway, whose tunnels were excavated by British army engineering units from New Zealand and South Africa in 1941 and 1942. Unsurprisingly, the line has been out of commission since 1948.

At the ticket windows, it's possible to hire a **bike** (including the grottoes 72NIS) for the 5km round-trip ride to **Betzet Beach**.

Up top, you can peer through a camouflaged border gate on the Israel–Lebanon border. A few kilometres north is the Naqoura base of the 12,000-member **United Nations Interim Force in Lebanon** (Unifil), which has been patrolling the border since 1978.

If you're hungry, there's a snack bar down below and a cafeteria next to the border gate.

Nateev Exprees bus 31 links Rosh HaNikra with Nahariya (7.40NIS, 17 minutes, every 1½ to two hours except Shabbat).

❶ Getting There & Away

Trails to Montfort can be picked up about 18km northeast of Nahariya, either from Goren Park, 9km east of the town of Shlomi (along Rte 899), or from a car park 3km northwest of Mi'ilya, a village that's about 16km east of Nahariya (along Rte 89). The hike to the castle from either trailhead takes about 45 minutes.

Akhziv
אכזיב שاطئ الزيب

The stretch of coastline north of Nahariya is known as Akhziv.

◉ Sights & Activities

Akhziv National Park　　　　BEACH
(www.park.org.il; adult/child 35/21NIS, camp per person 63/53NIS; ⊗8am-5pm Sep-Jun, to 7pm Jul & Aug) About 5km north of the centre of Nahariya, Akhziv National Park has two parts. Broad lawns, traces of a Phoenician port, a small, shallow, family-friendly beach, and changing rooms are situated on and around a little hill, site of an Arab village whose residents fled in 1948. A few hundred metres to the south, on a spot once occupied by a long-closed Club Med, is a much longer and wider beach with sunshades, showers and a snack bar.

🛌 Sleeping

Akhzivland　　　　　　HOSTEL $$
(📞04-982 3250; s/d/tr without breakfast 200/450/600NIS, camping per person 85NIS; 🅿🛜) The self-proclaimed micronation of Akhzivland, founded in 1951 and declared independent in 1971, has more than a whiff of *Robinson Crusoe* to it. Steps from the beach (part of Akhziv National Park), 10 airy wooden shacks come with rough-hewn furnishings, kitchens (BYO food) and a hippie vibe; seven have private showers. To get here, follow the signs to 'Eli Avivi'.

A sprawling, chaotic **museum** (admission 20NIS) of archaeology and bric-a-brac occupies the stone-built home of the *mukhtar* (leader) of the Arab village that stood here until 1948.

Lower Galilee & Sea of Galilee הגליל התחתון ים כנרת الخليل الاسفل بحيرة طبريا

Best Places to Eat

➡ AlReda (p191)
➡ Abu Ashraf (p190)
➡ Muhtar Sweets (p191)
➡ Shirat Ro'im (p197)
➡ Ein Camonim (p216)

Best Places to Stay

➡ Fauzi Azar Inn (p189)
➡ Al-Mutran Guest House (p190)
➡ Pilgerhaus Tabgha (p216)
➡ Ein Harod Guest House (p201)
➡ Genghis Khan in the Golan (p219)

Why Go?

Blessed with rugged hills cloaked in wildflowers in spring, ancient stone synagogues and archaeological sites from the early centuries of Christianity, the Lower Galilee – the part of northern Israel south of Rte 85 (linking Akko with the Sea of Galilee) – is hugely popular with hikers, cyclists, Jewish- and Arab-Israeli families on holiday, Tel Aviv epicureans and, of course, Christian pilgrims.

Green, lush and chilly in winter (the perfect time for a hot-spring dip) and parched in summer (you can beat the heat in the Sea of Galilee), this is where Jesus of Nazareth lived, preached and is believed to have performed some of his most famous miracles. But these days even Nazareth is much more than a place of Christian pilgrimage – it now boasts one of Israel's most sophisticated dining scenes. The shimmering Sea of Galilee (in Hebrew, the Kinneret), too, juxtaposes holiday pleasures with archaeological sites linked to Jesus's ministry.

When to Go
Nazareth

Dec–Mar Mt Gilboa is carpeted with daffodils, red poppies and, in March, purple Gilboa irises.

Jul–Sep Oppressively hot at the Sea of Galilee and in the Beit She'an Valley.

Early Dec & early May The twice-yearly Jacob's Ladder Festival brings music to Ginosar.

NAZARETH

الناصرة   נצרת

📷 04 / POP 74,000

Nazareth has come a long way since its days as a quiet Jewish village in Roman-ruled Galilee, so if you're expecting bucolic rustic-ity be prepared for a surprise. These days, Israel's largest Arab city is a bustling mini-metropolis with shop-lined thoroughfares, blaring car horns, traffic jams and young men with a penchant for showing off at the wheel. The Old City, its stone-paved alleys

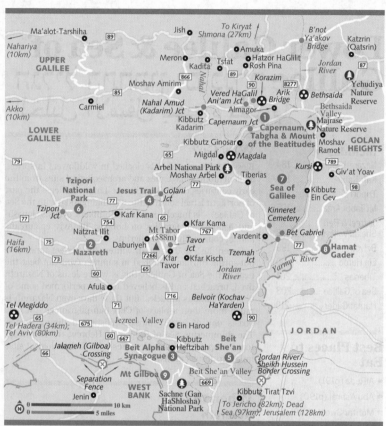

Lower Galilee & Sea of Galilee Highlights

1 Visiting the sites of Jesus's ministry at **Capernaum** (p214), **Tabgha** (p209) and **Mount of the Beatitudes** (p209).

2 Dining in the Arab-fusion restaurants of **Nazareth**, the Galilee's culinary capital (p184).

3 Identifying the zodiac signs, Jewish symbols and biblical personages depicted on the mosaic at the 6th-century **Beit Alpha Synagogue** (p199).

4 Hiking from Nazareth to the Sea of Galilee along the **Jesus Trail** (p188).

5 Imagining what Roman-era life was like as you explore the colonnaded streets of ancient **Beit She'an** (p198).

6 Admiring the brilliant mosaics of **Tzipori National Park** (p195).

7 Taking a dip in the refreshing waters of the **Sea of Galilee** (p208) on a scorching summer's day.

8 Lolling about in the steaming mineral-water pools of **Hamat Gader** (p219) on a chilly winter's day.

9 Getting lost among the spring wildflowers atop **Mt Gilboa** (p199).

lined with crumbling Ottoman-era mansions, is in the process of reinventing itself as a sophisticated cultural and culinary destination.

According to the New Testament, it was in Nazareth (al-Naasira in Arabic, Natzrat or Natzeret in Hebrew) that the Angel Gabriel appeared to Mary to inform her that she would conceive and give birth to the Son of God, an event known as the Annunciation (Luke 1:26-38).

Like Capernaum, Nazareth and its residents were treated rather dismissively in the Gospels. The disdainful words of Nathanael of Cana, 'Nazareth! Can anything good come from there?' (John 1:46) are believed to reflect most Nazarenes' lack of enthusiasm for their town's most famous preacher.

Everything in Nazareth is open for business on Shabbat (Friday night and Saturday). On Sunday, on the other hand, while attractions and pastry shops are open, stores and most restaurants are not.

History

In the 6th century, Christian interest in Nazareth was rekindled by reports of miracles, but a century later the Persian invasion brought massacres of Christians. After the arrival of Islam in 637 CE, many locals converted to Islam, but a significant Christian minority remained.

The Crusaders made Nazareth their Galilean capital in 1099 but were driven out a century later by Saladin (Salah ad-Din). In the mid-1200s the Mamluk Sultan Baybars banned Christian clergy, and by the end of the century Nazareth was no more than an impoverished village.

Churches were re-established in Nazareth in the 17th and 18th centuries. Napoleon Bonaparte briefly captured the town in 1799. By the end of the Ottoman period, Nazareth had a sizeable Christian community and a growing array of churches and monasteries (there are now about 30).

Today about 30% of the population of Nazareth is Christian (the largest denominations are Greek Orthodox, Melkite Greek Catholic and Roman Catholic), down from about 60% in 1949. Tensions between Christians and Islamists occasionally flare up and have caused some Christians to leave the city.

◎ Sights & Activities

★ **Basilica of the Annunciation** CHURCH
(✔04-565 0001, 04-565 0001; www.basilica nazareth.org; Al-Bishara St; ⊘ Upper Basilica 8am-

ℹ GET LOST

You are going to get lost in the maze of alleyways that make up the Old City, so you may as well relax and enjoy! Complicating matters is the lack of street signs – though given that most street names are four-digit numbers, it should come as no surprise that locals don't use them. On the brighter side, free colour maps of Nazareth are available at all of the Old City's guest houses.

6pm, Grotto of the Annunciation 5.45am-6pm, for silent prayer 6-9pm) FREE Dominating the Old City's skyline is the lantern-topped cupola of this Franciscan-run Roman Catholic basilica, a modernist structure that's unlike any building you've ever seen. Constructed from 1960 to 1969, it's believed by many Christians to stand on the site of Mary's home, where many churches (but not the Greek Orthodox) believe the Annunciation took place.

The **Upper Basilica**, its soaring dome shaped like an inverted lily, 'glorifies Mary as the Mother of God'. With lovely mid-20th-century flair, the bare cast concrete is adorned with indented dots.

In the dimly lit lower church, a sunken enclosure shelters the **Grotto of the Annunciation**, the traditional site of Mary's house, and remnants of churches from the Byzantine (4th century) and Crusader (12th century) eras.

The walls of the courtyard and the upper church are decorated with a series of vivid **mosaic panels**, donated by Catholic communities around the world, depicting Mary and the infant Jesus in styles that boldly reflect the cultures of their countries of origin. Panels from Ethiopia, Italy and France were added in 2013.

Confessions can be made in a variety of languages from 8.30am to 11.30am and 3pm to 5pm. Weekly events:

Marian Prayer 8.30pm Tuesday

Eucharistic Adoration 8.30pm Thursday

Candlelight Procession 8.30pm Saturday

There are plans to begin webcasting services in 2016.

Free brochures in a dozen languages – and shawls to cover exposed shoulders and knees (deposit required) – are available at the **Pilgrims Office** (⊘9am-noon & 2-6pm Mon-Sat), 20m to the left of the basilica's main gate.

Nazareth

St Joseph's Church CHURCH
(Al-Bishara St; ⊘7am-6pm) Across the court-yard from the upper level of the Basilica of the Annunciation, this neo-Romanesque Franciscan church, built in 1914, occupies a site believed by popular tradition to be that of Joseph's carpentry workshop. It was built on top of the remains of a Crusader church. Down in the crypt, signs explain in situ archaeological discoveries.

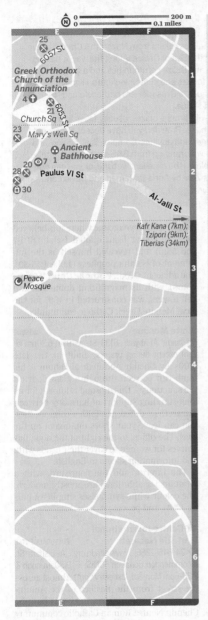

LOWER GALILEE & SEA OF GALILEE NAZARETH

situated directly under this richly frescoed, 17th-century church (other denominations hold that she was at home during the Annunciation). The barrel-vaulted **crypt**, first constructed under Constantine (4th century CE), shelters Nazareth's only year-round spring, a place everyone in the village obviously visited often. Check out the centuries-old **graffiti** carved around the outside doorway.

★**Greek Orthodox
Church of the Annunciation**   CHURCH
(St Gabriel's Church; Church Sq; ⊙7am-noon & 1-6pm) According to Greek Orthodox tradition, the Annunciation took place while Mary was fetching water from the spring

THE JESUS TRAIL

The 65km **Jesus Trail** (www.jesustrail.com) takes walkers from Nazareth's Church of the Annunciation to Tabgha and Capernaum on the Sea of Galilee. Along the way, it passes through Jewish, Christian, Muslim, Bedouin and Druze communities and a gorgeously varied landscape: rugged hills, olive groves, forests and clifftop lookouts. Highlights include Christian holy sites, ancient synagogues, a Crusader-era battlefield and Nebi Shu'eib, the Druze religion's most important shrine.

Walking the entire trail, which is marked with orange blazes, usually takes four days, but shorter sections can be enjoyed as day hikes. Provided you have decent shoes and plenty of water, the route is suitable for all ages and abilities. Camping is an option, and there is plenty of accommodation along the way, ranging from B&Bs to top-end hotels. The itinerary and GPS waypoints are available on the excellent website, or you can purchase two first-rate guides: *Hiking the Jesus Trail* by Anna Dintaman and David Landis, and *Jesus Trail and Jerusalem* by Jacob Saar.

LOWER GALILEE & SEA OF GALILEE NAZARETH

★ Ancient Bathhouse ARCHAEOLOGICAL SITE

(☑04-657 8539; www.nazarethbathhouse.com; Mary's Well Sq; tour 120NIS, per person 5 or more people 28NIS; ⊙9am-7pm Mon-Sat) When Elias Shama and his Belgian-born wife, Martina, set about renovating their shop in 1993, they uncovered a network of 2000-year-old clay pipes almost identical to ones found in Pompeii – and then, under the floor, an almost perfectly preserved Roman bathhouse once fed by water from Mary's Well. The 30-minute tour, which draws you into the excitement of serendipitous discovery, ends with refreshments.

Mary's Well SPRING

(Mary's Well Sq) Eastern Orthodox Christians believe that this spring – whose actual source lies under the nearby Greek Orthodox Church of the Annunciation – was the site of the Annunciation (al-Bishara in Arabic). The structure known as Mary's Well is a modern reconstruction and the water does not actually come from Mary's Spring. The litter, however, is genuine.

Cave of the 40 Holy Monks CAVE

(☑Odeh Jubran 052 324 2119; No 21, 6198 St; donation requested; ⊙tours 9.30am-2pm Mon-Sat) Under the compound of the Greek Orthodox Bishopric, this network of caves is named after 40 monks killed here by the Romans in the 1st century. To find the street entrance, look for a sign reading 'Ancient Holy Cave'; if the door is closed, call.

Synagogue-Church CHURCH

(⊙8am-noon & 3-7pm except during prayers, closed Sun morning) Hidden away in an alleyway off the souq, this humble Crusader-era structure, now a Catholic church, stands on the site of the synagogue where it is believed that the young Jesus quoted Isaiah (61:1-2 and 58:6) and revealed himself as the fulfillment of Isaiah's prophesy (Luke 4:15-30). The adjacent **Greek Catholic Church** (same hours), with its magnificent dome and two bell towers, was constructed in 1887 for the local Melkite Greek Catholic community.

White Mosque MOSQUE

(Al-Jaami' Al-Abyad; 6133 St; ⊙9am-6.30pm or 7pm except during prayers) Built in the late 1700s by Sheikh Abdullah al-Fahum – his tomb can be seen through a glass door off the sanctuary – this mosque is known for its long-standing support of harmony between Nazareth's different faith communities. You can leave your shoes on, except on the rugs. The office, to the right of the door, has scarves for women to cover their heads with, and information sheets in English.

The interior and the courtyard, with a fountain for ablutions, are mostly modern. The colour white symbolises simplicity, purity, unity and peace.

★ Centre International Marie de Nazareth CULTURAL CENTRE

(☑04-646 1266; www.cimdn.org; Al-Bishara St; recommended donation 50NIS; ⊙9.30am-noon & 2.30-6pm Mon-Sat, last entry 5pm) Almost across the street from the Basilica of the Annunciation, this stunning complex was built by Chemin Neuf, a Roman Catholic community based in France, as a venue for ecumenical work among Christians and for inter-religious dialogue. The peaceful rooftop gardens, landscaped with plants mentioned in the Bible, afford 360-degree panoramas, while in the basement there are in situ ruins from as far back as the First Temple period.

A four-room multimedia presentation, available in 11 languages, illustrates biblical highlights (from Creation through to the Resurrection), with an emphasis on the lives of Mary and Jesus. Films in 16 languages are shown; some can also be watched on www. netforgod.tv. Prayers (in French) are held at 6pm daily. Wheelchair accessible.

Nazareth Village   FARM
(☑04-645 6042; www.nazarethvillage.com; Al-Wadi al-Jawani St/5050 St; adult/child 50/25NIS; ⊗8.30am-5pm, last tour 3.30pm Mon-Sat) Run by an ecumenical NGO, this re-creation of a 1st-century Galilean farmstead is great at helping visitors imagine Nazareth and its economic life in the time of Jesus. The wine press and vineyard terraces are authentically ancient, but everything else – the threshing floor, the burial cave, the olive press, the carpenter's and weaver's studios, the synagogue – are recreations that accurately portray 1st-century life. Crafts are demonstrated by actors and volunteers in period costume.

Call ahead to find out when guided tours (1¼ hours), available in nine languages, are scheduled.

Basilica of Jesus the Adolescent   CHURCH
(☑04-646 8954, 04-646 8954; Salesian St/5004 St; ⊗2-6pm Sun-Fri, 8am-6pm Sat) Built between 1906 and 1923, this neo-Gothic church, with commanding views of Nazareth, has a clean, almost luminescent limestone interior whose delicate arches and soaring vaults can only be described as 'very French'. It owes its name to the fact that Jesus spent much of his early life in Nazareth.

Located along the Jesus Trail, the church is inside École Jésus Adolescent, a school run by Catholic religious order the Salesians of Don Bosco. If possible, call ahead before visiting.

The church is a steep, 20-minute walk from the Old City. From the gate to the parking lot, head left up the stairs and, at the top, enter the door to your right; the church is at the end of the hall.

👉 Tours

Fauzi Azar Inn   WALKING TOUR
(☑04-602 0469; www.fauziazarinn.com; ⊗9.15am daily) FREE Offers free two-hour cultural tours of the Old City, focusing on things you can't see on your own, to guests and nonguests alike. Can also arrange dinner with local families (80NIS to 90NIS per person).

Sharif Sharif-Safadi   TOUR
(☑054 541 9277, 04-601 3717; sharifla@zahav. net.il; 3-4hr tour for up to 10 people US$200) An expert on the preservation of historic monuments, Sharif offers excellent tours of the 'hidden city', including the interiors of Old City mansions normally closed to the public.

🛌 Sleeping

Demand for accommodation from pilgrimage groups is at its highest in March, April, October, November and around Christmas and New Year. Backpackers tend to be most numerous from late June to October and around Christmas and New Year.

Simsim Backpackers   GUESTHOUSE $
(☑04-628 3511; www.simsim-backpackers.com; 6132 St; dm excl breakfast 70NIS) Opened in 2014, this attractive guesthouse has 23 dorm beds (mostly bunks), seven of them in an all-female room. Amenities include kitchen facilities. Great value. Reception is down the block at Samira Guesthouse.

Vitrage Guesthouse   B&B $
(☑052 722 8424, 04-657 5163; www.vitrage-guest house.com; No 4 6083 St; dm/s/d/tr without bathroom 70/120/200/220; 🅿🅰) More a homestay than a B&B, with nine simply furnished rooms that were renovated in 2013. Bishara, the retired *vitrage* ('stained glass' in French) artisan who runs the place with his wife, grew up here – and, in fact, was baptised in the garden pool. Superb value.

Sisters of Nazareth Guest House   GUESTHOUSE $
(☑04-655 4304; 6167 St; dm/s/d/tr excl breakfast 75/220/260/330NIS) Set around a flowery courtyard with archaeological excavations underneath, this 46-room establishment, in a building that dates from 1855, is run by the Sisters of Nazareth, a French Catholic order. Dorm beds (16 for men, six for women) are in spotless, barrackslike rooms. The gate is locked for the night at 10.30pm sharp.

Breakfast costs 25NIS. Reservations are possible up to three weeks ahead; walk-ins are welcome.

★ Fauzi Azar Inn   GUESTHOUSE $$
(☑04-602 0469; www.fauziazarinn.com; dm 90NIS, d 350-500NIS; 🅿@🅰) Hidden away in a gorgeous, two-century-old stone house in the Old City, this place has oodles of charm – and so do the staff. The 14 rooms are simple but tasteful, though they're no match for the lounge's arched windows, marble floors and 5m-high

frescoed ceiling. A great place to meet other travellers – or to volunteer (see website).

Anyone with a passport stamp from Lebanon, Iraqi Kurdistan or Iran gets the first night free. A load of laundry costs 15NIS.

★ Al-Mutran Guest House
GUESTHOUSE $$

(📞 04-645 7947; www.al-mutran.com; Bishop's Sq; d US$108-128, ste US$220; 🟦 @ 🛜) Adjacent to the residence of Nazareth's Greek Orthodox *mutran* ('bishop' in Arabic), this family-run gem occupies a gorgeous, 200-year-old mansion with 4.5m-high ceilings, Ottoman arches and antique floor tiles. Nonguests are welcome to drop by the stylish lobby, with its Ottoman pillows and Bedouin textiles, for a coffee (7NIS).

Samira Guesthouse
GUESTHOUSE $$

(📞 077-551 7275; www.samira-guesthouse.com; 6089 St; d/q excl breakfast 400/580NIS; @ 🛜) This delightful, five-room guesthouse, in a marble-floored building from the 1860s, is run by Nazareth-born Sami – a great source of information about the city – and Stuttgart-born Silke. The rooftop balcony is great for chilling out. Breakfast costs 20NIS. Accepts volunteers.

Abu Saeed Hostel
GUESTHOUSE $$

(📞 04-646 2799; www.abusaeedhostel.com; 6097 St; dm excl breakfast 80NIS, d/tr 350/430NIS, r without bathroom 250NIS; 🟦 🛜) Staying here is like being the guest of a local family in their slightly chaotic, 350-year-old house, outfitted with two ancient cisterns, hand-me-down furniture, a family 'museum' and a plant-filled courtyard whose residents include a land turtle, goldfish and lovebirds. Showers are basic. Has a chill-out area on the roof.

AlReda Guesthouse
B&B $$$

(📞 04-608 4404; 21 Al-Bishara St; d/tr/q 800/900/1000NIS; 🟦) On the top floor of an Ottoman mansion, this vast, all-wood studio apartment affords breathtaking views. Unbelievably romantic!

🍴 Eating & Drinking

Connoisseurs around Israel and beyond know that Nazareth's dining scene has become so drop-dead delicious in recent years that it's worth staying the night (or weekend) for. The buzzword is 'fusion', with European-inspired dishes pimped with local seasonings and then served – with an extra helping of Arab hospitality – in atmospheric Old City mansions. Traditional Levantine specialities, tweaked for the Nazareth palate, are another highlight. Portions are copious.

Also famous are Nazareth's hummus joints, Oriental pastry shops, tahina (look for Al-Arz brand) and Kewar, the local arak (anise liqueur).

Friday is Nazareth's big night out so booking ahead is a good idea; restaurants may also be crowded on Thursday night and Saturday (lunch and dinner). Locals tend to eat late, often beginning dinner at 9pm or even 10pm. Wine, beer and spirits are widely available in Christian areas.

Many of Nazareth's trendiest spots for dining and sipping can be found at or around Church Sq, the focal point of the city's flourishing nightlife zone.

★ Abu Ashraf
HUMMUS $

(Diwan al-Saraya; 6134 St; mains 20NIS; ⊙ 8am-8pm Mon-Sat, noon-3pm or 4pm Sun; 🍴) This old-time hummus joint and coffeehouse (the beans are roasted on the premises) is famous all over town for its *katayef* (sweet pancakes folded over Umm Ashraf's goat's cheese or cinnamon walnuts, then doused with geranium syrup; three for 12NIS, including coffee or tea 19NIS). Has excellent vegetable salads. Ebullient owner Abu Ashraf loves to share stories about Nazareth.

Felafel Abu Haani Jabali
FELAFEL $

(Church Sq; felafel 15NIS; ⊙ 10am-midnight Mon-Sat, 5pm-midnight Sun; 🍴) Superfresh felafel since 1968.

Al-Taboun
MIDDLE EASTERN $

(Paulus VI St; ⊙ 9am-10pm daily; 🍴) The decor is unspeakably tacky, but the shwarma (28NIS), hummus (20NIS) and veggie salad-and-starters spread (25NIS, as a side dish 18NIS) are tops.

Mama Salt Room & Cafe
CAFE $

(📞 04-637 7807; 6089 St; cakes 20-25NIS; ⊙ 8am-8pm Mon-Sat; 🛜) Decorated with colourful photos by local artists, this mellow cafe serves sandwiches, fresh-squeezed juices and homemade baked goods, including brownies and pecan pie. The floor, ceiling and walls of a side room are coated with salt; breathing in the air for 50 minutes (40 minutes for children; 140NIS) is said to be healthful for people with respiratory problems such as asthma.

Situated one block northeast of the post office.

Souq
MARKET $

(Market Sq & 6152 St; ⊙ 8am-3pm Mon-Sat) Fruit, veggies, bread and even pita pizzas (6NIS) are on sale along the narrow, winding alleys of the Old City's market.

Muhtar Sweets
SWEETS $

(Paulus VI St; per kilogram 70NIS, with pistachios 80NIS; ⊙9am-11pm) A brightly lit sweets emporium that could be in Beirut or Cairo. Has a huge selection of mouthwatering baklava and superb *kunafeh* (a hot, thin, syrupy cheese cake; 10NIS).

Mahroum Sweets
SWEETS $

(www.mahroum-baklawa.com; cnr Paulus VI & Al-Bishara Sts; per kilogram 85NIS; ⊙8.30am-11pm) Run by the same family since 1890, this is one of the best places in Israel for baklava and other syrup-soaked Arab pastries, as well as *kunafeh* and Turkish delight.

Tishreen
MEDITERRANEAN $$

(⏰04-608 4666; 56 Al-Bishara St; mains 49-105NIS; ⊙10am-11pm; ⏹) The wood-fired oven at this homey restaurant, adorned with antiques and wine bottles, turns out Arab- and Mediterranean-inspired dishes such as aubergine stuffed with pesto and cheese, as well as excellent muhammar (Arab pizza topped with chicken and onion). Also worth trying: freekeh (cracked green wheat), a traditional Galilean dish; tabouleh; and breakfast.

Sudfeh
FUSION $$

(⏰04-656 6611; No 35 6083 St; mains 46-110NIS; ⊙noon-midnight Mon-Sat, may open Sun evening) Traditional Nazarene cuisine, a few dishes of North African inspiration and original creations such as shrimp baked with tahina, onions, ginger and arak – made with only the finest local ingredients – are served either in an enchanting inner courtyard or under Ottoman-era arches and vaults. Has live music (Arabic, jazz, Western classical) on most Thursdays and some Saturdays from 8.30pm.

Sudfeh means 'coincidence', a reference to the serendipity of encountering new people, unfamiliar music and undreamt-of flavours.

Olga
FUSION $$

(⏰04-656 7755; No 57, 6057 St; ⊙11am-11pm) This modern, airy establishment serves European, American and Arab dishes in a 200-year-old former school, presided over by the legendary Principal Olga for 42 years. Has garden seating and, upstairs, a sleek, modern bar with floor-to-ceiling windows.

★AlReda
FUSION $$$

(⏰04-608 4404; 21 Al-Bishara St; mains 60-128NIS; ⊙1pm-2am Mon-Sat, 7pm-2am Sun; ⏹)

In a 200-year-old Ottoman-era mansion, this atmospheric restaurant – the songs of Umm Kalthoum are on high rotation after 8pm – serves traditional Nazarene recipes with a Mediterranean twist. Specialities include seasonal dishes made with okra (*bamya*) and wild thistle (*akub*), and fresh artichoke hearts filled with chopped beef and pine nuts (owner Daher Zeidani loves nuts of all sorts).

Guests are encouraged to share portions in order to taste different dishes. Has a bar.

🛍 Shopping

★Elbabour
FOOD

(Galilee Mill; ⏰04-645 5596; www.elbabour.com; entrances on Al-Bishara St & Paulus VI St; per 100g 20NIS; ⊙8.30am-7pm or 7.30pm Mon-Sat) The otherworldly aroma inside this spice emporium, run by the same family for four generations, has to be inhaled to be believed. Shelves, sacks, bins and bottles display more than 2500 products, from exotic spice mixtures (including Pierina's Spice, based on a secret recipe passed down by owner Tony's mother) to herbal teas, and from dried fruits to aromatic oils.

The name is the local pronunciation of *al-vapeur* ('the steam' in Arabicised French), the name given in the 1890s to the steam engine that once ran the company's infernally noisy, German-made flour mill.

Shababik
CRAFTS

(⏰04-645 9747; Bishop's Sq; ⊙8am-10pm) Sells one-of-a-kind crafts from Nazareth and nearby villages, local Musmar pottery, embroidery from Ramallah and Bethlehem, and handmade jewellery. The name means 'windows', as in 'windows open to the world'. It's inside Al-Mutran Guest House.

Cactus Gallery
CRAFTS

(www.nazarethcactus.com; Mary's Well Sq; ⊙9am-7pm Mon-Sat) The shop above Nazareth's sensational Roman-era ancient bathhouse (p188) sells creative modern jewellery and gorgeous Palestinian embroidery, made in a convent in Jerusalem.

Sport HaMa'ayan
OUTDOOR EQUIPMENT

(⏰052 353 5362; Paulus VI St; ⊙9am-7.30pm Mon-Sat) If you'll be camping along the Jesus Trail or on the shores of the Sea of Galilee, this is a good place to buy inexpensive sleeping bags (70NIS to 100NIS), tents (100NIS to 150NIS) and travel mattresses (30NIS to 70NIS). Situated 150m down Paulus VI St from Mary's Well.

1

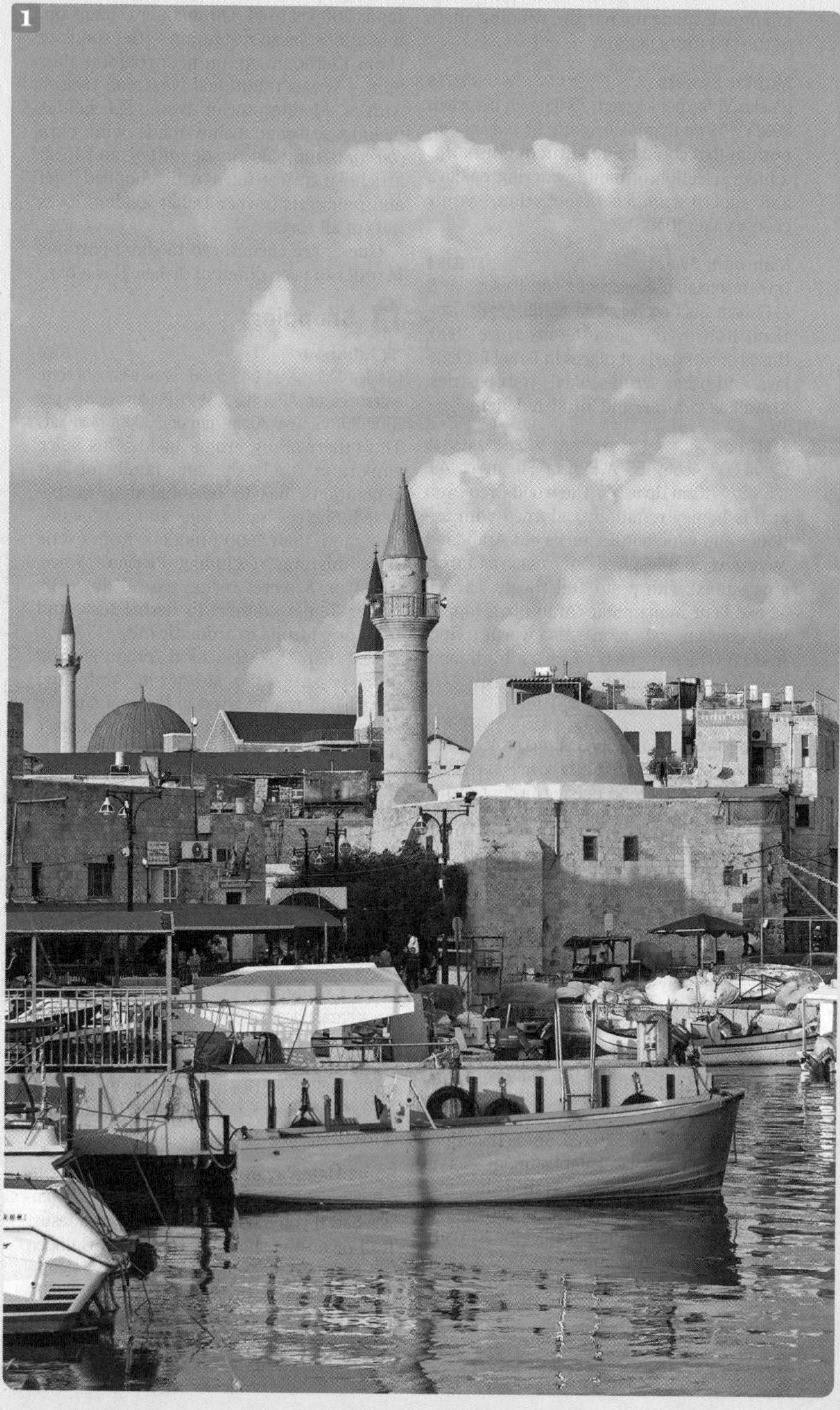

KORD.COM / GETTY IMAGES ©

HANAN ISACHAR / GETTY IMAGES ©

1. Akko (p175)
Green-domed mosques and church towers serve as a backdrop to colourful fishing boats in the marina.

2. Tiberias (p201)
Resort town and holy city, Tiberias is a mishmash of architecture, beliefs and beaches.

3. Basilica of the Annunciation (p185)
Christmas lights are displayed at the basilica believed by many to stand on the site of Mary's home.

4. Sea of Galilee (p208)
Israel's largest freshwater lake.

FREDFROESE / GETTY IMAGES ©

ℹ️ Orientation

Nazareth's main commercial thoroughfare is Paulus VI St, a traffic nightmare that runs roughly north-to-south along the eastern edge of the Old City. Almost parallel Al-Bishara (Annunciation) St, the main road through the Old City, links Mary's Well Sq with the Basilica of the Annunciation. Most guesthouses are situated along the narrow, pedestrians-only alleyways west of Al-Bishara St.

ℹ️ Information

There are several ATMs near the Basilica of the Annunciation. Bank HaPoalim is on Paulus VI St, while Bank Discount is at City Sq.

Cash and travellers cheques can be changed at the **post office** (6089 St) and at several exchange places on Paulus VI St.

Al-Mutran Guest House (Bishop's Sq; per hr 15NIS) Has wi-fi and an internet computer.

Ministry of Tourism Information Office (☑ 04-657 0555; www.goisrael.com; 58 Casanova St; ☺ 8.30am-5pm Mon-Fri, 9am-5pm Sat) Has brochures about Nazareth and the Galilee in 10 languages.

Nazareth Cultural & Tourism Association (www.nazarethinfo.org) Has a useful website. Publishes *Nazareth Today*, a free monthly magazine with feature articles and listings; Arabic, Hebrew and English versions are available in hotels and restaurants.

Police (☑ emergency 100; 6089 St) In the Moskubiya, a Russian pilgrims hostel built in 1904.

ℹ️ Getting There & Away

BUS

Nazareth does not have a proper bus station. Rather, intercity buses stop along traffic-plagued Paulus VI St between Mary's Well and the Basilica of the Annunciation – on the north-

---

VISITING JENIN

The Gilboa Regional Council, in the Jezreel Valley, and the municipality of the West Bank city of Jenin are working together to improve cross-border 'peace tourism', especially for Christian pilgrims. Travel to/from the Jenin area of the northern West Bank, through the Separation Barrier, is via the Israel Defence Forces' **Jalameh (Gilboa) crossing** (www.cogat.idf.il/1362-en/Cogat.aspx), 10km south of Afula along Rte 60.

---

bound side for Kafr Kana, Tiberias and Akko (Acre), on the southbound side for Haifa, Tel Aviv and Jerusalem. One bus company, **Nazarene Transport & Tourism** (Paulus VI St; ☺ 5.30am-6.30pm), has an office in town.

Tiberias (Nazareth Tourism & Transport bus 431, 19NIS, one hour, hourly except Friday evening and Saturday) Some buses stop on Nazareth's ring road, Rte 75, instead of on Paulus VI St.

Akko (Egged bus 343, 31.50NIS, 1½ hours, hourly except Saturday)

Haifa (Merkazit HaMifratz and/or Merkaz HaShmona Train Station, buses 331 and 339, shared by Nazareth Tourism & Transport and GB Tours, 17.20NIS, one hour, twice an hour Sunday to Friday, hourly Saturday)

Jerusalem (Egged bus 955, 40NIS, two hours, twice in the morning Sunday to Thursday, one Friday, two Saturday night)

Tel Aviv (Egged bus 826, 36NIS, 2¼ hours, several times an hour) Stops on Rte 75.

To get to Kfar Tavor and the base of Mt Tabor, you have to change in Afula (20 minutes) – take hourly Kavim bus 356 from Rte 75.

Buses to Amman are run by **Nazarene Tours** (☑ in Israel 04-601 0458, in Jordan 079-692 7455; Paulus VI St, Nazareth).

SHERUT

Sheruts (shared taxis) leave from 4066 St, just off Paulus VI St (across the street from Nazarene Transport & Tourism) – look for a tiny **office** (☑ 04-657 1140; 4066 St) on the right with a faded red-on-white sign in Arabic and Hebrew.

Destinations include:

➡ **Tel Aviv** (Central Bus Station, 32NIS Sunday to Friday morning, 40NIS Friday afternoon and Saturday, 1½ hours, departures 5am or 6am to 4pm)

➡ **Jenin (West Bank)** (25NIS, 40 minutes, departures 8am to 4pm or 5pm) Via the Jalameh (Gilboa) crossing, 10km south of Afula.

TAXI

Cabs can be ordered from **Mary's Well Taxi** (☑ 04-656 0035, 04-655 5105).

KAFR KANA   כפר כנא كفر كنا
☑ 04

About 8km northeast of central Nazareth on the road to Tiberias (and on the Jesus Trail), the Arab town of Kafr Kana (Cana) is believed to be the site of Jesus's first miracle (John 2:1-11), when he changed water into wine at a wedding reception. About 10% of the population is Christian.

◉ Sights

Most of Kafr Kana's Christian sights are on or near stone-paved Churches St, which intersects the main road through town (Rte 754) at an oblique angle, at a point just north of a special parking lane on the eastern side of the street. The intersection is marked by a large white-on-black sign.

Cana Catholic Wedding Church   CHURCH
(Churches St; ◷ 8am-5.30pm Mon-Sat, noon-5.30pm Sun) This late-19th-century, green-domed Franciscan church stands on the site believed by Catholics to be that of Jesus's miracle at a wedding. In the basement is an ancient jar that may have been among the six used by Jesus when he turned water into wine. Under the church floor, through a glass tile, you can see an ancient Jewish inscription in Aramaic.

**Cana Greek Orthodox
Wedding Church**   CHURCH
(First Miracle Church; Rte 754; ◷ 9am-5pm) This richly decorated, late-19th-century church – topped by a copper-brown dome – shelters two ancient jars believed to have been used by Jesus to perform the wedding miracle. Visitors are welcome to come and see the church scout troop's **drum and bagpipe band** practice on Friday and Saturday from 5pm to 7pm.

⌊ Sleeping

Cana Guest House   GUESTHOUSE $
(☏ 04-651 7186, Su'ad 052 409 8001; www.canaguesthouse.com; dm/d/tr/q excl breakfast 120/300/430/500NIS; ☀ @ ☎) The welcoming Billan family has turned four apartments into 18 comfortable, clean rooms, many quite spacious, some with private bathroom. Guests can use the kitchen and hang out in the lemon-tree-shaded courtyard. Dorms have three or four beds. Breakfast costs 35NIS, a packed lunch 35NIS and a hearty, home-cooked dinner 70NIS. Situated behind the Cana Catholic Wedding Church compound.

❶ Getting There & Away

Lots of short-haul buses, including 24, 26, 27, 28, 29, 30 and 31, connect Kafr Kana with Nazareth, 8km to the southwest; most buses go to Paulus VI St in Nazareth's Old City. A sherut to/from Nazareth's Paulus VI St costs 8NIS.

Nazareth Tourism & Transport's bus 431 (hourly except Friday evening and Saturday) links Kafr Kana with both Tiberias (19NIS, 30 minutes) and Nazareth (8.80NIS, 20 minutes); most, but not all, stop on Paulus VI St.

TZIPORI   צִיפּוֹרִי صفورية
📖04

Now one of Israel's most impressive archaeological sites, **Tzipori National Park** (Zippori, Sepphoris; www.parks.org.il; adult/child 29/15NIS; ◷ 8am-5pm daylight-saving time, to 4pm winter time, closes 1hr earlier Fri, last entry 1hr before closing) was, in ancient times, a prosperous and well-endowed city with stone-paved roadways (rutted over time by wagons and chariots), an amazing water-supply system, a marketplace, bathhouses, synagogues, churches and a 4500-seat theatre. For many modern visitors, though, the star attraction is a mosaic portrait of a contemplative young woman nicknamed the **Mona Lisa of the Galilee**, one of several superb early-3rd-century mosaics discovered here in the 1980s.

In the 2nd and 3rd centuries CE – a generation or two after the Bar Kochba Revolt (132 CE to 135 CE) against Rome – Tzipori was one of the most important centres of Jewish life in Israel. It was here that Rabbi Yehuda HaNassi is believed to have redacted the Mishnah (the earliest codification of Jewish law), and later on Tzipori scholars contributed to the Jerusalem (Palestinian) Talmud.

⌊ Sleeping

Zippori Village Country Cottages   B&B $$
(☏ 04-646 2647; www.zippori.com; Moshav Tzipori; d without breakfast from 400NIS; ☀ ☎ ☀) Run by the knowledgeable Suzy and Mitch, the spacious cottages here come with gorgeous Galilean views, comfortable cane furniture, cheerful decoration and a hot tub. The well-equipped kitchenettes are kosher dairy. Breakfast costs 100NIS for two.

❶ Getting There & Away

The village of Tzipori and Tzipori National Park are 11km northwest of Nazareth, a few kilometres north of Rte 79. There's no public transport.

MT TABOR AREA
📖04

Rising from the Jezreel Valley like an enormous breast, remarkably symmetrical Mt Tabor (588m) dominates the landscape between Nazareth and the Sea of Galilee.

Mt Tabor הר תבור جبل الطور

You don't have to be a Christian pilgrim to enjoy the beauty of Mt Tabor, the biblical site of the Transfiguration of Jesus (Matthew 17:1-9, Mark 9:2-8 and Luke 9:28-36), in which 'his face became as dazzling as the sun; his clothes as radiant as light' and he spoke with the prophets Moses and Elijah. Two compounds crown the mountain, one Catholic (Franciscan), the other Greek Orthodox (closed to the public).

According to the Hebrew Bible, Mt Tabor was where the Israelites, led by the prophetess Deborah, defeated a Canaanite army under the command of Sisera (Judges 4).

The mountain was much contested during the Crusader period. The Benedictine monks of that era would have been astounded to hear that one day it would be used to launch hang-gliders.

◉ Sights & Activities

Franciscan Monastery & Church   CHURCH
(◷ 8-11.30am & 2-5pm) An avenue of cypresses leads through this Catholic compound to a monastery, home to three Franciscan monks, a small garden of plants from around the world, the ruins of a Byzantine-era monastery, and the Roman Syrian–style **Basilica of the Transfiguration**, one of the Holy Land's most beautiful churches. Consecrated in 1924, it is decorated with lovely mosaics and has a crypt reached by 12 broad steps. Women are asked to dress modestly (no sleeveless shirts or miniskirts).

Up to the right from the entrance to the church, a **viewing platform** offers spectacular views of the Jezreel Valley's multihued patchwork of fields.

Hiking Trails   HIKING
The **Israel National Trail** goes up and over Mt Tabor, intersecting two marked trails that circumnavigate the mountain: **Shvil HaYa'aranim** and, up near the summit, the recently upgraded **Sovev Har Tavor** (Mt Tabor Circuit). The topographical map to have is SPNI Map No 3 (HaGalil HaTachton HaAmakim v'HaGilboa).

ⓘ Getting There & Away

Mt Tabor is about midway between Tiberias and Afula, just off Rte 65. From Rte 7266 – which goes all the way around the base of the mountain, connecting the Arab villages of Shibli and Daburiyeh with Rte 65 – it's a teeth-clenching 3km ride (with 16 hairpin turns) up to the summit.

Kfar Tavor כפר תבור كفر تافور

Founded in 1901, the Jewish village of Kfar Tavor is the area's main commercial and tourism hub.

◉ Sights & Activities

Tabor Winery   WINERY
(☎ 04-676 0444; www.twc.co.il; Kfar Tavor Industrial Zone; ◷ to 4pm Fri) Known for its reds (merlot, cabernet sauvignon, shiraz, cabernet franc) and whites (chardonnay, sauvignon blanc, roussanne and gewurztraminer), this well-regarded winery produces two million bottles a year. Offers free tastings and sales and, for groups of 10 or more, tours.

From late July to August, the winery runs 1½-hour **grape harvests** (child/accompanying adult 30/20NIS; ◷ 10am Sun-Fri) for children aged three and up. After using pruning shears and baskets to pick bunches of grapes, the kids stomp on them (yes, with their feet and yes, feet are washed first!) to turn them into juice, which they then bottle and take home. Reserve ahead.

Trails   HIKING, CYCLING
Kfar Tavor and nearby villages such as Kfar Kisch make a great base for hiking along the **Israel National Trail** and a spur of the **Jesus Trail** – for instance, northeast to the Yardenit baptism site on the Sea of Galilee or west up Mt Tabor. Sections of both trails are cyclable. For cyclists there's also a single track through **Beit Keshet Forest** and some fine routes on the **Sirrin Heights**.

✕ Eating

Cafederatzia   CAFE $$
(☎ 04-676 6233; 82 HaMeyadsim St; mains 38-62NIS; ◷ 8.30am-midnight Sun-Thu, to 4pm Fri, 10am-midnight Sat; ✎) This stylish cafe serves generous salads, pasta, gourmet sandwiches, hamburgers, roast beef and boutique hot dogs. In good weather you can eat outside in the olive-tree garden. Also offers gluten-free bread, homemade baked goods and local wines by the glass (from 25NIS). Breakfast costs 58NIS. Situated in the village centre, next to the library, post office and council building.

ⓘ Getting There & Away

Lots of buses, including Kavim line 43 and Egged lines 442, 541 and 542, link Kfar Tavor (the stops are on Rte 65) with Afula (16.80NIS, seven to 17 hourly, 25 minutes). From there, there are frequent buses to Tel Aviv, Beit She'an and Nazareth's ring road (Rte 75), a short bus or sherut ride (6NIS) from Paulus VI St. To get to Tiberias (19NIS, 35 minutes, two or three an hour), take Egged buses 442 and 541, among others.

Kfar Kisch   כפר קיש   كفر كيش

Surrounded by open fields where gazelles are a common sight, this moshav (cooperative settlement), 6km southeast of Kfar Tavor, is on both the Israel National Trail and a spur of the Jesus Trail.

🛏 Sleeping

Tabor Land Guest House   B&B **$$**
(✆050-544 1972; www.taborland.com; s/d excl breakfast 280/400NIS, d without bathroom 350NIS; ✻🏠) You're ensured a warm welcome at this two-storey villa. The four bedrooms (one with direct bathroom access) are homey, and the spacious living room will make you feel like a guest at a friend's house. A copious Israeli breakfast costs 50NIS per person. Owner Sarah is happy to take travellers on short walks of the area.

Situated 6km east of Rte 65 in Kfar Kisch's new neighbourhood, out past the petrol pump.

🍴 Eating

⭐**Shirat Ro'im**   CHEESE **$$**
(www.shiratroim.co.il; ⏱9.30am or 10am-4.30pm Fri, Sat & Jewish holidays, to 6pm daylight-saving time) Michal's award-winning cheeses – including Inbar, delicately flavoured with rosemary; Kinneret, an unbelievable blue; and Nirit, sprinkled with chestnut ash – astound even veteran foodies, leaving them gasping for superlatives.

Havat HaYatzranim   CHEESE **$$**
(✆052 250 6203; www.havat.co.il; cheese meals for 2 118NIS, cheese per kilogram 220NIS; ⏱9.30am-sundown Fri, Sat & holidays) This cheese shop and restaurant sells 19 types of cheese, including Katshota, Tomme, Valencia and St-Maur, and offers free tastings of varietal olive oils, the best sun-dried almonds you've ever encountered, and four boutique wines so exclusive that only one barrel (300 bottles) of each is made per year. Housed in a one-time chicken coop.

Sirrin   FRENCH **$$$**
(✆04-676 0976; mains 85-135NIS, 15% off noon-5pm except Fri & Sat; ⏱noon-9.30pm or later Sun & Tue-Thu, from 9am Fri & Sat) Inspired by a long-ago meal in Paris' St-Germain-des-Prés, this family-run restaurant, its decor evocative of the belle époque, specialises in French- and Italian-inflected steak (locally sourced) and fish; the goat and sheep cheeses come from France, Italy and Israel. Children's portions cost 35NIS to 45NIS. Breakfast (75NIS) is available on Friday and Saturday.

ℹ Getting There & Away

Kavim bus 42 links Kfar Kisch with Afula (16.80NIS, 35 minutes, five or six daily Sunday to Friday).

Kfar Kama   כפר כמא   كفر كما

As the Russian empire expanded southward in the mid-1800s, at least half a million Circassians (a Caucasian people of the Muslim faith) were forced out of their homes in the northern Caucasus – between the Black and Caspian Seas – and found refuge in the Ottoman lands. In 1876 some of them settled in Kfar Kama (population 3100), one of only two Circassian villages in Israel (the other is Rehaniya). The Circassians have always enjoyed good relations with their Jewish neighbours, and all Circassian men – long famed as fierce warriors – are drafted into the Israel Defense Forces (IDF). Signs around the prosperous town are in Hebrew, Circassian (spoken at home and taught in school) and English.

◉ Sights

Circassian Heritage Center   MUSEUM
(✆050 585 7640; www.circassianmuseum.co.il; adult/child 25/20NIS; ⏱9am-5pm) Housed in a complex of century-old basalt houses, this modest museum features a 20-minute film (in Hebrew, Arabic and English), traditional Circassian clothing and antique agricultural implements. Admission includes a tour in English. To get there from the eastern entrance to Kfar Kama (on Rte 767), follow the signs to 'Shami House'.

🍴 Eating

Cherkessia   CIRCASSIAN **$$**
(✆04-676 9608, 050 261 9996; Rte 767; 7-dish meal 57NIS; ⏱noon-9pm Sun-Thu, 10am-9pm Fri & Sat; 🍴) Run by a mother-and-son team, this Circassian restaurant's specialities include lentil soup, *haluzh* (a deep-fried crêpe filled with homemade Circassian cheese) and *mataza* (boiled ravioli stuffed with Circassian cheese and green onion). In a private

house 100m west along the frontage road from the western entrance to Kfar Kama (on Rte 767); look for a Cyrillic sign.

JEZREEL & BEIT SHE'AN VALLEYS עמק יזרעאל עמק בית שאן

مرج ابن عامر مرج بيسان

♪ 04

Stretching for about 45km from a bit west of Nazareth southeast to the Jordan River, the largely agricultural Jezreel Valley (also known as the Plain of Esdraelon) and the Beit She'an Valley, part of the Great Rift Valley, are bounded on the south by Mt Gilboa.

Beit She'an بيسان בית שאן

Founded sometime in the 5th millennium BCE, Beit She'an – strategically situated at the intersection of the Jezreel Valley and the Jordan Valley – has the most extensive Roman-era ruins in Israel. It was levelled in the massive earthquake of 749 CE. The struggling modern town (population 17,200) has little to offer the visitor.

◉ Sights

★ Beit She'an
National Park   ARCHAEOLOGICAL SITE
(☑04-658 7189; Rte 90; adult/child 40/24NIS; ☺8am-4pm Oct-Mar, to 5pm Apr-Sep, closes 1hr earlier Fri, last entry 30min before closing) Beit She'an's extraordinary Roman ruins are the best place in Israel to get a sense of what it was like to live, work and shop in the Roman Empire. Colonnaded streets, a 7000-seat theatre that looks much as it did 1800 years ago (the original public bathrooms are nearby), two bathhouses and huge stone columns that lie right where they fell during the 749 earthquake evoke the grandeur, self-confidence and decadence of Roman provincial life in the centuries after Jesus.

The path to the theatre and the Cardo, the hugely impressive colonnaded main street, is wheelchair accessible.

REALLY, REALLY HOT

The hottest temperature ever recorded anywhere in Asia, a sizzling 53.9°C (129°F), was registered at Kibbutz Tirat Tzvi (8km south of Beit She'an) on 21 June 1942.

Towering over the Roman city, known in Greek as Scythopolis, is Tel Beit She'an, created by at least 20 cities built and rebuilt one on top of the other. The viewpoint atop offers near-aerial views of the Roman ruins.

She'an Nights (Leilot She'an; ☑04-648 3639, 04-648 1122; adult/child 55/45NIS; ☺sundown Mon-Thu approximately Apr-Nov), an after-dark multimedia spectacular in English or Hebrew, brings alive the ruins with projected images but is not a satisfactory substitute for a daylight visit – it's too dark to read the signs and most of the site is off-limits. The show is cancelled if it rains. Call ahead for reservations.

To get to the park entrance, head down the hill for a few hundred metres from the Bank Leumi branch at 81 Sha'ul HaMelech St.

🛏 Sleeping & Eating

HI – Beit She'an Guest House   HOSTEL $$
(☑02-594 5644; www.iyha.org.il; 129 Menahem Begin Ave/Rte 90; s/d 385/510NIS, additional adult/child 160/125NIS; @🛜🏊) Within easy walking distance of Beit She'an's antiquities, this 62-room hostel has attractive public areas, a great rooftop patio and a pool (open April to September). Rooms are practical and clean and have five beds; individual dorm beds are not available. Situated a bit south of the intercity bus stops. Wheelchair accessible.

Shipudei HaKikar   MIDDLE EASTERN $$
(☑04-606 0198; 1 Shaul HaMelech St; mains 34-120NIS; ☺11.30am-midnight Sun-Thu, from 30min after sundown-midnight Sat, closed Fri; ☑) Widely acclaimed as Beit She'an's best restaurant. Excellent shish kebab (60NIS to 120NIS) is served with freshly baked laffa (flat pita) – and is preceded by 18 superfresh salads, including eggplant, hummus and tahina. If you're not ordering a main, the salads cost 26NIS – a superb veggie meal! Grilled meat in laffa or a baguette, without salads, costs 34NIS to 50NIS.

Situated 1km northwest of the Roman antiquities in a buiding with a clock tower on top (just past the police station).

ℹ Getting There & Away

Beit She'an doesn not have a proper bus station. Rather, buses stop along Menahem Begin Ave, aka Rte 90, about 100m north of the Beit She'an Guest House (youth hostel).

Tiberias (Afikim bus 28, 16.50NIS, 30 minutes, 15 daily Sunday to Thursday, six Friday, two

MT GILBOA

The rugged, 18km-long ridge known as Mt Gilboa (highest point 536m), which runs along the southern edge of the Jezreel Valley, makes for a great nature getaway. After the winter rains (December to March or April), the area is carpeted with wildflowers, including the purple Gilboa iris (blooms in late February and early March). According to the Bible, this was where King Saul and his son Jonathan were slain in battle with the Philistines (1 Samuel 31:1-13).

For a lovely hilltop drive with stupendous views of the Jezreel Valley (in the other direction, you can see the Palestinian villages around Jenin and, in the foreground, the Separation Fence between Israel and the West Bank), take 28km-long Rte 667 (Gilboa Scenic Rd), which links Rte 675 (8km southeast of Afula via Rte 71) with the Jordan Valley's Rte 90.

For a hearty, country-style meal in a rustic setting, head to the family-run **Herb Farm on Mt Gilboa** (☑04-653 1093; www.herb-farm.co.il; Rte 667; mains 67-135NIS; ☻noon-10pm Mon-Sat; ☑), which has both meat dishes (eg Cornish hen) and good veggie and vegan options. It's a good idea to reserve ahead on Friday and Saturday. Situated on Rte 667 3.5km southeast of Rte 675; follow the yellow signs to 'Country Restaurant'.

Saturday night) Has stops along the southwestern coast of the Sea of Galilee.

Jerusalem (Egged bus 961, 44NIS, two hours, six daily Sunday to Thursday, five Friday, three Saturday night) Via the Jordan Valley.

Afula (Kavim buses 411 and 412, 30 minutes, two or three times an hour except Friday evening and Saturday before sundown)

To get to Nazareth and Tel Aviv, change buses in Afula.

Travellers headed to Jordan can make use of the Jordan River/Sheikh Hussein border crossing, 8km east of town.

Belvoir כוכב הירדן حصن بلفوار

Set on a hilltop 550m above the Jordan River, this **Crusader fortress** (☑04-658 1766; www.parks.org.il; adult/child 22/10NIS; ☻8am-5pm Apr-Sep, to 4pm Oct-Mar, closes 1hr earlier Fri, last entry 1hr before closing), measuring an impressive 110m by 110m, consists of concentric ramparts, gates, courtyards and towers that afford spectacular views of the Jordan and Jezreel Valleys and Jordan's Gilead Mountains. Highlights include a dining room topped by a Gothic vault, a huge stone cistern and, along the western side, a deep dry moat. It's noticeably cooler up here than in the valley below. There's excellent signage in English and Hebrew.

Built by the Knights Hospitaller starting in 1168, Belvoir ('beautiful view' in French; the Hebrew name, Kochav HaYarden, means 'star of the Jordan'; the Arabic name, Kawkab al-Hawa, means 'star of the wind') was forced to surrender to Muslim forces in 1189

after a 1½-year siege. The defenders were permitted to retreat to Tyre unharmed, in acknowledgment of their courage.

The panoramic, 1.2km-long **Wingate Trail**, outlined with rocks, goes along the slope below the ruins. Posted maps explain what you're seeing on both sides of the border, including details on local plate tectonics and the route of the pre-1948 oil pipeline from Kirkuk (Iraq) to Haifa.

Next to the ruins stands a **sculpture garden** of works – made of cut steel plates – by the award-winning Israeli artist Yigal (Igael) Tumarkin (b 1933), creator of the Holocaust memorial at Tel Aviv's Rabin Sq.

Belvoir is 20km north of Beit She'an and 20km south of the Sea of Galilee, 6km off Rte 90 along a one-lane road.

Beit Alpha Synagogue
בית הכנסת בית אלפא كنيس بيت الفا

No one was more surprised than the members of Kibbutz Heftzibah when they went to dig an irrigation channel in 1928 and uncovered a Byzantine-era mosaic floor. Further excavation revealed the rest of the **Beit Alpha Synagogue** (www.parks.org.il; adult/child 22/10NIS; ☻8am-5pm daylight-saving time, 8am-4pm winter, closes 1hr earlier Fri), whose mosaics are extraordinarily evocative of ages past.

The three mosaic panels depict traditional Jewish symbols such as a Torah ark, two menorahs (seven-branched candelabras) and a shofar (ram's horn) alongside a spectacular, 12-panel **zodiac circle**, a pagan element if there ever was one. At the bottom, above inscriptions in Aramaic and Hebrew, Jacob (holding a knife) is shown about to sacrifice his son Isaac, alongside the ram that God (represented by a hand from heaven) sent to be sacrificed in the boy's stead; each character is labelled in Hebrew. A 14-minute film (in six languages), projected above and onto the mosaic, provides an excellent introduction. Wheelchair accessible.

Up the hill from the synagogue, inside Kibbutz Heftzibah, is something unexpected: a lovely little Shinto-style **Japanese garden** (☑ Na'ama 054 663 4348; tour adult/child 20/10NIS) with a serene koi pond, built by members of the Makoya, a Japanese Christian movement whose members have been studying Hebrew at the kibbutz since 1962. Call for a tour.

people's shirts and licking their neck sweat for its salt content. Opened in 1996, this fully accredited **zoo** (☑ 04-648 8060; http://www.nir tours.co.il/Gan_Garoo; Rte 669, Kibbutz Nir David; adult/child under 2yr 46NIS/free; ⊙ 9am-4pm Sun-Thu, to 3pm Fri, to 5pm Sat Sep-Jun, 9am-8pm Sat-Thu, to 3pm Fri Jul & Aug), run by Kibbutz Nir David, is also home to cassowaries, emus, flying foxes and Israel's only **koalas**.

Situated 6.5km west of Beit She'an, next to Sachne (Gan HaShlosha) National Park.

ⓘ Getting There & Away

Kibbutz Heftzibah is 8km west of Beit She'an along Rte 669. Kavim bus 412 (at least hourly except Friday night and during the day Saturday) goes both to Afula (17 minutes) and to Beit She'an (12 minutes).

Gangaroo Animal Park

פארק אוסטרלי 'גן גורו'
حديقة استرالية "جن جرو"

Kids will love this delightful little corner of Australia, where – amid Aussie vegetation – they can pet and feed friendly, free-range **kangaroos**. Another hit: in the aviary (open for 20 or 30 minutes every hour or two) they can feed apple slivers to colourful **lorikeets** and **cockatiels**; ever resourceful, the birds have developed a habit of hopping onto

Ein Harod   עין חרוד عين حرود

Ein Harod is actually two kibbutzim, torn apart 60 years ago by their shared socialist ideology.

⊙ Sights

Museum of Art, Ein Harod　MUSEUM
(Mishkan Le'Omanut; www.museumeinharod.org.il; Kibbutz Ein Harod Meuchad; adult/child 26/13NIS; ⊙ 9am-4.30pm Sun-Thu, to 1.30pm Fri, 10am-4.30pm Sat) Almost as remarkable for its

---

SOCIALIST PASSIONS

Life at Kibbutz Ein Harod, midway between Afula and Beit She'an (about 14km from each), carried on in relative tranquillity from its founding in 1921 until the very early 1950s. That was when an ideological dispute over Israeli Prime Minister David Ben-Gurion's strategic preference for the capitalist United States over the socialist Soviet Union flared into a full-fledged ideological conflagration. Complicating matters was the fact that, at the time, Stalin was staging anti-Semitic show trials in which prominent Jews were being accused of trumped-up counter-revolutionary crimes and then executed. Stalin's devotees at the kibbutz, who were of the 'you can't make an omelette without breaking a few eggs' school of hard-line socialism, stood by their man.

Passions flared – these were, after all, people who lived by their socialist ideals – and soon barricades went up in the dining hall, good friends stopped speaking to each other, fisticuffs were exchanged and couples broke up. Finally, Ein Harod split into two separate kibbutzim, Ein Harod Meuchad, run by the Stalin loyalists, and Ein Harod Ichud, under the control of the Ben-Gurionists (both *meuchad* and *ichud* mean 'united').

Resentments smouldered for decades, and even today some old-old-timers are angry about their rivals' craven betrayal. It was only 25 years ago that the first 'mixed' Ichud-Meuchad couple tied the knot, and just 15 years ago that agricultural and cultural co-operation between the two kibbutzim resumed. Today, Kibbutz Ein Harod Ichud – whose souces of income include wheat, cotton, milk cows and the production of ultra-advanced miniature cryocoolers – is still a traditional 'collective' kibbutz, while Kibbutz Ein Harod Meuchad, controlled by the hard left 60 years ago, has chosen the route of capitalist privatisation.

modernist building (inaugurated in 1948, with additions from the 1950s) as its outstanding art collection (over 16,000 works, mainly by Jewish and Israeli artists), this pioneering museum puts on highly regarded temporary exhibits (explanatory sheets available in English) in its 14 halls. Also has a permanent exhibition of Judaica. By car, take Rte 71 to Kibbutz Ein Harod Meuchad and follow the signs to 'Museums'.

🛏 Sleeping

★ **Ein Harod Guest House** GUESTHOUSE **$$**
(📞 04-648 6083; www.ein-harod.co.il; Kibbutz Ein Harod Ichud; d Sun-Wed from 490NIS, Thu-Sat from 570NIS, chalets 940-1300NIS, additional child 160NIS; 🕸@🛜🏊) Perched on a hilltop with clear-day views of Mt Carmel, Mt Hermon and the mountains of Gilead in Jordan, this 42-room guesthouse offers traditional kibbutz rooms and romantic wooden 'Iris' chalets with 50 sq metres of luxury. Amenities include a 50m swimming pool. By car, take Rte 716 to Kibbutz Ein Harod Ichud; the entrance is 1km north of Rte 71.

Tours of the kibbutz's agricultural branches are available on request.

TIBERIAS   טבריה   طبريا

📞 04 / POP 41,700

Tiberias is one of the four holy cities of Judaism, the burial place of venerated sages, and a very popular base for Christians visiting holy sites around the Sea of Galilee. It's also one of the most aesthetically challenged resort towns in Israel, its sunbaked lakeside strip marred by 1970s architectural monstrosities. So, not for the first time, the sacred and the kitsch – plus beaches and hot springs – coexist side by side in a whirl of holiness, hawkers and hedonism.

If you've got a car, the Golan, the Galilee panhandle, Beit She'an, Nazareth and even Akko are an hour or less away. Tiberias is often oppressively hot in July and August.

History

Tiberias' 17 hot springs have been luring pleasure seekers since well before 20 CE, when Herod Antipas, son of Herod the Great, founded the town and named it in honour of the Roman emperor Tiberias (r 14–37 CE).

After the Judeans' disastrous Bar Kochba Revolt (132–135 CE), Tiberias became one of the most important centres of Jewish life in

---

THE MONGOLS WERE HERE

The year was 1260, the place very near present-day Kibbutz Ein Harod. The belligerents were the mighty Mongol empire and the Egyptian Mamluks. In a cataclysmic clash known to history as the **Battle of Ein Jalut**, the Mongols were decisively and enduringly defeated for the first time in their history, bringing their expansion into the Middle East to a screeching halt.

Israel, playing a key role in the redefinition of Judaism after Temple sacrifices in Jerusalem were halted by the Roman victory of 70 CE. Some of the greatest post–Second Temple sages, including Yehuda HaNassi, chief editor of the Mishnah, lived here, and much of the redacting of the Jerusalem (Palestinian) Talmud also seems to have taken place in Tiberias. From the late 2nd century, the Sanhedrin (ancient Israel's supreme court) was based in the town. The system still used today to indicate vowel sounds in written Hebrew was developed in – and named after – Tiberias.

The Crusaders took Tiberias in 1099, building a massive fortress a bit north of the town's Roman-Byzantine centre. In 1187 Saladin captured the town and shortly thereafter devastated Crusader forces at the Horns of Hattin, 8km due west of Tiberias.

In 1558 the newly arrived Ottomans granted tax-collecting rights in the Tiberias area to Dona Gracia (www.donagracia project.org), a Lisbon-born Conversa (outwardly Catholic but secretly Jewish) woman who had found refuge from the Inquisition in Istanbul.

In the early 1700s a Bedouin sheikh named Daher al-Omar established an independent fiefdom in the Galilee, with Tiberias as its capital, and invited Jewish families to settle in the town. By the end of the Ottoman period, Jews constituted the great majority of Tiberias' 6500 residents.

Tiberias was almost completely demolished in the great earthquake of 1837.

⊙ Sights

⊙ Yigal Allon Promenade

Most of Tiberias' sights are along the boardwalk (of sorts) that runs along the lakefront. Parts are tacky and faded, and the area can

Tiberias

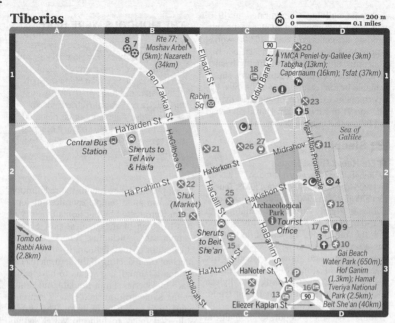

Tiberias

feel forlorn in winter, but the views of the Sea of Galilee and the Golan never get old. Sites below are listed from north to south.

Tiberias Open Air Museum PUBLIC ART
(HaYarden St; ⊙24hr) FREE A pedestrian park featuring creative modern sculptures. Some people's nostalgic favourite: a blow-up of a 1950s one-lira banknote. Situated along a walkway perpendicular to the shoreline.

St Peter's Church CHURCH
(📞04-672 0516; www.saintpeterstiberias.org; Yigal Allon Promenade; ⊙visits 8.30am-12.30pm & 2.30-5.30pm Mon-Sat, Mass in English 6.30pm Mon-Fri, 8.30am Sun) This rare Crusader church – administered by Koinonia Giovanni Battista, a Catholic community based in Italy – has a roof shaped like an upturned boat, a nod to Peter, a Sea of Galilee fisherman. The inter-

ior paintings date from 1902. A replica of the Vatican's famous statue of St Peter stands in the courtyard near the carved-stone **Monument to the Virgin of Czestochowa**, erected in 1945 by Polish soldiers billeted here during WWII. Runs a hostel for Catholic pilgrims.

Galilee Experience   FILM
(☑04-672 3620; www.thegalileeexperience.com; admission US$8; ⊗8.30am-10pm Sun-Thu, to 2pm Fri, 5-10pm Sat) On the upper floor of a 1970s monstrosity, the Galilee Experience screens a half-hour, Christian-oriented film on the history of Galilee.

Al-Bahr Mosque   MOSQUE
(Sea Mosque) Built of basalt in the 18th century, the Sea Mosque had a special entrance for the faithful who arrived by boat. This is one of the few reminders of the city's pre-1948 Arab community.

**Church & Monastery
of the Apostles**   CHURCH
(⊗8am-4pm Mon-Sat) From the peaceful, flowery courtyard, steps lead down to the church, its air of mystery enhanced by gilded icons, brass lamps and elaborately carved wood. The three chapels are dedicated to the 12 disciples, Sts Peter and Paul, and Mary Magdalene. To see if a monk is available to show you around, ring the bell high up on the right side of the red door 10m west of the overhead pedestrian bridge.

⊙ Tombs of Jewish Sages

Many of Tiberias' Jewish visitors are drawn to the city at least partly by the desire to pray – and ask for divine intercession – at graves believed to belong to some of Judaism's most eminent sages. If you were assembling an all-star team of the most influential Jewish thinkers of all time, the four rabbis mentioned below would certainly be on it.

**Tomb of Rabbi
Meir Ba'al HaNess**   RELIGIOUS SITE
(⊗6am-10pm or later Sun-Thu, in summer/winter to 5/3pm Fri) A complex of religious buildings has grown around the reputed burial place of Rabbi Meir Ba'al HaNess, a 2nd-century sage often cited in the Mishnah (*ba'al haness* means 'master of miracles'). The tomb itself, with separate, curtained entrances for men and women, is inside a domed Sephardi synagogue, situated just down the slope from its Ashkenazi counterpart, topped with a taller dome. The complex is 2.5km south

of the city centre, 200m up an asphalt road from Hamat Tveriya National Park.

Behind the Sephardi section, market stalls sell holy amulets, including specially blessed olive oil and arak.

Rabbi Meir's *hilula* (a celebration held by Hasidim on the anniversary of a sage's death) is just three days before that of Shimon Bar Yochai, who's buried at Mt Meron, so some pious Jews travel to the Galilee to take in both hugely popular events.

Tomb of the Rambam   RELIGIOUS SITE
(Ben Zakkai St; ⊗24hr) Rabbi Moshe Ben Maimon (1135–1204) was a Cordova-born polymath famous for his rationalist approach to religion and life (he was fond of quoting Aristotle). The nearby **Maimonides Heritage Center** (www.mhcny.org; ⊗10am-3pm Sun-Thu) has exhibits on the sage's life and writings.

The Rambam's most famous works are the *Mishneh Torah,* the first systematic codification of Jewish law; *Guide to the Perplexed,* a work of theology, written in Arabic, that is still hugely influential today; and various books on medicine (he served as the personal physician of the sultan of Egypt, where he spent the last decades of his life).

**Tomb of Rabbi
Yohanan ben Zakkai**   RELIGIOUS SITE
(Ben Zakkai St; ⊗24hr) Rabbi Yohanan ben Zakkai, Judaism's most eminent 1st-century sage, played a central role in replacing animal sacrifices – the raison d'être of the Temple in Jerusalem, destroyed in 70 CE – with prayer. His grave site is just a few metres from the grave of Cordova-born sage the Rambam.

Tomb of Rabbi Akiva   RELIGIOUS SITE
(HaGevura St; ⊗24hr) Rabbi Akiva, a leading Mishnaic sage (and teacher of Rabbi Meir Ba'al HaNess), played a major role in establishing rabbinic (ie post–Second Temple) Judaism. He was tortured to death by the Romans because of his support for the Bar Kochba Revolt – indeed, his enthusiasm for resistance to the Romans was such that he declared Bar Kochba to be the Messiah. What is believed to be his dome-topped tomb is on the hillside about 1.5km west of the town centre.

⊙ Elsewhere in Town

Hamat Tveriya National Park   PARK
(Eliezer Kaplan Ave/Rte 90; adult/child 15/7NIS; ⊗8am-5pm daylight-saving time, to 4pm winter

time, closes 1hr earlier Fri) Back in Roman times the fame of Tiberias' hot springs was such that in 110 CE the Emperor Trajan struck a coin dedicated to them – it depicted Hygeia, the goddess of health, sitting on a rock and enjoying the waters. Today, you can get a sense of Roman-era Tiberias at this grassy hillside park, whose star attraction is a **4th-century synagogue** decorated with a beautiful **zodiac wheel** mosaic. Situated 2.5km south of the centre; served by local bus 5 and sheruts.

Al-Amari Mosque   MOSQUE
(Ha-Banim St) With its black basalt walls and white dome, this mosque looks a bit lost squeezed between all the eateries and shops. Built by Daher al-Omar in 1743, it has not been in use since Tiberias' Arab minority was evacuated by the British in April 1948.

🏃 Activities

Along the Yigal Allon Promenade, half-a-dozen operators, including **Tiberias Water Sports** (☑ 052 807 7790) and **Water Sports Center** (☑ 052 349 1462; ⊘ closed Sat), offer pricey motorboat rental (150NIS per 30 minutes), water skiing (300NIS for 15 minutes) and rides on motorboats (30NIS per person) and banana boats (50NIS for 15 minutes). Closed on cold, rainy days, Shabbat and Jewish holidays.

Tiberias Hot Springs   SPA
(Ma'ayanot Hammei Tveriya; ☑ 04-612 3600; Eliezer Kaplan Ave/Rte 90; adult/child 3-12yr 80/40NIS, incl lunch adult 135NIS; ⊘ 8am-8pm Sun, Mon & Wed, to 10pm Tue & Thu, to 3.45/5pm Sat winter/summer) For the sort of relaxing soak and *shvitz* (steam bath) so appreciated by the Romans, head to this modern spa.

Emerging from the ground at 52°C, the mineral water gets cooled a bit before it's piped into four pools. Situated 2.5km south of the town centre, across the street from Hamat Tveriya National Park; served by bus 5 and sheruts.

The complex also has two saunas (one wet, one dry) and a heated outdoor swimming pool (open year-round), or you can indulge yourself with a Swedish massage (195NIS for 30 minutes). Locker rental costs 15NIS; a towel is 10NIS.

Gai Beach Water Park   SWIMMING
(☑ 04-670 0713; www.gaibeachhotel.com; admission over 3yr 80NIS; ⊘ 9.30am-5pm approx Passover-Sukkot) Has a fine beach, giant water slides (including one at a terrifying 70-degree pitch), a wave machine and a special section for small kids. Situated about 1km south of the town centre.

Tiberias Rowing Club   WATER SPORTS
(☑ 04-679 0243; www.rowgalilee.org; Yigal Allon Promenade; ⊘ 8-11am & 3pm or 4-8pm, closed Fri & Sat evenings) Members of Oxford- and Cambridge-style rowing (crew) clubs are welcome to drop by.

🛏 Sleeping

Tiberias has some of the Galilee's cheapest dorm beds as well as one of northern Israel's most luxurious hotels. Boisterous domestic tourists take over in July and August, when the weather is too hot for all but the hardiest foreign visitors.

It's possible to camp at almost all of the beaches that ring the Sea of Galilee, including the municipal **Hof Ganim** (Rte 90; per person 20NIS), 1.5km south of the centre of Tiberias.

CYCLING

The Sea of Galilee is great cycling territory. Completely circumnavigating the lake (60km) takes about six hours – for about 70% of the way you can follow the Kinneret Trail (Shvil Sovev Kinneret), but the rest (including from Ein Gev on the east coast to Arik Bridge at the Sea of Galilee's northern tip) has to be done on highways for now.

For a nice half-day ride from Tiberias, you can head 8km south to Yardenit, from where an 8km circuit follows the Jordan River.

Start early to beat the heat and take plenty of water. When riding on roads, make sure you're highly visible and stay on the verge (shoulder), as far as possible from traffic. Do not ride after sundown.

Aviv Hostel Bike Rental (☑ 04-672 0007; 66 HaGalil St; per day 70NIS; ⊘ 7am or 8am-sundown, to 7pm summer) rents out 300 24-speed mountain bikes. Prices include helmet, lock and maps. Staff are happy to provide information on itineraries and routes. If your bike has mechanical problems, they'll come out and do repairs.

Aviv Hostel HOSTEL $

(☎04-672 0007; 66 HaGalil St; dm 80NIS, d without excl US$65; ✳@🅟) Best thought of as a cheap hotel. Staff are indifferent, the 26 rooms are slightly scuffed and the sheets are polyester, but amenities include proper spring mattresses and fridges. Dorm beds are all nonbunk; women-only dorms are available. Lift-equipped. Breakfast costs US$11.

Galil Hostel HOSTEL $

(☎050 722 5181, 077-924 1404; gallilehostel@ gmail.com; 46 HaGalil St; dm/d 70/200NIS; ✳@🅟) This old-time hostel, in an airy 1930s basalt building, has 12 very basic rooms with three to five beds, a balcony sprinkled with bird droppings, a kitchen and a washing machine.

★ Arbel Guest House GUESTHOUSE $$

(☎04-679 4919; www.4shavit.com; Moshav Arbel; dm/d excl breakfast 120/350NIS, Fri, Aug & holidays 150/560NIS; ✳🅟🅟) Moshav Arbel is just 8km northwest of central Tiberias, but this tranquil B&B feels a world away when you're lazing in a hammock by the pool or relaxing among bougainvilleas, grape arbours and 60 kinds of fruit tree. The six two-room units, each with space for four or five, are eclectically decorated, and all have hot tub and kitchenette. Excellent value.

Superb breakfasts cost 48NIS. Arbel is 80m above sea level, so it's cooler than Tiberias in summer and warmer than the Golan in winter.

YMCA Peniel-by-Galilee GUESTHOUSE $$

(☎04-672 0685; www.ymca-galilee.co.il; Rte 90; s/d 450/550NIS; ✳🅟🅟) Built in the 1920s as a holiday home for the founder of the Jerusalem YMCA, this guesthouse is a gem. Set on a secluded, shady lakeshore, it has a clean pebbly beach, a natural pool fed by a warm spring and a richly decorated lobby with a distinctly Mandate-era vibe. The 14 rooms are forgivably simple; some have kitchenettes.

Situated on the east side of Rte 90 about 3km north of Tiberias; served by all buses heading north from Tiberias.

Russian Pilgrim's Residence GUESTHOUSE $$

(☎04-672 6625; www.domsosvodami.com; 248 Yigal Allon Promenade; s/d/tr from US$100/150/ 210; @) Icons, paintings of the Russian winter (a welcome visual relief from the shimmering summer heat) and the sort of furniture you'd expect to see in Moscow give this place – open to people of all religions –

a distinctly Russian vibe. Situated right on the waterfront in the Arched House, built in 1892.

Superior rooms are huge and have balconies. The good news: most of the 14 rooms have breathtaking sea views. The less-good news, at least for the romantically inclined: all but two of the doubles have separate twin beds.

Aviv Holiday Flats HOTEL $$

(☎04-671 2272; http://aviv-hotel.xwx.co.il; 2 HaNoter St; s/d/tr/q US$78/98/113/128) The 30 handsome, modern studio apartments have at least 30 sq metres of space, balconies, kitchenettes and new sheets and mattresses for 2014. One of the best deals in town.

Rimonim Galei Kinnereth HOTEL $$$

(☎04-672 8888; www.rimonim.com; 1 Eliezer Kaplan St; d Sat-Wed from US$270, Thu & Fri from US$350; ✳@🅟🅟) A favourite of David Ben-Gurion back in the 1950s, the doyen of the Tiberias hotel scene – opened in 1946 – retains some of its late-Mandate-era charm. Amenities include a spa and a kids' club for children aged five to 10. See if you can identify some of the hotel's more famous guests in the mural behind reception.

There's a small exhibition on the hotel's storied history in the Hermon Room (2nd floor).

Scots Hotel HOTEL $$$

(☎04-671 0710; www.scotshotels.co.il; 1 Gdud Barak St/Rte 90; d weekday/weekend from US$415/ 545; ✳@🅟🅟) Built in the 1890s as a hospital, this sumptuously restored complex – still owned by the Church of Scotland – is graced by landscaped gardens, breezy courtyards and a dazzling lake-view pool (open April to November). Has 69 rooms and a spa with Turkish hammam, hot tub and massage. Discounts are often available.

Nonguests can visit the gorgeous, tranquil gardens from about 10am to 4pm Sunday to Wednesday.

THE RED LINE

Israelis follow the water level of the Sea of Galilee – in newspapers, on the radio and on TV – at least as closely as they do stock-market indexes. As winter rains flow into the lake, news reports follow its progress towards full capacity (208.8m below sea level), while in summertime, the lake's descent towards (and sometimes even below) the 'red line' (213m below sea level) – beyond which pumping may adversely impact water quality – generates news flashes and, at times, screaming, doom-laden headlines. If not for the desalinisation plants along the Mediterranean coast that have come on line in recent years, the condition of the Sea of Galilee would be severely compromised.

To find out the current state of the lake, stop by the Water Level Surveyor (Yigal Allon Promenade; ☉24hr), a 5m-high sculpture shaped like the land surrounding the Sea of Galilee.

🍴 Eating & Drinking

The Yigal Allon Promenade has a number of places to grab a bite or sip a beer, as does the perpendicular Midrahov (a pedestrian mall) and a nearby section of HaBanim St.

Only a handful of in-town eateries are open on Shabbat, making Friday night a great time to check out Nazareth's dazzling dining scene.

Chiburichnaya   JEWISH $
(mains 35-38NIS; ☉8am-4.30pm Sun-Thu, to 3pm Fri) This hole-in-the-wall eatery is a great place to try the Jewish comfort food of Uzbekistan. Specialities include *manteh* (steamed dumpling filled with chopped mutton, onion and spices), *chiburiki* (deep-fried, meat-filled turnover), *belasheh* (jelly doughnut filled with meat instead of jam) and *plov* (rice with meat, onion and carrots). Near the market's upper end; look for a Cyrillic sign. Owned by a couple from Samarkand.

Fruit and Vegetable Market   MARKET $
(☉6am-8pm Sun-Thu, to 1hr before sundown Fri; 🖉) Some of the stall owners may be a bit, shall we say, uncouth, but their produce is top quality and cheap.

Supersol Sheli   SUPERMARKET $
(HaBanim St; ☉8am-9pm Sun-Thu, to 2.30/3.30pm Fri winter/summer) Picnic supplies and food for Shabbat.

Felafel & Shwarma Stalls   FELAFEL $
(HaGalil St; felafel 15NIS, shwarma 24NIS; ☉6am or 7am-8pm or 9pm Sun-Thu, 8am-1hr before sundown Fri; 🖉) Truly excellent meals-in-a-pita are served up by four stalls – long-time competitors for Tiberians' shwarma shekel – situated on the ground floor of a new, six-storey building made of black basalt.

Guy   ISRAELI $$
(📞04-672 3036; HaGalil St; mains 38-75NIS; ☉noon-9pm or 10pm Sun-Thu, to 1hr before sundown Fri; 🖉) An unpretentious, old-time Mizrahi (Oriental-Jewish) restaurant featuring home-style grilled meats, soups (winter only; 17NIS to 22NIS) and a delicious array of stuffed vegetables, as well as Ashkenazi-style chopped liver, Iraqi-style kibbeh (spiced meat balls in tangy soup) and Lebanese-style kibbeh (a fried cracked-wheat dumpling stuffed with chopped meat).

Galei Gil   SEAFOOD $$
(📞04-672 0699; Yigal Allon Promenade; mains 65-105NIS; ☉11am-10pm or later daily; 🕿) Has tables on a romantic wooden deck overlooking the waterfront – the sea views are unbeatable. Nine varieties of fish are available either grilled or fried, along with meat and soups. Open Shabbat.

Little Tiberias   INTERNATIONAL $$
(📞04-679 2806; www.littletiberias.com; HaKishon St; mains 69-149NIS; ☉noon-midnight or later daily; 🖉) Serves fish (grilled, baked or fried), meat, seafood, quiche, a cheese platter and pasta, on solid pine tables. Open Shabbat.

★ Yisrael's Kitchen   ISRAELI $$$
(📞04-679 4919; www.4shavit.com; Arbel Guest House, Moshav Arbel; mains 76-128NIS; ☉8-10am & 6-9pm daily) An 8km drive from Tiberias (take Rte 77 to Rte 7717), this rustic, family-run restaurant features local produce and warm, from-the-heart country cooking. Specialities include huge (500g) portions of Galilee-raised steak and lamb served in terracotta casseroles, baked St Peter's fish and scrummy desserts, including home-made ice cream. Particularly jolly on Friday night. Call to reserve.

Has a good selection of wines from the Galilee and the Golan.

Decks
STEAK $$$

(☎04-671 0800; www.decks.co.il; Lido Beach, Gdud Barak St; mains 75-155NIS; ⊙noon-midnight Sun-Thu, noon to 1½hr before sundown Fri, opens after sundown Sat) Legendary for grilled meats – including filet mignon, baby lamb and goose liver (not force-fed) – prepared outdoors over a mixture of five kinds of wood: olive, lemon, cherry, walnut and eucalyptus. Occupies a hangarlike space built out over the sea, offering gorgeous views. Has an excellent wine list. It's a good idea to reserve for dinner, especially on Thursday. Kosher.

Big Ben
PUB

(Midrahov; ⊙8am-1am or later daily; ☜) Decked out – despite the name – like an Irish-style pub, this old-timer serves eight beers on tap (including Murphy's), Illy coffee and uninspiring food. Screens international footy matches. Open Shabbat.

❶ Orientation

Tiberias' main commercial thoroughfare, north–south HaGalil St, is three blocks east of the Yigal Allon Promenade.

❶ Information

Banks with ATMs can be found around the intersection of HaYarden and HaBanim St.

Magen David Adom (☎04-671 7611; cnr HaBanim & HaKishon Sts; ⊙first aid 7pm-midnight Sun-Thu, 2pm-midnight Fri, 10am-midnight Sat, ambulance 24hr) Provides after-hours first aid and can arrange house (and hotel) calls by doctors.

Poriya Hospital (Baruch Padeh Medical Center; ☎04-665 2211; www.poria.health.gov.il; Rte 768; ⊙emergency room 24hr) Tiberias' government hospital is 8km southwest of the city centre. Linked to Tiberias by bus 39 (40 minutes, hourly except Friday afternoon and Saturday).

Post Office (HaYarden St) Exchanges currency.

Solan Express (3 Midrahov; per hr 20NIS; ⊙9am-10pm Sun-Thu, to 4pm Fri, opens after Shabbat Sat) Has two internet computers, sells prepaid SIM cards and changes foreign currency.

Tiberias Hotels Association (www.tiberias-hotels.com) Publishes a monthly events guide, B'Tveriya (Hebrew only), and has a moderately useful website that isn't necessarily up-to-date.

Tourist Office (☎04-672 5666; HaBanim St; ⊙8.30am-4pm Sun-Thu, to noon Fri) Has loads of free brochures on the Sea of Galilee, including Christian sites, and excellent hiking and cycling maps (eg for the Kinneret Trail). Run by the municipality. Situated in an open-air archae-ological park with the ruins of a 5th-century synagogue and mosaics depicting a lulav (palm frond) and etrog (a kind of citrus fruit). The Tourist Police has an office in the same building.

❶ Getting There & Away

BUS

Most intercity buses stop at the rather forlorn **central bus station** (www.bus.co.il; HaYarden St); some short-haul lines also stop along Ha-Galil St. Destinations:

Beit She'an (Afikim bus 28, 16.50NIS, 30 minutes, 15 daily Sunday to Thursday, six Friday, two Saturday night) Has stops along the southwestern coast of the Sea of Galilee.

Haifa-Merkazit HaMifratz (Egged bus 430, 25NIS, 1¼ hours, twice an hour except Friday afternoon to sundown Saturday)

Jerusalem (Egged buses 959, 961 and 962, 40NIS, 2½ to three hours, every one or two hours except Friday evening to sundown Saturday) Goes via Beit She'an.

Katzrin (Rama bus 52, 35 minutes, three or four daily except mid-afternoon Friday to sundown Saturday) Goes via the Sea of Galilee's north shore, including Capernaum. You can also take Rama bus 57 (50 minutes, seven daily except mid-afternoon Friday and Saturday), which follows the lake's southern and eastern shores, passing by Ein Gev and Kursi National Park.

Kfar Tavor (Egged buses 442, 541 and others, 19NIS, 35 minutes, two or three an hour except Friday evening and Saturday)

Kiryat Shmona (Egged buses 541 and 840, 31.50NIS, one hour, hourly except Friday evening to Saturday sundown) Via Rosh Pina.

Nazareth (Nazareth Tourism & Transport bus 431, 19NIS, one hour, hourly except Friday evening and Saturday) Some buses stop on Rte 75 instead of in central Nazareth. Goes via Kafr Kana.

Tel Aviv (Egged bus 836, 40NIS, 2¾ hours, hourly except Friday afternoon to Saturday afternoon)

Tsfat (Afikim bus 450, 16.90NIS, 40 minutes, hourly Sunday to Friday afternoon, one Saturday night)

---

❶ AROUND THE LAKE BY BUS

On Friday and Saturday in July and daily during much of August, the free **Kav Sovev Kinneret bus** (☎*55477; www.kineret.org.il) circumnavigates the Sea of Galilee – stopping at every beach – every two hours from 10am to 8pm. Check the website (in Hebrew) for exact dates.

CAR

Tiberias is the best place in the Galilee to hire a car. Rental companies:

Avis (☑ 04-672 2766; www.avis.co.il; 2 Ha-Amakim St, cnr HaYarden St)

Eldan (☑ 04-672 2831; www.eldan.co.il; 1 HaBanim St)

SHERUT

The fastest way to get to Tel Aviv (40NIS, two hours, departures about hourly 5am to 8.30pm Sunday to Thursday, to 2.30pm Friday) is to take a **sherut** (☑ 050-755 9282; ⊙ 5am-7pm Sun-Thu, to 2pm Fri) – a 10-seat minibus – from the parking lot just below the central bus station. Less regular services go to Haifa-Merkazit Ha-Mifratz (25NIS, one hour).

Sheruts to Beit She'an (17NIS, departures 7am to 7pm or 8pm Sunday to Thursday, to 3pm Friday) – via the Sea of Galilee's southwest coast and Yardenit (8NIS) – leave from HaGalil St, across the street from the Paz petrol station.

TAXI

Tiberias' taxi services include **Moniyot Tveriya** (☑ 04-655 5550).

SEA OF GALILEE

بحيرة طبريا   ים כנרת

The shores of the Sea of Galilee (in Hebrew, Yam Kinneret or HaKinneret), by far Israel's largest freshwater lake, are lined with great places to relax: beaches, camping grounds, cycling trails and walking tracks.

Jesus is said to have spent most of his ministry around the Sea of Galilee. This is where he is believed to have performed some of his best-known miracles (the multiplication of the loaves and fishes, walking on water), and it was overlooking the Kinneret that he delivered the Sermon on the Mount.

SEA OF GALILEE STATS

➡ Surface area when full: 170 sq km

➡ Length of shoreline: 53km

➡ Maximum depth: 44m

➡ Volume of water when full: 4.3 cu km

➡ Average surface water temperature in February: 14.7°C

➡ Average surface water temperature in August: 28.6°C

➡ Supplies a quarter of Israel's water needs

The Jordan River flows into the Sea of Galilee near the ruins of the ancient city of Bethsaida, providing three-quarters of the lake's annual intake. It exits the lake, on its way to the Dead Sea, next to the Yardenit baptism site, at the lake's far southern tip.

North of Tiberias

As you drive, cycle or walk north from Tiberias, Hwy 90 and the parallel Kinneret Trail (Shvil Sovev Kinneret) curve around the northwestern shore of the lake, passing some of Israel's most significant New Testament sites.

The places in this section are listed from southwest to northeast.

◉ Sights

Arbel National Park   PARK
(☑ 04-673 2904; www.parks.org.il; adult/child 22/10NIS; ⊙ 8am-5pm daylight-saving time, 8am-4pm winter, closes 1hr earlier Fri) Towering over the Sea of Galilee and offering mesmerising views of the Golan Heights and Mt Hermon, Arbel Cliff is 181m above sea level, making it 390m above the vast blue lake below. It is on both the Israel National Trail and the Jesus Trail, and **hikes** of various lengths are possible within the park.

The park is 11.5km northwest of Tiberias; take Rte 77, Rte 7717 and then the Moshav Arbel access road, from where a side road leads northeast for 3.5km.

For great views, you can walk to the **Carob Tree Lookout** (30 minutes return) and, a few minutes further along the ridge, the **Kinneret Lookout**. A three-hour circuit that requires some cliff clambering with cables and hand-holds takes you past the **Cave Fortress**, apparently built by a Druze chieftain in the 1600s. It's also possible to do a circuit (five to six hours) that heads down to the **Arbel Spring** and then back up to park HQ via the ruins of a 6th-century **synagogue** – the latter is 800m towards Moshav Arbel along the park's sole access road.

In 1187 Saladin inflicted a devastating defeat on the Crusaders at the **Horns of Hattin**, the ridge a few kilometres west of Arbel Cliff.

Magdala   ARCHAEOLOGICAL SITE
(☑ 04-620 0099; www.magdalacenter.com; Migdal Junction, Rte 90; admission 10NIS; ⊙ 9am-6pm daily) When the Legionnaires of Christ, a Catholic congregation based in Mexico, began to build a spiritual retreat in 2009, they

were astonished to discover a synagogue from the 1st century CE, dated to the time of Jesus by a local coin minted in 29 CE. The ongoing excavations were opened to the public as an open-air museum in 2014. Situated 6km north of Tiberias on the site of the ancient town of Magdala (Migdal in Hebrew), home of Mary Magdalene.

Inside the synagogue archaeologists found the **Magdala Stone**, a rectangular altar – discovered facing south towards Jerusalem – decorated with a seven-branched menorah that is unique because it was carved when the Temple in Jerusalem was still standing. The altar may have been used to read the Torah. The original is at the Israel Museum in Jerusalem; here you can see a copy.

Visitors can also see the elegant **Spirituality Center** and its five mosaic-adorned chapels, one financed by Catholics from Singapore. Volunteers conduct free tours in English, Spanish and French.

★**Ancient Galilee Boat**   HISTORIC SITE
(Jesus Boat; ☑04-672 7700; www.bet-alon.co.il; Kibbutz Ginosar, Rte 90; adult/child 20/15NIS; ⊘8am-5pm Sun-Thu, to 4pm Fri, to 5pm Sat; 🛱) In 1986, when the level of the Sea of Galilee was particularly low, a local fisherman made an extraordinary discovery: the remains of a wooden boat later determined to have plied these waters in the time of Jesus's ministry. The 8.2m fishing vessel, made of 12 kinds of (apparently recycled) wood, can be seen inside Kibbutz Ginosar's **Yigal Alon Centre**. Wall panels and three short films tell the fascinating story of its discovery and preservation (so does the website).

Another part of the complex houses a museum (open Sunday to Thursday) dedicated to the settlement of the Galilee by early Zionist pioneers. There's a viewing platform with fine views up on the 5th floor. Outside, the lovely shoreline site is surrounded by expanses of waving reeds and a garden of sculptures by Jewish and Arab artists. The museum has a cafeteria.

Tabgha   CHURCH
Two Catholic churches a few hundred metres apart occupy the stretch of Sea of Galilee lakefront known as Tabgha (an Arabic corruption of the Greek *hepta pega,* meaning 'seven springs'). An attractive walkway links Tabgha with Capernaum, a distance of about 3km.

The austere, German Benedictine **Church of the Multiplication of the Loaves &**

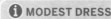

① MODEST DRESS

The Christian sites along the Sea of Galilee's northern shore require that visitors dress modestly (no tank tops or shorts above the knee).

Fishes (www.heilig-land-verein.de; ⊘8am-5pm daily), built in 1982, stands on the site of a 5th-century Byzantine church whose beautiful mosaic floor, depicting flora and feathered fauna, can still be seen. (Original tiles are in vivid colours; repaired sections are in shades of grey.) The rock under the altar is believed by some to be the 'solitary place' where Jesus is said to have laid the five loaves and two fishes that multiplied to feed 5000 faithful listeners (Mark 6:30-44). Excellent brochures (1NIS) are available along one wall. The church is wheelchair accessible.

A few hundred metres to the east, a shady, fragrant garden leads down to the water's edge and the Franciscan **Church of the Primacy of St Peter** (⊘8am-4.50pm), a chapel – lit by the vivid colours of abstract stained glass – built in 1933. The flat rock in front of the altar was known to Byzantine pilgrims as Mensa Christi (Christ's Table) because it was believed that Jesus and his disciples breakfasted on fish here (John 21:9). On the side of the church facing the lake, a few steps cut out of the rock are said by some to be where Jesus stood when his disciples saw him. (On the other hand, the steps may have been cut in the 2nd or 3rd century, when the area was quarried for limestone.) Just west of the church, a path leads to three serene **outdoor chapels** surrounded by the reeds and trees that grow along the lakeshore.

★**Mount of the Beatitudes**   CHURCH
(Har HaOsher; ☑04-6711225; Rte 90; per car 10NIS; ⊘8-11.45am & 2-4.45pm) This breathtaking Roman Catholic church, built in 1937, stands on a site believed since at least the 4th century to be where Jesus delivered his Sermon on the Mount (Matthew 5-7), whose opening lines – the eight Beatitudes – begin with the phrase 'Blessed are...' The sermon also includes the Lord's Prayer and oft-quoted phrases such as 'salt of the earth', 'light of the world' and 'judge not, lest ye be judged'.

Inside the octagonal church, looked after by Franciscan nuns, the Beatitudes are commemorated in stained glass just below the dome, while the seven virtues (justice,

COSMO CONDINA / GETTY IMAGES ©

DAN PORGES / GETTY IMAGES ©

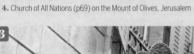

1. Dome of the Rock (p49), Jerusalem **2.** Western Wall (p59),
Jerusalem **3.** Pilgrims on the Via Dolorosa (p56), Jerusalem
4. Church of All Nations (p69) on the Mount of Olives, Jerusalem

CULTURA TRAVEL / LAURA ARSIE / GETTY IMAGES ©

Religious Sites

Modern-day travellers can visit places of monumental importance to the three great Abrahamic religions: Judaism, Christianity and Islam. Both believers and the merely curious often find themselves surprised, inspired and moved by these time-honoured sites.

Via Dolorosa

Threading through Jerusalem's Old City, the 'Way of Sorrows' (p56) follows the path that Jesus, bearing the cross, is believed to have taken on the way to Calvary. The 14 Stations of the Cross commemorate important events along the way.

Dome of the Rock

Topped by a shimmering golden dome, this 7th-century Islamic shrine (p49) stands atop the massive stone from which the Prophet Mohammed is believed to have ascended to Heaven during his Night Journey.

Western Wall

Many visit Judaism's holiest site (p59) to press their hands against the wall and stuff a prayer into the cracks between the stones.

Mount of Olives

Jews come to the Mount of Olives (p68) to visit the world's oldest Jewish cemetery, while Christian pilgrims are drawn here by dome- and mosaic-adorned churches and the 2000-year-old olive trees of the Garden of Gethsemane.

Jericho

Possibly the world's oldest city, Jericho (p266) is best known in the Bible as the place where Joshua's trumpets brought down the walls and Jesus was both tempted by the Devil and baptised by John the Baptist.

RELIGIOUS IMAGES / UIG / GETTY IMAGES ©

1. Church of the Holy Sepulchre (p54). 2. Ibrahimi Mosque/Tomb of the Patriarchs (p273) 3. St Catherine's Church (p256) 4. Church of the Multiplication of the Loaves & Fishes (p209). Tabgha

Church of the Holy Sepulchre

Incense, candles, icons and the hushed prayers of pilgrims set the mood inside Christianity's holiest site (p54), believed since at least the 4th century to be the site of Jesus's crucifixion, burial and resurrection.

Mt Zion

A single structure on Mt Zion (p65) is believed to shelter both the Room of the Last Supper, one of Christianity's holiest sites, and King David's Tomb, sacred to Jews.

Tomb of the Patriarchs

According to both Genesis and the Quran, Abraham and his family are buried in the highly contested Tomb of the Patriarchs (p273), the Holy Land's second-most-sacred site for both Muslims and Jews.

Ashkenazi Ari Synagogue

This ancient synagogue (p223) stands on the spot where the great 16th-century Kabbalist Yizhak Luria (aka the Ari) used to greet the Shabbat.

Church of the Nativity, Bethlehem

Duck through the low stone entrance (p255), intended to inspire humility, and make your way down to the traditional site of Jesus's manger, marked by a silver star with 14 points.

Tabgha

Situated on the shores of the Sea of Galilee, Tabgha (p209) is where Jesus is believed to have miraculously multiplied five loaves of bread and two fishes to feed a congregation of 5000.

LOWER GALILEE & SEA OF GALILEE NORTH OF TIBERIAS

JACOB'S LADDER

Jacob's Ladder (www.jlfestival.com; adult/5-12yr 395/270NIS, Fri only 320/220NIS, Sat only 195/130NIS; ⊙ Dec & May) Founded by a group of Anglo-Saxim (English-speaking immigrants) back in 1978, this twice-a-year festival features bluegrass, folk, country, blues, Irish jigs and world music. Performances by Israeli and international artists take place around the Nof Ginosar Hotel (10km north of Tiberias). Events are wheelchair accessible.

Winter Weekend takes place on a Friday night and Saturday in early December. The Spring Festival is staged over a long weekend (Thursday to Saturday) in early May.

charity, prudence, faith, fortitude, hope and temperance) are represented around the altar. The balcony and tranquil gardens have breathtaking views of the Sea of Galilee.

Monte delle Beatitudini (as it's known in Italian), situated on the Jesus Trail, is a 3.1km drive up the hill from Tabgha's Church of the Multiplication of the Loaves & Fishes. Walking is also an option – from just outside the mount's entrance booth, a 1km path leads down the hill to Tabgha, hitting Rte 87 at a point about 200m east of the Church of the Primacy of St Peter.

Capernaum   ARCHAEOLOGICAL SITE
(Kfar Nachum, Kfar Nahum; admission 3NIS; ⊙8am-5pm, last entry 4.30pm) The New Testament relates that the prosperous lakeside village of Capernaum (estimated population 1500), on the imperial highway from Tiberias to Damascus, was Jesus's base during the most influential period of his Galilean ministry (Matthew 4:13, Mark 2:1, John 6:59). It is mentioned by name 16 times: this is where Jesus is believed to have preached at the synagogue (Mark 1:21), healed the sick and recruited his first disciples, fishers Peter, Andrew, James and John, and Matthew the tax collector.

The Franciscan friars who run the site, dressed in brown cassocks with a white rope around the waist, are happy to answer questions. An explanatory sheet is available at the ticket window.

Capernaum's renowned synagogue, whose facade faces south towards Jerusalem, consists of two superimposed structures. The reconstructed building that can be seen today, known as the 'White Synagogue' because it's made of light-coloured limestone, was built in the late 4th century atop the dark basalt foundations of the 'Synagogue of Jesus', which – despite its name – appears to have been built at least a century after the Crucifixion.

On the other side of the tree-shaded benches from the synagogue, 10m to the right of the olive press, a menorah decorates the upper lip of a column. A nearby column bears a 5th-century inscription in Hebrew commemorating a donation made by someone named Alpheus, son of Zebidah.

A modern, glass-walled church (1991), used for hourly Masses in a variety of languages, is dramatically suspended over the ruins of an octagonal, 5th-century church that partly obscures St Peter's House, where Jesus is believed to have stayed.

At the entrance to the site, along the fence to the right of the statue of St Peter, is a row of impressive stone lintels decorated with fruit and plant motifs but, in accordance with the Third Commandment (Exodus 20:4), no images of people or animals.

Capernaum is 16km northeast of Tiberias and 3km northeast of Tabgha. Hwy 87 has three signs indicating turn-offs to Capernaum – to get to the archaeological site, take the westernmost of the three.

Monastery of the Twelve Apostles   CHURCH
(⊙9am-about 5pm, to about 6pm daylight-saving time) Peacocks strut around the serene, deeply shaded lakefront garden of this Greek Orthodox site, 200m as the crow flies (1.6km on foot or by car) northeast of the Capernaum synagogue, at the eastern edge of the ancient city. The chapel-sized church, its distinctive red domes visible from afar (including from the Mount of the Beatitudes), dates from 1925, but the whole complex – from the grape trellises to the rich interior iconography (redone for the millennium) – casts a very Byzantine spell.

To get there, follow the signs to 'Capernaum (Orthodox)'.

Korazim National Park   ARCHAEOLOGICAL SITE
(Rte 8277; adult/child 22/10NIS; ⊙8am-5pm daylight-saving time, to 4pm rest of year, closes 1hr earlier Fri, last entry 1hr before closing) On a hillside overlooking the Sea of Galilee, Korazim is a good place to get an idea of the layout of a prosperous, midsized Galilean town in the time of Jesus and of the Talmud (3rd to 5th centuries CE). The site – especially the

synagogue – is known for its extraordinary basalt carvings, which depict floral and geometric designs – permitted by Jewish law – as well as Hellenistic-style representations of animals, humans (eg people stomping on grapes) and mythological figures (Medusa!).

Two extraordinary objects were found inside the synagogue: a richly decorated column thought to have held up the table used to read the Torah; and an armchair bearing an inscription in Aramaic. The originals are now in the Israel Museum in Jerusalem (in situ you can see replicas). The people of Korazim – along with the inhabitants of Capernaum and Bethsaida – were denounced by Jesus for their lack of faith (Matthew 11:20-24).

Korazim is on Rte 8277, 2.5km east of Rte 90 (Korazim junction, i.e. Vered HaGalil), and 8km west of the ruins of Bethsaida (in Park HaYarden). There is no public transport.

Bethsaida ARCHAEOLOGICAL SITE
(Beit Tzayda; ☎04-692 3422; www.parkyarden.co.il; Rte 888 just north of Rte 87; per car 60NIS; ⊙last entry 5pm) These excavations, inside HaYarden Park Nature Reserve (Jordan River Park), are believed to be those of the ancient fishing village of Bethsaida, where Jesus is said to have fed 5000 people with just five loaves of bread and two fish (Luke 9:10-17), walked on water (Mark 6:45-51) and healed a blind man (Mark 8:22-26) – and where he also issued a stern rebuke to the town (Luke 10:13-15).

Two **walking circuits** are trail marked in black: a 500m route around the basalt ruins, which don't look like much to the untrained eye (signs help visitors imagine the original structures), and a 1km route down to the spring and back. The site is surrounded by pre-1967 Syrian trenches and minefields.

The **Bethsaida Excavations Project** (http://world.unomaha.edu/bethsaida), which accepts volunteers for its summer digs, is based at the University of Nebraska in Omaha.

Bethsaida is in the far northeastern corner of the Sea of Galilee, about 6km from Capernaum. In ancient times the lake, now 2km away, probably came up to the base of the tel.

🏃 Activities

Vered HaGalil Stables HORSE RIDING
(☎050 238 2225, 04-693 5785; www.vered hagalil.com; cnr Rte 90 & Rte 8277; 1/2hr rides 135/250NIS, children's rides 5/10min 20/35NIS; ⊙7am-6pm daily) Stickers reading 'Shalom, y'all' greet visitors to this Western-style ranch, established in 1961 by an immigrant from Chicago. Offers horse riding (minimum age: 10) and introductory rides for children (minimum age: three). Call for availability. Situated 6.7km (by road) up the hill from Tabgha. To get there from Tiberias, take any bus heading to Tsfat, Rosh Pina or Kiryat Shmona.

Also has 30 guest rooms.

SEA OF GALILEE BEACHES

Environmental organisations and local authorities have been waging a successful legal battle to claw beachfront land around the Sea of Galilee – which by law belongs to the public – back from the clutches of private operators. Beaches offering special facilities – lifeguards, security, changing rooms, showers, lawns, chairs, water slides and the like – are still authorised to charge, either per-person admission or per-car parking fees. In the latter case, access to the beach is free if you come on foot, though nonpaying guests aren't allowed to take advantage of the amenities.

Admission to pay beaches, many open 24 hours a day, usually costs either 20NIS to 30NIS per person or, if fees are for parking, 5.90NIS per hour for the first three hours and 2.10NIS per hour after that. Beaches north of Tiberias include **Tamar** and the lake's first 'green beach', **Hukuk**. South of town, there's municipal **Hof Ganim** (1.5km south of the centre) as well as **Sironit**, **Shikmim**, **Berniki**, **Tzinbari** (Zinabberay) and **Tzemah**. Along the eastern shore, beaches include (from north to south) **Dugit**, **Tze'elon** (Zelon), **Kursi**, **Lavnun**, **Halukim**, **Susita**, **Shittim**, **Shezaf** and **Rotem**.

In addition, there are plenty of free, unguarded stretches of coastline just off Rtes 90, 87 and 92, though these may be specked with rubbish and even glass shards. Winds can be surprisingly strong, especially in the afternoon, so make sure you don't get blown out to sea.

Camping is permitted at almost all Sea of Galilee beaches, including those that charge fees.

> ### ⓘ KINNERET TRAIL
>
> Part of an energetic campaign by environmentalists to ensure unrestricted, fee-free public access to the entirety of the Sea of Galilee shoreline, this trail – known in Hebrew as the Shvil Sovev Kinneret – will eventually make it possible to walk all the way around the lake, a distance of about 60km. For now, about 35km – including the southern half of the lake, from Tiberias to Ein Gev, and the northeastern coast – are trail marked (with purple and white blazes) and ready for use. The Tiberias tourist office (p207) can supply you with a map and updates.

🛏 Sleeping

Camping is possible on almost all Sea of Galilee beaches.

Sea of Galilee Guesthouse GUESTHOUSE **$$**
(📞04-693 0063; www.seaofgalileeguesthouse.com; Almagor, off Rte 8277; dm excl breakfast 100NIS, d 550NIS, 5-bed apt 750NIS; ❄@🛜) Lovely gardens with panoramic views of the Sea of Galilee surround the simple, cheery rooms and photo-adorned breakfast room of this 30-bed guesthouse, suffused with an old-time Israeli vibe. Serves great breakfasts (40NIS extra if you're in a dorm bed). Cooking facilities are available. If you've got a tent, you can camp. Wheelchair accessible. Situated 4km east of Korazim National Park in Moshav Almagor; call if the gate is closed.

Frenkels B&B B&B **$$**
(📞04-680 1686; www.thefrenkels.com; Kfar Korazim, off Rte 8277; s/d 500/600NIS; ❄🛜) Run by friendly American immigrants who arrived in Israel way back in 1960, this sweet tzimmer (B&B) has three homey suites, including one that's wheelchair accessible. Breakfast includes homemade goodies, served in a light, airy breakfast room. Situated 8km northeast of Capernaum Junction – take Rte 90 and then Rte 8277.

HI – Karei Deshe Guest House & Youth Hostel HOSTEL **$$**
(Kare Deshe; 📞02-594 5633, reservations 1-599 510 511; www.iyha.org.il; dm 130NIS, d 410-520NIS; ❄🛜) This sparkling-white facility, right on the lake, has 82 double, family and dorm rooms (with four or six beds), a sandy beach and lots of trees and grass. It's often full,

especially at the weekend. Hukuk Beach is next door.

The nearest bus stop, on Rte 90 next to the Sapir water-pumping station (3km southwest of Capernaum Junction), is served by all buses heading north from Tiberias; from there it's a 1.2km walk to the hostel.

★**Pilgerhaus Tabgha** GUESTHOUSE **$$$**
(📞04-670 0100; www.heilig-land-verein.de; s/d Sat-Wed 100/680NIS, Thu & Fri 600/880NIS; ❄@🛜) Opened in 1889, this 70-room German Catholic guesthouse – geared to Christian pilgrims but open to all – is a tranquil place with glorious gardens, right on the shores of the Sea of Galilee. Sumptuously renovated in 2001, it's ideal for meditation and reflection amid exemplary Germanic cleanliness and order. Wheelchair accessible. Situated about 500m from Capernaum Junction.

Reserve well in advance from March to May and mid-September to mid-November.

Nof Ginosar Hotel HOTEL **$$$**
(📞04-670 0320; www.ginosar.co.il; Kibbutz Ginosar, Rte 90; d/tr/f Sat-Wed US$200/285/300, Thu & Fri US$236/321/336; ❄@🛜🏊) Redolent with classic '70s charm, this kibbutz oldtimer has about 260 hotel and cottage rooms (including 12 deluxe rooms added in 2014), flowery grounds and its very own Sea of Galilee beach. Situated 200m from the Ancient Galilee Boat and 8km north of Tiberias.

🍴 Eating

★**Ktzeh HaNahal** LEBANESE **$$**
(📞04-671 7776; www.katsyhanahal.com; Rte 90; mains 70-115NIS, 4-course set meal 129NIS; ⏱noon-11pm; 🅿) From the outside you'd never guess that this unassuming restaurant serves up a sumac-accented Lebanese feast. After a parade of 11 mezze (30NIS), you might want to try *shishbarak* (meat-stuffed dumplings cooked in tangy goat's milk, 70NIS) or Antabli kebab with roasted tomatoes (70NIS).

Situated at the intersection of Rte 90 and the access road to the Ancient Galilee Boat, next to the Delek petrol station (look for a red, green and white sign).

Ein Camonim CHEESE **$$**
(En Kammonim; 📞04-698 9680, 04-698 9894; www.eincamonim.rest-e.co.il; Rte 85; all-you-can-eat meals 88NIS, breakfast 60NIS; ⏱9.30am-8pm Sat-Thu, to 10pm Fri; 🅿) Surrounded by Galilean brushland, this family-run 'goat cheese restaurant' serves up a gourmet vegetarian feast that includes 10 kinds of goat's cheese,

freshly baked bread, salads and wine that you can enjoy outside in the shade. Has a few kids (baby goats) for the kids (children) to pet. It's a good idea to reserve ahead on Friday and Saturday.

Situated 20km northwest of Tabgha, just off Rte 85 at a point 4.8km west of Nahal Amud Junction.

Tibi's Steakhouse & Bar STEAK $$
(☏ 04-633 0885; www.veredhagalil.com/restaurant; cnr Rtes 90 & 8277; steaks 118-145NIS, other mains from 59NIS; ☺ 8-11.30am & noon-11pm or later; ☏) Opened in 2013 by renowned chef Chaim Tibi, formerly of Muscat restaurant, this place in Vered HaGalil Stables specialises in steaks from the Golan but also has good options for vegetarians, such as salads and pasta. The sleek dining room has an alpine-chalet vibe.

ℹ Getting There & Around

All the buses (Egged and Afikim) that link Tiberias with points north via Rte 90, including Tsfat, Rosh Pina and Kiryat Shmona, pass by Magdala (Migdal Junction; 6.60NIS), Ginosar (the Ancient Galilee Boat), Capernaum Junction (Tzomet Kfar Nahum, which is a short walk from Tabgha but about 4km west of Capernaum) and the Mount of the Beatitudes' 1km-long access road.

Rama bus 52 (three of four daily except mid-afternoon Friday to sundown Saturday), which links Tiberias with the Golan town of Katzrin (1¼ hours), continues from Capernaum Junction east along the northern edge of the lake (Rte 87), passing by Capernaum.

South of Tiberias

The places mentioned in this section are listed from north to south.

◉ Sights

Kinneret Cemetery CEMETERY
(Rte 90; ☺ 24hr) Shaded and serene, this luxuriantly green lakeside cemetery, established in 1911, is the final resting place of socialist Zionist pioneers such as **Berl Katznelson** (1887–1944), famous for being at the centre of a celebrated love triangle (his grave is flanked by those of his first and second wives), and **Shmuel Yavnieli** (1884–1961), who worked to bring Yemenite Jews to Israel. It is 9km south of Tiberias and 300m south of Kinneret Junction.

Also buried here is the Hebrew poet **Rachel** (Rachel Bluwstein; 1890–1931); books of her hugely popular poems – many of which

have been set to music – can be found in a stainless-steel container attached to her grave. She appears on the Bank of Israel's new 20NIS banknote, released in late 2014.

In the spring of 1917 the Ottomans expelled the entire Jewish population of Tel Aviv and Jaffa. Of the 2000 refugees who fled to the Galilee, 430 died and 10 are buried here, commemorated by 10 anonymous gravestones and a stone plaque, erected in 2003, bearing their names.

Yardenit RELIGIOUS SITE
(www.yardenit.com; ☺ 8am-6pm, to 5pm Dec-Feb, to 4pm Fri) FREE This hugely popular, eucalyptus-shaded baptism site, run by Kibbutz Kinneret, is 100m south of where the Jordan River flows out of the Sea of Galilee. No one knows if this is the exact spot where Jesus was baptised, but groups of Christian pilgrims line up here – praying and singing – to be baptised in white robes (rental/purchase US$10/25, including towel and certificate). Changing rooms are provided.

Those furry rodents paddling around the fish-filled Jordan are nutrias (coypus), natives of South America. The site has a restaurant and a large religious-souvenir shop.

Yardenit is 10km south of Tiberias and 1km northwest of Kibbutz Degania Alef, the world's first-ever kibbutz (founded in 1910).

Bet Gabriel NOTABLE BUILDING
(☏ 04-675 1175; www.betgabriel.co.il; Rte 92; ☺ closed Sun) Opened in 1993, this lakeside cultural centre – one of Israel's most beautiful buildings – is known for its art exhibitions, first-run cinema (two screens), cafe and truly spectacular sea views. In November 1994 it served as the venue for a ceremony reconfirming the peace treaty between Israel and Jordan. Situated at the southern tip of the Sea of Galilee, 300m east of Tzemah Junction.

King Hussein's red-and-white keffiyeh and a sword given to Shimon Peres by Yasser Arafat can be seen in the **Peace Room** (free tours 10-11.30am Tue; call ahead), whose mirrors ensured that everyone, no matter where around the six-sided, eight-seat table they sat, could see the Sea of Galilee.

⌂ Sleeping

HI – Poriya Guest House & Youth Hostel HOSTEL $$
(Poriya Taiber Youth Hostel; ☏ 02-594 5720, reservations 1-599 510 511; www.iyha.org.il; dm US$33, d US$90-125, additional adult/child US$29/23; ✸ @ ☎) Perched on a hillside high above the

THE JEZREEL VALLEY RAILWAY

From shortly before WWI until 1951, you could hop on the legendarily slow **Jezreel Valley Railway** in Haifa at 8am and pull into Hamat Gader at 11.45am – or, until 1946, arrive in Damascus at 7.47pm. Or you could transfer to the Hejaz Railway in the Syrian town of Daraa, 60km east of Hamat Gader, and roll south. (Daraa is where the first confrontations of the Syrian civil war took place in 2011.) Until the Hejaz Railway was knocked out of commission during WWI by Lawrence of Arabia and his Bedouin fighters, you could take the train all the way to Medina, now in Saudi Arabia.

In the 1930s, the Jezreel Valley Railway helped transport construction materials for the 942km **Kirkuk–Haifa Pipeline** that, until 1948, carried crude oil from Iraq to the refineries of Haifa Bay. Remains of the pipeline can still be seen on the Golan Heights. Regional peace would make rebuilding the pipeline very attractive both economically and strategically – and turn Haifa into the major Mediterranean port the British intended it to be.

Proposals to place the Jezreel Valley Railway back into service have been mooted for decades, but the construction of a 4.5-billion-NIS standard-gauge line (the Ottoman tracks were narrow gauge) from Haifa to Beit She'an (61km) is finally under way. At a later stage, there are plans to extend the line to Irbid, Jordan, allowing the Hashemite Kingdom to take advantage of Haifa's Mediterranean port facilities.

For details on cycling the 150km route of the original Jezreel Valley Railway, pick up a copy of the guidebook *Shvil Rakevet HaEmeq* by Aharon Brindt (in Hebrew).

Sea of Galilee, the lovely Poriya (Poria) campus boasts a glass-walled lobby with spectacular views, 58 rather spartan rooms, and proximity to the Switzerland Forest. Dorm rooms have six beds. Also offers tile-roofed wooden cabins. Situated 9km south of Tiberias, a steep 4km up Rte 7877 from Rte 90. No public transport.

ℹ Getting There & Around

Rte 90 between Tiberias and Tzemah Junction (at the Sea of Galilee's southern tip; 30 minutes) is served by Afikim buses 26, 28 and 53, all Tiberias–Beit She'an buses, and Rama bus 57, which continues around to the lake's eastern shore and, finally, northeast to Katzrin (on the Golan).

Eastern Shore

As you cross Arik Bridge on Rte 87 and continue northeast, the highway moves away from the Kinneret coast and runs around the edge of the verdant Bethsaida Valley, Israel's largest natural wetlands.

Moshav Ramot is 3km up the hill from Rte 92. Like Giv'at Yoav, 13km southeast of Kursi Junction, it's on the western edge of the Golan.

◉ Sights & Activities

Majrase Nature Reserve PARK
(☏04-679 3410; www.parks.org.il; adult/child 29/15NIS; ☺8am-6pm daylight-saving time, to 7pm Aug, to 4pm winter time, closes Fri 1hr or 1½hr

earlier, last entry 1hr before closing) Located in the northeastern corner of the Sea of Galilee, the spring-fed streams and junglelike wetlands of this reserve are ideal for a refreshing 'water hike'. The **wet circuit** (there's also a dry one) takes 40 to 60 minutes; be prepared for water that's up to hip height (60cm deep in summer). The lagoons near the lake are off-limits, to allow fish and water turtles to breed.

Changing rooms are available; bring shoes suitable for walking in water. Some trails are wheelchair accessible. Situated 2km off Rte 92; follow the signs to 'Daliyyot Estuary' or 'Bethsaida Valley'.

Kursi National Park ARCHAEOLOGICAL SITE
(☏04-673 1983; www.parks.org.il; cnr Rtes 92 & 789; adult/child 15/7NIS; ☺8am-4pm Oct-Mar, to 5pm Apr-Sep, closes 1hr earlier Fri, last entry 30min before closing) Mentioned in the Talmud as a place of idol worship, this Gentile fishing village – discovered by chance in the early 1970s – is where Jesus is believed to have cast a contingent of demon spirits out of two men and into a herd of swine (Mark 5:1-13, Luke 8:26-39). The beautifully conserved ruins feature an impressive 5th-century Byzantine monastery.

Near the entrance, an audioguide gadget with buttons for English and Hebrew provides excellent historical background. The site should be fully wheelchair accessible by the end of 2015. This is considered a Christian holy site, so dress modestly (no bathing suits). Situated 30km from Tiberias if you go around the southern side of the Sea of Galilee and 33km if you take the highway along the northern side.

🛏 Sleeping

Leafy **Moshav Ramot** (www.ramot4u.co.il), a favourite with domestic tourists, has several dozen upmarket tzimmerim (B&Bs); the website has details (in Hebrew). There are more B&Bs in nearby Golan villages, including Giv'at Yoav.

⭐ **Genghis Khan in the Golan**   HOSTEL $
(☑052 371 5687; www.gkhan.co.il; Giv'at Yoav; dm/6-person tents 100/600NIS, linen & towel per stay 20NIS; ❄) Hosts Sara and Bentzi Zafrir offer the warmest of welcomes and a fantastic independent-travel vibe here. Inspired by the yurts (gers) used by the nomads of Mongolia, they designed and handmade five colour-coded yurts, each of which sleeps six or 10 on comfortable foam mattresses. Powerful heating/air-con makes sure you stay toasty warm in winter and cool in summer.

In the kitchen, the pans, plates and fridge space are, like the tents, colour-coded, and guests can cook with fresh thyme, lemongrass and mint grown in the herb garden (a row of recycled tyres). The Golan Trail is just one of the hiking paths that pass by here.

Situated on the western slopes of the Golan 13km southeast of Kursi (Kursy) Junction (the intersection of Rtes 92 and 789). Bus 51 links Giv'at Yoav with Tiberias (35 minutes, eight daily Sunday to Thursday, six on Friday, one on Saturday night); Sara is happy to pick up guests at the bus stop.

Ein-Gev Holiday Resort   HOTEL $$$
(☑04-665 9800; www.eingev.com; Kibbutz Ein Gev, Rte 92; d 850-1000NIS; ❄@🛜) From 1948 to 1967, when most of the Sea of Galilee's eastern coast was under Syrian control, the only way to get to Kibbutz Ein Gev was by boat. Today, the kibbutz owns banana, avocado, mango and lychee orchards, a cowshed and this delightful 166-room hotel, which boasts the Sea of Galilee's only natural sand beach.

Options include sunny beachfront family units (1300NIS to 1700NIS) that can sleep five. Situated about 1.5km south along Rte 92 from the vehicle entrance to Kibbutz Ein Gev and its port area.

🍴 Eating

Moshbutz   STEAK $$
(☑04-679 5095; www.moshbutz.com; Dalyot St, Moshav Ramot; mains 62-139NIS, breakfast 60NIS; ⊙8.30am-10pm) This cosy restaurant – the name is a contraction of 'moshav' and 'kibbutz' – serves up fabulous Golan-raised steaks, juicy burgers and creative salads as well as starters such as grilled aubergine with tangy goat's-milk yoghurt – complemented by boutique Golan wines and micro-brews, charming service and great views down to the Sea of Galilee.

Reservations are highly recommended, especially on Friday and Saturday. To get there from the moshav's gate, take the third right.

HAMAT GADER
الحمة السورية   חמת גדר

A favourite of the Romans, whose impressive **2nd-century bath complex** can still be seen, this 42°C **natural hot spring** (☑04-665 9999; www.hamat-gader.com; adult/child from 1m to 16yr 83/62NIS, Fri & Sat 96/72NIS; ⊙8.30am-10.30pm Mon-Fri, to 5pm Sat & Sun Oct-May, 8.30am-5pm Sat-Wed, to 10.30pm Thu & Fri Jun-Sep) – elevation: 150m below sea level – is hugely popular (except in the summer heat) with Jewish (especially Russian), Arab and Druze Israelis. Has picnic facilities and places to eat. You generally need to book ahead for spa treatments. Wheelchair accessible.

Kids will love the **splash pool** (open June to September); the **zoo**, which has baboons, ibexes, ostriches, alligators (feeding at 1.30pm from May to October) and cuddly rabbits in the **petting corner**; a troupe of performing parrots (shows at 11am, 1pm and 3pm); and the free-range peacocks. The temperature of the main open-air pool is about 37°C; staying in for more than 10 minutes is inadvisable.

Hamat Gader, part of British Mandated Palestine, was occupied by the Syrians in 1948, thoroughly enjoyed by Syrian army officers during the 1950s and 1960s, and recaptured by Israel in 1967.

ℹ Getting There & Away

Hamat Gader is 9.5km southeast of Tzemah Junction along Rte 98, which affords fine views across the Yarmuk River (a major tributary of the Jordan) into the Hashemite Kingdom.

Rama bus 24 links Tiberias with Hamat Gader (22 minutes) once a day except Saturday; departures are at 9.15am from Tiberias and 2.30pm from Hamat Gader.

Upper Galilee & Golan

הגליל העליון רמת הגולן
الجليل الاولى هضبة الجولان

Why Go?

The rolling, green hills of the Upper Galilee (the area north of Rte 85) and the wild plateaus and peaks of the Golan Heights offer an incredible variety of activities to challenge the body and the soul and to nourish the stomach and the mind. Domestic tourists flock to the area – some are looking for luxurious tzimmerim (B&Bs), boutique wineries and gourmet country restaurants, while others come in search of superb hiking, cycling and horse riding, white-water rafting and even skiing. The region has still more attractions, including dazzling carpets of spring wildflowers, some of the world's best birdwatching and the spiritual charms of Tsfat, the most important centre of Kabbalah (Jewish mysticism) for over five centuries. The entire region, its summits refreshingly cool in summer, is just a short drive from the Christian sites and refreshing beaches of the Sea of Galilee.

Best Places to Eat

→ Dag Al HaDan (p240)

→ HaAri 8 (p230)

→ Shiri Bistro & Wine Bar (p235)

→ Misedet HaArazim (p232)

→ Villa Lishansky (p238)

Best Places to Stay

→ Villa Tehila (p235)

→ Villa Lishansky (p238)

→ Ohn-Bar Guesthouse (p231)

→ Golan Garden Hostel (p241)

When to Go
Tzfat

Dec–Mar Skiing on Mt Hermon – if there's enough snow.

Feb–Aug Spring flowers bloom earliest in the Hula Valley, latest on Mt Hermon.

late Mar–Oct Adventure kayaking and rafting on the Jordan River.

ℹ️ Getting There & Around

The best way to explore the region is by car – distances are relatively short and the buses run to many lovely villages and nature reserves run just a few times a day. There's a rental agency in Kiryat Shmona (Eldan) but you'll probably be better off hiring a vehicle in Tiberias, Haifa, Tel Aviv or Jerusalem.

The main bus hub is Kiryat Shmona.

Although it's not recommended, many Israelis hitchhike their way around, especially on the Golan.

THE UPPER GALILEE

Tsfat (Safed)   צפת صفد

🎵 04 / POP 32,100

The mountaintop city of Tsfat is an ethereal place to get lost for a day or two. A centre of Kabbalah (Jewish mysticism) since the 16th century, it's home to an otherworldly mixture of Hasidic Jews, artists and devout-but-mellow former hippies, a surprising number of them American immigrants.

In the old city's labyrinth of cobbled alleys and steep stone stairways, you'll come across ancient synagogues, crumbling stone houses with turquoise doorways, art galleries, artists' studios and Yiddish-speaking little boys in black kaftans and bowler hats. Parts of Tsfat look like a *shtetl* (ghetto) built of Jerusalem stone, but the presence of so many mystics and spiritual seekers creates a distinctly bohemian atmosphere.

On Shabbat (Friday night and Saturday until sundown), commerce completely shuts down. While this may be inconvenient if you're looking for a bite to eat, the lack of traffic creates a meditative, spiritual atmosphere through which joyful Hasidic tunes waft from hidden synagogues and unseen dining rooms. Do not photograph observant Jews on Shabbat and holidays.

In July and August and during the Passover and Sukkot holidays, Tsfat is packed with tourists – both Israeli and foreign – and the city's restaurants and cafes buzz until late at night. Winter, on the other hand, is very quiet, giving the city's many artists a chance to get some work done.

History

Founded in the Roman period, Tsfat was fortified by Yosef ben Matityahu (later known as Josephus Flavius), commander of Jewish forces in the Galilee in the early years of the Great

Jewish Revolt (66–70 CE). According to the Jerusalem Talmud, Tsfat was the site of one of the hilltop fire beacons used to convey news of the sighting of the new moon in Jerusalem.

The Crusaders, led by King Fulk of Anjou, built a vast citadel here to control the highway to Damascus. It was later captured by Saladin (1188), dismantled by the Ayyubids (1220), rebuilt by the Knights Templar (1240) and expanded by the Mamluk Sultan Beybars (after 1266).

During the 15th and 16th centuries, Tsfat's Jewish community increased in size and importance thanks to an influx of Sephardic Jews expelled from Spain in 1492. Among the new arrivals were some of the Jewish world's pre-eminent Kabbalists. During this period, Tsfat was an important stop on the trade route from Akko to Damascus and was known for its production of textiles. A Hebrew printing press – the first such device anywhere in the Middle East – was set up in Tsfat in 1577.

In the late 1700s, Tsfat welcomed an influx of Hasidim from Russia.

Tsfat was decimated by the plague in 1742, 1812 and 1847, and devastated by earthquakes in 1759 and 1837. The latter disaster killed thousands and caused all but a handful of buildings to crumble.

In 1948 the departing British handed the town's strategic assets over to Arab forces, but after a pitched battle Jewish forces prevailed and the Arab population fled – among them, 13-year-old Mahmoud Abbas, now president of the Palestinian Authority. These days, Tsfat's residents include more than a few American Jews who turned to mysticism in a 1960s-inspired search for spirituality and transcendental meaning.

◉ Sights

Central Tsfat's main thoroughfare, lined with shops and eateries, is north–south Yerushalayim St (Jerusalem St). West of here, a broad staircase called Ma'alot Olei HaGardom divides the Synagogue Quarter (to the north) from the Artists' Quarter (to the south). The main alley in the Synagogue Quarter, famous for its many art galleries, is called Alkabetz St and Beit Yosef St (Yosef Caro St). The Kabbalists' tombs are further down the slope.

Most of Tsfat's sights are in the Synagogue Quarter and the adjacent Artists' Quarter.

◉ Synagogue Quarter

Tsfat's long-time Jewish neighbourhood spills down the hillside from HaMaginim Sq (Kikar HaMaginim; Defenders' Sq),

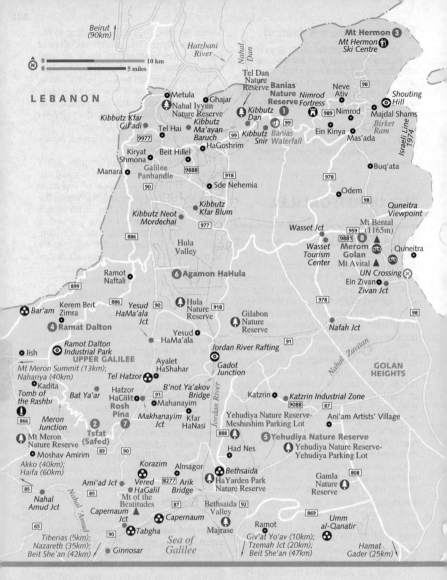

Upper Galilee & Golan Highlights

① Gazing into the burbling, spring-fresh water below the Suspended Trail at **Banias Nature Reserve** (p246).

② Getting lost in the ancient stones and mysticism of Tsfat's **Synagogue Quarter** (p221).

③ Breathing in the crisp alpine air high atop **Mt Hermon** (p248).

④ Visiting award-winning wineries on the Golan Heights and **Ramat Dalton** (p233).

⑤ Hiking into the canyons and past the waterfalls of **Yehudiya Nature Reserve** (p242).

⑥ Getting a close-up view of migrating cranes from the Safari Wagon at **Agamon HaHula** (p236).

⑦ Staying at a luxury B&B in a flowery, old stone house in **Rosh Pina** (p234).

⑧ Going **horse riding** (p245) with a genuine Israeli cowboy from Kibbutz Merom Golan – up a volcano.

which dates from 1777; all of Tsfat's historic Kabbalist synagogues are a quick (if often confusing) walk from here. If you're short on time, the two to visit are the Ashkenazi Ari and Caro synagogues. Galleries filled with exuberant art line the main alleyway, known as Alkabetz St and Beit Yosef St.

Synagogue hours tend to be irregular, especially in winter, and unannounced closings (eg for Monday and Thursday morning bar mitzvahs) are common. Visitors should wear modest clothing (no shorts or bare shoulders); kippas/yarmulkes are provided for men (or you can wear any hat). Caretakers appreciate a small donation (5NIS). Synagogues are closed to tourists on Shabbat and Jewish holidays.

★ **Ashkenazi Ari Synagogue** SYNAGOGUE
(Najara St; ⊙9.30am–about 7pm Sun-Thu, 9.30am-1pm Fri, closed during prayers) Founded in the 16th century by Sephardic Jews from Greece, this synagogue was destroyed in the 1837 earthquake and rebuilt in the 1850s. It stands on the site where the great Kabbalist Yitzhak Luria (Isaac Luria; 1534–72; often known by the name Ari) used to greet the Sabbath. In the 18th century it came to serve Tsfat's Ashkenazi Hasidic community, hence the synagogue's name (the Jerusalem-born Ari had a Sephardic mother and an Ashkenazi father).

High atop the 19th-century holy ark (where the Torah scrolls are kept), carved and elaborately painted according to the traditions of Galicia (Poland), the lion has a humanlike face that worshippers speculate may be that of the Ari (the Hebrew word *ari* means 'lion').

In 1948, the synagogue was packed with worshippers when an Arab mortar round slammed into the courtyard, sending shrapnel crashing into the side of the *bimah* (central platform) facing the door (the hole is still there). It was a miracle, say locals, that there were no casualties.

★ **Caro Synagogue** SYNAGOGUE
(☑04-692 3284, Eyal 050 855 0462; Beit Yosef St; ⊙9am-5.30pm Sun-Thu, 9am-3pm or 4pm in winter, 9am-noon Fri) Named (like the street it's on) in honour of the author of the *Shulchan Aruch* (the most authoritative codification of Jewish law), Toledo-born Rabbi Yosef Caro (1488–1575), this synagogue was founded as a house of study in the 1500s but rebuilt after the earthquakes of 1759 and 1837 – and again in 1903. To the right as you face the ark, hanging in one of the windows, you can see the twisted remains of a Katyusha rocket from Lebanon that landed just outside in 2006.

In the 16th century, Caro, the head of Tsfat's rabbinical court, was the most respected rabbinical authority not only in Palestine but in many parts of the Jewish Diaspora as well. According to tradition, an angel revealed the secrets of Kabbalah to Caro in the house below the synagogue.

Abuhav Synagogue SYNAGOGUE
(☑04-692 3885; Abuhav St; ⊙usually 9am-5pm Sun-Thu, 9am-noon Fri) Named after the 15th-century Spanish scholar Rabbi Yitzhak Abuhav, this synagogue was founded in the 16th century but moved to its present location after the 1759 earthquake. The ornately carved courtyard, restored in the late 20th century, is often used for weddings.

Inside, the four central pillars represent the four elements (earth, air, water and fire) that, according to Kabbalists (and ancient Greeks such as Aristotle), make up all of creation. The oval dome has 10 windows, one for each of the Ten Commandments; representations of the 12 Tribes of Israel; illustrations of musical instruments used in the Temple; pomegranates (said to have the same number of seeds as there are Jewish commandments, 613); and the Dome of the Rock, a reminder of the Temple in Jerusalem.

Sephardic Ari Synagogue SYNAGOGUE
(Synagogue Ha'Ary Sefaradi; Ha'Ari St; ⊙1-7pm Sun-Wed, 1-5pm Thu in summer, shorter hours rest of year) Tsfat's oldest synagogue – it's mentioned in documents from as far back as 1522 – was frequented by the Ari, who found inspiration in the panoramic views of Mt Meron and the tomb of Shimon bar Yochai. To the left of the raised *bimah* (platform) is the small room, glowing with candles, where he is said to have studied mystical texts with the prophet Elijah. The present structure is partly the result of rebuilding after the earthquake of 1837.

HaMeiri Museum MUSEUM
(☑04-697 1307; www.bhm.org.il; 158 Keren Ha-Yesod St; adult/child 6-18yr 20/13NIS; ⊙8.30am-2.30pm Sun-Thu, 9.30am-1.30pm Fri) Housed in a 150-year-old building that once served as the seat of Tsfat's rabbinical court, this museum illustrates Jewish life in Tsfat during the 19th and early 20th centuries. Exhibits include unique household and Jewish ritual objects made by local tinsmiths using empty kerosene cans (some even incorporate the Shell logo into the design). To get there, go all the way to the bottom of the Ma'alot Olei HaGardom staircase and turn right.

Tsfat (Safed)

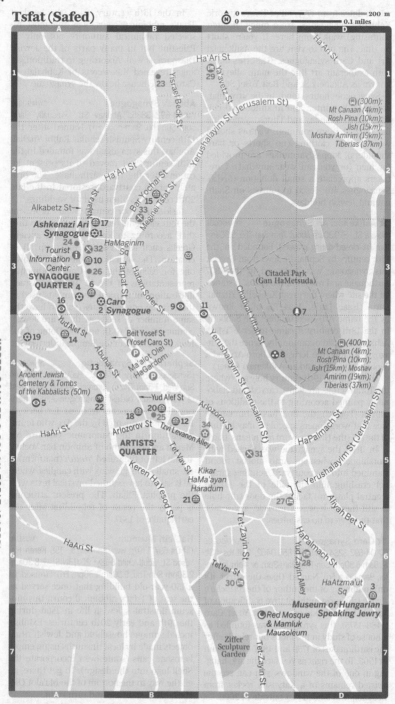

Ha'Ari St

0 ————— 200 m
0 ————— 0.1 miles

Ha'Ari St

Yisrael Beck St

Ya'avetz St
23
29

Ha'Ari St

(300m);
Mt Canaan (4km);
Rosh Pina (10km);
Jish (15km);
Moshav Amirim (19km);
Tiberias (37km)

Ha'Ari St

Alkabetz St

Bar Yochai St

Meginei Tsfat St

15
33

Ashkenazi Ari
Synagogue 1
17

24
32
Tourist
Information 10
Center 26
SYNAGOGUE
QUARTER 4 6

Caro
2 Synagogue

HaMaginim
Sq

Tarpat St

Hatam Sofer St

9

11

Citadel Park
(Gan HaMetsuda)

7

16

Yud Alef St

14

19

Abuhav St

Beit Yosef St
(Yosef Caro St)

Ma'alot Olei
HaGardom

Chativat Yiftah St

(400m);
Mt Canaan (4km);
Rosh Pina (10km);
Jish (15km); Moshav
Amirim (19km);
Tiberias (37km)

8

Ancient Jewish
Cemetery & Tombs
of the Kabbalists (50m)

13

5

22

Yud Alef St

18
20
25
12
34

HaAri St

Arlozorov St

Tzvi Levanon Alley

ARTISTS'
QUARTER

Arlozorov St

Keren HaYesod St

Tet Vav St

Kikar
HaMa'ayan
Haradum

21

31

HaPalmach St

Yerushalayim St (Jerusalem St)

27

Aliyah Bet St

HaAri St

Tet-Zayin St

TetVav St

30

HaPalmach St

Yud Zayin Alley

28

HaAtzma'ut
Sq

3

Museum of Hungarian
Speaking Jewry

Red Mosque
& Mamluk
Mausoleum

Ziffer
Sculpture
Garden

Tet-Zayin St

Tsfat (Safed)

Top Sights
1	Ashkenazi Ari Synagogue A3
2	Caro Synagogue A3
3	Museum of Hungarian Speaking Jewry D6

Sights
4	Abuhav Synagogue A3
5	Ari's Mikveh A4
6	Canaan Gallery A3
7	Citadel Park D3
8	Citadel Ruins C4
9	Davidka Memorial B3
10	Fig Tree Courtyard A3
11	Former British Police Station C3
12	General Safed Exhibition B5
13	HaMeiri Dairy A4
14	HaMeiri Museum A4
15	Kabbalah Art B2
16	Kadosh Dairy A3
17	Safed Candles Gallery A3
18	Safed Craft Pottery B5
19	Sephardic Ari Synagogue A4
20	Sheva Chaya Glassblowing Gallery B4
21	Tzfat Gallery of Mystical Art B5
22	Yehezkel HaMeiri Viewpoint A4

Activities, Courses & Tours
23	Ascent Institute of Safed B1
24	Livnot U'Lehibanot A3
25	Path of the Heart B5
26	Tzfat Kabbalah Center A3

Sleeping
27	Adler Apartments C5
28	Artist Quarter Guest House D6
29	Carmel Hotel C1
30	Ruth Rimonim C6

Eating
31	Coöp Shop Supermarket C5
	HaAri 8 .... (see 29)
32	Lahuhe Original Yemenite Food Bar A3
	Maximilian .... (see 12)
33	Tree of Life Vegetarian Cafe B2

Entertainment
34	Khan of the White Donkey C5

UPPER GALILEE & GOLAN TSFAT (SAFED)

Upstairs is a re-creation of a one-room apartment inhabited by a family with six children. The mother got to sleep in the one bed, and the shower consisted of a hanging bucket made of reused tin with a showerhead welded to the bottom.

Visitors are asked to check in their backpacks so they don't knock anything over. Signs are in English.

HaMeiri Dairy   DAIRY
(☑Yaniv 052 372 1609; www.hameiri-cheese.co.il; Keren HaYesod St; ⊙9am-3pm Sun-Thu, 9am-1.30pm Fri) Run by the same family for six generations, this small dairy takes about 50,000L of sheep's milk a year and turns it into delicious cheeses, including soft, creamy Bulgarian cheese (aged for a full year) and a variety of *gvina Tzfatit* (Tsfat-style cheese; aged for six months) that's harder, saltier and sheepier than the supermarket variety – both can be purchased at the deli counter. To get there, go to the bottom of the Ma'alot Olei Ha-Gardom staircase, turn right and walk 50m.

There are 45-minute **tours** (adult/child 20/15NIS, in Hebrew) at noon on Friday; a cafe is planned. Cheeses are made each Thursday.

Kadosh Dairy   DAIRY
(Kadosh Cheese; ☑04-692 0326; 34 Yud Alef St; ⊙8am-8pm Sun-Thu, 8am-1hr before sundown Fri) Run by the Kadosh family for seven generations, this microdairy produces minuscule quantities of deliciously sharp, salty *gvina Tzfatit* as well as a variety of other cheeses, including blue cheese, *kashkaval* (a semihard yellow sheep's milk cheese) and pecorino. You can usually watch cheese being made on Sunday, Tuesday and Thursday from 8am to 3pm. To get there from the Synagogue Quarter, follow the signs down the hill to 'Safed Cheeze' or 'Zefat Cheeze'.

The dairy sells cheeses, as well as halva made with honey, stuffed grape leaves and local wines. A sampler plate with about 10 cheeses and bread – enough for a meal – costs 40NIS.

◉ Artists' Quarter

The neighbourhood south of the Ma'alot Olei HaGardom stairway used to be Tsfat's Arab quarter, as you can see from the minarets, but after the 1948 war the area was developed as an Israeli artists' colony. To help things along, the government declared that any artist who was willing to live in Tsfat for at least 180 days a year would be given a free house and gallery.

In the '50s and '60s, some of the country's most celebrated painters (Moshe Castel, Yitzhak Frenkel, Simcha Holtzman, Arieh Merzer and Menahem Shemi), inspired by Tsfat's stunning landscapes and mystical traditions, opened studios and held exhibitions in the town. Art-lovers escaped the heat of Tel Aviv and spent their summers holidaying in the city's two dozen hotels.

Most of the galleries and studios around the quarter are open to visitors, with many artists happy to talk about their work and even happier to make a sale.

General Safed Exhibition GALLERY

(Ta'arucha Klalit; ☑04-692 0087; 2 Arlozoroff St; ⊙10am-5pm Sun-Thu, 10am-2pm Fri & Sat) Opened in 1952, this group gallery – housed in the white-domed, Ottoman-era Market Mosque – displays, sells and ships works by about 50 painters and 10 sculptors, including some very talented immigrants from the former Soviet Union. If you find yourself intrigued by a particular work, ask for directions to the artist's studio.

◉ Ancient Jewish Cemetery

The weed-covered, rock-strewn jumble of sun-baked graves below the Synagogue Quarter doesn't look like much, but for followers of Jewish mysticism, the spirits of the great 16th-century Kabbalists buried here make this hillside an exceptional place to connect with the divine spark through prayer and meditation.

A wander through the area is a bit otherworldly at any time, but it's particularly magical in the early evening, when you can walk in the flickering glow of memorial candles, often to the haunting echoes of chanted prayers and psalms.

Anyone who is remotely famous has had their stones painted 'Tsfat blue', a light hue that reminds passers-by that the Kabbalists' spiritual role is to connect the heavens and the earth.

To avoid impure thoughts among the pious men who come to pray in Tsfat's ancient Jewish cemetery, Hebrew signs direct women to separate walkways and platforms. But it's not always clear where you're supposed to go, and even strictly Orthodox people often ignore the contradictory signage, which is part of a growing trend among some ultra-Orthodox groups to separate the sexes to a degree unprecedented in Jewish history.

If you can't read Hebrew, all you need to know to keep the signs straight is that the word for 'women' (*nashim*, written נשים) includes the letter *Shin*, which looks like a three-branched candelabra.

As at any holy site, visitors should dress modestly.

Ari's Mikveh RELIGIOUS

(south of the southern end of Ha'Ari St; ⊙24hr) A boldface Hebrew sign on the gate reads 'entry for men only'. The reason is not gynophobia but the fact that inside there are naked men taking a quick, ritually purifying dip in the icy waters of a natural spring. Once used by the Ari, the site is run by the Breslov (Bratzlav) Hassidic movement.

Tombs of the Kabbalists CEMETERY

(below Ha'Ari St; ⊙24hr) The graves of many of Tsfat's greatest sages and Kabbalists are about one-third of the way down the slope, just below a solitary pine tree in an area where the converging double walkways are covered with transparent roofing. If you can't read Hebrew, ask passers-by for help in finding the tombs of **Yitzhak Luria** (Isaac Luria; born in Jerusalem in 1534, died in Tsfat in 1572), aka HaAri, the father of modern Jewish mysticism (Lurianic Kabbalah).

Near the tomb of Luria is that of **Shlomo Alkabetz** (born in Thessalonika c 1500, died in Tsfat in 1580), best known for composing the hymn 'Lecha Dodi'. **Yosef Caro** (born in Toledo in 1488, died in Tsfat in 1575), the most important codifier of Jewish law, is buried about 100m further down the hill.

◉ Elsewhere Around Town

Citadel Park PARK

(Gan HaMetsuda; Chativat Yiftach St; ⊙24hr) The highest point in central Tsfat (834m), now a breeze-cooled park, was once part of the largest Crusader fortress in the Middle East (its outer walls followed the line now marked by Jerusalem St).

Near the park's southern tip, the **ruins** of one of the inner walls can be seen along Chativat Yiftach St. From there, a path leads up the slope and under an old water pipe to a dark, flat, 30m-long tunnel that takes you into an ancient stone **cistern**. Stand in the middle and see what happens when you clap. Other footpaths lead up to the **ridge line**, which affords panoramic views in all directions.

Yerushalayim Street HISTORIC SITE

(Jerusalem St) About 50m south of City Hall, the **Davidka Memorial** recalls the role played by the homemade, notoriously inaccurate Davidka mortar in sowing panic among the Arab population, possibly because of rumours that its incredibly loud 40kg warhead was an atomic bomb. About 3km to the left, a free audioguide tells the dramatic tale of the battle for Tsfat in 1947 and 1948 – from the Israeli perspective, of course.

TSFAT'S GALLERY SCENE

A retreat and inspiration for Israeli artists since the 1950s, Tsfat is home to one of Israel's largest collections of artists' studios and art galleries, making it the best place in the country (along with Jerusalem) to shop for Judaica (Jewish ritual objects). You'll find jaw-dropping original art, commercial semikitsch and everything in between, and almost all the works – menorahs, mezuzahs, illuminated Hebrew manuscripts, jewellery, glasswork, sinuous modern sculpture, paintings – are imaginative and upliftingly colourful. Most, in the mystical Hasidic tradition, are also joyous.

In the Synagogue Quarter, dozens of galleries can be found along **Alkabetz St**, an alleyway that stretches south from the Ashkenazi Ari Synagogue; further south it is known as **Beit Yosef St** (Yosef Caro St). More galleries, as well as artists' studios, are hidden away in the Artists' Quarter along the alleys around the General Exhibition, including Tet-Vav St.

The galleries mentioned below are listed from north to south.

Kabbalah Art (☏04-697 2702; www.kosmic-kabbalah.com; 38 Bar Yochai St, Synagogue Quarter; ◷9am-7pm Sun-Thu, 9am-2hrs before sundown Fri) Denver-born David Friedman uses the mysteries of the Hebrew alphabet, Kabbalistic symbols such as the Tree of Life, and the universal language of colour and geometry to create striking visual representations of Kabbalah, and is happy to give visitors a short introduction to Kabbalah. Situated about 100m northwest of HaMaginim Sq.

Safed Candles (Najara St, Synagogue Quarter; ◷9.15am-6.30pm Sun-Thu, 9.15am-12.30pm Fri, 9.15am-1.45pm Fri in summer) If you've ever wondered how Shabbat, Havdalah and Chanukah candles are braided and decorated, drop by this emporium to watch an expert candlemaker at work – she's often here from noon to 4pm Sunday to Thursday. Other waxy highlights include the world's largest braided Havdalah candle (it's got 180 strands) and a gloriously gory minidiorama showing David holding aloft the severed head of Goliath – a masterwork of kitsch! Situated 50m down an alley from the Ashkenazi Ari Synagogue.

Fig Tree Courtyard (28 Alkabetz St, Synagogue Quarter; ◷9am-7pm Sun-Thu Apr-Oct, 9am-5pm Sun-Thu Nov-Mar, 9am-2pm or 3pm Fri) Set around a centenarian fig tree and a 9m-deep cistern (visible through a glass floor panel), this collection of galleries and silversmiths' ateliers is one of Tsfat's classiest. From the rooftop patio you can see half the Galilee, from Mt Meron all the way south to Mt Tabor, with the cliffs of Amud Stream (Nahal Amud) in the depths below. Restrooms available.

Canaan Gallery (☏04-697 4449; www.canaan-gallery.com; Fig Tree Courtyard, 28 Alkabetz St, Synagogue Quarter; ◷9am-7pm Sun-Thu Apr-Oct, 9am-5pm Sun-Thu Nov-Mar, 9am-2.30pm Fri) Continuing Tsfat's centuries-old textile tradition, begun by Jews fleeing the Inquisition, Orna and Yair Moore's studio produces richly textured tapestries, wall hangings and Jewish ritual objects (*talitot, kippot,* challah covers) made from cotton and chenille. You can see weavers at work at their upstairs studio.

Safed Craft Pottery (☏054 434 5206; www.haaripottery.blogspot.com; 63 Yud Alef St, Artists' Quarter; ◷10am-6pm Sun-Thu, 10am-3hrs before sundown Fri) UK-born potter Daniel Flatauer works in the English studio pottery tradition, producing tableware, kitchenware and Judaica that is both functional and extraordinarily beautiful. He has the only salt kiln in Israel – if you're not sure what that means, ask him!

Sheva Chaya Glassblowing Gallery (☏058 714 7640; www.shevachaya.com; 7 Tet Vav St, Artists' Quarter; ◷9am-6pm Sun-Thu, 9am-2pm or 3pm Fri) Kabbalistic concepts and women's themes in Judaism are represented in the art of Denver-born painter and glass-blower Sheva Chaya Shaiman. She does glass-blowing demonstrations on most days in July and August, and often the rest of the year. Situated across the street from the General Safed Exhibition.

Tzfat Gallery of Mystical Art (☏04-692 3051; www.kabbalahart.com; 35 Tet Vav St, Artists' Quarter; ◷usually 9am-4pm Sun-Thu, 9am-noon Fri) Avraham Loewenthal, who hails from Detroit, is happy to explain the symbolism of his colourful, abstract works, which are based on Kabbalistic concepts. Call ahead for a private viewing. Situated across the street from HaMa'ayan HaRadum Sq.

MA'ALOT OLEI HAGARDOM

Leading southwest from the Mandate-era police station on Yerushalayim St, this broad, arrow-straight **stairway** was built by the British in the late 1930s to serve as a buffer between the Arab community (living mainly in what's now the Artists' Quarter) and the Jewish community (in the Synagogue Quarter). Much of the rioting of 1929 took place on what is now Tarpat St, which is about halfway down the hill.

From the top of the staircase, look at the rooftop directly across Yerushalayim St and you'll see an old British fortification, still topped by a **searchlight**. At the bottom, the **Yehezkel HaMeiri Viewpoint** (Ma'alot Olei HaGardom), opened in 2014, affords views of the Kabbalists' tombs and Mt Meron.

Across the street is the **former British police station**, riddled with bulletholes from 1948, which is now used by the Tsfat Academic College.

★ **Museum of Hungarian Speaking Jewry** MUSEUM
(☑04-692 3880; www.hjm.org.il; HaAzma'ut Sq; admission 20NIS, incl tour 35NIS; ☺9am-2pm Sun-Thu, 9am-1pm Fri) Evocative artefacts, photographs and documents do a masterful job of evoking the lost world of pre-WWII Hungarian-speaking Jewry. A 17-minute film provides context. If you're interested, museum co-founder (along with her husband) Chava Lustig will tell you about the Budapest ghetto, which she survived as a 14-year-old. The museum has extensive archives for those interested in doing family research. Signs are in Hebrew, Hungarian and English.

🍃 **Courses**

A variety of organisations work to connect Jews – and, in some cases, non-Jewish travellers as well – with Jewish mysticism and traditional Hasidic life. For a list of options, see the 'Learning Centers' section of http://safed.co.il.

Note that some places have an ulterior agenda (turning secular Jews into Orthodox ones) that they're not completely above-board about, so while questioning is ostensibly encouraged, those in search of truly open and intellectually honest give-and-take may come away disappointed.

Tzfat Kabbalah Center KABBALAH
(International Center for Tzfat Kabbalah; ☑04-682 1771; www.tzfat-kabbalah.org; 1st fl, Fig Tree Courtyard, 28 Alkabetz St, Synagogue Quarter; ☺9am-6pm Sun-Thu, 9am-1pm Fri) Adherents of all religions, or none at all, are welcome to drop by for an introduction to Jewish mysticism and on-the-spot meditation. Hour-long personalised workshops with Eyal Riess, who lectures around the world on the Tsfat Kabbalah tradition, cost 150NIS to 250NIS. Screens films (18NIS) on Tsfat in Hebrew, English, Spanish and Russian.

Livnot U'Lehibanot JEWISH
(☑052 429 5377; www.livnot.org; 17 Alkabetz St, Synagogue Quarter) Offers well-regarded classes, hikes, inexpensive accommodation and community service opportunities to Jewish adults aged 21 to 30. Orthodox-run but pluralistic. The name means 'to build and be built'.

Ascent Institute of Safed KABBALAH
(☑077 360 1101; www.ascentofsafed.com; 2 Ha'Ari St; ☺classes Sun-Thu) Offers Jews interested in 'spiritual discovery' drop-in classes on the Torah and Jewish mysticism. Run by members of the Chabad Hasidic movement. Staff have a variety of opinions on whether Menachem Mendel Schneerson (1902–94), aka the Lubavitcher Rebbe, is in fact the Messiah.

For 200NIS a rabbi will sit with you for an hour (also possible via phone and Skype) to find your 'personal Torah code', based on your birth date, which Ascent promises will 'reveal matters connected to your personality and purpose in life' and give you 'tools for success and fruition'. A scam? You decide.

👉 **Tours**

While it's easy to float around Tsfat on your own little trip, it's a town where stories and secrets run deep.

Baruch Emanuel Erdstein WALKING TOURS
(☑052 251 5134; www.safedexperience.com; per hour 180NIS) Offers spiritual walking tours, generally of three to five hours. Baruch, a storyteller and musician who grew up near Detroit, describes Tsfat as having a 'tremendous gift' to offer, that it's a place that 'opens people up to themselves, to their potential and to beginning to understand the meaning of their lives and of creation'.

Path of the Heart WALKING TOURS
(B'Shvil HaLev, Tzfat Experience; ☑050 750 5695, 04-682 6489; www.shvilhalev.co.il; 7 Tet-Vav St, Artists' Quarter; 2hr tour up to 8 people 350NIS) Runs experiential walking tours of the old city ac-

companied by Hasidic guitar melodies, tales of the Kabbalists and an exploration of their spiritual message.

Festivals

Tsfat Klezmer Festival MUSIC
(www.klezmerf.com) Eastern European Jewish soul music fills the old city for three days in mid-August. Accommodation is in very short supply so book far ahead.

Sleeping

Tsfat has lots of B&Bs and holiday apartments, some rented out by artists. Most places keep Shabbat so some B&Bs have a two-night weekend minimum; it's not usually possible to check-in on Saturday until after sundown.

Room prices rise precipitously during the Tsfat Klezmer Festival (mid-August) and around the Jewish holiday of Lag BaOmer (33 days after Passover); at these times, reserve many months ahead.

Back before air-conditioning, 950m-high Mt Canaan (Har Kna'an) – now a neighbourhood of Tsfat – offered a welcome 'hill station' escape from the summer heat. The area is about 4.5km northeast of the city centre.

Adler Apartments APARTMENTS $
(☎052 344 7766; adler1.4u@gmail.com; office in Adler's Change, 88 Yerushalayim St; d excl breakfast 300NIS, Fri night & all day Sat 350NIS, additional bed 100NIS; ❄) Has 10 clean, practical, simply furnished apartments with kitchenette, in or near the centre of town. If you're arriving on Saturday, easy-going Baruch can arrange key pick-up.

★ **Safed Inn** GUESTHOUSE $$
(Ruckenstein B&B; ☎04-697 1007; www.safedinn.com; 1 Merom Kna'an St; dm/s/d/q without breakfast US$29/100/129/158, cheaper Sun-Wed, additional person US$29; ⏲reception 8am-8pm; ❄@📶) Opened in 1936, this garden guesthouse has comfortable rooms untouched by interior design theories, a sauna, an outdoor hot tub (open 8pm to 11pm) and washing machines (15NIS). Riki and Dov get rave reviews for their local knowledge and tasty continental/Israeli breakfasts (30/60NIS). Call ahead if you'll be arriving after 8pm.

To get there, turn off Rte 8900 onto HaGdud HaShlishi St 250m towards Rosh Pina from the Tsfat police station (in a Tegart Fort built by the British in the late 1930s). Served by local bus 3 (4.80NIS, 22 minutes, twice an hour until 9pm Sunday to Thursday and to 2.30pm Friday) from the central bus station, or you can take a taxi (25NIS during the day).

Carmel Hotel HOTEL $$
(☎050 242 1092, 04-692 0053; 8 Ha'Ari St, ie 8 Ya'avetz St; s/d/q excl breakfast US$75/100/150; ❄@📶) Thanks to owner Shlomo – who is likely to insist that you try his limoncello – staying here is like having the run of a big, old family house. Some of the 12, simply furnished rooms are romantic and some aren't but they're all clean and practical and some have fantastic views.

Artist Quarter Guest House B&B $$
(☎054 776 4877, 077 524 0235; www.artistquarterguesthouse.com; 43 Yud Zayin Alley, Artists' Quarter; d 600-750NIS, additional person 100NIS; ❄📶) Northern Californians Joy and Evan warmly welcome guests to their two spacious, Ottoman-era rooms, both with high, vaulted stone ceilings and Moroccan-style furnishings. Swedish massage available for women.

Beit Yosef Suites B&B $$$
(☎04-692 2515; www.beityosef.co.il; d 650NIS, additional person 175NIS; ❄📶) Rents out nine one-, two- and three-bedroom apartments, with cosy, eclectic decor, in old stone buildings in the Artists' Quarter. The same family, originally from Los Angeles, runs a cafe, which is where breakfast is served. Reserve by phone or online; when you arrive, Sharon will meet you with the key.

Ruth Rimonim HOTEL $$$
(☎04-699 4666, reservations 03-675 4591; www.rimonim.com; Tet-Zayin St, Artists' Quarter; d 700-800NIS; ❄@📶🏊) Housed in part in a one-time Ottoman-era post house, this hotel has stone-walled common areas with wrought iron furnishings and fresh-cut flowers, expansive gardens, a spa and 76 elegant, modern rooms with sparkling marble bathrooms. Wi-fi costs 10/40NIS per two/24 hours.

Eating

Places selling pizza, felafel and shwarma can be found along Yerushalayim St and on the edge of the Synagogue Quarter, at HaMaginim Sq.

All of central Tsfat's restaurants close on Shabbat. If you decide not to drive to settlements such as Rosh Pina, Jish and Amirim to dine, you can order meals from several places on Yerushalayim St, with pick-up on Friday in the early afternoon – ask your B&B for details. Another option is to self-cater at **Coöp Shop Supermarket** (102 Arlozoroff St; ⏲7.30am-9pm Sun-Wed, 7.30am-10pm Thu, 7.30am-1pm or 2pm Fri). At Ruth Rimonim Hotel, a kosher buffet lunch or dinner on Shabbat costs 140NIS; reserve and pay in advance.

Lahuhe Original
Yemenite Food Bar   YEMENITE $

(22 Alkabetz St, Synagogue Quarter; mains 25-35NIS; ☺9am-7pm Sun-Thu, 9am-2hrs before sunset Fri) Decked out in a gown and kaftan that Abraham might have worn, Ronen flips pan-fried 'Yemenite pizza' called *lachuch* (35NIS).

★ **HaAri 8**   ISRAELI $$

(☑04-692 0033; 8 Ha'Ari St; mains from 58NIS; ☺11am-11pm Sun-Thu, closed Fri, sometimes opens after sundown Sat; ☑) When the mayor has VIP guests, this is where he brings them. Specialities include steak, grilled meats, 'cigars' filled with chopped meat, fish and fresh salads. Vegetarians options include salads, soups and pasta. Has a playroom for kids.

Maximilian   CAFE $$

(☑077 788 2887; 2 Arlozoroff St, Artists' Quarter; mains 42-58NIS; ☺8.30am-10pm Sun-Thu, 8.30am-2hrs before sundown Fri; ☎☑) Serves a range of tasty pasta, quiches (48NIS), salads and freshly squeezed juices as well as creative fare such as figs (fresh when in season) filled with local goat's cheese and topped with a berry sauce. Has a sunny courtyard. Situated right next to the General Safed Exhibition.

Tree of Life Vegetarian Cafe   VEGETARIAN $$

(☑050 696 0239; HaMaginim Sq, Synagogue Quarter; mains 38-48NIS; ☺9.20am-10pm Sun-Thu, 9.20am-11pm or later in summer, 9.20am-2hrs before sundown Fri; ☑) If you're in the mood for something very healthy – portobello mushroom quiche, for instance, or quinoa pilaf, or whole-grain desserts sweetened with date syrup – LA-raised Feiga and her tiny eatery may be the perfect destination. Specialities include homemade veggie burgers and quesadillas. Lots of dishes are vegan and/or gluten-free.

Gan Eden   ITALIAN $$$

(☑04-697 2434; www.be-ganeden.com; 33 Ha-Gdud HaShlishi St, Mt Canaan; mains 57-89NIS; ☺9am-10.30pm Sun-Thu, 9am-2.30pm Fri; ☑) It's worth the 3km ride from the town centre (about 25NIS by taxi) for the scrumptious antipasti and oven-baked fish served here, prepared under the supervision of chef Rafi; and the fabulous desserts (35NIS), many of them chocolate-based, made by his wife, pastry chef Yael. Set in an early-20th-century house with a lovely garden and views to Mt Meron. Kosher-dairy.

☆ **Entertainment**

Back in the 1970s Tsfat had half-a-dozen nightclubs, but these days the increasingly haredi city goes to bed fairly early, except in summer when tourists keep the old city's streets and cafes lively until late.

Almost everything is closed on Shabbat – except, of course, for the synagogues, some of which sing their prayers, such as **Shlomo Carlebach** (☑054 804 8602; http://carlebach. intzfat.info), or hold Hassidic *farbrengen* (joyous community gatherings).

★ **Khan of the**
White Donkey   CULTURAL EVENTS

(☑077 234 5719, Maxim 054 449 4521; www.thekhan. org; 5 Tzvi Levanon Alley, Artists' Quarter; ☺9am-4pm Sun-Thu) This centre hosts a variety of cultural, environmental and health-oriented community activities, including concerts (50NIS to 70NIS), open-mic jam sessions (20NIS, on some Thursdays at 9pm) and a low-cost holistic medicine clinic (Sunday from 8am to 4pm). The alternative vibe attracts a mix of hippies, backpackers and strictly observant Jews. The centre occupies a 700-year-old khan (caravanserai), beautifully restored with all-natural materials. Rents out three B&B rooms.

ℹ **Information**

For info on Tsfat's history, attractions, accommodation and study options – and some colourful local personalities – check out www.safed.co.il.

There are banks with **ATMs** along Yerushalayim St at Nos 34, 35 and 72.

ℹ **LOST ON THE WAY TO ETERNITY**

If you ask a local for directions, explaining that you're lost, you may be told: 'You're not lost, you're in Tsfat!' Providing details on where you're going is likely to elicit the desired directions – the locals, though otherworldly in their spiritual yearnings, are generally a friendly and helpful lot (and many are native English speakers).

Even the geographically gifted visitor is almost sure to get lost in the old city's tangle of alleyways. Most have names (or at least Hebrew-letter designations), but signs are few and far between and, in any case, few locals use – or even know – the official street names. Making matters worse is the fact that street numbers, where they exist, are not always sequential. Oh, and the signs pointing the way to various landmarks are designed to provide directions for drivers, not pedestrians.

Adler's Change (88 Yerushalayim St; per hour 15NIS; ⊙10am-1am Sun-Thu, 10am-1½hr before sundown Fri) Tsfat's only cybercafe is basically an exchange bureau with two computers. Owner Baruch is happy to dispense tourist information. Situated almost under the Palmach St bridge.

Post Office (37 Yerushalayim St)

Rivka Ziv Hospital (Sieff Hospital, Ziv Medical Center; ☑04-682 8811; www.ziv.org.il; HaRambam St; ⊙emergency 24hr) Founded in 1910, this large government hospital is 3km southwest of the central bus station. Served by buses 6 and 11.

Tourist Information Center (☑04-692 4427; info@livnot.com; 17 Alkabetz St, Synagogue Quarter; ⊙8.30am-5pm Sun-Thu, 9am-1pm Fri) English-speaking staff are happy to provide information on visiting Tsfat and on local volunteering opportunities for both non-Jews and Jews. Run by the outreach organisation Livnot U'Lehibanot (www.livnot.org).

ⓘ Getting There & Away

The **central bus station** (www.bus.co.il; Ha-Atzma'ut St), situated about 700m west of the Synagogue Quarter, has services linked to:

Tiberias (Afikim bus 450; 16.50NIS, 40 minutes, hourly Sunday to Friday afternoon, one Saturday night)

Jerusalem (Nateev Express bus 982; 40NIS, 3¼ hours, eight daily Sunday to Thursday, five Friday, at least three Saturday night)

Haifa-Mercazit HaMifratz (Nateev Express bus 361; 1¾ hours, twice an hour) Goes via Akko (one hour).

Kiryat Shmona (Nateev Express bus 511; 20.70NIS, one hour, hourly) Goes via Rosh Pina (10.20NIS, five minutes) and the Hula Valley.

Tellingly, there are a lot more direct buses to the ultra-Orthodox Tel Aviv suburb of Bnei Brak than to Tel Aviv itself (Egged bus 846; 49.50NIS, 3½ hours, one or two daily Sunday to Friday). In fact, to get to Tel Aviv it's faster to take Egged bus 361 to Akko and then hop on a train.

Mt Meron Area

جبل الجرمق   הר מירון

West of Tsfat, antenna-topped Mt Meron (1204m), Israel's second-tallest peak (after Mt Hermon), looms over the Dalton Plateau and scattered Jewish, Druze and Arab villages. Until recently, the area was planted with fruit trees such as pear and apple, but more and more land is being given over to grapevines for the thriving wineries of Ramat Dalton, sometimes called (with some exaggeration) the 'Israeli Napa Valley' or 'Israel's Tuscany'.

Moshav Amirim   أميريم   אמירים

Founded in 1958 by pioneers of the Israeli vegetarian movement, Amirim (elevation 600m) is still 100% veggie – no one here cooks, eats or serves meat, fowl or fish. Set on the southeastern slopes of the Mt Meron massif, the moshav is known for its clean air (no chicken coops or cow sheds), excellent organic food and rustic guesthouses – a beautiful place to bliss out.

⊙ Sights & Activities

Amirim is a quiet settlement of single-family homes with a few artists' galleries, a sculpture park in the centre of the moshav, and a **swimming pool** (open approximately mid-June to mid-September) situated in an enchanting canyon. Trails lead into the nearby **Mt Meron Nature Reserve**. Everything is signposted.

Many locals are as passionate about alternative medicine as they are about vegetarianism, and yoga teachers, shiatsu practitioners and naturopaths abound – for details, see http://amirim.com/health/en.

ⓘ Sleeping

Amirim has an (over)supply of about 170 tzimmer (B&B) rooms. In winter prices drop by as much as 30%.

Campbell Family Guest Rooms   B&B $$
(☑054 532 2640, 04-698 9045; alitamirim@hotmail.com; d1/2 nights 400/700NIS; ❋ ⊛) Friendly British expat Phillip Campbell and his wife, Alit, rent out two unpretentious double rooms with kitchenette, patio and spa bath. A great spot for some peace and quiet.

★**Ohn-Bar Guesthouse**   GUESTHOUSE $$$
(☑04-698 9803; www.amirim.com; d/q excl breakfast from 660/920NIS, additional child 50NIS; ❋ @ ⊛) Perched on a terraced hillside, these 14 wooden units come with balcony, spa bath and fully equipped kitchenette. Outside, hammocks swing among the fruit trees and there's an organic vegetable garden. In-room breakfast costs 94NIS to 140NIS per couple. Discounts are offered if you stay three or more nights, are a student or arrive by public transport. American-educated owners Ohn and Anva are excellent sources of information on the area. The guesthouse is wheelchair accessible.

✕ Eating

Amirim has three vegetarian and vegan restaurants. Having breakfast/dinner delivered to your B&B generally costs 100/200NIS per couple.

If you get desperate, here's a little secret: there's a hamburger joint up on Rte 866, across from the access road to Amirim.

Bait 77
VEGETARIAN $

(Bayit 77; ☎04-698 0984; www.bait77.com; 77 Mitzpeh Menahem St; mains 24-38NIS; ☺8.30am-6pm Fri-Sun, 8.30am-9pm Thu, open daily in Aug; ☑) This attractive little bakery and cafe, run by Melbourne-raised Joy and her son Ariel, specialises in light, healthy meals: soup, salad, quiche, pasta, pizza and foccacia, complemented with homemade cakes, pastries and gluten-free muffins. Breakfast costs 100NIS for two, Thursday is pizza night in the garden, and there is whole-wheat bread and pitas for sale and, on Friday, sweet challah bread.

Dalia's Restaurant
VEGETARIAN $$

(☎04-698 9349; http://dalia-rest.co.il; breakfast/ brunch 50/65NIS, set menu 100NIS; ☺8am-10pm daily; ☑) Dalia has served a hearty set menu featuring soups, stuffed vegetables, 'meatballs' made of almonds, walnuts and peanuts, and delicious salads since 1974. The relaxing, old-time dining room has panoramic views of the Sea of Galilee. Children three years and under eat for free.

☆ Entertainment

Hemdat Yamim
MUSIC

(☎04-698 9423; www.hemdatyamim.com; Moshav Shefer) A much beloved music venue, with frequent concerts of Israeli pop, jazz, Western classical etc, especially on Thursday and Friday nights and Saturday mornings. Situated across Rte 866 from Amirim.

❶ Getting There & Away

Nativ Express bus 361 (twice hourly) links Amirim Junction, 1km to 1.5km from the moshav, with Haifa's Merkazit HaMifratz bus station (26.50NIS, 1¼ hours) and Tsfat (15.40NIS, 20 minutes).

Jish
גוש חלב الجش

The only village in Israel with a Maronite (Eastern Catholic) majority, serene hillside Jish (population 3000) was settled by migrants from Lebanon in the 18th and 19th centuries. Today it is the site of a pioneering effort to revive the use of Aramaic, the language of Jesus and an important source of identity for Maronites. Most shops are closed on Sunday.

During the Great Jewish Revolt (66-70 BCE) – then, as now, known in Hebrew as Gush Halav – was the last place in the Galilee to fall to the Romans, according to Josephus Flavius.

◉ Sights & Activities

Near the entrance to the village, you can visit a large, modern Maronite church and, across the street, the tombs of Shamaiya and Avtalion, Jewish sages who served on the Sanhedrin in Jerusalem during the 1st century BCE. In a small valley 800m east of the entrance to Jish, hikers can explore the remains of an ancient synagogue (3rd or 4th century CE) amid fig and olive groves.

A paved, 2.5km hiking and cycling path known as the Coexistence Trail (wheelchair accessible) heads east from Jish, leading to Moshav Dalton via Dalton Reservoir.

At local farms you can pick your own cherries (May), peaches (starting in June), raspberries (summer) and apples (late August to October).

🛏 Sleeping & Eating

Several area restaurants serve authentic Lebanese cuisine.

Ruah Glilit
B&B $$

(☎052 281 0433; swojish@yahoo.com; d 500NIS) George Samaan, a well-known oud, *saz* and violin player (you can see him on YouTube) who often appears with Ehud Banai, and his wife, Eva, offers guests a warm, musical welcome in a cosy sitting room outfitted with an upright piano, an old gramophone and a wood-burning stove. The three upstairs rooms feature wooden balconies and gorgeous views. It's 600m up the main street from the entrance to town.

★ Misedet HaArazim
LEBANESE $$

(☎Wiam 054 552 5590; Rte 89; mains 45-98NIS; ☺10am-10pm or 11pm; ☑) Scrumptious offerings include eight kinds of hummus, stuffed grape leaves (45NIS), grilled meats, *shishbarak* (meat dumplings in goat yoghurt sauce; 50NIS) and *sheikh al-mahshi* (zucchini stuffed with ground beef and lamb and cooked in yoghurt sauce; 55NIS). Situated at the entrance to Jish; the sign features a green cedar of Lebanon.

A selection of two dozen different veggie salads costs 45NIS per person (35NIS if you also order a main dish; minimum two people). For dessert, try the chocolate shwarma (25NIS).

Baladna
MIDDLE EASTERN**$$**

(☑04-699 1151; mains 40-80NIS; ⊙10am-2am, closed Mon) Ensconced in two 19th-century stone houses, this atmospheric restaurant specialises in authentic Galilee-style Arab cuisine, including *shishbarak* (40NIS) and dishes made with *freekeh* (roasted green wheat). Other offerings include pork schnitzel (50NIS) and seven cocktails (35NIS to 40NIS). It often has live music on Saturday night. Situated 600m up the main street from the town entrance.

ℹ Getting There & Away

Jish is 13km northeast of Tsfat, right where Rte 89 does a 90-degree turn. It is linked to Tsfat (20 minutes, every one or two hours) by buses 43 and 367; the latter also goes to Nahariya (45 minutes).

Ramat Dalton רמת דלתון هضبة دالتون

The area around Moshav Dalton, known as Ramat Dalton (Dalton Plateau), produces some highly regarded wines. Several wineries do their thing in the Ramat Dalton Industrial Park, 4km northeast of Jish on Rte 886.

🏃 Activities

Dalton Winery
WINERY

(☑04-698 7683; www.dalton-winery.com; Ramat Dalton Industrial Park; admission 15NIS; ⊙10am-4pm Sun-Thu, 10am-2pm Fri) Using cabernet sauvignon, merlot, petit syrah, shiraz and zinfandel grapes, this winery produces about one million bottles a year. It has a log-cabin-style tasting centre across the car park from the modern production facilities. Offers 45-minutes tours (call ahead if you can), the last one hour before closing.

Adir Winery
WINERY

(☑04-699 1039; www.adir-winery.com; Ramat Dalton Industrial Park; ⊙9am-5pm Sun-Thu, 9am-2pm or 3pm Fri, closes later in summer) Inside the all-white visitors centre, you can sample Adir's award-winning wines (30NIS; free if you buy a bottle); production is just 100,000 bottles a year. Also has a cheese shop that serves sublime frozen yoghurt (8NIS to 32NIS depending on cup size). At the cafe, breakfast (130NIS for two), based on goat's cheeses, is served from 9am to 3pm (to 1pm Fri).

WINERY TOURS

Israeli wines are attracting growing attention on the world wine scene – and winning top international awards. Among those that are kosher, the best are those that are not *mevushal* (flash pasteurised), a process that can degrade a wine's delicate flavours and aromas.

Israel now has some 300 wineries of all sizes, including about 30 on the Golan, with its well-drained volcanic soils, cool breezes and varied elevations and microclimates; 90 in the Upper Galilee; 30 in the Western Galilee; 30 in the Lower Galilee and on Mt Carmel; 70 in the Judean Hills; and 30 in the deserts of the Negev.

Quite a few Galilee and Golan wineries are happy to welcome visitors. Create your own 'wine route' out of the following wineries:

➡ Adir Winery

➡ Bahat Winery (p244)

➡ Dalton Winery

➡ Golan Heights Winery (p241)

➡ Odem Mountain Winery (p245)

Wine connoisseurs might want to look out for three excellent wine guides:

➡ *The Ultimate Rogov's Guide to Israeli Wines* (Daniel Rogov, 2012) A comprehensive guide by Israel's premier wine critic, who died in 2011.

➡ *The Wine Routes of Israel,* 3rd edition (Eliezer Sacks, Yaron Goldfischer and Adam Montefiore, 2012)

➡ *Wines of Israel* (Eliezer Sacks and Adam Montefiore, 2012) A lighter, smaller version of *The Wine Routes of Israel.*

Useful websites covering the Israeli wine scene include www.winesisrael.com and www.israelwines.co.il. Shiri Bistro & Wine Bar (p235) in Rosh Pina is a great place to taste hard-to-find boutique vintages.

✖ Eating

Nalchik　　　　　　　　　　　　　　CIRCASSIAN $
(☏04-699 0548; Rehaniya; dishes 25-35NIS; ⏲noon-8pm daily; ☏) This unpretentious, family-run restaurant is a great place to try dishes brought from the North Caucasus by Circassian refugees in the 1870s. The village of Rehaniya is 4.5km north of the Dalton Industrial Park; from Rte 886, follow Nalchik's white, black and red signs (in Hebrew).

Specialities include *majmak* (lentil paste, eaten with pita), *shush barak* (ground-meat-filled dumplings served in light tomato soup), *k'ulak'* (chickpea-filled dumpling served with yoghurt), *haloj* (pastry filled with Circassian cheese and deep-fried in olive oil) and *mataza* (dumplings filled with Circassian cheese and green onions and served with yoghurt).

Tomb of the Rashbi

קבר הרשב״י　قبر الحاخام شمعون بار يوشاي

Authorship of the *Zohar*, the most important work of Kabbalah, is traditionally credited to the 2nd century CE Jewish sage Rabbi Shimon bar Yochai, who is often known by his acronym, the Rashbi (Rashby). Scholars believe the work was compiled in Spain in the 13th century. By tradition, the **tomb of the Rashbi** (Rte 866; ⏲24hr) is 5km northwest of Tsfat on the slopes on Mt Meron, somewhere under a rigorously sex-segregated complex (men to the left, women to the right) that appears to date, in part, from the Crusader period. Since his precise burial place is unknown, there is no actual tomb, just a *tziun* (marker) – inside a multi-alcove synagogue – above which candles flicker behind smoke-darkened glass.

Other important sages who are believed by some to be buried in the immediate vicinity include the Rashbi's son **Rabbi Elazar**; the renowned 1st-century BCE sage **Hillel the Elder**, who summed up Judaism with the single commandment 'What is hateful to thee, do not unto thy fellow man'; and Hillel's great rival in legal disputations, **Shammai**.

On the eve of the holiday of **Lag BaOmer**, tens of thousands of mostly haredi pilgrims flock to the tomb of the Rashbi, spending the whole night in fervent prayer, with singing and dancing around bonfires. Some pilgrims perform a ceremony known as Upsherin in Yiddish and Halaaka in Judeo-Arabic, at which three-year-old boys are given their first haircuts.

The Rashbi's blue-domed grave complex, situated inside the Orthodox Moshav Meron (gate locked from sundown on Shabbat and Jewish holidays), is run rather chaotically by squabbling haredi groups. Adding to the hair-trigger atmosphere is the fact that the complex serves as a place of refuge for homeless people (some with psychiatric issues) and criminals recently released from prison. To get to the tomb you may have to run a gauntlet of beggars. Non-Jews, as well as anyone who's not modestly dressed or who arrives on Shabbat, may encounter hostility, as did Madonna, who had rocks thrown at her.

Bikta BeKadita

Bikta BeKadita　　　　　　　　　　B&B $$$
(☏04-692 1963; www.kadita.co.il; cabin US$182-415; ❄🐾🛏) Perched on a hilltop, artsy, rustic Bikta BeKadita – inspired by the American back-to-nature movement of the 1960s – has an ecological philosophy and a hippy vibe. It's situated 4.5km northeast of Meron Jct, 1km off Rte 89 along a one-lane gravel road.

The five eclectic and very creative cabins, surrounded by fruit orchards, are built of sustainable materials; each has room for two to four people and comes with – what else? – a hammock. Hosts Doron and Mika serve lavish homemade breakfasts and wine from Kadita's own vineyard, which produces just 500 bottles a year.

Rosh Pina　ראש פינה روش بينا

☏04 / POP 2800
Rosh Pina's 19th-century stone houses, oozing with charm, were discovered years ago by Tel Aviv chicsters. The town now plays host to artists' studios and some of the most upscale sleeping and dining in the Upper Galilee.

◉ Sights

**Rosh Pina Pioneers
Restoration Site**　　　　　　　HISTORIC SITE
(⏲galleries 10am-noon & 2-5pm or 6pm, later in Jul & Aug, some closed Sat) Rosh Pina's old town was settled in the 1870s by Jews from Tsfat and after 1882 by immigrants from Romania. It consists of just three short cobblestone streets, one of them, with Parisian pretension, called HaBoulevard. It has been turned into a pedestrian zone, and visitors can explore the quiet lanes, lined with pretty, restored (and unrestored) stone houses, visit the **old synagogue** and pop into about a dozen **galleries** selling jewellery, ceramics and paintings. In **Professor Mer's House**

(1887) there's a small museum with exhibits on Rosh Pina's early years.

Follow the signs to the **Baron's Garden** (founded 1886), across HaRishonim St from Shiri Bistro; and the **Old Cemetery** (via Ben Arieh St).

The Pioneers Restoration Site is at the upper edge of Rosh Pina – it's at the top of Ha-Halutzim St, which heads up the hill (west) from the roundabout next to the Centre HaGalil shopping mall on Rte 90.

🛏 Sleeping

Rosh Pina's many B&Bs, great for a romantic getaway, are the most crowded – and priciest – on Thursday and Friday nights.

★ Villa Tehila   B&B $$$
(☎04-693 7788; www.villa-tehila.co.il; HaHalutzim St; d from 670NIS; ✴@🛜🛝) You may spot a few old-time Israeli celebrities at this fabulous B&B, whose shaded, 19th-century stone courtyards shelter bubbling fountains, glittering fairy lights, stained glass, a veritable menagerie and a cosy bar. During the British Mandate, they hid a secret weapons cache. Villa Tehila has 11 rooms, all of them exquisite. Book well ahead. It's situated 150m down the hill from the Restoration Site.

Pina Barosh   B&B $$$
(☎04-693 6582; www.pinabarosh.com; HaHalutzim St; d weekday/weekend from 600/750NIS; ✴🛜) The seven atmospheric rooms (there's also a luxury villa) arrayed around the central courtyard of a one-time livestock yard, feature vaulted ceilings, spa bath and exposed brick- and stonework. Breakfast is served at Shiri Bistro until 1pm.

Hotel Mizpe Hayamim   RESORT $$$
(☎04-699 4555, reservations 1 800 555 666; www.mizpe-hayamim.com; d incl half-board US$420-620; ✴@🛜🛝) Set in 15 hectares of gorgeous gardens, this is one of Israel's most exclusive hotels. Amenities include a spa, a 25m heated indoor pool and rooms that are as comfortable as they are romantic – that is, very. Mobile phone use is prohibited in public areas. Situated 3km towards Tsfat from Rosh Pina along Rte 8900.

🍴 Eating & Drinking

Rosh Pina has about 60 places to eat. Some are hidden inside and behind the old houses of the Pioneers Restoration Site, others – including shwarma joints – are 1.5km down the hill in and around the modern Centre HaGalil mall just off Rte 90.

Amburger   BURGERS $$
(☎04-680 0044; Centre HaGalil mall, Rte 90; mains 43-149NIS; ◷11.30am-11pm or later; 🛜) An excellent family choice for burgers (43NIS to 63NIS), steaks, lamb chops and other meaty dishes, most of them made with aged Golan-raised meat (the entrecôte, though, is from Uruguay). Has pasta for vegetarians. Lunch deals (49NIS to 61NIS) are served until 5pm.

★ Shiri Bistro & Wine Bar   BISTRO $$$
(☎04-693 6582; www.pinabarosh.com; Pina Barosh B&B, HaHalutzim St; mains 65-150NIS; ◷8.30am-11pm or later; 🍴) Fresh-cut flowers, flickering candles and spectacular views greet you at this Mediterranean-inflected French bistro, named after the chef, whose great-great-great-grandparents built the place in the late 1870s. This is an excellent spot to sample rare Israeli boutique wines – at least 250 Galilee and Golan wines are available by the glass – and learn about the vibrant Israeli winery scene.

Tangerine   BAR
(◷7.30pm-2am or later daily) Down a stairway from the Pioneers Restoration Site, this vaulted, three-room pub is run by local blokes. From May to September it hosts live concerts every Saturday from 8pm and a jam session each Tuesday from 7.30pm; the rest of the year there are concerts one Saturday a month.

ℹ Information

The Centre HaGalil mall on Rte 90 has three banks with ATMs, a pharmacy, a Steimatzky bookshop and two petrol stations.

ℹ Getting There & Away

All long-haul buses going to or coming from the Hula Valley and Kiryat Shmona (eg to/from Tiberias or Tel Aviv) pass the entrance to Rosh Pina on Rte 90. From there it's 1.5km up to the Pioneers Restoration Site.

Nateev Express bus 511 (hourly) goes up the hill, along Rte 8900, to Tsfat (10.20NIS, 30 minutes) and north to Kiryat Shmona (35 minutes) via the Hula Valley. It stops near the outskirts of the Pioneers Restoration Site.

Around Rosh Pina

Tel Hatzor   ARCHAEOLOGICAL SITE
(Tel Hazor; ☎04-693 7290; adult/child 22/10NIS; ◷8am-4pm or 5pm Sat-Thu, 8am-3pm or 4pm Fri, last entry 30min before closing) At this spot, archaeologists have uncovered no fewer than 21 layers of settlement from the 3rd millennium BCE to 732 BCE, when the Israelite

city that stood here – whose 10th-century BCE gate may have been built by Solomon – was destroyed by the Assyrians. In times of siege, the supply of water was ensured by an extraordinary underground system whose 40m-deep shaft is accessible via a spiral staircase. Excavations are ongoing and signage is excellent. Tel Hatzor has been a Unesco World Heritage site since 2005.

The tel is 7km north of Rosh Pina on Old Rte 90. From Rte 90, get off at Ayelet Ha-Shahar; the access road is about 400m south of the kibbutz.

Hula Valley

וادي الحولة   עמק החולה

The swamps of the Hula Valley were once notorious for malaria, but a massive drainage program completed in 1958 got rid of the anopheles mosquitoes – and destroyed one of the country's most important wetlands, a crucial stopping point for the millions of migratory birds who pass through Israel on their way between Europe and Africa. In recent years about 10% of the old lake has been restored.

The Society for the Protection of Nature in Israel (SPNI) was founded in 1953 by people galvanised into action by the draining of the Hula.

★ **Agamon HaHula**   PARK

(☑ 04-681 7137; www.agamon-hula.co.il; admission 5NIS; ☺ 9am-7pm, last entry 6pm) This is one of the best places in Israel to see flocks of cranes, pelicans and storks. By road, the site is 7.5km north of the Hula Nature Reserve, and 1.2km off Rte 90.

In the 1990s, the Hula's cotton fields were converted to growing peanuts – the soil here is ideal and Israel needs a massive supply of peanuts to produce Bamba, Israeli children's favourite junk food. Unfortunately, cranes love peanuts as much as Israeli kids love Bamba, so conflict between the birds, protected by law, and local farmers was inevitable.

Happily, an elegant solution was found. It turns out that the best way to encourage the birds to continue on their way to Ethiopia and Sudan is to feed them – if they can't find nibblies, research shows, they stick around longer and end up munching even more peanuts. Or they may stop migrating altogether – 35,000 cranes have already decided to become wintertime couch potatoes. An entire field is now given over to supplying the migrating birds with 6 to 7 tonnes of corn daily, delivered by tractor.

Seeing wild cranes up close is notoriously difficult because under normal circumstances the entire flock will take to the sky en masse if anyone comes near, landing in the safety of a neighbouring (peanut) field. A local farmer noticed that the one moving object that the cranes showed no fear of was their great benefactor, the corn tractor. So he had a brilliant idea: the corn tractor could be used to transport not only corn but also birdwatchers – without the cranes paying the slightest attention. That's how the 50-seat **Safari Wagon** (Aglat Mistor; adult/child 57/49NIS, at dawn 85/65NIS; ☺ hourly 9am-1hr before dark late Sep-Apr, often also 6am and 7.30pm) was born. Camouflaged and pulled by an utterly unremarkable (from a crane's point of view) John Deere tractor, it offers visitors unparalleled crane-watching opportunities – you can see the birds without even having to crane your neck! Reserve ahead if possible.

Other birds that can be seen here seasonally include **pelicans** (September, October and March to mid-April), 65,000 of which fly between the Danube Delta in Romania and the Blue Nile and Lake Victoria in Africa; and **storks** (August, September, April and May), a stunning 500,000 of which pass by twice a year.

To cover the 8.5km path around the restored wetlands, you can either walk or rent a mountain bike (50NIS), four-wheeled pedal cart (185NIS for up to five people), seven-seat 'conference bike' (50NIS per person) or golf cart (149NIS for two people). Don't expect to see many birds in the summer. The entire site is wheelchair accessible.

Call ahead to coordinate a visit to the site's banding (ringing) station.

★ **Hula Nature Reserve**   PARK

(☑ 04-693 7069; www.parks.org.il; adult/child 35/21NIS; ☺ 8am-5pm Sun-Thu, 8am-4pm Fri, last entry 1hr before closing) Migrating birds flock to the wetlands of Israel's first nature reserve, founded in 1964. More than 200 species of small waterfowl mingle happily with cormorants, herons, pelicans, raptors, storks and cranes, while water buffalo (*jamoose*) roam certain areas of the reserve, their grazing important to the preservation of open meadows. The main 1.5km **Swamp Trail**, which passes birdwatching hides, is wheelchair accessible. Situated 15km north of Rosh Pina, at a point 2km west of Rte 90.

The visitors centre offers an excellent, 40-minute **3D film** (available in English) on bird migration and dioramas on Hula wildlife. In the shallow lake, you may spot fur, shells and fins in addition to feathers – these will be attached to nutrias, otters, swamp turtles or catfish weighing up to 20kg. Unlike the rest of Israel, the Hula is at its greenest in summer. Around sunset in the winter, you can see birds returning from their daytime feeding. Renting binoculars costs 10NIS.

Kiryat Shmona & Tel Hai

קרית שמונה תל חי   كريات شمونة تل حاي

☑ 04 / POP 23,100

Kiryat Shmona is a sunbaked, hardscrabble 'development town' with little to offer the visitor except the promise of transport from the faded, grungy bus station. The town is almost completely shut on Shabbat.

The name, which means 'Town of the Eight', honours eight Zionist pioneers, including Josef Trumpeldor, killed in 1920 at Tel Hai, 3km to the north.

◉ Sights & Activities

Open Museum of Photography   MUSEUM
(☑ 04-681 6700; www.omuseums.org.il; Tel Hai, east side of Rte 90; adult/child 3-18yr 20/16NIS; ☉ 8am-4pm Sun-Thu, 10am-4pm Sat, closed Fri) Temporary exhibitions, by renowned local and international photographers, change three times a year. This is a good place to explain the 'ancient' technologies of predigital photography to your kids.

It's situated inside the high-tech Tel Hai Industrial Park, next to a landscaped sculpture garden. To get there from the centre of Kiryat Shmona, head north on Rte 90 for 3km and follow the signs to 'Photography'.

⌂ Sleeping

HI – Tel Hai Youth Hostel   HOSTEL $$
(☑ 02-594 5666; www.iyha.org.il; Tel Hai, east side of Rte 90; dm/s/d 152/292/400NIS; s/d Fri 355/450NIS; ▣ @ ☎) These modern, well-kept facilities include 83 rooms with 350 beds. Dorm rooms have four to six beds and are excellent value. Situated opposite the vehicle gate to the Open Museum of Photography.

❶ Getting There & Away

BUS

Kiryat Shmona is the major bus junction in the Galilee Panhandle. Destinations include:

Majdal Shams (Rama bus 58; 30 minutes, five daily Sunday to Thursday, three on Friday until early afternoon, one Saturday night) Stops along Rtes 99 and 989 include the Banias Nature Reserve, Nimrod Fortress and Neve Ativ.

Katzrin (Rama bus 59; one hour, four or five daily Sunday to Thursday, one Saturday night) Goes via Merom Golan and Ein Zivan.

Tsfat (Nateev Express bus 511; 20.70NIS, one hour, hourly) Travels via Rosh Pina's Pioneer Restoration Site (30 minutes) and the turn-offs for Agamon HaHula (12.40NIS, 12 minutes) and the Hula Nature Reserve (13.70NIS, 15 minutes).

Tiberias (Egged buses 541 and 840; 31.50NIS, one hour, hourly) Passes by Rosh Pina.

Tel Aviv (Egged buses 840 and 845, 49.50NIS, 3¾ hours, at least hourly)

Jerusalem (Egged bus 963; 49.50NIS, 3¼ hours, twice a day Sunday to Thursday, one Friday)

CAR

The area's only car-rental agency is run by **Eldan** (☑ 04-690 3186; www.eldan.co.il; 4 Sinai St).

TAXI

For a taxi based at Nehemia Mall (at the intersection of Rte 90 and Rte 99), call ☑ 1 800 304 141. For taxis based at the bus station, call ☑ 04-694 2333/77.

Metula

מטולה   مطولة

☑ 04 / POP 1560

Situated at the Galilee's northernmost tip, this picturesque, hilltop village – surrounded on three sides by Lebanon – was founded in 1896 with help from the French branch of the Rothschild family. In 1920 its location played a crucial role in the decision to include the Galilee Panhandle in the British Mandate of Palestine rather than the French Mandate of Lebanon. Today, the economy is based on tourists in the mood for a Swiss alpine vibe and on fruit orchards growing apples, pears, peaches, nectarines, apricots, kiwifruit and lychees.

⊙ Sights & Activities

Strolling up and down Metula's quaint main street, you'll pass lots of solid stone houses built a century or more ago; ceramic panels explain their history

Dado Lookout VIEWPOINT
Perched high atop the hill southwest of HaRishonim St – the one with the red-and-white antenna tower on top – this lookout offers spectacular, often windy views. To the south you can see the Hula Valley, to the east the Golan (including Mt Hermon and the twin volcanoes of Avital and Bental) and to the north the fields and hills of Lebanon. Inside Israel's northern neighbour, you can see the Ayoun Valley in the foreground, while on the horizon it's easy to spot the **Beaufort**, a Crusader fortress. To get to the lookout, follow the signs – it's about 1km above the centre

★ **Nahal Iyyun Nature Reserve** HIKING
(☑04-695 1519; www.parks.org.il; adult/child 29/15NIS; ⊙8.30am-5pm Apr-Sep, 8.30am-4pm Oct-Mar) One of the Galilee's loveliest creekside trails, about 3km long, follows the Iyyun (Ayun) Stream from its crossing from Lebanon into Israel, through a cliff-lined canyon, to four waterfalls, including the 31m-high Tanur (Chimney) Waterfall. The park has two entrances: one in Metula's northeastern corner, just 100m from the border fence (last entry 1½ hours before closing), the other – offering an easy circuit to the Tanur Waterfall – on Rte 90 3km south of town (last entry 30 minutes before closing).

The lower entrance has a wheelchair-accessible trail.

Canada Centre ICE SKATING
(☑04-695 0370; www.canada-centre.co.il; 1 HaRishonim St; ice skating 65NIS, pool 50NIS, bowling 35NIS, combo ticket 105NIS; ⊙closed Sun except Jul & Aug) This modern sports complex, a bit down the hill (south) from the village centre, houses Israel's largest ice rink (10am to 5pm), indoor and outdoor swimming pools, a 10-lane bowling alley (10am to 5pm), a spa and an impressive fitness centre.

🍽 Sleeping & Eating

The historic houses along HaRishonim St are home to a number of rustic restaurants and a few places to stay.

★ **Villa Lishansky** HISTORIC HOTEL $$
(☑04-699 7184; www.rest.co.il/lishansky; 42 HaRishonim St; d 450-500NIS; ⊙restaurant 9am-noon, 1-4pm & 6.30-10pm or later; ❊ 🐾) Built in

the Bauhaus style in 1936 by the family of a famous WWI spy, this place – still owned by the Lishanskys – retains the original floor tiles, mouldings and lamps. Hearty beef, lamb, chicken and fish dishes are prepared with Galilean herbs and spices in the hotel's **restaurant** (2-course meals 99NIS to 138NIS). Upstairs, the three very spacious guest rooms connect to a sitting room that's straight out of the 1930s.

Travel Hotel Metulla HOTEL $$
(☑04-824 8801, reservations 04-688 3040; www.travelhotels.co.il; 52 HaRishonim St; d/apt 500/650NIS, Thu & Fri extra 100NIS, additional child 100NIS; ❊ 🐾) Opened in 2014, this attractive and thoroughly modern place – right in the centre of the village – has 23 rooms and four apartments with space for five. Wheelchair accessible. Guests get free use of the Canada Centre swimming pools from June to mid-October.

HaTachanah STEAK $$$
(☑04-694 4810; 1 HaRishonim St; mains 65-230NIS; ⊙1-10pm or later Mon-Sat; 🐾) Modern and airy, with wood-panelled walls and panoramic views, this highly regarded restaurant serves first-rate steaks as well as hamburgers, pasta, soups, salads and lamb chops. A 0.5L glass of German beer costs 33NIS. Kiddie portions are available (of the mains, not the beer). Reserve ahead on Thursday night, Friday, Saturday and holidays, and in August.

ℹ Getting There & Away

Egged buses 20 and 20א link Metula with Kiryat Shmona (12.40NIS, 20 minutes, eight daily Sunday to Thursday, four on Friday), via Tel Hai.

East of Kiryat Shmona

Heading east from Kiryat Shmona to the Golan, Rte 99 passes a number of worthwhile sites and villages with plenty of B&Bs. The Banias Nature Reserve (p246) is just 5km east of the Tel Dan Nature Reserve.

⊙ Sights & Activities

Tel Dan Nature Reserve PARK
(☑04-695 1579; adult/child 29/15NIS; ⊙8am-4pm or 5pm Sat-Thu, 8am-3pm or 4pm Fri, last entry 1hr before closing) This 50-hectare reserve, 1.6km north of Rte 99, boasts two major attractions. The first, an area of lush forests, is fed by year-round **springs** that normally gush 8 cu metres of water per second into

RAFTING THE JORDAN

First-time visitors may be surprised at the Jordan's creek-size proportions, but first-time rafters are often bowled over – sometimes into the soup – by how powerful its flow can be. The wildest bit of the river, a 13km stretch known as the **Yarden Harari** (Mountainous Jordan), runs from B'not Ya'akov Bridge (on Rte 91) to Karkom (about 6km north of Rte 87's Arik Bridge, near the Sea of Galilee). The season begins as soon as the river's springtime flow isn't so powerful that it's dangerous.

All the outfits we list have changing rooms (bring a bathing suit) and lockers for valuables (10NIS or 20NIS); some places will hold your car keys and mobile phone for no charge. Unless you're told otherwise, assume that you'll get either wet or drenched.

Discounts of 20% or more are often available on the internet if you book at least 24 hours ahead, or from locally distributed coupon books. A dry winter caused some companies to cancel their 2014 season – call for details on weather and river conditions.

Jordan River Rafting (☑04-900 7000; www.rafting.co.il; Rte 918; ☺ regular route late Mar or Apr-Sep or Oct, Yarden Harari Mar–mid-Jun) The regular route (one to 1½ hours; minimum age five years) costs 90NIS per person in a two-person inflatable kayak or a raft with room for three to eight. Taking on the Yarden Harari (16km in three to five hours) costs 400NIS per person (minimum age 15). Also offers a zipline (25NIS) and cycling (80NIS; not available when the riverside track is too muddy).

Situated 11km northeast of Rosh Pina and 1.6km north of Gadot Junction on Rte 91; from the northeastern corner of the Sea of Galilee, take Rte 888.

Kfar Blum Kayaks (☑04-690 2616; www.kayaks.co.il; ☺10am-3 or 4pm, open late Mar or early Apr-Oct or Nov) In an inflatable two-person kayak or a raft (for up to six), a tame, 4km (1¼-hour) descent costs 90NIS, while a more challenging 8km (2½-hour) route costs 120NIS. Both start on the Hatzbani River and end on the Jordan. The minimum age is usually five years. There is also an 'active amusement' park for kids. To get there from Gomeh Junction on Hwy 90, follow the signs to Kfar Blum and go a bit past the kibbutz entrance.

Ma'ayan-Hagoshrim Kayaks (☑077-271 7500; www.kayak.co.il; Kibbutz Ma'ayan Baruch; ☺Apr-Oct) Based up near the Lebanese border at the entrance to Kibbutz Ma'ayan Baruch (on Rte 99), this veteran outfit – run by two neighbouring kibbutzim – offers trips in inflatable kayaks (for two people) and rafts (for up to six). The Family Route (5km) costs 90NIS per person; the wilder Challenge Route (6km) is 109NIS. Runs begin from 9am or 10am to 3pm or 4pm.

the Dan River, the most important tributary of the Jordan. The second is the remains of a grand **ancient city** inhabited by the Canaanites in the 18th century BCE and the Israelites during the First Temple period (from the 12th century BCE).

You can explore the reserve on three trails, parts of which are virtual tunnels through thick brambles and undergrowth: the **Short Trail** (40 minutes), the **Long Trail** (1½ hours) and the **Ancient Dan Trail** (two hours); significant sections are wheelchair accessible. All pass a 40cm-deep wading pool, a great place to cool your feet (swimming is prohibited elsewhere in the reserve).

Because the reserve is a meeting place of three ecosystems, it supports a surprisingly varied selection of flora and fauna, including the Indian crested porcupine and the endangered fire salamander, a speckled orange and black critter with five toes on its back

feet but only four on its front feet. Some of the reserve's non-native tree species, including eucalyptus (gum) and silver poplar, have been cut to make room for native species.

The **Tel Dan Stele**, found by an archaeology team from Hebrew Union College in 1993, is a fragment of a 9th-century BCE tablet in which the king of Damascus boasts of having defeated the 'king of Israel' and the king of the 'House of David'. This is the earliest known reference to King David from a source outside the Bible. The original is at the Israel Museum in Jerusalem.

Galil Nature Center   MUSEUM
(Beit Ussishkin; ☑04-694 1704; adult/child 20/15NIS; ☺8am-4pm Sun-Thu) This first-rate regional museum, run by the SPNI, has two sections. In the old-fashioned but informative (and, in its own way, beautiful) natural history room, you can get a close-up look at

(stuffed) butterflies, birds and mammals that you're not likely to encounter in the wild. The archaeology section focuses on nearby Tel Dan and includes a copy of the Tel Dan Stele. The museum is situated just east of Kibbutz Dan, 800m north of Rte 99 and 300m off the access road to Tel Dan Nature Reserve.

The museum screens a 17-minute film on the area in eight languages. The 940km Israel National Trail, which goes all the way to the Red Sea, begins in the parking lot. The Syrian tank on the nearby lawn was knocked out by kibbutz members at the beginning of the 1967 Six Day War.

Mifgash HaOfanayim CYCLING
(Bike Place; ☑04-689 0202; www.bikeplace.co.il; Rte 9888, Moshav Beit Hillel; half-/full day 55/90NIS; ☺8am-7pm daily) Rents and repairs bikes and can supply you with route tips and cycling maps. The woman who runs it is from Detroit. Situated 2km south of Rte 99.

✖ Eating

At the Gan HaTzafon (HaTzafon Garden) shopping mall, on Rte 99 4km east of Rte 90 (Kiryat Shmona), fast food joints sell felafel (15NIS), pizza and hamburgers, and there are several decent, seven-day-a-week restaurants, including Focaccia (Italian and Mediterranean) and Klompus (American burgers).

Restaurants in the Galilee Panhandle cater to weekend vacationers so it's a good idea to reserve ahead on Friday night and Saturday.

Lechem'keh BAKERY $$
(Little Bakery; ☑04-644 1978; Rte 99; sandwiches 18-45NIS, light meals 40-50NIS, breakfast 35-60NIS; ☺8am-7pm Sun-Thu, 8am-3pm Fri) Opened in 2013, this is the region's finest gourmet bakery; it also has a tiny cafe. It's situated in a run-down little strip mall, Nofit Hermon, on the south side of Rte 99 1.5km east of the intersection of Rte 99 and Rte 90.

Cheese ITALIAN $$
(☑04-690 4699; Rte 9888, Beit Hillel; mains 28-84NIS, breakfast 38-52NIS, set lunch 55-65NIS; ☺9.30am-11pm daily; ☑) Serves delicious Italian- and Mediterranean-inspired dishes, including a fine selection of pasta and pizza (including gluten-free). Situated in Beit Hillel about 2.5km south of Rte 99.

★ Dag Al HaDan FISH $$$
(☑04-695 0225; www.dagaldan.co.il; off Rte 99; mains 86NIS; ☺noon-10.30pm or later daily) One of Israel's best fish restaurants, renowned for grilled trout (99NIS) – raised in ponds just 50m away (and open to visitors) – served

with superb oven-roasted potatoes. Also has first-rate starters such as smoked trout and, for vegetarians, pasta. Except in winter, diners sit outside under gorgeous fig trees with the cold, clear waters of the Dan burbling by. Situated 1km north of Rte 99, across the highway from Kibbutz HaGoshrim.

THE GOLAN HEIGHTS

هضبة الجولان   רמת הגולן

Offering commanding views of the Sea of Galilee and the Hula Valley, the volcanic Golan plateau is dry and tan in the summer, and lush, green and carpeted with wildflowers in the spring. Its fields of basalt boulders – and, on its western edge, deep canyons – are mixed with cattle ranches, orchards, vineyards and small, middle-class communities. The area is a favourite destination for holidaying Israelis. Accommodation – mostly B&Bs – tends to cost more than in the Galilee; prices are highest from June to August and on Jewish holidays.

Israel captured the Golan Heights from Syria during the 1967 Six Day War, when 90% of the inhabitants fled. In the bitterly fought 1973 Yom Kippur War, Syrian forces briefly took over much of the Golan before being pushed back; a 1974 armistice set the current ceasefire lines. All around the Golan – unilaterally annexed by Israel in 1981 – you'll see evidence of these conflicts: abandoned Syrian bunkers along the pre-1967 front lines; old tanks, left as memorials, near the battlefields of 1973; and ready-for-action Israeli bunkers facing the disengagement zone, staffed by the blue-helmeted soldiers of the UN Disengagement Observer Force troops (Undof).

❶ Getting Around

Bus services around the Golan and down to Kiryat Shmona, Hatzor HaGlilit (near Rosh Pina) and the entire shoreline of the Sea of Galilee (including Capernaum, Kursi and Tiberias) are run by Katzrin-based **Rama** (☑1 900 721 111; www.bus.gov.il). The main lines run two to five times a day from Sunday to Thursday, two to four times on Friday until midafternoon, and once on Saturday afternoon or evening; feeder lines (kav hazana) serve destinations off the main roads.

Katzrin

קצרין   كتسرين

☑04 / POP 6725

Katzrin (Qazrin), 'capital of the Golan', makes an excellent base for exploring the central Golan and stocking up on picnic supplies. Founded in 1977, it is the region's only real town.

The lively little commercial centre, **Merkaz Eitan**, is a classic 1970s complex that was spruced up considerably in 2013 – adding a tile-covered sculpture that is as whimsical as it is colourful. In addition to a bank and some eateries, it has a first-rate museum. Everything closes on Shabbat.

◎ Sights & Activities

★**Golan Archaeological Museum**   MUSEUM
(☑04-696 1350; www.mpkatzrin.org.il; Merkaz Eitan; adult/child 19/16NIS, incl Ancient Katzrin Park 28/20NIS; ☺9am-4pm Sun-Thu, 9am-2pm Fri) A real gem! Highlights include extraordinary basalt lintels and Aramaic inscriptions from 30 Byzantine-era Golan synagogues; coins minted during the Great Jewish Revolt (66–70 CE); a model of Rujum al-Hiri, a mysterious Stone Age maze 156m across, which was built some 4500 years ago; and a film (available in English) that brings to life the Roman siege of Gamla. Wheelchair accessible. Situated 100m west of the Merkaz Eitan commercial centre, next to the library.

Ancient Katzrin Park   ARCHAEOLOGICAL SITE
(☑04-696 2412; http://parkqatzrin.org.il; adult/child 26/18NIS, incl Golan Archaeological Museum adult/child 28/20NIS; ☺9am-4pm Sun-Thu, 9am-2pm Fri, 10am-4pm Sat, closes 1hr later in Aug) To get a sense of life during the Talmudic period (3rd to 6th centuries), when the Golan had dozens of Jewish villages, drop by this partly restored Byzantine-era village, whose highlights include a basalt synagogue and an audiovisual presentation on Talmudic luminaries (not shown on Saturday). On Jewish holidays such as Passover and Sukkot and in August, there are reenactments by actors in period costumes. Situated 1.6km east of Merkaz Eitan.

Kesem Hagolan   VISITORS CENTRE
(Golan Magic; ☑04-696 3625; www.magic-golan.co.il; Hutzot HaGolan Mall, Katzrin Industrial Zone; adult/child 25.50/20.50NIS; ☺screenings 9am-5pm Sat-Thu, 9am-4pm Fri) An excellent introduction to the Golan, this centre takes you on a half-hour virtual journey around the region, projected on a 180-degree panoramic screen (in English hourly on the half hour). Also has a 1:5000-scale topographic model of the Golan. Situated in the shopping mall 2km east of Merkaz Eitan, next to the Industrial Zone.

Golan Heights Winery   WINERY
(☑04-696 8435, 04-696 8409; www.golanwines.co.il; Katzrin Industrial Park; tasting 10NIS, incl tour

ⓘ MINEFIELDS

Some parts of the Golan Heights – particularly those near the pre-1967 border and the 1974 armistice lines – are still sown with antipersonnel mines. For more information, see p400.

20NIS; ☺8.30am-at least 5.30pm Sun-Thu, 8.30am-2.30pm or 3.30pm Fri, last tour 4pm or 5pm Sun-Thu, 1.30pm or 2pm Fri) Winner of many international awards, this outstanding winery offers guided cellar tours (advance reservations highly recommended) and wine-tasting. The shop sells more than 40 wines bottled under its Yarden, Gamla (Gilgal), Hermon and Galil Mountain labels. All wines are kosher but, mercifully, not *mevushal* (flash pasteurised).

⊨ Sleeping

★**Golan Garden Hostel**   HOSTEL $
(☑072 230 3565; www.golangarden.com; 13 Hofit St; dm 100NIS, d without bathroom 285NIS; ❄@☎) Katzrin finally has a hostel. Opened in 2013, this place – run by superfriendly Alon and Milou – has a lounge with bean-bag chairs, dorms with four or six beds, a hammock on the back terrace, and guitars and drums for guests to play. Situated 1km southeast of Merkaz Eitan – take Si'on and then Gilabon St.

Laundry costs 15NIS, including drying. Rents out camping equipment (eg a sleeping bag for 15NIS a day).

SPNI Golan Field School   HOSTEL $$
(☑04-696 1234; www.natureisrael.org; 2 Zavitan St; r 438-504NIS, additional adult 140-164NIS, child 98-114NIS; ❄@☎) Housed in an unpretentious, 1970s complex on the edge of town. The 33 simple rooms, all with fridge, can sleep up to nine and so are a good option for families and groups of friends. Does not rent individual dorm beds. Sometimes (eg on Jewish holidays) offers free group hikes. Situated 1km from Merkaz Eitan – head down Daliyot St and then turn left on Zavitan St; follow the signs to 'Field School'.

✕ Eating & Drinking

Fast food (hummus, shwarma, bad pizza and the like) is available in Merkaz Eitan – except on Shabbat, when your eating options shrink to two restaurants 2km or 3km east of Merkaz Eitan in the Industrial Zone.

Co-op Shop   SUPERMARKET $
(Lev Katzrin Mall; ☺8am-9pm Sun-Thu, 7am-2.30pm or 4pm Fri) Picnic supplies for a hike or Shabbat.

UPPER GALILEE & GOLAN KATZRIN

★ **Golan Brewhouse** BREWERY $$
(☑04-696 1311; www.beergolan.co.il; Hutzot HaGolan Mall, Katzrin Industrial Zone; mains 49-126NIS; ☺11.30am-11pm daily; ☑) This pub-restaurant, with a circular wooden bar and panoramic windows, serves red meat, chicken, fish, soup, salad, veggie mains and some damn fine microbrews.

The Brewhouse Beer Sampler (14NIS) gets you a whisky tumbler of each of the Brewhouse's four beers (an amber ale, a pilsner, a Doppelbock and a wheat beer), brewed in the copper vats in the corner. For 48NIS you can sample 200mL of each and munch on olives and sauerkraut.

Meatshos STEAK $$$
(☑04-696 3334; www.meatshos.co.il; Katzrin Industrial Zone; mains 65-169NIS, 15% off Mon-Thu; ☺noon-11pm Mon-Sat) Renowned for its flavoursome steaks, chops, kebabs and hamburgers (400g to 750g), all made with Golan-raised, kosher-slaughtered (but not certified) 1½-year-old calf and lamb. Also serves Salokiya boutique wine (red/white per glass 42/32NIS), made right on the premises. Situated at the far northern end of the Industrial Zone next to the fire station, 1km past the Golan Heights Winery.

Pub Savta PUB
(Ancient Katzrin Park; ☺9pm-2am or later Sat-Thu) Inside the archaeological site, this beer pub is popular with both locals and young Israeli travellers.

ℹ Information

Information Centre (☑04-696 2885; www.tourgolan.org.il; ☺9am-4pm Sun-Thu) Run by the regional council, this tourist information office has brochures and free maps in Hebrew, English and Russian, and can supply information on accommodation, hiking and winery visits. Situated in the shopping centre 2km east of Merkaz Eitan, behind the round fountain next to Kesem HaGolan.

SPNI Hiking Information (☑04-696 5030; www.teva.org.il; SPNI Golan Field School, 2 Zavitan St; ☺8.30am-5pm Sun-Thu) Free consultations with experienced SPNI guides about Golan hiking options. You can also phone with questions.

ℹ Getting There & Away

Katzrin is the Golan's public transit hub. **Rama buses** (☑1 900 721 111; www.bus.co.il) head to virtually every part of the Golan, as well as to Tiberias, Hatzor HaGlilit (near Rosh Pina) and Kiryat Shmona. Bus 57 follows the Sea of Galilee's eastern and southwestern coasts (eg Kursi) on its way to Tiberias; bus 52 goes to Tiberias via the lake's northwestern coast (eg Capernaum). To get to Neve Ativ, Majdal Shams and other places near Mt Hermon, you have to change in Kiryat Shmona.

Egged bus 843 (49.50NIS, four hours, one or two daily) links Katzrin with Tel Aviv. On weekdays there are departures from Katzrin early in the morning and from Tel Aviv at 4pm.

South of Katzrin

The southern Golan – the area between Katzrin and the Sea of Galilee and the hills overlooking the Sea of Galilee from the east – has some excellent hiking. For details on Moshav Ramot and staying in Giv'at Yoav, see p219.

Yehudiya Nature Reserve

שמורת טבע יהודיה   محمية طبيعية يهودية

One of the most popular hiking areas in all of northern Israel, the 66-sq-km **Yehudiya Nature Reserve** (☑Meshushim entrance 04-682 0238, Yehudiya entrance 04-696 2817; adult/child 22/10NIS; ☺7am-4pm or 5pm Sat-Thu, 7am-3pm or 4pm Fri) offers walks suitable for casual strollers as well as experienced hikers, especially those who aren't averse to getting wet. Mammals you might encounter include gazelles and wild boar; its cliffs are home to birds of prey as well as songbirds.

Most of the trails follow three cliff-lined wadis, with year-round water flow, that drain into the northeastern corner of the Sea of Galilee. **Wadi Yehudiya** and **Wadi Zavitan** are both easiest to access from the Yehudiya Parking Lot (Chenyon Yehudiya), which is on Rte 87 midway between Katzrin and the Sea of Galilee.

Wadi Meshushim, easiest to get to from the Meshushim Parking Lot, is situated 2.8km along a gravel road from Rte 888, which parallels the Jordan River. The parking lot is 8km northeast of the New Testament site of Bethsaida.

The rangers at both entrances to Yehudiya (pronounced 'yeh-hoo-*dee*-yah') are extremely knowledgeable and can point you in the right direction, as well as register you, for your own safety. The only map you'll need is the excellent colour-coded one provided at ticket booths. At both entrances, snack counters sell sandwiches and ice cream.

Stick to marked trails – people have fallen to their deaths while attempting to negotiate treacherous makeshift trails, and there's an army firing zone east of Wadi Yehudiya (across Rte 87).

⊙ Sights & Activities

New Upper Yehudiya Canyon Trail   HIKING
This new circuit, which replaces a trail closed by a cliff collapse, takes 2½ to three hours. Blazes are red, then black.

The trail begins at the ruins of the pre-1967 Syrian settlement of **Yehudiya**, built – as its Arabic name hints – on the remains of a 3rd- and 4th-century Jewish village.

To get there from the Yehudiya Parking Lot, cross the highway via the tunnel in the lot's southern corner.

One section of the New Upper Yehudiya Canyon Trail involves 20 to 40 minutes of walking in water 50cm to 1m deep. A variant is the **Yehudiya Waterfall Trail** (red blazes; 45 minutes one-way from park HQ).

Upper Zavitan Canyon Trail   HIKING
This three-hour circuit offers great views of 27m-high **Zavitan Waterfall**, spectacular in the rainy season. The descent begins at the ruins of the Arab village of **Sheikh Hussein**, northeast of the Yehudiya Parking Lot. An easy trail with blue, then black, then red, then blue blazes, the path heads downstream to link with the **Lower Zavitan Canyon Trail** and, eventually, Meshushim (Hexagons) Pool.

If you begin hiking after 11am, don't plan on making it all the way to the pool.

Branches of the Upper Zavitan Canyon Trail can be picked up near Katzrin and on Rte 9088 between Katzrin and Katzrin Darom Junction.

Meshushim (Hexagons) Pool   HIKING
Surrounded by extraordinary, six-sided basalt pillars (thus the name), this chilly (19°C), 7m-deep pool makes for a refreshing dip. Getting there from the Meshushim Parking Lot, which has changing rooms, requires a delightful, 20-minute downhill walk; getting back up takes 30 to 40 minutes. The **Stream Trail** (Shvil HaNahal), which hits Wadi Meshushim further upstream (and has a 3m cliff ladder), takes 20 to 30 minutes downhill.

Begin these routes before 2pm (3pm during daylight savings).

At the pool, remember that there is no lifeguard – and jumping and diving are absolutely forbidden (people have died here from hitting their heads).

It's possible to hike down to Meshushim Pool from the Yehudiya Parking Lot (four to six hours, depending on your route) but transiting from Wadi Zavitan to Wadi Meshushim involves a steep ascent and then an equally steep descent; and getting back up to your car (assuming you have one and parked it at Ye-

> **SPRING WILDFLOWERS**
> ....
> The fields, hills and wadis of the Golan plateau burst into bloom from about February to mid-May (the exact dates depend on the rains). The higher up Mt Hermon you go, the later the wildflowers bloom (until August).

hudiya) could be a problem. This route cannot be started, in either direction, after 11am.

🛏 Sleeping

Yehudiya Camping Ground   CAMPGROUND $
(Orchan Laila; ☎ 04-696 2817; www.campingil.org.il; Yehudiya Parking Lot; per person incl next-day park admission 50NIS; ⊙24hr) Open year-round, this well-lit camping area is securely fenced (against wild boars and jackals) and has hot showers, barbecue pits and shade constructions. If there's no one around, just make yourself at home and pay in the morning. Bags can be left at the information desk (when it's open); nearby there are lockers (10NIS) for valuables.

ℹ Getting There & Away

Rama buses 52 and 57 (10 daily Sunday to Thursday, six on Friday), which connect Katzrin with Tiberias, stop at the Yehudiya Parking Lot (20 minutes from Katzrin). Egged bus 843, linking Katzrin with Tel Aviv, also passes the Yehudiya Parking Lot. A bus schedule is posted to the right of the Yehudiya snack counter.

Gamla Nature Reserve

שמורת טבע גמלא   محمية طبيعية جملا

The site of a thriving Jewish village during the late Second Temple period, **Gamla** (Rte 808; www.parks.org.il; adult/child 22/15NIS; 8am-4pm or 5pm Sat-Thu, 8am-3pm or 4pm Fri, last entry 1hr before closing) – perched atop a ridge shaped like a camel's back (*gamla* is the Aramaic word for camel) – defied the Romans during the Great Jewish Revolt (66–70 CE) and was besieged by Vespasian's legions. In 67 CE, historian Josephus Flavius recorded the seven-month siege, the defenders' valiant stand and the bloody final battle, and reported a Masada-like mass suicide of thousands of Jews. The town was identified in 1968 based on Josephus' descriptions, and excavations unearthed an enormous quantity of Roman siege weaponry (some can be seen in Katzrin's Golan Archaeological Museum) as well as one of the world's oldest synagogues, believed to date from the 1st century BCE. Walking down to, and around, ancient Gamla takes two to three hours.

Gamla is known for the dozens of **Griffon vultures** (wingspan: an astonishing 2.7m) that nest in the reserve's cliffs and soar majestically over the valley below. Sadly, they are becoming rarer, victims of high-voltage electrical lines and poisoned carrion that ranchers set out – illegally – to kill wolves and jackals. Half-hour guided walks (in Hebrew) begin daily at 11am and 1pm at the **Vulture Lookout**.

Israel's highest perennial waterfall, which drops 51m to a pool, can be seen from the **Waterfall Overlook** (Tatzpit HaMapal); the trail (1½ hours return) passes a field dotted with **dolmens** (basalt grave markers) erected by nomads 4000 years ago.

On the plateau around the parking lot, the **Vulture Path** (Shvil HaNesharim; 20 to 30 minutes) affords a fine panorama of the ancient city. It was made wheelchair accessible in 2014.

Gamla is 20km south of Katzrin, to which it's linked by Rama buses 10, 11 and 17.

Ani'am Artists Village

This quiet moshav, 9km southeast of Katzrin (and about 1km off Rte 808), is home to eight attractive ateliers and galleries arrayed along a brick-paved pedestrian street. The artists – including two ceramicists and a New York–born goldsmith, Joel Friedman of **Golan Gold**, who makes exquisite braided gold jewellery – are happy to tell visitors about their crafts. Most places are open Sunday to Thursday from 11am to 4pm or 5pm (7pm or later in August); Friday and Saturday hours tend to be 10am to about 3pm (4pm in summer).

Ani'am has two kosher restaurants that are closed on Friday night and Saturday.

North of Katzrin

The north-central Golan includes several nature reserves and the twin volcanoes of Avital and Bental, which tower over the UN disengagement zone. In 2014 artillery shells and rockets from Syria landed in the area, leading to periodic closures of parts of Rte 98.

Ein Zivan עין זיוון عين زيوان

Kibbutz Ein Zivan, 19km northeast of Katzrin, was the first kibbutz in the country to undergo privatisation, starting in 1992.

Bahat Winery WINERY
(☑ 04-699 3710; www.bahatwinery.co.il; tour adult/child 20/10NIS; ☺9am-5pm Sun-Thu, 9am-3pm or later Fri) A true boutique operation, Bahat (the name means 'alabaster') – housed in a one-time flip-flop factory – produces just 10,000 bottles of wine a year, including a blend of cabernet sauvignon and sangiovese. Short tours of the one-room production facilities, in Hebrew and English, leave every half-hour and end with a tasting session. Kids can learn how wine bottles are corked (30NIS).

De Karina Chocolatier CHOCOLATE MAKER
(☑ 04-699 3622; www.de-karina.co.il; tour adult/child 24/20NIS, incl workshop 65/55NIS; ☺9am-5pm Sun-Thu, 9am-3pm Fri, last tour 1hr before closing) An artisanal chocolate maker that offers tours and chocolate-making workshops. Reservations are a must.

Quneitra Viewpoint

תצפית קוניטרה موقع المراقبة القنيطرة

From high atop **Mt Avital**, top-secret IDF electronics peer deep into Syria, but the Quneitra Viewpoint, on the volcano's lower flanks, also affords fine views into Israel's troubled northern neighbour. The site – at which an 'audio explanation station' describes the battles fought here in 1973 – overlooks the ruined town of Quneitra, one-time Syrian 'capital of the Golan', just 2km away.

At the end of the Six Day War, Quneitra, at the time a garrison town defending Damascus (60km to the northeast), was abandoned in chaos by the Syrian army after Syrian government radio mistakenly reported that the town had fallen. It changed hands twice during the 1973 Yom Kippur War, which Israel began with just 177 tanks against the attacking Syrians' 1500. Inside the UN buffer zone since 1974, Quneitra was captured by Syrian rebel forces in mid-2014.

Just beyond the apple orchards and vineyards of Kibbutz Ein Zivan, you can see the only **crossing** between the Golan and Syria, run by the UN and – until the civil war – used by Golan Druze students and brides heading to Syria to study and/or get married (the subject of the 2004 Israeli film *The Syrian Bride*) and by Druze-grown Golan apples being trucked to Syria.

A path leads down the slope from the viewpoint to the **Avital Volcanic Park** (HaPark HavVolkani; ☺10am-4pm daily), situated in an old quarry whose excavations exposed many layers of the Golan's eventful geological history. Signs are in Hebrew, Arabic and English.

The viewpoint and park are next to a small parking lot on the eastern side of Rte 98, 1.3km north of Zivan Jct.

Merom Golan מרום גולן مروم جولان

♪ 04

Nestled at the base of the western slopes of Mt Bental, this kibbutz was the first Israeli settlement established on the Golan Heights after the 1967 Six Day War.

Head into them thar (volcanic) hills with the *bokrim* (cowboys) of **Havat Habokrim** (☑ 057 851 4497; www.mgtour.co.il; 1hr ride 140NIS; ⊗ rides usually begin 10am, noon & 2pm), which offers horse-riding. Reserve ahead by phone.

Then rest your saddle-weary body at **Merom Golan Resort Village** (☑ 04-696 0267; www.mgtour.co.il; d 720-760NIS, chalets 880-980NIS; ❋ ☞ ☎), whose 45 wood-and-basalt, spa-equipped chalets and 33 very comfortable guestrooms are surrounded by lovely gardens. Wheelchair accessible.

Habokrim Restaurant (☑ 04-696 0206; www.mgtour.co.il; mains 60-136NIS, Fri buffet adult/child 125/60NIS; ⊗ noon-10pm Sun-Thu, noon to 3pm & 7-9pm Fri), its ranch-style dining room expanded in 2014, serves mouth-watering, Golan-raised steaks, lamb and hamburgers. Opened in 1989, this veteran meatery also has fish, quiche and a good selection of children's meals (49NIS). Local wines cost 28NIS per glass. Kosher, so Friday dinner is a buffet.

Mt Bental הר בנטל جبل بنطل

Part of a nature reserve, the summit of this volcanic ash cone (elevation 1165m; open 24 hours) affords fantastic panoramas. From old Israeli trenches and bunkers, ready to be used at a moment's notice, you can see the Hula Valley, Lebanon, Mt Hermon, Syria and nearby Mt Avital, sprouting IDF antennas. The clearest views of the Quneitra area are just before sunset; recent visitors have reported hearing distant gunfire from Syria's civil war. Two 'audio explanation stations' provide historical information in Hebrew and English. Signposts show the way to Damascus (60km), Haifa (85km), Amman (135km), Jerusalem (240km), Baghdad (800km) and Washington, DC (11,800km).

Named in honour of former UN Secretary General Kofi Annan, once in charge of the UN troops on patrol down below, **Coffee Anan** (☑ 04-682 0664; www.meromgolantour ism.co.il; sandwiches 32-39NIS; ⊗ 9am-6pm summer, 9am-5pm rest of year) serves sandwiches, salads, homemade cakes, bourekas, shak-

shuka (45NIS) and ice cream. In Hebrew, the name means 'cafe in the clouds'.

Odem אודם اودم

This small moshav, 33km north of Katzrin, has some of the Golan's most reasonably priced accommodation, making it a great place to meet other travellers.

Odem Mountain Winery　　　　WINERY
(☑ 04-687 1122; www.harodem.co.il; ⊗ 10am-4pm Sun-Thu, 10am-1hr before sundown Fri) At this family-run boutique winery, which produces just 80,000 bottles a year, sampling three/five wines costs 30/50NIS – keep an eye out for their light, summery rosé, made with cabernet sauvignon, and their cabernet franc red, which is gaining international recognition. Call ahead for a tour (10NIS).

Ya'ar HaAyalim　　　ZOO, AMUSEMENT PARK
(☑ 050 522 9450; www.yayalim.co.il; child 2-12yr/accompanying adult 60/35; ⊗ 9am-5pm, 9am-7pm Jul & Aug) Kids will love this gravelly, tree-shaded hillside, home to three species of deer (from Northern Europe, the Himalayas and Japan), ibexes, rideable mini-ponies, a petting zoo, pedal cars, a trampoline and a rope park with a 15m zipline.

Golan Heights Hostel　　　HOSTEL **$**
(☑ 054 260 0334; Odem; dm 100NIS, d 350NIS, d without bathroom 250NIS; ☞) Opened in 2014, this friendly, purpose-built hostel has six rooms, three of them dorms with six bunk beds, and all the amenities you'd expect, including cooking and laundry facilities and plenty of public spaces for socialising. Heating is underfloor, a blessing in winter. For details, see its Facebook page.

Khan Har Odem　　　GUESTHOUSE **$**
(☑ 050 566 2673; www.hanharodem.co.il; per person excl breakfast Sun-Wed 110NIS, Thu-Sat 135NIS; ☞) Think of it as luxury camping: up to 50

SYRIAN CIVIL WAR SPILLOVER

In 2014 Syrian opposition groups took control of the Syrian side of the frontier, holding a group of Fijian UN Disengagement Observer Force (UNDOF) soldiers hostage. In a not-unrelated development, a number of shells and rockets landed on the Israeli side of the disengagement lines. Check into local security conditions before you venture near the border, especially around Mt Bental and the Quneitra Viewpoint.

guests sleep on mattresses on the floor of a large hall, subdivided by curtains for privacy. The kitchen facilities, a focus of social interaction, are airy and spacious. Sheets, pillows and blankets can be rented for 30NIS.

Ya'ar HaAyalim HUTS **$**
(☑ 050 522 9450; www.yayalim.co.il; per person excl breakfast 120NIS) Cheap sleeps in simple tin huts.

Northern Golan

The area along and north of Rte 99 includes some superb nature reserves and towering Mt Hermon, which has four Druze villages on its southern slopes.

Tel Dan Nature Reserve (p238) is just 5km west of Banias Nature Reserve.

Banias Nature Reserve
שמורת טבע הבניאס محمية طبيعية بنياس

The gushing springs, waterfalls and lushly shaded streams of **Banias Nature Reserve** (☑ Banias Springs 04-690 2577, Banias Waterfall 04-695 0272; www.parks.org.il; Rte 99; adult/child 29/15NIS, incl Nimrod Fortress 40/20NIS; ☉ 8am-4pm or 5pm Sat-Thu, 8am-3pm or 4pm Fri) form one of the most beautiful – and popular – nature spots in Israel. The park has two entrances on Rte 99 that are about 3.5km (1½ hours on foot) apart. The name 'Banias' derives from Pan, Greek god of the countryside, to whom the area was dedicated.

Many sections of the park's four trails (trail map provided) are shaded by oak, plane, fig and carob trees. Near the Banias Waterfall (lower) entrance, the **Suspended Trail**, a boardwalk cantilevered out over the rushing Banias (Hermon) Stream, gives a pretty good idea of what the Garden of Eden might look like. A bit upstream is the 10.5m **Banias Waterfall**, with its sheer, thundering drop into a deep pool. Tempting as it may look, swimming is prohibited.

Near the Banias Springs (upper) entrance, the excavated ruins of a **palace complex** built by Herod's grandson, Agrippa II, can be seen on a 45-minute walking circuit.

Both entrances are served by Rama bus 58 from Kiryat Shmona to Majdal Shams.

Nimrod Fortress
قلعة الصبيبة מבצר נמרוד

Built by the Muslims in the 13th century to protect the road from Tyre to Damascus, **Nimrod Fortress** (☑ 04-694 9277; www.parks.org.il;

Rte 989; adult/child 22/10NIS; ☉ 8am-4pm or 5pm Sat-Thu, 8am-3pm or 4pm Fri, last entry 1hr before closing) towers fairy-tale-like on a long, narrow ridge (altitude 815m) on the southwestern slopes of Mt Hermon. The work that went into building such a massive fortification – 420m long and up to 150m wide – on the top of a remote mountain ridge boggles the mind. If you're going to visit just one Crusader-era fortress during your trip, this should be it.

Background on the fortress' colourful medieval history, including its destruction by the Mongols, can be found in the excellent English map-brochure given out at the ticket booth. Highlights include an intact 13th-century hall, complete with angled archers slits, in the **Northern Tower**.

The castle, visible from all over the Hula Valley, is protected by near-vertical cliffs and canyons on all sides but one. South of Nimrod is Wadi Sa'ar, which divides the Golan's basalt plateau (to the south) from the limestone flanks of Mt Hermon (to the north).

The fortress is served by Rama bus 58 from Kiryat Shmona to Majdal Shams.

Ein Kinya
עין קנייא عين قنية

The smallest and quietest of the Golan's Druze villages is in a valley just up the hill from Nimrod Fortress, 2km south of Rte 989.

The four doubles and two spacious apartments of **Snabl Druze Hospitality** (☑ 050 577 8850; sanabl.tal@gmail.com; d 600-750NIS, additional person 100-150NIS, 6-/10-bed apt 1500/2000NIS) – the name, which means 'ear of wheat' in Arabic, is pronounced *snah*-bel – afford fine views of Nimrod Fortress and the Hula Valley. Great for families, it's situated in a chocolate-brown house with Jerusalem-stone trim on the northern side of town, up the hill from the main street. To get there, follow the white-and-green signs.

Neve Ativ
נווה אטי''ב نيف اتيف

☑ 04 / POP 115

The closest thing Israel has to a Swiss Alpine village, this moshav, on the flanks of mighty Mt Hermon, is a good base for hiking in summer and skiing in winter. B&B prices rise in winter because of heating costs.

Particularly cosy – and very popular with families – is the B&B **Chez Stephanie** (☑ 04-698 1520; mauriceski@gmail.com; upper section of Naftali St; d/q 580/860NIS; ❋). Owners Reine and Maurice were born in Marseille but their three log-built chalets, which can sleep up to six, and four doubles feel like they're in Chamonix.

The Golan's most visited nature reserves issue excellent trail maps when you pay your admission fee, but if you'll be hiking further afield, the map to get – if only to avoid minefields and firing zones – is the Hebrew-only **SPNI Map 1**, a 1:50,000-scale topographical trail map which covers Mt Hermon, the Golan and the Galilee Panhandle (ie the Hula Valley and surrounds). It is sold at most of the area's national parks.

In nature reserves with entry fees, up-to-the-minute details on trail conditions are available at information counters. For certain routes you'll be asked to register, possibly by leaving a card on your dashboard so if rangers find your car after dark they'll know where to send the rescue teams.

Other safety tips:

➡ Bring plenty of water.

➡ Wear a hat and sturdy shoes.

➡ Never dive into the pools of water often found at the base of waterfalls (every year people are killed when they hit underwater boulders).

➡ Make sure you get back by nightfall.

Neve Ativ is 4km west down Rte 989 from Majdal Shams. Served by Rama bus 58 from Kiryat Shmona to Majdal Shams.

Nimrod   נמרוד   نمرود
☎ 04

This isolated hilltop hamlet off Rte 98 (and on the Golan Trail), with its staggering views and winter snows, is a great place to bliss out. The total population is only six families.

Rama bus 58 linking Kiryat Shmona with Majdal Shams stops at Nimrod Junction, on Rte 989 2km below Nimrod. Accommodation owners are happy to pick you up, or you can walk.

Ohel Avraham   CAMPGROUND $
(Abraham's Tent; ☎ 052 282 1141, 04-698 3215; tepee 100NIS plus per person 60NIS, prefab cabin 350NIS, camp sites per person 60NIS; ☺ approx Passover–Sukkot, prefab units year-round) Hippyish hillside accommodation in three tepees, a Mongolian-style tent and some shacks – a great spot to chill out. Bring a sleeping bag; mattresses are supplied. Very basic.

Bikta BaArafel   GUESTHOUSE $$
(☎ 04-698 4218; www.bikta.net; cabins 500-1000NIS, camping per person 50NIS) Ten rustic rooms, built of recycled wood, are surrounded by an organic cherry, apple and apricot orchard. For dinner you can order meat or veggie stew cooked on an open fire (70NIS). To camp, bring your own tent and sleeping bag; renting a mattress costs 15NIS. It no longer has dorm beds but does accept volunteers interested in ecological construction techniques and organic gardening.

Majdal Shams   מג'דל שמס   مجدل شمس
☎ 04 / POP 10,200

The largest of Golan's four Druze towns – big enough to have traffic jams – Majdal Shams serves as the commercial and cultural centre of the Golan Druze community. Druze flags flutter in the wind, and you often see men with elaborate curling moustaches sporting traditional Druze attire, including a black *shirwal* (baggy pants) and a white fez. That said, the town is considerably less conservative than most Druze villages: young women dress like typical secular Israelis and alcohol is available in several pubs.

Higher education is hugely important here. Before civil war engulfed Syria, some 400 Golan Druze studied at Syrian universities. Now most young locals choose to pursue university studies in either Israel or Germany.

◉ Sights

Shouting Hill   HISTORIC SITE
Druze families separated by the conflict between Israel and Syria long used megaphones to communicate with relatives and friends assembled on opposite sides of a UN-controlled ravine on the eastern outskirts of town. In recent years Skype and cellphones have pretty much replaced this ritual, which featured prominently in the award-winning 2004 film *The Syrian Bride*.

🛏 Sleeping

Narjis Hotel   HOTEL $$
(Malon Butik Narkis; ☎ 04-698 2961; www.narjis hotel.com; Rte 98, Majdal Shams; d 450-650NIS; ❋❄) This stylish, locally owned hotel has 21 huge, modern rooms with Jacuzzi, balcony

and fridge. Situated 200m up towards Mt Hermon from Hermon Junction, the roundabout at the intersection of Rte 989 and Rte 98.

✗ Eating & Drinking

There's a strip of little eateries selling felafel, shwarma (28NIS; open 11am to 8pm or 9pm) and Druze pita with labneh (*pita druzit;* 15NIS) at the western entrance to Majdal Shams. From the intersection of Rte 98 and Rte 989, head towards the traffic circle that has a heroic equestrian statue in the middle, erected to commemorate the 1925 uprising against French rule in Syria.

Two rival places selling scrumptious baklava (70NIS per kg) and soft, warm *kunafeh* face each other on opposite sides of the roundabout at the intersection of Rte 98 and Rte 989: Abu Jabal (look for a red-and-white sign with Hebrew and Russian lettering) and Abu Zeid (the sign has pink Hebrew lettering).

The bars are liveliest on Thursday and Friday nights.

Nisan   DRUZE $$
(☎ 04-687 0831; Rte 98; mains 29-95NIS; ☺ 10am-11pm; ☎ 🍴) A brightly lit, sparklingly clean place that serves both Druze favourites (grilled meats, hummus, kebab and salads) and Western standards (pasta, pizza and something called a 'California salad'). Wheelchair accessible. Situated 400m up the hill, towards Mt Hermon, from the Narjis Hotel.

Why?   BAR
(Rte 98; mains 38-95NIS; ☺ 10am-1am or later) A simpatico spot for a beer (there are four on tap) or a bite (grilled meats, pizza, ravioli). Situated 50m east of the Narjis Hotel.

Green Apple Bar & Cafe   PUB
(☎ 052 666 2285; Rte 98; ☺ 11am-11pm or later daily) This new, Irish-style pub could be in Chicago. Has live music on every other Thursday from 9pm. Situated next to the Narjis Hotel.

ℹ Information

Majdal Shams' banks have ATMs.

ℹ Getting There & Away

Majdal Shams is 30km east of Kiryat Shmona. Served by Rama bus 58 from Kiryat Shmona, which passes Neve Ativ, Nimrod Fortress and Banias Nature Reserve.

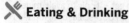

Mt Hermon خبل الشيخ הר החרמון

Israel's only ski station (☎ 1 599 550 560, 03-606 0640; www.hermonski.com; Rte 98; winter adult/child 49/44NIS, summer free; ☺ 7am or 8am-4pm, last entry 3.30pm) is at the far northern tip of the Golan, high atop Mt Hermon, known for its crisp mountain air (even in summer), delicate alpine plants and unpredictable snowfall. The mountain's 2814m summit is in Syrian territory; the highest point controlled by Israel is 2236m. Once you're inside the site, you can stay until sundown.

The facilities at Mt Hermon look like a low-altitude, low-budget ski station in the Alps, circa 1975, which is why you'll be greeted by cheesy, giant snowmen made of styrofoam. In good years there are 30 to 40 ski days between December and March, not enough to meet demand, so the pistes are often crowded. In bad years, the pistes may hardly open at all. Edibles are available at a number of snack bars, only one of which stays open in summer.

In winter, there's usually 3m or 4m of snow at the top of Mt Hermon; the record, set in 1992, was 10m. Details on ski conditions are available by phone or online.

Hitting the slopes of Mt Hermon can be pricey – but for Israelis it's a lot cheaper than flying to Austria (before 1948, Palestinian Jews with a passion for winter sports used to head to Lebanon). In addition to entry fees (paid at toll booths on the road up), costs include a ski pass (all-day/afternoon 245/200NIS) and equipment rental, which can include skis (adult/child 140/120NIS), a snowboard (170NIS) and a ski suit (120NIS).

The site has three blue (easy) runs, seven red (difficult) runs and two runs rated black (very difficult). The longest is 1248m, with a vertical drop of 376m; the highest begins at 2036m. To get you uphill, there are 11 lifts, including five chair lifts and five T-bars.

If you decide to ski, make sure your travel insurance covers 'high-risk' sports and includes evacuation.

In the warm season, there's access to the summit – and its riot of alpine wildflowers – by chair lift (adult/child 3-12 years 49/42NIS; last descent 3.30pm). The ride is a blast, with great views, but there's not much to see up top except Israeli bunkers in the distance, so it's worth timing your ascent to coincide with a free, 1½-hour guided walk (11am and 1pm daily from late May to Sukkot), led by an SPNI guide, that takes a look at plants, flowers and local military history; get to the lift a half hour ahead. The blooming season up here lasts from late May to August, which is three or four months later than on the coast.

The ski station is about 9km up the hill from Majdal Shams along Rte 98.

West Bank
הגדה המערבית الضفة الغربية

Best Places to Eat

➡ La Vie Cafe (p264)
➡ Afteem (p258)
➡ Al Essawe (p269)
➡ Al Aqsa (p277)
➡ Peace Center Restaurant (p258)

Best Historic Sites

➡ Mar Saba Monastery (p262)
➡ Hisham's Palace (p268)
➡ Sebastiya (p275)
➡ Nabi Musa (p268)

Why Go?

'Welcome' is a word you hear a lot in the West Bank. Whether it is shouted by a street trader in a bustling souk, expressed with a smile over a plate of felafel or roared from a taxi over booming Arabic music, Palestinians are forever wanting to make tourists feel appreciated.

Given the popular conception of the West Bank as a poster-child for strife and violence, this might surprise some visitors; and it is true that dirt-poor refugee camps, barbed-wire checkpoints and the towering separation wall are rarely far from the eye. But there is another Palestine too, one of bustling cities and chaotic souks, rolling hills and traditional villages, olive groves and chalky desertscapes, where biblical sites abound.

But perhaps most appealing is the chance to meet Palestinians who remain hopeful of peace and stability even under untold pressures. The West Bank may not be the easiest place in which to travel – but the effort is richly rewarded.

When to Go
Bethlehem

°C/°F Temp — Rainfall inches/mm
40/104 — — 8/200
30/86 — — 6/150
20/68 — — 4/100
10/50 — — 2/50
0/32 — — 0
J F M A M J J A S O N D

Oct There's a festive air as city dwellers return to their native villages for the olive harvest.

Nov A harvest festival is held at Burqi'in in early November.

Late Dec Bethlehem is electric, with lights, decorations, carolling and Christmas Eve Mass.

West Bank Highlights

❶ Wandering the serene stone streets of **Bethlehem** (p253), from the Old City to Manger Sq and the Church of the Nativity.

❷ Keeping cool over cocktails in one of **Ramallah's** (p262) trendy gathering spots.

❸ Dangling aloft in a cable car above **Ancient Jericho** (p267), the sandy remains of the oldest continuously inhabited civilisation on earth.

❹ Visiting the troubled city of **Hebron** (p272) and its contentious resting place of the monotheist patriarchs.

❺ Coming clean at a soap factory and Turkish bath in **Nablus** (p274).

❻ Meeting the inspiring actors at the world-renowned **Freedom Theatre** (p277) in Jenin.

❼ Clambering up to the platform on **Mt Gerizim** (p276), believed by Samaritans to be God's first creation on Earth.

History

The West Bank, as a geographical designation, was a creation of the 1948 Arab–Israeli War, which resulted in areas north, east and south of Jerusalem – the 22% of Mandatory Palestine now known as the West Bank – falling under Jordanian control. The name is derived from the area's position on the western bank of the Jordan River (the Hashemite Kingdom of Jordan is sometimes known as the East Bank).

Historically, Jews have called the area Judea (Yehuda) and Samaria (Shomron), in reference to the West Bank's southern and northern lobes, respectively. Contemporary use of this expression – the preferred nomenclature among Jewish settlers and right-wing Israeli governments – is contentious since it suggests a belief that contemporary Israeli policy should be based on the biblical boundaries of the Land of Israel. You may also hear the terms 'the Occupied Palestinian Territories' or 'the Territories'.

West Bank Palestinian culture still bears the stamp of 400 years of Ottoman Turkish rule, during which the area was part of the Ottoman province of Syria. Shorter occupations, such as the post-WWI British Mandate (1917–48), have also left their mark (English is still taught widely in Palestinian schools).

Although few in number, Jews maintained a presence in the West Bank (particularly in Hebron) throughout the Ottoman period. In the late 19th and 20th centuries large numbers of Jews immigrated from Russia, Yemen and other countries to Palestine but few settled in the mountainous parts of Palestine that would later become the West Bank.

During the 1948 Arab–Israeli War, Jordan captured (and later annexed) the West Bank, only to lose control of the area to Israel in the 1967 Six Day War. During the 1970s and 1980s Jordan sought to reunify the West Bank with the East Bank but relinquished all claims to the Palestine Liberation Organisation (PLO) in 1988.

In the wake of the First Intifada (Arabic for 'uprising' or 'shaking off'), from 1987 to 1993, the Oslo Accords were set. These interim agreements between the Israeli government and the PLO gave control of some areas (such as Jericho, Ramallah and Jenin) to the newly created Palestinian Authority, and implied the possibility of a future Palestinian state.

Both sides were unhappy with the accords and their aftermath. Violence continued,

with both Israeli and Palestinian deaths. The failure of US-sponsored peace talks at Camp David in 2000 paved the way for the outbreak of the Second Intifada that year.

The Second Intifada (2000–05) brought the worst violence in a generation. High-profile killings shocked both sides. Bloody battles and military attacks caused thousands of casualties inside the West Bank and Gaza and there were scores of suicide bombings inside Israel. In response, Israel constructed a sophisticated separation wall (p267), sealing off the West Bank from Israel.

In 2006 Hamas, a militant Islamic group, won parliamentary elections, causing the prompt scale-back of international aid (because many countries consider Hamas a terrorist organisation) and squeeze of financial lifelines. After a struggle for power with Fatah, isolated Hamas did not take control of the West Bank, which was taken by Fatah leader Mahmoud Abbas, but did hold control of Gaza.

That division remains today, as does a state of affairs under which the vast majority of West Bank Palestinians are unable to trade and travel freely or visit relatives either in Israel or Gaza.

The spectacular failure of the US-sponsored peace initiative between Israel and Palestine in April 2014 meant that, for the first time in decades (outside of wartime) there was no ongoing peace process.

The kidnapping and murder of three Israeli teenagers outside a West Bank settlement in June 2014 led to a massive military crackdown in Palestinian cities, with hundreds of arrests, and Israel Defense Forces (IDF) incursions into Ramallah, Nablus and Hebron on a scale not seen since the Second Intifada. The action led to demonstrations across the West Bank, which intensified during the 2014 war in Gaza, when West Bank Palestinians took to the streets to protest civilian casualties in the strip.

Across the cities of the Fatah-ruled Palestinian Authority, you'll spot big banners proclaiming the Palestinians' right to a seat at the United Nations as well as calls for Palestinian rights to return to land lost in 1948. At the same time, their discontent simmers as the Israeli government continues to expand Jewish settlements in the region. In the meantime, the Palestinians maintain efforts to build their institutions and economy – and to push for an independent homeland.

Climate

Bethlehem, like Jerusalem, can be snowy in winter and enjoys cooler climes in the midst of the otherwise sweltering summer. If you're seeking Yuletide spirit, bring your woolly jumper and don't miss out on a crisp, cold Bethlehem Christmas. Balmier Jericho is the place to escape chillier winter days, and can be oppressively hot during the summer months. If you're considering doing some hiking around Wadi Qelt or elsewhere, spring and autumn are the best times.

☞ Tours

Backpacker hostels, including those in Jenin, Nablus, Ramallah and Bethlehem, are excellent places to ask about tours, and for those travelling solo they provide good opportunities to meet others and share costs.

Those who want to set up a tour before they leave should contact one of a number of organisations that offer tours; Green Olive Tours (p85) is particularly recommended. The Beit Sahour–based Siraj Center for Holy Land Studies runs cycling and walking trips. Two other recommendations:

Bike Palestine CYCLING
(☏02-274 8590; www.bikepalestine.com) Seven-day bike tour from Jenin to Jerusalem.

Walk Palestine WALKING
(☏02-274 8590; www.walkpalestine.com) Brings tourists on walking tours that last three to 14 days, staying with locals in villages on a route that makes up part of the Abraham Path (www.abrahampath.org).

❶ Getting There & Around

The West Bank is served by an excellent and easy-to-use public transport network, and buses and shared taxis (pronounced ser-vees) run from the major cities to most – if not all – sites and cities you will want to visit. Most signs are in Arabic but as long as you know the name of where you are going, it is relatively easy to get on the right bus or shared taxi and it will set you back a fraction of the cost of a private taxi. To Taybeh from Ramallah, for example, a service taxi is 7NIS while a private car is 70NIS. Most buses, even between cities, will cost between 5NIS and 20NIS.

Since distances are short (and local knowledge of roads essential) many tourists choose to hire a taxi by the hour or for the day. Ask a tour operator to set you up with a reliable driver. Most taxi drivers in Bethlehem are used to the needs of tourists and can run ad hoc day trips all over the West Bank. They hang around Bab iz-Qaq or the entrance to the Bethlehem checkpoint. Prepare to haggle hard.

If you're considering driving yourself, bear in mind that most Israeli rental-car agencies won't allow you to take their cars into Palestinian-controlled areas. Dallah (p415) and Goodluck (www.goodluckcars.com) are notable exceptions; both are based close to Jerusalem's American Colony Hotel. Palestinian roads are a mixed bag; potholes and bad signage can be a problem, but it is the quirks of Palestinian driving that may prove the biggest challenge, especially for first-time Middle East drivers. A general rule is every man or woman for him/herself.

Israeli licence plates are yellow, while Palestinian plates are green and white. Yellow-plated cars, while fine to drive throughout most of the West Bank – especially in more peaceful times – might cause you to be mistaken for an Israeli or Jewish settler and treated with hostility. Some tourists place a keffiyeh on the dashboard to avoid trouble in the more fraught areas.

Since roadblocks, settlement construction and separation wall building work are all ongoing, accessibility and roads can change quickly. It pays to buy an up-to-date road map (maps bought in Israel cover the West Bank, too). GPS is largely useless on the Palestinian side of the green line, and the best way to find your destination is to roll down the window and ask someone.

Bethlehem   בית לחם   بيت لحم

🎵 02 / POP 47,000

Most visitors come to Bethlehem with a preconceived image – a small stone village, a manger and shepherds in their fields – thanks to memories of a childhood nativity, perhaps, or years of scenic Christmas cards.

The reality is quite different. Bethlehem positively hums with activity, its winding streets congested with traffic and its main square filled with snap-happy tourists scrambling to keep up with their guides.

Churches now cover many of the holy sites but there is plenty to see and do for even the non-religious. There's a lively Old City and bazaar, plus sites around town including the incredible Herodium (p260). At the numerous cultural centres you can critique local art, watch performances and talk politics.

Most travellers come on a day trip but to get the most out of your visit it's best to stay overnight – accommodation and food are both cheaper than in Jerusalem.

JEWISH SETTLEMENTS

Israeli Jewish colonies set up in the Palestinian Territories are most often referred to as 'settlements'. There are currently approximately 350,000 Israeli settlers in the West Bank, living in more than 100 settlements, with hundreds of thousands more living in parts of Jerusalem captured by Israel in 1967.

Settlements range in size from a collection of caravans on a remote hilltop to large urban areas, such as Ma'ale Adumim near Jerusalem, home to tens of thousands of Israelis and now effectively a suburb of Jerusalem. There are a variety of reasons cited by settlers for why they live on the West Bank: most commonly, cheaper housing prices than in Israel and, among the religious, the fulfilment of biblical prophecy and an extension of the will of God.

Under almost all interpretations of international law, which forbids the transfer of civilians to land under military occupation, all Israeli settlements on the West Bank and in East Jerusalem are illegal. The Israeli right disputes this interpretation of international law. Key complaints against Jewish settlements are that they often occupy private Palestinian land (as opposed to state-owned land), divert precious water resources from surrounding Palestinian cities, towns and villages and, most significantly, fragment the territory of the West Bank, making the establishment of a coherent, contiguous and viable Palestinian state impossible.

The USA and European Union have declared the settlements an obstacle to peace, but Israeli Prime Minister Binyamin Netanyahu's right-wing coalition government has continued to construct housing in West Bank settlements and East Jerusalem, announcing plans throughout 2014 to build thousands of new settlement units on Palestinian land.

To find out more, visit the websites of Palestinian NGO Al-Haq's (alhaq.mits.ps) or left-wing Israeli organisation B'Tselem (www.btselem.org). For a settler's perspective, the settlement of Gush Etzion, near Bethlehem, has a visitor centre and museum (www.gush-etzion.org.il).

Bethlehem

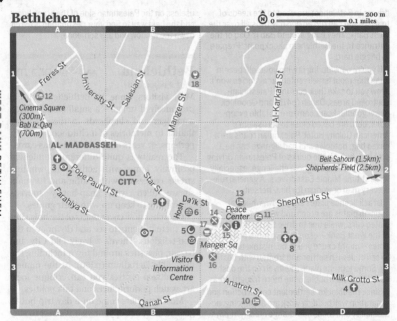

Bethlehem

◉ Sights

Cave	(see 2)
1 Church of the Nativity	C3
2 International Center of Bethlehem (Dar Annadwa)	A2
3 Lutheran Christmas Church	A2
4 Milk Grotto Chapel	D3
5 Mosque of Omar	B3
6 Old Bethlehem Museum	B2
7 Souq (Market)	B3
8 St Catherine's Church	C3
9 St Mary's Syrian Orthodox Church	B2

⊜ Sleeping

10 Bethlehem Youth Hostel	C3
11 Casanova Orient Palace	C2
Dar Annadwa	(see 2)
12 Grand Hotel Bethlehem	A1
13 Manger Square Hotel	C2

⊗ Eating

14 Afteem	C3
15 Peace Center Restaurant	C3
16 Square	C3

⊚ Drinking & Nightlife

17 Star Bucks	C3
18 Sultana	B1

History

Built along ancient footpaths, the little town where Mary and Joseph went for a census and returned with a son has had residents since as far back as the Palaeolithic era. The town is thought to have first developed in the 14th century BCE as a city state named Beit Lahmu (after Lahmu, goddess of protection), and later took the Hebrew Bible name, Ephrata.

Then in 313 CE, three centuries after the birth of Jesus, the Roman Emperor Constantine made Christianity the official state religion. Bethlehem soon became a popular, well-to-do pilgrimage town, with flourishing monasteries and churches. In 638 the city was conquered by Muslims, but a treaty was signed guaranteeing Christians property rights and religious freedom, and Bethlehem continued to prosper for the next millennium or so.

Bethlehem's numbers swelled after the 1948 Arab–Israeli War, when Palestinian refugees from the newly created State of Israel poured into town. Many continue to live, along with their descendants, in the refugee camps of Aida, Dheisheh and Al-Azzah on the edges of town.

Today Bethlehem continues to rely – as it has for the last 1700 years or so – on the tourist and pilgrim trade. It is easily the most visited city in the West Bank, especially around Christian holidays, with crowds flocking here for Easter and for the traditional Christmas Eve midnight Mass.

⊙ Sights

From Bab iz-Qaq (where bus 121 from Jerusalem stops) walk up Pope Paul VI St for five minutes to Cinema Sq, from where it's a 10-minute walk to Manger Sq. For those who took the bus to the checkpoint, there are taxi drivers waiting to bring you into the city for around 20NIS.

If you get a taxi to Manger Sq, walk from here up along bustling Pope Paul VI St (taking in the souq to the left), then take a right to loop around and return down charming Star St for an atmospheric taste of the Old City.

Most of the city's other sights are within walking distance of the town centre; pick up a taxi down on Manger St or on Manger Sq to venture to Shepherds' Field, Mar Saba Monastery or Herodium.

Opening hours of churches and other sites in (and outside) Bethlehem can change without notice, but a general rule in the West Bank is to start early and expect most sites to close their doors at sunset or an hour before.

Manger Square & Old City   HISTORIC SITE
The narrow limestone streets and exotic storefronts are a scene from another age, particularly Pope Paul VI St, Star St and the narrow alleys connecting the two. Visit on a Sunday to experience some church services. Most in attendance will be Palestinians and resident monks and nuns, but visitors are welcome to attend or stop in for a few moments of contemplation.

Spend a Sunday morning dropping discreetly in and out of the sights. Set out early to the 19th-century **Lutheran Christmas Church** (Pope Paul VI St, Madbasseh Sq) to experience a Lutheran service. Then head towards Manger Sq to the more modern **St Mary's Syrian Orthodox Church** (⊙ 9am-5pm), where Sunday Mass is held in Syriac. Descend the stairs to Manger Sq and enter the Church of the Nativity to find a Greek Orthodox service in session. Tiptoe through the cloisters around to the left and through a passage to St Catherine's Church for a Roman Catholic Mass.

And finally, don't miss a visit to the little **souq**, with its range of fruit and vegetables, meat and fish, junk, shoes and some mighty tasty snacks. Known to locals as the Green Market, the souq was established in 1929.

Church of the Nativity   CHURCH
(⊙ 6.30am-7.30pm spring-autumn, 6.30am-6pm winter) Though many have argued over whether X (or, in this case, a star) really does mark the spot, the Church of the Nativity nevertheless makes an imposing marker for the birthplace of Jesus. Also called the Basilica of the Nativity, it's the oldest continuously operating church, commissioned in 326 CE by Emperor Constantine. To really get the most out of a visit, negotiate a price for a tour from one of the handful of tour guides you'll find milling outside (around 50NIS per hour is a decent price): they know all the nooks and crannies intimately, and may even introduce you to some of the resident priests and monks.

A major restoration project recently took place on its exterior – as of September 2014 the church had been restored to its former glory.

You might be surprised, if you've never seen pictures, to find that the facade of the church is only a tiny Ottoman-era front door, aptly named the Door of Humility. Watch your head as you bow through – originally the entrance was much larger, but the Crusaders reduced its size to prevent

WEST BANK BETHLEHEM

ONE-WEEK ITINERARY

With a growing number of hotels and an excellent transport network in the West Bank, travellers no longer need to use Jerusalem as a base for excursions. Not only does staying overnight avoid having to deal with time-consuming daily checkpoints and rush-hour traffic, but it pumps much-needed shekels into the West Bank economy.

Get in a full day of sightseeing around **Bethlehem** before a day trip to **Hebron**. Then, from Bethlehem take a service taxi to **Jericho**, and tour the city and surrounding desert sites. Next travel to **Nablus** (via Ramallah) for a city tour and much-needed visit to the bathhouse. In **Jenin** see the Freedom Theatre and Burqi'in, before heading back to spend a day around **Ramallah**, checking out its hip bars and cafes, and **Taybeh**, where you can visit the Palestinian Territories' only brewery.

STREET ART IN BETHLEHEM

When British graffiti artist Bansky first daubed his now world-famous pictures close to the heavily fortified concrete wall that separates Bethlehem from Jerusalem he did more than give Palestinian tour guides another feather in their cap.

The artist – who has tagged a number of locations in Bethlehem since visiting in 2005 – started a trend that, a decade on, has seen swathes of the separation wall covered in colourful, political graffiti by both local and foreign street artists.

From Checkpoint 300 it is an easy walk tracing the wall through now-deserted Palestinian neighbourhoods to the entrance to Aida refugee camp. Along the way you will see huge portraits of Palestinian fighters, flags and all manner of slogans.

At Bansky Shop, started by local entrepreneur Yamen Elabed, you can pick up all manner of street-art-themed merchandise, and arrange tours with local street artists. The shop also has spray paint, so you can add your own mark to the wall.

Banksy's own three offerings are still visible but are not on the wall itself. Locals will point the way, and taxi drivers are always happy to include a viewing as part of their package.

attackers from riding in. Later, either during the Mamluk or Ottoman periods, the portal was made even smaller – you can still see the outline of the original 6th-century doorway and, within it, the pointed Crusader-era arch. Proceed to the cavernous nave. Renovations over the centuries have included a new floor here, beneath which lies Constantine's original 4th-century mosaic floor, rediscovered in 1934 and now viewable through wooden trapdoors in the central aisle.

The 6th century saw the church rebuilt almost entirely by Emperor Justinian, after the majority of it was destroyed in a Samaritan revolt. The mammoth red-and-white limestone columns that still grace the nave are probably the only surviving remnants of the original structure, their stone quarried from nearby. Some of them are decorated with frescos of saints, painted by Crusaders in the 12th century. To the right of the Door of Humility, a doorway leads to the Armenian Monastery, these days housing just six monks to service the needs of Bethlehem's 300-strong Armenian congregation. The Armenians flourished during the 1600s, when they were noted for their transcribed and illuminated versions of the Bible.

At the front of the nave, descend the stairs to enter the Grotto of the Nativity. It's popular with tour groups, but if you time your visit over lunchtime midweek, you'll likely have the grotto entirely to yourself (on a weekend you may have to stand in line for an hour or more). There is a rather zealous security guard who has been known to physically eject pilgrims that he thinks are staying too long. Atmospherically lantern-lit and

redolent with mystery, this is where Jesus is said to have been born, the 14-pointed silver star marking the spot. The Chapel of the Manger or 'the Crib' to one side of the grotto represents the scene of the nativity, while the chapel facing it houses the Altar of the Adoration of the Magi, which commemorates the visit of Caspar, Balthazar and Melchior. The Persians spared the church and grotto when they sacked Palestine in 614 CE, ostensibly because they saw a depiction of the magi in their own native costume.

Though all might seem serene down here, conflict has actually rocked this cradle for ages. The 14-pointed star was stolen in 1847, each of the three Christian communities in residence (the Greek Orthodox, the Armenians and the Catholics, who have bitterly and ceaselessly fought for custodianship of the grotto) blaming the others. A copy was subsequently supplied to replace it, but the fights didn't end there, and administrative domination of the church changed hands repeatedly between the Orthodox and Catholics. To this day, management of the church is divvied up metre for metre between the Orthodox, Catholic and Armenian clerics (this system of management for holy places is known as the 'status quo'). Take the grotto lanterns for example: six belong to the Greek Orthodox, five to the Armenians and four to the Catholics.

St Catherine's Church   CHURCH
Midnight Mass at this pink-toned church, next door to the Church of the Nativity, is broadcast across the world on Christmas Eve, but there's nothing like being there in person for an atmospheric – if rather lengthy – Christmas experience. Access the

church via the Church of the Nativity to first wander through the Crusader-era Franciscan cloister with a statue of St Jerome.

Milk Grotto Chapel CHURCH
(Milk Grotto St; ⊙8am-6pm summer, 8am-5pm winter) A short walk from Manger Sq is the lesser-known Milk Grotto Chapel. The white rock inside this stony chapel is said to bring milk to a mother's bosom and enhance fertility in women who swallow a morsel of the chalky substance. Legend has it that Mary and Joseph stopped here to feed the baby during their flight to Egypt; a drop of milk touched the red rock, turning it white.

Mosque of Omar MOSQUE
(Manger Sq) Opposite the Church of the Nativity, is this mosque, named after the 2nd Muslim caliph, Omar Ibn al-Khattab. It is the sole mosque in Bethlehem's Old City. It was built in 1860 on land granted by the Greek Orthodox Church in honour of Omar, the Prophet Mohammed's father-in-law, who in 637 took Jerusalem from the flagging Byzantines and then stopped for prayer at the Christian Church of the Nativity. He declared, in his Pact of Omar, that the basilica would remain a Christian shrine, and that Christians, even under Muslim rule, would remain free to practise their faith.

Rachel's Tomb RELIGIOUS
(⊙12.30-10.30pm Sun-Wed, 24hr Thu) In a desolate corridor created by Israel's separation wall, near the main checkpoint into town on the Israeli side of the wall, stands Rachel's Tomb. Another Bethlehem sojourner during labour, Rachel is said to have died here in childbirth, on the way south to Hebron, after which her husband, Jacob, 'set a pillar upon her grave' (Genesis 35:20).

Today the tomb is completely surrounded by the separation wall, and visiting the site is difficult. The gate can be reached on Arab bus 24, and Egged bus 163 from Jerusalem's Central Bus Station goes all the way to the tomb.

Once at the tomb there are separate sides for men and women (kippas for men are available at the door).

Revered by followers of all three Abrahamic religions – Jews and Muslims in particular – it has been enshrined and guarded for centuries, from the Byzantine and Islamic eras through to the Crusaders, and during the epochs of the Ottomans and Israelis.

Old Bethlehem Museum MUSEUM
(☑02-274 2589; www.arabwomenunion.org; Star St; admission 8NIS; ⊙8am-noon Mon-Sat

& 2-5pm Mon-Wed, Fri & Sat) This museum is located in a typical Palestinian home of the 19th century. See native costumes, peruse the collection of early-20th-century photos of Palestine, and purchase embroidery produced by the Bethlehem Arab Women's Union, at the embroidery centre upstairs.

International Center of Bethlehem (Dar Annadwa) CULTURAL CENTRE
(☑02-277 0047; www.annadwa.org; Pope Paul VI St, Madbasseh Sq; ☎) This Lutheran-run centre puts on concerts, plays, films, English-language documentaries, workshops and lectures. There's also a coffee shop, guesthouse, art gallery and gift shop, known as the Cave (Al-Kahf; thecave@annadwa.org), where local artists show off their work. Attached to the gallery is a small, underground dwelling, hence the name of the gallery.

🛏 Sleeping

Most hotel rooms in Bethlehem are rather nondescript, though comfortable nonetheless. Since most cater to a pilgrim crowd, expect to pay 30% to 50% more at Christmas or Easter time, and book your room well in advance.

Bethlehem Youth Hostel HOSTEL $
(☑02-274 8466, 059 964 6146; byh@ejepal.org; Anatreh St; dm 70NIS; @☎) Once a backpacker staple in Bethlehem, this hostel has moved to a smaller building next door and now has just one dorm for men and one for women. The former, bizarrely, looks over a prison yard, where armed guards watch inmates playing ping pong. Still, staff are helpful and it is great value.

Ibdaa Cultural Centre Guesthouse GUESTHOUSE $
(☑02-277 6444; www.ibdaa48.org; Dheisheh Refugee Camp; dm 50NIS; @☎) This multipurpose facility is a lively, happening place, treating travellers to free internet, cheap eats, simple dormitory lodging, a host of activities and a fascinating window into Palestinian refugee life. It is just off the Jerusalem–Hebron Rd, next to the taxi stand.

★Casanova Orient Palace HOTEL $$
(☑02-274 3980; www.casanovapalace.com; s/d/tr from US$45/60/90; @☎) The closest you'll get to sleeping in the manger itself, this perennially popular place offers reasonable rooms and a buzzing atmosphere, particularly around Christmas. The lobby, just off Manger Sq next to the Church of the Nativity, is as

ⓘ TIMES & DATES

The West Bank day of rest is Friday, but in Bethlehem and Ramallah some shops might close on Sundays due to Christian ownership. During the Muslim holy month of Ramadan, shopkeepers scale back opening hours, as do some attractions, and in the daytime you will only find food in Christian establishments (it's unlikely you'll go hungry in Bethlehem or Ramallah).

much a gathering place for transient tourists and devout dignitaries as it is for hotel guests. The hotel has two sections: a nicer wing closer to the square and a more basic wing around the corner (next to the church).

Dar Annadwa GUESTHOUSE $$
(Abu Gubran; ☑ 02-277 0047; www.diyar.ps; 109 Pope Paul VI St, Old City; s/d US$66/92; ☜) Students from the International Center's art school provide decor in this very comfortable, Lutheran-sponsored, boutique guesthouse with all the amenities. Each of its 13 tasteful rooms is named after a Palestinian village. Book ahead because reception is often closed.

Arab Women's Union GUESTHOUSE $$
(☑02-277 5857; www.elbeit.org; Beit Sahour; s/d/tr US$30/60/80; @) ☝ The women who run this guesthouse in beautiful Beit Sahour recycle paper, run community programs and produce olive-wood artefacts. The rooms are clean and modern although it is a little out of the way.

Manger Square Hotel HOTEL $$
(www.mangersquarehotel.com; Manger St; s/d US$80/120) This four-star hotel over the road from Manger Sq was built in 2012 and is excellent value considering the location. Some rooms have views over the valley behind Bethlehem, others over the Old City. Staff are polite and helpful and in summer there is a rooftop pool. Breakfast is pretty depressing.

Grand Hotel Bethlehem HOTEL $$
(☑02-274 1440; www.grandhotelbethlehem.com; Pope Paul VI St; s/d/tr US$70/90/120; ☜) Neat, clean, efficient and in the middle of the action, the Grand Hotel might not have bags of character, but rooms are comfy and central. Breakfast is served at the hotel's Mariachi Bar and the coffee shop serves Mexican dishes and seafood daily until midnight.

✖ Eating & Drinking

For fast food, stroll along Manger St or head up to the small souq just off Pope Paul VI St. Here you'll find fist-size felafel, sizzling shwarmas and lots of tempting produce for picnics or self-catering. Many of the restaurants and midrange hotels in Bethlehem serve alcohol, and there are a handful of bars just outside the Old City.

★ **Afteem** MIDDLE EASTERN $
(Manger Sq; felafel 6NIS, hummus from 15NIS) A Bethlehem institution for decades. Top-notch hummus and *masabacha* (warm hummus with whole chickpeas) are dispensed to locals' delight, just down the ramp from Manger Sq. For something a little different, go for a delectable bowl of *fatteh* – a sort of soupy hummus topping submerged pieces of pita and finished with roasted pine nuts.

Square MIDDLE EASTERN, WESTERN $
(Manger Sq; mains from 35NIS; ☾9am-midnight; ☜) A swish lounge-style place right in the heart of Bethlehem, this makes a great respite from a long walking tour around the city. Sip a cappuccino or order a light lunch (salads and pastas) in the basement dining room. Also available are beers and wines, cocktails and shisha, best enjoyed on the terrace overlooking the square.

Peace Center Restaurant SANDWICHES, ITALIAN $
(Manger Sq; mains 20-45NIS; ☾9am-6pm Mon-Sat) This spacious, central spot is great for a light snack or something more refined such as Mediterranean salmon or *shish tawooq* (chicken skewers). The restaurant has daily specials, including traditional Palestinian dishes such as *mansaf,* a joint of meat served on rice with fatty broth. Staff are friendly and helpful.

Dar al-Balad INTERNATIONAL $
(Beit Sahour; mains 25-50NIS; ☾noon-midnight) This atmospheric restaurant with arched ceilings and stone walls serves tasty grilled dishes, salads and pastas. It's located down a narrow alley, a pleasant find in Beit Sahour's restored old town, 1.2km east of Manger Sq. The family who run it have opened a lovely hotel upstairs, with a dozen tidy rooms (single/double 215/300NIS).

Sultana BAR
(Manger St; ☾10am-midnight; ☜) The walls of this tiny locally run bar just outside the Old City are emblazoned with flags from across

the world. It serves a range of wines and beers until around midnight in the backroom behind an off-license and is one of a number of small nightspots on the street.

Star Bucks   CAFE
(Manger Sq; ⊙7am-midnight) No relation to Ramallah's famous Starbucks copycat, Star Bucks Bethlehem is a small coffee kiosk with great views across Manger Sq to the Church of the Nativity. It has excellent filter coffee, a rarity in the West Bank, and mugs and T-shirts for sale.

❶ Information

Peace Center (☑02-276 6677; ⊙8am-3pm Mon-Thu & Sat) This information desk gives away city maps and provides helpful hints on accommodation and transport. It often holds art and photography exhibitions.

Visitor Information Centre (☑02-275 4235; vic.info.palestine@gmail.com; Manger Sq; ⊙8am-4pm Tue & Wed, 8am-5pm Thu-Sat) A Vatican-sponsored tourist office run by international volunteers.

❶ Getting There & Away

Bus 21 from Jerusalem to Bethlehem (30 minutes) departs every 15 minutes between 6am and 9pm (until 6.30pm in winter) from the Damascus Gate bus station. Alternatively, take bus 24 from Jerusalem to the main Bethlehem checkpoint, from where there are taxis into Bethlehem.

The best way to get from Bethlehem to the sites that surround it is by taxi, and drivers will clamour to offer visits to multiple sites for a fixed price (something around 50NIS an hour is standard, but you'll need to haggle). It is actually pretty good value, especially if you are in a small group, and many drivers speak good English and can answer your questions. Drivers generally congregate outside Checkpoint 300, Manger Sq or the 21 bus stop to Jerusalem.

VISITING A REFUGEE CAMP

The term 'refugee camp' brings to mind crowded tents, food riots and waterborne disease. But the refugee camps in the West Bank have existed for more than 60 years, time enough to transform them into established neighbourhoods with housing, schools, hospitals and other infrastructure. The camps were developed – and are still run – by the United Nations Relief and Works Agency but limited funding has allowed the UN to only build the most basic facilities.

Although the camps are not a hotbed of tourism, some travellers are keen to visit them to experience a different side of Palestinian life. While the camps are generally safe, it's best to be aware of the risks, as the security situation can change at a moment's notice. One minute it's all clear but the next minute violence might break out between demonstrators and Israeli soldiers, filling the air with tear gas, hurled stones and rubber bullets.

Israel Defense Forces raids are more likely in Nablus, Hebron and Jenin but have occurred in Bethlehem too. In any refugee camp it's best to visit with a Palestinian guide who understands the security situation – these guides are easily sourced, either through your hotel or hostel or through one of the numerous organisations that work in the camps.

Aida Refugee Camp

This camp is located in the shadow of Israel's separation wall, near Rachel's Tomb. A cornerstone of the community is the **Al Rowwad Centre** (☑02-275 0030; www.alrowwad. org), which offers drama, music, computer and arts training, as well as arranging special classes and workshops for women, the blind and residents with disabilities. A taxi from the city centre should cost 20NIS.

Dheisheh Refugee Camp

Located 3km west of Bethlehem, this camp was founded in 1948 to house refugees from 45 villages around Jerusalem and Hebron. The camp is home to the **Ibdaa Cultural Centre** (www.ibdaa48.org), the headquarters for a world-renowned youth folk-dance troupe. It also supports a media centre, trade school, women's leadership initiative, basketball league, restaurant and the Ibdaa Cultural Centre Guesthouse. The centre has a gift shop where you can purchase bags, clothing and other items produced by residents of the camp. It also runs tours of the camp; payment is by donation. To get to Dheisheh, catch a private taxi (20NIS) from the city centre, or a service taxi (3NIS) at Bab iz-Qaq in Bethlehem.

Central West Bank

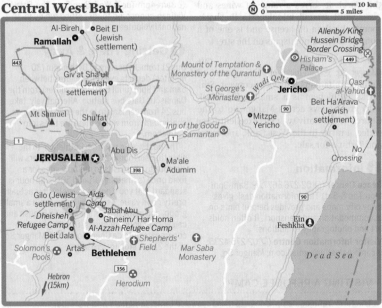

Alternatively, it's possible to get shared taxis from the main bus station to Jericho and Hebron. Share taxis to Hebron also leave from Bab iz-Qaq.

Around Bethlehem

Bethlehem makes a good base for excursions to other West Bank cities, especially Hebron, but there are also some worthwhile sights close to home.

Shepherds' Field

If you've always wondered where exactly 'shepherds watched their flocks by night' (Luke 2:8), drop into Shepherds' Field, a parklike area just outside Beit Sahour, to see for yourself. While the Beit Sahour Shepherds' Field isn't the only Bethlehem location earmarked as the exact spot the heavenly host visited to announce Jesus's birth to a group of shepherds, it's certainly the most frequented. As well as the strollable grounds, you'll find a Byzantine **cave** housing a chapel and the 1953 Italian-designed **Church of the Angels**, with its lovely, light interior.

To reach Shepherds' Field take a private taxi from Bethlehem (15NIS) or catch Beit Sahour–bound bus 47 (2NIS) from Shepherd's St, just below Manger Sq.

Herodium ﻦﻭﻳﺩﻭﺭﻳﻫ הרודיון

King Herod's spectacular fortress-palace, **Herodium** (adult/child 27/14NIS; ☉ 8am-5pm Apr-Sep, 8am-4pm Oct-Mar), built between 23 and 15 BCE, was known through the centuries to Arab inhabitants as the Mountain of Paradise.

Even from a distance, you won't miss the site: it rises from the Judean Desert like a flat-topped caricature of a volcano (the top is actually an extension of the natural hill, hollowed out to hold Herod's palace), 9km south of Beit Sahour. The complex features a series of stunning remains of Herod's own personal 'country club' (which included a bathhouse and rooftop pool) and also includes King Herod's own tomb, discovered in 2007. Though it was sacked by the Romans in 71 CE, around the same time as Masada was similarly assaulted, much remains at the site, with still more awaiting further excavation – including a network of tunnels used by Jewish rebels during their uprising against Rome. You can clamber through many of the tunnels today.

Note that Herodium falls under 'Area C' and is thus under full Israeli control (you'll see the military base at the foot of the hill); the site itself is administered by the Israeli

CHECKPOINTS

Checkpoints (in Hebrew, *machsomim*) control the flow of travellers between the West Bank and Israel. There are also some checkpoints inside the West Bank, although these tend to be less stable, shifting locations, shutting down altogether or popping up in new locations. Most checkpoints are run by the IDF, although some have been outsourced to private contractors. The latter tend to be more troublesome and more likely to question foreigners and search their bags.

Operating hours of checkpoints vary, often depending on whether the primary users are settlers or Palestinians. For example, the checkpoint leading south from Jerusalem on Rte 60 near Bethlehem is open 24/7, while Bethlehem checkpoint 300 (which leads into Bethlehem city) is sometimes closed at night (but not always). Checkpoints used by Palestinians are subject to random closures, especially around Jewish holidays, when the West Bank is sometimes sealed for security reasons.

Checkpoints range in size from small pedestrian-only checkpoints, such as Abu Dis, to larger ones that accommodate vehicles and resemble an international border crossing, such as the Bethlehem 300 checkpoint. 'Flying checkpoints' are temporary IDF road-blocks set up inside the West Bank. Delays depend on the volume of traffic. Checkpoints set up by Palestinian police exist too (for example, near Jericho) but traffic generally flows smoothly through them.

In general, travellers are not checked when going into the West Bank, only when travelling from the West Bank back into Israel. Foreign-passport holders are allowed to travel through IDF checkpoints into areas under the control of the Palestinian Authority but by military order, Israeli citizens are (theoretically) forbidden from doing so.

There is no cost involved with crossing a checkpoint and foreign-passport holders do not need any special documentation. Just show your passport and visa and put your bags through an X-ray machine. The procedure is generally fast but with waiting time you can expect to be at a checkpoint for 15 to 20 minutes (or longer if lines have formed).

Try to avoid passing through a checkpoint in the early morning (7am to 9am) or on Muslim or Jewish holidays due to long lines.

Foreigners can take a vehicle into and out of the West Bank (if you've got a rental car, make sure your insurance policy covers travel to the Palestinian Authority – most don't) but there can sometimes be delays upon your return to Israel because the soldiers may inspect the vehicle for explosives.

The following are some of the main checkpoints into and out of the West Bank:

Qalandia – Between Jerusalem and Ramallah. Use this checkpoint for Ramallah, Nablus and Jenin. This is one of the busiest checkpoints and it sports some fairly grim metal corrals and locking turnstiles of the sort you'd expect to see at a maximum-security prison. There is actually a checkpoint on both sides of the road – one for pedestrians and the other for bus travellers.

Bethlehem 300 – Located south of Jerusalem at the entrance to Rachel's Tomb. One road leads to the checkpoint for cars and one for pedestrians. This is an indoor checkpoint and the conditions are better than the one at Qalandia, but opening hours are not reliable and it is sometimes closed at night.

Bethlehem (highway) – You will go through this checkpoint if you take bus 21 from Bethlehem. It resembles a toll gate and security is very light. Tourists may remain on the bus during the passport check (Palestinian passengers are asked to line up outside the bus). It's open 24/7.

Jalameh – Located 10km south of Afula, this checkpoint is one of the best in terms of ease and accessibility. However, long lines have been reported and it is only open between 8am and 5pm.

Abu Dis – This checkpoint connects East Jerusalem to Abu Dis, from where travellers can connect to Jericho. It is a pedestrian-only checkpoint and is usually closed at night.

For more details on the conditions at individual checkpoints, visit the website of the left-wing Israeli group Machsom Watch, www.machsomwatch.org.

Parks and Nature Authority (www.parks.org.il). To get here, take a private taxi from Bethlehem (around 50NIS per hour), and negotiate at least an hour's waiting time. Try to avoid Fridays, when Herodium fills with tour buses from Israel.

Al-Khader Church

كنيسة الخضر   כנסיית אלח'דר

Just outside Bethlehem, on the road to Hebron, Al-Khader Church (St George's; Jerusalem–Hebron Rd; ⊙8am-noon & 3-6pm Sun & holidays) is dedicated to St George, famous enemy to dragons and patron saint of travellers and the sick. St George is also known as the patron saint of Palestine, or St George the Green; his feast day is celebrated annually on 5 May with a pilgrimage out to the church, attended by both Christians and Muslims.

Someone from the Muslim family entrusted with the keys to the small Greek Orthodox church will perform a chaining ritual at your request, ceremonially chaining and unchaining any visitor desiring to release bad energy, cleanse the soul, cast off illness or prepare for a long journey. It's said that this derives from the practice (thankfully no longer undertaken) of chaining the mentally disturbed to the walls in the hope that St George might cure their insanity.

You can take a private taxi from Bethlehem (20NIS) to Al-Khader.

Solomon's Pools

بركة السلطان سليمان القانوني   בריכות שלמה

A prominent site in the Al-Khader area is Solomon's Pools. During Roman times a system of springs filled three mammoth rectangular reservoirs supplying water via aqueducts to Jerusalem and Herodium. King Solomon enjoyed respite beside their serene shimmer, where he is said to have written the sensuous *Song of Solomon*. The springs were used into the 20th century for irrigating crops in the surrounding fertile valley, while successive armies have also set up camp here. An Ottoman fortress is still evident, the historic last stop for pilgrims on their way to Jerusalem.

Unfortunately, the pools are now fenced off and the water largely drained, so it's no longer a very picturesque place. Only travellers with a serious interest in history make it this way. A new conference centre was recently built next to the site.

To reach Solomon's Pools from Bethlehem take Dheisheh bus 1 (3NIS) from Manger Sq, or private taxi (20NIS).

Mar Saba Monastery

دير مار سابا   מנזר מר סבא

A must-see on any journey through the Holy Land is Mar Saba Monastery (⊙8am-sunset Sat-Tue & Thu), a bleak and beautiful 20km drive east of Bethlehem (beyond Beit Sahour). This phenomenal cliff-clinging copper-domed hermitage, founded in 439 CE, is best seen from the opposite slope, but men can exercise their privilege by going inside and getting a tour with one of the 15 monks still in residence. Women can get a bird's-eye view from the Women's Tower, a rather squat structure opposite the monastery itself.

Also residing here (rather more eternally) are the remains of 5th-century ascetic St Sabas, whose body lies in the church's second chapel, and the skulls of some 120 monks massacred here in 614 CE.

For those who are driving, the monastery is well signposted from Beit Sahour. Otherwise you'll need to take a private taxi out to Mar Saba from Bethlehem; plan on around a three-hour journey, costing around 120NIS to 150NIS.

Ramallah & Al-Bireh

رام الله البيرة   רמאללה אל בירה

📍02 / POP 65,000

Ramallah (the name means God's Mountain) and Al-Bireh were once separate villages, but now make up one urban conglomerate, a mere 10km north of Jerusalem. Though Al-Bireh's history can be traced back to the Canaanites, Ramallah was only settled by Christians in the 1500s, and these days is a bustling, cosmopolitan city, with a thriving art scene and vibrant nightlife.

Ramallah may lack the religious fervour of Nablus, Hebron or, indeed, Jerusalem, but the Palestinian flags and graffiti that adorn every wall leave you in no doubt about where you are. While Israeli incursions into the city are unusual (although not unheard of), Ramallah has suffered greatly over the past few decades: much of the city was levelled during the Second Intifada, and it was here that Palestinian leader Yasser Arafat spent the last weeks of his life, under siege.

But Ramallah is not all about politics. The tiny shops, cafes and eateries that line

Ramallah

Ramallah

the arteries that lead off Al-Manara Sq – with its iconic four lions – are fascinating places to wander around, and the nearby Al-Muntazah neighbourhood is packed with trendy cafes and bars. As the economic and political heart of the West Bank, Ramallah is home to a good deal of expatriates, English is widely spoken and transport links are

superb. As such, it makes an excellent base for further forays into the West Bank.

◉ Sights & Activities

Most tourists begin their exploration of Ramallah in Al-Manara Sq, which is a short walk downhill from the bus station where buses arrive from Jerusalem.

The streets that branch off Al-Manara lead to the city's other neighbourhoods. Al-Ra'eesy St (also known as Main St) and Palestine St (directly opposite) lead to the Old City and the entrance to the street market respectively, and are packed with coffee shops and kebab houses.

To reach the Al-Muntazah neighbourhood, head down the Jaffa Rd; take a right at the HSBC bank and head up Eisah Zeyada St, which has a host of chic cafes, bars and dining destinations.

Set on a steep hill, Ramallah can be a disorientating and tiring place to get lost but locals can generally point you in the right direction. Taxis are also relatively cheap; a journey within the city should cost no more than 10NIS.

Muqata'a HISTORIC BUILDING
(Al-Itha'a St; ⊙tomb 9am-9pm daily) Those interested in modern history might want to stop at the now-rebuilt Muqata'a, Yasser

Arafat's large presidential compound, where he was based during the last days of the Second Intifada. He was evacuated from his base in 2004 while under Israeli siege and later died in a Paris hospital. In 2014 his body was briefly exhumed for tests after speculation that he had been poisoned. Arafat's enormous **cubicle tomb** is guarded by soldiers and adorned with wreaths.

The compound's buildings have been restored, with the exception of some holes from tank shelling. The Muqata'a is around 1km from Al-Manara on the road to Birzeit and Nablus, and is easily walkable from downtown. Soldiers will not let tourists stray from the short path between the entrance and the tomb, but Muslims will be allowed to enter the modern mosque erected in Arafat's honour.

Al-Kamandjati   CONCERT HALL
(✆ 02-297 3101; www.alkamandjati.com; Old City) This small conservatory, which features an ancient arch with an edgy, modern copper entryway, offers intimate concerts and recitals.

🛏 Sleeping

Ramallah does not have a huge amount of accommodation for tourists, but it has at least one good option in each budget.

★ Area D Hostel   HOSTEL $
(✆ 056 934 9042; http://ramallahhostel.com; Vegetable Market St; dm 70NIS, d 160-200NIS) With cosy, spotless dorms and a number of private rooms, Area D makes a great hub for tourists – not least because its position on the top floor of Ramallah's service taxi garage means you can get a ride to most parts of the West Bank without having to leave the building. Staff are helpful, the location is fantastic and the open plan lounge is a lovely place to relax.

Royal Court Suites Hotel   HOTEL $$
(✆ 02-296 4040; www.rcshotel.com; Jaffa St; s/d/ste 305/355/445NIS; ❋ @ ⚥) This is a reliable midrange option 15 minutes' walk downhill from the centre of town. Many of the rooms come with kitchen facilities and balconies and all have wi-fi and breakfast. The suites are enormous. Consider asking for a room at the back of the hotel where it is quieter.

Beauty Inn   HOTEL $$
(✆ 02-246 4040; www.beautyinn.ps; Al Muntazah; s/d/ste US$90/120/180; ❋ @ ⚥ ⚥) Tucked away on a quiet street close to the Khalil

Sakakini Cultural Centre, this is a smart, clean midrange option with a pool and a gym and corridors lined with pictures of Palestine. Some rooms are a little dark, so ask to see a couple when you check in.

Mövenpick Ramallah   HOTEL $$$
(✆ 02-298 5888; www.moevenpick-hotels.com/en/middle-east; Al Masyoun; s/d US$180/200) One of only a handful of Western-branded hotels in the West Bank, the Mövenpick has become a hub for Palestine's great and good – as evidenced by the flashy cars that pull up outside its imposing glass-fronted lobby. It has huge rooms, excellent staff and great facilities, including a gym and pool (summer only). Book online for better rates.

🍴 Eating

The area around Al-Manara Sq is packed with cheap hole-in-the-wall eateries and kebab and felafel stands, but Ramallah has a range of restaurants, from fast food to Italian, from organic to sushi. The trendier spots – congregated close to Jaffa St – chop and change, but there are a few stalwarts.

Ameed Al Zain   RESTAURANT $
(Palestine St; mains 15-50NIS; ⏱ 9am-6pm Sat-Thu) This tiny restaurant just off Al Manara Sq is the best of the kebab and felafel joints that dominate this part of town. Sit down at one of the three tables and point either to the grill or the felafel. Their speciality is kofta-style kebabs cooked with pine nuts and fresh mint (40NIS). Staff speak little English but make life very easy nonetheless.

★ La Vie Cafe   RESTAURANT, BAR $$
(✆ 02-296 4115; info@lavie-cafe.com; Castel St; mains 35-70NIS; ⏱ 10am-midnight Sat-Thu, 4pm-midnight Fri) Tucked away on a quiet street just 10 minutes' walk from Al-Manara, this place has a diverse menu of pasta, pizza and sandwiches, with much of its produce grown in owners Saleh and Morgan's roof garden. On weekends, La Vie is a popular nightspot, serving a range of beers, wines and cocktails.

Pronto Resto-Café   ITALIAN $$
(Al-Muntazah; mains 45-75NIS; ⏱ 7am-11pm) This dark and cosy little trattoria is a popular spot for musicians, filmmakers, professionals and peacemakers. The pizzas are top notch and a handful of pasta options make it the only place for real Italian food in Ramallah. Pronto prides itself on local ingredients, from the fish (caught in Jaffa) to the wine (from Bethlehem).

Zamn   CAFE $$

(Al-Tireh; coffee from 10NIS, mains 35-60NIS; ⊙7am-11pm; 🛜) The hippest spot in Ramallah and meeting ground for reporters and NGO workers, Zamn is a fun place for a morning croissant and cuppa or a lunchtime sandwich. Walk down Dar Ibrahim and bear right at the roundabout.

🍷 Drinking & Nightlife

Ramallah is packed with trendy bars and restaurants, many of which stay open until the wee hours and are usually far cheaper than Jerusalem. For those of a more sober disposition, Al-Manara is well served with local coffee houses, where older Ramallans congregate to play cards, smoke shisha and gossip.

★ Al-Snobar   CLUB

(Pine; 📋02-296 5571; www.al-snowbar.com; ⊙May-Oct) This entertainment complex has a flashy restaurant, a swimming pool and one of the hottest nightclubs in the city. Note that it's only open in high season. It's located 2km northwest of Al-Manara Sq. Take a taxi, everyone knows it.

Lawain   BAR

(📋059 763 6003; Al-Manara; ⊙6pm-late; 🛜) Situated above the Qasaba Theatre just off Al-Manara, Lawain is a late-night party spot, with live music, DJs and a young crowd of both locals and expats hanging out on weekends into the early hours. Be warned that unless there is a show on, Lawain doesn't get going until 9pm or 10pm. Ask for the theatre if you can't find it.

Sangria's   BAR

(📋02-295 6808; Jaffa Rd, Al-Muntazah; ⊙noon-midnight; 🛜) A veteran Ramallah hang-out, Sangria's beer garden is the place to be on Thursday and Saturday nights. The Mexican and international menu is ambitious, but you are here for the drinks menu – arguably one of the best in the city, with everything from local Taybeh beer (15NIS) to a range of cocktails (35NIS to 40NIS) to sangria, of course, at 80NIS a litre.

La Grotta   BAR

(Old City; ⊙6pm-late) La Grotta is a tiny, grungy, alternative hangout, close to posh Mexican restaurant Fuego in the Old City. There are a few tables outside but the main bar is up the steps on the 1st floor of a traditional Palestinian house. It doesn't get going until late and can be tricky to find: walk down Main St and turn left at the garage.

Stars & Bucks   CAFE

(Al-Manara; ⊙8am-late) A Ramallah institution and not just because of its mischievous take on the logo – or indeed, the entire concept – of the US coffee giant, Stars & Bucks is a great place to hang out with coffee or cocktails (non-alcoholic) overlooking the bustle of Al-Manara Sq.

☆ Entertainment

There is a lot going on in Ramallah, but you tend to need to be in the know to find out what is on when. Ask at your hotel, check online or pick up the entertainment listing *This Week in Palestine*.

Al-Kasaba
Theater & Cinematheque   CINEMA

(📋02-296 5292; www.alkasaba.org; Al-Manara) A magnet for artists, musicians and film and theatre buffs. It's well worth catching a performance or screening here while you're in town.

Khalil Sakakini Centre   CULTURAL CENTRE

(📋02-298 7374; www.sakakini.org; Al-Muntazah) Hosts art exhibitions by the locally and internationally renowned, along with a whole host of other cultural pursuits. Check the website for upcoming events.

ⓘ Getting There & Around

From the old Arab bus station in East Jerusalem take bus 18 (30 minutes) all the way to Ramallah.

As a rule of thumb; the smaller the bus the faster the journey. Buses to/from Ramallah operate from 6am to 9pm in summer or until 7pm in winter, after which you can take a service taxi from Ramallah to Qalandia and then a taxi to Jerusalem, or vice versa.

You will not need to get off the bus on the way into the West Bank, but on the way out all passengers disembark and go through airport-style security. Have your passport and Israeli visa ready to show the soldiers behind the bulletproof glass.

Also hold onto your ticket to show to the driver once you're on the other side of the checkpoint.

Everything within the Ramallah area is 10 minutes or less by private taxi and should cost 10NIS to 20NIS; but be sure to agree on the final price with the driver before setting off.

The main bus station where buses arrive from Jerusalem has services to Nablus and Hebron, and the service taxi parking garage across the road (below Area D Hostel) has dirt cheap shared taxis to almost everywhere you could want to go in Palestine.

Around Ramallah

When a small Christian village is known more for its beer than for its Bible stories, one might think the past is forgotten. But the townsfolk in **Taybeh** hold fast to their heritage, raising a glass to the place they believe Jesus stayed with his disciples in his final hours (John 11:54). Sample its nectar at the **Taybeh Beer Brewery** (☑02-289 8868; www. taybehbeer.net); call to arrange a tour, or drop by for its annual two-day **Oktoberfest**, a must-visit if you are anywhere in the region.

Taybeh is around 15km from Ramallah, on a reasonably remote – and very picturesque – hillside. The village is home to a number of interesting churches and chapels as well as fascinating Byzantine ruins. Take a shared taxi (7NIS) from the service taxi garage below Area D Hostel. In 2014 Taybeh began producing and bottling its own wine at the cavernous Taybeh Winery just a short walk from the brewery. Call ahead to arrange a tasting.

Jericho & Around
اريحا　　　　　　　　　　　　יריחו

☑02 / POP 20,300

Local authorities proudly call Jericho the 'world's oldest continuously inhabited city'

> ### WEST BANK AREAS
>
> The West Bank is divided into three areas, designating the amount of civil and military power exercised by Israelis and Palestinians.
>
> ➡ Area A (around 17%): under full Palestinian civil and military control; you'll see Israeli signs forbidding Israelis from entering. Includes the cities of Ramallah, Nablus, Tulkarem, Jenin, Qalqilya, Bethlehem, Jericho, parts of Hebron and some other small towns and villages.
>
> ➡ Area B (around 24%): under Palestinian civil control but Israeli military control. Includes many rural Palestinian areas.
>
> ➡ Area C (about 59%): under full Israeli control. Includes many sparsely populated areas, outskirts of towns and villages, and the West Bank's highway network.

and this is no idle boast – archaeological evidence traces the city's history back over 10,000 years. But despite the biblical stories, it was earthquakes rather than trumpets that proved Jericho's biggest challenge, levelling some of its most fantastic sites – such as Hisham's Palace – over the centuries.

Jericho has modernised somewhat since the Canaanite period, but not much. Small-scale farming still makes up a significant portion of the local economy, although tourism is making inroads. The town is rather scruffy and unkempt but retains a raffish charm and a smiley demeanour. Most visitors just stay long enough to ascend the Mount of Temptation and marvel at the archaeological remains of Tel al-Sultan (Ancient Jericho).

History

Settled history in Jericho dates to around 10,000 BCE when hunter-gatherer groups settled here around a spring. Mudbrick buildings were erected at the site and by 9400 BCE it's believed that some 1000 people lived here.

For the biblically astute, Jericho is known as the first city the Israelites captured after wandering for 40 years in the desert: shaken by horn blasts and the Israelites' shouts, the city walls came crashing down (Joshua 6). Following Alexander the Great's conquest of the region in the 4th century BCE, Jericho became his personal fiefdom.

Further waves of occupiers arrived and departed until Jericho fell into the hands of Mark Antony, who gave it to Cleopatra as a wedding gift. Herod later leased it from Cleopatra and improved its infrastructure with aqueducts and a hippodrome. The 1st-century aristocracy of Jerusalem used the city as a winter getaway.

Christians celebrate Jericho as the place where John the Baptist received his own baptism in the Jordan River and where the temptation of Jesus took place on the mountain.

In the 1967 Six Day War Israel captured Jericho from Jordan. After the signing of the 1993 Oslo Accords, it became the first city to be handed over to Palestinian Authority control. During the Second Intifada, the Israeli army attacked the Palestinian Authority prison and security headquarters in Jericho.

Today Jericho has returned its attention to tourism and daily trade, and though you won't find a great many foreign visitors in town, it makes an interesting stop for a night or two.

ISRAEL'S SEPARATION WALL

From 1967 until the Second Intifada (2000–05), most Palestinians were still able to cross into Israel from the West Bank with relative ease, many commuting on a daily basis.

But in the mid-1990s and even more so during the Second Intifada, scores of suicide bombers crossed into Israel from the West Bank, killing hundreds of Israeli civilians. Israel responded with military incursions into areas controlled by the Palestinian Authority, and both security experts and the Israeli public called on the government to build a security barrier to prevent infiltration.

From the point of view of the Israeli left, a barrier would only further the Oslo Accords process (which had as its goal the establishment of two separate states), along the lines of 'good fences make good neighbours'. But there was opposition, from Jewish settlers not wanting to find themselves on the West Bank side of the wall, and from West Bank Palestinians, whose villages and fields were bisected by the wall, and whose access to Jerusalem the borders made difficult or impossible.

Except in Jerusalem, most of the barrier (about 5% of which is a concrete antisniper wall up to 8m high) matches the Green Line (the 1949 armistice between Israel and Jordan) – but only roughly. Quite a few sections loop and scoop around Jewish settlements, separating Palestinians from their communities, businesses, schools and crops. Palestinians call the separation wall the 'Apartheid Wall' and see it as part of a concerted campaign to grab land wherever possible. Israel – where the barrier is seen as a security success – says that the route of the wall can always be modified, eg if there is a final status accord on borders.

Demonstrations are periodically held in parts of the West Bank where the wall cuts through villages. The Israel Defense Forces (IDF) regularly disperse the crowds with tear gas and rubber bullets – as well as live ammunition, according to both local and international NGOs. Protestors have frequently been injured and some killed.

◉ Sights & Activities

A gaggle of storefronts and restaurants with colourful bouquets of household products, fresh produce and roasting snack foods spilling into the streets marks Jericho's diminutive and dusty town centre. The **Tree of Zacchaeus**, nearby on Ein as-Sultan St (a sycamore said to be more than 2000 years old) received its name from the story of the wealthy tax collector who was too short to see Jesus amid the crowds and thus climbed this very tree to get a better view. Seeing this, Jesus asked the tax collector if he could visit his home, a gesture that so moved Zacchaeus that he decided to dedicate himself to a life of charitable deeds.

Many of Jericho's sights are outside the city, making for good drives, hikes or cable car rides into the surrounding area. The best way to see these sites is to hire a driver for the day – 30NIS to 40NIS an hour is a fair price.

The new **tourist information centre** in Jericho's main square is an excellent place to stop at early in your visit. Staff speak fluent English and have a huge variety of information about sights and tours, as well as very useful maps of the area. It is open every day.

★ **Tel al-Sultan (Ancient Jericho)** RUIN
(adult/child 10/5NIS; ⊘8am-5pm) It is impossible not feel a sense of history strolling around the mounds and ruins at Tel al-Sultan, where remains of dwellings and fortifications dating back some 10,000 years have been unearthed. You will see what look like sand dunes and stairways (the oldest known stairways in the world); underneath, the layers of civilisation beneath go back even further into the mists of history.

The remains of a round tower, thought to date from 8000 BCE, indicates that Jericho was possibly the world's first fortified city; legend has it that the tower withstood seven earthquakes.

Though a large portion of ancient Jericho remains unexcavated, Tel al-Sultan is an essential part of any trip to the city, and what has already been identified here is very well explained on signposts throughout the site.

Mount of Temptation & Monastery of the Qurantul RELIGIOUS
(round trip 55NIS; ⊘8am-9pm) It was on the Mount of Temptation where, so we're told, Jesus resisted Satan after his 40-day fast in the desert. The Monastery of the Qurantul marks the spot where the Devil urged

Jesus to make a loaf of bread out of a stone (Matthew 4:1–11). It's an incredible feat of engineering, cut into the cliff face with dramatic views over the Dead Sea to Jordan.

Opening times for the monastery are sporadic but as with all tourist attractions in Palestine it is best to go early – or at least a couple of hours before sunset. Note that the caretaker may lock the door if he is showing big groups around, so it is worth hanging around a few minutes if you find it closed.

Cable cars (p269) stop just before the monastery, and even the short climb up the stairs to the front gate can be a struggle in the midday heat. They sometimes stop running without notice, making for a sweaty 400m climb. The juice sellers and a couple of restaurants provide a good spot to catch your breath.

Hisham's Palace   RUIN
(Khirbet al-Mafjar; admission 10NIS; ◷8am-6pm)
A short drive north of Tel al-Sultan, this is a spot not to be missed. The sprawling winter hunting retreat of Caliph Hisham Ibn Abd al-Malik must have been magnificent on its creation in the 8th century, with its baths, mosaic floors and pillars – so much so that archaeologists have labelled it the 'Versaille of the Middle East'. It was not fated to last, however – it was destroyed by an earthquake soon after its creation.

The caretaker will direct you to a cinema, where you will be shown a 20-minute video on the history of the site, which gives much-needed perspective for a walk around the ruins. A high point is an amazingly well-preserved 'tree of life' mosaic in the entertaining room of the bathhouse. On one side of the tree two deer graze peacefully, while on the other a deer is attacked by a lion. There are various interpretations of the mosaic, including the struggle between good and evil, peace and war, as well as good versus bad governance.

Wadi Qelt & Nabi Musa   HISTORIC SITE
The steep canyon of Wadi Qelt links Jerusalem to Jericho and has a number of interesting religious sites along its course, as well as springs, plants and wildlife, and often breathtaking views over the mountains and desert. The whole canyon is hikeable, although it would take a full day, and even in the spring and autumn the heat can be intense. The key sites of the wadi are linked to the highway that connects Jerusalem with Jericho and the Dead Sea, and are well signposted in both directions.

Beware of extreme heat in summer and flash floods in winter.

The spectacular St George's Monastery (9am to 1pm daily) is a must see in Wadi Qelt, built into the cliff face in the 5th century. Turn right off the access road and park in the car park, from where it is a steep 10-minute walk to the monastery – expect to be hassled by donkey-taxi vendors the entire way. The paintings inside the main chapel are worth the walk, and parts of the original mosaic floors are visible below perspex screens. Up another flight of stairs there is a beautiful cave chapel.

Drinking water is available at the monastery. You'll see signposts along the way for the three main springs (Ein Qelt, Ein Farah and Ein Fawwar) but don't drink the spring water.

Another road off the highway towards Jericho will take you to the complex of Nabi Musa (Prophet Moses; 8am till sunset). About 10km north of the Dead Sea, this is where Muslims believe Moses (Musa in Arabic, Moshe in Hebrew) was buried. A mosque was built on the site in 1269, under Mamluk Sultan Baybar (it was expanded two centuries later) and annual week-long pilgrimages set out from Jerusalem to Nabi Musa – they continue today. The road beyond the mosque takes you past a Muslim graveyard – including the tomb of a former imam of Nabi Musa, sadly today covered in graffiti – and then into the Judean desert for some 20km. The road passes solitary camels, abandoned tanks and vast open desert.

Qasr al-Yahud   RELIGIOUS
(◷9am-4pm Apr-Oct, 9am-3pm Nov-Mar) At an isolated spot on the Jordan River, on the border between Jordan and the West Bank, stands the reputed spot of Jesus's baptism by John (Matthew 3), which began his ministry. John was based here because it was an important crossroads for passing traders, business people and soldiers, but the same cannot be said of the site today. It was only reopened to pilgrims in 2011; you must pass an Israeli checkpoint and drive through a deserted landscape surrounded by barbed wire and minefields to reach a car park, from where it is a short walk down to the river.

Expect to see dozens of pilgrims, most in white T-shirts or smocks, taking turns in walking to the water and submerging themselves. The Jordan River is divided in the middle by a piece of wood – which denotes the border and prevents people from wading to the other side. Just metres away, armed Jordanian soldiers loll on a bench, facing their Israeli counterparts. Whether you are religious or not, it is a beautiful spot, and the site has been fully renovated with changing facilities, a gift shop, a food and drink outlet and shaded areas where you can sit and admire the view.

Inn of the Good Samaritan
HISTORIC SITE

(adult/child 21/9NIS; ⊗ 8am-5pm Apr-Oct, 8am-4pm Nov-Mar) Located just off the main road between Jerusalem and Jericho, this site is associated with the popular parable told in Luke 10: 25-37. In the story, Jesus describes a man who is robbed, beaten and left for dead on the road between Jerusalem and Jericho. A priest passes by and then a Levite but neither lends a hand to the stricken traveller. Finally, a Samaritan stops to help the stranger, dressing his wounds and bringing him to a nearby inn; thus 'good Samaritan' became a byword for 'compassionate individual'.

Historians suggest that an Israelite rather than a Samaritan was the original hero of the story, and that a Greek translator mistakenly swapped the words while compiling the book of Luke.

Archaeologists have unearthed a Second Temple-era palace, presumably constructed by Herod, which may have been converted into the inn mentioned in the Bible. A church was added under the Byzantines, and during the Crusader period a khan (travellers inn) was erected. The ruins you can see today are a confection of foundations and mosaics from the different eras of construction. Also on the site is a new Israeli museum housing a collection of mosaics.

Jericho Cable Car
CABLE CAR

(www.jericho-cablecar.com; 60NIS; ⊗ 8am-8pm) The Swiss-made red cable cars that ply the route between Tel al-Sultan and the Mount of Temptation are visible from throughout Jericho. Although they may appear dated, the 20-minute ride is a great way to see the city and the farms that dominate its outskirts. Even when the site is quiet, cars leave fairly regularly.

Look out for the network of irrigation ditches that intersect the groves growing bananas and oranges, a technique used in this city for thousands of years.

🛏 Sleeping

Jericho's accommodation scene is hardly burgeoning, but there is a handful of options for each price category.

★ Sami Youth Hostel
GUESTHOUSE $

(☏ 02-232 4220; eyad_alalem@live.com; r 120NIS; 🛜) The best budget option in Jericho, this guesthouse is nestled deep in the refugee camp, with a dozen private rooms in a clean, quiet and enigmatically furnished two-storey hostel. Coming into Jericho from Highway 90, take a left at the first roundabout, then continue straight – the guesthouse will be on your right. Failing that, ask any local for 'Hotel Sami' and they will point the way.

The owner, Sami, speaks perfect English, and can advise on tours to the sights around Jericho.

Oasis Hotel
HOTEL $$$

(☏ 02-231 1200; www.intercontinental.com; d US$120-140, ste US$200; ❄@🛜♨) Until 2014 this cavernous hotel was the Intercontinental Jericho, and the logo is still visible on the side of the building, one of the tallest in the city. Much of the decor has remained the same, and rooms are clean and modern, with baths and TVs. The hotel also has two pools, a bar and helpful staff.

Jericho Resort Village
RESORT $$$

(☏ 02-232 1255; www.jerichoresorts.com; s/d 350/450NIS, bungalows 500-550NIS; @🛜♨) Out in the north of the city by Hisham's Palace, this resort hotel has two pools and a range of comfortable and well-furnished rooms, including modern chalets, doubles and singles. In 2014, the owners added two storeys to the main building. It is popular with tour groups so be sure to book ahead.

🍴 Eating

The roads surrounding Jericho's central square are packed with kebab and felafel stands, as well as small coffee shops. A kebab or sandwich is unlikely to cost more than 10NIS, and the park in the centre of the roundabout is a lovely spot to sit, eat and watch the locals playing cards and smoking shisha.

★ Al Essawe
RESTAURANT $

(Main Sq; mains 15-45NIS; ⊗ 6am-11pm daily) On a corner overlooking Jericho's main square, Al Essawe's lovely 2nd-floor terrace is an excellent place to watch the world go by. The owner speaks English and the restaurant serves the usual Arabic fare, kebabs, felafel and mezze. Al Essawe's speciality is barbequed chicken in lemon sauce. Coffee and shisha are served on the roof terrace.

REMI BENALI / GETTY IMAGES ©

1. Around Bethlehem
A shepherd minds his flock near Bethlehem.

2. Nablus (p274)
Nablus is an exciting metropolis where the Old City coexists with bustling modern life.

3. Street Art (p256), Bethlehem
The separation wall is adorned with colourful street art by local and international artists.

4. Nabi Musa (p268)
Muslims believe Moses (Musa in Arabic, Moshe in Hebrew) was buried in Nabi Musa.

ⓘ MEDIA

This Week in Palestine (www.thisweek inpalestine.com) is a free monthly booklet with listings, articles, events and maps related to the West Bank.

Abu Omar MIDDLE EASTERN $

(Ein al-Sultan St; mains 20-50NIS; ⊘ 6am-midnight) Next to the main square, this local favourite serves everything from felafel in pita (4NIS) to a half-chicken dinner for two people (50NIS).

Rosanna Restaurant and Café RESTAURANT $$

(Jericho-Jerusalem Rd; mains 35-70NIS; ⊘ 10am-late) A good option for those staying either at Sami's or the Oasis, Rosanna is walking distance from both hotels and serves Arabic and Western food in massive portions. In the evenings, films are projected onto a screen outside in the leafy garden, the centrepoint of which is a bubble fountain. Despite the signs, Rosanna no longer appears to serve alcohol, but the Oasis over the road has a good bar open 24 hours.

ⓘ Getting There & Away

There are no direct service taxis from Jerusalem to Jericho. A private taxi ride from Jerusalem to Jericho (or vice versa) should cost around 400NIS.

The best way to reach Jericho via public transport is from Ramallah, where buses leave regularly throughout the day. Ask around for the bus times, since they vary; they generally take around 90 minutes via a circuitous route to avoid the Qalandia checkpoint.

Remember to bring a passport; you'll need to show it on the way back to Jerusalem.

Hebron חברון الخليل

📲 02 / POP 183,000

For Jews, Christians and Muslims alike, Hebron (Al-Khalil in Arabic) is considered the cradle of organised religion. For thousands of years the major holy site has been the Tomb of the Patriarchs – the collective tomb of Abraham, Isaac and Jacob, along with their wives (except Rachel). In addition, Islamic tradition states that Adam and Eve lived here after being exiled from the Garden of Eden. Sadly, the common thread of beliefs has done little to improve relations between the major monotheistic religions, and Hebron has long been the location of religious violence.

What distinguishes Hebron from other Palestinian towns is the presence of Jewish settlers within the city centre. There are five microsettlements there, with other, larger ones on the outskirts, effectively dividing the city into two pieces. Many streets are barricaded and/or off limits to Palestinians. There are also regular flare-ups between Israeli soldiers – of which there are thousands stationed in the city – and Palestinian youths, particularly on Fridays.

The murder of three Israeli teenagers kidnapped outside a settlement near Hebron in 2014 brought the city back into the limelight, with the two men accused of the killing – both said to be members of Hamas – later killed in an Israeli raid on a Hebron house. These events had followed months of raids, riots and arrests in the city as well as renewed settler activity, with hardline Israeli settlers occupying a new building in an Arab neighbourhood for the first time in decades.

The security situation in Hebron has created palpable tension and the city remains fairly unstable. Obviously, if you see a situation developing – particularly around Al-Manara Sq – go the other way. Hiring a local guide can help explain the situation in the city, but be aware that Palestinian guides probably won't be allowed in settler areas. If you arrive independently, expect local kids to offer you a tour, but agree on the price before you set off.

Despite its woes, Hebron continues to flourish as a business leader among Palestinian communities. Situated on a former trade route to the Arabian Peninsula, the city is celebrated for its grapes, its skilled traders and its artisans' production of blown glass, leather and hand-painted pottery, just as it has been since antiquity.

History

According to the Hebrew Bible, Hebron was founded around 1730 BCE, its biblical name, Kiryat Arba (the Village of Four), perhaps referring to its position on four hills on which four Canaanite tribes settled.

For the few centuries before the 20th, Hebron had been home to a small Jewish community, but in 1929, Arab nationalists attacked the city's Jews – all of them non-Zionist ultra-Orthodox – and killed 67 of them. The rest of the community fled.

After 1967, Orthodox Jews returned to the city, and a prominent feature of today's Hebron is the presence of Israeli soldiers guarding Jewish enclaves – populated by some of the West Bank's most hardline settlers – in the town centre. The suburb of Kiryat Arba, now home to more than 7000 Jews, was established nearby.

In 1994, during the Muslim holy month of Ramadan and on the Jewish holiday of Purim, Brooklyn-born physician Baruch Goldstein opened fire on Palestinians while they prayed in the Ibrahimi Mosque, killing 29 men and boys and injuring a further 200. Moderate settlers, like the average Israeli, view Goldstein as a cold-blooded killer. However, extremist Jewish settlers, who see local Palestinians as foreign interlopers in the Land of Israel, consider him a hero and his gravesite remains a popular place of pilgrimage.

◉ Sights & Activities

For most travellers, there are three main parts to Hebron. The first is Ras al-Jora (Jerusalem Sq), set on Hebron Rd (also known as Shari'a al-Quds) as it comes in from Bethlehem. The area is a commercial hub with plenty of restaurants and workshops that produce glass and ceramics.

About 3km further, Hebron Rd becomes Ein Sarah St, which eventually runs into Al-Manara Sq (really just an intersection). From Al-Manara Sq, turn right for about 200m, to reach the bus station, or turn left and walk for 10 minutes to reach Bab al-Zawieh, the entrance to the Old City souq and further to the Ibrahimi Mosque.

The Jewish section of town lies south of the Old City, beyond high walls and barbed-wire fences. You can easily walk there from the Ibrahimi Mosque/Tomb of the Patriarchs. You can also cross at the checkpoint at Al-Manara Sq. Have your passport handy to cross through checkpoints between the Arab and Jewish parts of town.

Hebron is not an easy place to visit by anyone's standards. It feels notably more tense than any other area of the West Bank, and fending off the myriad stall holders and touts plying their trade in the souk can be draining. At the same time, a visit is crucial for anyone wishing to understand the root of the settlement issue. The best way to visit the city – as with any politically sensitive area – is on an organised tour.

Ibrahimi Mosque/
Tomb of the Patriarchs   MOSQUE, SYNAGOGUE
(☉ 8am-4pm Sun-Thu, except during prayers) The focal point of Hebron for most visitors is the Tomb of the Patriarchs (Cave of Machpelah), known to Muslims as the Ibrahimi Mosque (Ibrahim is the Arab name for Abraham).

The site is sacred to both Muslims and Jews – be aware of the strict security and separate prayer spaces for each.

When entering the mosque, you will be asked to remove your shoes, and women will be handed a head covering.

Looking rather like decorated tents, the mostly Mamluk-era cenotaphs commemorate the patriarchs Abraham, Isaac and Jacob, and their wives, but it's the cave below that both Jews and Muslims believe was chosen by Abraham as the actual final resting place of his family.

You can peer into the cave through a metal grate in the corner of the mosque. As you walk into the room that allows viewing of the cenotaph of Abraham, note the small niche near the door where you can see a footprint. The Muslims believe this to be Mohammed's footprint while Jews say Adam created it.

Built by Herod (notice the Herodian stones at the base of the walls), the complex was altered by the Byzantines in the 6th century – they added a church, beside which a synagogue was built. When the Arabs conquered the area in the following century, the church was converted to a mosque but the synagogue remained intact. After the Crusaders left the scene, the Mamluks built another mosque.

Old City   ARCHITECTURE
The Old City's stunning, often crumbling, Mamluk-styled Ottoman architecture includes a souq, but merchants have been moved to an outdoor area due to friction with Jewish settlers. Look out for the nets hung over the narrow streets to catch trash thrown from the upstairs windows (home to settlers) at the Palestinian shops below. You can also peer through the barbed wire at Hebron's gold souk, once renowned throughout the region but now completely off limits, with the doors to the shops welded shut during the Second Intifada.

For shops and food, it generally makes sense to head away from the Tomb of the Patriarchs, where more of the stalls are open.

Glass & Ceramic Workshops   ARTS CENTRE
At the northern entrance to Hebron, in the area called Ras al-Jora, several traditional blown-glass and ceramic factories are open for viewing and shopping. Al-Natsheh and Al-Salam glass factories receive visitors and shoppers, as does the smaller Tamimi Ceramics. All are open between 9am and 7pm daily except during Friday-morning prayers.

🛏 Sleeping & Eating

Very few tourists spend the night in Hebron, not only because of the security situation but because the city makes an easy day trip from Bethlehem. If you're keen, contact the **Association d'Échanges Culturels Hebron-France** (AECHF; ☎02-222 4811; www.hebron-france.org), which can arrange homestays with local families. Another good option is www.womeninhebron.com; its founder, Nawal Slemiah, has a small guesthouse not far from her stall in the souk. Ask around the other stalls if you can't find her.

Hebron doesn't boast many top-notch culinary choices, though there are plenty of places for a quick, tasty bite on the go, particularly along Nimra St.

Abu Salah   MIDDLE EASTERN $
(Bab-e-Zawi; mains 10-35NIS; ⊘7am-10pm) Perched on the edge of Hebron's Old City, this busy restaurant is a good bet for shwarma or a plate of chicken, rice and potatoes served buffet-style.

❶ Getting There & Away

The best way to reach Hebron from Jerusalem is to go via Bethlehem, in one of the regular service taxis. From the bus station in Hebron, it's possible to catch service taxis to Jericho, Bethlehem and Ramallah between 5am and 6pm. Vehicles leave when full.

For a very different perspective – that of Hebron's Jewish settlers – take Egged bus 160 from Jerusalem's Central Bus Station. It stops right by the Ibrahimi Mosque/Tomb of the Patriarchs, from where you can walk into the Arab side of the city.

Nablus   שכם نابلس

☑09 / POP 126,000

Situated in and around a lush valley between Mt Gerizim (Jarzim in Arabic) and arid Mt Ebal, Nablus (known as Shechem in Hebrew) has historically been a significant exporter of olive oil, cotton, soap and carob. Best known these days for its olive-oil soap factories, olive-wood carving and *kunafeh* (a warm, syrupy cheese-based pastry), the city is layered with millennia of plunder and glory.

Nablus is a bustling, exciting and vibrant metropolis, with a stunningly beautiful Old City that even rivals Jerusalem's – not least because of the lack of tour groups clogging its narrow alleyways. Nablus is also a hotbed of Palestinian activism, and more often than not its central square is covered in flags,

banners and posters of martyrs, those killed in the decades-long struggle against Israel.

The northern West Bank is still known to Jews as Samaria, from which the term 'Samaritan' is derived. Among the most fascinating elements of the Nablus area is its tiny Samaritan community, set on Mt Gerzim and overlooking the city.

History

After the 12 tribes of Israel split into two rival kingdoms in the 10th century BCE, Shechem was briefly the capital of the northern faction, ie of the 10 tribes who would eventually be lost to history.

In 70 CE the Romans obliterated ancient Shechem and set up Flavia Neapolis (New City), whose name the Arabs would later pronounce as Nablus. Graeco-Roman cults developed, only to be destroyed in 636 CE when the city was conquered by Arab forces. Christian shrines were converted to Muslim mosques, and Nablus developed the character it still displays today. The Old City dates back to Ottoman times, though relics from as long ago as the Roman occupation can still be spotted.

Nablus is now surrounded by some of the West Bank's most hardline Jewish settlements. On nearby hilltops you'll see Bracha, Itamar, Yitzhar and Elon Moreh, often in the news because local Jewish extremists have clashed either with Palestinians or with Israeli soldiers.

◉ Sights & Activities

For more information on things to do and see, go to www.nablusguide.com.

Al-Qasaba   NEIGHBOURHOOD
The focal point for visitors to Nablus is Al-Qasaba (Casbah or Old City), where you'll find an Ottoman-era rabbit warren of shops, stalls and pastry stands, spice sacks and vegetable mounds. Amid the clamour, you'll find dozens of contemplative mosques, including the **Al-Kebir Mosque** (Great Mosque), which is built on the site of an earlier Crusader church and Byzantine and Roman basilicas. Bits and pieces of its earlier incarnations have survived; look out for the huge columns and capitals, traces of the Byzantine structure.

Soap Factories   SOAP FACTORIES
If cleanliness is next to godliness, then the Old City offers plenty of opportunities for both. Nablus has seven or eight functioning

Nablus

soap factories that produce olive-oil-based suds, carrying on an 800-year-old Nablus tradition. **Mofthen Factory**, on Martyrs Sq, is just one of those happy to receive visitors.

Jacob's Well   CHURCH
(donations appreciated; ⏰8am-noon & 2-4pm) Near the entrance to Balata (population 20,000), the largest United Nations Relief and Works Agency refugee camp in the West Bank, you'll find the spot where Christians believe a Samaritan woman offered Jesus a drink of water, and that he then revealed to her that he was the Messiah (John 4:13–14).

A Byzantine church destroyed in the Samaritan revolt of 529 CE was replaced by a Crusader church, which itself fell into ruins in the Middle Ages. The current church, St Photina the Samaritan, was built in the 1860s by the Greek Orthodox Patriarchate.

Go down the steps close to the altar to see the well itself. The church grounds are a stunningly beautiful spot, the immaculate chapel set in lush, quiet gardens filled with neighbourhood cats.

About 300m southeast, a compound known as Joseph's Tomb has in recent years been a source of considerable friction between Jews, who come here to pray under IDF escort (in coordination with the Palestinian Authority), and local Arabs. A

Nablus

◉ Sights
1 Al-Qasaba D3

◉ Activities, Courses & Tours
2 Hammam Al Shifa C3

◉ Sleeping
3 Al-Yasmeen Hotel C3
4 International Friends
   Guesthouse A2

◉ Eating
5 Al Aqqad B2
6 Al Aqsa D3
7 Assaraya C2

nervous security guard will allow visitors to enter the eerily deserted tomb.

Tell Balata   RUIN
FREE Close to Joseph's Well and well sign-posted from the main road into Nablus from Ramallah, Tell Balata is the remains of what is believed to be the first settlement in Nablus, based around a spring in the valley between two mountains. It boasts some interesting ruins and an excellent – albeit tiny – museum.

Sebastiya   RUIN
FREE Located uphill from a village of the same name, Sebastiya is a collection of

DON'T MISS

MOUNT GERIZIM

הר גריזים جبل جرزيم

The Samaritans (members of an ancient religion closely related to Judaism) believe that Mt Gerizim, which overlooks Nablus from the south, was not only the first piece of land ever created, but is also the land out of which Adam was made, the only place spared in the great flood, the place Abraham went to sacrifice his son Isaac (Judaism holds that this event took place on Jerusalem's Temple Mount) and the location chosen by God for the Temple.

One of the world's last communities of Samaritans (there's another in Holon, Israel) lives on the mountain. Learn more about their community at the excellent **Samaritan Museum** (☑02-237 0249; samaritans-mu@hotmail.com; admission 15NIS; ☺9am-3pm Sun-Fri, 9am-1pm Sat), where an English-speaking guide will show you a video and answer any questions you have about the Samaritans. From the museum, continue further down the main road to the **Good Samaritan Center** (☺9am-4pm Sun-Fri, 9am-1pm Sat) **FREE**, which contains a library and information desk.

After a short walk, take the left fork to reach the **Platform** (adult/student 22/19NIS; ☺9am-sunset daily), the ancient site of the Samaritan Temple. A guard will unlock the gate to let you inside and will give a brief tour of the site. Once at the top, you'll see the lowered floor that Samaritans say was the foundation of their Temple, which was built in the 5th century BCE. It only survived about 200 years before being destroyed by the Maccabees (a Jewish rebel army) in 128 BCE. The remains of a church, first constructed in 475 CE, have also been found here. You can rent binoculars for an extra 10NIS.

From the centre of Nablus, Mt Gerizim can be reached by taxi in around 10 minutes. It's a 50NIS journey including wait time. Taxis have to wait outside the village at a military checkpoint, so be prepared to pay your driver in advance to keep them waiting.

ruins that includes an amphitheatre (which once held 7000, making it the largest in Palestine) and a Byzantine church, built upon a site considered to be the grave of John the Baptist. In the mid-4th century the grave was desecrated and the bones were partly burned; surviving portions were taken to Jerusalem and later to Alexandria where they were interred at a Coptic monastery. Sebastiya is 11km from Nablus; a taxi with waiting time will cost around 100NIS.

Sebastiya's old city has recently been restored and is a nice place to walk, and there are a couple of restaurants close to the ruins that cater to the tour buses that call in occasionally.

Hammam Al Shifa BATHHOUSE
(35NIS; ☺9am-11pm, Thu women-only) This can be hard to find but locals will point the way. Hand over your valuables before changing into a towel (or swimming costume, if you have one). The hammam has a hot room – a heated platform for lying on – a sauna and steam room. Massages (NIS10) are not for the faint-hearted.

🛏 Sleeping

Nablus makes a great place to stop for a couple of nights, especially as a base for excursions in the northern West Bank.

⭐ **International Friends Guesthouse** HOTEL **$**
(www.guesthouse.ps; dm/d 85/200NIS; 🛜) Set in a leafy garden, this is a clean, smart hostel just 10 minutes' walk from the walls of the Old City. Manager Jihad is a local lad who returned from overseas three years ago and is a wealth of knowledge on Nablus. The hostel has four large dorms and one double room. It is often booked by groups so be sure to call ahead.

Al-Yasmeen Hotel HOTEL **$$**
(☑02-233 3555; www.alyasmeen.com; s/d/tr US$70/80/100; 🅿🛜) Tucked away in the heart of the bustling Old City, this has long been the preferred choice for journalists, diplomats and NGO types. Helpful and polite staff, clean rooms and traditional architecture make it a great midrange choice in the city. It is worth splashing out the extra US$10 for a double room.

🍴 Eating & Drinking

In addition to confectioners selling Turkish delight, halvah (squares of fruit and nuts covered with a sweet sesame paste) and syrupy pastries, Nablus is full of cafes for sipping and puffing – but the clientele is usually male. The best spot for a kebab is Martyr's Sq, where vendors also sell thick black Arabic coffee for 2NIS. Most of the Old City closes down at sunset, but the restaurants and cafes that line the streets around the square are open later. An essential part of any trip to Nablus is trying *kunafeh*, the Palestinian dessert that is famous throughout the Middle East.

★**Al Aqsa**   RESTAURANT $
(Old City; 4NIS; ⊘8am-sunset) This tiny eatery next door to the Al-Kebir Mosque in the kasbah is unanimously considered to produce the finest *kunafeh* in Palestine, and every day the warm, elastic cheese and syrup-soaked wheat shreds (it works, trust us) is divvied up from huge circular trays and dispensed to a throng of hungry customers. Do as the locals do and eat standing in the street outside.

Al Aqqad   RESTAURANT $
(Hitten St; mains 10-30NIS; ⊘9am-late) Somewhere between kebab stand and diner, this tiny local eatery just outside the Old City serves huge shwarmas and sides, including salads and fries. A chicken or lamb wrap will cost you just 12NIS, a fraction of what it would in even a midrange restaurant. It only has a handful of tables inside.

Assaraya   MIDDLE EASTERN $$
(Hitten St; mains 40-70NIS; ⊘10am-10pm) For a more formal sit-down meal, ascend Assaraya's wood-panelled staircase from the main gate into the Old City and take a seat in the restaurant's two-storey glass atrium, which overlooks Martyrs Sq. The tables are adorned with folded white napkins and wine glasses (although there is no wine, this being Nablus), and the restaurant serves a mixture of Western and Arabic fare.

❶ Getting There & Away

There is no direct bus service to Nablus from Jerusalem. The best way to reach the city is from Ramallah, where buses leave from the central bus station throughout the day. A taxi from Qalandia checkpoint will cost around 100NIS.

Jenin   جنين   ג'נין

☑ 04 / POP 40,000

The northernmost city in the West Bank, Jenin is home to religious sites, a bustling souq, a unique performing-arts scene and the Arab-American University, but its isolation has traditionally left it off the tourist trail.

That is starting to change, due to the opening of the Jalameh (Gilboa) Border Crossing, just 10km south of Afula, allowing easier access for travellers from Nazareth and Haifa.

◉ Sights

**Masjid Jenin al-Kabir
& Downtown**   MOSQUE, NEIGHBOURHOOD
With its unmissable green roof, Masjid Jenin al-Kabir (Jenin Great Mosque), was built in 1566 on the orders of Fatima Khatun, then wife of the Governor of Damascus. Cross the street and enter a dense network of alleys that form the **Old City**, today largely occupied by furniture makers, barbers and machinists. Two blocks south of the mosque is King Talal St, which leads to Jerusalem Sq, the main bus station and the **Jenin Cinema**. It's fun to wander into the **souq**, North of King Talal St, which is absolutely bursting with activity.

★**Freedom Theatre**   THEATRE
(☑04-250 3345; www.thefreedomtheatre.org; ⊘9am-4pm daily) This world-renowned theatre group has persevered in the face of difficult circumstances since it was founded in 2006. Its founder, Juliano Mar Khamis, was assassinated in 2011 by masked gunmen outside the theatre building in the heart of Jenin's refugee camp and his killer has never been identified. The Palestinian filmmakers, actors, photographers and directors who have moved through the theatre have also had to put up with significant Israeli restrictions on movement.

Despite this, the Freedom Theatre holds regular performances in both Arabic and English, and foreign visitors are always warmly received whether there is a show on or not.

**Greek Orthodox
Church of St George**   CHURCH
Located in Burqi'in village, this church was built upon the site where it is believed Jesus healed 10 lepers (Luke 17: 11–19). It's said to be one of the world's oldest surviving churches (dating to the 4th or 5th century CE) and contains the cave that sheltered the lepers. Service taxis (3NIS) go here from a station about 300m west of the Masjid Jenin. The church is often locked but the caretaker family should be able to unlock the gates for you.

In front of the church a shaft has been uncovered that leads to another cave where early Christians took shelter from the Romans. Ask if you can climb down the ladder to have a nose inside.

THE LAST PALESTINIAN ZOO

The city of Qalqilya, with its lush tree-lined boulevards demonstrating its proximity to the coast, feels very different than the dry and often arid cities of the northern West Bank – as well as than Israeli settlements and the separation wall, which surrounds it on most sides. Little surprise, perhaps, that this city was the first to vote Hamas into power in the local elections of 2006.

Politics aside, Qalqilya is famous as the home of the last surviving zoo in Palestine, housed within the sprawling Qalqilya Park, which is also home to a space museum and a small theme park.

A half dozen lions, black bears and various species of baboons sit idly in small green cages towards the rear of the park, as well as a sad looking hippo in just a couple of feet of water. It is also home to spectacular, if a little cramped, aviary.

That said, the conditions of the animals are not bad by Middle Eastern zoo standards, and head vet Dr Sami Khader's struggle to keep the park going through two intifadas and an ongoing Israeli blockade is commendable.

Dr Sami – who was featured in Amelia Thomas's book *The Zoo on the Road to Nablus* – is happy to greet foreign visitors; if he is absent, you can meet other staff members who speak English. Tickets are 7/5NIS for adults/children and Qalqilya can be reached via service taxi from Nablus. The park is open from 8am to midnight.

Canaan Fair Trade FACTORY
(☑04-243 1991; www.canaanfairtrade.com; ⊙8am-5pm Sat-Thu) 🖉 Located 2km beyond Burqi'in, this newly built olive-oil factory practises fair-trade policy with its olive farmers. A tour of the factory (40NIS) includes a free bottle of olive oil and if you want to get to know the olive farmers, they can set you up with a homestay. A good time to visit is the first Friday of November, when the factory holds its annual harvest festival.

🛏 Sleeping & Eating

⭐**Cinema Guesthouse** GUESTHOUSE $
(☑059 931 7968; www.cinemajenin.org; 1 Azzaytoon St; dm/s/d 75/125/250NIS; @🛜) A quiet spot in the heart of chaotic Jenin, this is a great place to meet other travellers (or NGO workers, journalists, activists and the like) and unwind for a day or two. It has three spacious dorm rooms, a couple of tiny private rooms and a nice kitchen for cooking communal meals. Breakfast is an extra 10NIS. The English-speaking manager is a font of information on the area. It's opposite the central bus station.

North Gate Hotel HOTEL $$
(☑04-243 5700; www.northgate-hotel.com; Palestine St; s/d 200/300NIS; @🛜) The high-end option in Jenin, North Gate has a pool and clean, modern rooms but its location, a 20-minute walk from the Old City and amidst half a dozen unfinished apartment buildings, counts against it. It is one of only a handful of midrange options in the city. Breakfast and wi-fi are included in the room rate.

Awtar WESTERN, MIDDLE EASTERN $
(Cinema Circle; dishes 20-60NIS; ⊙8am-midnight) Head up to Awtar's spacious roof garden for a choice of Arabic and Western dishes under the stars. Even on cool evenings, the terrace is packed with groups of men and women drinking, eating and chatting over shisha. Downstairs, the restaurant has bay windows overlooking the street and serves Arab staples as well as pizza, burgers and enormous salads.

❶ Information

Jenin Tourism Office (⊙10am-2pm Sat-Thu) Don't be put off by the rather ramshackle tower block that houses this excellent tourism centre, opened in 2013 with the aid of funding from the Spanish government. The centre has a number of fascinating rooms, which include a timeline of Jenin's history from 7000 BCE to 2002, touch-screen photography exhibitions and examples of handicrafts. English-speaking staff are a wealth of advice on what to do in Jenin and the surrounding area.

❶ Getting There & Away

There are frequent buses during the day to/from Nablus for 10NIS. From the north (Nazareth or Haifa), it's possible to take a direct share taxi from Nazareth or Afula to Jenin, passing through the Jalameh border crossing (open daily, 8am to 5pm). Expect a long delay if you cross with your own car.

The Gaza Strip

رצועת עזה   قطاع غزة

Gaza in Numbers

➡ Total population: 1.81 million

➡ Estimated refugees in Gaza: 1.1 million

➡ Total area: 360 sq km

➡ Average age: 18 years

➡ Unemployment: 45%

Gaza throughout History

➡ 1516–1917: Ottoman Empire

➡ 1917–48: British Mandate

➡ 1948–67: Egyptian occupation

➡ 1967–2005: Israeli occupation

➡ 2006–present: Hamas control

Introduction

Gaza has been off the to-do list for travellers for some time – and for good reason. Israel has blockaded the tiny strip from land, air and sea since just after Islamist party Hamas took control in 2006, keeping Gaza's 1.8 million residents in and, with the exception of a handful of journalists, politicians and aid workers, the world out. Even if it were possible to visit Gaza, it would not be recommended: Hamas fought three wars with Israel between 2006 and 2014 and the strip remains unstable and dangerous.

At 45km long and 10km wide, Gaza is one of the most densely populated places in the world – but it remains desperately poor, with hundreds of thousands of people living either in ramshackle refugee camps or heavily bombed towns and cities. It doesn't need to be this way: literacy levels are upwards of 97% and its seas hold untapped natural gas reserves worth up to US$7 billion. Its historic sites go back three millennia and it is home to one of the most beautiful coastlines in the Mediterranean.

At the end of 2014, billions were pledged internationally to rebuild the strip, but it was difficult to see how any serious change could take place while the blockade continues and while many Palestinian militants remained committed to establishing a Palestine 'from the river to the sea' (the Jordan to the Mediterranean) – leaving little room for their Israeli neighbours.

Further Reading

➡ *Gaza, a History,* by Jean Piere-Filiu (2014)

➡ *Footnotes in Gaza: a Graphic Novel,* by Joe Sacco (2010)

➡ *Gaza Writes Back: Short Stories from Young Writers in Gaza,* edited by Rafeet Alareer (2014)

➡ *The Book of Gaza: a City in Short Fiction (Reading the City),* edited by Atef Abu Saif (2014)

The Gaza Strip

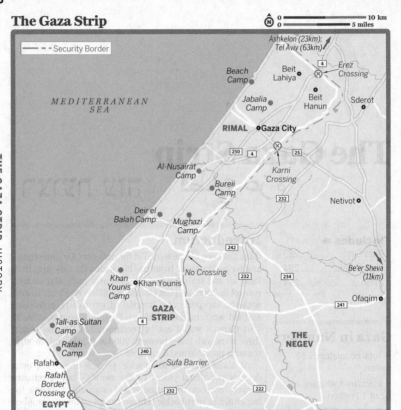

- - - Security Border

MEDITERRANEAN
SEA

Ashkelon (23km);
Tel Aviv (63km)

Beach
Camp

Beit
Lahiya

Erez
Crossing

Sderot

Jabalia
Camp

Beit
Hanun

RIMAL   Gaza City

250   4

25

Karni
Crossing

232

Netivot

Al-Nusairat
Camp

Bureii
Camp

Deir el
Balah Camp

Mughazi
Camp

242

Be'er Sheva
(11km)

No Crossing

232

234

Khan
Younis
Camp

Khan Younis

241

Ofaqim

GAZA
STRIP

4

THE
NEGEV

Tall-as Sultan
Camp

Rafah
Camp

240

Sufa Barrier

Rafah

Rafah
Border
Crossing

232

222

EGYPT

0 — 10 km
0 — 5 miles

History

Commerce & Conquerors

Settlement in Gaza is thought to date back to the Bronze Age, when it was used by the ancient Egyptians as a centre of trade. As far back into antiquity as 1500 BCE, an inscription on the Egyptian Temple of Amun at Karnak noted that Gaza was 'flourishing'.

By the time Alexander the Great arrived, in 332 BCE, the land had already passed through the hands of the Philistines, the Israelites (under Kings David and Solomon), the Assyrians and the Persians. In 63 BCE Gaza became part of the Roman province of Judea (later named Syria Palaestina) and was governed by a diverse 500-man senate. In the late 4th century, the Bishop Porphyrius forced Gazans to convert to Christianity and burned down the pagan Temple of Marna to replace it with a church.

Islam arrived in 635 CE, turning churches into mosques, a process that was briefly reversed in 1100 by the Crusaders, who built a cathedral that now forms part of the Great Mosque. During the 14th century, Mamluk rule came to Gaza but the population dwindled due to a deadly plague in the 1340s. In 1516 Ottoman Empire rule began, lasting until the British arrived in 1917.

Withdrawal & War

During WWI, the British air force under General Edmund Allenby pounded Gaza while taking Palestine from the Turks, reducing much of the city to rubble. Then, in 1927, a huge earthquake finished off much of what was left standing after the war.

Gaza was under British Mandate administration until 1948 when, with the creation of the State of Israel, Palestinian refugees flooded into the area, swelling its population from 35,000 to 170,000 in a matter of months. Egypt immediately responded to the declaration of Israel's independence in 1948 by occupying Gaza. During the occupation housing projects were expanded but after President Nasser closed the Straits of Tiran in 1967, the Six Day War began and Israel took control of Gaza.

Israeli settlers arrived in the 1970s and growing tensions ignited Palestinian activism and riots. The radical Islamic organisation Hamas was formed in 1987 and the First Intifada began. A brief period of calm followed the Oslo Peace Accords and in 1994 the Palestinian Authority (PA) assumed administrative control of parts of Gaza. But talks to transfer permanent control to the PA failed and a Second Intifada began in September 2000, causing a series of Hamas suicide bombings and IAF strikes.

Under international pressure and in a bid to improve Israel's home security, Prime Minister Ariel Sharon ordered Israel's disengagement from Gaza and removed all of the strip's 21 Jewish settlements, with their 8000 inhabitants, in August 2005. Afterwards, a power struggle within Palestinian ranks began, culminating in the victory of Hamas in the January 2006 PA elections and the subsequent withdrawal of much international aid.

In June 2006, Israel Defense Forces soldier Gilad Shalit was kidnapped at the Gaza–Israel border. Several days afterwards, Israel launched 'Operation Summer Rains', a series of attacks that killed some 280 Palestinian militants and more than 100 Palestinian civilians. In 2007 violent clashes broke out within Palestinian ranks as Hamas took control from Fatah.

Meanwhile, from 2005 to 2008, thousands of Kassam and Grad rockets and mortars were fired on southern Israel from within Gaza, culminating in 87 rockets in just 24 hours on 24 December 2008. In response, Israeli forces launched 'Operation Cast Lead' by air and then by land. The Gaza War resulted in the deaths of more than 1400 Palestinians, with thousands made homeless. Israel lost 10 soldiers and three civilians. Many NGOs declared a humanitarian crisis and Israel declared a ceasefire after three weeks of fighting.

Recent Events

In 2011, kidnapped soldier Shalit was handed over as part of a prisoner swap that saw 1027 Palestinians released from Israeli jails. The deal was a major coup for Hamas, increasingly unpopular in Gaza due to ongoing economic malaise. The Islamist party got a further boost in June 2012 with the election of Muslim Brotherhood leader Mohammed Morsi in Egypt. As the flow of goods through tunnels that linked the strip with Sinai surged, Gaza experienced a rare period of economic growth.

THE GAZA STRIP HISTORY

ACCESS TO GAZA

Gaza is inaccessible to all but a tiny minority of journalists and aid workers. The foreign ministries of most countries advise against all nonessential travel to the strip. As a result of the 2014 Hamas–Israel war, Lonely Planet was unable to visit Gaza during our research trip to Israel and the Palestinian Territories.

Both Israel and Hamas – or, often, more extreme elements in Gaza – routinely break ceasefire agreements, the former with its controversial targeted assassinations of senior militants and the latter through rocket attacks, which often provoke Israeli air strikes.

Foreign journalists and aid workers have been killed in recent years while working in Gaza, including an Italian activist who was kidnapped and murdered by an Islamist group in 2011 and an Associated Press cameraman who was killed by unexploded Israeli ordinance while reporting on the aftermath of the 2014 war.

The Israeli authorities have made it clear that they will prevent any vessels from breaching the naval blockade, so participating in any sort of protest flotilla is not advised. In 2010, an Israeli commando raid on a Turkish protest ship aiming to land in Gaza left nine dead, with a 10th activist dying in hospital four years later after a protracted coma.

International journalists and aid workers who want to enter Gaza not only need to gain permission from Israel, but also from Hamas, who control the entry and exit of reporters on the other side of the formidable Erez crossing. On the occasions when the border at Rafah from Egypt is open, this crossing is a long, complicated and often dangerous process, not least because of the ongoing instability in Sinai.

GAZA IN PEACETIME

Gaza does not feel like the rest of the Palestinian Territories – the traffic-snarled streets and general aura of chaos are more reminiscent of Cairo than Ramallah – but even in peacetime the strip is an intensely political place. It is not unusual to see armed militants at pro-Hamas rallies, while the first rocket Hamas fired at Tel Aviv in 2012 is memorialised in a monument on one of Gaza City's main thoroughfares. Many homes are riddled with shrapnel and bullet holes, and posters of 'martyrs' killed in the fighting with Israel are ubiquitous.

That said, life goes on for most Gazans. They are an incredibly young population: over 43% are under 14 and the whole population has a median age of 18 (compared to 40 in most European nations). While much attention is paid to their attendance at the infamous 'Hamas summer camps' (where children barely out of nappies pose with machine guns and go through military drills), most young Gazans dream of being entrepreneurs, business people and journalists rather than militants.

The strip is football-mad, home to some 30 domestic clubs and dozens of beachfront shisha bars that show European games late into the night. Like many other Arab countries, and Israel, most Gazans are either die-hard fans of Real Madrid or Barcelona, and when the two clubs meet the atmosphere is electric.

Gaza is home to a small surf club, although the inability to smuggle more than a handful of haggard boards from Egypt has hindered its growth. But it is at the beach where Gaza really comes to life in peacetime. In the evenings, mothers clad in long black robes bathe toddlers in the shallows, families huddle in tents and the local kids scream and play in the booming surf. At these moments, Gazans can get a glimpse of what life was like before the wars, the hatred and the violence, and what, *insh'allah* (God willing), it will one day be again.

But the boom, like Morsi's government, was to be short-lived.

On 10 November 2012, a mortar fired from Gaza hit an Israeli military jeep, wounding four soldiers, and a retaliatory Israeli air strike killed four Palestinian teenagers while they played football. The killings provoked dozens of rockets which, in turn, led to Israel's assassination of Hamas military commander Ahmed Jabari. By the time Egypt was able to negotiate a ceasefire on 21 November, more than 100 Gazans had been killed and almost 1000 wounded.

Rebuilding Gaza's shattered infrastructure in the wake of the war was easier than in 2009 due to Hamas's Egyptian allies as well as significant financial aid from Qatar. But the coup that overthrew Morsi and installed the Egyptian military in Cairo in July 2013 was a hammer blow for Hamas, as the tunnels were gradually dismantled and the Rafah border once again slammed shut. As the year rumbled on, Hamas's popularity in Gaza once again began to wane.

In early 2014, with both Hamas and Fatah in the West Bank facing rising anger for their failure to improve the lives of Palestinians in either territory, the two parties signed a unity deal ending their seven-year split. Although welcomed internationally, the deal was greeted with horror by Israeli Prime Minister Binyamin Netanyahu, who accused Abbas of choosing Hamas over peace with Israel.

At the end of April, peace negotiations between Israel and the PA – doomed for some time – finally broke down. By the time war broke out between Israel and Hamas in June 2014, relations between Israelis and Palestinians were at their lowest ebb since the Second Intifada (2001–05). Over the next 50 days, 73 Israelis and more than 2100 Palestinians would be killed and tens of thousands made homeless, while the limited infrastructure that Gaza had been able to develop was levelled by Israeli air strikes. As 2014 came to a close, Gaza's future looked bleaker than ever.

Gaza Today

For over a decade Gaza has been a byword for conflict and hardship, and though the strip has had periods of optimism and even growth in that time, in 2014 it was difficult to see an end to this dark period of its long history.

Even veteran Gaza-watchers were shocked at the range and ferocity of the rockets that Hamas had stockpiled and then fired during the 50-day war in 2014, as well as the complex network of tunnels it had built, some of which led into Israel and had been used to attack and kill Israeli soldiers. Equally, the fierceness of the Israeli response and massive civilian casualties in Gaza brought condemnation from across the world, with thousands-strong protests in European cities, the US and even Israel itself, where citizens took to the streets in Tel Aviv, Jerusalem and Haifa.

As 2014 ended, the situation in Gaza seemed to be little changed – except that one hundred thousand of its people were now homeless and its infrastructure largely non-existent. Although Hamas made wide-reaching demands during peace negotiations in Cairo, it was only able to secure a meagre extension to the fishing zone off Gaza's coast – quite a price, many Palestinians argued, for the more than 2100 who died. Its demands for an end to the blockade and permission to build a port and airport were shelved for future talks in Cairo – at the time of writing these had failed to materialise.

It may be optimistic to think that the massive media coverage of the war could help prevent the outbreak of further conflict, but the fact remains that the 2014 Hamas–Israel war was easily the most-covered yet. Dozens of journalists inside Gaza produced often-harrowing reports from the battles, such as that in the Gaza City neighbourhood of Shejaiya, in which 120 Palestinians (a third of them women and children) and 13 Israeli soldiers were killed. Meanwhile social media was abuzz with Gazans tweeting as their buildings were under fire, giving a whole new reality to the war.

The impact on Israel also suggests that hopes for peace are over-optimistic. Although there were anti-war protests inside Israel, the regularity and range of Hamas rockets was such that even many liberal Israelis got behind the war effort. In liberal Tel Aviv, residents were shocked by the almost constant barrage of rockets, and although most were shot down by Israel's Iron Dome missile defence system, a handful landed inside the city for the first time. Even Israeli Prime Minister Binyamin Netanyahu, a staunch right-winger, began

to look moderate in the face of some of the comments from his cabinet members, some of whom urged an even harsher military response and even a re-occupation of the strip.

A 2014 report published in the *Arab Journal of Psychiatry* claimed that more than half of 15- to 18-year-olds in Gaza suffered from post-traumatic stress disorder, while UNRWA reports that more than 100,000 people were homeless. The tragedy remains that, beyond the aspirations and rhetoric of leaders on both sides, and the violence it inevitably leads to, Gaza and its people continue to live lives shattered by violence.

Reconstruction Efforts

At a summit in Cairo in October 2014, international donors promised US$5.4 billion for rebuilding Gaza following the war, with Qatar alone promising US$1 billion and the US offering US$212 million. The EU put forward US$568 million. The United Nations Relief and Work Agency had called for donations of US$1.6 billion – the biggest sum it had ever sought to raise, claiming that even before the war Gaza had a shortage of 75,000 homes, as well as deficient water, sewage and power infrastructure.

Of course, the commitment of funds was only the beginning of a long and uncertain process of reconstruction. Israel has restricted the importation of construction materials to Gaza since Hamas took power, arguing that they are used to construct tunnels and weapons depots. Reconstruction will also rely on renewed cooperation between Hamas and Fatah, which controls the Palestinian Authority. Improved relations with Egypt will also be crucial to allow import of materials through the Egypt–Gaza border.

Gaza City   غزة   עזה

The exact meaning of the name Gaza has been obscured through time. The ancient Egyptians called it Ghazzat ('the prized city') and, as one of the oldest functioning cities in the world, Gaza has always been considered a treasure for invaders and emperors.

Gaza City is based around the long Omar al-Mukhtar St, which runs north to south from the sea to the main Salah ad-Din St. At the southern end of Omar al-Mukhtar, the town's main focus is Palestine Sq. At the opposite end, the Rimal (Sands) area of town has the city's beaches and some hotels. Directly to the east of Rimal is the Beach Refugee Camp, also called the Al-Shati Camp.

Khan Younis

חא'ן יונס   خان يونس

Once a stopping point on the ancient trade route to Egypt, Khan Younis is primarily a market town and is Gaza's second-largest urban centre. It incorporates the neighbouring Khan Younis refugee camp, home to around 72,000 people. The ruined khan

in the square nearby – from which the town got its name – dates back to 1387, and was built by the Mamluks.

Rafah

רפיח   رفح

Rafah was traditionally the gateway between Egypt and the Middle East. It became infamous in 2011 for its subterranean network of tunnels – the main route for goods and weapons into Gaza. According to the United Nations Relief and Work Agency, 99,000 people live in the Rafah and Tall-as-Sultan refugee camps, which are no longer distinguishable from Rafah town.

The Dead Sea
البحر الميت

ים המלח

Best Places to Stay

➜ Shkedi's Camplodge (p302)

➜ Ein Gedi Kibbutz Hotel (p291)

➜ Hod HaMidbar (p299)

Best Family Hikes

➜ Wadi David (p289)

➜ Wadi Arugot (p290)

➜ Wadi Bokek (p298)

Why Go?

The lowest place on the face of earth, the Dead Sea (428m below sea level) brings together breathtaking natural beauty, compelling ancient history and modern mineral spas that soothe and pamper every fibre of your body. The jagged bluffs of the Judean Desert, cleft by dry canyons that turn into raging tan torrents after a cloudburst, rise from the cobalt-blue waters of the Dead Sea, heavy with salt and oily with minerals. In oases such as Ein Gedi, year-round springs nourish vegetation so lush it's often been compared to the Garden of Eden. Atop the bluffs lies the arid moonscape of the Judean Desert; down below, human beings have been at work for millennia, building Masada and Qumran (where the Dead Sea Scrolls were found) in ancient times and, more recently turning their hands to creating hiking trails, bike paths, kibbutzim, luxury hotels and even a world-famous botanic garden.

When to Go
Ein Gedi

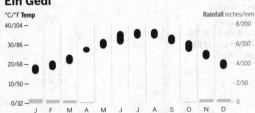

Nov–Apr Warm and sunny. Judean Desert cloud-bursts cause flash floods in wadis.	**Jul–mid-Sep** Oppressively hot. Record temperature: 49.2°C. Begin hikes at dawn.	**Passover & Sukkot** Completely booked with domestic tourists.

Dead Sea Highlights

1 Floating in the briny, soothing waters of the Dead Sea at sandy **Ein Bokek Beach** (p298).

2 Ascending Masada's **Snake Path** (p297) before dawn and watch the sunrise from the top.

3 Taking a refreshing dip in the waterfall-fed plunge pools of **Ein Gedi Nature Reserve** (p288).

4 Soaking in a hot sulphur pool and glop on black mud at **Mineral Beach** (p293).

5 Imagining life among the defenders of Roman-besieged Masada at the evocative **Masada Museum** (p296).

6 Cycling one of the wide wadis around **Neot HaKikar** (p301).

7 Descending **Wadi Daraja** (p293) with the help of ropes and the breast stroke.

8 Shooting the breeze around the campfire at **Shkedi's Camplodge** (p302) in Neot HaKikar.

9 Pampering yourself at one of the hotel day spas at **Ein Bokek** (p298).

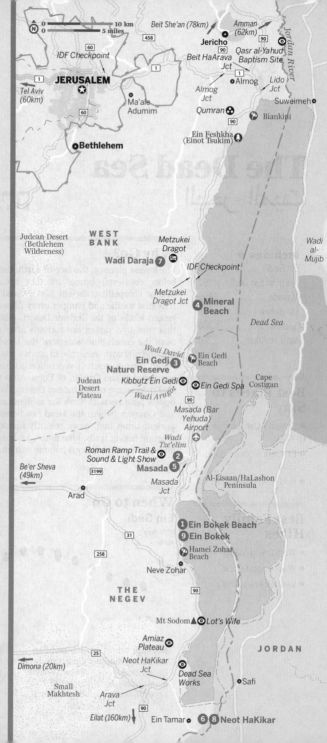

History

Awareness of the Dead Sea's unique qualities goes back to at least the 4th century BCE; luminaries such as Aristotle, Pliny and Galen all made mention of the sea's physical properties. The Nabataeans collected bitumen from the surface of the water and sold it to the Egyptians, who used it for embalming.

For most of history, though, the Dead Sea – today shared by Israel, the West Bank and Jordan – has been regarded as unhealthy and hence shunned; popular lore had it that no bird could fly over its waters without dropping from the sky. This made the area a favoured retreat of religious ascetics and political fugitives: the future King David, King Herod, Jesus and John the Baptist are all said to have taken refuge along its shoreline or in nearby mountains and caves.

Because it was seen as the 'Sea of the Devil', the area remained uncharted until it was finally explored by a team from the United States Navy in 1848. The Palestine Potash Company (now the Dead Sea Works) was established in 1930 by Moshe Novomeysky, a Siberian-born engineer and Zionist pioneer. The 1948 war left Israel with a quarter of the Dead Sea's shoreline and Jordan with the rest. Israel captured the lake's northwestern shore in 1967.

Geography

The Dead Sea (Yam HaMelach, ie the Salt Sea, in Hebrew; Bahr al-Mayit, ie Sea of the Dead, in Arabic), whose surface is now about 428m below sea level, is the lowest point on the face of the earth. Connected to the Mediterranean Sea until about two million years ago, it forms part of the 6000km-long Great Rift Valley (Syrian-African Rift), which stretches from Syria south to Mozambique and includes the Sea of Galilee and the Red Sea.

About 65km long and 18km across at its widest point, the Dead Sea is fed mainly by the Jordan River, and supplemented by underground springs, seasonal wadis and flash floods. With no outlet, the in-flow has historically been balanced, more or less, by evaporation. Water arrives with normal mineral concentrations (mainly magnesium, sodium, calcium and potassium chlorides) – but, over the millennia, evaporation has removed vast quantities of H_2O but left behind everything else, causing mineral concentrations in the lake to rise dramatically. The Dead Sea's salt concentration is about 34%, making it 10 times more saline than the ocean.

Because some 95% of the water from the Jordan River basin is now diverted to agriculture in Israel, Jordan, Syria and Lebanon, the Dead Sea is drying up. Every year its surface drops by approximately 1m, and the shore, depending on its gradient, recedes by up to 5m. The Med-Dead Project, a plan to refill the Dead Sea by reconnecting it with the Mediterranean, generating electricity by taking advantage of the 400m drop, was proposed in the 1980s, but was eventually shelved. In 2013 an agreement was signed by Israel, Jordan and the Palestinian Authority to build a 180km-long 'Red-Dead Canal' that would partly refill the Dead Sea with seawater from the Red Sea. Policy-makers, economists and environmentalists – such as Friends of the Earth Middle East (www.foeme.org) – are engaged in a spirited debate over the virtues and risks of the plan.

The Dead Sea's shores are dotted with springs and oases that provide water for 90 species of birds, 25 species of reptiles and amphibians, and 24 species of mammals, as well as more than 400 species of plants, some of them at the extreme northern or southern edge of their natural distribution.

These days the Dead Sea is in fact two separate lakes connected by an artificial channel. The larger northern basin (fronting Mineral Beach and Ein Gedi Beach) is a proper, if shrinking, lake whose deepest point is about 300m below the surface. The shallow southern section (fronting Ein Bokek) – actually an expanse of artificial evaporation pools – would be completely dry if not for the water pumped in by the Dead Sea Works. Whereas the level of the northern lake is dropping, that of the southern section is actually rising – to the point of threatening the Ein Bokek hotels – due to the accumulation of salt deposits on the bottom of the evaporation pools. The two lakes are separated by a peninsula that juts from the Dead Sea's eastern shore and is known as HaLashon in Hebrew and Al-Lisaan in Arabic (both names mean 'the Tongue').

ℹ Getting There & Around

BUS

It's possible, though a bit fiddly, to explore the Dead Sea by public bus. To avoid hanging around wilting under the sun, it's a good idea to plan your itinerary in advance.

Egged buses (www.bus.co.il) link sites along Rte 90 (including, from north to south, Qumran, Ein Feshkha, Metzukei Dragot Junction, Mineral Beach, Ein Gedi Nature Reserve, Ein Gedi Beach, Kibbutz Ein Gedi, Ein Gedi Spa, Masada, Ein Bokek, Neve Zohar, Neot HaKikar Junction and Arava Junction) with the following destinations:

Jerusalem – buses 421, 444 and 486; 25NIS to 49.50NIS, one to two hours, about hourly 7am to 5pm Sunday to Thursday, hourly until about 2pm Friday, at least one Saturday night.

Eilat – bus 444; 49.50NIS to 82NIS, 2½ to four hours, four per day Sunday to Thursday, three on Friday, one to three Saturday afternoon and night.

Tel Aviv – bus 421; 46NIS to 49.50NIS, 1¾ to 3¼ hours, departs Tel Aviv at 8.45am and Neve Zohar at 2pm Sunday to Friday. In Tel Aviv departs from the Central (Arlozoroff/Savidor) train station; goes via Jerusalem.

Be'er Sheva – buses 384 and 385; 31.50NIS to 44NIS, 1¼ to 2¼ hours, four per day Sunday to Thursday, two on Friday.

All of these lines can be used for travel north and south along the Dead Sea's Rte 90, which runs along the Dead Sea's western shore (eg from Masada to Ein Gedi Beach).

If you're short on time, it's possible to do a one-day circuit from Jerusalem on weekdays (Sunday to Thursday). Take bus 444 from Jerusalem to Masada (first departure at 7am); after visiting Masada, hop on any northbound bus to Ein Gedi Nature Reserve; walk over to Ein Gedi Beach for a dip; and finally take bus 486 back up to Jerusalem (last bus at about 7.30pm).

CAR

The Dead Sea's western coast is served by Rte 90 – Israel's longest highway, it continues north to the Lebanese border and south to the Red Sea. There's an army roadblock about 14km north of Ein Gedi at the junction below Metzukei Dragot.

The Dead Sea is served by three east–west highways:

→ **Rte 1** – Thanks to this modern, divided highway (and a stretch of Rte 90), Ein Gedi is only 75km from Jerusalem. Rte 1 passes through the West Bank but rarely has security issues. For Jerusalem-bound traffic, there's an army roadblock between the large settlement of Ma'aleh Adumim and Jerusalem.

→ **Rte 31** – Connects Arad with Rte 90 at a point a few kilometres south of Ein Bokek. To get to the back (western) side of Masada, take Rte 3199 from Arad.

→ **Rte 25** – Passes through Be'er Sheva and Dimona on its way to the Dead Sea's southern tip, near Neot HaKikar.

Locals recommend that you arrive in the Dead Sea area with a full tank as the only petrol stations are (from north to south) at Lido junction (40km north of Ein Gedi near Jericho), Ein Gedi Beach, Neve Zohar junction and Arava junction (11km west of Neot HaKikar).

Most hikes are circuits so you end up where you began. For one-way hikes, you can arrange (for a fee) to be dropped off and picked up, eg by the kind folks in Neot HaKikar.

Only one car rental company (Hertz) has an office at the Dead Sea (at Ein Bokek).

Ein Gedi עין גדי عين جدي

📍 08 / POP 530

Nestled in two dramatic canyons that plunge from the arid moonscape of the Judean Desert to the shores of the Dead Sea, Ein Gedi is one of Israel's most magical desert oases. The area's freshwater pools, cool streams, Eden-like waterfalls and luxuriant vegetation, fed by four year-round springs, are a haven for wildlife such as the majestic Nubian ibex (*ya'el* in Hebrew) and the boulder-dwelling hyrax (*shafan sela* in Hebrew; also known as a dassie or rock rabbit), both of which you're very likely to encounter (the ibex is easiest to spot during the first and last hours that the reserve is open). Ein Gedi is the northernmost natural habitat of a number of plants that are more usually found on the savannahs of East Africa, thousands of kilometres south along the Great Rift Valley.

Ein Gedi (literally 'Spring of the Kid', as in 'young goat') was first settled during the Chalcolithic Age (5000 years ago), when people just out of the Stone Age built a temple here. In the Bible, David fled to Ein Gedi to escape the wrath of Saul (I Samuel 23:29), and the oasis crops up again in the love poetry of the Song of Songs (1:14): 'My beloved is to me as a cluster of henna blossoms in the vineyards of Ein Gedi'. More recently, the erotic waterfall scene in one of Brooke Shields' worst movies, *Sahara* (1983), was filmed at Ein Gedi.

◎ Sights & Activities

⭐ **Ein Gedi Nature Reserve** NATURE RESERVE (📞 08-658 4285; www.parks.org.il) This reserve consists of two roughly parallel canyons, Wadi David and Wadi Arugot, each of which has its own entrance complex and ticket office.

The key to a successful hike in the reserve is the excellent colour-coded map-brochure given out when you buy your ticket. It has invaluable details on the area's many trails (indicated using the same colours as the trail markings), how long each route takes, and the times by which you need to begin and finish each circuit.

Park rangers make sure that visitors do not enter the park before it opens or stick around after closing time (in theory, they can fine violators 730NIS). The reason: desert animals such as the wolf, jackal and fox need some people-less peace and quiet in order to search for food and drink (the reserve has the only year-round water sources in the entire area).

The last time a critically endangered Arabian leopard (*Panthera pardus nimr*) was spotted in the Ein Gedi area – carrying off Kibbutz Ein Gedi house pets for dinner – was in 2006. The species is now presumed to be extinct here.

Eating, smoking and pets are not allowed in the reserve.

Ancient Synagogue ARCHAEOLOGICAL SITE
(Ein Gedi Antiquities National Park; adult with/ without nature reserve 29/15NIS, child 15/7NIS; ⊙8am-4pm or 5pm) Situated about midway between the Wadi David and Wadi Arugot ticket offices, this 5th-century CE synagogue sports a superb mosaic floor decorated with the 12 signs of the zodiac and three Aramaic inscriptions, one of which calls down a curse on anyone who is quarrelsome, slanderous or larcenous.

Ein Gedi Botanical Garden GARDENS
(☏08-658 4220; www.ein-gedi.co.il; Kibbutz Ein Gedi; adult/child 20/15NIS; ⊙8.30am-4pm Sat-Thu, 8.30am-2pm Fri) These famous botanic gardens are home to a thousand species of indigenous and exotic plants, from near-mythological biblical species such as frankincense and myrrh to the highly poisonous Sodom apple, and from gargantuan baobab trees to tiny plants that can survive with minuscule quantities of water. Situated in Kibbutz Ein Gedi, 3km south of Ein Gedi Nature Reserve.

Ein Gedi Beach BEACH
(Rte 90) **FREE** This hugely popular but steep and unpleasantly stony public beach (bring flip-flops) fulfils the bare requirements of those seeking a Dead Sea float in that it has **toilets and changing rooms** (2NIS; 6am to 7pm or 8pm) and a 24-hour snack bar. Situated 1km south (a 20-minute walk) along Rte 90 from the Ein Gedi Nature Reserve turn-off.

THE FOUR EIN GEDIS

The area known as Ein Gedi stretches for 6km along Rte 90, with separate turn-offs (and bus stops) for the following spots (from north to south):

➡ Ein Gedi Nature Reserve (p288) – This is the turn-off to use for Wadi David, Wadi Arugot, the Ein Gedi Youth Hostel and the Ein Gedi Field School.

➡ Ein Gedi Beach – 1km south of the nature reserve.

➡ Kibbutz Ein Gedi – 3km south of the nature reserve (800m off Hwy 90).

➡ Ein Gedi Spa (p291) – 6km south of the nature reserve.

Wadi David HIKING
(Nahal David; adult/child incl Ein Gedi Antiquities 29/15NIS; ⊙8am-4pm or 5pm, last entry 1hr before closing) Ein Gedi Nature Reserve's most accessible – and popular – pools and waterfalls are situated along **Lower Wadi David** (Nahal David Tachton), ie the area downstream from **David's Waterfall** (Mapal David; one hour return). The entrance pavilion has bathrooms where you can change into your bathing suit, free lockers (ask staff for a key) and free cooled drinking water (if you don't have an empty bottle, ask staff for one that's on the way to being recycled).

The refreshments counter sells sandwiches, ice cream and drinks, including espresso.

To get to **Upper Wadi David** (Nahal David Elyon), which is significantly less crowded, head up the trail that climbs the south wall of the canyon. A bit past tiny **Shulamit's Spring** (Ma'ayan Shulamit) is a T-junction: go right and you'll head down the slope to the section of Wadi David above David's Waterfall, including **Dodim Cave** (Lovers' Cave); hanging a left takes you to a **Chalcolithic Temple** (3000 BCE), the pools of **Ein Gedi Spring** (most of whose mineral water is diverted and bottled by Kibbutz Ein Gedi) and, near the base of Wadi Arugot, an archaeological site known as **Tel Goren** (7th to 8th century BCE).

Wadi David can get very crowded, especially on Jewish holidays and on days when raucous coach loads of schoolkids are around. The first 400m of the trail, to the first waterfall, are fully accessible to wheelchairs.

ⓘ SAFE HIKING

A few tips on staying safe and healthy in the Dead Sea's unique climate and geography:

➡ Don't hike without a 1:50,000-scale **SPNI topographical trail map** (87NIS; not necessary at Ein Gedi unless you climb up to the plateau above the wadis). The maps to have – available only in Hebrew – are No 11 *(Ein Gedi v'Daroma)* for Ein Gedi and places south of there; and No 8 *(Tzfon Midbar Yehuda v'Yam HaMelach)* for Ein Gedi and points north. Both can be purchased at the Ein Gedi Field School and the Wadi Arugot entrance to Ein Gedi Nature Reserve.

➡ Bring along *lots* of **water** – at least 5L per person per day.

➡ To **beat the heat** of summer, hit the trail shortly after dawn. If you're still out at midday, you're unlikely to run into anyone other than 'mad dogs and Englishmen'.

➡ **Flash floods** can turn the dry canyons above the Dead Sea into raging torrents. In the late autumn, winter and spring, keep an eye on the weather reports and stay well away from narrow channels (eg those along Wadi Daraja) if there's any chance of a cloudburst up in the Judean Desert.

➡ Temperatures can drop precipitously at night so bring along a fleece jacket to avoid **hypothermia** in case you get stuck.

➡ Keep away from areas (eg south of Ein Gedi Beach and across Rte 90 from Ein Gedi Youth Hostel) where signs warn of **sinkholes** *(bol'anim)*, which can open under your feet with no warning and swallow you alive (yes, this has happened to people!). Caused by the dissolution of underground salt deposits, sinkholes have been found at 37 different sites around the Dead Sea; there are now several thousand of them up to 30m across and 25m deep, with hundreds more formed each year.

➡ Stay out of the area's **caves**, all of which (including the famous Flour Cave) are closed to the public because various geological factors, including high salt content, make them susceptible to sudden collapse.

Wadi Arugot　　　　　　　　　　HIKING

(Nahal Arugot; adult/child incl Ein Gedi Antiquities 29/15NIS; ⊗ 8am-4pm or 5pm, last entry 2hr before closing) Generally less crowded but no less lovely than Wadi David, Wadi Arugot offers a number of excellent trails, some of them quite challenging. The ticket office complex, a 20- to 30-minute walk or a five-minute drive from the Wadi David car park, has free lockers, a small refreshment counter with ice cream and cold drinks, and a shop that sells SPNI 1:50,000-scale trail maps.

Hikers must leave the upper reaches of **Wadi Arugot** (Nahal Arugot), ie the area above the **Hidden Waterfall** (HaMapal HaNistar), including the **Upper Pools** (Ha-Breichot HaElyonot), by 2pm (3pm during daylight savings time).

Desert Plateau Hikes　　　　　　HIKING

The plateau above Ein Gedi – the eastern edge of the Judean Desert – is about 200m above sea level, ie 625m above the Dead Sea. Five trails head from Ein Gedi Nature Reserve up to the plateau and its spectacular panoramas, taking you well away from the madding crowds.

The reserve's most difficult hike (six to eight hours), marked by black blazes, links Wadi Arugot with Wadi David via the Desert Plateau, Ein Gedi Lookout (Mitzpeh Ein Gedi) and Ein Gedi Spring. It should only be attempted by very experienced hikers.

From north to south, the trails leading up to the plateau are the **Yishay Ascent** (from Ein Gedi Field School); the **Ein Gedi Ascent** (from Ein Gedi Spring, on the hillside between Wadi David and Wadi Arugot); **Bnei HaMoshavim Ascent** (an especially difficult route that begins at the upper section of Wadi Arugot); **Ha'Isiyyim Ascent** (from near the top of Wadi Arugot); and the **Tzruya (Zeruya) Ascent** (from near Kibbutz Ein Gedi).

A 1:50,000-scale SPNI trail map, sold at the entrance to Wadi Arugot, is a must for all these routes, which are closed from about June to September because of the extreme heat. Park staff are happy to help with planning; before heading out, let them know your route.

Ein Gedi Spa
SPA

(☏08-659 4813; www.eingediseaofspa.co.il; Rte 90; without/with lunch 95/155NIS, child 5-12yr 61/110NIS; ☺8am-5pm or 6pm Sat-Thu, 8am-4pm or 5pm Fri) Owned by Kibbutz Ein Gedi, this spa is a popular place to catch a float and get coated with invigorating natural black mud. The shoreline has receded 1.2km since the spa opened in 1984 so beach-goers take a little train to the water's edge. Wheelchair accessible. Situated 6km south of Ein Gedi Nature Reserve.

The spa has six sulphur pools and a fresh-water pool and offers a range of natural beauty and massage treatments. There's also a coffee shop and a restaurant.

🛏 Sleeping

The field school and hostel are usual-ly totally full (Friday night is booked out months ahead) so don't show up without reservations.

Ein Gedi Youth Hostel
HOSTEL $

(Beit Sarah; ☏02-594 5600, reservations 1-599 510 511; www.iyha.org.il; Rte 90, near Ein Gedi Nature Reserve; dm/s/d 124/301/381NIS, additional adult/child 2-17yr 110/85NIS; 🅿@🛜) The sensational setting and contemporary rooms, with four or five beds and brand new air-con units, make this 68-room hostel madly popular (more rooms are planned). Dinner is 58NIS (67NIS on Friday) and it offers discounts to various area attractions. Situated 200m up the slope from the Rte 90 turn-off to Ein Gedi Nature Reserve. Reserve well ahead.

Ein Gedi Beach
CAMPGROUND $

(Rte 90; ☺24hr, changing rooms 6am to 7pm or 8pm) FREE Camping is free. Toilets and changing rooms cost 2NIS per entry. Bring flip-flops and a torch. There's a 24-hour snack bar in the car park. Situated 1km south of the Ein Gedi Nature Reserve turn-off from Rte 90.

SPNI Field School
HOSTEL $$

(☏08-658 4288; www.natureisrael.org; near Ein Gedi Nature Reserve; dm/s/d 132/381/421NIS, ad-ditional adult/child 7-14yr 137/96NIS; 🅿🛜) The 50 rooms, each with five to seven beds, are not as swish as at the youth hostel, but this is an excellent launching point for hikes. Guests are greeted by signs – not a joke – reading 'please don't feed the ibex'. Dinner (57NIS, on Friday 68NIS) is served pretty much daily. Reception sells hiking maps.

Situated 800m up the hill from the Rte 90 turn-off to Ein Gedi Nature Reserve.

Ein Gedi Kibbutz Hotel
HOTEL $$$

(☏08-659 4222; www.ein-gedi.co.il; d from US$212-316; 🅿@🛜) This low-rise campus, lushly planted with exotic trees and plants (including two immense baobab trees), offers an on-site spa and a deliciously cool-ing pool, along with five categories of very comfortable rooms, some with space for two adults and two children. The Rte 90 turn-off to Kibbutz Ein Gedi is 2.3km south of Ein Gedi Nature Reserve.

The bar and cafe (dairy) attract a mix of tourists and *kibbutznikim* (kibbutz mem-bers). A copious, kosher meat buffet dinner costs 130NIS from Saturday to Wednesday and 170NIS on Thursday and Friday.

🍴 Eating

There are few dining options in the Ein Gedi area so arrive with picnic supplies and con-sider having dinner at your hotel or hostel.

Pundak Ein Gedi Kiosk
SANDWICHES $

(Ein Gedi Beach; sandwiches 18NIS; ☺24hr) Serves decent baguette sandwiches, ice cream and beer. Situated across the car park from the entrance to the beach, behind the petrol station.

Kolbo Grocery
GROCERIES $

(Kibbutz Ein Gedi; ☺8am-8pm Sun-Thu, 8am-2pm Fri, 11am-2pm Sat) The only proper food shop in the area. Situated next to Kibbutz Ein Gedi's dining hall.

ℹ Information

ATM Inside the Ein Gedi Kibbutz Hotel.
SPNI Field School (☏08-658 4288; www.teva.org.il; ☺8.30am-4pm Sun-Thu) Free consultations by expert staff on area hikes, including family-friendly Wadi Mishmar and Wadi Tze'elim. Sells 1:50,000-scale SPNI topo-graphical trail maps (87NIS). Situated 800m up the hill from the Rte 90 turn-off to the Ein Gedi Nature Reserve.

ℹ Getting There & Away

Bus schedules are posted at both entrances to the Ein Gedi Nature Reserve, at the SPNI Field School and at Ein Gedi Kibbutz Hotel. For infor-mation on bus services to/from the Dead Sea, see p287.

North of Ein Gedi

🎧02

Highlights along the Dead Sea's northwestern coast include the Qumran Caves, where the Dead Sea Scrolls were discovered, and some wild, unspoilt nature sites. Captured by Israel from Jordan in 1967, this almost uninhabited corner of the West Bank is just a short drive from Jericho.

Qumran National Park

גן לאומי קומראן   خربة قمران

World-famous for having hidden the **Dead Sea Scrolls** for almost 2000 years, **Qumran** (02-994 2235; www.parks.org.il; Rte 90; adult/child 29/15NIS, incl entry to Ein Feshkha 43/24NIS; ⊙ 8am-4pm or 5pm Sat-Thu, 8am-3pm or 4pm Fri, last entry 1hr before closing) was the site of a small Essene settlement around the time of Jesus – specifically, from the late 1st century BCE until 68 CE, when it was destroyed by the Romans. The ruins are not that extensive, but from an elevated wooden walkway you can clearly make out the aqueduct, channels and cisterns that ensured the community's water supply. Elsewhere are ritual baths (the Essenes were zealous about ritual purity); the refectory, in which communal meals were eaten; and the scriptorium, where some of the Dead Sea Scrolls may have been written. One of the caves where the scrolls were discovered can be visited on a two-to-three-hour walking circuit (not recommended in summer). The small museum and its seven-minute multimedia program will give you basic historical background. Wheelchair accessible.

Qumran is a safe vantage point for watching wintertime flash floods. Walking from Qumran to Ein Feshkha takes about five hours one-way. Park HQ has a restaurant.

Qumran is 35km east of Jerusalem and 35km north of Ein Gedi. All Jerusalem–Dead Sea buses pass here.

Ein Feshkha (Einot Tsukim)

עינות צוקים   عين فشخة

These spring-fed freshwater ponds and the lush greenery around them were a favourite holiday spot of Jordan's King Hussein in the 1950s and 1960s. Today, the oasis and its veritable forest of salt-resistant plants, including tamarisks and reeds, are an agreeable place to spot birds and take a cooling dip, though the **pools** (open Friday and Saturday late March to November) can be crowded.

There is no access to the rapidly receding Dead Sea shoreline – note the sign, some 4km from the water's edge, reading 'The sea was here in 1967'. However, you can see a Second Temple–period **farm** where the Essenes of Qumran apparently produced date wine and afarsimon oil and raised sheep and goats.

The southern **Hidden Reserve** is off limits – for reasons of conservation – unless you join a one-hour **guided tour** (⊙ 9am & 1pm Fri & Sun Sep-Jun).

THE DEAD SEA SCROLLS

Few discoveries in the history of archaeology have elicited as much enduring worldwide fascination as the Dead Sea Scrolls, accidentally found at Qumran in 1947 inside earthenware jars hidden in a cliffside cave by a Bedouin shepherd boy searching for a stray goat. Eventually, about 950 different parchment and papyrus documents written during the Second Temple period and the earliest years of Christianity (200 BCE to 68 CE) were found in 11 caves. Most of the documents, which include the oldest known manuscripts of the Hebrew Bible, texts that didn't make it into the Bible and descriptions of life in Judea around the time of Jesus, are in Hebrew, some are in Aramaic and a few are in Greek. Many are in tiny fragments, making the process of reassembling and deciphering them long and arduous.

The scrolls are believed to have belonged to the Essenes, a separatist, ascetic Jewish sect – mentioned by Josephus Flavius – that moved to the desert to escape the decadence they believed was corrupting their fellow Jews.

The Israel Museum in Jerusalem, where some of the scrolls are on display, runs, with some help from Google, the Dead Sea Scrolls Digital Project (http://dss.collections.imj.org.il), which makes searchable, high-resolution digitised images of the scrolls available to the general public.

For some interesting facts on the scrolls, see www.centuryone.com/25dssfacts.html.

Ein Feshkha is 3km south of Qumran. Thanks to the local geography, the site is never closed due to flash floods.

Metzukei Dragot

מצוקי דרגות

منحدرات درجة (متسوقي درجوت)

Perched on a cliff 600m above the Dead Sea – the views are truly spectacular – this no-frills, hippyish holiday village (☑ 08-622 2202, reservations 1-700-707 180; www.metzoke.co.il; dm huge tent 110NIS, d/q private tent 250/500NIS, d with bathroom 400-650NIS, basic q 400NIS; ☺ reception 8am-8pm) is like a quick trip back to the 1970s, with bare-bones infrastructure, worn furnishings and very basic bathrooms. There are 50 basic rooms and hundreds of sleeping spots in large tents that can be subdivided to keep members of a family or group together.

You can pitch your own tent for 50NIS per person (90NIS including an excellent Israeli breakfast). Sleeping bags can be rented for 30NIS. If you want to cook, bring your own food. Dinner is available for 95NIS (65NIS for kids aged three to 12 years). You must check in before 8pm. It's situated 18km north of Ein Gedi; a steep 5.5km up the hill (it may be possible to hitch) from the army roadblock on Rte 90, where you can ask any Jerusalem–Dead Sea bus to stop.

Wadi Daraja   נחל דרגה   وادي درجة

One of the more difficult hikes in the area, this steep canyon descent (five to six hours not including stops), known in Hebrew as Nahal Darga, requires you to climb down about two dozen waterfalls (30m climbing rope required) and swim across year-round pools up to 4m deep – all your kit will get wet so leave those mobile phones and cameras somewhere safe. Wear proper shoes (ones you don't mind getting wet), not sandals. The minimum age is 10 years.

The Israel Nature and Parks Authority has an information booth (www.parks.org.il; ☺ Fri, Sat & Jewish holidays Sep-Jun, daily Jul & Aug) right outside Metzukei Dragot, which is 1.5km from the trailhead; schematic maps are available there or at the Metzukei Dragot reception desk. Begin this hike no later than 9am (10am during daylight savings) – and don't begin it at all if there's any chance of rain in the Judean Desert. The bottom of the trail intersects Rte 90 near Kibbutz Mitzpe Shalem.

SOOTHING & HEALTHFUL

The waters of the Dead Sea contain 20 times as much bromine, 15 times more magnesium and 10 times as much iodine as the ocean. Bromine, a component of many sedatives, relaxes the nerves; magnesium counteracts skin allergies and clears the bronchial passages; and iodine has a beneficial effect on certain glandular functions – or so it's claimed.

If this were not enough, the Dead Sea's extremely dense air – the area has the world's highest barometric pressure – has 10% more oxygen than sea-level air. Other healthful properties, especially for people with breathing problems, include high temperatures, low rainfall, low humidity and pollen-free air.

The Dead Sea Medical Research Centre (www.deadsea-health.org), affiliated with Ben-Gurion University of the Negev, conducts scientific analyses of the sea's health benefits.

Several circular, family-friendly hikes (which don't require you to get soaked) start at the same point. These include the Wadi Tekoa Circuit (five hours) and the Mashash-Murba'at Circuit (three hours), which passes caves in which letters personally signed by Bar Kochba (leader of the Bar Kochba Rebellion of 132 to 135 CE) were found in 1952.

Mineral Beach

חוף מינרל   شاطئ مينرال (شاطئ معدني)

Run by Kibbutz Mitzpe Shalem, this is one of the nicest of the Dead Sea beaches (☑ 02-994 4888; www.dead-sea.co.il; adult/child 50/30NIS, on Sat 60/35NIS; ☺ 9am-5pm or 6pm Sun-Fri, opens 8am Sat). After having a float and glopping black mud onto your skin, you can soak in naturally sulphurous spring water (39°C) or indulge in a Tibetan or Swedish massage. Lockers and towels each cost 10NIS (plus a 10NIS deposit). Has a cafeteria and transport down to the receding water line. Wheelchair accessible. Camping is not permitted.

Had you dropped by here on 18 September 2011, you would have seen more than a thousand completely nude Israelis being photographed by the artist Spencer Tunick.

1. Muddy Fun
Bathers can slather themselves in natural black mud on many Dead Sea (p285) beaches.

2. Salt fields
The Dead Sea's salt concentration is about 34%, making it 10 times more saline than the ocean.

3. Relaxing
With high levels of magnesium, iodine and bromine, the briny waters will relax your nerves and soothe your skin.

4. Floating
Floating in the Dead Sea is a great natural experience. Just don't shave your legs (p298)!

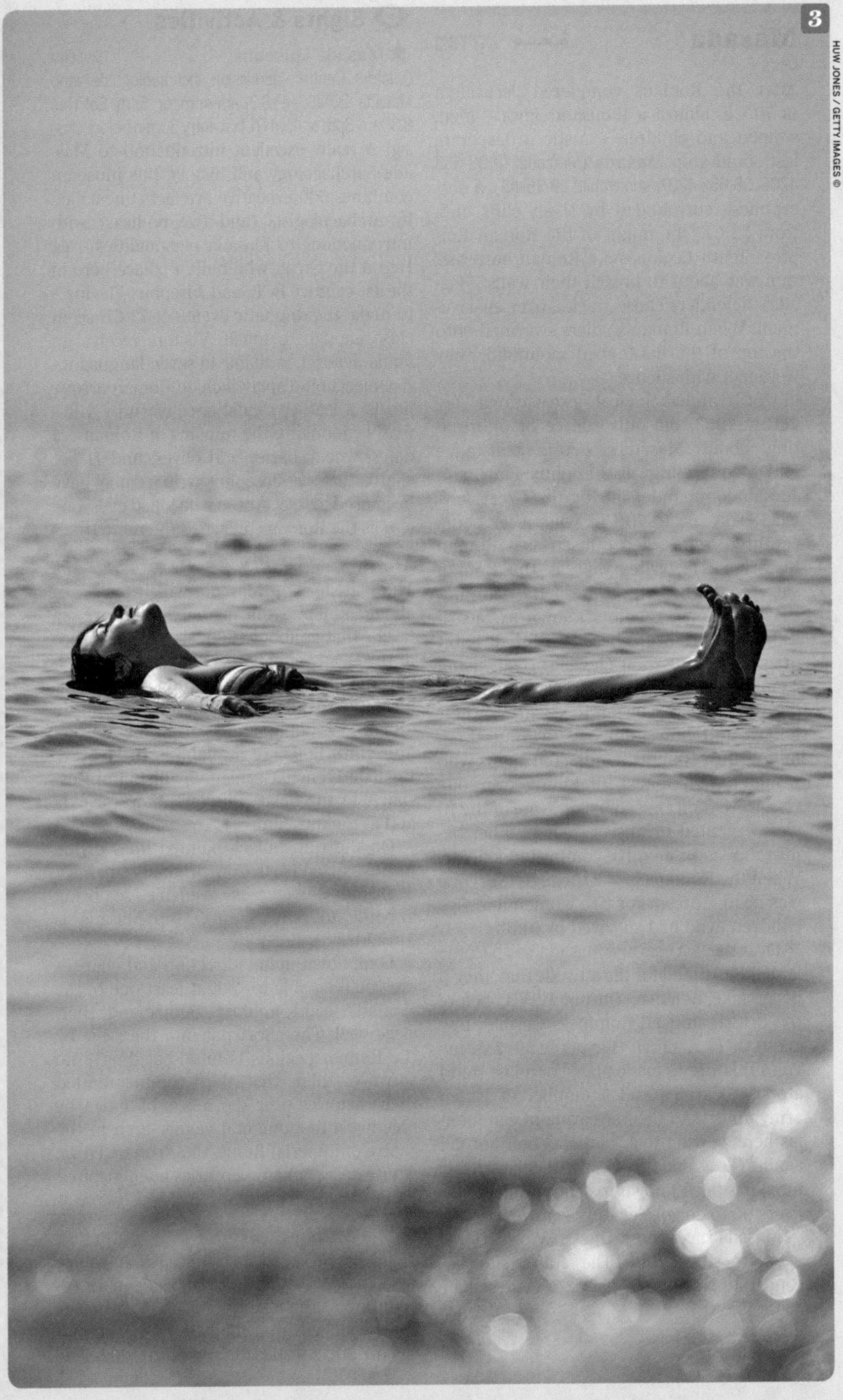

HUW JONES / GETTY IMAGES ©

Masada

מצדה מسعدة

☑ 08

After the Romans conquered Jerusalem in 70 CE, almost a thousand Jews – men, women and children – made a desperate last stand atop **Masada** (Metzada; ☑ 08-658 4208, 08-658 4207; adult/child 29/15NIS), a desert mesa surrounded by sheer cliffs and, from 72 CE, the might of the Roman Empire's Tenth Legion. As a Roman battering ram was about to breach their walls, Masada's defenders chose suicide over enslavement. When Roman soldiers swarmed onto the top of the flat-topped mountain, they were met with silence.

Until archaeological excavations began in 1963, the only source of information about Masada's heroic resistance and bloody end was Josephus Flavius, a Jewish commander during the Great Jewish Revolt (66 to 70 CE) who, after being captured, reinvented himself as a Roman historian. He writes that as the Roman siege engine inched towards the summit, the defenders – Zealots known as Sicarii (Sikrikin in Hebrew) because of their habit of assassinating their (Jewish) rivals using a curved dagger (*sica* in Greek) hidden under their cloaks – began to set fire to their homes and possessions to prevent them falling into Roman hands. Ten men, who would have the task of killing everyone else, were then chosen by lot. Nine of the 10 were executed by one of their number before the last man alive committed suicide. When the Romans broke through everyone was dead – except for two women and five children, who had survived by hiding.

Over the last century, Masada has become Israeli shorthand for the attitude that 'they'll never take us alive'. During WWII, before the British stopped Rommel's German divisions at El Alamein (Egypt) in 1942, some Palestinian Jews made plans for a last stand atop Mt Carmel, and a number of Israeli army units hold their swearing-in ceremonies here, vowing that 'Masada shall not fall again'. (Less apocalyptically, the Israeli air force has been known to send groups of officers up to do yoga at sunrise.)

Masada has been a Unesco World Heritage Site since 2001. The entire site, except the Northern Palace, is wheelchair accessible.

◉ Sights & Activities

★ Masada Museum

MUSEUM

(Visitors Centre; admission incl audioguide atop Masada 20NIS; ☺ 8.30am-4pm or 5pm Sat-Thu, 8.30am-3pm or 4pm Fri, last entry 30min before closing) A really excellent introduction to Masada's archaeology and history, this museum combines 500 evocative artefacts unearthed by archaeologists (and five replicas) with introductions to Masada personalities – eg Herod the Great, who built a palace here in the 1st century BCE, and Josephus Flavius – to make the dramatic events of 73 CE seem close enough to touch. Visitors receive an audio headset, available in seven languages.

Objects on display include Roman arrowheads; a leather sandal once worn by a Roman legionnaire; the remains of Roman-era dates, wheat, barley and olives; and 11 pot shards that – as Josephus writes – may have been used to select those who killed everyone else as the Romans breached the ramparts.

Atop Masada

ARCHAEOLOGICAL SITE

The plateau atop Masada, which measures about 550m by 270m, is some 60m above sea level – that is, about 488m above the surface of the Dead Sea. Visitors are given an excellent map-brochure of the ruins; similar information can be had from an **audioguide** (20NIS, including admission to the Masada Museum). Both are available – in Hebrew, English, French, German, Spanish and Russian – at the ticket windows, atop Masada and at the museum.

On the ruins, black painted lines divide reconstructed parts from original remains.

Drinking water is available so bring a bottle to refill. Eating atop Masada is forbidden.

Look down in any direction and chances are you'll be able to spot at least one of the Romans' eight military camps and their siege wall. The effort put into the siege by the Roman Legions is mind-boggling – no surprise, then, that they commemorated their victories over the rebels of Judea by erecting a monumental victory arch in the centre of imperial Rome, the **Arch of Titus**, whose design, many centuries later, inspired Paris's Arc de Triomphe.

Sound & Light Show

LIGHT SHOW

(☑ 08-995 9333; adult/child 45/35NIS; ☺ 9pm Tue & Thu Mar-Oct) This dramatic, open-air recounting of the history of Masada is meant to be watched from the base of the Roman siege ramp on Masada's western side. The narration is in Hebrew but you can rent **earphones** (15NIS) for simultaneous translation into five languages. Access is via Arad and then Rte 3199; from the Visitors Centre, it's a 68km drive. Get there by 8.30pm.

★ Trails Around Masada HIKING

Paths link the remains of the eight Roman military encampments that still encircle Masada, making it possible to circumnavigate the mesa in part or in full. To get a sense of the area's geography, check out the 3D relief map facing the Visitors Centre ticket windows.

From the Visitors Centre, a trail heads west up **Mt Eleazar** to Camp H (30 minutes). From here, Roman legionnaires could peer down at Masada, gathering aerial intelligence on the Zealots' activities. The path continues to the bottom of the siege ramp on Masada's western side.

Alternatively, you can walk north from the Visitors Centre, following the siege wall on a trail known as **Shvil HaRatz** (the Runner's Trail). It, too, eventually goes to the siege ramp on the western side.

Another trail links Camp D (north of Masada) with the eminently hikeable **Wadi Tze'elim**, 4km to the north.

★ Snake Path HIKING

This famously serpentine footpath winds its way up Masada's eastern flank, starting from near the Visitors Centre. Walking up takes about 60 minutes; count on spending 30 minutes to come back down. If you'd like to watch sunrise from the summit, get to the base an hour before the sun comes up, ie sometime between 4.30am (in June) and 5.30am (in December). Before 8am, access is from the security barrier near the youth hostel.

On particularly hot summer days, park authorities sometimes close the trail at 10am or 11am (9am when conditions are extreme) for the rest of the day.

Ramp Trail HIKING

The Romans wimped out and so can you – the path up the spine of their siege ramp takes only about 15 minutes to climb. The catch is that the ramp (ie western) side of the mountain is accessible only from the town of Arad, a 68km drive from the Visitors Centre via Rte 31 and then Rte 3199.

If you'd like to watch sunrise from the summit, get to the base of the ramp half an hour before the sun comes up.

Cable Car CABLE CAR

(return/one-way 76/57NIS, child 43/29NIS; ☉ every 15min 8am-4pm or 5pm Sat-Thu, 8am-3pm or 4pm Fri, last trip up 45min before closing) Whisks you from the Visitors Centre to the top, in Swiss comfort, in just three minutes. Each car holds 65 people. Wheelchair accessible.

🛏 Sleeping

Some visitors, especially those heading to the Ramp Trail, stay up in Arad.

Chenyon Layla Metzada Ma'arav CAMPGROUND $

(✆ 08-628 0404 ext 1; www.parks.org.il; western entrance, Masada; camping adult/child 53/42NIS, tent rental incl mattress 75/65NIS, 5-person hut with bathroom 450NIS) A modern, well-equipped camping area on Masada's western side, near the base of the Roman ramp. Prices include the use of kitchen facilities and admission to Masada. Mattresses and sleeping bags can be rented for 10NIS. Road access is via Arad.

Camping Zone CAMPGROUND $

FREE Camping is permitted in a parking area, signposted 'Nature's Cultural Hall' (because operas are staged here), on Masada's eastern access road at a point 1km west of the junction with Rte 90 and a bit under 2km east of the Visitors Centre. There are no amenities, not even water; bring a flashlight/torch.

Masada Guest House HOSTEL $$

(✆ 02-594 5623/4; www.iyha.org.il; dm/s/d 145/305/424NIS; ☉ reservations 8am-6pm Sun-Fri; ✳@🛜🏊) This 350-bed hostel is ideal if you'd like to see sunrise from atop Masada. The six-bed, single-sex dorm rooms border on luxurious. Staff do their best to separate travellers from the packs of noisy schoolkids. The swimming pool is open from Passover to October. Dinner (US$16.80, on Friday US$19.60) is served most nights until 8pm. Frequently booked out, especially on Friday, so reserving is a must. Situated a few hundred metres below the Visitors Centre. Wheelchair accessible.

🍴 Eating & Drinking

Free drinking water is available atop Masada.

Visitors Centre Food Court FOOD COURT $

(mains from 24NIS; ☉ until 4pm or 5pm; 🍴) Stalls serve felafel (24NIS), shwarma (35NIS), sandwiches and cold beer (26NIS); also has a cafe, McDonald's and a cafeteria charging

46NIS to 78NIS for a meal. Situated downstairs from the ticket windows.

Getting There & Away

Masada's Visitors Centre, on the eastern side of the mountain, is 21km south of the Ein Gedi Nature Reserve; the access road from Rte 90 is 3km long. All intercity buses serving the Dead Sea (see p287) stop a few hundred metres from the Visitors Centre; bus times are posted at Visitors Centre ticket windows.

The Roman siege ramp, on Masada's western side, is accessible from Arad (via Rte 3199). As the crow flies, the Visitors Centre is a bit over 1km from the siege ramp; by car the distance is 68km! To get there from Arad, you can take a **taxi** (☎08-997 4444; day/night 120/150NIS).

Ein Bokek عين بوقيق עין בוקק

☎08

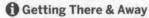

Sandwiched between the turquoise waters of the southern Dead Sea and a dramatic tan bluff, Ein Bokek's strip of luxury hotels is the region's main tourist zone. Ein Bokek (also spelled En Boqeq) has the area's nicest free beaches, and is the Dead Sea's main centre for treating ailments such as psoriasis, arthritis and respiratory conditions with naturally occurring minerals and compounds.

The three most commonly heard languages here are Hebrew, Arabic and Russian – the area is hugely popular both with Israelis (Jews and Arabs) and Russians (immigrants and tourists).

Unlike beaches further north, Ein Bokek fronts evaporation pools (kept full by Dead Sea Works pumps) rather than the open sea, which is why its lakeshore is not receding.

There are no left-luggage facilities at Ein Bokek.

Sights & Activities

A 3km-long **pedestrian promenade** and occasional buses (5.80NIS) link Ein Bokek's two hotel zones, Ein Bokek (the main, northern one) and Neve Hamei Zohar.

★ Ein Bokek Beach — BEACH

(24hr) FREE This broad, clean beach, in the middle of Ein Bokek's main (northern) hotel zone, is gloriously sandy. It has lifeguards, shade shelters, beach showers, changing rooms and bathrooms (closed at night). Camping is permitted – this is a much more comfortable option than Ein Gedi Beach. Wheelchair accessible.

As of 2014, the entirety of the Ein Bokek beachfront, including areas that once belonged to specific hotels, is open to the public, with access along a lovely, shaded promenade. Facilities such as beach chairs are still reserved for paying guests.

Wadi Bokek — HIKING

This is one of just three wadis on the Dead Sea's western shore that are fed year-round by spring water (the other two are at Ein Gedi). The narrow gorges, lush vegetation and waterholes make for an easy and refreshing hour-long hike. Access is through a tunnel under Rte 90, between the David and Leonardo Inn Hotels – or you can park at the trailhead.

PREPARING FOR A DEAD SEA DIP

The waters of the Dead Sea have some fantastic healing powers, but unless you respect their bromines and chlorides you may find yourself in significant pain – or even danger. As a result, a few preparations are in order before you slip into the slimy brine. First off, don't shave the day before you swim or you may find out more than you'd like to know about the meaning of the phrase 'to have salt rubbed into your wounds'. Other nicks and cuts – whether you realised you had them or not – are also likely to call attention to themselves.

What to wear when swimming in the Dead Sea:

- Do not wear jewellery – silver will turn jet black (don't worry, it can be cleaned) and other metals (including gold that isn't 24 carat) may also be affected.
- Wear waterproof sandals to protect your feet from sharp stones, both on shore and in the water, and from burning the soles of your feet on the sun-scorched sand.

The Dead Sea's dense, low-elevation air naturally filters the sun's harmful ultraviolet rays, making it much harder to get sunburnt than at sea level, despite scorching temperatures.

ⓘ SWIMMING SAFELY

Staying safe while bobbing and paddling requires a bit more caution than at the sea shore.

➡ Do not under any circumstances dunk your head! If water gets in your eyes, it will sting horribly and temporarily blind you. Do not thrash around – calmly get out of the water and ask someone to help you rinse your eyes under a tap or shower.

➡ Swallowing just a few gulps of sea water – or inhaling it – is extremely dangerous and can even be fatal. Seek immediate medical attention (eg from lifeguards) if this happens.

➡ Drink *lots* of potable water – not only will the heat dry you out, but the water of the Dead Sea is so saturated with minerals that it will suck out your body's fluids like a thousand leeches. Remember what happened in high school physics class when you learned about osmosis by putting a slice of potato in saltwater?

➡ The Dead Sea can be so relaxing that some people don't notice when westerly winds gently blow them out towards the middle of the lake (ie towards Jordan). Broadsheet readers are in special danger – a newspaper makes an excellent sail!

Day Spas   SPA

Almost every Ein Bokek hotel boasts a spa with swimming pools, saunas, spa baths, a long menu of treatments and an army of predominantly Russian therapists. Most places charge non-guests 100NIS to 260NIS to use their facilities for the day, including beach chairs but not including special treatments. Some deals include lunch.

🛏 Sleeping

Unless you camp on the beach (free), there's no budget or even midrange accommodation in Ein Bokek's two hotel zones. But if you're up for a splurge there are loads of options – the area's dozen hotels offer crisply air-conditioned facilities (a life-saver during the summer), gorgeous swimming pools, state-of-the-art spas and buffet bonanzas. Some offer direct beach access. All the hotels, except two of the four places branded as Leonardo (www.fattal.co.il) and Herod's, are in Ein Bokek's lively northern zone.

Many hotels charge high-season prices from April to mid-June and from September to mid-November. Significant discounts are often available on the web, especially in the off-season.

About 1.5m south of Ein Bokek's southern hotel zone, the charmless row houses of beachless Neve Zohar (Newe Zohar) shelter some of the Dead Sea's cheapest B&Bs – we're talking 350NIS to 500NIS per room. For phone numbers, see www.deadsea.co.il (click 'Zimmers' under 'Accommodation').

Tsell Harim   HOTEL $$

(☑ 08-668 8124; www.holitel.co.il; d with half-board from 690NIS) One of Ein Bokek's least expensive options, this modest, low-rise complex, built in 1979, was renovated in 2014. Has 160 rooms, direct beach access, a freshwater pool, a pool with Dead Sea water and a sauna.

Hod HaMidbar   HOTEL $$$

(☑ 08-668 8222; www.hodhotel.co.il; d incl half-board US$280-340; ❋@🛜🏊) Right on the waterfront, this 213-room hotel is known for its high-quality service. The swimming pool overlooks the sea, while downstairs the glass-enclosed spa offers sulphur pools and saunas. Offers free use of bicycles and free international phone calls.

Crowne Plaza   HOTEL $$$

(☑ 08-659 1919; www.h-i.co.il; d US$250-450; ❋@🛜🏊) Highlights include a doughnut-shaped freshwater swimming pool, a kiddie pool, a pool with Dead Sea water, a luxurious spa and lots of activities for adults and kids. Some of the 304 spacious rooms can sleep two adults and two children. Has two floors just for couples.

🍴 Eating & Drinking

Most of Ein Bokek's restaurants are inside hotels and cannot be described as inexpensive. Budget options in the northern zone include cafes that serve sandwiches and, in the Petra Shopping Centre, a McDonald's (open daily from 11am to 9pm or 10pm). Both Sky Blue Mall and Petra Shopping Center have mini-markets with a small selection of proper food.

Ein Bokek doesn't have much nightlife.

Taj Mahal GRILLED MEAT **$$**
(☏057 650 6502; mains 35-119NIS; ☺noon-midnight daily; ☏🖉) Completely unconnected with anything Indian, this non-aircon restaurant – in a Bedouin tent outfitted with rugs, pillows and low couches – serves Middle Eastern grilled meats, *nargilehs* (water pipes; 35NIS) and East Jerusalem baklava (25NIS). A belly dancer gyrates on Friday from 10pm. Situated on the grounds of the Leonardo Inn Hotel, at the end facing Isrotel Ganim.

🛍 Shopping

The **Sky Blue Mall** (Kanyonit Ein HaT'chelet) in the northern zone is the best place in Israel to buy Dead Sea beauty products. Shops also sell beach supplies, including flip-flops.

ⓘ Information

There are several **ATMs** at the Sky Blue Mall and one in the Petra Shopping Center (inside the mini-market). The **exchange bureaus** in the malls offer mediocre rates.

Dead Sea Tourist Information (☏08-997 5010; www.deadsea.co.il; ☺9am-4pm Sun-Thu, 9am-3pm Fri; ☏) Sarah and Hanita are an excellent source of maps and information on hotels, B&Bs, restaurants and outdoor activities in the area from Ein Gedi south (the area north of there, in the West Bank, belongs to a different regional council). Situated across the street from the Daniel Hotel, inside the Solarium-400 complex.

ⓘ Getting There & Away

Street parking at Ein Bokek, marked with kerbs painted blue and white, costs 5NIS per hour or 25NIS per day. Hotels have limited free parking. For bus information, see p287.

Sodom סدوم סדום

By tradition, this area is the site of Sodom and Gomorrah, the biblical cities that were destroyed in a storm of fire and brimstone, punishment from God because of their people's depravity (Genesis 18-19). These days, Sodom is much better known for its desert hiking and cycling trails than for sodomy.

◉ Sights & Activities

'The Situation of Man' SCULPTURE
(Rte 90) Atop a bluff overlooking the Dead Sea Works stands this modern sculpture, a rusty steel column with old steel railway ties striving to climb it like desperate worms.

Next to the sculpture, a **viewpoint** looks out over a crazy juxtaposition of smoke-spewing heavy industry, electric-blue evaporation pools, green farm fields (over in Jordan) and the wild, tawny beauty of the desert. Views are best in the late afternoon, when the setting sun turns the mountains of Moab a reddish gold.

The 600m-long access road intersects Rte 90 250m north of the main entrance to the Dead Sea Works. Turn off at the white-on-brown sign reading 'Plant Viewing Point' (ignore the yellow 'no trespassing' sign) and follow the green signs marked (in Hebrew) 'LaMitzpeh' ('to the scenic lookout'). Beyond the sculpture, a 4WD road continues to the **Amiaz Plateau**.

Lot's Wife ROCK FORMATION
About 11km south of the southern end of Ein Bokek, high above the west side of Rte 90, a column of salt-rich rock leans precariously away from the rest of the Mt Sodom cliff face. It is popularly known as Lot's Wife because, according to the Bible, Lot's wife was turned into a pillar of salt as punishment for looking back to see Sodom as it burned (Genesis 19:17 and 19:26).

Dead Sea Works INDUSTRIAL COMPLEX
(DSW; www.iclfertilizers.com; Rte 90) Israel's only major natural resource – other than sunlight and the gas fields off the Mediterranean coast – is the Dead Sea, from which products ranging from magnesium chloride and anhydrous aluminium chloride to table salt and cosmetics are extracted. Founded in the 1930s, the DSW is now the world's fourth-largest producer of potash, an important component of agricultural fertiliser.

By day, the rusty (from the salt air) smokestacks, pipes and holding tanks of the DSW complex look like a mid-20th-century industrial dystopia, but by night, when the sprawling facilities are lit by thousands of yellowish lights, the site has a mysterious, otherworldly beauty.

Mt Sodom HIKING, CYCLING
Two trails head down the steep flanks of Mt Sodom from a **lookout point**, reachable by 4WD, whose views are at their best in the

late afternoon. **Ma'aleh HaSulamot** (Ladders Ascent; 1½ hours to walk down), named after its many stairs, connects with Rte 90 across the highway from the sun-blasted huts of the Dead Sea Works' first workers' camp, built in 1934.

Another descent to Rte 90 is **Shvil HaDagim** (Fishes Trail; 1½ hours down), so named because of the many fossilised fish you can see in the rocks.

Mt Sodom, 11km long and up to 2km wide, is one of the world's stranger geological formations. Start with the fact that it's made almost entirely of rock salt, a highly soluble material that in any other climate would have melted away. In fact, over the millennia the area's rare rainfalls have dissolved some of the salt, creating deep in the bowels of the mountain a maze of **caves** (closed to the public) up to 5.5km long. Many are connected to the surface by shafts that hikers need to make sure they don't fall into, and some are filled with delicate, eerie salt stalactites. And then there's the matter of Mt Sodom's summit. A respectable 250m above the surface of the Dead Sea – the views of Jordan's Moab Mountains are gorgeous – it also happens to be 176m below sea level.

West of Mt Sodom, **Wadi Sodom** is ideal for mountain biking. If you start at the top (accessible by 4WD), it's about two hours, mostly downhill, to the Neve Zohar area. A round-trip circuit that connects with beautiful **Wadi Pratzim** (Wadi Perazim), whose upper reaches pass the famous **Flour Cave** (closed to the public), is another option.

🛏 Sleeping

The Mt Sodom area has several well-marked **camping zones** (chenyonei layla) without facilities, including one up on the Amiaz Plateau (Mishor Amiaz) and another further north at Wadi Tze'elim.

Neot HaKikar

ناؤت هاكيكار ⁣⁣ נאות הכיכר

☑ 08 / POP 400

Snuggled up against the Jordanian border in one of Israel's most remote corners, this agricultural moshav is the perfect base for exploring the wadis, plateaus and bluffs around the southern Dead Sea. Tranquil and laid-back, Neot HaKikar and its sister moshav, Ein Tamar, have some mellow B&Bs and all sorts of options for mountain biking, hiking, birdwatching and exploring the des-

ert by jeep. The nearest beach is 20 minutes away at Ein Bokek. Because of the intense summer heat, some places close from July to mid-September.

The moshav's main source of income is agriculture, with 70% of the produce destined for export. Crops – grown with the help of some 500 Thai farm-workers, in salty soil using saline well water – include red, green, yellow and orange peppers, winter-ripening vegetables and melons, and organic medjool dates. The latter are sorted using the world's most advanced sorting machine: eight digital cameras take portraits from three angles of every single date, shuttled by air guns to this or that box according to a sophisticated algorithm. Back in the 1960s, Neot HaKikar was the site of some of the earliest experiments with modern drip irrigation.

◉ Sights & Activities

Hikeable and cyclable **wadis** (nechalim) within a 20-minute 4WD drive of here include Arava, Tzin (Zin), Amatzya (Amazyahu), Peres, Tamar, Tzafit and Ashalim. Other great places to pedal or hoof it include **Mt Sodom** and the **Amiaz Plateau** (Mishor Amiaz). The **Small Makhtesh** – the smallest of Israel's three great erosion craters – is a 25-minute drive west. Your place of lodging can arrange to have someone take you out to the trailhead by 4WD (for a fee).

The moshav has newly refurbished **tennis and basketball courts**, a **children's playground** and a public **swimming pool** (adult/child 30/15NIS; open 11am to 2pm and 5pm to 8pm except Sunday mornings from May to Sukkot).

Local **artists** produce pottery and metal sculptures. A number of farmers offer tours of their fields that include an introduction to **desert agriculture**.

Desert Cycling   CYCLING
Mountain biking is a fantastic way to experience the wild wadis that drain into the Syrian-African Rift around Neot HaKikar. A wide variety of off-road circuits, including one called **HeCharitz** ('the slit') and another that follows Wadi Sodom to Wadi Pratzim, can be found within a 30-minute drive of Neot HaKikar. Mountain bikes can be rented from **Cycle Inn** (☑ 052 899 1146; www.cycle-inn.co.il; per day 50NIS); Uzi and Barak are happy to supply you with maps and the low-down on area trails.

DEAD SEA FESTIVALS

➡ Tamar Festival: www.tamarfestival. com

➡ Ein Gedi International Semi-Marathon: www.deadsea-race.co.il

➡ Mt Sodom International Bike Race: www.desertchallenge.co.il

Jeep Tours   ADVENTURE TOUR

Tooling along wadis, up hills and around cliffs in the company of a knowledgeable local guide is a great way to get acquainted with the desert, its flora and – if you're lucky – its fauna. Operators include **Gil Shkedi** (☑052 231 7371; www.shkedig.com; per person 150NIS, minimum 4 people; ☻year-round), owner of Shkedi's Camplodge, and one-time camel herder **Barak Horwitz** (☑052 866 6062; barakhorwitz@gmail.com). Reserve ahead.

🛏 Sleeping

Neot HaKikar has about 50 B&B units, none of which offer breakfast unless you specifically order it (100NIS per couple).

★**Shkedi's Camplodge**   TENTS, CABINS **$**

(Khan Shkedi; ☑052 231 7371; www.shkedig.com; dm/d/q with shared bathroom & without breakfast 100/350/450NIS; ☻closed Jul–mid-Sep; ❈🤶) A wonderful place to linger for a couple of days, this desert retreat is especially enchanting at night, when guests hang out around the campfire or sip beers in the chill-out tent before heading to one of the cosy new dorm lodges, equipped with air-con and quality mattresses. The clean, modern bathroom block feels vaguely Mexican. Has a well-equipped kitchen. Inform owner Gil Shkedi ahead of time if you need to be picked up from the bus stop on Rte 90.

Melach HaAretz   B&B **$$**

(☑050 759 4828; http://madmonynh.com; d without breakfast 450-500NIS; ❈🤶) Two studio apartments off a garden (great for kids)

decorated with owner Asaf Madmony's extraordinary stone, wood and metal sculptures.

Nof Tamar   B&B **$$**

(☑052 899 1170; www.noftamar.co.il; Ein Tamar; d 500-600NIS, additional person 75NIS) All-wood suites at the highest point in Ein Tamar, with views of the Jordanian villages of Fifa and Safi.

Korin's Home   B&B **$$$**

(☑050 680 0545; www.korins.co.il; d without breakfast 650NIS, additional person 100NIS; ❈🤶) Like having your own, spa-equipped, two-bedroom apartment; each unit sleeps up to six.

Mul Edom   B&B **$$$**

(☑052 395 1095; muledom@gmail.com; Ein Tamar; d without breakfast 600-700NIS, additional person 100NIS; ❈🤶) Two 75-sq-metre, spa-equipped units up in Ein Tamar's old (but recently refurbished) hillside neighbourhood.

🍴 Eating

Neot HaKikar and Ein Tamar each have a grocery store; the latter, which has an ATM, is even open for two hours on Saturday morning.

Lunch and dinner can be ordered a day ahead from local families; mains cost 55NIS to 90NIS.

ℹ Getting There & Away

Neot HaKikar is 8km southeast of Rte 90's Neot HaKikar Junction and 11km southeast of Arava Junction, where Rte 25 from Dimona and Be'er Sheva intersects Rte 90.

All buses linking Eilat with Be'er Sheva, Tel Aviv, the Dead Sea and Jerusalem (and vice versa) stop at Arava Junction; accommodation owners are usually happy to pick you up.

The only bus that goes all the way into Neot HaKikar is bus 321, which does two circuits a day – one in the early morning, the other in the mid- to late afternoon – linking Neot HaKikar with Dimona (19NIS, one hour) and Ein Bokek (19NIS, 45 minutes).

The Negev

הנגב النقب

Best Places to Eat

➡ Kaparuc'hka (p305)
➡ Chez Eugéne (p316)
➡ Kornmehl Farm (p311)
➡ Pastory (p326)

Best Places to Stay

➡ Midbara (p320)
➡ Carmey Avdat Winery (p310)
➡ Desert Shade (p315)
➡ iBike (p315)
➡ Beresheet (p315)
➡ Orchid Reef Hotel (p326)

Why Go?

Visitors have been making their way across the arid landscape of the Negev desert for millennia, following in the footsteps of incense traders who transported precious cargo of frankincense and myrrh from south Arabia to the Mediterranean in ancient times. Today it's possible to visit the ruins of dramatically sited Nabataean cities that were built along this trade route, before heading south to the sybaritic summer playground of Eilat on the Red Sea coast.

Archaeological sites aren't the only diversions on offer in this part of the country. So many vineyards and artisanal food producers have established themselves here in recent years that the region near the extraordinary geological phenomenon of the Makhtesh Ramon is now marketed as a wine route and is a popular weekend getaway for city slickers. As well, there are activities aplenty, including hiking, cycling, camel riding and 4WD desert drives. Put simply, this majestic southern desert region is one of the country's greatest attractions – don't miss it.

When to Go
Eilat

Mar–May, late Sep–Nov The best time for desert treks; sunny in the daytime but cold at night.

Aug The Red Sea Jazz Festival adds a cool note to a sweltering Eilat summer.

Dec–Feb Occasional rainstorms lead to waterfalls flowing in En Avdat National Park.

The Negev Highlights

1 Starting at the ancient Nabataean settlement of **Avdat** (p308) and then follow the Unesco-listed Incense Route.

2 Hiking a trail past natural springs, pools and waterfalls in **En Avdat National Park** (p310).

3 Sampling the viticultural lifestyle and local wines when overnighting on the **Ramat Hanegev Wine Route** (p310).

4 Witnessing millions of years of evolution beneath your feet from the lookout at **Makhtesh Ramon** (p312).

5 Investigating the communal, sustainable and creative ways of life being forged by kibbutz residents in the **Arava** (p318).

6 Diving and snorkelling under the Red Sea waves at **Eilat** (p320).

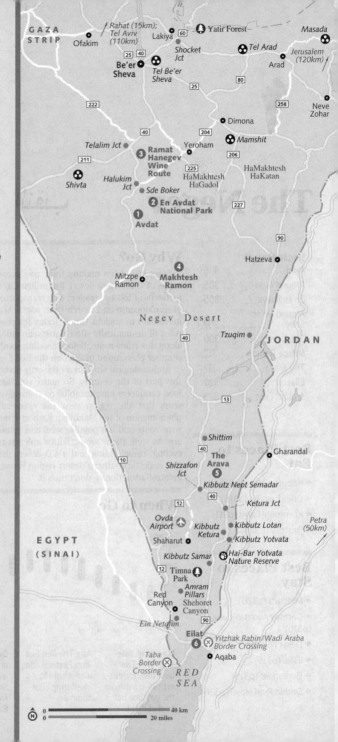

Arad ערד عراد

☑ 08 / POP 23,900

A popular base for those visiting nearby Masada, Arad sits on a high plateau between Be'er Sheva and the Dead Sea. There are no sights worthy of mention in the town.

🛏 Sleeping & Eating

Blau Weiss Youth Hostel HOSTEL $$

(☑ 08-995 7150; arad@iyha.org.il; 34 Atad St; dm/s/d 150/355/450NIS; ❄) From the outside, this recently refurbished IYHA-affiliated hostel resembles an army barracks. But inside, the 53 clean and comfortable rooms are set within a lush and attractive garden. All have fridge, kettle and cable TV. To get here, walk east from the bus station up Yehuda St, turn right into HaPalmach St and then left at the skate park.

Yehelim BOUTIQUE HOTEL $$$

(☑ 052 652 2718, 077 563 2806; www.yehelim.com; 72 Moav St; d 850-950NIS; f 1200NIS; ste 1500-1800NIS; ❄🛜) A recent renovation and expansion of this family-friendly hotel has certainly raised the bar in the Arad accommodation stakes – nothing else even comes close in the areas of comfort and style. Located on the residential edge of town, it has 15 large rooms with cable TV and a kettle; suites sport a spa bath and coffee machine.

★ Kaparuc'hka PIZZA, CAFE $$

(☑ 08-860 6615; 19 Ahwa St; pizzas 29-36NIS; ⏰9am-9pm Sun-Thu, 9am-3pm Fri) Travel writers tend to overuse the word 'gem', but here it really does apply. Opened in 2014, this tiny place is run by Lisa and Uriga, seasoned travellers and committed foodies, and it is far and away the best eating option in town. The limited menu includes an antipasti platter, caprese salad, pizzas, calzones and delicious home-made desserts and cakes.

There's a good range of imported beers, local wine and good espresso coffee to enjoy with your meal, and a choice of indoor and outdoor seating. To find it, head east along Elazar Ben Yair and turn right into Ahwa St after the park.

Muza PUB $$

(☑ 08-997 5555; www.muza-arad.co.il; Rte 31; burgers 37-62NIS; pasta 42-52NIS; ⏰8am-1am) Decked out with team scarves and pennants from around the world, this big sports-oriented pub near the petrol stations serves huge plates of hearty food including burgers, pasta and sandwiches. The simplest dishes are the best choices.

❶ Getting There & Away

Metropoline bus 388 travels frequently between the central bus terminal on Yehuda St in Arad and Be'er Sheva (19NIS, 40 minutes). Services operate from 6am to 11.40pm Sunday to Thursday, to 4.45pm on Friday and from 6.45pm on Saturday.

Egged bus 384 links Arad with the main (eastern) entrance to Masada (one hour, three or four daily Sunday to Thursday, two on Friday). To get to Masada's western (Roman ramp) entrance and its sound-and-light show by car or taxi (day/night 120/150NIS), take Rte 3199 from the back of Arad. The drive takes approximately 30 minutes.

Around Arad

Tel Arad National Park ARCHAEOLOGICAL SITE

(☑ 057 776 2170; www.parks.org.il; adult/child/student 15/7/13 NIS; ⏰8am-4pm Sat-Thu year-round, 8am-3pm Fri Apr-Sep, 8am-2pm Fri Oct-Mar) The remains of two ancient settlements can be found at this archaeological site 13km northwest of the modern city of Arad. The lower city was inhabited in the Early Bronze Age (3150–2200 BCE) and the upper city was first settled in the Israelite period (1200 BCE). Highlights include the remains of an Israelite temple.

To reach the site from Arad, take Hwy 31 and turn right (north) at the Tel Arad junction onto Hwy 80 (direction: Jerusalem).

Be'er Sheva

بئرالسبع באר שבע

☑ 08 / POP 197,300

Developed in the 1960s and still rapidly expanding, the industry and university hub of Be'er Sheva (Beersheba) is the major city in the Negev. The only compelling reason for travellers to visit is to transfer between the train service that comes from the north and the bus services heading south.

History

Be'er Sheva was mentioned in the Bible (Judges 20:1; I Samuel 3:20; II Samuel 3:10, 17:11, 24:2), though few traces of that time are detectable today.

During WWI the small town fell to Allenby's Allied forces after a charge by units of the Australian Light Horse. The Egyptian

Be'er Sheva

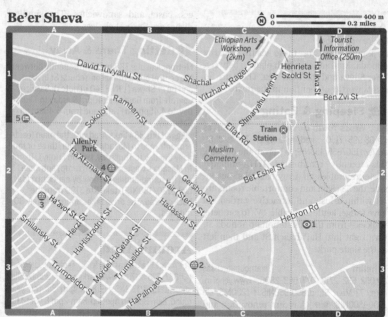

Be'er Sheva

◎ Sights

1 Bedouin Market	D3
2 Be'er Avraham	B3
3 Negev Artists' House	A2
4 Negev Museum of Art	B2

⌂ Sleeping

5 Beit Yatziv	A1

army conquered Be'er Sheva after the State of Israel was declared, but in October 1948 the Israel Defense Forces (IDF) regained the town and a new era of immigration began.

◎ Sights

Be'er Avraham
MUSEUM

(Abraham's Well International Visitor's Centre; ☑ 08-623 4613; www.abraham.org.il; 2 Dereh Hevron; adult/concession 30/16NIS; ⊙ 8am-5pm Sun-Thu, 8am-1pm Fri) Opened in 2013, this visitor centre is located near the banks of Nahal Be'er Sheva and showcases a reconstruction of a well that Abraham, the first of the three Biblical patriarchs, is said to have dug here (Genesis 21:22-34). There is also an audio-visual presentation and an Ottoman-era well with a water-drawing wheel and a drainage pool.

Negev Museum of Art
MUSEUM, GALLERY

(☑ 08-699 3535; www.negev-museum.org.il; 60 Ha'Atzmaut St; adult/child 15/10NIS; ⊙ 10am-4pm Mon, Tue & Thu, noon-7pm Wed, 10am-2pm Fri & Sat) This small art gallery on the edge of the Old City is housed in the elegant Ottoman governor's mansion, which was built in 1906. The building, which has been beautifully restored, comprises three galleries hosting temporary exhibitions.

Negev Artists' House
GALLERY

(☑ 08-627 3828; www.b7omanim.com; 55 Ha'Avot St; ⊙ 10am-1.30pm Mon-Fri, 4-7.30pm Mon-Thu, 11am-2pm Sat) FREE Originally built in 1933, this grand colonial-style building is now a compact art gallery showcasing works by artists from the Negev.

Ethiopian Arts Workshop
ARTS CENTRE

(☑ 08-623 5882; 50 Arlozorov St; ⊙ 9am-1pm Sun-Wed) Preserving the unique culture of the Ethiopian Jews, this arts and crafts workshop in the Taubel Community Centre has a small exhibition and shop and holds pottery workshops. To get here, continue up Yitzhack Rager St past the hospital, turn right on Ben-Gurion Blvd and again onto Arlozorov St, or take bus 5 from Ha'Atzmaut St in the Old City.

Bedouin Market MARKET

(☉ 7am-4pm Thu) Every week a car park in the southeast of town is transformed into a market where Bedouin vendors and merchants from neighbouring villages sell clothing, footwear, kitchenware and food. The merchandise isn't particularly interesting, but it gives a taste of contemporary Bedouin culture. It's a 10-minute walk south of the Kenyon HaNegev shopping centre on the main Eilat Rd.

🛏 Sleeping

If you have a car, stay elsewhere – the hotels here are mightily unimpressive.

Beit Yatziv HOSTEL $$

(☑ 08-627 7444; www.beityatziv.co.il; 79 Ha'Atzmaut St; s/d 300/400NIS, deluxe r 450NIS; ❋ 🛜 🛉) If transport connections leave you stuck in town overnight, this hostel will be your best bet. It offers standard rooms that are small, but each comes with a fridge, TV and kettle. If you are not on a tight budget, it is worth paying the extra 100NIS for one of the newer 'deluxe' rooms, which have wi-fi.

The pleasant gardens and swimming pool (open June to August) are a blessed relief on a scorching desert day. Take bus 12 or 13 from the bus station and look for the three large radio antennae.

ℹ Information

Tourist Information Office (☑ 08-646 4978; mgmtoc@br7.org.il; Municipality, Menachem Begin Sq) Cross the road opposite the train station and walk up HaTikva St to the municipality complex.

ℹ Getting There & Away

BUS

From Sunday to Thursday, Metropoline buses run every 30 minutes or so from 1am to 10.40pm heading to Tel Aviv's Central Bus Station (17.80NIS, 1½ hours). The last bus on Friday departs mid-afternoon and the first on Saturday is in the late afternoon or early evening.

Egged buses to Jerusalem's Central Bus Station leave at least half-hourly between 5.50am and 10.30pm (31.50NIS, 1¾ hours). The last bus on Friday departs mid-afternoon and the first on Saturday is in the late afternoon or early evening.

Frequent Metropoline buses 60 and 64 travel between Be'er Sheva and Mitzpe Ramon (17NIS, 1½ hours) via En Avdat and Sde Boker. Bus 65 is a faster service that only stops on the highway. None of these services operate during Shabbat.

Egged buses to Eilat (60NIS, 3¾ hours) depart every 90 minutes between 7.30am and 7.25pm Sunday to Thursday. The last bus on Friday departs mid-afternoon and the first on Saturday is in the late afternoon or early evening.

Egged bus 384 to the Dead Sea, including Ein Gedi (44NIS, 2¼ hours), leaves three times daily from Sunday to Thursday, and twice on Friday; there is no service on Saturday. All stop at Arad (19NIS, 45 minutes) en route.

TRAIN

Northbound trains from Be'er Sheva's central **train station** (www.rail.co.il) start at 5am and run at least hourly until 10pm, stopping at stations including Tel Aviv (31.50NIS, 1¼ to 1½ hours), Haifa (62NIS, 2¼ to 2¾ hours), Akko (70.50NIS, 2¾ to 3¼ hours) before terminating at Nahariyya (77NIS, three to 3¼ hours). The last train on Friday leaves in the early afternoon and the first on Saturday is in the late evening.

ℹ Getting Around

You can easily walk from the central bus station to the Old City and the market. Local bus tickets cost 5.80NIS.

Around Be'er Sheva

Museum of Bedouin Culture MUSEUM

(☑ 08-991 3322; www.joealon.org.il; admission 28NIS; ☉ 8.30am-5pm Sun-Thu, 8.30am-2pm Fri) 🖉 With the fast-paced social and technological changes of the 21st century, preservation of indigenous Bedouin culture is becoming increasingly important. This museum, which is located in the Joe Alon Center for Regional Studies, aims to promote Bedouin culture and heritage with exhibits that include traditional clothes, household utensils, carpets, tools, jewellery and photographs. There's also a hospitality tent where visitors can sit with a local Bedouin, drink coffee and talk.

The complex stands behind Kibbutz Lahav, near Kibbutz Dvir, 20km north of Be'er Sheva. Both are off a side road that intersects with Rte 31.

Israeli Air Force Museum MUSEUM

(☑ 08-990 6888; http://iaf.co.il; Hatzerim; ☉ 8am-4.30pm Sun-Thu, 8am-11.30am Fri) Set in the Hatzerim Israeli Air Force (IAF) base, this outdoor museum displays more than 100 aircraft including Spitfires, Phantoms, Hawkeyes and Cobra helicopters. First

THE INCENSE ROUTE

Often overlooked in school history lessons, the Nabataeans were ancient Arabs known to have lived in the Negev from the 4th century BCE. They were a nomadic people until Rome became aware of the profitability of their trade in spices and incense, and decided to muscle in on their territory and activities. After the Roman conquest, the Nabataeans took on more 'European' attributes, built permanent settlements and eventually adopted Christianity. They spoke a form of Aramaic, the lingua franca of the region some 2000 years ago, and were innovative engineers –.despite the hostile desert environment, they developed sophisticated irrigation methods and their kings lavishly wasted water in front of guests to show off.

At one point, the incense and spice trade route stretched from Yemen and Oman to the Mediterranean, passing through Saudi Arabia, Petra and Judea. As a result, the Negev cities of Avdat, Mamshit, Shivta and Haluza became prosperous, and the desert around them flourished.

The atmospheric ruins of these settlements were declared Unesco World Heritage sites in 2005 under the collective designation of the Incense Route – Desert Cities in the Negev. Three of them are maintained and opened to the public by the Israel Nature and Parks Authority.

Avdat
עבדת   عبدات

A beautifully preserved site, this ancient city 650m above sea level dominates the surrounding desert skyline. Named after the Nabataean monarch Obada, it was built in the 3rd century BCE as a caravan stop on the road from Petra to the Mediterranean. Prosperous throughout the Byzantine period, the city was deserted following an earthquake in 630 CE and the Muslim takeover of the Negev six years later.

The ruins include a Roman bathhouse, catacombs, several 4th-century churches, a pottery workshop and a Byzantine winepress.

Buy your tickets at the visitor centre next to the petrol station, where you can also watch a 10-minute film about the Incense Route. Then visit the nearby bathhouse before driving up the hill to a carpark next to the ruins. Those travelling by public transport will need to follow the steep walking track from the bathhouse.

On Rte 40, Avdat lies 10km south of Sde Boker and 23km north of Mitzpe Ramon. Buses pass by in each direction about every hour from Sunday to Thursday.

Shivta (Subeita)
שיבטה   شبطا

The most isolated of the Nabataean towns, Shivta (⊘ 8am-5pm Apr-Sep, 8am-4pm Oct-Mar) FREE was founded during the early Roman period (1st century BCE). Its ruins date from the Byzantine period (4th to 7th centuries CE), when it was an important stop on the caravan route between Egypt and Anatolia. They include churches, houses, tiled streets and an impressive irrigation system.

Shivta is 58km southwest of Be'er Sheva. From Rte 40 continue from Telalim Junction on Rte 211 for about 15km. At the junction near the petrol station, drive 9km south.

Mamshit
ממשית   ممشيت

Much easier to reach than Shivta, Mamshit National Park (☏ 08-655 6478; www.parks. org.il; adult/child/student 22/10/19NIS; ⊘ 8am-4pm Sat-Thu year-round, 8am-3pm Fri Apr-Sep, 8am-2pm Fri Oct-Mar) is the ancient city also known as Memphis or Kurnub. It is the smallest but best-preserved Nabataean city in the Negev.

Overlooking Wadi Mamshit, the settlement dates from the 1st century CE; it was later used by the Romans. The excavations include ancient reservoirs, watchtowers, churches and Roman and Byzantine cemeteries. One highlight is the large mosaic floor at the courtyard of the Church of St Nilus.

Mamshit is on Rte 25, about 8km from Dimona. Any of the buses heading to Eilat via Dimona will drop you at the turn-off for the site.

opened in 1977, it was closed at the time of research for a major renovation. It will levy an admission charge when it re-opens.

Hatzerim (sometimes spelt Khatserim) is 6km west of Be'er Sheva. From the central bus station take Egged bus 31 (9.50NIS, 15 minutes, every 40 minutes or so); the IAF museum is the last stop.

Sidreh – Lakiya Negev Weaving ARTS CENTRE
(☑08-651 9883; www.lakiya.org; tour 20NIS; ☺8am-5pm Sun-Thu, 10am-4pm Sat) ♪ Located in the Bedouin village of Lakiya, about 6km north of Be'er Sheva off Rte 31, this centre was established in 1991 as an income-generating project for Bedouin women living in villages in the Negev, providing them with an opportunity to develop the tradition of spinning and weaving, and to acquire new skills in dyeing, production and business management. It conducts tours (reserve in advance) and sells the carpets, cushions and accessories that are produced by its members.

Tel Be'er Sheva ARCHAEOLOGICAL SITE
(☑08-646 7286; www.parks.org.il; adult/child/student 15/7/13NIS; ☺8am-4pm Apr-Sep, 8am-3pm Oct-Mar) One of a group of three *tels* (prehistoric hilltop ruins) included on the Unesco World Heritage List in 2005, these ruins include two-thirds of a fortified city dating from the early Israelite period (10th century BCE) and are an important example of biblical-period urban planning. The site is 5km northeast of Be'er Sheva on the Shocket Junction road, near the Bedouin settlement of Tel Sheva.

Like the other Unesco-listed *tels* (Megiddo and Hazor), the ruins show traces of underground water-collecting systems that were created to serve dense urban communities; the best-preserved elements are the cisterns and a 70m well, the deepest in Israel. There are great views to be had from an observation tower.

Khan Be'erotayim CAMEL TOURS
(☑08-655 5788; www.beerotayim.co.il; Ezus, near Nizzana; tours US$20-108) To get a taste of the traditional Bedouin lifestyle, head to this desert inn in the western Negev highlands near the Egyptian border. It offers guided camel rides (choose from one-hour, half-day, eight-hour or overnight options), serves Bedouin meals and provides simple accommodation in cabins and tents (dorm including two meals US$78).

Sde Boker

سديه بوكير ▪ שדה בוקר

☑08 / POP 1895

Initially famous as the home of Israel's first prime minister, David Ben-Gurion, **Kibbutz Sde Boker** (aka Sede Boquer), established in 1952, remains one of the best known of all Negev kibbutzim. Now home to around 400 residents, it welcomes visitors to Ben-Gurion's Desert Home, a small house museum on the kibbutz that is an important pilgrimage destination for many residents and supporters of Israel.

The kibbutz was established by young pioneers who planned to breed cattle in the desert; its name is Hebrew for 'Cowboy's Field'. Ben-Gurion joined this lush oasis the following year at the age of 67, to practice what he preached by cultivating the Negev. Only 14 months later he returned to the political scene as minister of defence and went on to serve a second term as prime minister, returning to kibbutz life in 1963.

About 5km southwest (by road) of the kibbutz is the university settlement of **Midreshet Ben-Gurion** (Midreshet Sde Boker; www.boker.org.il), a satellite campus of Be'er Sheva's Ben-Gurion University of the Negev. The campus is well known for its environmental research and incorporates institutions including the Jacob Blaustein Institutes for Desert Research and the Ben-Gurion National Solar Energy Centre. There is a small commercial centre with cafes, a pub and a supermarket, as well as a number of accommodation options that are particularly handy for those wanting to explore En Avdat National Park.

⊙ Sights

Ben-Gurion's Desert Home MUSEUM
(www.bgh.org.il; Kibbutz Sde Boker; adult/concession 18/12NIS; ☺8.30am-3pm Sun-Thu, 8.30am-1pm Fri, 10am-3pm Sat) In his will, Israel's founding father asked that the modest kibbutz quarters where he lived with his wife Paula remained exactly as he left them, and that's what you see when you visit this house museum. A short animated film about the great man's life is shown near the entrance, recounting his birth in Poland, immigration to Palestine and dedication to the establishment of the state of Israel ('My greatest desire – the air I breathe – is Zionism').

At the entrance to the museum is a visitor centre housing a cafe, a retail outlet for the Mitzpe Ramon–based Faran Natural Cosmetics company and a stand selling wines made by the Sde Boker Winery (www.sdebokerwinery.com).

The entrance to the visitor centre and museum is next to the petrol station on Hwy 40.

Ben-Gurion Graves MEMORIAL

(Midreshet Ben-Gurion) The graves of David (1886–1973) and Paula (1892–1968) Ben-Gurion lie in a spectacular clifftop setting overlooking the stunning Wadi Zin and the Avdat plain. A desert flora park has been planted next to the tombs, and wild ibexes often wander here.

The site is on the southern edge of Midreshet Ben-Gurion, near the northern entrance of En Avdat National Park.

★ En Avdat National Park PARK

(☏08-655 5684; www.parks.org.il; adult/child/student 29/15/25NIS; ◷8am-3.45pm Sun-Thu, 8am-2pm Fri Apr-Oct, 8am-2.45 Sun-Thu, 8am-1pm Fri Nov-Mar) En Avdat is a freak of nature in this otherwise bone-dry desert – a freshwater spring that flows via a waterfall into a narrow and winding ravine with steep sides of soft white chalk. Reached via an easy hike past caves that were inhabited by monks during the Byzantine period, it is home to Euphrates poplars and to fauna including ibex. Unfortunately, swimming in the ravine and its pools is prohibited.

There are two entrances to the park – southern and northern. The main ticket office is at the northern entrance, at Midreshet Ben-Gurion (next to the Ben-Gurion Graves and the Wilderness of Zin nature trail).

The most popular trail to the spring covers 7km and takes around four hours. Note that eating in the park is not allowed, and the only toilet facilities are at the main ticket office. Start from the inner parking lot and follow the blue markers into the ravine and on to the first waterfall. Climb

---

RAMAT HANEGEV WINE ROUTE

In recent years the number of vineyards in the valleys and hills between Mitzpe Ramon and Be'er Sheva has grown significantly. These vineyards mark the first attempts to nurture grapes in the desert since the ancient Nabataeans made wine at Shivta and Avdat. Using innovative computerised watering methods (eg drip irrigation), today's winegrowers have converted arid areas of dust into fertile land.

Located on the kibbutz of the same name, the **Sde Boker Winery** was established in 1999 in association with the School of Agriculture Rehovot to test the possibility of growing wine grapes with brackish water. Winemaker Zvi Remak hails from San Francisco and concentrates on making handcrafted, barrel, red wines from cabernet sauvignon and merlot grapes. You can taste his wines at a stand in the visitor centre next to the Ben-Gurion Desert Home.

Located close to the Avdat ruins, the **Carmey Avdat Winery** (☏08-653 5177; www.carmeyavdat.com; ☏) ◢ is a family-run vineyard built on the ruins of an ancient agricultural settlement. It harvested its first yield in 2002, and now produces a rosé, merlot, cabernet sauvignon and cabernet sauvignon/merlot blend. This is a lovely spot to spend a few nights; it offers rustic cabins with kitchen and private dipping pool (per double on weekdays 560NIS to 890NIS, on the weekend 670NIS to 890NIS). Breakfast is delivered to guests, and there's a produce shop where local cheeses and other products can be purchased.

As well as producing organic wine, olives and fruit, the **Boker Valley Vineyards Farm** (☏052-578 6863, 052-862 2930; www.bokerfarm.com; d weekday/weekend US$160/190, f weekday/weekend $US270/300; ❋) offers comfortable accommodation. Operated by a friendly Israeli-Dutch family, it has five safari-style cabins sleeping between two and five; each comes with a small kitchenette and outdoor barbecue area. Guests love the spa-bath hut and the lavish home-cooked breakfasts. The farm is a 3.5km drive north of Kibbutz Sde Boker on Rte 40, between the Telalim and Halukim Junctions.

Other local wines to sample include those produced by Nana (try its impressive chardonnay), Kadesh Barnea, Ashba, Rota, Sdema, Rujum and Derech Erez. For more information about the Ramat Hanegev region and the wine route, go to www.rng.org.il.

the stairs on the right wall of the ravine and follow the markers to the grove of poplars at the upper end. The trail follows a series of stairs until it reaches two ladders attached to the ravine wall. Once you make it to the top, follow the cliff to the left (south) until you reach a spectacular observation point. Continue south along the dry creek, looking out for rock art on the western bank. In the winter, the waterholes at this point are full and quite beautiful. From here, you can make your way to the petrol station on Hwy 40 near the ruins of Avdat, from where you'll need to hitch or take a bus back to your starting point or to Mitzpe Ramon.

Another popular trail leads to En Akev, a freshwater spring on the other side of Wadi Zin. Starting from the car park next to the petrol station and the ticket office for the ruins, follow the blue markers as they circle the park fence on the north side, cross two shallow valleys and then take a short descent to the En Akev Elyon (Upper Akev Spring) trail crossing, where there are natural pools. From here, follow the black markers and walk north down the canyon for 3km until you reach a waterfall and large pool at En Akev. Then follow the green markers on the west side of the canyon to go along the Divshon Pass (Maale Divshon), a 6km trail along the plateau and down a steep windy trail (be careful!) to the paved entrance road to the national park. Take the road north (uphill) to Midreshet Ben-Gurion, where you will be able to take a bus back to your starting point or to Mitzpe Ramon. In all, this trail covers 13km and will take around seven hours.

A combined ticket to Avdat National Park and the En Avdat National Park costs adult/child/student 46/24/39NIS. All of these trails are best explored during winter, when the waterfalls flow.

🏃 Activities

Geofun Desert Cycling
CYCLING

(☑08-655 3350; www.geofun.co.il) Based in Midreshet Ben-Gurion's small shopping centre, Geofun runs a four-day cycling tour visiting Negev wineries, a seven-day all-mountain tour of the Negev and a seven-day cross-country tour from Sde Boker to Eilat. It also hires bikes and sells cycling gear. See its website for useful descriptions of cycling trails in the area.

GOURMET GOATS

Along with camels and migrating birds, the Negev Highlands region has traditionally been a home for mountain goats. These animals are usually associated with Bedouin herders, but a number of new Israeli gourmet goat farms are cropping up along the wine route.

Naot Farm (☑054-421 8789; www. naotfarm.co.il; ⊗9am-7pm) has 150 goats and a shop selling its own labneh (thick yoghurt), *dulce de leche* and cheese. Try its *noam*, a delicious camembert-style mould cheese.

On the other side of the highway, **Kornmehl Farm** (☑08-655 5140; www. kornmehl.co.il; ⊗10am-6pm Tue-Sun) has a cute hillside shack and terrace in which it serves cheese platters (66NIS), goat's-cheese pizzas and calzones (44NIS) and a refreshing homemade yoghurt drink (19NIS).

Both farms offer the chance to see goat milking and are on Rte 40 between the Telalim and Halukim Junctions near Sde Boker.

🍴 Sleeping & Eating

Eating options are limited to Midreshet Ben-Gurion and are geared towards the resident student community. You can choose from a pub, pizzeria, felafel joint and deli/coffee shop, all of which can be found at the shopping centre.

Hamburg House
Field School Hostel
HOSTEL $

(☑08-653 2016; www.boker.org.il; Midreshet Ben-Gurion; s/d weekday 240/290NIS, weekend 290/360NIS; ❄) The Hamburg House Field School runs a hostel next to its office/guesthouse. Often filled with noisy school groups during the week, it's relatively tranquil on weekends. Rooms are very basic but come with kettle and en-suite bathroom. Hikers following the Israel Trail can organise a dorm bed for 70NIS per night.

From June to September guests have use of one of the university swimming pools. Wifi and internet are available in the next-door field-school office foyer.

Makom Ba'Tzel
PENSION $$

(Desert Shade; ☑050 662 2665; makombatzel1@ gmail.com; Midreshet Ben-Gurion; d weekday/

weekend 400/450NIS; ❄️🛜) Operated by friendly young couple Michal and Tal, these two small self-catering suites are on the top floor of a villa in a residential cluster in Midreshet Ben-Gurion. Each has a balcony, kitchenette and cable TV – the 'desert room' is larger than its 'classic room' neighbour. A home-made breakfast costs an extra 50NIS.

Hamburg House
Field School Guesthouse   GUESTHOUSE $$
(📞08-653 2016; www.boker.org.il; Midreshet Ben-Gurion; s/d weekday 320/370NIS, weekend 420/500NIS; ❄️@🛜) Run by the Sde Boker Field School and located on the edge of Wadi Zin, this guesthouse offers clean and comfortable rooms with tiled floors, hard beds, cable TV, kettle and fridge. During June to September guests have use of one of the university swimming pools. Wi-fi is available in the foyer only.

ℹ️ Information

Hamburg House Field School (📞08-653 2016; www.boker.org.il; ⏰7.30am-4.30pm Sun-Thu, 7.30am-noon Fri) The guides at this field school are extremely knowledgeable and can supply information about hikes in the desert, as well as about the local mammals, reptiles and birds of prey that you might spot.

ℹ️ Getting There & Away

Metropoline buses 60, 64 and 69 between Be'er Sheva and Mitzpe Ramon stop at the kibbutz, Ben-Gurion's Desert Home, the main gate to Midreshet Ben-Gurion and the petrol station below the Avdat ruins, and bus 65 stops at the petrol station (17NIS, 70 minutes, frequent). Inform the driver in advance where you want to get off. None of these services operate during Shabbat.

Mitzpe Ramon

متسبي رمون   מצפה רמון

📍08 / POP 5100

You'll feel like an extra in a sci-fi movie when exploring the massive Makhtesh Ramon Nature Reserve. The landscape resembles Tatooine (the fictional desert planet in *Star Wars*) and the wide, open spaces, far from city lights and crowds, are equally suited to those seeking solitude or an activity-triggered adrenaline rush.

In Hebrew the word 'mitzpe' means 'lookout', and the town of Mitzpe Ramon, spectacularly sited on the *makhtesh's* northern edge, well and truly lives up to its name. Views are of the take-your-breath-away variety and draw a constant stream of tourists – as a result the town is well set up with tourism infrastructure.

Sometimes described as Israel's very own Grand Canyon, the reserve is the largest protected area in Israel and is home to a huge number of hiking, cycling and horse-riding trails, as well as cliffs offering rappelling opportunities. If you're keen on outdoor activities, you'll be in your element.

Despite being in the heart of the desert, Mitzpe (as it's often called) is also one of the coldest places in Israel due to its elevation (900m above sea level), so pack appropriately.

◉ Sights

⭐ **Makhtesh Ramon**   PARK
Israel is a small country, but the Makhtesh Ramon is one place where it feels vast. Featuring multicoloured sandstone, volcanic rock and fossils, this geological phenomen-

---

WHAT EXACTLY IS A MAKHTESH?

Usually translated as 'crater' and occasionally as 'canyon', a more accurate definition of a *makhtesh* is an 'erosion cirque' – a large, asymmetrical hole formed by erosion as the Negev made the transition from ocean to desert. Providing a peep into the Earth's crust, the *makhteshim* found in the Negev and Sinai are thought to be unique geological phenomena because each is drained by a wadi (valley), although similar rock features have been found in Turkmenistan and Iran. Makhtesh Ramon is the largest *makhtesh* in Israel.

There are two other *makhteshim* in the Negev: **Makhtesh HaKatan** (Small Makhtesh) and **Makhtesh HaGadol** (Big Makhtesh). Makhtesh HaKatan, almost perfectly circular, can be found off the highway linking Dimona with the Dead Sea (Rte 25). The entrance to Makhtesh HaGadol is near the sleepy town of Yeroham (take Rte 204 south from Dimona towards Sde Boker). There is a beautiful drive right through the crater on Rte 225; look out for the coloured sands.

Mitzpe Ramon

on is 300m deep, 8km wide and 40km long and is best viewed from the lookout jutting over its edge 300m south of the Ramon Visitor Centre.

Ramon Visitor Centre MUSEUM, INFORMATION
(☎08-658 8691; mm.ramon@npa.org.il; museum adult/child/student 5-18yr 29/15/25NIS; combined ticket museum & Bio Ramon adult/child 35/18NIS; ◷8am-4pm Sat-Thu, 8am-3pm Fri Apr-Sep, 8am-3pm Sat-Thu, 8am-2pm Fri Oct-Mar) 🖉 Perched on the *makhtesh* rim, this visitor centre operated by the Israel Nature and Parks Authority has an extremely helpful information desk providing information about the Makhtesh Ramon Nature Reserve. It also contains a museum with four exhibition spaces, the most interesting of which are the hall with a 3D exhibition about the creation of the *makhtesh* and the audiovisual hall where a movie about desert animals is screened. Bookings are essential if you wish to visit the museum.

The Israel Nature and Parks Authority also offers private guided tours of the nature reserve. Telephone or email the visitor centre for details.

Bio Ramon WILDLIFE RESERVE
(adult/student/child 22/19/10NIS; ◷8am-4pm Sat-Thu, 8am-3pm Fri Apr-Sep, 8am-3pm Sat-Thu, 8am-2pm Fri Oct-Mar) This tiny desert wildlife park located next to the visitor centre

Mitzpe Ramon

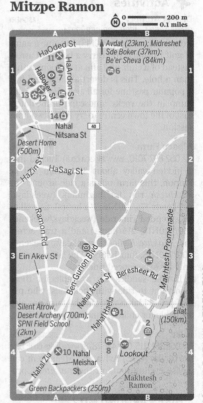

shows how nature can find a way to survive even in the harshest desert conditions. It offers an integrated approach to the geology, flora and fauna that represent the six habitats of the Negev's desert dwellers (insects, mammals and reptiles) and numbers scorpions, tortoises and snakes among its residents.

Spice Route Quarter ARTISTS' QUARTER
Located on the northern edge of town, this cluster of hangars and warehouses was once used by the military but now houses artisanal factories, artists' studios, boutique hotels, cafes and a dance workshop. With a pronounced hippy (as opposed to hipster) vibe, its arts and crafts aren't going to be to everyone's tastes, but the presence of Faran Cosmetics, Lasha Bakery and the Hadasaar and Hakatze cafes mean that it's worth a stop.

⚡ Activities

Desert Archery
ARCHERY

(☏050 534 4598, 08-658 7274; www.desert-archery.co.il; per group 250NIS) Imagine a game of golf in which you carry a bow and arrow instead of a club, and aim at balloons rather than a hole. This is desert archery, and it is a popular pastime for all ages. Head to this camp in the rocky landscape immediately east of the town centre to try it in a two-hour session.

Alpaca Farm
HORSE RIDING

(☏052 897 7010; www.alpaca.co.il) Tucked into a hidden valley about 3km from Mitzpe Ramon, this farm offers a ride around the *makhtesh* rim for beginners (weekdays/weekends 175/190NIS, 1½ hours), as well as an extended rim ride (weekdays/weekends 250/320NIS, 2½ hours) and a trail across the *makhtesh* floor (weekdays/weekends 600/750NIS, four hours). The latter two are only for experienced riders.

Double saddles are available for those who want to ride with their kids, who pay half price. Llama rides at the farm are also available for children under 25kg (20NIS).

iBike
BICYCLE RENTAL

(☏052 361 1115, 052 436 7878; www.ibike.co.il; bike hire per day 70NIS) Aviva and Menachem can devise cycling tours of the *makhtesh*, pro-

---

HIKES AROUND MITZPE RAMON

Some of the best hiking in the country is available in and around Mitzpe. Choose from an easy, 5.5km, two-to-three-hour 'Green Trail' descent into the *makhtesh;* a medium-to-difficult hike to an ancient ammonite wall; and a highly recommended 16km, five-hour hike from Mitzpe to the Hemet Cistern. The latter follows a trail along the cliff edge, down into a lush canyon and on to a 4000-year-old cistern.

Other walks in the area include a 3.5km loop to Wadi Ardon, a 7km loop to Wadi Ardon and the Nekarot Horseshoe and a hardcore five-to-six-hour climb up and down Mt Ardon.

Shvil Net publishes a handy 1:40,000 map covering the Makhtesh Ramon Area for cyclists and hikers, which can be bought from the Ramon Visitor Centre.

---

vide advice and information about trips in the upper Negev and supply logistic support including camping and transportation of cyclists and their gear.

☞ Tours

★ Astronomy Israel
ASTRONOMY TOURS

(☏052 544 9789; www.astronomyisrael.com; adult/child 150/75NIS; ⊙Sat-Thu) Ira Machefsky, the self-proclaimed 'Starman of Mitzpe Ramon', runs nightly two-hour astronomy tours of what locals claim to be the clearest and darkest skies in Israel, using both the naked eye and telescopes. Ira has a great sense of humour, and his well-honed and dramatic presentations include plenty of jokes, fascinating information and musical vignettes.

Yoash Limon
OUTDOOR TOURS

(☏08-653 2319; www.thegreenbackpackers.com) One of the most enthusiastic and experienced outdoors guides in the Negev, Yoash Limon has worked as a ranger at Bandelier National Monument in New Mexico and as a teacher at the national school of tourism in Tel Aviv. A hiking and rappelling enthusiast, he leads guided hikes and rappelling tours around the region and can customise private programs.

Adam Sela
JEEP TOURS

(☏050 530 8272; www.adamsela.com) Specialising in organising and operating desert adventure tours, Adam Sela's company offers guided jeep tours, desert treks and mountain bike trips, as well as rappelling and camping trips.

Ramon Desert Tours
OUTDOOR TOURS

(☏052 396 2715; www.ramontours.com) An experienced operator of jeep tours into the Negev desert and Jordan, this local outfit can organise anything from a short tour of the *makhtesh* or the Zin Vally through to multiday desert journeys in the Negev, Judean desert and Jordan.

Chakra Desert Camel Tours
CAMEL TOURS

(☏052 570 7752, 054 525 9717; http://cameltours.co.il/tag/mitzpe-ramon; 1hr/90min/overnight camel trek 120/160/480NIS) Based in the Spice Routes Quarter, this company offers a range of camel tours in the desert around Mitzpe.

🛏 Sleeping

There are a huge number of accommodation options in and around Mitzpe. Backpackers can often take up 'volunteering' stints where they barter work for accommodation and meals at the town's budget lodges or hostels.

★ **Desert Shade** DESERT LODGE $
(☑054 627 7413, 08-658 6229; http:// desert-shade.com; dm 80-90NIS, s/d/tr tent 180/250/360NIS; ☜) Right on the edge of the *makhtesh*, with simply extraordinary views, this place offers accommodation in a Bedouin tent sleeping 20, in smaller dorms or in private 'ecotents'. Showers and toilets are in a clean barracks-like block. Communal areas include an attractive lounge/bar, a guest kitchen and a huge campfire area on the crater's edge. A light breakfast costs 30NIS.

This must be the only hostel we've encountered with an on-site winery – be sure to sample its Rujum red blend.

Green Backpackers HOSTEL $
(☑08-653 2319; www.thegreenbackpackers.com; 2/2 Nahal Sirpad St; dm/d/tr without bathroom 95/285/405NIS; ❄@☜) Run with enthusiasm and expertise by keen hikers Lee and Yoash, this home-style hostel on the edge of town is the local backpacker hub. There's a tiny lounge with DVD library, a book exchange, communal kitchen, travellers' message board, laundry facilities (25NIS per load) and plenty of activities, including guided hikes. Free tea and coffee, but breakfast costs extra.

If arriving by bus, ask to alight at the Har Gamal (Camel Mountain) stop, which is in front of the hostel.

Silent Arrow DESERT LODGE $
(☑052 661 1561; www.hetzbashekt.com; Hetz BaSheket; Bedouin tent dm 80NIS, dome tent s/d/tr 150/250/300NIS) Seeking desert tranquillity? This place may fit the bill. A 20-minute walk from town, it offers simple accommodation and true Negev hospitality. Choose a mattress in the Bedouin-style tent or a private dome tent (BYO sleeping bag). There are clean but limited bathroom facilities and a communal kitchen where free coffee and tea are provided. Breakfast isn't included.

★ **iBike** HOTEL $$
(☑052 361 1115, 052 436 7878; www.ibike.co.il; 4 Har Ardon St, Spice Route Quarter; s/d/ste weekday 395/440/555 s/d/ste weekend 485/540/640NIS; ❄☜) Its mantra is 'selling the experience, not just the room', and this convivial place does just that. Hosts and keen cyclists Avi-

va and Menachem offer 10 small rooms, three suites with kitchenette, a spacious and comfortable lounge area, and a communal dining table at which they dispense a homemade breakfast, good coffee and advice on activities in the *makhtesh*.

Mitzpe Ramon Youth Hostel HOSTEL $$
(☑08-658 8443; mitzpe@iyha.org.il; 4 Nahal HaEla; dm/s/d 152/320/450NIS; ❄☜) A short downhill walk from the visitor centre, this large hostel is right on the edge of the crater, but unfortunately not all rooms offer views. Like all IHYA hostels, it is mainly geared towards student groups. Rooms are clean and come with satellite TV, kettle and fridge.

★ **Beresheet** LUXURY HOTEL, RESORT $$$
(☑08-638 7799; www.isrotelexclusivecollection. com/beresheet; 1 Beresheet Rd; r US$340-520, villas US$540-790; ❄☜❄) Ask any Israeli where they would most like to head for a weekend getaway, and they are likely to nominate this luxury resort hotel overlooking the *makhtesh*. Designed to blend in with the surrounding landscape, it has one of the most spectacularly sited infinity pools that you are ever likely to dive into, two restaurants and a busy activities program.

It's definitely worth paying extra for a room with crater view – enjoying a sunset drink from your private balcony is really very special. Note that a two- or three-night minimum applies on weekends.

Chez Eugène BOUTIQUE HOTEL $$$
(☑052 664 6939, 08-653 9595; www.mitzpe-ramonhotel.co.il; 8 Har Ardon St, Spice Route Quarter; d/ste weekday 670/840 d/ste weekend 840/1090NIS; ❄☜) Mitzpe's only boutique hotel opened in 2010 and its designer-chic rooms are starting to look a bit worn. It's extremely well run, though, and charming manager Naomi Dvora is a font of information about the region. The on-site restaurant is a definite plus.

Desert Home B&B $$$
(Bait BaMidbar, ☑052 322 9496; www.baitbamid-bar.com; 70 Ein Shaviv St; d Sun-Wed 650NIS, Thu & Sat 700NIS, Fri 850NIS; ❄) On the edge of a quiet residential neighbourhood, this place is for travellers who enjoy their creature comforts. Each of the five units has a kitchenette and is decorated in a minimalist style with locally produced arts and crafts. Top marks for the view and the breakfast, but the lack of reliable wi-fi is a problem.

Alpaca Farm B&B   B&B $$$

(☑08-658 8047, 052 897 7010; www.alpaca.co.il; d weekday/weekend 600/1250NIS; ❄) If you love animals and are travelling with children, this place will be just the ticket. The farm itself isn't particularly attractive, but the on-site hillside cabins are very comfortable, with wooden floors, satellite TV, kitchenette and a balcony with hammock. On-site animals include llamas, alpacas, camels and horses. Two-night minimum on weekends.

 Eating

Lasha Bakery   BAKERY $

(☑050 361 1488; off Har Boker St, Spice Route Quarter; ⊙9am-sunset Thu & Fri) Baking challah for Shabbat as well as a range of artisan breads made with full grains and without preservatives, this bakery is known throughout the Negev and is a great stop for self-caterers.

Hadasaar   ORGANIC, VEGETARIAN $$

(☑08-940 8473; 23 Har Arif St; sandwich 30NIS, soup 35NIS, salads 30-40NIS; ⊙8am-8pm Sat-Wed, 8am-11pm Thu & Fri; ☑) ☞ Set up as a community gathering place, this laid-back operation includes an open cafe kitchen, indoor and outdoor dining areas and a grocery selling organic produce. Staff are friendly and fully committed to sustainability. The menu features treats including locally made goats cheese and home-made granola with goat yoghurt, but there are plenty of vegan options on offer too.

Hakatze   ISRAELI $$

(☑08-659 5273; 2 Har Ardon St; mains from 35NIS; ⊙noon-8pm) Locals rate this simple place at the entrance to the Spice Route Quarter hangar highly, and often head here to enjoy lunch on its rear covered patio. The menu is home-style, featuring labneh, hummus, salads, and curried or stewed meats served with rice or couscous.

Hahavit   INTERNATIONAL, PUB $$

(☑050 684 0396; 8 Nachal Ziya; sandwiches 48NIS, pastas 38-50NIS, salads 45-70NIS; ⊙noon-late Sun-Thu, noon-3pm Fri) 'The Barrel' serves hefty portions of fresh salad, burgers, sandwiches and pasta dishes in a pub-like atmosphere and is the only decent eatery in the town centre. There's a good range of beers on tap and a predilection for loud rock music later in the evening.

★**Chez Eugéne**   EUROPEAN $$$

(www.mitzperamonhotel.co.il; 8 Har Ardon St, Spice Route Quarter; mains 68-153NIS; ⊙7pm-midnight Mon-Sat) Serving sophisticated alternatives to standard desert cuisine, the restaurant at this boutique hotel serves steak, pasta and other Mediterranean-influenced dishes. The desserts are particularly impressive.

☆ **Entertainment**

Mitzpe Ramon Jazz Club   JAZZ

(☑050 526 5628; http://jazzramon.wordpress. com; Spice Route Quarter; ⊙from 9.30pm Thu & Fri) Mitzpe's only club hosts jam sessions on Thursdays and live sets on Fridays.

🔒 **Shopping**

Faran Natural Cosmetics   BEAUTY

(☑08-675 7312; www.faran.com; 22 Har Ardon St, Spice Route Quarter; ⊙9.30am-7pm Sun-Thu, 9.30am-6pm Fri) ☞ The soaps, shampoos and skincare products sold at this factory store are made using plant oils and other extracts, and the relatively new line of 100% natural and organic mineral makeup was inspired by the richly coloured mineral sands of the *makhtesh*. There's another outlet at the visitor centre next to the Ben-Gurion Home in Sde Boker.

ℹ **Information**

There is a small commercial concourse with a bank and **post office** (⊙8am-6pm Sun-Thu, 8am-noon Fri) in the shopping centre at the entrance to Ben-Gurion Blvd.

Tourist information is available at the Ramon Visitor Centre (p313).

ℹ **Getting There & Away**

Mitzpe Ramon lies 23km south of Avdat and 136km north of Eilat. Frequent Metropoline buses 60 and 64 travel between Mitzpe and Be'er Sheva (17NIS, 1½ hours) from 5am to 9.30pm via En Avdat and Sde Boker. Bus 65 is a faster service that only stops on the highway. None of these services operate during Shabbat.

Metropoline bus 660 travels from Mitzpe to the Central Bus Station in Tel Aviv at 6.05am (24.80NIS, 2½ hours), and from Tel Aviv to Mitzpe at 4.05pm. Both services operate Sunday to Thursday only.

From Sunday to Thursday Egged bus 392 travels from Be'er Sheva to Eilat via Mitzpe four times per day (49NIS, three hours).

HIKING IN THE NEGEV

There are some excellent hikes in the Negev region, taking in a surprisingly wide variety of landscapes. Particularly recommended are those around Sde Boker, Mitzpe Ramon and Eilat.

The Society for the Protection of Nature in Israel (SPNI) has field schools with lodging at Mitzpe Ramon, Eilat and Hatzeva, 50km south of the Dead Sea on Rte 90; reserve ahead for a bed. Although they predominantly serve school groups, they will usually be able to sell detailed hiking maps and give up-to-date information about local hiking trails, but unfortunately they don't always have multilingual staff. A better bet is to chat with staff at hostels – Green Backpackers in Mitzpe Ramon and the Hamburg House Field School in Sde Boker are particularly helpful. The Israel Nature and Parks Authority staff at the Ramon Visitor Centre in Mitzpe Ramon provide advice and sell plenty of maps.

A new outfit called **Self Guided Negev Trek** (☏054-533 0948; www.sgnegevtrek.com) can organise food, lodging, maps, transportation and camping gear for those wanting to hike a 61km Negev section of the Israel Trail. The five-day trek starts in Mitzpe Ramon and crosses desert expanses, hidden canyons, cool springs and breathtaking scenery.

The Negev is a harsh environment but due to its rapid development visitors can easily be lulled into a false sense of security and forget to follow safety guidelines. It is best to make an early start, cover your head and use sunscreen, drink plenty of water, follow marked trails and avoid physical exertion in the middle of the day (noon to 3pm) and during the summer months. Don't hike by yourself and be sure to inform someone of where you are going so that they can sound the alarm if you don't return from your hike as scheduled.

The Arava

وادي عربة   הערבה

☏08

Part of the Great Rift Valley that runs for some 5000km from northern Syria to central Mozambique, this austerely beautiful and sparsely populated desert stretches from the Dead Sea to the Red Sea and has as its backdrop the majestic multi-hued Jordanian mountain range known in Israel as the Edom (Red) Mountains. The desert scenery is most spectacular around the settlement of Tzukim (aka Zuqim, or Zukim) on Hwy 90 between the Dead Sea and Zihor Junction.

The Arava is becoming known as a centre for outdoor activities, especially cycling. A popular 33km bike trail runs along a wadi (dry river bed) between Zofar and Paran, and the desert terrain is a favourite destination for 4WD enthusiasts. In rainy years, Eshet Lake near Paran is a popular swimming spot.

◉ Sights & Activities

Kibbutz Neot Semadar   KIBBUTZ
(☏054 979 8966 (gallery), 08-635 8170 (tours); www.neot-semadar.com; Shizafon Junction; gallery entrance 18NIS, 2hr guided tour 250NIS; ⊙tours & gallery entrance 11am-2pm Sun-Fri) A true oasis in the desert, this kibbutz has lush green surrounds and a bizarre pink tower in which residents have established an arts centre and a gallery where artisan crafts are sold to the public. The community was established in 1989 and focuses on promoting cooperation, creativity and learning in daily life. It supports itself through agriculture (orchard and olive grove), a winery, a solar field and the workshops it runs on self-awareness and eco-building.

The kibbutz is located on Hwy 40, halfway between Mitzpe Ramon and Eilat (10km up Hwy 40 from Ketura Junction on Hwy 90).

Timna Park   PARK
(☏08-631 6756; www.parktimna.co.il; day ticket adult/child 44/36NIS; ⊙8am-4pm Sat-Thu, 8am-3pm Fri) The colourful sands and craggy mountains of the Timna Valley, 25km north of Eilat, are full of minerals including copper, iron and manganese. This park incorporates traces from one of the world's first copper mines, and is home to thousands of ancient mining shafts, the remains of smelting furnaces dating back to ancient imperial Egypt, temple remnants and ancient rock drawings depicting ostriches, ibex and Egyptian battle chariots.

Other attractions are geological phenomena including Solomon's Pillars (two huge columns of granite formed by rainwater some 540 million years ago) and the Mushroom, an eroded monolith in the shape of... you guessed it.

You could easily spend a whole day hiking here, but the park is so spread out that you'll also need a car. Information about walks is available at the visitor centre, accessed off Hwy 90.

Hai-Bar Yotvata Nature Reserve
WILDLIFE RESERVE

(☑ 08-637 6018; www.parks.org.il; adult/child/student 29/15/25NIS; ☺ 8.30am-4pm Sun-Thu, 8.30am-3pm Fri & Sat) Wild animals that are mentioned in the Bible are bred at this nature reserve 35km north of Eilat, as are other endangered desert species. Divided into three areas – an area where herds of desert herbivores live in conditions similar to the wild; enclosures containing large predators, reptiles and small desert animals; and a 'dark room' to view nocturnal animals when they are active – it can be thoroughly explored in two hours if you have your own car.

The reserve's inhabitants include asses, oryx, addax and ostriches, and its flora includes acacia groves. You'll find it on Hwy 90 about 42km north of Eilat, between Kibbutz Yotvata and Kibbutz Samar.

Kibbutz Ketura
KIBBUTZ

(www.ketura.org.il) One of the most interesting of Israel's kibbutzim, Ketura has transformed itself from an agricultural kibbutz into a leader in innovative eco-technology. Founded in 1973, it is unusual in that it is a multinational, religiously pluralistic community. Home to the internationally renowned Arava Institute (http://arava.org), which researches and draws attention to ecological problems in the region, it runs businesses including a date plantation, a dairy farm, a photovoltaic solar field and an algae factory producing the powerful antioxidant Astaxanthin.

The kibbutz is located on Hwy 90, 50km north of Eilat.

ISRAEL'S KIBBUTZIM

Back in 1909, when the first kibbutz was established in Palestine, the idea was both practical – growing crops in a harsh climate required collective action – and utopian. The word 'kibbutz' means gathering or clustering, and the original kibbutzniks (members of a kibbutz) were driven by equally weighted beliefs in socialism and Zionism. Committed to establishing a Jewish homeland, they believed that farming collectively owned land in their new place of residence would provide a sound economic and political underpinning for an eventual Jewish state.

At the outbreak of WWII there were 79 kibbutzim in Palestine, all of which relied on agriculture for their livelihoods. The movement reached its apogee in the 1950s and 1960s, when many new kibbutzim were established by Nahal, an Israel Defense Forces program that combined military service and establishment of new agricultural settlements. In the 1980s, as a more individualist ethos gained currency, increasing numbers of residents started to leave their kibbutz homes and forge new lives and careers in Israel's rapidly expanding cities. A number of kibbutzim ended up in debt and, eventually, were forced to privatise. The others had no choice but to reinvent themselves by adopting new ways of structuring the kibbutz economy and finding new sources of income. Many diversified into non-agricultural endeavours including manufacturing, artisanal industries, tourism and innovative environmentally sustainable businesses.

Today, there are approximately 270 kibbutzim in Israel. Of these, 75% function according to an economic model known as 'renewing' (mitchadesh), under which kibbutzniks generate and keep their own income. The remaining 25% are run according to the traditional collective model (kibbutz shitufi), whereby members are compensated equally, regardless of what work each member does. Eight of these collective kibbitzim are located in the Negev and most of them have adopted a business plan that includes sustainable agriculture and tourism.

For some interesting musings on the history of the kibbutz movement, consider reading Walking Israel, a travelogue written by Israel-based former NBC correspondent Martin Fletcher.

Kibbutz Lotan
KIBBUTZ

(☑08-635 6935; www.kibbutzlotan.com) ✈ Embracing an ecological vision known in Hebrew as *tikun 'olam* (repairing the world), this kibbutz is known for its sincere and long-demonstrated commitment to sustainability and cooperative action. Visitors can take a guided daily tour at 9.30am (20NIS), spot wildlife in the kibbutz's nature and bird reserve, discover the therapeutic delight of watsu (water shiatsu) in the kibbutz's heated pool, or sign up for a one-week 'eco-experience', four- to seven-week 'green apprenticeship' or short permaculture workshop at the ecology education centre.

Regional bus 20 from Eilat stops at the kibbutz, and Egged buses to/from Tel Aviv stop on Hwy 90, nearby.

Samar Bike
CYCLING

(☑052 551 8904, 052 304 0640; www.samarbike.com; Kibbutz Samar) Based at Kibbutz Samar, 34km north of Eilat, this outfit runs bike tours across a variety of trails in the Arava and can supply pick-up and drop-off services and logistics for those wanting to cycle part of the Israel National Trail. It operates a small guesthouse on the kibbutz that is tailored specifically towards bike tourism.

🛏 Sleeping & Eating

Desert Routes Inn
HOSTEL $$

(☑052 366 5927, 08-658 1829; www.shvilimbamidbar.com; Hatzeva; dm/d/tw/f US$27/208/208/285; ☎) The owners of this khan (desert inn) close to the Jordanian border in the Northern Arava are a mine of information about the area and can organise jeep, hiking and rappelling tours. They offer private and dorm rooms, and also operate a nearby camping ground. There's a communal kitchen and hospitality tent, making it a great option for self-caterers.

Desert Days: Negev Eco Lodge
CABIN $$

(☑058 484 2357, 052 617 0028; www.negevecolodge.com; Tzukim; d weekday/weekend 450/525NIS, per child extra 50NIS; ☎🖵) ✈ Nine cabins made of straw bales and mud provide a base for city dwellers seeking a tranquil desert escape. The surrounds are stony and stark, but there is an unusual string of desert pools to soften the overall effect. Each cabin can sleep up to six, and green features include self-composting toilets, recycled grey water and solar-generated power.

Breakfast costs an extra 50/30NIS per adult/child. To reach the lodge, turn off Rte 90 at Tzukim and follow the 'Desert Days' sign.

Neot Semadar Guesthouse
GUESTHOUSE $$

(☑054 979 8433; www.neot-semadar.com; d weekday/weekend 430/480NIS) A minimalist aesthetic is the hallmark of these sustainably built and attractive cabins, which are set in a garden on the edge of an olive grove. Each is equipped with a fridge and kettle, and the room charge includes a breakfast basket. Other meals can be taken at the nearby inn.

Kibbutz Ketura Country Lodge
KIBBUTZ $$

(☑057 941 9109; www.keren-kolot-israel.co.il; s/d weekdays 350/440, s/d weekends 400/530NIS; ✳@🛜🖵) ✈ Ketura's guesthouse is comfortable and extremely well maintained. Three types of room are on offer: the 'Marulla', which sleeps up to four and has a private terrace; the two-room 'Pitaya' family suite, which sleeps up to eight; and the four-room 'Argania', which can also sleep eight. All have kitchenette and cable TV, and there are communal BBQs.

Facilities include a basketball court, football field, alternative health centre (treatments from 180NIS), bicycle hire, and on-site coffee shop (open 8am to 11pm every day except Shabbat). Guests receive a free tour of the kibbutz and are welcome to join members for a dairy dinner (adult/child 35/30NIS) in the communal dining hall.

Egged buses travelling along Hwy 90 will drop passengers at Ketura (40 minutes from Eilat; be sure to specify Kibbutz Ketura, not Ketura Junction). From Eilat, Regional Council bus 20 also stops here.

Kibbutz Lotan Guesthouse
GUESTHOUSE $$

(☑08-635 6935; www.kibbutzlotan.com; s/d weekdays 300/370NIS, s/d weekends 370/440NIS; ✳🛜🖵) ✈ There are two types of accommodation on offer at this kibbutz: simple but comfortable guesthouse cabins with kitchenette, bathroom, air-con and outdoor seating area; and hippy-ish mud eco-domes (some with private bathroom and some with shared facilities). Prices include breakfast in the kibbutz teahouse, and other meals may be enjoyed with kibbutz residents in the communal dining room.

Lotan is known as a 'baby-butz' because it is relatively small and many of its residents are young (the average age is 40), so there's a lively atmosphere. Facilities include shady gardens, a playground, a basketball court and a soccer field. Meals make the most of home-grown vegetables and dates, as well as dairy products made on site, and both vegans and vegetarians are catered for.

Egged buses travelling to/from Eilat will drop passengers on Hwy 90 near the 1.5km-long access road to the kibbutz (45 minutes from Eilat); Regional Council bus 20 comes to the kibbutz itself.

★ **Midbara** CABINS $$$
(☏052 701 0444; www.midbara.co.il; Tzukim; d/q weekdays 800/1200NIS, d/q weekends 900/1500NIS; ✲⊙) The settlement of Tzukim is becoming a tourism hotspot, with a boom in construction of desert lodges. Midbara is definitely the most attractive of these, offering 11 well-spaced, comfortable and stylish mud cabins scattered along a valley planted with fruit trees. All its cabins have kitchens, a few have indoor fireplaces and most have a private relaxation pool and hammock.

Children love the free bike hire and on-site animals (chickens, a camel), so it's a great spot for a family holiday. Note that prices drop for stays of multiple nights.

Tzukim is 113km north of Eilat. To reach the lodge, turn off Rte 90 at Tzukim and follow the 'Desert Days' sign.

Nof Zuqim CABINS $$$
(☏08-658 4748; www.nofzuqim.co.il; Tzukim; standard d weekdays/weekends 820/1130NIS, d with panoramic view weekdays/weekends 1040/1430NIS; ✲⊙) A great deal of thought has gone into the design of these mud cabins overlooking a stony wadi in Tzukim. Each is extremely well equipped and tastefully decorated, and has an outdoor BBQ and private balcony with hot tub. It's worth paying extra for a cabin with a panoramic view, as the mountain vistas are magnificent.

A delicious breakfast can be delivered to your cabin for 54NIS per person.

Neot Semadar Inn CAFE $$
(Pundak Neot Semadar; ☏08-635 8180; www.neot-semadar.com; Shizzafon Junction; labneh 26NIS, cheese platter 50NIS, mains 40-45NIS; ⊙7am-7pm Sun-Thu, 7am-3pm Fri; ☏) A lush rear garden gives this roadside inn its name (*neot* means 'oasis'). Operated by the kibbutz of the same name, it serves home-made goats cheese and labneh, as well as a range of salads, egg dishes, dips, pasta and cakes made using organic produce. Be sure to try one of the home-made fruit nectars or juices.

Eilat אילת ايلات
☏08 / POP 47,700

It's incumbent upon travel writers to tell it as it is, so we won't pull our punches when describing this resort town on Israel's southern tip. Hugely popular with Israeli families looking for an affordable beach break and with Eastern European tourists seeking a refuge from the bone-chilling winters back home, Eilat is brash, ugly and almost inevitably crowded, a place where being scantily clad and sunburned is the rule rather than the exception, and where cocktails are about as close to culture as the local scene gets.

However – and it's a big however – Eilat is also a place where visitors seem to have a great time and where children in particular tend to be blissfully happy. The turquoise-tinted waters of the Red Sea offer snorkelling, diving and swimming opportunities galore, and there are plenty of other attractions on offer, including an aquarium, a theme park, tax-free shopping and an array of outdoor activities showcasing the spectacular local desert scenery.

Average winter temperatures are between 21°C and 25°C, but come summer the temperature averages 40°C. Fortunately, humidity levels are low (15%).

History

Four thousand years ago the desert landscape surrounding Eilat was rich in copper, and trade between Eilat and the Theban sea port of Elim flourished. As well, frankincense and myrrh from Ethiopia and Punt passed through the port of Eilat, as did bitumen and natron from the Dead Sea. In the Roman era, a road was built from Eilat to Petra, opening a new trade route with the Nabataeans.

Trade declined after the Roman era, but Eilat stayed in touch with the wider world courtesy of its location on the Darb el-Hajj (Muslim Pilgrim's Road) between Africa and Mecca. The settlement remained small and life relatively uneventful until the modern city and port were built after the 1948 Arab–Israeli War.

◉ Sights

Underwater Observatory Marine Park AQUARIUM
(☏08-636 4200; www.coralworld.co.il; South Beach; adult/child 104/84NIS; ⊙8.30am-4pm; ☐15) For as much aquatic action as you can

Eilat

Eilat

See Eilat Town Centre Map (p322)

THE NEGEV EILAT

get without entering the water, visit this marine park near Coral Beach. As well as standard aquarium features such as shark and sea turtle pools, there are two glassed-in observation halls in an oceanarium 12m below the surface of the Red Sea, a children's adventure park where little ones can pet and feed koi, and a theme-park-style 'Journey into the World of Sharks' movie experience. Tickets are valid for three days.

Cruises on the park's Coral 2000 glass-bottomed deep-hulled boat leave hourly between 10.25am and 1.25pm (adult/child 35/29NIS).

Botanical Garden of Eilat   GARDENS
(Map p321; ☑08-631 8788; www.botanicgarden.
co.il; adult/child 25/20NIS; ⊙8.30am-6pm Sun-Thu, 8.30am-3pm Fri, 9.30am-3pm Sat; ☐5 & 6) Built on stone terraces in ancient biblical style, this garden on the northern edge of town is planted with more than 1000 different types of tropical trees, plants and bushes and also features a stream, waterfalls, walking tracks and rainforest (certainly a novelty in this arid landscape!). Take the first right as you enter Eilat on Rte 90; the garden is behind the petrol station.

International Birding &
Research Center Eilat Park   WILDLIFE RESERVE
(☑050 767 1290; IBRCEilat.blogspot.com; ⊙24hr) FREE Each year, tens of millions of migrating birds pass through the Arava and Eilat when travelling between Africa and

Europe. The largest migrations occur from February to May, but autumn/fall migration also sees interesting species visiting. Head to this lakeside reserve directly opposite the Yitzhak Rabin–Wadi Araba Border Crossing to see species including the Namaqua Dove, Hoopoe Lark, Bar-tailed Desert Lark, Desert Warbler, Barbary Falcon, Hooded Wheatear and Desert Finch, as well as pelicans, storks and raptors galore.

It is possible to book special private birder tours of the park (350NIS, 90 minutes) or of the park and Southern Arava (900NIS, four hours) – email or call the park for details.

Eilat Town Centre

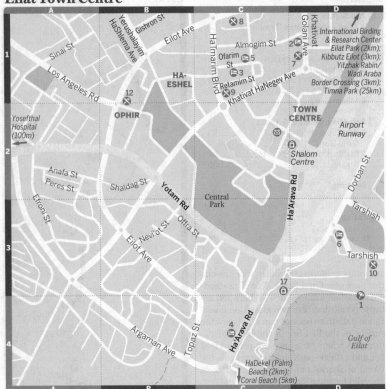

King's City & Funtasia
AMUSEMENT PARK

(Map p321; ☑08-630 4444; www.kingscity.co.il; East Lagoon; adult/child 125/100NIS; ◷10am-6pm Mon-Sat, 2-6pm Sun) Holy proselytising prophets! This biblical Disneyland took four years and US$40 million to build and features mazes, kaleidoscopes, 3D films and a heart-thumping water ride inspired by King Solomon's life (yes, really). Also here is Funtasia – a more conventional outdoor amusement park with bumper cars, a small roller coaster and carousel. The King's City entrance fee includes three rides in Funtasia; extra rides cost 10NIS each.

☂ Beaches

Eilat's central beaches can be crowded, so many tourists prefer to laze around their hotel pools. South of the lagoons, the coastline is initially dominated by the ugly naval base and port but improves south of Dolphin Reef.

★Coral Beach Nature Reserve
DIVE SITE

(Map p321; ☑057 855 2381; adult/child/student 35/21/30NIS; ◷9am-5pm Apr-Sep, 9am-4pm Oct-Mar; ☐15) The beach at this marine reserve overseen by the Israel Nature and Parks Authority is definitely the best on this part of the coast, and the protected waters are a utopia for snorkellers. A wooden bridge leads from the shore to the beginning of the reef, which is over 1km in length and is home to a diverse array of coral and tropical fish. Underwater trails are marked by buoys, and snorkelling equipment can be hired for 19NIS.

Dolphin Reef
WATER PARK

(Map p321; ☑08-630 0111; www.dolphinreef.co.il; South Beach; adult/concession 67/46NIS; ◷9am-5pm Sun-Thu, 9am-4.30pm Fri, relaxation pools 9am-11.30pm Mon-Sat; ☐15) Head to this private beach to see – and sometimes interact with – its resident pod of bottlenose dol-

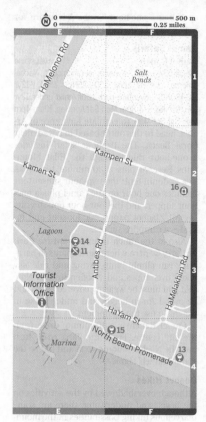

Eilat Town Centre

cafes and restaurants means that it is perennially crowded and full of action.

HaDekel (Palm) Beach BEACH
(Map p321) Just south of town, HaDekel is less crowded than North Beach but is wedged between the ugly port and naval base. It's a popular snorkelling spot.

Village Beach BEACH
(Map p321) Just north of Coral Beach, this stretch of sand has free umbrellas, clean water for snorkelling and a bar hosting loud parties during summer.

🏃 Activities

Eilat offers activity options for every age and level of expertise.

Water Sports
The Red Sea offers some great diving opportunities and Eilat has no shortage of dive clubs. However, due to the sheer volume of divers, the reef has seen some inevitable damage over the years. Over the past decade, steps have been taken to rehabilitate the coral and thousands of young coral colonies have been grown in aquariums and attached to the existing reef.

phins. They can be observed from floating piers or during guided snorkelling (290NIS) or diving (339NIS) experiences. The admission charge includes beach use, but for a surcharge (98NIS for a two-hour slot including refreshments) you can also chill out in three heated relaxation pools (rainwater, seawater and Dead Sea water) surrounded by lush greenery.

Advance booking is advised for swimming or snorkelling with the dolphins or using the relaxation pools. Note that diving is restricted to those over eight years, snorkelling for those over 10 and the pools for those over 18.

North Beach BEACH
(Map p322) The main stretch of beach in town, North Beach stretches from the Meridien Hotel past the lagoons and all the way to the Jordanian border. Its backdrop of high-rise hotels and a promenade of bars,

It is true that all you need to do is pop your head underwater in Eilat to see all sorts of colourful fish and coral (there are thought to be 1200 species of fish and 250 of coral). This accessibility makes it a great place for kids as well as for beginners looking to do a PADI course. The best dive sites are at Coral Beach Nature Reserve, Lighthouse Reef, Neptune's Tables (aka Veronica's Reef) and the Caves.

Prices vary, but average around 250NIS for a guided snorkel or introductory dive and 450NIS for a dive lesson (all including equipment hire). To hire equipment and dive or snorkel independently you will be looking at around 60NIS for snorkel, mask and fins, and 170NIS for a wetsuit, tank and breathing equipment.

Most dive centres open daily from 8.30am to 5pm.

Manta Isrotel
Diving Center
DIVING, SNORKELLING
(Map p321; ☑08-633 3666; www.divemanta.com; Coral Beach) Manta has been in business for over 30 years and offers introductory dives, diving courses and guided snorkelling and diving. The fact that it operates out of Isrotel's Yam Suf Hotel means that it can also offer services such as babysitting.

Aqua Sport International
DIVING, SNORKELLING
(Map p321; ☑08-633 4404; www.aqua-sport.com; Coral Beach) One of the oldest dive outfits operating in the Red Sea, this British-owned company offers open water diving courses (including introductory courses), three-day dive cruises, a full-day snorkelling cruise and a two-hour sunset cruise. Based at Coral Beach, it also operates out of the Hilton and Mövenpick Hotels in Taba.

Reef Diving Group
DIVING, SNORKELLING
(☑Marina Divers 08-637 6787, Dolphin Reef 08-630 0111; www.reefdivinggroup.co.il) A well-regarded outfit with two branches in Eilat and another in Tel Aviv, Reef Diving Group incorporates the Dolphin Reef Dive Centre and Marina Divers at Coral Beach.

Deep Siam
DIVING, SNORKELLING
(Map p321; ☑08-632 3636; www.deepdivers.co.il; Coral Beach) This outfit offers guided snorkelling, introductory dives and scuba courses.

Snuba
DIVING
(Map p321; ☑08-637 2722; www.snuba.co.il; South Beach) Popular with Russian tourists, Snuba offers introductory dives to the Caves Reef, as well as a one-hour 'Snuba Adventure' for novices aged over eight (200NIS).

Camel Safaris
Camel Ranch
CAMEL RIDING
(☑08-637 0022; www.camel-ranch.co.il; Nachal Shlomo; safaris adult 150-225NIS, child 7-12yr 110-180NIS, adventure park adult/child under 12yr 106/96NIS; ☉4-8pm Mon-Sat Apr-Sep, 10am-4pm Mon-Sat Oct-Mar) To emulate Lawrence of Arabia, head to this outfit based in a wadi near Coral Beach. The 1½-hour safari includes a one-hour ride through the Eilat Mountains Reserve plus a 30-minute tea break in a Bedouin tent; the two-hour sunset tour includes one hour on the camel plus a one-hour supper; and the four-hour option visits the Mt Zfachot panoramic lookout and includes a campfire supper.

Also at the ranch is an **Adventure Park Activity Centre** where participants in harnesses can climb, jump, swing and ride 'sky bikes' over ropes and wooden towers. Note that you must be wearing covered shoes and be over 1.2m in height and under 120kg in weight to use the equipment.

Camel Ranch is a 10-minute drive from the city centre. From the Taba road, turn into the Nachal Shlomo road and follow the 'Camel Ranch' signs.

Desert Hikes
Although overshadowed by the activities on the beach and underwater, there are some marvellous hiking possibilities in the mountains and valleys just outside Eilat.

When you go hiking in the desert be sure to abide by these safety guidelines: follow a marked path, take sufficient water, cover your head, don't hike in high summer and avoid the Israel–Egypt border area.

Hiking maps and advice are available at the **SPNI Field School** (Map p321; ☑08-637 2021, 08-637 1127; eilat@spni.org.il) on the Taba road at Coral Beach.

Mt Tzfachot Circular Trail
HIKING
This almost circular 4km hike culminates in superb views of the four countries whose borders meet around the Gulf of Eilat/Aqaba: Israel, Egypt, Jordan and Saudi Arabia. Within reach of non-drivers and suitable for all ages and most fitness levels, the hike takes 2½ hours and is best enjoyed at sunrise or towards the end of the day.

Take bus 15 from the central bus station and get off at the Camel Ranch stop opposite the Isrotel Yam Suf Hotel at Coral Beach. Follow the sign pointing to Wadi

Shlomo, walk along the dirt road for about 2km past Camel Ranch and head left along Wadi Tzfachot (aka Zefahot, or Zfachot), following the green trail markers. You'll pass a dry waterfall on your right. After 300m the path forks with a black-marked trail veering to the right. Keep going straight ahead on the green marked trail for another 200m. It then turns to the left and starts to climb quite steeply. Head up this path and keep climbing for about 15 minutes to reach the Mt Tzfachot summit at about 278m.

From this vantage point, Sinai and the Crusader castle on Coral Island are visible to the south, while across the gulf are the Jordanian port city of Aqaba and the Saudi Arabian border. To the northeast is the greenery of Kibbutz Eilot. Although sunset can be beautiful here, hikers are advised not to return after dark as the trail can be difficult to follow. The path ends at the SPNI Field School on the main road.

Birdwatching

Alaemon Birding BIRDWATCHING
(☑ 052 368 9773; www.eilatbirding.blogspot.com; full-day tour 1400NIS) Until 2014, keen birder Itai Shanni was the Eilat & Arava regional coordinator of the Israel Ornithological Centre. Now running this outfit with bird photographer Avi Meir, he operates ecotours focusing on birds and birding in the Arava. Advance bookings are essential for tours during the main migration season (February to May).

☞ Tours

Desert Eco Tours ADVENTURE TOUR
(☑ 052 276 5753, 08-632 6477; www.desertecotours.com) This highly regarded outfit offers jeep tours around Eilat, through the Negev Desert and to the Makhtesh Ramon, as well as extremely popular tours to Jordan including a one-day tour to Petra and a two-day tour to Petra and Wadi Rum.

✵ Festivals & Events

Isrotel Classic Music Festival MUSIC
(www.isrotel.co.il/events) Bringing an annual and sorely needed touch of class to Eilat, this long-running festival is held in late January.

Eilat Chamber Music Festival MUSIC
(www.eilat-festival.co.il) Held in February, this international festival hosts new productions, renowned soloists and unique collaborations.

★ Red Sea Jazz Festival MUSIC
(www.redseajazzeilat.com) Going strong since 1987, the Red Sea Jazz Festival is an international four-day jazz festival held annually in the last week of August. Outdoor performances are staged around the Eilat Sea Port. The festival's legendary jam sessions are free and take place at Dekel Beach next to the Port. It also stages a winter event in February.

🛏 Sleeping

Eilat's accommodation ranges from the good to the bad to the downright ugly – this is not a place to expect a charming or unique hotel experience.

As is the case with most resort towns, the cost of hotel rooms rises by about 25% at weekends and 50% (or more) during Israeli school holidays and in July/August. Reserve ahead during these times. The prices we have cited in our reviews are at the higher end of the mid-season range.

If you enjoy staying in five-star chain hotels, you'll be spoiled for choice. There are more than 50 options around the lagoons at North Beach and along the road to Taba, including nine Isrotels, two Dan Hotels and seven hotels in the Leonardo/Herod group. Most have bland decor, restaurants where the fixed-price buffet reigns supreme, large pool areas and decent but not exceptional levels of service. All are predominantly geared towards families and can be noisy.

Many of the recently opened hotels in town are in less-than-salubrious locations overlooking the airport or behind the lagoons or Hayam Shopping Mall – do your location research before booking.

Light sleepers should note that the North Beach promenade is noisy well into the wee small hours, and most of the town's hotels are directly under the flight path for Eilat Airport.

Camping is illegal on most of Eilat's beaches. Exceptions are the areas east of Herod's Beach, towards the Jordanian border.

Arava Hostel HOSTEL $
(Map p322; ☑ 08-637 4687; www.a55.co.il; 106 Almogim St; dm/s/d 70/200/220NIS; ✹@🛜) The only Eilat hostel with an authentic backpacker vibe, the Arava wouldn't win any awards for its dated rooms and dark, cramped dorms or for its location far from the beach. There are compensations, though: a front garden perfect for sunset

THE NEGEV EILAT

beers, communal kitchen, laundry (15NIS per load) and free parking. Internet costs 16NIS per hour; wi-fi is free.

Note that the prices we have given here apply for most of the year but almost double in July and August.

Motel Aviv   HOTEL $
(Map p322; ☑ 08-637 4660; www.avivhostel.co.il; 126 Ofarim Lane; dm/r 100/300NIS, small/large ste 350/500NIS; ✳ 🛜 ☒) It may have an institutional feel, but the Aviv is clean, secure and in proud possession of a small swimming pool. Standard rooms are cramped and dark – we suggest opting for a suite as some have sea views and all offer better value for money. Note that breakfast isn't served and dorm beds aren't available in summer.

Eilat Youth Hostel & Guest House   HOSTEL $$
(Map p322; ☑ 02-594 5605; www.iyha.org.il; 7 Ha-Arava Rd; dm/s/d 130/292/400NIS; ✳ @ 🛜) If it weren't for the ubiquitous groups of noisy schoolkids staying here, this huge hostel with its expansive front balcony overlooking the Gulf of Eilat would be one of our top accommodation picks. Even with the school-group factor in play, it's an extremely attractive option due to its modern, clean and comfortable rooms and dorms. Free parking and wi-fi; internet 1NIS per minute.

Blue Hotel   HOTEL $$
(Map p322; ☑ 08-632 6601; www.bluehotel.co.il; 123 Ofarim Lane; s/d weekdays 305/360NIS, s/d weekends 350/420NIS; ✳ @ 🛜) Run by a friendly Israeli/Irish couple, this three-star choice is located in a characterless budget accommodation enclave near the city centre but is worth considering for its well-priced, recently renovated rooms with excellent amenities (fridge, cable TV, kettle). There are bicycles for hire and guests receive discounts on diving packages with the Reef Diving Group.

Soleil Boutique Hotel   HOTEL $$
(Map p322; ☑ 08-633 4004; www.soleil-hoteleilat. com; 12 Tarshish St; s/d/ste 420/500/680NIS; ✳ 🛜 ☒) Its size (only 70 rooms) and stylish decor give credence to this recently opened hotel's claim to boutique status, but its location overlooking the runway at Eilat Airport falls well short. That said, the reasonable prices, proximity to North Beach and facil-

ities including a bar, restaurant, spa, gym and pool make it worthy of consideration.

★ Orchid Reef Hotel   HOTEL $$$
(Map p321; ☑ 08-636 4444; www.reefhoteleilat. com; Coral Beach; r standard/sea view/superior sea view 620/730/1050NIS; ✳ 🛜 ☒) Recently refurbished, this place overlooks a lovely stretch of sand right next to the Coral Reef Nature Reserve. It has a huge pool area, fitness room, spa and restaurant. Beach activities include snorkelling and sea kayaking, and bike hire is free (parking costs 25NIS per day). The comfortable rooms are spacious and most have a balcony or terrace with sea view.

✗ Eating

Most of the town's restaurants, cafes and bars can be found on North Beach Promenade or in the streets around the lagoons, although the better-quality options tend to be located away from these mega-touristy areas.

★ Paulina IceCreamy   ICE CREAM $
(Map p322; www.paulina.co.il; King Solomon Promenade; 1/2/3 scoops 13/18/22NIS; ☺ 11am-1am) Ice cream and the seaside go together like Posh and Becks, and in Eilat there's only one place to come to for a cup or cone – lagoon-side Paulina. Made fresh each day using quality ingredients, the icy confections served here have nearly as many devoted fans as the aforementioned celebrities, making it an essential stop.

Family Bakery   BAKERY $
(Map p322; cnr Sderot HaTmarim Blvd & Retamim St; pastries 4-10NIS; ☺ 24hr) Consider yourself warned: these bakers work around the clock, meaning that the sweet and savoury pastries are fresh and oh-so-addictive. The signage is all in Hebrew, but the 'Supermarket Galgal' sign works as a locator. Take-away only, but the cafe next door is happy for you to BYO pastries if you order a tea or coffee.

★ Pastory   ITALIAN $$
(Map p322; ☑ 08-634 5111; 7 Tarshish St; pizza 48-68NIS, pasta 58-96NIS, mains 72-168NIS; ☺ 1-11pm) *Mamma mia!* Who would have thought that an authentic Italian-style trattoria serving *molto delizioso* cuisine would be found in a North Beach back street? This family-friendly place behind the Leonardo Plaza Hotel serves antipasti platters packed with flavourful morsels, al dente pasta with

rustic sauces, piping-hot pizza with quality toppings and an irresistible array of home-made desserts and gelato. Go.

Shibolim
BAKERY **$$**

(Map p322; ☑08-632 3932; 39 Eilot Ave; breakfast plates 20-42NIS, sandwiches 39-43NIS; ☺7am-9pm Sun-Thu, 7am-2pm Fri; ☑) Shibolim's ye-olde-Bavarian-inn decor strikes a somewhat bizarre note, but this long-timer in the city centre is a decent option if you're after breakfast or a light lunch. The bread and pastries are home-made, and everything is kosher.

Giraffe
ASIAN **$$**

(Map p321; ☑08-631 6583; www.giraffe.co.il; Herods Promenade; sushi 27-41NIS, noodles 51-58NIS, mains 51-63NIS; ☺noon-11.30pm) This giraffe can be found lurking under the Herods Hotel at the end of the North Beach Promenade. A newcomer to the local eating scene, it's a branch of a popular chain based in Tel Aviv and has been quick to build a loyal local following. We prefer the noodles, soups and curries to the sushi and sashimi.

Last Refuge
SEAFOOD **$$$**

(Map p321; ☑08-637 3627; www.hamiflat.co.il; Coral Beach; mains 88-110NIS; ☺12.30pm-midnight) Stuck in a 1970s time warp (kitsch fishing nets dangle from the ceiling, Tom Jones rules the sound system and garlic butter figures heavily on the menu), this place opposite the SeaCoral Hotel promises little on first inspection but confounds the sceptic with its delicious catch of the day grilled over coals. A taxi from North Beach costs around 40NIS.

Eddie's Hide-A-Way
INTERNATIONAL **$$$**

(Map p322; ☑08-637 1137; www.eddieshide-away.rest.e.co.il; 68 Aghmonim St; mains 46-125NIS; ☺6-11.30pm Mon-Fri, 2-11.30pm Sat) The surrounds and menu have hardly changed since this ramshackle place opened back in 1979, so it's a testament to Eddie's abilities as a host that it's been packed most nights since. The food is hit and miss, but you're sure to be happy with a steak and a bottle from the unexpectedly impressive wine list. Enter off Eilot Ave.

Casa do Brasil
STEAK **$$$**

(Map p322; ☑08-632 3032; www.casadobrasil.co.il; Sderot Hativat Golani 3; set meat menu 170NIS; ☺noon-late) Simpsons fans and hungry carnivores should head here to emulate Homer's all-you-can-eat antics at the 'Frying Dutchmen'. As far as we know, no one has ever had the ignominy of being banished for eating too much. The set meat menu includes 11 cuts – some of these were over-cooked when we visited but others were fine.

Drinking & Nightlife

The drinking scene in Eilat is largely confined to raucous pubs in the North Beach precinct. The club scene is healthy but venues have short lifespans and hotspots change every season – staff at your hotel or at the tourist office on North Beach Promenade will be able to give you the lowdown.

Mike's Place
SPORTS BAR

(Map p322; ☑08-864 9550; www.MikesPlaceBars.com; King Solomon Promenade; ☺11am-late) Mike certainly gets around. Here in Eilat he has staked a claim to a space under the King Solomon Hotel and opened yet another branch of his national sports bar empire. There are a few outdoor tables overlooking the marina, but most of the action – including big TV screens and live music after 10pm on weekends – occurs inside.

Three Monkeys Pub
PUB

(Map p322; ☑08-636 8877; www.threemonkeys pub.co.il; North Beach Promenade; ☺9pm-3am) Inevitably packed with sunburnt tourists, this place is popular due to its location on the boardwalk and the fact that it hosts live bands most nights from 11pm in high season. Be warned that drinks are expensive and service can be both slow and abrupt.

Café Café
BAR, CAFE

(Map p322; www.cafecafe.co.il; North Beach Promenade; ☺8am-1am) There are two branches of this Israeli chain in Eilat, the best of which is undoubtedly this venue in front of the Dan Eilat Hotel. Its expansive terrace overlooks the beach action and is scattered with umbrellas and comfy couches. It's a pleasant spot to enjoy a coffee, beer or cocktail.

Shopping

Eilat is a VAT-free city, so prices should be lower than elsewhere in the country. It must be said that our experience doesn't necessarily attest to this.

Ice Park Mall
MALL

(Map p322; http://ice-mall-eilat.com; cnr Kampen & Piestany Sts; ☺9.30am-11.45pm) The main draw at this glass-domed complex behind the Eilat Lagoon is an Olympic-size

SECURITY ALERT

Always check the security situation with the tourist office in Eilat before driving along route 12, which hugs the border with Egypt and has been the site of terrorist incidents in the past. Hikers should do the same with the SPNI Field School near Coral Beach before setting out anywhere in the border region.

ice-skating rink that is popular with families. Shops are clustered around the rink and offer stock-standard mall fare.

Mall HaYam   MALL

(Map p322; http://mallhayam.co.il; Ha-Palmakh St 1; ⊙9am-11pm Sat-Wed, 9am-midnight Thu, 9am-6pm Fri) Eilat's major mercantile draw, Mall HaYam is right on the seafront and is where locals and tourists come to buy up big in high-street stores including Zara, Mango and the local equivalent, Castro.

ℹ Information

EMERGENCY

Police Station (☑08-636 2444, 100; Hativat HaNegev Ave)

Tourist Police (North Beach Promenade; ⊙hours vary) This station is near the tourist information office at North Beach.

Yoseftal Hospital (☑08-635 8015; cnr Yotam Rd & Argaman Ave; ⊙24hr emergency dept)

MONEY

To change money, head for one of the many exchange bureaus in the old commercial centre off HaTmarim Blvd, the post office in the Red Canyon Centre or branches of Bank Leumi.

POST

Post Office (Map p322; Red Canyon Mall; ⊙8am-6pm Sun-Tue & Thu, 8am-1.30pm Wed, 8am-noon Fri)

TOURIST INFORMATION

Tourist Information Office (Map p322; ☑08-630 9111; eilatinfo@tourism.gov.il; Bridge House, North Beach Promenade; ⊙8.30am-5pm Sun-Thu, 8am-1pm Fri) This extremely helpful office answers questions, supplies free maps and brochures and sells second-hand English, French and German books.

ℹ Getting There & Away

The Yitzhak Rabin–Wadi Araba border crossing between Israel and Jordan is about 5km north-

east of Eilat, and the Taba border crossing with Egypt is about 8.5km southwest.

AIR

Eilat's municipal **airport** (☑1 700 705 022; www.iaa.gov.il/Rashat/en-US/Airports/Eilat) is right in the heart of town. There are plans for a new airport to be built in Timna, north of Eilat – when completed (estimated dates vary wildly, and some cynical locals doubt if it will ever happen) it will replace the current civil airports in Eilat and at the Ovda air-force base.

Both **Arkia** (☑08-638 4888; www.arkia. com; Red Canyon Mall) and **Israir** (☑1 700 505 777; www.israirairlines.com; Shalom Centre) fly several times daily between Eilat and Sde Dov and Ben-Gurion airports in Tel Aviv (from US$25, 35 minutes).

Ovda Airport (p412) is about 67km north of the centre of Eilat. It serves occasional charter flights from Europe as well as Arkia and El Al flights, but its distance from town means it's not the most convenient landing post.

BUS

Egged services to Tel Aviv (bus 393, 394 or 790, 82NIS, five hours) depart from the central bus station every 90 minutes or two hours from 5am to 7pm, with an additional overnight service at 1am. Services on Fridays and Saturdays are greatly reduced. It's a good idea to reserve long-haul bus tickets for travel to/from Eilat via www. egged.co.il or by calling ☑2800; reservations can be made up to two weeks ahead.

Bus 392 to Be'er Sheva (60NIS, three hours) stops at Ovda Airport (25NIS, 45 minutes) and Mitzpe Ramon (49NIS, 2¼ hours). To Jerusalem (bus 444, 82NIS, five hours) there are four buses per day between 7am and 5pm; these pass through Ein Gedi (49.50NIS, three hours). Services on Fridays and Saturdays are greatly reduced.

There are no direct buses from Eilat to Cairo.

ℹ Getting Around

The town centre is walkable, but you'll need a bus or taxi for locations along the Taba road. Bus 15 leaves from the central bus station and travels to the Taba border crossing via Coral Beach (4.90NIS, 30 minutes) every hour from 8am to 9pm Sunday to Thursday, 8am to 3pm Friday and 9am to 7pm Saturday. It changes to bus 16 for the return trip. A taxi from the town centre to the border crossing costs around 60NIS.

To reach the Yitzhak Rabin–Wadi Arava border crossing into Jordan, you'll have to take a taxi (45NIS).

CAR

You can rent a car by calling Eldan, Hertz or Budget, located with a number of other car-hire companies in the Shalom Centre opposite the airport.

Budget (☏ 03-935 0016; www.budget.co.il)
Eldan (☏ 08-637 4027; www.eldan.co.il)
Hertz (☏ 08-637 5050; www.hertz.co.il/en)

TAXI
Although distances are short, the heat means that using taxis to get around can be a good option. A taxi from the airport to most parts of the city centre or North Beach will cost around 20NIS; to Coral Beach you'll be looking at 45NIS.

Around Eilat

Eilat is surrounded by jagged, red-rock mountains created by the tectonic movements of the Great Rift Valley (Syrian-African Rift). The desert environment, blazing with glorious colours (especially at sunrise and sunset), is home to a huge variety of wildlife, flora and fauna.

Hikers will want to head for the Eilat Mountains. Popular treks include the six-hour climb up **Mt Shlomo**, which rewards hikers with views to Jordan, across the Arava Valley and (on a clear day) across the Gulf of Eilat. The start and end points of this walk are different, so you'll need two cars. A handout with map and directions is available from the SPNI Field School.

An excellent six- to seven-hour hike will take you through the spectacular **Nakhal Gishron** (part of the Israel National Trail) from Har Yoash to the Egyptian border. Details are available at the field school.

Petra

البتراء

Best Places to Eat & Drink

➡ Cave Bar (p339)

➡ Al-Saraya Restaurant (p339)

➡ Petra Kitchen (p336)

➡ Red Cave Restaurant (p339)

➡ Basin Restaurant (p333)

Best Places to Stay

➡ Mövenpick Hotel (p337)

➡ Amra Palace Hotel (p339)

➡ Petra Palace Hotel (p337)

➡ Petra Guest House Hotel (p337)

➡ Cleopetra Hotel (p337)

➡ Rocky Mountain Hotel (p337)

Why Go?

The ancient Nabataean city of Petra, with its elaborate architecture chiselled out of the pink-hued cliffs, is not just the leading highlight of Jordan, a country blessed with more than its fair share of top sites: it's a wonder of the world. It lay forgotten for centuries, known only to the Bedouin who made it their home, until the great Swiss explorer Jean Louis Burckhardt happened upon it in 1812.

Built partly in honour of the dead, the Petra necropolis retains much of its sense of hidden mystery thanks to its inaccessible location in the heart of a windblown landscape. Reached via the Siq, a narrow rift in the land whose cliffs cast long shadows across the once-sacred way, the path suddenly slithers into sunlight in front of the Treasury – a spectacle that cannot fail to impress. Add to this the cheerfulness of the Bedouin people, and it's easy to see what makes Petra a must-visit.

When to Go

Wadi Musa

Mar–May It's peak tourist season and for good reason, with flowering oleanders and safe hiking.

Mid–Oct–end Nov A last chance to visit Petra in good weather before rains put some routes off limits.

Dec–Jan Bitterly cold by night and bright blue skies by day, Petra is almost empty in winter.

History

Petra was established in the 4th century BCE by the Nabataeans, a nomadic tribe from Arabia. In its heyday, the city was home to around 30,000 people, including scribes and engineers who built a city of sophisticated culture with an emphasis on the afterlife. Around 100 CE, the Romans assumed control, leaving trademark features such as the colonnaded street.

Earthquakes in 363 and 551 ruined much of Petra and it became a forgotten outpost, known only to local Bedouin who preferred to keep its whereabouts secret. In 1812, a young Swiss explorer, JL Burckhardt, ended Petra's splendid isolation, riding into the city disguised as a Muslim holy man.

During the 1950s, Petra achieved near-mythological status in Israel, and a number of young Israelis risked – and in some cases lost – their lives trying to visit the site surreptitiously.

A Unesco World Heritage Site since 1985, Petra was elected one of the 'New Seven Wonders of the World' by an international public poll in 2008, proving that its allure has survived two centuries worth of outside scrutiny.

❶ Getting There & Away

It's almost impossible to cover Petra as a day trip from Israel or the West Bank by public transport.

The **Yitzhak Rabin–Wadi Araba border crossing** (☑ 08-630 0555; ☺ 6.30am-10pm Sun-Thu, 8am-8pm Fri & Sat) provides the easiest access to Jordan. From Eilat it's a short taxi ride (50NIS) to the border. On the Jordanian side, a taxi to Petra costs around JD60 (JD80 return). Alternatively, take a taxi into Aqaba (JD10) and a minibus to Petra (JD5, 2½ hours, 120km); these leave when full between 6am and 7am, and there is also an occasional service between 11am and noon.

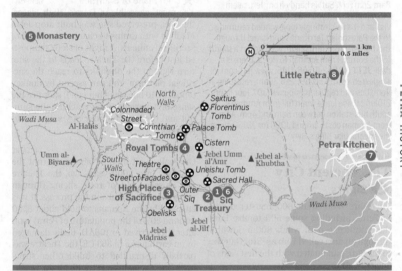

Petra Highlights

❶ Treading the path of history by winding through the **Siq** (p332) leading to an ancient world.

❷ Catching the early morning sun slanting off the pillars of the **Treasury** (p332), a sublime spectacle.

❸ Climbing to the **High Place of Sacrifice** (p332), pause for tea with the Bedouin and return to the valley floor through a garden of wildflowers.

❹ Searching the **Royal Tombs** (p332) for spirits lurking in the rainbow-coloured hollows.

❺ Making the pilgrimage to the **Monastery** (p333) and watching the stones catch alight at sunset.

❻ Letting your soul glide through the Siq's shadows, guided by music and candlelight on tour with **Petra by Night** (p336).

❼ Preparing your own traditional Jordanian supper at **Petra Kitchen** (p336).

❽ Visiting **Little Petra** (p342) and enjoying Nabataean tombs and temples in a miniature siq without the company of tour groups.

FAST FACTS ON JORDAN

Capital Amman

Country code ✑962

Petra area code ✑03

Language Arabic

Visas Most nationalities can get a two-week Jordanian visa free of charge at the Yitzhak Rabin crossing. An exit tax of 100NIS is payable on leaving Israel. The Allenby–King Hussein Bridge border crossing does not issue Jordanian visas. It costs JD40 to enter Jordan through Queen Alia Airport. Jordanian exit tax costs JD10.

The **Allenby–King Hussein Bridge border crossing** (✑02-548 2600; ☺8am-8pm Sun-Thu, 8am-2pm Fri & Sat) is handy from Jerusalem (45 minutes), but you must have a pre-arranged visa and it's frustratingly long-winded returning to the Palestinian Territories and Israel through this border. From Jerusalem, you can get a *sherut* to the border. From Amman to Petra, there is a daily **JETT** (✑962-6-566 4146; www.jett.com.jo; single/return JD9.50/19; ☺6.30am, returning at 4pm) bus and regular minibuses (JD7, four hours, 210km); these leave when full from Amman's south bus station between 6am and 4pm. A taxi from Amman costs around JD90 (or JD130 along the spectacular King's Hwy).

The Ancient City
◉ Sights

There are more than 800 registered sites in Petra, including some 500 tombs. From the entrance, a path winds 800m downhill through an area called **Bab as-Siq** (Gateway to the Siq), punctuated with the first signs of ancient Petra.

Beware that Petra is crowned with 'high places' of ancient religious significance. These locations, affording magnificent views, usually involve steep steps to a hilltop where there is no railing or other safety features.

★ Siq   CANYON
The 1.2km siq, or canyon, with its narrow, vertical walls, is undeniably one of the highlights of Petra. The walk through this magical corridor, as it snakes its way towards the hidden city, is one full of anticipation for the wonders ahead – a point not wasted on the Nabataeans who made the passage into a sacred way, punctuated with sites of spiritual significance.

★ Treasury (Al-Khazneh)   TOMB
Known locally as the Treasury, this tomb is where most visitors fall in love with Petra. The Hellenistic facade is an astonishing piece of craftsmanship. Although carved out of iron-laden sandstone to serve as a tomb for the Nabataean King Aretas III, the Treasury derives its name from the story that an Egyptian pharaoh hid his treasure here (in the facade urn) while pursuing the Israelites.

Street of Facades   TOMB
From the Treasury, the passage broadens into what is commonly referred to as the Outer Siq. Riddling the walls of the Outer Siq are over 40 tombs and houses built by the Nabataeans in a 'crow step' style reminiscent of Assyrian architecture. Colloquially known as the Street of Facades, they are easily accessible, unlike many tombs in Petra.

★ High Place of Sacrifice   VIEWPOINT
The most accessible of Petra's 'High Places', this well-preserved site was built atop Jebel Madbah with drains to channel the blood of sacrificial animals. A flight of steps signposted just before the Theatre leads to the site: turn right at the **obelisks** to reach the sacrificial platform. You can ascend by donkey (about JD10 one way), but you'll sacrifice the sense of achievement on reaching the summit and the good humour of your poor old transport.

Theatre   THEATRE
Originally built by the Nabataeans (not the Romans) over 2000 years ago, the Theatre was chiselled out of rock, slicing through many caves and tombs in the process. It was enlarged by the Romans to hold about 8500 (around 30% of the population of Petra) soon after they arrived in 106AD. Badly damaged by an earthquake in 363 CE, the Theatre was partially dismantled to build other structures but it remains a Petra highlight.

★ Royal Tombs   TOMB
Downhill from the Theatre, the wadi widens to create a larger thoroughfare. To the right, the great massif of Jebel al-Khubtha looms over the valley. Within its west-facing cliffs are burrowed some of the most impressive burial places in Petra, known collectively as the 'Royal Tombs'. They look particularly stunning bathed in the golden light of sunset.

Colonnaded Street   ANCIENT THOROUGHFARE
Downhill from the Theatre, the Colonnaded Street marks Petra's city centre. The street was built in about 106 CE and follows the

standard Roman pattern of an east–west *decumanus*, but without the normal *cardo maximus* (north–south axis). Columns of marble-clad sandstone originally lined the 6m-wide carriageway, and covered porticoes gave access to shops.

Qasr al-Bint   TEMPLE

One of the few free-standing structures in Petra, Qasr al-Bint was built in around 30 BCE by the Nabataeans. It was later adapted to the cult of Roman emperors and destroyed around the 3rd century CE. Despite the name given to it by the local Bedouin – Castle of the Pharaoh's Daughter – the temple was built as a dedication to Nabataean gods and was one of the most important temples in Petra.

★ Monastery (Al-Deir)   TOMB

Hidden high in the hills, the Monastery is one of the legendary monuments of Petra. Similar in design to the Treasury but far bigger (50m wide and 45m high), it was built in the 3rd century BCE as a Nabataean tomb. It derives its name from the crosses carved on the inside walls, suggestive of its use as a church in Byzantine times. The ancient rock-cut path of more than 800 steps starts from the Nabataean Museum and follows the old processional route.

🏃 Activities

It costs from JD30 for a two- to three-hour horse ride around the surrounding hills. Book a ride through a tour agency in town, or for an adventure, ask the animal handlers near the entrance to take you to their favourite haunt.

Wadi Muthlim to Royal Tombs   HIKING

(moderate; guide mandatory, JD50; 1½ hour one-way) This adventurous 1½-hour canyon hike is an exciting alternative route into Petra if you've already taken the main Siq path. Flash floods are a serious issue in the area and a guide is mandatory. The hike is not difficult or too strenuous, but there are several boulder blockages and in winter you may need to wade through pools of water.

Umm al-Biyara   HIKING

(strenuous; self-guided; 3 hour one-way) The strenuous hike from Qasr al-Bint to Umm al-Biyara (1178m) offers stunning mountain-top views. Legend has it that the flat-topped mountain was once the Edomite capital of Sela, from where the Judaean king Amaziah (r 796–81 BCE) threw 10,000 prisoners to their deaths over the precipice.

Jebel Haroun   HIKING

(strenuous; self-guided or JD150 with guide; 6 hour return) This hike via **Snake Monument** starts from Qasr al-Bint. Jebel Haroun (1350m) is thought to be biblical Mt Hor – burial site of Moses's brother Aaron; a white shrine built in the 14th century marks the site.

🍴 Eating

In addition to the two main restaurants, there are several **stalls** selling tea, soft drinks and snacks scattered around Petra.

★ Basin Restaurant   BUFFET $$

(lunch buffet JD17, fresh orange juice JD4; ⏱noon-4pm; 🌿) The Basin serves a wide spread of international dishes, including a healthy selection of salads, fresh felafel and barbecued spicy sausage. Lots of deserts are also on offer, including fruit and *umm ali* (bread-pudding-like dessert). There's a fully air-conditioned interior seating area or groups sit by the ravine under canvas while

PETRA THE ANCIENT CITY

ℹ️ FINDING YOUR OWN PACE IN PETRA

Instead of trying to 'see it all' (the quickest way to achieve monument fatigue), make Petra your own by sparing time to amble among unnamed tombs or sip tea at a Bedouin stall.

Half day (five hours) Stroll through the Siq, savouring the moment of revelation at the Treasury. Climb the steps to the High Place of Sacrifice and take the path through Wadi Farasa, passing a paintbox of rock formations.

One day (eight hours) Complete the half-day itinerary, but pack a picnic. Visit the Royal Tombs, walk along to Qasr al-Bint and hike the wadi that leads to Jebel Haroun as far as Snake Monument – an ideal perch for a snack and a snooze. Save some energy for the climb to the Monastery, a fitting finale for any Petra visit.

Two days Spend a second day scrambling through exciting Wadi Muthlim and restore energies over a barbecue at the Basin Restaurant. Sit near the Theatre to watch the Royal Tombs at sunset –"the best spectacle in Petra. Reward your efforts with a Turkish bath and a drink in the Cave Bar – the oldest pub in the world.

Petra

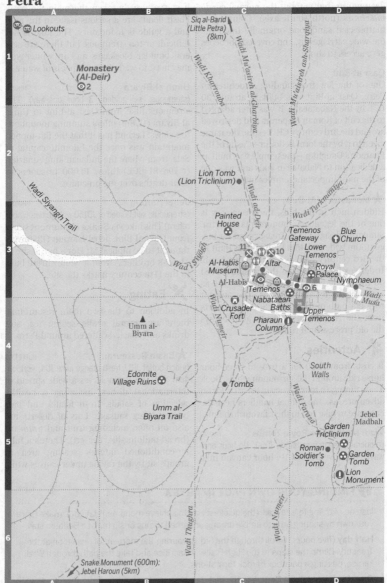

Lookouts

Monastery
(Al-Deir)
◉ 2

Siq al-Barid
(Little Petra)
(8km)

Wadi Kharrouba

Wadi Mu'aisreh al-Gharbiya

Wadi Mu'aisreh ash-Sharqiya

Wadi Siyagh Trail

Lion Tomb
(Lion Triclinium) ●

Wadi ad-Deir

Wadi Turkmaniyya

Wadi Siyagh

Painted
House
☢

11
☢ ☯ ⑪ 10
Al-Habis
Museum 🏛 ⑪ Altar
7 🗿
Al-Habis
☢ Temenos 🏛
Nabataean
Baths
🗿
Crusader
Fort
Pharaun
Column

Temenos
Gateway
Lower
Temenos
Royal
Palace
Upper
Temenos
⊙ 6

Blue
✝ Church

Nymphaeum
*Wadi
Musa*

Wadi Numeir

▲
Umm al-
Biyara

Edomite ◉
Village Ruins

● Tombs

Umm al-
Biyara Trail

South
Walls

Wadi Farasa

Jebel
Madbah

Garden
Triclinium

Roman
Soldier's
Tomb

◉ Garden
Tomb

ⓘ Lion
Monument

Wadi Thughra

Wadi Numeir

Snake Monument (600m);
Jebel Haroun (5km)

independent travellers are given tables under the trees.

Nabataean Tent Restaurant   BUFFET **$$**
(lunch buffet JD10, drinks JD2; ⊙11am-3pm) With simple Jordanian dishes and one or two international favourites, this casual restau-

rant occupies a lovely spot under blue-flowering jacaranda trees (they flower in May). The proprietors rustle up a generous packed lunch with a sandwich, boiled egg, yoghurt and cake for a bargain JD6 and you can eat it on the spot with a Turkish coffee if you wish.

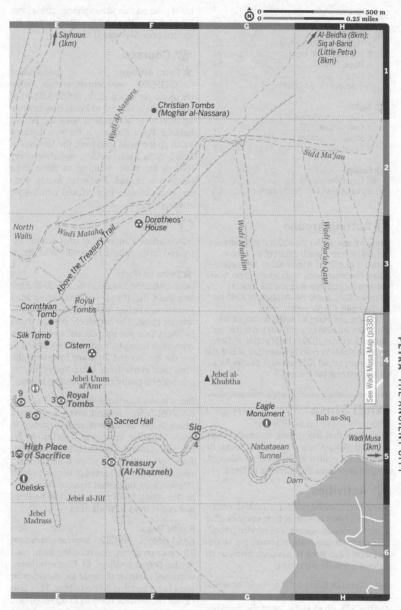

PETRA THE ANCIENT CITY

ℹ Information

Ticket Office (📠/fax 2156044; for one-/two-/three-day passes JD50/55/60; admission free for children under 15 years; 🕐 6am-4pm, to 6pm in summer) The ticket office is in the visitor centre at the entrance to Petra. Although tickets are not sold after 4pm, you can remain in Petra until sunset (5pm in winter). Entry fees are payable only in Jordanian currency and multiday tickets are non-transferable. If visiting Petra as a day trip from Israel and the Palestinian Territories the entry fee is JD90.

Petra

❶ Getting Around

A return horse ride for the 800m stretch between the main entrance and the start of the Siq is included in your ticket. A tip of JD3 or JD4 is appreciated. Horse carriages, seating two people, travel between the main entrance and the Treasury (2km) for JD20, and to the museum for JD40 per carriage, plus JD5 per person in tips.

Donkeys, and mules for longer distances, are available from JD10 for a one-way trip to the High Place of Sacrifice (JD30 to the Monastery). Camels are available for rides between Qasr al-Bint and the Treasury (about JD15 one way), pausing for a photograph near the Theatre.

Wadi Musa وادي موسى

✏ 03 / POP 30,050 / ELEV 1150M

The village that has sprung up around Petra is called Wadi Musa (Valley of Moses). Its commercial centre is Shaheed roundabout, around 3km from the entrance to Petra.

🏃 Activities

Many hotels in Petra offer a Turkish bath – the perfect way to ease aching muscles after a hard day's sightseeing. The service typically includes steam bath, massage, hot stones and scrubbing. Book in advance; women can request a female attendant.

Petra Turkish Bath BATHHOUSE
(✉03-2157085; ⊘3-10pm) In the passage under the Silk Road Hotel, near the entrance of Petra, this hammam has a completely separate bath area for women, with female attendants.

Salome Turkish Bath BATHHOUSE
(✉03-2157342; ⊘4-10pm) Entered via a grotto displaying old farming implements, this

bathhouse has an atmospheric sitting area for relaxing with a herb tea after bathing. It's located near Al-Anbat II Hotel.

🍃 Courses

★ **Petra Kitchen** COOKING COURSE
(✉03-2155700; www.petrakitchen.com; cookery course per person JD35; ⊘6.30-9.30pm) If you've always wanted to know how to whip up wonderful hummus or bake the perfect baklava, Petra Kitchen is for you. Located 100m up the main road from the Mövenpick Hotel, Petra Kitchen offers nightly cookery courses for those wanting to learn from locals how to cook Jordanian mezze, soup and main courses in a relaxed family-style atmosphere.

☞ Tours

Hotels arrange simple day trips around Petra and further afield, especially Wadi Rum.

★ **Petra by Night** TOUR
(adult/child under 10yr JD12/free; ⊘8.30-10.30pm Mon, Wed & Thu) If you were wondering what Petra would be like under the stars, then you are not alone. The extremely popular Petra by Night Tour was introduced in response to numerous requests from visitors wanting to see the siq and Treasury by moonlight. The 'tour' starts from Petra Visitor Centre (cancelled if raining), and lasts two hours.

Petra Moon Tourism Services TOUR
(✉07-96170666; www.petramoon.com) Petra Moon is the most professional agency in Wadi Musa for arranging trips inside Petra and around Jordan (including Wadi Rum and Aqaba). The office is on the main road to Petra. It can arrange horses to Jebel Haroun, fully supported treks to Dana (four to five days), hikes from Tayyibeh to Petra and camel treks to Wadi Rum.

Raami Tours TOUR
(✉03-2154551, 2154010; www.raamitours.com) This tour company, based on the main road in the Bedouin village of Umm Sayhoun, organises traditional meals for visitors who want to try genuine homecooking. They also design tailor-made tours to fit all schedules, special interests and budgets (email at least three days ahead of arrival).

🛏 Sleeping

You can't stay overnight in Petra itself. The prices quoted here are for high-season accommodation with bathroom and breakfast and include taxes.

🛏 Lower Wadi Musa

Many hotels are located within walking distance of the entrance to Petra.

★ Petra Palace Hotel HOTEL $$
(📞 03-2156723; www.petrapalace.com.jo; s/d/tr JD49/70/95; ✱@🛜🏊) Located on the main street, 500m from the entrance to Petra, this attractive and well-established hotel – with its palm-tree entrance, big bright foyer and helpful management – is an excellent choice. A whole suite of rooms open onto the outdoor swimming pool. The lively bar and restaurant are also drawcards.

Silk Road Hotel HOTEL $$
(📞 03-2157222; www.petrasilkroad.com; JD40/65/85; ✱) Hand-painted panels of Bedouin camps stretch across the foyer and restaurant walls of this old favourite, 300m from the entrance to Petra. The common areas in lavender hues may not be to everyone's taste but the rooms all sport decent furniture and big bathtubs. Some rooms are very dark so ask for one with a view.

★ Petra Guest House Hotel HOTEL $$$
(📞 03-2156266; www.guesthouse-petra.com; s/d/tr JD90/105/125; ✱🛜) You can't get closer to the entrance to Petra without sleeping in a cave – and indeed the hotel's bar (the famous Cave Bar) is located in one. Choose from spacious, motel-like chalets or sunny (if cramped) rooms in the main building. The staff are unfailingly delightful and the breakfast buffet is superior to most. Offers excellent value for money.

★ Mövenpick Hotel LUXURY HOTEL $$$
(📞 2157111; www.moevenpick-hotels.com; r from JD185; ✱@🛜🏊) This beautifully crafted Arabian-style hotel, 100m from the entrance to Petra, is worth a visit simply to admire the inlaid furniture, marble fountains, wooden screens and brass salvers. As the hotel is in the bottom of the valley, there are no views but the large and super-luxurious rooms all have huge windows regardless. The buffet breakfast and dinner are exceptional.

🛏 Wadi Musa Town Centre

Many hotels are near the bus station. Free transport to and from the entrance to Petra is usually offered once a day.

★ Cleopetra Hotel HOTEL $
(📞 03-2157090; www.cleopetrahotel.com; s/d/tr JD20/30/40; @🛜) This continues to be the friendliest and most efficient budget hotel in town. It has bright, fresh rooms with private bathrooms and hot water. There's a communal sitting area in the lobby which is ideal for meeting fellow travellers and rooftop developments are planned. Wi-fi is available for JD2.

Rocky Mountain Hotel HOTEL $
(📞 03-2155100; rockymountainhotel@yahoo.com; s/d/tr/q JD26/39/50/60, buffet dinner JD8; ✱@🛜) This backpacker-friendly hotel near the junction with the main road into town has caught just the right vibe to make it a successful travellers' lodge. The hotel is 'big on cleanliness' and there's a cosy communal area with free tea and coffee and a majlis-style roof terrace makes the most of the impressive sweeping views.

WALKING TIMES

These are indications of one-way walking times at a leisurely pace. At a faster pace without stopping, you can hike from Petra Visitor Centre to the Treasury in 20 minutes, and the museum in 40 minutes, along the main thoroughfare. Don't forget to double the time for the uphill return journey.

DIRECT ROUTE	TIME	DIFFICULTY
Visitor Centre to Siq Entrance	15min	easy
Siq Entrance to Treasury	20min	easy
Treasury to Royal Tombs	20min	easy
Treasury to Obelisk at High Place of Sacrifice	45min	moderate
Obelisk to Museum (via main thoroughfare)	45min	easy
Treasury to Museum	30min	easy
Museum to Monastery	40min	moderate

Wadi Musa

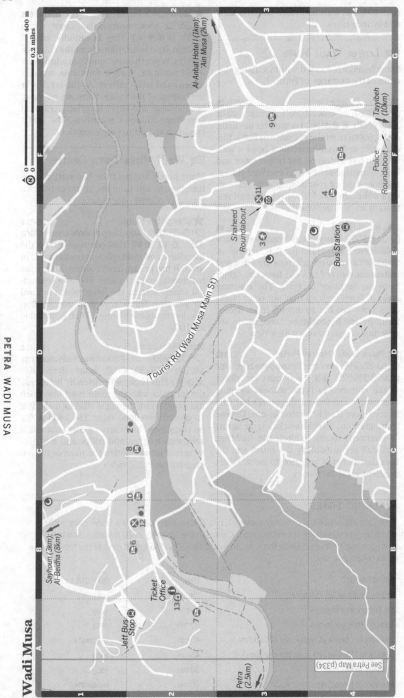

0 400 m
0 0.2 miles

Sayhoun (3km);
Al-Beidha (8km)

Jett Bus Stop

Ticket Office

Petra (2.5km)

See Petra Map (p334)

Tourist Rd (Wadi Musa Main St)

Shaheed Roundabout

Bus Station

Police Roundabout

Tayyibeh (10km)

Al-Anbat Hotel I (1km);
'Ain Musa (2km)

Wadi Musa

Al-Anbat Hotel I   HOTEL $
(☏ 03-2156265; www.alanbat.com; s/d/tr JD20/35/45, buffet lunch or dinner JD10; ❄ @ ⑂ ☒) Located some way out of town, on the road between 'Ain Musa and Wadi Musa, this three-storey resort with a beautiful, brand new lobby with sofas spanning the magnificent view, offers midrange quality for budget prices. The large rooms (many with gorgeous sunset views) have satellite TV and come with a balcony.

★ **Amra Palace Hotel**   HOTEL $$
(☏ 03-2157070;www.amrapalace.com;s/d/trJD44/64/84; ❄ @ ⑂ ☒) This lovely hotel with its pretty garden of roses and jasmine, marble-pillared lobby, giant brass coffeepots and homely furniture offers a more Jordanian sense of hospitality than many of the rather bland hotels in town. The brothers who have run this establishment for many years take a personal interest in the details and it shows.

✕ Eating

Al-Wadi Restaurant   JORDANIAN $
(☏ 03-2157151; salads JD1, mains JD4-5; ☺ 7am-late) Right on Shaheed roundabout, this lively spot offers pasta, as well as a range of vegetarian dishes and local Bedouin specialities such as *gallayah* (meat, rice and onions in a spicy tomato sauce) and *mensaf* (lamb on a bed of rice topped with a lamb's head), most of which come with salad and rice.

★ **Red Cave Restaurant**   JORDANIAN $$
(☏ 2157799; starters JD1, mains from JD5; ☺ 9am-10pm) Cavernous and friendly, this restaurant specialises in local Bedouin specialities including *mensaf* and *maqlubbeh* (steamed rice with meat, grilled tomato and pine nuts). It's a cosy place to come on a chilly evening or to catch the breeze on a hot summer's day.

Al-Saraya Restaurant   INTERNATIONAL $$$
(☏ 2157111; lunch/dinner JD20/JD25; ✎) Serving a top-notch international buffet in an elegant banquet hall, this fine-dining restaurant offers a quality of dishes that matches the general opulence of the Mövenpick Hotel in which it is located. Leave time for a nightcap in the grand, wood-pannelled bar afterwards which sports a roaring fire in the hearth in winter.

☕ Drinking

★ **Cave Bar**   BAR
(☏ 03-2156266; ☺ 4-11pm) You can't come to Petra and miss the oldest bar in the world. Occupying a 2000-year-old Nabataean rock tomb, this blue-lit Petra hot spot has been known to stay open until 4am on busy summer nights. Sit among the spirits, alcoholic or otherwise, and you'll soon get a flavour of Petra you hadn't bargained on (not least the 26% tax and service charge!).

Al-Maqa'ad Bar   BAR
(☏ 03-2157111; ☺ 4-11pm) The Mövenpick Hotel bar has a superb Moroccan-style interior with carved wooden grills and a chandelier: it's worth having a cocktail or an ice-cream special just to enjoy the ambience. A 26% tax and service charge is applied.

Wranglers Pub   BAR
(☏ 03-2156723; ☺ 2pm-midnight) The Petra Palace Hotel runs this sociable bar, decorated with assorted local memorabilia.

🛍 Shopping

The **Wadi Musa Ladies Society** (☺ 6am-9pm) and the **Society for the Development and Rehabilitation of Rural Women** (☺ 6am-9pm) both have shops at the visitor centre selling a range of souvenirs, books and crafts.

Petra

WALKING TOUR

Splendid though it is, the Treasury is not the full stop of a visit to Petra that many people may imagine. In some ways, it's just the semicolon – a place to pause after the exertions of the Siq, before exploring the other remarkable sights and wonders just around the corner.

Even if you're on a tight schedule or worried the bus won't wait, try to find another two hours in your itinerary to complete this walking tour. Our illustration shows the key highlights of the route, as you wind through Wadi Musa from the Siq ①, pause at the Treasury ② and pass the tombs of the broader Outer Siq ③. With energy and a stout pair of shoes, climb to the High Place of Sacrifice ④ for a magnificent eagle's-eye view of Petra. Return to the Street of Facades ⑤ and the Theatre ⑥. Climb the steps opposite to the Urn Tomb ⑦ and neighbouring Silk Tomb ⑧: these Royal Tombs are particularly magnificent in the golden light of sunset.

Is the thought of all that walking putting you off? Don't let it! There are donkeys to help you with the steep ascents and Bedouin stalls for a reviving herb tea. If you run out of steam, camels are on standby for a ride back to the Treasury.

TOP TIPS

» **Morning Glory** From around 7am in summer and 8am in winter, watch the early morning sun slide down the Treasury facade.

» **Pink City** Stand opposite the Royal Tombs at sunset (around 4pm in winter and 5pm in summer) to learn how Petra earned its nickname.

» **Floral Tribute** Petra's oleanders flower in May.

Treasury

As you watch the sun cut across the facade, notice how it lights up the ladders on either side of Petra's most iconic building. These stone indents were most probably used for scaffolding.

Jebel Madbah

Jebel al-Khubtha

To Entrance to Petra

Siq

This narrow cleft in the land forms the sublime approach to the ancient city of Petra. Most people walk through the corridor of stone but horse-carts are available for those who need them.

DOWN DIFFERENTLY

A superb walk leads from the High Place of Sacrifice, past the Garden Tomb to Petra City Centre.

High Place of Sacrifice

Imagine the ancients treading the stone steps and it'll take your mind off the steep ascent. The hilltop platform was used for incense-burning and libation-pouring in honour of forgotten gods.

Outer Siq

Take time to inspect the tombs just past the Treasury. Some appear to have a basement but, in fact, they show how the floor of the wadi has risen over the centuries.

Street of Facades

Cast an eye at the upper storeys of some of these tombs and you'll see a small aperture. Burying the dead in attics was meant to deter robbers – the plan didn't work.

Stairs to High Place

Souvenir shops, teashops & toilets

Wadi Musa

5

6

Wadi Musa

To Petra City Centre →

7

Jebel Umm al'Amr (1066m)

Royal Tombs

8

Royal Tombs

HEAD FOR HEIGHTS

For a regal view of Petra, head for the heights above the Royal Tombs, via the staircase.

Urn Tomb

Earning its name from the urn-shaped finial crowning the pediment, this grand edifice with supporting arched vaults was perhaps built for the man represented by the toga-wearing bust in the central aperture.

Silk Tomb

Perhaps Nabataean builders were attracted to Wadi Musa because of the colourful beauty of the raw materials. Nowhere is this more apparent than in the weather-eroded, striated sandstone of the Silk Tomb.

Theatre

Most stone amphitheatres are freestanding, but this one is carved almost entirely from the solid rock. Above the back row are the remains of earlier tombs, their facades sacrificed in the name of entertainment.

Made in Jordan
HANDICRAFTS

(☑2155700) This shop sells quality crafts from local enterprises. Products include olive oil, soap, paper, ceramics, table runners, nature products from Wild Jordan in Amman, jewellery from Wadi Musa, embroidery from Safi, camel hair shawls, and bags from Aqaba as well as Jordan River Foundation goods. The fixed prices reflect the quality and uniqueness of each piece; credit cards are accepted.

ⓘ Information

EMERGENCY

Main Police Station (☑ 03-2156551, emergency 191) Adjacent to the police roundabout.
Tourist Police Station (☑ 03-2156441, emergency 196; ⊘8am-midnight) Opposite Petra Visitor Centre.

INTERNET ACCESS

Rum Internet (per hr JD1; ⊘10am-midnight)
Seven Wonders Restaurant (per hr JD3.500; ⊘9am-11pm)

MEDICAL SERVICES

Queen Rania Hospital (☑ 03-2150628) High-standard healthcare; open for emergencies without referral. Located 5km from the police roundabout on the road to Tayyibeh.
Wadi Musa Pharmacy Located near the Shaheed roundabout.

MONEY

The banks on Shaheed roundabout have ATMs. For changing money, banks are open from about 8am to 2pm Sunday to Thursday and (sometimes) 9am to 11am on Friday.

POST

Main Post Office (⊘8am-5pm Sat-Thu) Located inside a miniplaza on the Shaheed roundabout.

TOURIST INFORMATION

The best source of information is Petra Visitor Centre. The easiest way to find information about transport is to ask at your hotel or log on to **Jordan Jubilee** (www.jordanjubilee.com).

ⓘ Getting Around

Wadi Musa bus station is in the town centre, a 10-minute walk uphill from the entrance to Petra. Private (yellow) unmetered taxis shuttle between the two (around JD3).

Siq al-Barid (Little Petra)
السيق البارد (البتراء الصغيرة)

Siq al-Barid (Cold Canyon), a resupply post for caravans visiting Petra, is well worth a visit. Nearby camps offer a rural alternative to hotels in Wadi Musa.

◉ Sights

★ Little Petra Siq
RUIN

(⊘daylight hours) **FREE** From the car park, an obvious path leads to the 400m-long siq, which opens out into larger areas. The first open area has a **temple**, which archaeologists know little about. Four **triclinia** – one on the left and three on the right – are in the second open area, and were probably used as dining rooms to feed hungry merchants and travellers. About 50m further along the siq is the **Painted House**, another small dining room, which is reached by some exterior steps.

Al-Beidha
RUIN

(⊘daylight hours) **FREE** The Neolithic ruins of **Al-Beidha** date back 9000 years and, along with Jericho, constitute one of the oldest archaeological sites in the Middle East. The remains of around 65 round (and later rectangular) structures are especially significant because they pinpoint the physical transition from hunter-gatherer to settled herder-agriculturalist communities. The settlement was abandoned around 6000 BCE.

A 15-minute walking trail, starting left of the entrance to Little Petra, leads to the site.

🛏 Sleeping & Eating

Seven Wonders Bedouin Camp CAMP $
(☑ 079 7958641; rockymountainhotel@yahoo.com; half board per person in tent JD30, B&B JD20) Signposted along a track off the road to Little Petra, and tucked discreetly into a hillside, this relaxed and good-value camp looks particularly magical at night when the open fires are burning and the rocks behind the camp are illuminated. Accommodation is in simple but cosy cabins with electric light, carpets and mosquito nets. Hot water and towels are available.

Ammarin Bedouin Camp CAMP $$
(☑ 079 5667771; www.bedouincamp.net; half board per person in tent JD52) A 10-minute walk from Little Petra and signposted off the approach road, this camp is in Siq al-Amti, hidden in a spectacular amphitheatre of sand and hills, and run by the local Ammarin tribe. Accommodation comprises mattress and blankets in a sectioned Bedouin tent with concrete floors, with a clean shower and toilet block. Reservations are essential.

ⓘ Getting There & Away

From Wadi Musa, a private taxi costs about JD22 one way or JD32 return, including an hour's waiting time. Alternatively, Little Petra is a pleasant 8km walk following the road.

Understand Israel & the Palestinian Territories

Israel & the Palestinian Territories Today

There's no denying that Israel and the Palestinian Territories are currently in a very difficult time, as the Hamas–Israel war of 2014 left tensions running high. Attacks, riots and violent outbreaks across the region continue and the possibility of reconciliation seems low. However, many Israelis and Palestinians still hope for a more stable future and get on with their lives as peaceably as they can.

Best Non-Fiction

My Promised Land: The Triumph and Tragedy of Israel (Ari Shavit, 2013) A penetrating personal look at Israel's existential fears.

The Iron Cage: The Story of the Palestinian Struggle for Statehood (Rashid Khalidi, 2007) Delves into Palestinian attempts to achieve independence and their failure.

Best Films

Sallah Shabbati (Ephraim Kishon, 1964) Satire about immigrant life in a 1950s transit camp.

Yossi & Jagger (Eytan Fox, 2002) Secret love between two IDF officers.

Omar (Hany Abu-Assad, 2013) Oscar-nominated thriller and love story set in the West Bank.

Best Documentaries

The Flat (2011) A filmmaker looks at his German-Jewish roots.

Strangers No More (2010) A South Tel Aviv elementary school takes in refugee children.

Precious Life (2010) A Gaza baby fights for medical treatment in Israel.

Top Football Teams

Maccabi Haifa Twelve-time Israeli champions.

Hapoel Ironi Kiryat Shmona Surprise Premier League powerhouse.

Palestine National Football Team Represents the Palestinian Territories internationally.

Prospects for Peace

The Hamas–Israel war ended with few real gains for either side. Although both parties claimed victory, the open-ended, Egyptian-sponsored ceasefire did little to solve the underlying causes of the conflict, including the partial Israeli and Egyptian blockade of Gaza, the continuing occupation, the statelessness of Palestinians and Hamas's implacable opposition to peace with Israel. Israel's economy suffered from the direct costs of the conflict and a significant drop in tourism, while Gazans' dire economic situation and living conditions were made worse than ever; they have many years of rebuilding ahead of them. With Israelis now feeling more vulnerable both militarily and in the court of world public opinion (and possibly, along with Hamas, in the International Criminal Court in the Hague), and Palestinian Islamists further radicalised by the death and destruction, moderates are facing an uphill battle.

Israeli Prime Minister Binyamin Netanyahu publicly abandoned what had already been a questionable commitment to a two-state solution to the conflict during his most recent election campaign. His statements ruling out an eventual Palestinian state put him further at odds with the US and much of the international community.

Netanyahu, who won his fourth consecutive term in March 2015, also declared that his latest right-wing coalition government will continue to expand Jewish settlements.

The leadership of the Palestinian Authority, President Mahmoud Abbas and his prime minister, Rami Hamdallah, have a long record of support for a two-state solution, but have seemed reluctant to make any bold moves. Abbas has been putting his efforts into having the State of Palestine recognised by international bodies such as the United Nations, and has demanded that the international community set a date for an end to Israel's occupation.

Both sides' antipathy towards each other is currently as deep as it has ever been and both are even more entrenched in irreconcilable positions. It remains to be seen whether the bleak postwar atmosphere will present any diplomatic opportunities.

'Price Tag' Attacks

Hardline Jewish settlers in the West Bank see the outcome of the 1967 Six Day War as a miracle that proves we are living in the messianic age, and view the 1993 Oslo Accords and the 2005 Gaza withdrawal as nothing short of apostasy against God and his commandments. Since 2008, some of them have been employing violence to deter the Israeli government from implementing certain policies – for instance, against settlement outposts deemed illegal by the Israeli courts. These 'price tag' *(tag mechir)* attacks, as they are known, involve defacing mosques, smashing Palestinians' car windshields, setting fire to Palestinian fields and cutting down olive trees, and – more recently – vandalising churches and harassing Christian clergy in Jerusalem.

'Price tag' activists do not shy away from using threats and violence against their fellow Israeli Jews, and on several occasions have defaced the homes of left-wing activists, stoned the Israeli police and vandalised IDF vehicles and equipment.

In the aftermath of the 2014 Hamas–Israel war, as deadly Palestinian attacks on Jews in Jerusalem soared, so did attacks on Palestinians by bands of Jewish extremists, some of them inspired by the radical 'price tag' logic of revenge and intimidation.

The source of the 'price tag' ideology is the 'Hilltop Youth', second-generation settlers who believe that Halacha (Jewish law) takes precedence over laws enacted by the Knesset or decisions by Israeli courts, and see themselves as uncompromising patriots and self-sacrificing heroes. Most Israelis see them as messianic fanatics who imperil Israeli democracy – and worry that their aggression will lead to another Israeli-on-Israeli political assassination and tit-for-tat violence by radical Palestinians.

POPULATION ISRAEL:
8.2 MILLION (INCLUDING 550,000 JEWS WHO LIVE IN THE WEST BANK AND EAST JERUSALEM)

POPULATION WEST BANK:
2.7 MILLION

POPULATION GAZA:
1.8 MILLION

if Israel were 100 people

75 would be Jewish
17 would be Muslim
2 would be Christian
2 would be Druze
4 would be Other

if West Bank were 100 people

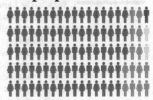

83 would be Muslim
14 would be Jewish
2 would be Christian
1 would be Other

population per sq km

Israel   West Bank   Gaza

👤 ≈ 400 people

History

The land that holds Israel and the Palestinian Territories has been inhabited – and contested – since the dawn of civilisation. A litany of the empires and kingdoms that have ruled the country reads like a Who's Who of Western and Middle Eastern history: there are Egyptians and Canaanites, Israelites and Philistines, Greeks and Judeans, Romans and Byzantines, Arabs and Crusaders (and, briefly, Mongols), Ottomans and British. Each left behind fascinating evidence of their aspirations and follies for modern-day travellers to explore.

Ancient Times

Because the terms BC (Before Christ) and AD (Anno Domini, ie the 'Year of Our Lord') assume Christian belief, we use the religion-neutral abbreviations BCE (Before the Common Era) and CE (Common Era), standard practice in most academic writing.

The land now occupied by Israel and the Palestinian Territories has been inhabited by human beings and their forebears for some two million years. Between 10,000 and 8000 BCE – a little later than in nearby Mesopotamia – people in places such as Jericho switched from hunting to the production of grain and the domestication of animals.

During the 3rd millennium BCE, the area was occupied by semi-nomadic tribes of pastoralists. By the late 2nd millennium BCE urban centres had emerged, and it is clear from Egyptian documents that the pharaohs had significant interests and influence in the area. Around 1800 BCE, Abraham is believed to have led his nomadic tribe from Mesopotamia to a land the Bible calls Canaan, after the local Canaanite tribes. His descendants were forced to relocate to Egypt because of drought and crop failure, but according to the Bible Moses led them out of slavery and back to the Land of Israel in about 1250 BCE. Conflicts with the Canaanites and Philistines pushed the Israelites to abandon their loose tribal system and unify under King Saul (1050–1010 BCE) and his successors, King David and King Solomon.

Myth and history intersect on the large, flat rock that now lies beneath Jerusalem's golden Dome of the Rock. Originally an altar to Baal or some other pagan deity, the rock is known to Jews as the Stone of Foundation, the place where the universe began and Adam was created out of dust. It's also said to be where Abraham bound his son Isaac in preparation to sacrifice him, as a sign of obedience to God. King Solomon built the First

TIMELINE	2 million BCE	9000 BCE	4500–3500 BCE
	Hominids inhabit Tel Ovadia, 3km south of the Sea of Galilee. Around 780,000 BCE their successors set up camp on the Jordan River 13km north of the Sea of Galilee.	Abundant water and a good climate attract early Neolithic people to Jericho, where they establish a permanent settlement surrounded by a mud-brick wall, grow food crops and flax, and raise goats.	Chalcolithic (pre-Bronze Age) people inhabit small villages in Jordan Valley and on the Golan, producing pottery and stone tools. Food sources include agriculture and domesticated goats and sheep.

Temple (Solomon's Temple) here in the 10th century BCE to serve as the centre of Jewish sacrificial worship.

After Solomon's reign (965–928 BCE), the Jews entered a period of division and periodic subjugation. Two rival entities came into being: the Kingdom of Israel, in what is now the northern West Bank and the Galilee; and the southern Kingdom of Judah, with its capital at Jerusalem. After Sargon II of Assyria (r 722–705 BCE) destroyed the Kingdom of Israel in 720 BCE, the 10 northern tribes disappeared from the historical record (even today, groups around the world claim descent from the 'Ten Lost Tribes').

The Babylonians captured Jerusalem in 586 BCE, destroying the First Temple and exiling the people of Judah to Babylonia (now Iraq). Fifty years later Cyrus II, king of Persia, defeated Babylon and allowed the Jews to return to the Land of Israel. The returning Jews immediately set about constructing the Second Temple, consecrated in 516 BCE.

The earliest extra-biblical mention of Israel is on the Egyptian Museum's Israel Stela (1230 BCE), inscribed with the victory hymn of the Pharaoh Merneptah: 'Plundered is Canaan, carried is Ashkelon, Israel is laid waste.'

Greeks & Maccabees, Romans & Christians

When Alexander the Great died in 323 BCE, Ptolemy, one of his generals, claimed Egypt as his own, founding a line of which Cleopatra would be the last. He also took control of the Land of Israel, but in 200 BCE the Seleucids, another dynasty descended from one of Alexander's generals, captured it.

The 'Hellenistic' period – so called because of the Greek origin of the Seleucids and the Olympian cults they promoted – was marked by conflict between the Sadducees, mostly urban, upper-class Jews who were open to Greek culture and the refined Greek lifestyle, and the Pharisees, who resisted Hellenisation. When the Seleucid king Antiochus IV Epiphanes banned Temple sacrifices, Shabbat and circumcision, the Jews, led by Judah Maccabee, revolted. Using guerrilla tactics, they captured Jerusalem and rededicated the Temple.

ISRAEL BY ANY OTHER NAME

The land on which the State of Israel and the Palestinian Territories are situated has been known by a variety of names. Among those you may come across are Canaan, the Land of Israel (Eretz Yisra'el) and Judah (Yehudah), in the Hebrew Bible; Judea (Provincia Iudaea) and, after 135 CE, Syria Palaestina, used by the Romans; Al-Sham (Syria) and Filastin (Palestine), in Arab sources; and the Holy Land (Terra Sancta in Latin) and Palestine, in texts by Christians, Muslims and Jews.

1250 BCE	10th century BCE	late 10th century BCE	586 BCE
Estimated date of the Israelites' biblical exodus from Egypt. Archaeologists have found no evidence of Egyptian slavery, desert wandering or military conquest and posit that the Israelites originated in Canaan.	King Solomon, legendary for his wisdom, rules Israel and builds the First Temple in Jerusalem to house the Ark of the Covenant, containing the original Ten Commandments tablets.	The northern Kingdom of Israel splits from the southern, Jerusalem-based Kingdom of Judea. The 10 northern tribes are eventually lost to history; today's Jews are descended from the Judeans.	Nebuchadnezzar, King of Babylon, destroys the First Temple and exiles the Jews to Babylonia. Cyrus II, King of Persia, allows them to return to Judea 48 years later.

The Hasmoneans – as the dynasty founded by the Maccabees is known – became a useful buffer for the Roman Empire against the marauding Parthians, whose empire was based in what is now Iran. But the Hasmoneans fought among themselves and in 63 BCE Rome stepped in. The Romans sometimes ruled the area – which became the Roman province of Judea (also spelled Judaea or Iudaea) – directly through a procurator, the most famous of whom was Pontius Pilate, but preferred a strong client ruler such as Herod the Great (r 37–4 BCE), whose major construction projects included expanding the Temple.

The 1st century CE was a time of tremendous upheaval in the Roman province of Judea, not least between approximately 26 and 29 CE, when it is believed that Jesus of Nazareth carried out his ministry. The tension exploded in 66 CE, when the Jews launched the Great Jewish Revolt against the Romans, also known as the First Jewish–Roman War. Four years later, Titus, the future emperor, crushed the rebels and destroyed the Second Temple, leaving only one outer wall standing, now known as the Western Wall. Masada fell in 73 CE, putting an end to even nominal Jewish sovereignty for almost two millennia. However, although the Jews were expelled from Jerusalem, a large Jewish population remained in other parts of the Land of Israel.

Just 60 years after Josephus Flavius wrote *The Jewish War,* his firsthand, decidedly pro-Roman account of the Great Jewish Revolt, another insurrection broke out. The Bar Kochba Rebellion (132–35 CE) was led by Simon Bar Kochba, whose guerrillas lived in caves near the Dead Sea; some Jews even considered him to be the Messiah. The Romans, under Hadrian, suppressed the rebellion with difficulty – and with great ferocity, essentially wiping out the Jewish population of Judea.

After his victory, Hadrian sought to erase both Judaism and any traces of Jewish independence: statues of Jupiter and of Hadrian himself were placed on the site of the Temple, Jews were barred from living in Aelia Capitolina (his new name for Jerusalem), and the Roman province of Judea was renamed Syria Palaestina after the Philistines, a coastal people of Mycenaean Greek origin who had been arch-enemies of the Jews for a millennium.

> The Temple in Jerusalem was so central to Jewish life that some scholars estimate only 270 of the 613 Commandments that religious Jews are obligated to perform can actually be carried out in the absence of the Temple's priesthood and animal sacrifices.

ARCH OF TITUS

In 82 CE the Romans celebrated Titus's hard-fought victory over Judea by constructing an impressive triumphal arch just off the Roman Forum in Rome. Still standing today, its friezes depict a procession of Roman legionnaires carrying off the contents of the Temple in Jerusalem, including a seven-branched *menorah* (candelabra).

516 BCE	4th century BCE	167–161 BCE	63 BCE
The Second Temple is consecrated in Jerusalem. Though without the Ark of the Covenant, lost to Nebuchadnezzar, it serves as the focus of Jewish worship through animal sacrifices.	Nabataeans, a nomadic tribe from Arabia, establish Petra, now in Jordan. They wax wealthy from the incense trade between Yemen and the Horn of Africa and Greece and Rome.	Outraged by Seleucid king Antiochus' imposition of pagan sacrifices, the Jews, led by Judah Maccabee, revolt. Their victory, celebrated by the holiday of Hanukkah, establishes the Hasmonean dynasty.	The independent Kingdom of Judea becomes a Roman client state after Pompey captures Jerusalem. Roman proconsuls rule Judea but Temple sacrifices continue.

THE JEWISH DIASPORA

During the 3300 or so years since the Children of Israel entered Canaan – according to the Bible after the Exodus from Egypt – there have always been Jews in the Land of Israel. But for about two-thirds of that time, most Jews lived outside the Holy Land, dispersed among other nations in communities collectively known as the Jewish Diaspora (from the Greek word for 'dispersion' or 'scattering').

The first major Diaspora community was established in Babylonia (now Iraq) after Nebuchadnezzar destroyed the First Temple and exiled the Jews in 586 BCE. When Cyrus II of Persia allowed them to return to Judea 48 years later, many stayed in Babylonia.

From the 3rd to the 6th centuries CE, Jewish sages in Palestine and Babylonia vied for supremacy in establishing Jewish law. Babylonia eventually won out.

In the 11th century, the seat of the Jewish world's greatest legal authorities shifted to North Africa (Cairo and Kairouan, Tunisia) and, more improbably, to the Rhineland, in a faraway land that the Jews called Ashkenaz. From the 13th to 15th centuries, many of the greatest sages lived in Spain, known in Hebrew as Sfarad.

Persecuted in Western Europe, Ashkenazi Jews began moving eastward into the Slavic lands from the 14th century, bringing with them a German-Hebrew patois known as Yiddish. By the 17th century the world's main centre of Jewish scholarship was in Lithuania and Poland. In the 18th century, for the first time in Jewish history, more Jews lived in Europe than in North Africa and Asia.

The Jews of Eastern Europe were again dispersed in the late 19th century when czarist pogroms forced many of them to flee. The expulsion of the Jews from Spain in 1492 scattered Sephardic Jews to the lands of the Ottomans (who welcomed the exiles) as well as the Netherlands, from where some eventually went to England. Of the Jews who remained in Europe and found themselves under Nazi occupation during WWII, the vast majority died in the Holocaust; most were either shot, their bodies dumped in mass graves, or killed in the gas chambers.

A few Sephardic Jews lived in colonial America before 1776, but most of the American Jewish community is descended from 19th-century Ashkenazi immigrants. Today, the United States and Israel, each with about six million Jews, vie for Jewish cultural and religious pre-eminence, just as Babylonia and the Land of Israel did 17 centuries ago.

With the Temple destroyed and the elaborate animal sacrifices prescribed in the Torah suspended, Jewish religious life was thrown into a state of limbo. In an effort to adapt to the new circumstances, Jewish sages established academies around Roman Palestine and Galilee and set about reorienting Judaism towards prayer and synagogue worship, though the direction of Jewish prayer remained (as it does today) towards Jerusalem. The 'Rabbinic Judaism' practised today is almost entirely a product of the principles, precepts and precedents laid down by sages and rabbis after the destruction of the Second Temple.

37 BCE	c 4 BCE	66–70 CE	67
The Roman Senate appoints Herod the Great as king of Judea. To win popular support, he rebuilds the Second Temple, including the Western Wall. He also constructs palaces atop Masada and at Herodium.	A Jew known to history as Jesus is born in Bethlehem. He grows up in Nazareth, preaches in Galilee and is tried and crucified in Jerusalem by Pontius Pilate.	Jewish anger at Roman oppression sparks the Great Jewish Revolt, crushed by Roman legions under Vespasian and Titus. Jerusalem and the Second Temple are destroyed, ending sacrifices.	Yosef ben Matityahu, commander of the Great Jewish Revolt in Galilee, is captured by the Romans and re-invents himself as the great Roman historian Josephus Flavius.

In the years following Jesus's crucifixion, which some experts believe took place in 33 CE, Jews who believed him to be the Messiah and those who didn't often worshipped side by side, observing Jewish rituals with equal meticulousness. But around the time the Gospels were being written (late 1st century CE), theological and political disagreements emerged and the two communities diverged. Christian polemical tracts against the Jewish faith from this period, delivered from a position of weakness – at this time Christianity, unlike Judaism, was treated as an illegal sect by the Romans – would be used to justify anti-Semitism in subsequent centuries.

Christianity was generally suppressed by the Romans until 313 CE, when the Roman Empire's Edict of Milan granted tolerance to all previously persecuted religions, including Christianity. Shortly thereafter, Constantine the Great's mother, Helena, set about identifying and consecrating sites associated with Jesus's life. Many of the most important Christian sites, including the Church of the Holy Sepulchre in Jerusalem, date from this period.

The Byzantine Empire – the Christian successor to the eastern part of the Roman Empire – ruled Palestine from the 4th to the early 7th centuries CE. During this time, there were three revolts – one by the Jews of Galilee and two by the Samaritans – but as can be seen from the opulent ruins of Beit She'an and the Galilee's many beautiful Byzantine-era synagogues, the country was quite prosperous and, for the most part, at peace.

In 611 CE the Persians invaded, capturing Jerusalem, destroying churches and seizing the True Cross. Byzantine rule was restored in 628 CE – but it didn't last long.

Some Jews believe that when the Messiah comes, the Temple will be rebuilt on Jerusalem's Temple Mount. In the Old City's Jewish Quarter, you can find artists' renderings of the 'Third Temple'. Muslims, of course, prefer to keep the Dome of the Rock right where it is.

Muslims & Crusaders

Islam and Arab civilisation came to Palestine between 636 and 638 CE, when Caliph Omar (Umar), the second of the Prophet's successors, accepted the surrender of Jerusalem from the Byzantines. This was just six years after the death of the Prophet Mohammed, whose followers had initially been told to pray facing Jerusalem; in 624 they were instructed to face Mecca.

The Temple Mount was holy to the newly arrived Muslims because they believed it to be the site of Mohammed's Night Journey (Mi'raj) to behold the celestial glories of heaven. In the Quran, the ascension is described as happening in a 'faraway place', which Muslims interpret as meaning Jerusalem. It is for this reason that Jerusalem is considered to be Sunni Islam's third-holiest city (after Mecca and Medina).

Omar's successors built the Dome of the Rock and Al-Aqsa Mosque on the Temple Mount, which had been a derelict trash dump during

73	132–35	2nd century	313
Three years after the fall of Jerusalem, the desert stronghold of Masada succumbs to the might of the Roman legions, marking the end to all Jewish resistance in Judea.	After Hadrian bans circumcision, Bar Kochba leads the catastrophic Bar Kochba Rebellion, leading to a crushing Roman victory and the near-annihilation of Jewish communities of Judea.	With Jerusalem in ruins and sacrifices halted, centres of Jewish learning are established in Yavneh, Tzipori and Beit She'arim. Oral traditions are written down in the Mishnah and, later, Talmud.	Constantine the Great, the Roman Empire's first Christian emperor, issues the Edict of Milan, granting freedom to all religions, including Christianity.

Byzantine times. Jews were again permitted to settle in Jerusalem. With Christianity respected as a precursor of Islam, the shrines of previous generations were preserved, though over time many Christians converted to Islam and began speaking Arabic.

Omar issued a famous promise to the Christians of Jerusalem that 'the security of their persons, their goods, their churches, their crosses' would be guaranteed. This promise was largely kept until 1009, when the mentally disturbed Fatimid Caliph Al-Haakim destroyed many churches and persecuted Christians and Jews.

Christian pilgrimage to the holy sites in Jerusalem was possible until 1071, when the Seljuk Turks captured the city and travel became difficult and often dangerous due to political turmoil. In 1095 Pope Urban II issued a call for a crusade to restore to Christianity the site of Jesus's Passion. By the time the Crusades began, the Seljuks had been displaced by the Fatimid dynasty, which was quite happy to allow the old pilgrimage routes to reopen – but it was too late for the Christian armies to turn back. In 1099 the Crusaders overwhelmed Jerusalem's defences and massacred the city's Muslims and Jews. It would be 200 years before the bloodshed came to a halt.

When the Crusaders took Jerusalem, they founded what even Arab chroniclers acknowledged was a prosperous state with an effective administration, based on the feudal system in force in Europe. The first King of Jerusalem was Baldwin I (r 1100–18), who saw himself as restoring the kingdom of the biblical David and who had himself crowned on Christmas Day in David's hometown of Bethlehem.

In 1187 the celebrated Kurdish-Muslim general Saladin (Salah ad-Din) defeated a Crusader army at the Horns of Hattin in Galilee (near Arbel) and captured Jerusalem. Even Saladin's enemies acknowledged his decent treatment of prisoners and the honour with which he observed truces – not something that could be said for the Crusader chiefs.

The final Crusader left the Middle East with the fall of Akko in 1291, but the bloody symbolism of the Crusades lived on. When Britain's General Edmund Allenby entered Jerusalem in 1917 to become its first Christian ruler since Saladin's victory, he declared: 'now the Crusades are over'.

For a highly readable account of what the Arabs thought of the Crusaders, try *The Crusades Through Arab Eyes*, by Lebanese writer Amin Maalouf.

Ottomans, Zionists & British

The Ottoman Turks captured Constantinople in 1453 and built an empire that extended to the Balkans, the Middle East and North Africa. In 1516 Palestine was added to their territory, and two decades later Sultan Süleyman the Magnificent (r 1520–66) built the present massive walls around Jerusalem's Old City. For most of the 400 years of Ottoman rule, Palestine was a backwater run by pashas more concerned with tax collection than good governance.

358	614–28	638	749
The lunisolar Hebrew calendar still in use today is adopted by the Sanhedrin right before its dissolution. It fits lunar months into the solar year by inserting seven leap months every 19 years.	Palestine is occupied by the Sasanian Empire of Persia.	Just six years after the death of the Prophet Mohammed, Muslim armies capture Jerusalem from the Byzantines, bringing Islam, Arab culture and the Arabic language to Palestine.	A massive earthquake destroys Beit She'an and Tiberias. In Jerusalem it kills thousands and seriously damages Al-Aqsa Mosque.

MYSTIC JUDAISM

The leading thinkers of Spain's illustrious medieval Jewish community were rational philosophers whose interests encompassed both science and medicine. In 1492 Spain's Christian rulers expelled all the country's Jews, causing a crisis of faith to which the rationalists had no answer. (The expulsion, after all, seemed deeply irrational, unless you were the Spanish king and queen, who confiscated considerable property from departing Jews.) As a result, some Jews developed a new, mystical understanding of why bad things happened to them. The centre of this new mysticism was the hilltop Galilee town of Tsfat, where a number of eminent Spanish rabbis found a home. Its greatest figure was Jerusalem-born Yitzhak Luria (1534–72), who expanded an old form of mysticism called Kabbalah (pronounced kah-bah-*lah*) so that it could provide answers to the vexing spiritual questions haunting Jews after the Expulsion.

Lurianic Kabbalah (the word means 'receiving') was inspired by earlier texts such as the 13th-century *Zohar*, but Luria's adaptations and innovations had such an impact that many are now part of mainstream Jewish observance. Luria left no writings, but his assistant recorded the essence of his teachings. Luria asserted that in order to create the world, the Infinite (the Eyn-Sof) was damaged – to make a space in which to fit Creation. As a result, sparks from the Divine Light fell from their original position and were at risk of being used for evil purposes. Jews, he argued, could restore the Divine Light and repair the Infinite by performing the 613 Commandments (the 10 on Moses' tablets plus 603 others). This mystical approach gave Jews a way to understand the horror of the Expulsion from Spain and the Inquisition – as well as later persecution – because it asserted that evil was inherent in the world. It also directed them to look inward to build a higher degree of spiritual awareness and, in so doing, to 'repair the world'.

The lack of effective administration in Palestine reflected the gradual decline of the Ottoman Empire, which would cease to exist at the end of WWI. But the final decades of the empire saw other forces taking shape in Palestine that remain strong today. Zionism arose largely in response to post-Napoleonic nationalism in Western Europe and waves of pogroms in Eastern Europe. At least small numbers of Jews had remained in Palestine continuously since Roman times (eg in the Galilee town of Peki'in) and pious Jews had been immigrating whenever political conditions permitted, but organised Zionist immigration to agricultural settlements began in 1882 – for slightly different reasons, Jews from Yemen began arriving the same year. Known as the First Aliya (the Hebrew word for emigrating to the Land of Israel, *aliya* literally means 'going up'), this group was joined from 1903 by the Second Aliya, made up largely of young, secular-minded socialists. But until after WWI, the vast majority of Palestine's Jews belonged to the old-line Orthodox com-

1095–99	1187	1291	16th century
The First Crusade brings Christian armies from Europe to Muslim-ruled Jerusalem, which is defended by both Muslims and Jews. Crusaders massacre Jews in both Europe and the Holy Land.	Saladin (Salah ad-Din) defeats the Crusaders at the hugely important Battle of Hattin, in the Galilee, and captures Jerusalem, allowing Jews to return to the city.	The Mamluks take Akko, the Crusaders' last stronghold, ending Christian rule in Palestine until the arrival of the British in 1917.	Tsfat (Safed) becomes a centre of Jewish scholarship and Kabbalah (Jewish mysticism) with the arrival of Jerusalem-born Isaac Luria (the Ari) and Sephardic rabbis fleeing the Spanish Inquisition.

munity, most of it uninterested in Zionism, and lived in Judaism's four holy cities: Hebron, Tsfat (Safed), Tiberias and Jerusalem, which had a Jewish majority since about 1850.

In 1896 a Budapest-born Jewish journalist named Theodor Herzl, convinced by the degrading treatment of Captain Alfred Dreyfus (court-martialled in Paris on trumped-up treason charges) that Jews would never achieve equality and civil rights without self-determination, formulated his ideas in *The Jewish State*. The next year, he opened the first World Zionist Congress in Basel, Switzerland. Inspired by political Zionism, young Jews – many of them secular and socialist – began emigrating to Palestine, mostly from Poland and Russia.

In November 1917 the British government issued the Balfour Declaration, which stated that 'His Majesty's Government view with favour the establishment in Palestine of a National Home for the Jewish People'. The next month, British forces under General Edmund Allenby captured Jerusalem.

Immediately after the end of WWI, Jews resumed immigration to Palestine, this time to territory controlled by a British-run mandatory government – approved by the League of Nations – that was friendly, modernising and competent. The Third Aliya (1919–23) was made up mostly of young, idealistic socialists, many of whom established kibbutzim (communal settlements) on marginal land purchased from absentee Arab landlords, deals that sometimes resulted in the displacement of Arab peasant farmers. But the Fourth Aliya (1924–29) was made up largely of middle-class merchants and tradespeople – not exactly the committed pioneers that the Zionist leadership had hoped for. In the 1930s they were joined by the Fifth Aliya, made up largely of refugees from Nazi Germany, many of them from comfortable bourgeois backgrounds.

The rise in Jewish immigration angered Palestinian Arabs, who were beginning to see themselves in Arab nationalist terms and to see Palestine's growing Jewish population as a threat to Arab interests. Anti-Zionist riots rocked the country in 1921 and 1929, but Jews continued to arrive, especially after Hitler's rise to power in 1933. In 1931 Palestine's 174,000 Jews constituted 17% of the total population; by 1941, there were 474,000 Jews, 30% of the total.

Growing Palestinian Arab opposition to Zionism and the policies of the British Mandate, especially regarding Jewish immigration, led to the Arab Revolt (1936–39), in which about 400 Jewish civilians and 200 British soldiers were killed. The Mandatory government suppressed the uprising with considerable violence, killing some 5000 Palestinian Arabs. Palestinian Jews took advantage of the Arab economic boycott to increase their economic autonomy – for instance, by establishing an independent

Baptist lay preacher Thomas Cook led a party of middle-class English tourists to Jerusalem in 1869. At the time, criminals were still being publicly decapitated by sword at Jaffa Gate.

Zionism struck a heroic chord in 1960s Hollywood. Paul Newman starred in *Exodus* (1960), based on Leon Uris's bestseller about a boat carrying illegal Jewish immigrants; and Kirk Douglas played an American war hero who joined the war for Israel's independence in *Cast a Giant Shadow* (1966).

1536	1799	1837	1882
Ottoman Sultan Suleiman the Magnificent begins building the present-day walls of Jerusalem's Old City.	Napoleon captures Gaza, Jaffa (where he massacres thousands of POWs) and Haifa but fails to take Akko and doesn't get anywhere near Jerusalem. Abruptly leaves his army and returns to France.	Massive earthquake hits the Galilee, flattening much of Tsfat, where more than 2000 people are killed, as well as 600 in Tiberias.	Pogroms in Russia spark the First Aliya, the first organised Zionist immigration to Palestine. Agricultural settlements such as Metula, Rosh Pina, Zichron Ya'acov and Rishon LeZion are soon established.

ZIONISM

The Jewish Virtual Library (www.jewishvirtuallibrary.org) defines Zionism as 'the national movement for the return of the Jewish people to their homeland and the resumption of Jewish sovereignty in the Land of Israel'. The biblical word 'Zion' (Tziyon) refers both to Jerusalem, towards which Jews have prayed since the time of the Temple, and to the Land of Israel.

According to the historian Binyamin Neuberger, 'political Zionism, the national liberation movement of the Jewish people, emerged in the 19th century within the context of the liberal nationalism then sweeping through Europe. Central to Zionist thought is the concept of the Land of Israel as the historical birthplace of the Jewish people, and the belief that Jewish life elsewhere is a life of exile'.

This theme also appears in Israel's Declaration of Independence (1948), which states:

The Land of Israel was the birthplace of the Jewish people. Here their spiritual, religious and political identity was shaped. Here they first attained to statehood, created cultural values of national and universal significance and gave to the world the eternal Book of Books. After being forcibly exiled from their land, the people kept faith with it throughout their dispersion and never ceased to pray and hope for their return to it and for the restoration in it of their political freedom.'

Among Zionism's practical goals: to provide the Jewish people – seen by Zionists as no less a nation than the Czechs, the Hungarians or the French – with national self-determination in a world made up of nation-states; and to offer individual Jews a place of refuge from anti-Semitic discrimination and persecution.

The history of Palestine during the British Mandate comes alive through individual stories in the excellent *One Palestine, Complete* (2001), by Israel's leading popular historian, Tom Segev.

---

port in Tel Aviv. However, the Arab Revolt succeeded in convincing the British – who, in case of war with Germany, would surely need Arab oil and political goodwill – to severely limit Jewish immigration to Palestine. Just as the Jews of Europe were becoming increasingly desperate to flee Hitler (the Nazis allowed Jews to leave Germany until late 1941 provided they could find a country to take them), the doors of Palestine slammed shut. Even after WWII, the British prevented Holocaust survivors from reaching Palestine, outraging Jewish public opinion in Palestine and the United States; refugees who tried to run the blockade were imprisoned on Cyprus.

By 1947 the British government, exhausted by WWII and tired of both Arab and Jewish violence in Palestine, turned the problem over to the two-year-old United Nations. In November 1947, in a moment of rare agreement between the United States and the Soviet Union, the UN General Assembly voted in favour of partitioning Palestine into two independent states, one Jewish, the other Arab, with Jerusalem under a 'special international regime'. Palestinian Jews accepted the plan in

1909	1910	1916	1917
Led by Meir Dizengoff, 66 families found Tel Aviv on sand dunes north of Jaffa. The 5 hectares purchased by the group are parcelled out by lottery.	The first kibbutz, Degania, is established by socialist 'pioneers' from Russia at the southern end of the Sea of Galilee, on land purchased in 1904.	The secret Sykes-Picot Agreement divvies up the Ottoman Empire into spheres of influence. Palestine, Trans-Jordan and southern Iraq are earmarked for Britain; France gets Lebanon and Syria.	In the Balfour Declaration, the British government expresses support for a 'Jewish national home' in Palestine. British forces under General Allenby capture Jerusalem from the Ottomans.

principle, but Palestinian Arabs and nearby Arab countries rejected it. Arab bands immediately began attacking Jewish targets. The protection of Palestinian Jewish communities, economic interests and transport was led by the Haganah, an underground military organisation that would soon become the Israel Defense Forces (IDF).

As soon as the British left, at midnight on 14 May 1948, the Jews proclaimed the establishment of an independent Jewish state, and the armies of Egypt, Syria, Jordan, Lebanon and Iraq invaded Palestine. British Field Marshall Bernard Montgomery, who won fame for his North African desert campaigns during WWII, commented that Israel would survive no longer than three weeks. But to the Arab states' – and the world's – surprise the 650,000 Palestinian Jews were not defeated but rather took control of 77% of Mandatory Palestine (the Partition Plan offered them 56%). Jordan occupied (and annexed) the West Bank and East Jerusalem, expelling the residents of the Old City's Jewish quarter; Egypt took control of an area that came to be known as the Gaza Strip.

Independence & Catastrophe

The 1948 Arab–Israeli War brought independence for Israel, a place of refuge for Holocaust survivors and Jewish refugees from the Arab countries, and a guarantee that Jews fleeing persecution would always have a country that would take them in. But for the Palestinian Arabs the 1948 war is remembered as Al-Naqba, the Catastrophe.

Approximately 700,000 of the Arabs living in what was to become Israel fled or were expelled by the end of the year. The impact of this pivotal point in the conflict cannot be underestimated, resulting as it did in humanitarian disaster and the unresolved issue of Palestinian refugees today.

Numerous causes have been attributed to the mass exodus. Jewish military assaults on towns and villages, mortar shelling and sniper attacks forced Arabs from their homes in many cases. Reports spread fast of fallen towns and atrocities, such as the Deir Yassin massacre, in which more than 200 villagers were killed by Zionist militia. Intimidation and widespread fear of a similar fate led others to leave, in the belief they could return at a later date. At the close of 1948, over 80% of Palestinians had become refugees. Shortly after the exodus, a series of laws were passed by the Israeli government that prevented both displaced Arabs within Palestine and abroad from returning to their homes.

After Israel became independent, impoverished Jewish refugees began flooding in – from British internment camps on Cyprus (set up by the British to hold Jews intercepted on the way to Palestine), from 'displaced persons' camps in postwar Europe (including hundreds of thousands of Holocaust survivors), from countries soon to be locked tight

Israelis call immigration to Israel *aliyah*, from a Hebrew root meaning 'to ascend'. Moving from Israel to another country is sometimes derisively called *yeridah* (going down).

1918	1925	1929	1939–45
British forces take northern Palestine from the Ottomans. In one of the world's last cavalry charges, an Indian cavalry brigade captures Haifa.	The Hebrew University of Jerusalem is founded atop Mt Scopus. Members of the first Board of Governors include Albert Einstein, Sigmund Freud and Martin Buber.	Arab–Jewish riots erupt due to a disagreement over Jewish access to the Western Wall. Many of Hebron's Jews are sheltered by Muslim neighbours but 67 are killed by mobs.	Six million European Jews are murdered by the Nazis. Many Palestinian Jews volunteer for service in the British Army. Zionists smuggle Jewish refugees into Palestine.

behind the Iron Curtain (eg Bulgaria), and from Arab countries whose ancient Jewish communities became targets of anti-Jewish violence (eg Iraq, Yemen and Syria). Within three years, Israel's Jewish population more than doubled.

War & Terrorism

In the spring of 1967 Arab capitals – especially Cairo – were seething with calls to liberate all of historic Palestine – in the name of pan-Arab nationalism – from what was seen as an illegitimate occupation by Israel. Egyptian President Gamal Abdel Nasser closed the Straits of Tiran to Israeli shipping (including oil shipments from Iran, at the time an ally of Israel), ordered UN peacekeeping forces to withdraw from Sinai, and made rousing speeches listened to with rapt attention by tens of millions across the Arab world. Jordan and Syria massed troops on their borders with Israel. Terrified Israelis took Nasser at his word – on 3 May he declared, 'our basic objective will be the destruction of Israel' – and wondered if their fate would be similar to that of the Jews of Europe during WWII.

On 6 June Israel launched a pre-emptive attack on its Arab neighbours, devastating their air forces and then, in a three-front land war, the armies of Syria, Egypt and Jordan. In less than a week – that's why the conflict came to be known as the Six Day War (for an Israeli perspective, see www.sixdaywar.co.uk) – Israel captured Sinai and Gaza from Egypt, the West Bank and East Jerusalem from Jordan, and the Golan Heights from Syria.

Israelis reacted to the victory with nothing less than euphoria, and many could find no other explanation for their astounding victory than divine intervention. Some saw the triumph as proof that the messianic process was well and truly underway and sought to settle the newly captured lands. At the time, few Israelis were able to see the demographic, political and moral difficulties that Israeli control of the Palestinian Territories would entail.

In 1973 Egypt and Syria launched a surprise, two-front attack on Israel on Yom Kippur, the holiest day of the Jewish calendar. Unprepared because of intelligence failures born of post-1967 hubris, Israel was initially forced to withdraw but soon rallied and, with enormous casualties on both sides, pushed the Arab armies back. However, initial Egyptian battlefield successes made it possible for Egyptian President Anwar Sadat to portray the Yom Kippur War as a victory; and although in tactical and strategic terms it was Israel that had won on the battlefield, Israelis never saw the war as a victory.

Thoroughly discredited by both the failures of the Yom Kippur War and the Labor Party's perceived corruption and lassitude, Prime Minis-

There are 20 refugee camps administered by the UN Relief and Works Agency (UNRWA) in the West Bank. The Gaza Strip has eight, and there's one in East Jerusalem. Over 50% of Palestinians are listed by the UN as refugees.

Considered by many to be the Palestinian national poet, Mahmoud Darwish (1941–2008) wrote works expressing Palestinian anguish at their dispossession and exile. He was active in the PLO from 1973 to the 1990s. In one of his best-known poems he wrote, 'We have a country of words.'

1946	1947	1948	1948–70s
Etzel (Irgun) underground paramilitary fighters under Menahem Begin blow up the south wing of Jerusalem's King David Hotel, a British military command centre, killing 91.	The UN General Assembly votes to partition Palestine into Jewish and Arab states, a plan accepted in principle by the Zionists but rejected by the Arabs. Fighting engulfs Palestine.	The British leave Palestine; Zionist forces hold five Arab armies and local militias at bay; 700,000 Palestinian Arabs become refugees; the State of Israel is declared.	Some 600,000 Jews leave, flee or are expelled from Arab countries such as Yemen, Syria, Iraq, Egypt, Libya and Morocco and find refuge in Israel; many endure years in transit camps.

ter Golda Meir ended her political career in 1974. Three years later, the Labor Party, which had been at the head of every government since 1948, was voted out of office, in part by Mizrahi (Asian and North African) Jews angry at their economic and political marginalisation. Likud Party leader Menahem Begin, a right-wing former underground fighter (some would say terrorist because of his organisation's attacks on Arab civilians and symbols of the British occupation), became prime minister. But when Egyptian President Anwar Sadat stunned the world by travelling to Jerusalem (1977) and offering to make peace with Israel in return for an Israeli withdrawal from Sinai and promises (never fulfilled) of progress towards Palestinian autonomy, Begin accepted. With a beaming US President Jimmy Carter looking on, Begin and Sadat signed the Camp David Accords in 1978.

Israel completed its evacuation of Sinai, including 7000 settlers, in spring 1982 – just six weeks before simmering tensions between Lebanon-based Palestine Liberation Organisation (PLO) forces and Israel, and the attempted assassination of the Israeli ambassador to the UK by an anti-PLO Palestinian faction, were used by Israel's defence minister Ariel Sharon to justify launching a full-scale invasion of Lebanon. His objective was to drive the PLO out of Lebanon and install a pro-Israel Christian government. The war divided Israelis to an unprecedented degree as it dragged on and on, until 1985 (Israeli forces occupied a 'security zone' on Lebanese territory until May 2000). Many Israelis believed that the war was launched without proper government approval, and even more felt that their country was tainted when IDF soldiers failed to stop their Christian Lebanese allies from massacring Palestinians in the Beirut refugee camps of Sabra and Shatila in September 1982. A mass demonstration against the war and the massacre attracted 400,000 people in Tel Aviv, the largest civil demonstration in Israel's history. (Israel's ongoing trauma from the First Lebanon War was the subject of the 2008 Oscar-nominated animated film *Waltz with Bashir*.)

Meanwhile, Palestinian refugees waited in the West Bank and Gaza, in refugee camps in neighbouring countries, and across the Arab world and beyond for a solution to their plight. The PLO was set up in 1964 by the Arab League, made up of representatives of 22 Arabic-speaking nations. But it wasn't until after the Arab defeat in the 1967 Six Day War that a Palestinian leader willing to defy the Arab League won control of the PLO.

Born in Cairo in 1929, Yasser Arafat was in Kuwait working as an engineer in the late 1950s when he founded Fatah, a reverse Arabic acronym for 'Palestine Liberation Movement' and also the word for 'victory'. It was through the Fatah faction that he took over the PLO in 1969. From exile in Jordan and later in Lebanon and Tunisia, he launched a

HISTORY WAR & TERRORISM

Yasser Arafat made the chequered *keffiyeh* (traditional Arab men's headgear) famous around the world. His was black and white, the colours favoured by Fatah, and he arranged the folds to form an elongated triangle shaped like Palestine. Red-and-white *keffiyehs* are often worn by Jordanian Bedouin, leftist Palestinian groups and Hamas.

1950	1951	1956	1964
Jordan annexes the West Bank and East Jerusalem, captured in the 1948 war. The Hashemite Kingdom renounces its claims to the territory in 1988.	Jordan's King Abdullah I is assassinated on Al-Haram al-Sharif/ Temple Mount in Jerusalem by a Palestinian nationalist. His grandson becomes King Hussein and rules until 1999.	After Egypt closes off the Red Sea to Israeli shipping, Israel captures Sinai. Britain and France try to use the conflict as a pretext to retake control of the Suez Canal.	The Arab League, meeting in Cairo, founds the PLO. Israel and Syria clash over water rights in the Jordan River basin.

campaign of hijackings, bombings and attacks against civilian targets designed to weaken Israel (which responded with a determined campaign that included cross-border commando operations and assassinations) and keep the Palestinian problem in the international headlines.

In 1987 a popular uprising against Israeli rule broke out in the West Bank and Gaza. Known as the First Intifada (Arabic for 'shaking off'), it was a spontaneous eruption of strikes, stones and Molotov cocktails. Arafat, based in Tunis, was at first out of touch with grass-roots events in the Palestinian Territories but he soon took control, garnering worldwide sympathy for the Palestinian cause.

In 1988 Arafat publicly renounced terrorism and effectively recognised Israel. Five years later, Israel (under Yitzhak Rabin) and the PLO signed the Oslo Accords, so named because secret negotiations in the Norwegian capital laid the basis for an agreement under which Israel would hand over control of territory to the Palestinians in stages, beginning with the major towns of the West Bank and Gaza. The toughest issues – the future of Jerusalem and Palestinian refugees' right of return – were to be negotiated at the end of a five-year interim period. The Oslo formula was, essentially, 'land for peace' based on the two-state solution proposed by the UN in 1947.

Israel's Arab citizens – Palestinian Arabs who remained in their homes in 1948 and their descendants – lived under military law until 1966. They now number some 1.6 million; most live in the Galilee. Arabs living in East Jerusalem have blue Israeli ID cards but most have not taken up Israel's offer of citizenship.

The Oslo Era

Yasser Arafat arrived in Gaza to head the new Palestinian Authority (PA) in July 1994. Over the next few years, Israel handed over most of Gaza and the major West Bank towns to Palestinian control. But the Oslo Accords didn't bring real peace. Rather, they drove those on both sides who opposed the compromises to greater acts of violence. Hamas and Islamic Jihad took their terrorism to new heights with suicide bombings against Israeli civilians. Israel hit back by assassinating Hamas and Islamic Jihad leaders, using tactics that often resulted in civilian casualties. Military incursions and settler violence against local Palestinians increased and their expectations of an improved economy and freedom of movement were not fulfilled.

Perhaps the greatest single blow to the peace process came in November 1995, when a right-wing Orthodox Israeli shot Prime Minister Yitzhak Rabin after a Tel Aviv peace rally. The assassination was the culmination of several years of incitement from nationalist Israelis (especially Jewish settlers) bitterly opposed to Rabin's agreement to give up part of the historic 'Land of Israel'. Many Orthodox Jews (though not the ultra-Orthodox, who are non- or anti-Zionist) believe that the biblical lands they call Judea and Samaria (ie the West Bank) and Gaza came under Israeli control as part of a divinely ordained process heralding the beginning of the messianic era. Relinquishing control of land they see

1967	1972	1973	1978
In six days, Israel defeats Egypt, Jordan and Syria, more than tripling its territory. Israelis can pray at the Western Wall for the first time since 1948.	Palestinian terrorists belonging to Yasser Arafat's Fatah kill 11 Israeli athletes and coaches at the Munich Olympics. Golda Meir gives the order to hunt down the killers and assassinate them.	Egypt and Syria launch a surprise attack against Israel on Yom Kippur, the holiest Jewish holiday.	Israel and Egypt sign the Camp David Accords. Israel opens an embassy in Cairo, Egypt establishes one in Tel Aviv, and Sinai is returned to Egypt.

as Israel's God-given birthright would do no less than put an end to the messianic process. For messianists there can be no greater crime.

For most Israelis Rabin's killing was nothing less than a national nightmare, but in the end it accomplished much of what the assassin had hoped by robbing the peace process of an advocate whose military background – as a brigade commander in 1948 and later as chief of staff in the 1967 war – inspired Israelis to trust him on security issues.

Rabin's death was followed by a string of Hamas suicide bombings that helped bring a right-wing coalition led by Binyamin Netanyahu to power. But in 1999 a centre-left coalition government led by former chief of staff Ehud Barak took office. Barak and Arafat agreed to a summit with US president Bill Clinton at Camp David, with the aim of striking a final peace deal. Negotiations, held against the backdrop of discontent since the Oslo Accords, failed. Widespread violence broke out, sparked by a controversial visit of Israel's Likud Party leader Ariel Sharon to Jerusalem's Temple Mount. Both Sharon and Arafat were accused of stoking the unrest.

At first Arafat considered unleashing violence as a way to pressure Israel into making concessions, but he quickly lost control of the situation to young, local Fatah leaders who felt he hadn't given them enough power since his return from exile – they accused him of giving all the top military and political jobs to corrupt, old party hacks who'd been with him in Beirut and Tunis. The young Fatah leaders quickly allied with Hamas and Islamic Jihad, eventually launching a wave of suicide bombings.

Israeli public opinion hardened and in 2001 Ariel Sharon, a tough-talking former general who spoke privately of the Intifada as an 'existential danger' to Israel, and who had opposed Barak's efforts to reach a deal with Arafat, was elected prime minister. Sharon sent tanks to occupy West Bank towns previously ceded to Arafat, made frequent, bloody incursions into Gaza, and carried out 'targeted assassinations' of presumed terrorist leaders. He confined Arafat to his Ramallah compound by surrounding it with tanks. Depressed and sick, Arafat's command of events and – according to some aides – reality weakened until he was airlifted to France for treatment and died in November 2004. Over the course of the Second Intifada (2000–05), more than 1000 Israelis, 70% of them civilians, were killed by Palestinians, and approximately 4700 Palestinians, more than 2000 of them civilians, were killed by Israelis, according to the Israeli human rights group B'Tselem (www.btselem.org).

With his old enemy out of the way, Sharon – contradicting his reputation as an incorrigible hardliner – forged ahead with a radical plan to 'disengage' from the Palestinians, building the Separation Fence around most of the West Bank (despite furious opposition from Jewish settlers) and pulling out of isolated settlements. In August 2005 he completed the

Arab men are often referred to as Abu (meaning 'father of') followed by the name of their eldest son. Arafat was known popularly as Abu Ammar – but not because he had a son (he had a daughter, Zahwa, born in 1995). He chose the name of a follower of the Prophet Mohammed as his *nom de guerre*.

1982	1987–93	1988	1991
Israel invades Lebanon, besieging Beirut. Lebanese Phalangists massacre Palestinians at Sabra and Shatila camps. Yasser Arafat and PLO fighters leave Beirut by sea, transferring their headquarters to Tunis.	Palestinian frustration with occupation explodes in the First Intifada. The IDF, trained to fight standing armies, responds ineffectively; Palestinian casualties generate international condemnation.	Arafat renounces terrorism in a speech to the United Nations General Assembly in Geneva.	Israel is hit by 39 Iraqi Scud missiles. Arafat supports Saddam Hussein's invasion and annexation of Kuwait; in response, Kuwait and other Gulf nations cut off PLO funding and expel Palestinians.

hugely controversial evacuation of all 8600 Israeli settlers from the Gaza Strip and four settlements in the northern West Bank. In January 2006 Sharon suffered a massive stroke; many Jewish settlers saw it as divine punishment for his betrayal of the Land of Israel. Sharon remained in a coma until his death in 2014.

Recent History

Ehud Olmert, Sharon's deputy, was elected as Israel's 12th prime minister in March 2006 on a platform that promised a further pull-back from much of the West Bank, but his plans were never implemented. A few months earlier, Hamas had won the Palestinian parliamentary elections, and the following year Hamas gunners took over the Gaza Strip by force; Fatah officials who didn't make it out were tortured and some killed – a few were thrown to their deaths from tall buildings. Since then the US and EU have continued to send significant aid to the Fatah-led Palestinian Authority in the West Bank, while Iran, despite disagreements over the civil war in Syria, has supplied weapons and money to Hamas in Gaza. Olmert was convicted of corruption and sentenced to six years in prison in 2014.

In summer 2006 Hezbollah guerrillas kidnapped two Israeli soldiers patrolling on the Israeli side of the Israel–Lebanon border. Israel entered a brief war with the Iranian-backed Lebanese militia, during which the latter launched thousands of rockets at Israeli cities, towns and villages, bringing northern Israel to a halt and killing 43 civilians. The scale of Israel's bombing attacks on Lebanese towns in return was widely condemned and the war was a diplomatic disaster for Israel, but eight years later the ceasefire agreed to at war's end was still holding.

In 2001 Hamas and Islamic Jihad began launching missiles from Gaza into nearby parts of Israel. These attacks escalated after Israel's 2006 withdrawal from Gaza, and over time homemade Qassam rockets were upgraded and supplemented by Iranian-supplied 122mm Grads capable of hitting Be'er Sheva, Rishon LeZion and perhaps Tel Aviv. However, the people of Sderot and nearby kibbutzim bore the brunt of the attacks. At the end of 2008 Israel launched a major offensive, dubbed Operation Cast Lead, aimed at halting the missile attacks. Battles raged for three weeks and, by the end, much of Gaza's infrastructure lay in ruins and thousands were homeless. According to the Israeli human rights organisation B'Tselem, during the operation 1397 Palestinians were killed by Israelis (Israel claims a large majority were militants) and five Israeli soldiers were killed by Palestinians. But Hamas remained in control and dug new smuggling tunnels to circumvent Israel's much-criticised blockade of Gaza (significantly eased for civilian goods in 2010). Egypt sealed

1993	1994	1995	2000–05
Israeli Prime Minister Yitzhak Rabin and PLO Chairperson Yasser Arafat, sworn enemies for decades, sign the Oslo Accords at the White House with an uneasy handshake.	Israel and Jordan sign a peace treaty, delimiting their long border and guaranteeing Jordan a share of Jordan River water. Embassies are opened in Amman and Ramat Gan.	After a peace rally in Tel Aviv, Israeli Prime Minister Yitzhak Rabin is assassinated by a right-wing Jewish extremist. The killing contributes to the breakdown of the Oslo peace process.	The Second Intifada brings scores of suicide bombings to Israeli cities and towns, leading to deadly IDF incursions into Palestinian towns and deepening bitterness on both sides.

the Gaza–Sinai border; in 2013 and 2014 the Egyptian army destroyed some 1200 smuggling tunnels, cutting off a significant source of revenue for Hamas.

Israel's 2013 general elections brought to power another coalition government headed by Binyamin Netanyahu; initially it focused on trying to force the men of Israel's growing ultra-Orthodox community to serve in the IDF and integrate into the workforce. Following the collapse of US-sponsored Israeli–Palestinian peace talks, in part because of continued settlement construction by the Netanyahu government, the PA applied for full membership as an independent state in a variety of international organisations, angering Israel. In 2014 Israeli president Shimon Peres (at age 90, the world's oldest head-of-state) was replaced in the largely ceremonial post by Reuven 'Ruby' Rivlin, a right-winger with a strong civil rights record.

In 2014 Fatah, which governs much of the West Bank, and Hamas, which controls Gaza, established a government of national unity, but differences and mistrust between the groups remain deep. Egypt, under President Abdel Fattah al-Sisi, is implacably hostile to Hamas, in part because of the Egyptian military's historic opposition to the Muslim Brotherhood.

The Hamas–Israel War

Three Israeli teenagers were kidnapped and murdered by Palestinians in June 2014, after which violence swiftly escalated. Israel launched a major crackdown on Hamas in the West Bank in response to the kidnappings, killing 10 Palestinians in raids and arresting hundreds more. Rockets were fired into Gaza, and from Gaza into Israel. The resulting 50-day Hamas-Israel war left more than 2100 Palestinians (69% of them civilians, according to a UN estimate) and 73 Israelis (67 of them soldiers) dead, large parts of the Gaza Strip (including 17,200 homes) in ruins, and hundreds of thousands of civilians – especially children – traumatised. Israel's Iron Dome anti-missile system virtually neutralised the threat to the Israeli population posed by Hamas.

Few Palestinian militants had long careers during the Second Intifada. At one point in 2003, 11 successive leaders of Islamic Jihad in the West Bank town of Jenin were either arrested or killed by Israeli troops within a week of taking their position – sometimes on the very day they were made leader.

2004	2005	2006	2008–14
Yasser Arafat dies at age 75, of unexplained causes, in a Paris hospital and is buried in Ramallah. Conspiracy theories abound; some claim he was poisoned.	Israel unilaterally withdraws from the Gaza Strip, evacuating 21 settlements; Jewish settlers are outraged and radicalised. Palestinians condemn Israel's continued control of Gaza's land, sea and air access.	Attacks on the Galilee by Iranian-backed Hezbollah lead to Israel's Second Lebanon War. The hard-line Islamist movement Hamas defeats pro-two-state Fatah in Palestinian parliamentary elections.	Radical Jewish settlers carry out 'price tag' attacks on Palestinians and the IDF in an effort to deter the Israeli government from policies detrimental to Jewish settlements in the West Bank.

People of Israel & the Palestinian Territories

Almost 13 million people live in Israel and the Palestinian Territories. Israel's population is 75% Jewish (almost half of today's worldwide population of 13.7 million Jews), 17.6% Muslim Arab and 1.7% Christian Arab. The West Bank population is made up of about 83% Sunni Muslims, 13% Jews and perhaps 2% Christians. The population of the Gaza Strip is almost all Sunni Muslims. According to the Palestinian Central Bureau of Statistics, there are about 11 million Palestinians worldwide, of which the United Nations Relief & Works Agency classifies 1.5 million (in the Palestinian Territories, Jordan, Lebanon and Syria) as refugees.

Since 1948 Israel has absorbed more immigrants than any country on earth, relative to its population. About 900,000 Jews from the former Soviet Union arrived in the 1990s; recent arrivals include thousands of Jews fed up with anti-Semitism in France.

Jews

During the Ottoman period, most Palestinian Jews lived in the holy cities of Jerusalem, Hebron, Tiberias and Tsfat (Safed), but starting in the 1880s Jews began immigrating to Palestine, not only for religious and spiritual reasons but also to further Jewish national self-determination – and to live and raise their children without fear of anti-Semitism.

Jews born in Israel are known as Sabras, after the prickly pear, a tenacious type of cactus (Opuntia ficus-indica) native to Mexico, whose fruit is prickly on the outside but soft and sweet inside.

Sephardim

In 1492, the Jews of Sefarad (the Hebrew name for Spain) were given the choice of conversion, death or expulsion. Some Sephardic Jews (Sephardim) fled to North Africa, while others found refuge in the Ottoman Empire, whose sultan welcomed them with open arms.

Until the late 19th century, the majority of the Jews of Ottoman Palestine were Sephardim, defined not only by their origins in Spain but also by their religious liturgy, rites and melodies. Many of the leading Kabbalists (Jewish mystics) in 16th-century Tsfat (Safed) were Sephardic.

Much has been written about the condescension of some Ashkenazi Jews towards their non-European brethren, but one group has long looked out on the rest of the Jewish world with supreme confidence in its innate cultural superiority: the 'pure' Sephardim who can trace their lineage back to medieval Spain.

For five centuries, the language of the old-line Sephardim in places such as Turkey, Greece, Bosnia and Bulgaria has been Ladino (Djudeo-Espanyol), which is essentially medieval Spanish (Castilian) mixed with words from Hebrew and – depending on where the exiles settled – elements of Turkish, Greek, Arabic and French.

For more information on Sephardic history and culture, see www.sephardicstudies.org. A site in Ladino (readable if you know Spanish), www.aki-yerushalayim.co.il, has useful links.

Ashkenazim

The ancestors of today's Ashkenazim arrived in Ashkenaz (the old Hebrew name for Germany) in the 10th century. As successive expulsions forced the Jews of Ashkenaz to flee eastward, they were welcomed into what later became the Russian and Austro-Hungarian Empires. A thousand years ago just 3% of the world's Jews were Ashkenazim; by the 1930s that number had risen to 92%. Today about half of Israeli Jews (and three-quarters of Jews worldwide) trace their ancestry – either directly or via North and South America – to Central and Eastern Europe, especially Russia, Poland, the Ukraine, Belarus, Lithuania, Hungary, Romania and, of course, Germany and Austria.

Starting in 1882, pogroms and other forms of persecution led millions of Ashkenazi Jews to emigrate from Eastern Europe to the Americas and Western Europe, but small groups of Jews from countries such as Romania and Russia chose instead to move to Ottoman Palestine in order to establish agricultural settlements (eg Zichron Ya'acov). Friction soon developed between these Zionists, some of them socialists, and the traditionalist, ultra-Orthodox communities of Palestine, a conflict that continues to this day.

One of the cultural markers of the Ashkenazim is Yiddish, a mixture of medieval German, Hebrew and words of Slavic origin that is written in Hebrew characters. Yiddish words that have made their way into English (thanks in part to *Seinfeld*) include bagel, blintz, chutzpah, dyubbuk, glitch, klutz, lox, maven, mensch, noodge, nosh, oy vey, putz, shlemazel, shlemiel, schlep, schlock, schmaltz, schmooze, schmuck, shpiel, shpritz, shtetl, shtik, shvitz and tush.

In 1939, 11 to 13 million Jews spoke Yiddish; today, as a result of the Holocaust and linguistic assimilation in countries such as Israel, the USA, the Soviet Union and Argentina, only perhaps one million do. Visitors to Israel can hear Yiddish being spoken in places such as Jerusalem's ultra-Orthodox Mea She'arim neighbourhood.

Mizrahim

Jews whose families came to Israel from North Africa (Morocco, Algeria, Tunisia and Libya), the Middle East (eg Iraq, Syria, Yemen, Iran and Afghanistan) and Central Asia (eg Uzbekistan, Azerbaijan and Georgia), as well as India, are known as Edot HaMizrah ('communities of the East') or Mizrahim ('easterners'). This definition reflects common liturgical traditions as well as geography.

Yemenite Jews began emigrating to Ottoman Palestine in 1881. The number of Mizrahim swelled after 1948 as some 600,000 Jews immigrated

> Judaism has three main liturgical and ritual traditions, Ashkenazi, Sephardic and Edot HaMizrah (Mizrahi), as well as a number of distinct local traditions from places such as Rome and Alsace (France).

> Because Mizrahi and Sephardi liturgy and ritual are similar in some ways, Mizrahim are sometimes subsumed under the umbrella term Sephardim – despite the fact that the Jews of Bagdhad, Damascus, San'a and Buchara never got anywhere near the Iberian Peninsula.

THE LAW OF RETURN

Passed by the Knesset in 1950, Israel's Law of Return grants Israeli citizenship to any Jew – defined as anyone with at least one Jewish grandparent or who has converted to Judaism – and their legally married spouse (heterosexual or, as of 2014, same-sex) who requests it. Because the law guarantees that all Jews, anywhere in the world, who are faced with persecution always have a place of refuge – something that was emphatically not the case in the 1930s – the law is seen as one of the bedrocks of Israel's mission as a Jewish homeland.

In 2013 and 2014, Portugal and Spain passed their own 'laws of return' offering citizenship to the descendants of Sephardic Jews expelled from the Iberian Peninsula 500 years ago.

A variety of countries, including Armenia, China, Greece and Germany, have laws conferring citizenship or residency rights on the descendants of émigrés.

to Israel from the Arab countries, many to escape violence and anti-Jewish decrees. In recent years, Mizrahi groups have begun demanding reparations for lost personal and communal property.

Mizrahim in Israel have long suffered discrimination at the hands of the Ashkenazim, and after 1948 many spent years in resettlement camps and/or were sent to live in remote 'development towns' in the Negev or Galilee. In recent years, intermarriage between Mizrahim, Sephardim and Ashkenazim has become common, and while Mizrahim – especially the descendants of immigrants from Morocco – are still underrepresented in universities and overrepresented in prisons, Israeli popular culture is now much more inclusive. The ultra-Orthodox Shas political party draws almost all of its support from religiously traditionalist Mizrahim.

For centuries Mizrahi Jews spoke a number of distinctive dialects and languages, including Maghrebi Judeo-Arabic, Iraqi Judeo-Arabic (Yahudi) and Judeo-Tat (Juhuri), a Persian language spoken by the Mountain Jews of Azerbaijan.

> Although Jews make up just 0.2% of the world population, they have been awarded 27% of the Nobel prizes for chemistry, physics, medicine and economics.

Ethiopian Jews

Also known as Beta Israel (House of Israel) and, somewhat derogatorily, Falashas ('exiles' or 'strangers'), the Jews of Ethiopia trace their origins back to King Solomon and the Queen of Sheba (I Kings 10:1–13), though other traditions suggest that they may have been converted to Judaism almost two millennia ago by Yemenite-Jewish traders. But no one is quite sure how, or when, Jews got to Ethiopia.

The first Ethiopian Jews arrived in Israel in the 1960s, but it wasn't until two airlifts, Operation Moses (1984–85) and Operation Solomon (1991), that large-scale immigration began. Today, there are about 121,000 Jews of Ethiopian descent in Israel, 2% of Israel's Jewish population.

The transition to life in Israel has proved difficult for many of the Beta Israel and collectively they are among the poorest people in the country, with educational achievements that are well below average. Well-known Ethiopian-Israelis include the model Esti Mamo, who has appeared in *Elle* and *Vogue,* and Miss Israel 2013, Yityish Titi Aynaw. Six Ethiopian Jews have served in the Knesset.

Muslims

Sunni Muslims make up 17.4% of the population of Israel, about 97% of the Arab population of the West Bank and over 99% of the population of Gaza. About 90% of Israeli Arabs are Muslim; Muslims constitute 38% of the population of the Galilee. The largest Muslim-majority city in Israel is Nazareth (population 66,000). About a third of the residents of Jerusalem are Muslims.

> About 2000 Ahmadiyya Muslims, members of a famously tolerant community founded in India in the late 1800s, live in the Haifa neighbourhood of Kababir on Mt Carmel. To improve relations with their Jewish neighbours, they published a Yiddish translation of the Quran in 1987.

Traditionally, Palestinian Muslims have been moderate in their beliefs and practices. The rise of Muslim fundamentalism among Palestinians since the 1970s, especially in evidence in Gaza and some parts of the West Bank (eg Hebron), has been attributed to a number of factors, including the 1979 Islamic Revolution in Iran; disillusionment with secular Palestinian groups such as Yasser Arafat's Fatah, in part because of corruption; and the increasing influence of Islamist groups across the Arab and Muslim worlds. Hamas, the Islamist movement that controls Gaza, is the Palestinian branch of the Egyptian Muslim Brotherhood. In Israel, the Muslim Brotherhood gave rise to the Islamic Movement, which has a hard-line 'northern' branch and a moderate 'southern' branch that supported the Oslo Accords and has representatives in the Knesset.

Palestinian Muslims, both in Israel and the Palestinian Territories, see themselves as the guardians of Islam's third-holiest site, Al-Aqsa Mosque in Jerusalem, and of sites such as the Ibrahimi Mosque (Cave of the Patriarchs) in Hebron. Muslim holy sites, including Jerusalem's

Al-Haram Ash-Sharif (the Temple Mount), are run autonomously by Muslim religious trusts known as *waqfs*.

Islam and Judaism have much more in common – in rituals, liturgy and jurisprudence – than either does with Christianity:

➡ Muslims pray five times a day, while Jews traditionally have three services a day.

➡ Muslim halal laws concerning which animals may be eaten and how they are to be slaughtered are very similar to Judaism's kosher laws (many Muslims consider kosher meat to be *halal*).

➡ The first part of the Shahada (Islamic creed), 'There is no God but Allah', is very similar to the Jewish Shema, 'Hear O Israel, the Lord is your God, the Lord is One' – both emphasise the absolute oneness and unity of God.

➡ The Arabic and Hebrew words for God, Allah and Elohim, derive from the same Semitic root.

Bedouin

About one in six Israeli Arabs is a Bedouin – that is, a descendant of one of the Arabic-speaking, Sunni Muslim nomadic groups that, historically, have raised sheep and goats in desert areas all over Arabia. About 220,000 Bedouin live in the Negev, in seven government-built townships and some 45 unrecognised villages; another 60,000 Bedouin live in villages in the Galilee. Although Bedouin are not drafted into the Israel Defense Forces (IDF), many volunteer, often serving as trackers.

There has long been tension between Negev Bedouin and the Israeli government as the latter, like its British and Ottoman predecessors, has tried to end the Bedouin's nomadic ways by moving them to permanent settlements. A controversial resettlement plan, bitterly opposed by many Negev Bedouin, was shelved in late 2013.

Some Bedouin men still practice polygamy although it is forbidden under Israeli law.

Circassians

As the Russian Empire expanded into the northern Caucasus (the area between the Black and Caspian Seas) in the mid-1800s, hundreds of thousands of Circassians, a Caucasian people of Sunni Muslim faith, were forced from their homes. Many found refuge in the Ottoman Empire, some in what is now Israel.

Today about 4000 Circassians live in two Galilee villages, Kfar Kama and Rehaniye. Male Circassians are the only Muslims for whom service in the Israeli army is obligatory.

Christians

In 1920, about one in 10 people in what is now Israel and the Palestinian Territories was Christian; today Christians make up about 2% of the population of Israel and 0.8% of the population of the Palestinian Territories. Part of the reason for this precipitous drop is the growth in the number of Jews and Muslims, but emigration to the majority-Christian countries of Europe and North and South America has played a significant role. In recent years, a major impetus for emigration by Christians from the West Bank and Gaza has been the rise in Islamic fundamentalism.

In Israel, 80% of the Christians are Arabs; most of the rest are immigrants from the former Soviet Union. The largest Christian denominations in Israel are Eastern-Rite (Melkite) Catholics (53%), Greek Orthodox (27%), Latin-Rite Catholic (10%) and Maronite Catholics (7.5%). Christians have the highest rates of high school graduation and eligibility for university study of any religious group in Israel, including

Some 60,000 Africans, most from Eritrea and Sudan, have sought asylum in Israel in recent years after crossing the border from Egypt. The Israeli government says almost all are economic migrants rather than bona fide refugees.

Often seen in Druze villages, the horizontally striped Druze flag – like the Druze star – has five colours: green (the mind), red (the soul), yellow (the word, mediator between the divine and the material), blue (the will and the realm of possibility) and white (the manifested will).

PEOPLE OF ISRAEL & THE PALESTINIAN TERRITORIES CHRISTIANS

BLACK HEBREWS

Also known as the African Hebrew Israelites of Jerusalem (www.africanhebrewisraelites ofjerusalem.com), the Black Hebrews are African Americans who claim descent from the ancient Israelite tribe of Judah and see Israel as their ancestral homeland. After spending time in Liberia, they began settling in Israel in 1969 under the leadership of Ben Carter, also known as Ben Ammi Ben-Israel. Although not recognised as Jews by any stream of Judaism (their traditions include a vegan diet, fasting on the Sabbath and polygamy), they were granted permanent residency in 2004 and a path to citizenship in 2009; many volunteer for service in the army.

About 2500 Black Hebrews live communally in the Negev town of Dimona. The community is known for its gospel choir and for singer Eddie Butler, who represented Israel in the Eurovision song contest in 1999 and 2006.

Jews. Over the last few years, an increasing number of Israeli Christian Arabs have been volunteering to serve in the IDF.

Major Christian centres include Nazareth, whose Christian population has dropped from 60% in 1949 to less than 30% today, and Bethlehem, which was 80% Christian in the 1940s but is now less than a quarter Christian. Other cities with sizable Christian communities include Jerusalem, Haifa and Nazareth.

Druze

The Druze speak Arabic but most don't consider themselves to be Arabs, and they believe in a strictly unitary God and accept many of the same prophets as Islam but they are not Muslims – in fact, Orthodox Muslims have sometimes persecuted them as heretics ever since their religion, an offshoot of Islam, was founded in Cairo in the early 11th century.

It was to escape persecution that the Druze established themselves in the remote mountains of southern Lebanon about a thousand years ago, and it is in order to prevent accusations of heresy that they keep the principles (eg reincarnation) and texts of their religion secret not only from outsiders but also from Druze laypeople *(juhhal)*, revealing them fully only to the community's *uqqal* (wise men and women). Only the *uqqal* attend Thursday-night religious ceremonies. The Druze religion has forbidden conversion, either in or out, since the mid-11th century.

Israeli Druze live mainly on Mt Carmel (eg in Daliyat al-Karmel), in various Galilee villages and on the Golan Heights, whose largest Druze village – most of whose residents identify at least nominally as Syrian – is Majdal Shams. Tradition dictates that the Druze be loyal to their country of residence so Israeli Druze men are drafted into the IDF, and many make careers in the army and the Border Police. During the 2014 Hamas–Israel war, a Druze colonel commanded the IDF's elite Golani infantry brigade.

Almost all Israeli and Palestinian Arabs are Sunnis but Israel has one Alawite (Alawi) village: Ghajar, 4km due east (by air) from Metulla, which is half in Lebanon and half in a sliver of land captured by Israel, along with the adjacent Golan, in 1967.

Samaritans

The Samaritan religion can probably best be described as an offshoot of Israelite-era Judaism. The Samaritans have a five-book Torah, written in Hebrew, but it differs in a number of significant ways from the Jewish Torah; for instance, regarding the place where God commanded that an altar for sacrifices be built – ancient Judaism established the Temple in Jerusalem, whereas the Samaritans built their Temple on Mt Gerizim, overlooking Nablus.

In Roman times, the Samaritans were powerful religious and political rivals of the Jews, which is why the New Testament's Parable of the Good Samaritan (Luke 10:25–37) is such a stinging rebuke of Judaism's Jerusalem-based priestly elite.

Today the Samaritans, who number just 760, are not considered Jews, but they are not exactly non-Jews either. Their religion and history are so closely tied to Judaism that they are eligible to receive Israeli citizenship based on the Law of Return, but in Israel they are considered – by themselves and by the Chief Rabbinate – to be a separate religious community.

Modern-day Samaritans (see www.thesamaritanupdate.com) live in two communities: one, Kiryat Luza, is on Mt Gerizim, near the West Bank city of Nablus; the other is in Israel, in the Tel Aviv suburb of Holon. While Israeli Samaritans are drafted into the IDF, their brethren in Kiryat Luza are Palestinian citizens. But every year the entire community joins together on Mt Gerizim to sacrifice sheep for Passover – so it was before 1967, when the two centres of Samaritan life were ruled by Jordan and Israel, and so it is today despite the complicated relationship between Israelis and Palestinians.

Israel's Vietnamese community of about 200 was established in 1977 when Prime Minister Menahem Begin welcomed Vietnamese boat people rescued in the South China Sea by Israeli merchant ships.

Hummus & Olives: Regional Food

Israelis and Palestinians disagree about many things, but food isn't one of them. Israel and the Palestinian Territories offer a vast smorgasbord of delicious dishes, some of them hard to find outside the region, many of them vegetarian and all of them – including innovative fusion variants – likely to intrigue your taste buds.

What to Eat

Heavenly Hummus

Ali Caravan, Jaffa

Hummus Said, Akko

Abu Shukhri, Abu Ghosh

Abu Shukri, Jerusalem

Felafel Hazkenim, Haifa

➜ **Hummus** Made of cooked chickpeas, this creamy paste is beloved across religious, political and cultural boundaries. Made to be dipped or scooped up with fresh pita bread, it is often served with warm *fuul* (fava beans), whole boiled chickpeas or tahina (sesame seed paste); Arabs sometimes serve it with ground meat. One difference: while Jews eat hummus all day long, Arabs traditionally take their (warm) hummus in the morning or early afternoon.

➜ **Olives** Especially popular for breakfast and dinner, olives come in a wide variety of styles very different than their Greek, Italian or Spanish cousins. Sold from vats in both markets and supermarkets, one particularly tasty variety to look for is *surim d'fukim* (cracked Tyre olives).

➜ **Felafel** Deep-fried balls made of ground chickpeas, best when piping hot. They are typically served inside a pita or wrapped in a *lafa* (flatbread) along with hummus and/or tahina, tomato, cucumber, pickle slices, a hot condiment such as Yemenite *s'chug* and, sometimes, sauerkraut.

➜ **Sabih** Felafel's upstart rival consists of deep-fried eggplant, egg, boiled potato, cucumber, tomato, chopped parsley and tahina tucked into a pita; traditionally eaten by the Jews of Iraq on Shabbat morning.

➜ **Shwarma** Chicken, turkey or lamb grilled on a giant spit and sliced in layers before being stuffed into a pita – the ultimate non-vegetarian street food.

➜ **Grilled meats** On sunny weekends you're likely to see families in parks gathered around a *mangal* (portable brazier) chargrilling red meat, served with pita and hummus. Many Jewish- and Arab-run restaurants specialise in grilled meats – keep an eye out for *kabab* (ground meat balls on a skewer), *shishlik* (lamb or chicken chunks on a skewer), *me'urav yerushalmi* ('Jerusalem mixed grill': heart, liver, spleen and other chicken bits grilled on a plancha) and goose liver.

A question you're likely to hear at breakfast time in Israel: would you like *betzei ayin* (sunny-side-up eggs), *beitzim mekushkashot* (scrambled), a *chavita* (omelette) or just a plain *beitza kasha* (hard-boiled egg)?

➜ **Labneh (labaneh)** A creamy, sour, yoghurt-type cheese, eaten with pita or *lafa*, that's smothered in olive oil and sprinkled with *za'atar* (a blend of local spices that includes hyssop, sumac and sesame).

➜ **Bourekas** Savoury, flaky Balkan pastries, often triangular, filled with salty Bulgarian cheese, mashed potatoes, mushrooms or spinach.

➜ **Shakshuka** A spicy Moroccan egg and tomato stew, usually eaten for breakfast.

➜ **Kubbeh** Minced lamb or beef encased in bulgur wheat to create a dumpling shaped like an American football. Iraqi and Kurdish Jews eat *kubbeh* made with semolina in a tangy soup.

VEGETARIAN BONANZA

Few countries offer a better selection of vegetarian options than Israel and the Palestinian Territories. Street food includes felafel, *sabih* and *bourekas;* almost all restaurants serve giant – and often creative – salads; and even in grilled-meat joints and meat-heavy Arab and Levantine eateries, the mezze-style appetisers can serve as a remarkably inexpensive vegetarian meal.

➔ **Jachnun** Rolled-up, buttery dough slow baked in a pot and served with grated tomatoes and *s'chug* hot paste; traditionally eaten by the Jews of Yemen on Shabbat morning.

➔ **Fruits** Locally grown, seasonal fruits include apricots, peaches, nectarines, plums, apples, pears, oranges, grapefruit, strawberries, cherries, kiwis, watermelon, mangoes, papayas and pomegranates.

➔ **Vegetables** The finest, freshest veggies are on offer in markets such as Jerusalem's Mahaneh Yehuda.

➔ **Dates** Varieties include the yellowish, translucent *dekel nur (deglet nur)* and the giant *medjoul*. In the fall you'll see plump, unripe yellow dates for sale – freezing them shortly before consumption takes away the pucker effect.

Kosher & Halal

Traditionally, Jews and Muslims observe strikingly similar sets of dietary laws, the former known as kosher *(kasher)*, the latter as halal. Both religions allow only certain species of animal to be eaten, with pigs considered to be the most unclean of all the beasts, and have the same basic rules for slaughter: a blessing is recited and animals are killed while fully conscious, their throats slit with a sharp, non-serrated blade.

In addition, keeping kosher involves:

➔ Refraining from the consumption of mammals that do not both have cloven hoofs and chew their cud (cattle, sheep and goats are fine); seafood (shrimp, lobster, squid etc); amphibians, reptiles and insects (except locusts); most birds that aren't ducks or geese; and those few types of fish that lack fins and/or scales (eg eels and catfish).

➔ Not mixing meat and dairy products (yes, cheeseburgers and pepperoni pizza are out).

Food that is neither milk nor meat, such as vegetables and fish, is called *parveh* (parve) and can be eaten with either milk or meat dishes. Foods to which especially strict standards have been applied are called *kasher l'mehadrin*. Meat labelled 'glatt kosher' comes from mammals whose lungs have been certified to be 'smooth', ie free of adhesions.

Israeli law does not require restaurants to be kosher – it's up to the owner to arrange (and pay for) kosher certification by the local Rabbinate branch. Kosher restaurants, which must close on Shabbat and Jewish holidays, are almost always either *basari* (*fleyshig* in Yiddish; 'meat') or *chalavi* (*milchig* in Yiddish; 'dairy', ie vegetarian plus fish). In Tel Aviv, kosher restaurants are the exception rather than the rule, whereas in Jerusalem it can be hard to find a place to eat on Shabbat.

Unlike Judaism, Islam strictly prohibits alcohol. Even foods with trace amounts of alcohol, or whose preparation involves alcohol (eg vanilla extract), are *haram* (forbidden).

Shabbat Foods

Israeli families from across the religious spectrum keep the ancient tradition of dining together on Erev Shabbat (Sabbath eve). On Friday

Local Brews

Goldstar, dark lager

Maccabee, pale lager

Taybeh, Palestinian beer

Bazelet Amber Ale, from the Golan

Alexander, boutique ale

Dancing Camel, microbrews from Tel Aviv

Shapiro, ales and stouts from Beit Shemesh

Negev, brewed in the south

evening, parents, children and grandchildren gather for a festive dinner, often after a battle of wills between in-laws over who gets to host the married children. In many homes, even secular ones, the lighting of the Shabbat candles is followed by Kiddush, the blessing over the wine. Traditional main dishes among Ashkenazim include chicken, or couscous for families with roots in North Africa.

All work, including cooking, is forbidden on Shabbat, which runs from 18 minutes before sundown on Friday (36 minutes before in Jerusalem) to one hour after sundown on Saturday. As a result, the only hot foods that could traditionally be eaten for Saturday lunch – we're talking about the time before the invention of the electric hot plate – were slow-cooked dishes put on the fire the night before. That's how Jews in different communities around the world came up with *hamin* (*tsholent* in Yiddish), a rich, stick-to-your-ribs stew usually made with potatoes, meat, beans, barley, chickpeas and hard-boiled eggs.

Festivals & Celebrations
Jewish

Food is a central feature of all Jewish festivals and celebrations, notable either for its omnipresence (eg on Passover and at weddings) or its absence (during fasts such as Yom Kippur, the Day of Atonement).

A few weeks before each Jewish holiday, you'll start seeing special foods and dishes in shops and markets. See p22 for dates of Israel's festivals.

➡ **Rosh HaShanah** The Jewish New Year begins sweetly with apples dipped in honey, honey cake, sweet round *challah* bread and pomegranates. Followers of Sephardi and Mizrahi traditions also eat foods such as leek, squash, beet, fritters and a fish head, each punningly associated with a blessing.

➡ **Yom Kippur** Nothing at all. About two-thirds of Israeli Jews, both religious and secular, refrain from eating or drinking for 25 hours, then dine in gatherings for a break-the-fast meal.

➡ **Sukkot** Commemorating the Israelites' 40 years of desert wandering after the Exodus, the eight-day holiday of Sukkot is noteworthy less for what is eaten than where: weather permitting, observant Jews take their meals in a *sukkah* (a rectangular hut with a flat roof made of branches); to find one, head to a kosher hotel or restaurant.

➡ **Hanukkah** Stuff yourself with *levivot* (*latkes* in Yiddish; fried potato pancakes) topped with sour cream or apple sauce and *sufganiot* (jelly-filled doughnuts), an Israeli contribution to the holiday.

➡ **Tu B'Shevat** On the New Year of the Trees, kids and adults eat dried fruits and nuts and plant trees.

➡ **Purim** *Oznei haman* ('Haman's ears'; *hamantashen* in Yiddish) are triangular pastries with a poppy-seed, prune or date filling; they are named after the arch-villain of the Purim story, Haman.

'Im hareef v'amba?' the busy felafel guy asks. What he wants to know is whether you'd like *s'chug* (fiery Yemenite hot pepper paste) and *amba* (Iraqi-style mango chutney) shmeared inside or dripped on your felafel. Unless you're an old hand or a masochist, the prudent answer is '*ktzat*' (a bit).

Favourite cheeses in Israel include *gvina Bulgarit* (Bulgarian cheese, similar to feta), *gvina Tsfatit* (a soft, set cheese, originally from Tsfat), *gvinat emek* (a yellow cheese), and deliciously creamy cottage cheese, so popular that price rises set off a consumer boycott and Knesset inquiries in 2011.

BREAKFAST IN ISRAEL

Israeli hotels, guesthouses and even hostels really shine come breakfast time. Most serve generous smorgasbords that include eggs, matias herring, pickled herring, soft and hard cheeses, Israeli-style vegetable salads, green olives, jams, breads, breakfast cereals and hot drinks.

Based on the dining traditions of the kibbutzim, whose members often worked in the still-cool fields for several hours before breakfast, the 'Israeli breakfast' has become a much loved feature of the local hotel scene; variants are on offer in cafes and restaurants.

FRUIT OF THE VINE

Local wines to look out for include those produced by:

Adir (www.adir-winery.com)

Domaine du Castel (www.castel.co.il)

Ella Valley (www.ellavalley.com)

Flam (www.flamwinery.com)

Golan Heights Winery (www.golanwines.co.il; labels include Yarden, Gamla, Hermon and Galil Mountain)

Odem Mountain (www.harodem.co.il)

Recanati (www.recanati-winery.com)

Tishbi (www.tishbi.com)

Tzora Vineyards (www.tzoravineyards.com)

Yatir (www.yatir.net)

➡ **Passover (Pesach)** Parsley, salt water, bitter herbs (usually horseradish or romaine lettuce), *charoset* (a sweet paste of grated apple, grated walnuts, sweet wine and chopped dates), a lamb shank bone and a roasted hard-boiled egg symbolise aspects of the Exodus story. Instead of bread, which – along with all leavened foods – is forbidden, there's *matzah*, unleavened crackers made of just two ingredients: flour and water. (During Passover, Israeli law forbids the sale of bread in Jewish areas.) In Ashkenazi communities, other festive treats include chicken soup with *matzah* balls (*kneydlakh* in Yiddish; dumplings made of ground matzah, eggs and oil or chicken fat) and gefilte fish (poached cod or carp balls).

➡ **Shavuot** Judaism's most vegetarian major holiday is a time to dine on dairy. Popular cheese-based dishes include *blintzes* (stuffed, folded-over crêpes), often topped with sour cream.

Muslim

During the month of Ramadan, observant Muslims refrain from eating or drinking (or smoking or having sex) during daylight hours, but it's what happens before and, especially, after the fast that turns Ramadan into a culinary festival – and a time when many Muslims actually gain weight! Fasters generally awaken before sunrise to eat because they won't take food or drink again until the *iftar,* the festive, break-the-fast family feast at dusk. (In some places, such as the Israeli seaside town of Jisr al-Zarka, organised programs invite paying, non-Muslim guests to the *iftar* meal.) The best-known Ramadan treat is *qatayif,* a pancake folded over a cluster of crushed nuts or small mound of cheese and drizzled with sugar syrup.

On Eid al-Adha (Feast of the Sacrifice), Muslims traditionally sacrifice an animal, often a lamb or sheep, as an act of thanksgiving for God's mercy. Not surprisingly, lamb or mutton are often on the menu.

When a baby is born, relatives might prepare *mughly,* a spice-laden rice pudding said to aid lactation. During periods of mourning, bitter Arab coffee replaces the sugared variety.

On major holidays and celebrations, sweet pastries are everywhere. Keep an eye out for *ma'amoul* (grainy cookies made of buttery semolina and stuffed with dates or nuts) and a host of honeyed pastries and sweets, including baklava, that are carried to the homes of relatives and friends in wrapped bakery trays.

Palestinian Arabs, Bedouin and Druze often bake their breads in a *taboun* (clay oven), also used for pizzas and *bourekas* (stuffed, flaky Balkan pastries) in Israel and the Palestinian Territories.

Where to Eat & Drink

In recent years, Tel Aviv and neighbouring Jaffa have become international-calibre dining destinations, with food options for every budget, including a bumper crop of high-end brasseries and *mis'adot shef* (restaurants whose decor and dishes reflect the chef's larger-than-life personality). Jerusalem, too, has plenty of dining choices but, with a few exceptions, the standard is far below that of Tel Aviv. In other parts of the country, dining experiences well worth trying include seafood in Akko, traditional Arab cuisine in Haifa and the Galilee, locally raised steak on the Golan and meat-free meals in vegetarian Moshav Amirim in the Upper Galilee.

Most Jewish restaurants are kosher, which means that, except for those in hotels, they're closed on Shabbat. Elsewhere in Israel and the Palestinian territories, the vast majority of establishments offering fine dining are not kosher and so stay open seven days a week – and may serve milk and meat together, seafood and even 'white meat' (the Israeli euphemism for pork).

Although Jerusalem, Be'er Sheva and Haifa have lively student scenes, the best bars are to be found in Tel Aviv. Aside from sports pubs and dance bars, the city is home to a new crop of boutique brewhouses serving local and international beers. For wine-tasting, head to the wineries of the Golan Heights, the Upper Galilee's Dalton Plateau, the Judean Hills or the Negev Highlands.

In the West Bank, Ramallah and Bethlehem offer the best top-end dining options, though the best food is generally cheap and cheerful: felafel, grilled meats and *ka'ek* (elongated sesame bagels). Nablus is justifiably famous for its sweets – come here for *kunafeh,* a thin cheese cake, served hot, made with melted white Nabulsi cheese topped with orange-coloured vermicelli-like pastry and soaked in rosewater syrup. While in Hebron, look out for *kedra* (a rice and lamb dish, infused with saffron and steamed inside a ceramic jar).

Lebanese and Palestinian specialities include the 'three Ms': *majadra* (rice and lentils garnished with fried onions), *mansaf* (lamb cooked in sour yoghurt and served atop rice) and *maklubeh* (layers of stewed chicken or lamb, rice and vegetables, turned 'upside down' before serving).

Daily Life

While you can learn quite a bit about a country by visiting historical sites, national parks and museums, the only way to get a sense of what really makes a place tick is to connect with the locals and their values, priorities and lifestyles.

Israelis
Values & Lifestyle

Although Israel is a Western-oriented liberal democracy with a booming high-tech economy, the country's incredible patchwork of ethnic groups, belief systems, languages and family stories make for a wide array of worldviews, personal priorities and lifestyles.

Israeli society was founded a century ago on socialist principles, exemplified by the shared communal life of the kibbutz (though even at the height of the kibbutz movement, only 3% of the Jewish population lived in one). These days, the vast majority of Israelis have shifted to a decidedly bourgeois and individualistic outlook, creating aspirations – including international travel – whose fulfilment depends in large part on finding good jobs with middle-class paychecks. These are increasingly hard to find, even in Tel Aviv, and have always been few and far between in the geographical 'periphery'.

In the bubble of Tel Aviv, secular Jews – alongside smaller numbers of Modern Orthodox Jews, Israeli Arabs and expats – work, shop, eat, play and create art with an intensity and panache that has more in common with Silicon Valley, Berlin and the booming cities of East Asia than with the city's poor suburbs or the development towns of the Galilee and Negev. Meanwhile, in Haredi (ultra-Orthodox) neighbourhoods such as Jerusalem's Mea She'arim, residents strive to preserve (or recreate) the lifestyle of 18th-century Eastern Europe. Although most kibbutzim have been 'privatised', with member-owned apartments and income determined by an individual's earning power, the residents of the country's 74 remaining 'communal' kibbutzim still live lives of 1950s-style socialist equality.

Hebrew culture and the arts are immensely important so reading literature and going out to concerts, the theatre and films are an integral part of life for many Israeli Jews. A longstanding love of the outdoors has helped make Israelis an active lot: hiking, cycling, windsurfing, backpacking, camping and other leisure activities are hugely popular.

In the Muslim Arab, Christian Arab, Bedouin, Druze and Circassian villages of the Galilee and the Negev, the pace of life is heavily influenced by religion (generally moderate and Western-oriented among Christians and Circassians, quite traditional among Muslims and Druze), economic realities (including job discrimination) and the latest, often disquieting, news from the Palestinian Territories and the Knesset. Many young people live at home until they get married.

Family is hugely important for virtually all Israelis. Young Jews may leave the nest at 18 to serve in the army, backpack through Southeast Asia, study, and live with a boyfriend or girlfriend, but even among the

> Among Israeli Jews, 42% define themselves as 'secular', 38% as 'traditional' to one degree or another, 12% as modern Orthodox and 8% as ultra-Orthodox (Haredi). Source: a 2009 survey by Israel's Central Bureau of Statistics.

> Gays and lesbians can pursue an open and, if they choose, flamboyant lifestyle in Tel Aviv, but the smaller gay scene in more conservative Jerusalem is low-key and circumspect.

THE ROLE OF JUDAISM

Judaism – as a religion, a national identity and a civilisation – has a significant impact on the daily lives of all Israeli Jews. For the Orthodox and especially the ultra-Orthodox (Haredim), virtually every action and decision is governed by Halacha (Jewish law), as interpreted by over 2000 years of legal precedent. Secular Jews pay little attention to the daily discipline of Jewish observance, but their lives are still shaped by the weekly rhythm of Shabbat and the annual cycle of Jewish holidays. Many Jewish Israelis define themselves not as 'secular' (ie ideologically secularist) but as 'traditional' *(masorti)* – for instance, young people may have Shabbat (Saturday) lunch with their family before heading out to a football match.

Studies show that in recent years, Israeli Jews have been showing increasing religiosity. Secular Jews are keeping more Shabbat rituals, often for cultural rather than theological reasons; traditional Jews are becoming a bit more traditional; and some Modern and ultra-Orthodox Jews are turning to ever-stricter interpretations of Halacha.

The exponential growth of the Haredi community is creating all sorts of frictions, for example, in formerly secular neighbourhoods in which new Haredi residents demand that roads be closed on the Sabbath and swimming pools be segregated by sex.

Most schools run by the ultra-Orthodox teach only religious subjects, providing virtually no education in science, mathematics, history, literature or English and producing generations of young people with few job skills. A significant majority of ultra-Orthodox men never work; instead they are supported by government subsidies while studying in *yeshivot* (religious seminaries) and *kollelim* (seminaries for married men). Haredi women, who are not bound by the Halachic command to spend every waking moment on religious study, are entering the workforce in increasing numbers, often as their family's sole breadwinner – despite also having to look after six, eight or more children.

most secular there is, for men as well as women, constant – some would say unrelenting – pressure to find a partner and bring children into the world.

In Israeli Jews' sense of themselves, the Holocaust is always hovering in the background: in the way they respond to missiles from Gaza and suicide bombings; in the way they assess Iran's nuclear program; in the way they react to reports of anti-Semitic violence in places such as France and Sweden; and in the way they wonder what a German tourist's grandfather was doing in 1943.

Hundreds of thousands of ultra-Orthodox Israelis use 'kosher' mobile phones that block access to 'inappropriate' content and lack cameras and text messaging, potentially tools for illicit flirting. Some models come with a Yiddish interface and Hassidic ringtones.

Military Service

Israel's military has been part of daily life since the country's birth, and for most young Israeli Jews being drafted – three years for men, two for women – is a rite of passage. Israel Defense Forces (IDF) service is also compulsory for Druze and Circassian men, and some Bedouin and Christian Arab men volunteer to serve. To the chagrin of many, draft exemptions are granted to the vast majority of ultra-Orthodox Jewish men and to most Orthodox and all ultra-Orthodox Jewish women.

Reservists can be called up (though most aren't) for training every year or two, generally until age 40 for men and until age 24 (or until the birth of their first child) for women. Soldiers are everywhere – especially, it seems, on buses and trains – and while it remains a jarring sight for first-time visitors, Israelis are unfazed by the proliferation of automatic weapons. If asked, some may answer that while being armed to the teeth is hardly ideal, it sure beats what their grandparents had to go through, hiding from Cossacks in Russia or anti-Jewish mobs in Iraq.

Women

Israeli women have personal freedom, social status and professional opportunities on a par with their European counterparts and have played significant roles in the economy, politics (eg Golda Meir) and the army (Israel is the only country to have a military draft for women). However, as in Ottoman times, marriage and divorce for Jews remain in the hands of the Chief Rabbinate, dominated by the ultra-Orthodox, whose all-male religious judges favour traditional male prerogatives over women's rights.

In recent years, some of Israel's ultra-Orthodox communities have become noticeably more concerned (some would say obsessed) with 'modesty', attempting to enforce ever-stricter rules aimed at separating men and women. Attempts to gender-segregate public transport (women, of course, are sent to the back of the bus) and even sidewalks, and to ban images of women from advertising billboards, have been met by protests and legislation forbidding the exclusion of women and images of women from the public sphere.

Palestinians
Values & Lifestyle

The ebb and flow of daily life in the Palestinian Territories depends largely on the security and economic situation. Gaza is in particularly dire straits as a result of the Israeli and Egyptian blockades, Egypt's sealing of hundreds of smuggling tunnels (2013–14) and Hamas's periodic confrontations with Israel. In the West Bank, Israel has removed most internal checkpoints in recent years, making it easier for Palestinians to travel between home and work or school, but day-to-day life can be profoundly frustrating, and residents never know when they may find themselves in a humiliating – or at least time-wasting – confrontation with the Israeli security forces or settlers.

Despite everything, the Palestinians are determined to make the best of their tenuous situation. Family bonds are unbreakable and are often made stronger by intra-family business partnerships. Many extended families pool their income to build a large home so everyone can live under one roof, with separate units for each nuclear family. Palestinian men often spend their leisure time in the local coffeehouse, where old-timers play backgammon.

Life in Gaza is tightly controlled by the precepts of fundamentalist Islam but much of the West Bank retains a moderate outlook, and Ramallah in particular exhibits the trappings of modern, Western living, including fancy cars, health clubs and late-night bars. Football and basketball are both popular sports, played by young Palestinians on makeshift fields and courts across the West Bank and Gaza.

Palestinians are steadfastly attached to their land, especially their olive groves, and many urban Palestinians return to their home villages to help with the harvest in October and November.

Inside Israel, there is increasing interest in documenting and preserving the ruins of villages lost in 1948. The app iNakba, launched in 2014, helps users find Palestinian villages destroyed since 1948.

Employment & Income

Despite restrictions imposed by Israel, the pragmatic policies of former Palestinian Authority Prime Minister Salam Fayyad, a PhD economist, and foreign aid have helped produce solid economic growth in the West Bank in recent years. But Palestinians still earn far less than Israelis (the annual per capita GDP is just US$2800 in the Palestinian Territories, compared to US$34,000 in Israel), and the lack of economic opportunity, especially for young people, has done much to keep Palestinians frustrated with their lot. With unemployment rates of 19% in the West Bank and 40% in Gaza and one of the

According to the United Nations Development Programme, Israel ranks 19 (out of 187 countries) on its 2014 Human Development Index; the State of Palestine is ranked 107.

Palestinian men are the bread-winners in most families, but in a typical household the wife handles the accounts. After budgeting her husband's earnings she hands him back some walking-around cash, called 'cigarette money'.

highest birth rates in the world (Muslim Palestinian women have an average of seven children each, as do ultra-Orthodox Jewish women in Israel), the average Palestinian home is both overcrowded and poor.

Women

Palestinian women have traditionally played the role of home-based caregiver, but recent years have seen more women entering higher education and working outside the home. Except in fundamentalist areas, women have slowly made their mark on Palestinian politics – Ramallah, for instance, had a female mayor, Janet Michael, from 2005 to 2012, and Hannan Ashrawi is well known as an eloquent spokeswoman for the Palestinian cause.

Government & Politics

Government policies and processes loom especially large in the lives of Israelis and Palestinians, whose century-old confrontation periodically sweeps everyone up in unpredictable and sometimes violent events. Even casual visitors are likely to come across frequent references to political parties, government decisions and policy failures.

Israel's System of Government

Because of longstanding disagreements over the most basic aspects of Israel's identity, including the role of religion, Israelis have been unable to agree on a constitution. Instead, the Knesset has cobbled together a set of laws with constitutional force, known as the Basic Law, that includes a partial Bill of Rights. The High Court of Justice has the power to judicially review laws passed by the Knesset, determining their constitutionality based on their compatibility with the Basic Law.

Legislative Branch & President

Israel is a parliamentary democracy whose unicameral legislature, the Knesset, has 120 members (MKs). It is elected by national proportional representation for a four-year term, though elections can be called early if the coalition loses a vote-of-no-confidence (on average, Israeli governments last a bit over two years).

Because of the fragmented nature of Israeli society – religiously, ideologically, ethnically and linguistically – and the fact that any party that receives a mere 3.25% of the vote wins parliamentary seats, the Knesset typically includes a dozen or more parties. Achieving a 61-vote majority requires forming a coalition, which means that smaller parties often wield significant power.

All Israeli citizens aged 18 or over can vote. There is no absentee voting (except for diplomatic staff and members of the merchant marine) so Israelis living abroad cannot cast ballots unless they are physically present in Israel on election day. Voters vote for political parties, not specific candidates; if a party gets, say, 10% of the national vote, the first 12 candidates on its ranked election slate enter the Knesset.

Israel's head of state is the president, whose role is largely ceremonial except that after elections he or she decides which party leader will be given the opportunity to form a coalition and must also consent to the dissolution of parliament. Another presidential prerogative: issuing pardons. The Knesset elects the president for a single term of seven years.

Executive Branch

The prime minister presides over the cabinet (government), whose members (ministers) are chosen by the prime minister based, in part, on the electoral power of their respective parties; their appointment must be approved by the Knesset. Most cabinet members also serve as the executive heads of government ministries, though some serve as 'ministers-without-portfolio'. The cabinet votes on the prime minister's security, foreign and domestic policies. Under the principle of

Golda Meir (1898–1978), the world's third female prime minister (1969–74), was born in Kiev, grew up in Milwaukee and Denver, where she became a socialist Zionist, and moved to Palestine in 1921.

'ministerial responsibility', ministers must support policies endorsed by the cabinet even if they voted against them. The weekly cabinet meeting – often featured in the news – is held every Sunday.

Some members of the cabinet also serve in the powerful Security Cabinet, led by the prime minister, whose members – including the ministers of defence, foreign affairs, internal security, interior and treasury – make decisions about urgent defence and foreign policy issues.

Judicial System

Israel has an independent judiciary with three tiers of courts: the Magistrates Courts, for ordinary criminal and civil trials; the District Courts, for appeals; and the Supreme Court, which serves as the highest court of appeal and, sitting as the High Court of Justice (known by its acronym, Bagatz), makes decisions concerning the legality of actions by government authorities.

Israel also has a system of religious courts – Jewish, Muslim and Christian – with jurisdiction over matters of personal status (mainly marriage and divorce). There is no provision in Israeli law for civil (ie secular) marriage and as none of the religious courts perform intermarriages, couples of mixed religious background wishing to wed can do so only outside Israel (eg in Cyprus). (Civil marriages abroad, including homosexual marriages, are recognised in Israel.)

Israeli President Reuven (Ruby) Rivlin of the right-wing Likud, inaugurated in 2014 to succeed Shimon Peres, opposes territorial compromise – but also has a strong civil rights record. As president he has spoken out forcefully against discrimination and political incitement against Israel's Arab citizens.

Israeli Political Parties: an Introduction

Can't keep all the Israeli political parties mentioned in the news straight? Here's a rundown of the 10 parties represented in the 20th Knesset, elected in March 2015:

➡ **Likud** (30 MKs) The centre-right party of Prime Minister Netanyahu includes far-right, populist elements. The 2015 election was viewed largely as a referendum on the leadership of Netanyahu, a divisive figure both at home and internationally. After a tight race, Likud won the 2015 elections with a decisive margin. The party takes a hard line on security issues and concessions to the Palestinians.

➡ **Zionist Union** (24 MKs) This centre-left alliance let by Isaac Herzog was formed between the Labor Party and Hatnuah ahead of the 2015 elections. Key issues include repairing relations with the US, negotiating with the Palestinians and addressing Israel's economic problems.

➡ **Joint Arab List** (13 MKs) The alliance of Hadash, Balad, United Arab List, and Ta'al became the third largest party in the Knesset after the elections, promising to represent the interests of the Arab minority. The party encompasses diverse ideologies.

➡ **Yesh Atid** (11 MKs) A centrist, free-market party founded in 2012 to represent the secular middle class; led by Yair Lapid.

➡ **Kulanu** (10 MKs) Influential right-leaning centre party led by Moshe Kahlon. The party's key issue is tackling the high cost of living in Israel.

➡ **Jewish Home** (eight MKs) Far-right party representing the national-religious Orthodox Zionists and the West Bank settlers. Led by software entrepreneur Naftali Bennet.

➡ **Shas** (seven MKs) A Mizrahi/Sephardi ultra-Orthodox party founded to fight discrimination against non-Ashkenazi Jews; supported by many 'traditional' Jews from North Africa.

➡ **United Torah Judaism** (six MKs) An alliance of two rival Ashkenazi-ultra-Orthodox parties, Degel HaTorah, which is Litvak ('Lithuanian'), and Agudat Yisrael, which is Hassidic. Focuses on securing funding for the ultra-Orthodox sector.

→ **Yisra'el Beitenu** (six MKs) A secular, nationalist, right-wing party led by Soviet-born Avigdor Lieberman. Supported by many Russian-speaking immigrants.

→ **Meretz** (five MKs) A left-wing party with strong social-democratic credentials and an upper-middle-class Ashkenazi base of support.

Palestinian Authority

The Palestinian Authority (Palestinian National Authority; PA or PNA) is an interim administrative body set up in 1994 under the Oslo Accords to rule parts of the West Bank and Gaza for five years, until the establishment of a Palestinian state. Final-status negotiations have dragged on – and so has the PA.

As part of the Oslo peace process, the PA assumed control of civil and security affairs in the major cities of the West Bank – known collectively as Area A, this covers about 3% of the land area of the West Bank. A further 25% of the West Bank (most built-up villages), known as Area B, is under PA civil control; Israel retains responsibility for security affairs. The rest of the West Bank (some 72% of the land area) is designated as Area C, under full Israeli civil and security control. About 300,000 West Bank Palestinians live in Area C, whose Israeli settlements, military bases and bypass roads fragment PA-controlled areas into dozens of tiny enclaves.

Since Hamas's violent takeover of Gaza in 2007, the West Bank and Gaza have been governed by separate governments. The internationally recognised and funded Fatah-controlled PA government continues to exercise authority in much of the West Bank, while Gaza is under the rule of a Hamas government that Israel, Egypt, the US and many Arab and European governments have sought to isolate.

The Palestinian Legislative Council (PLC), also known as the Palestinian parliament, has 132 members elected from 16 districts in the West Bank and Gaza. The last elections, won by Hamas, took place in 2006; under the Fatah-Hamas unity government sworn in in mid-2014, new general elections were due to take place within six months.

The PA is headed by an executive president, directly elected – at least in theory – once every four years. Yasser Arafat held the post from 1994 until his death in 2004. In January 2005 Mahmoud Abbas (also known

WHO'S WHO IN PALESTINIAN POLITICS

→ **Palestine Liberation Organisation (PLO)** Founded in 1964, the PLO is a coalition of Palestinian factions. The UN General Assembly recognised the organisation as the 'representative of the Palestinian people' in 1974 and gave it the status of a 'non-member observer state' in 2012.

→ **Fatah** Long the dominant political party in the PLO, Fatah ('conquest') – secular and nationalist in orientation – was founded by Yasser Arafat (1929–2004) and several young Palestinian refugees in 1959. During the 1970s and 1980s it engaged in international terrorism, but renounced violence in 1988 and recognised the 'right of the State of Israel to exist in peace and security' in 1993. After the Oslo Accords, Fatah, under Arafat, gained a reputation for corruption and undemocratic, non-transparent ways.

→ **Hamas** Both a militant movement and a political party, Hamas currently rules Gaza. The Hamas charter calls for the destruction of the State of Israel through 'armed struggle' and the establishment of a Palestinian Islamic state in what is now the territory of Israel, the Gaza Strip and the West Bank.

→ **Islamic Jihad** An armed Islamist movement in Gaza and a rival to Hamas. Considered a terrorist organisation by Israel and most Western countries.

FATAH–HAMAS RECONCILIATION

After the 2006 Palestinian legislative elections, which Hamas won with 76 seats to Fatah's 43, Fatah military commanders refused to take orders from their rivals and Hamas and Fatah were unable to reach an agreement on sharing power. The two sides were soon engaging in mutual kidnappings, attacks and assassinations. In 2007 Hamas forces ejected Fatah from Gaza in a bloody takeover that saw pitched street battles and party loyalists from both sides executed by their opponents. Fatah responded by cracking down on Hamas activities in the West Bank. Since then, the two discontiguous regions that make up the Palestinian Territories have been ruled by rival governments.

Several attempts at reconciliation foundered due to ideological differences, bitterness over past violence and deep mistrust, but in the spring of 2014 Fatah and Hamas signed an agreement providing for the formation of an interim unity government and parliamentary elections. Israel opposed the move but may after the 2014 Hamas–Israel war have no choice but to deal with both Fatah and Hamas.

as Abu Mazen) was elected and has served as PA president ever since – there has been an absence of subsequent elections. The president nominates the PA's prime minister, who must be confirmed by the PLC.

The PLC has had difficulty functioning, in part because of Israeli restrictions on its members (especially those from Hamas) and in part because of the Fatah-Hamas split of 2007.

What Is Hamas?

In 1987 Islamist leaders in Gaza set up the Palestinian wing of Egypt's Muslim Brotherhood, calling it Harakat al-Muqawama al-Islamiya (Islamic Resistance Movement). Better known by its acronym, Hamas, this Islamist organisation seeks to establish a Palestinian Islamic state in all of what is now Israel, the West Bank and Gaza. Because it has refused to renounce violence against Israeli civilians (eg suicide bombings and rocket attacks), Hamas is classified as a 'terrorist group' by some countries including Israel and the US.

Hamas: From Resistance to Government (2012) by Paola Caridi looks at the complexities of the organisation's history.

By the early 1990s, Hamas – funded by Gulf countries and, later, Iran – was gaining status among Palestinians, not only for its uncompromising opposition to Israel but also for running youth clubs, medical clinics and schools in poor neighbourhoods. Whereas Arafat's Fatah Party was seen as corrupt to the core, Hamas was considered both pious and honest.

In 2005 the group agreed with Arafat's successor, Mahmoud Abbas, to accept a role in Palestinian parliamentary politics. In the Palestinian Authority elections of January 2006, Hamas won a surprise majority in the Palestinian Legislative Council (the PA parliament), in large part because voters were sick of Fatah's corruption and failure to deliver on Palestinian national aspirations.

The new Hamas government refused to recognise Israel, renounce violence or accept agreements with Israel signed by the PA – as demanded by Western countries – and found itself shunned. It also faced internal opposition from Fatah members loath to give up their non-Islamist nationalism, and their prerogatives and power. In 2007, in a bloody coup, Hamas forced Fatah out of Gaza and clamped down on dissent and launched a campaign of missile attacks against Israeli towns and villages. In response, Israel instituted a partial blockade of Gaza (for its own reasons, so did Egypt). In the following years, Hamas and Israel had three bloody confrontations: around New Year 2009, in late 2012 and during the summer of 2014.

In the wake of the Arab Spring upheaval, Hamas has found itself more isolated than ever. Although it had long been a guest of the Assad regime in Damascus, Hamas's declaration of support for Syria's Sunni opposition damaged its ties with – and funding from – Assad's main ally, Shi'ite Iran. Relations with Egypt warmed up after Mohammed al-Morsi of the Muslim Brotherhood was elected president in 2012 but he still kept the Gaza–Sinai border largely closed. Under Abdel Fattah el-Sisi, Egypt has taken aggressive measures to isolate Gaza from Sinai. Domestically, the Hamas leadership in Gaza faces challenges to its authority from radical, Al-Qaida-inspired groups.

Religion

Israel and the Palestinian Territories are the birthplace of two of the three great monotheistic faiths, Judaism and Christianity. The youngest of the trio, Islam, considers Jerusalem to be its third-holiest city. And another world religion, the Baha'i faith, has its holiest sites in Haifa and Akko (see p156).

Judaism

One of the oldest religions still practised, Judaism is based on a covenantal relationship between the Jewish people and God. The most succinct summary of Jewish theology and Judaism's strict monotheism is to be found in the Shema prayer, which reads, 'Hear O Israel, the Lord is your God, the Lord is One'.

According to the Torah (the first five books of the Hebrew Bible), the covenant between God and the Jewish people began with the first monotheist, Abraham (19th century BCE), forefather of both Jews and Muslims. It was later confirmed and elaborated at Mt Sinai (13th century BCE), where the Israelites – in addition to receiving the Ten Commandments – were transformed from a tribal grouping into a people. The Jewish people is eternally bound by this covenant – this is the meaning of being 'chosen' – and is required not only to obey God's *mitzvot* (commandments) but also to demonstrate, through exemplary conduct, the truth of God's oneness to all the nations of the world.

Judaism holds that God is present in history and in the actions of human beings. Evil occurs when human beings wilfully and deliberately ignore God's will, good happens when they follow the rules he has laid down. Humans have both free will and moral agency: they can choose to follow either their evil impulses or their better natures.

Jewish history can be divided into two periods: before and after the destruction of the Second Temple in Jerusalem in 70 CE. Before that momentous year, Jewish ritual and service to God were focused on animal sacrifices carried out in the Temple in Jerusalem by the *kohanim* (members of the priestly class, from whom Jews with the family name of Cohen are descended). After the destruction of Jerusalem, sacrifices ceased and Judaism turned to prayer, meditation and study as the main methods of communication with the Divine. Over the next few centuries, Judaism's Oral Law was put into writing in the Mishna and further elaborated in the Talmud; much of the latter, written in Aramaic, reads like a shorthand protocol of legal deliberations.

Before the Holocaust, there were about 18 million Jews worldwide. Today, there are estimated to be about 13 million Jews, including about six million each in Israel and the US.

KEEPING SHABBAT

On the Sabbath, observant Jews refrain from performing 39 'creative activities', including lighting or extinguishing fires, using electricity, travelling by motorised vehicle, writing, cooking, baking, sewing, harvesting, doing business, handling money, and transporting objects between private and public spaces.

JEWISH HEADCOVERINGS

If you see a man wearing a small, round, convex skullcap, chances are he is a religious Jew (unless he's the Pope).

There is no commandment specifying that Jewish men cover their heads. Rather, wearing a *kippa* (*yarmulke* in Yiddish, skullcap in English) is merely a tradition, albeit one that is well entrenched. All male visitors to Jewish holy sites are asked to cover their heads – either with a *kippa* or any kind of hat.

It is often possible to infer a Jewish man's background, religious orientation and even political beliefs by the type of *kippa* he wears. Zionist Orthodox Jews, including West Bank settlers, usually go for crocheted *kippot* with designs around the edges, while ultra-Orthodox (Haredi) men, of both the Hasidic and Litvak streams, generally wear black velvet or cloth *kippot* of medium size. The Bukharian Jews of Central Asia wear pillbox caps decorated with embroidery. An extra-large crocheted *kippa* is a sign that the wearer is probably either a follower of the Braslav Hassidic movement or a messianic Jewish West Bank settler. (Don't confuse such *kippot* with the white, crocheted skullcaps worn by Hajjis, ie Muslims who have made the pilgrimage to Mecca.)

Over the next 1500 years, generation after generation of sages – issuing legal rulings and teaching in places such as Babylonia (Iraq), Egypt, Spain, Tsfat (in the Galilee) and Lithuania – debated and refined both Jewish theology and the 613 commandments of Halacha (Jewish law). Orthodox Judaism (the most conservative of the religion's streams) holds that the Oral Law, in its entirely, was given at Mt Sinai, while the Reform, Conservative and Reconstructionist Movements believe that Judaism has always been dynamic and proactive, changing and developing over the generations as it has had to deal with new ideas and new circumstances.

Today, ultra-Orthodox (Haredi) rabbis – many of whom are non-Zionist (ie are at best ambivalent about the role of the State of Israel in Jewish history) – have exclusive control of state-supported Jewish religious practice in Israel through the Chief Rabbinate, despite the fact that their followers constitute only a small minority of the country's Jewish population. In the Diaspora, the vast majority of Jews belong to the liberal (progressive) movements or are not affiliated with any movement.

Jerusalem, Zion and Israel have played a central role in Judaism ever since God promised the Land of Israel to the Children of Israel in the Torah. When praying, Jews face Jerusalem, and virtually all synagogues are built with the Torah ark facing the Holy City.

Christianity

Christianity is based on the life and teachings of Jesus of Nazareth, a Jew who lived in Judea and Galilee during the 1st century CE; on his crucifixion by the Romans; and on his resurrection three days later, as related in the New Testament.

Christianity started out as a movement within Judaism, and most of Jesus's followers, known as the Apostles, were Jews. Like many Jews of his time, Jesus was critical of the decadence and materialism of Jerusalem's ruling class and contemptuous of Roman authority. But after his death, the insistence of Jesus's followers that he was the Messiah caused Christianity to become increasingly distinct from Judaism. The anti-Jewish polemics of some early Christians, written at a time when Christianity was a beleaguered sect persecuted by the Romans, would have serious implications in later centuries, when Christianity became all-powerful in Europe.

In 1920, one in 10 Palestinian Arabs was Christian; today, just one in 75 residents of the Palestinian Territories is. Bethlehem, which in 1948 was 85% Christian, is now more than three-quarters Muslim.

According to the New Testament, the Angel Gabriel – in an event known as the Annunciation – appeared to Mary in Nazareth and informed her that she would conceive and give birth to the son of God. Jesus was born in Bethlehem (in Christian terminology and art, his birth is known as the Nativity) but grew up back in Nazareth, where he later preached. Much of his ministry – and many of his best-known biblical miracles – took place around the Sea of Galilee, in places such as Capernaum, Korazim, Bethsaida and Kursi. The Sermon on the Mount was delivered just up the hill from Capernaum on the Mount of the Beatitudes, while the Transfiguration took place on Mt Tabor. Places believed to correspond to all these venues can be visited.

At the age of 33 or so Jesus, whose growing influence had caused alarm among Jewish and Roman authorities alike, was accused of sedition and condemned to death by the Roman prefect of Judea, Pontius Pilate. Christians believe that his suffering was foretold in the Hebrew Bible. According to the New Testament, after the Last Supper Jesus was arrested in Gethsemane; put on trial before the Sanhedrin (Jewish supreme court), Pontius Pilate and even Herod the Great (the Roman-appointed king of Judea) himself; condemned to death; and mocked by Roman soldiers as he was led to Golgotha (Calvary), where he was crucified. Three days after his burial (Entombment), the New Testament says, his tomb was found to be empty, evidence of his resurrection.

The followers of Jesus came to be known as Christians (Christ is a Greek-derived title meaning 'Anointed One'), believing him to be the son of God and the messiah (the English word 'messiah' comes from the Hebrew *mashiach*, which also means 'anointed one'). Jews did not (and do not) accept Jesus as the messiah or as the son of God – this difference is the defining theological disagreement between the two faiths. Muslims consider Jesus to be a messenger of God and a prophet but do not believe that he was crucified or that he atoned for humankind's sins.

In about 325 CE, St Helena (Constantine the Great's mother) identified what she believed to be the location of Jesus's crucifixion and burial, marking the site with a predecessor of today's Church of the Holy Sepulchre. The First Crusade (1095–99) was launched in part to ensure Christian access to this site.

The ownership of holy sites in Israel and the Palestinian Territories has long been a subject of contention among the country's various Christian denominations. At a number of sites in Jerusalem and Bethlehem, relations are still governed by a 'status quo' agreement drawn up in Ottoman times. The Holy Land's largest denomination, the Greek Orthodox Church – almost all of whose local members are Arabic-speaking Palestinians – has jurisdiction over more than half of Jerusalem's Church of the Holy Sepulchre and a large portion of Bethlehem's Church of the Nativity.

> Only about 1400 Christians still live in Gaza. Since the Hamas takeover, Islamist hard-liners have killed the owner of a Gaza City Christian book-shop for alleged proselytising (2007), bombed the Gaza City YMCA (2008) and attacked several churches.

> Excellent primers on the Muslim faith include *Inside Islam* (2002), edited by John Miller and Aaron Kenedi, and *Islam: A Short History* (2000), by Karen Armstrong. *No God But God: The Origins, Evolution, and Future of Islam* (2005) by Reza Aslan received critical acclaim for its liberal interpretation of Islam.

Islam

Founded by the Prophet Mohammed (570–632 CE), who lived in what is now Saudi Arabia, Islam is based on belief in the absolute oneness of God (Allah) and in the revelations of his final prophet, Mohammed. The Arabic word *islam* means 'absolute submission' to God and his word.

Mohammed began preaching to the people of Mecca in about 610 CE, calling on them to renounce idolatry, believe in one God and prepare themselves for the Day of Judgement, when all humans would be held accountable for their actions.

Islam's sacred scripture is the Quran (Koran), which was revealed to Mohammed over the course of two decades. Believed by Muslims to be God's infallible word, it consists of 114 *suras* (chapters) written in high-

THE FIVE PILLARS OF ISLAM

➡ **Shahadah** Islam's confession of faith, the Shahadah sums up the Islamic belief in the absolute oneness of God and the finality of Mohammed's prophecy: 'There is no God but Allah, and Mohammed is the messenger of Allah'. Anyone who recites the Shahadah – which appears on the flag of Saudi Arabia – three times, in front of witnesses, becomes a Muslim.

➡ **Salat** The obligation to pray to God, without an intermediary, five times a day (dawn, midday, late afternoon, sunset and night). Prayers are performed facing Mecca and can be undertaken anywhere, except on Friday at noon, when men must attend congregational prayers in a mosque.

➡ **Zakat** Muslims are required to give alms to the poor worth one-fortieth of their income. The West Bank and Gaza have around 80 *zakat* committees that oversee the distribution of charitable donations.

➡ **Sawm** During Ramadan, the ninth month of the Islamic calendar, nothing must pass through the lips (food, cigarettes or drinks), and sex is prohibited, from dawn until dusk.

➡ **Hajj** The pilgrimage to Mecca, which every Muslim who is able should make at least once in their lifetime.

ly complex – and often poetic – classical Arabic. The Quran presents God as the omnipresent creator and sustainer of the world, infinite in his wisdom and power. Sayings and acts attributed to the Prophet, believed to illustrate correct Islamic behaviour and beliefs, are known as *hadith*.

Islam and Judaism share common roots, and Muslims consider Adam, Noah, Abraham, Isaac, Jacob, Joseph and Moses to be prophets. As a result, Jews and Muslims share a number of holy sites, including Al-Haram ash-Sharif/Temple Mount in Jerusalem and the Ibrahimi Mosque/Cave of Machpelah (Tomb of the Patriarchs) in Hebron. Because of their close scriptural links, Muslims consider both Jews and Christians to be an *ahl al-Kitab,* a 'people of the Book'. Judaism has always seen Islam as a fellow monotheistic faith (because of the Trinity, Jewish sages weren't always so sure about Christianity).

Muslims believe that Mohammed visited Jerusalem on his 'Night Journey', during which his steed Buraq took him from Mecca to Jerusalem in a single night. He then ascended to heaven from the stone around which the Dome of the Rock was later built, returning with revelations for the faithful. For a brief period, Mohammed instructed Muslims to pray towards Jerusalem.

Almost all Palestinian Muslims belong to Sunni Islam, by far the religion's largest branch; so do the vast majority of Egyptians, Jordanians and Syrians. The Lebanese Hezbollah movement, like its patrons in Iran, is Shiite (Shi'a). Syria's ruling elite belongs to a heterodox offshoot of Shiite Islam known as Alawite (Alawi).

In 1993 the late King Hussein of Jordan – out-manoeuvring the Saudis – donated funds to refurbish the golden dome of Jerusalem's Dome of the Rock. The exterior is now covered by 80kg of 24-carat gold leaf.

Arts

Both Israelis and Palestinians have been exceptionally creative in expressing their aspirations, joys and fears through literature and the performing, visual and musical arts. Travellers who enjoy connecting through the arts with the cultures they're visiting will find plenty opportunities to do so at festivals and in theatres, museums and bookshops.

Attended by 600 publishers from 30 countries, the huge Jerusalem International Book Fair (www.jerusalembookfair.com) has been held in odd-numbered years since 1963. It's here that the prestigious Jerusalem Prize for Literature is awarded.

Literature

Israeli Literature

Israelis across the political spectrum see the revival of the Hebrew language and the creation of modern Hebrew literature as the crowning cultural achievements of the State of Israel. Some names to keep an eye out for (their major works are available in English translation):

Shmuel Yosef Agnon (1888–1970) Israel's Nobel winner examined the dichotomy between traditional Jewish and modern life.

Yehuda Amichai (1924–2000) His poetry, written in colloquial Hebrew, captured the public's imagination with its gently ironic explorations of daily life.

Ephraim Kishon (1924–2005) The works of the brilliant Hungarian-born satirist skewer Israeli society and universal human foibles.

Aharon Appelfeld (b 1932) In novels such as *Badenheim 1939* (1978), the Holocaust hovers just off stage.

AB Yehoshua (b 1936) Caught between intentions and their implementation, his characters struggle to break out of their loneliness.

Amos Oz (b 1939) His works paint compelling, if sometimes bleak, pictures of an Israel few visitors encounter.

Meir Shalev (b 1948) Often set in Israel's recent past, Shalev's highly acclaimed novels deal with vengeance and masculinity.

David Grossman (b 1954) The novelist established his reputation with *The Yellow Wind* (1987), a blistering and prescient look at Israel's occupation of the Palestinian Territories.

Zeruya Shalev (b 1959) Through her characters' inner life, Shalev explores family ties, yearning, the compromises people make and the pull of the past.

Orly Castel-Bloom (b 1960) Known for postmodern sensibilities and irony, with characters suspended between meaninglessness and moments of belonging.

Etgar Keret (b 1967) Dubbed 'the voice of his generation' for his often humorous postmodern short stories, screenplays and graphic novels.

Sayed Kashua (b 1975) Israeli-Arab humorist known for his tongue-in-cheek portraits of the lives and travails of Arab Israelis.

Palestinian Literature

The most widespread form of literary expression among Palestinians has long been poetry, whose leading voice remains Mahmoud Darwish (1941–2008; www.mahmouddarwish.com). His lyrical collections, dealing with loss and exile, include *Why Did You Leave the Horse Alone?* (1995) and *Unfortunately, It Was Paradise* (2003). Prominent themes in the poetry of Tawfiq Ziad (Zayyad; 1929–94) include freedom, solidarity and Palestinians' connection with the land.

It wasn't until the 1960s that narrative fiction appeared on the Palestinian literary scene. Emile Habibi (1922–96) – like Ziad, a Knesset member from the Israeli Community Party – was the author of seven novels, including *Secret Life of Saeed the Pesoptimist* (1974), a tragicomic tale dealing with the difficulties facing Palestinians who became Israeli citizens after 1948.

The stunning debut work of Ghassan Kanafani (1936–72), *Men in the Sun* (1963), includes a novella and a collection of short stories that delve into the lives, hopes and shattered dreams of its Palestinian characters. In *The Inheritance* (2005), Nablus-born Sahar Khalifeh (b 1942) provides frequently chilling insights into the lives of Palestinian women, both in the Palestinian Territories and abroad.

Music

Israeli Music

Israeli music encompasses a rich tapestry of modes, scales and vocal styles inspired by the musical traditions of both the East and West.

Israelis of all ages listen to songs from decades past without necessarily thinking of them as 'retro'. Among the still-popular greats of the mid-20th century is the Yemen-born singer Shoshana Damari (1923–2006), renowned for her peerless pronunciation of the guttural letter *'ayn*. Naomi Shemer (1930–2004) composed much of the soundtrack of Israel's 1960s, 1970s and 1980s, including the iconic - though rarely heard - 'Jerusalem of Gold' (1967).

Despite the 1965 banning of a Beatles tour by Israel's cultural commissars, rock quickly made itself a fixture on the local music scene thanks to groups such as Poogy (Kaveret), Mashina, Teapacks (named after Tipp-Ex, the correction fluid) and Benzin. Rock has inspired many of the anthems of classic Israeli pop – names to listen for include Shlomo Artzi, Arik Einstein, Matti Caspi, Shalom Hanoch, Yehudit Ravitz, Assaf Amdursky and Aviv Geffen. Idan Raichel introduced Ethiopian melodies to a mainstream audience.

Among the Israeli hip-hop artists and groups you may come across are Shabak Samech, HaDag Nachash, Subliminal, and militant rightwing rapper The Shadow. One of the most exuberant performers of dance music has been Dana International (www.danainternational.co.il), a half-Yemenite transsexual who won the Eurovision Song Contest in 1998.

Mizrahi (Oriental or Eastern) music, with its Middle Eastern and Mediterranean scales and rhythms, has its roots in the melodies of North Africa (especially Umm Kulthum–era Egypt and mid-century Morocco), Iraq and Yemen. Many modern works, though, are inspired by musical styles from the Mediterranean basin, especially Turkey and Greece. For decades Mizrahi music was banned from the radio – the Ashkenazi cultural elite feared 'Levantinisation' – so to find the work of artists such as Zohar Argov (1955–87) and Haim Moshe (b 1956) you had to head to grungy cassette shops around Tel Aviv's (old) central bus station.

These days, though, Mizrahi music may be Israel's most popular genre. Old-timers Shlomo Bar (www.shlomobar.com) and Yair Dalal (www.yairdalal.com), inspired by the traditional Jewish music of Morocco and Iraq respectively, are still performing, joined more recently by superstars Sarit Hadad (www.sarit-hadad.com), who has been described as Israel's Britney Spears, and Amir Benayoun, whose genre-defying concerts mix love songs, medieval Jewish liturgical poems and strident nationalism. Moshe Peretz enjoys crossing the line from Mizrahi to mainstream and back again.

The Hebrew Book Week (www.sfarim.org.il), an incredibly popular carnival of the printed word, brings scores of publishers' book stalls – and steep discounts – to public squares in several dozen Israeli cities in mid-June.

Musical festivities in Israel include the twice-a-year Abu Gosh Vocal Music Festival (www.agfestival.co.il), Eilat's Red Sea Jazz Festival (www.redsea-jazzeilat.com) and, for dance music, Tel Aviv's annual Love Parade.

> ## TRADITIONAL & MODERN DANCE
>
> Israel has several world-renowned professional dance companies. The acclaimed Bat Sheva Dance Company (www.batsheva.co.il), founded by Martha Graham in 1964, is based at Tel Aviv's Suzanne Dellal Centre (p138); it is led by celebrated choreographer Ohad Naharin (b 1952). The Kibbutz Contemporary Dance Company (www.kcdc.co.il) performs around the country.
>
> For something completely different, catch a noisy, raucous, energetic performance by Jaffa-based **Mayumana** (Map p119; ☏03-681 1787; www.mayumana.com; 15 Louis Pasteur St), Israel's answer to Stomp.
>
> In the realm of folk dancing, Israel is famous for the hora, brought from Romania by 19th-century immigrants. The best place to see folk dancing is at the Carmiel Dance Festival (www.karmielfestival.co.il), held over three days in early July in the central Galilee.
>
> The most popular Palestinian folk dance is a line dance called the *dabke*. One of the best Palestinian dance groups is El-Funoun (www.el-funoun.org), based in Al-Bireh in the West Bank.

Another trend is to use Jewish religious vocabulary and soundscapes to express latent religious feelings. Over the last few years, performers such as Etti Ankri, Ehud Banai, David D'Or, Kobi Oz, Berry Sakharof and Gilad Segev have turned towards traditional – mainly Sephardic and Mizrahi – liturgical poetry and melodies to create works with huge mainstream popularity.

Mizrahi music's traditional Ashkenazi counterpart, Klezmer, has not enjoyed as much crossover popularity. Born in the shtetls of Eastern Europe, Jewish 'soul' can take you swiftly from ecstasy to the depths of despair – check it out at the Tsfat Klezmer Festival.

Israel has a strong Western classical tradition thanks to Jewish refugees from Nazism and post-Soviet immigrants from Russia. The Israel Philharmonic Orchestra (www.ipo.co.il) – whose first concert, in 1936, was conducted by Arturo Toscanini – is world renowned.

To hear some genuine Palestinian folk music, go to www.barghouti.com/folklore/voice. Many of the songs were recorded live at Palestinian weddings, where the art form is particularly appreciated.

Palestinian Music

In addition to catchy Arabic pop from Beirut and Cairo, visitors to the West Bank and Arab areas of Israel may come across traditional folk music featuring the sounds of the *oud* (a stringed instrument shaped like half a pear), the *daf* (tambourine) and the *ney* (flute), and the love ballads and nationalist hymns of Mohammed Assaf, a Gazan who won the second season of *Arab Idol* (the Arab world's version of *Pop Idol*).

Locally produced rap music has gained a big following in recent years. From Gaza's first hip-hop group, PR (Palestinian Rappers), to the genre's main exponents, DAM (www.damrap.com), Palestinian rap frequently deals with the themes of occupation, the difficulties of daily life, and resistance. The members of DAM are actually Israeli Arabs from the impoverished city of Lod, not far from Ben-Gurion airport. Identifying both with Palestinians and Israelis, they rap in a heady mixture of Hebrew, Arabic and English.

Theatre
Israeli Theatre

Israelis attend the theatre more often than almost any other people. Tel Aviv, Jaffa, Jerusalem and Haifa have a profusion of companies, venues and festivals both large and small. The Acco Festival of Alternative Israeli Theatre (www.accofestival.co.il) brings innovative productions to Akko each fall.

Most performances are in Hebrew, though you can also find plays in Arabic, Russian and Yiddish. Some companies offer English subtitled translations once a week or more.

Many contemporary Israeli plays tackle the hot political and social issues of the day. In recent years, the Holocaust, *refuseniks*, the West Bank occupation, suicide and homosexuality within Orthodox Judaism have all been explored onstage. Playwrights to keep an eye out for include Hanoch Levin (1942–99), provocative enough to have had several of his plays censored in the 1970s, Nissim Aloni (1926–98), Yehoshua Sobol (b 1939), Hillel Mittelpunkt (b 1952) and Shmuel Hasfari (b 1954).

Attending a musical performed by the Yiddish troupe Yiddishpiel (www.yiddishpiel.co.il) is like a quick trip to pre-Holocaust Warsaw, though performances are heavy on nostalgia and the subtitles are in Hebrew and Russian, not English.

For something unusual and poignant, head to Jaffa's **Nalaga'at Centre** (Map p119; ☎03-633 0808; www.nalagaat.org.il; Jaffa Port), home to the world's only deaf-blind theatre company.

Palestinian Theatre

Long an important expression of Palestinian national aspirations, Palestinian theatre has been censored by the British, suppressed and harassed by the Israelis, battered by conflict and closures and, most recently, targeted by Islamists. Nevertheless, Palestinian actors and directors carry on. Two of the main centres of Palestinian theatre are the Palestinian National Theatre (www.pnt-pal.org) in East Jerusalem, founded in 1984 by the El-Hakawati Theatre Company, and Al-Kasaba Theatre & Cinematheque (p265) in Ramallah.

Juliano Mer-Khamis (1958–2011), the Palestinian-Israeli founder of Jenin's Freedom Theatre (www.thefreedomtheatre.org), was murdered by unknown masked shooters in Jenin in 2011.

Visual Arts

Israeli Visual Arts

Jerusalem's Bezalel Academy of Arts & Design (www.bezalel.ac.il), established in 1906 to provide training for both European-educated artists and traditional Yemenite artisans, developed a distinctive style combining biblical themes with the sinuous lines of art nouveau (Jugendstil). Today, the academy remains one of the most exciting forces in Israel's art scene.

During the 1930s, German-Jewish artists fleeing Nazism brought with them the bold forms of German expressionism. The New Horizons group, which strove to create visual art in line with European movements, emerged after 1948 and remained dominant until the 1960s. Romanian-born Marcel Janco, one of the founders of the Dada cultural movement, immigrated to Palestine in 1941 and later established the artists' village of Ein Hod, where a museum features his work.

In Israel's cities, keep an eye out for modern sculpture – works range from provocative to whimsical.

Israel's leading art museums, Jerusalem's Israel Museum (p79) and the Tel Aviv Museum of Art (p110) have superb permanent collections and often showcase contemporary Israeli artists. For details on Israel's many museums, check out www.ilmuseums.com.

Palestinian Visual Arts

Contemporary Palestinian art became distinct from traditional craft-based art during the 1960s. In the West Bank, the best places to see visual

Israel's grandest performing arts festival, the Israel Festival (www.israel-festival.org.il), is held every year in May and June in Jerusalem.

The best places in Israel to find creative Judaica (Jewish ritual objects) are Jerusalem (eg Yoel Moshe Salomon St), Tsfat (the Synagogue Quarter and the Artists' Quarter) and Tel Aviv's Nahalat Binyamin crafts market (Tuesday and Friday).

ARTS VISUAL ARTS

CONFLICT FLICKS

A host of powerful, award-winning documentaries by Palestinians and Israelis – in some cases working together – have emerged from the Israeli–Palestinian conflict:

➡ *Arna's Children* (Juliano Mer-Khamis; 2003) – about a children's theatre group in Jenin.

➡ *Death in Gaza* (James Miller; 2004) – a harrowing film about the lives of Palestinian children and the death of the director, shot by an IDF soldier during production.

➡ *5 Days* (Yoav Shamir; 2005) – looks at the Israeli pullout from Gaza in 2005.

➡ *Precious Life* (Shlomi Eldar; 2010) – examines the relationships formed during a Gaza baby's medical treatment in Israel.

➡ *Law in These Parts* (Ra'anan Alexandrowicz; 2011) – about Israel's military legal system in the West Bank.

➡ *5 Broken Cameras* (Emad Burnat; 2011) – on the anti–Separation Fence protests at Bil'in.

➡ *The Gatekeepers* (Dror Moreh; 2012) – based on interviews with six former heads of Israel's Shin Bet security service.

To take the edge off these tension-filled flicks, check out Ari Sandel's zany *West Bank Story* (2005; www.westbankstory.com), a spoof of the musical *West Side Story*.

Each fall, the Israeli Academy of Film & Television (www.israelfilm-academy.co.il) chooses the winners of the Ophir Awards, Israel's equivalent of the Oscars.

art are Ramallah's Khalil Sakakini Centre (p265) and the International Centre of Bethlehem (p257).

Arab and Palestinian art is featured at the Umm el-Fahem Art Gallery (http://umelfahemgallery.org), in the Israeli-Arab town of Umm al-Fahm. Jerusalem's Museum on the Seam (p70) has made a special effort to exhibit works by Arab and Muslim artists.

Street art by local and international artists (yes, including Banksy) lines swathes of the Palestinian side of the Separation Wall (p256).

Cinema

Israeli Film

Israeli cinema has come a long way since the silent footage of the late Ottoman era, the heroic documentaries of the 1930s and 1940s, and the comic *borekas* movies (named after the flaky Balkan pastry) that dominated big screens during the 1970s. In recent years, Israeli feature films and documentaries – many of which take a highly critical look at Israeli society and policies – have been garnering prizes at major film festivals, including Cannes, Berlin, Toronto and Sundance. Israel's 10 Oscar nominees include Ephraim Kishon's *Sallah* (*Sallah Shabati*; 1964), a comedy set in a 1950s transit camp for Mizrahi Jewish immigrants, and Ari Folman's *Waltz with Bashir* (2008), an extraordinary animated documentary about Israel's 1982 First Lebanon War.

Shashat (www.shashat.org), a Palestinian NGO focusing on women in cinema, holds a Palestinian women's film festival each fall.

The country's first cinema, the Eden, opened in 1914 in Tel Aviv, on the edge of Neve Tzedek. Today, there are thriving cinematheques in Haifa (www.haifacin.co.il), Jerusalem (www.jer-cin.org.il) and Tel Aviv (www.cinema.co.il).

Israeli celebrations of the Seventh Art include the following:

➡ Docaviv International Documentary Film Festival (www.docaviv.co.il) – in Tel Aviv.

➡ Haifa International Film Festival (www.haifaff.co.il)

➡ Tel Aviv International Student Film Festival (www.taufilmfest.com)

➡ Jerusalem Film Festival (www.jff.org.il)

→ Other Israel Film Festival (www.otherisrael.org) – focuses on Israel's minorities, including its Arab citizens.

→ Tel Aviv International LGBT Film Festival (www.tlvfest.com)

For a complete database of made-in-Israel movies, see the website of the Manhattan-based Israel Film Center, www.israelfilmcenter.org.

Palestinian Film

Cinema in the Palestinian Territories is hampered by a dearth of resources and film schools and by threats from Islamists. Nevertheless, the Palestinian Social Cinema Arts Association (http://pscaa.word press.com) is working to develop the Seventh Art in the Palestinian Territories. Most feature-length Palestinian movies are international co-productions.

The first Palestinian film nominated for an Oscar was the controversial *Paradise Now* (2005), directed by Nazareth-born, Netherlands-based Hany Abu-Assad, which puts a human face on Palestinian suicide bombers. *Omar,* also by Hany Abu-Assad, a political thriller about trust and betrayal, garnered an Oscar nomination in 2014.

The West Bank has two movie venues, the Al-Kasaba Theater & Cinematheque (p265), in Ramallah, and the internationally supported Cinema Jenin (www.cinemajenin.org). In Gaza, Islamists have forced all the cinemas to close.

Environment

Situated at the meeting point of two continents (Asia and Africa) and very near a third (Europe), Israel and the Palestinian Territories are home to a mix of habitats and ecologies found nowhere else on earth. Asian mammals such as the Indian porcupine live alongside African tropical mammals such as the rock hyrax (dassie) and creatures more often found in European climes such as the stone marten.

A dozen species of bat, two of them critically endangered, have found cool, secluded warm-season shelter in abandoned Israel Defense Forces bunkers along the Jordan River, unused since the 1994 Israel-Jordan peace treaty.

In the Bible, the Land of Israel is described as teeming with life, and even the casual reader will notice that nature served as a central inspiration and motif for the prophets and psalmists. The Mediterranean forests of the Galilee (eg in the Carmel and Meron regions), with their oaks, almonds and sycamores, probably constitute the best extant examples of the kinds of biblical-era landscapes that inspired the vivid imagery of the Song of Songs and Isaiah's prophecies.

Some of Israel's most extraordinary habitats can be found in the arid deserts of the Negev, where travellers are likely to come across species usually often associated with Africa. These include dry-river-dwelling acacia trees – mentioned repeatedly in the Bible – and doum palms (eg at Ein Evrona in the Arava), as well as mammals such as the antelope and the ibex; the latter can often be spotted on the steep hillsides around Ein Gedi.

Habitats & Animals

Human beings have been having an impact on the habitats and creatures of Israel and the Palestinian Territories since the dawn of history, but the innovations of the past few centuries have been particularly damaging. The introduction of firearms during the 19th century led to the devastation of the country's large mammals and birds – cheetahs, bears, ostriches and crocodiles are just a few of the animals hunted to extinction in the area. Since the 1950s, Israeli ecologists have been working to protect the country's remaining biodiversity and have even reintroduced a few mammal species.

Much of the lush (and malarial) wetlands that once covered large areas of central and northern Israel were drained over the course of the 20th century, destroying important habitats for mammals and – especially – birds. Today, small sanctuaries such as the Hula Nature Reserve, Agamon HaHula and Ein Afek Nature Reserve (north of Haifa) preserve some of the original swamp habitats, providing important rest stops and feeding grounds for migrating birds. Like a number of other sites around the country, they are world-class spots for birdwatching.

Israel's 128 surviving indigenous mammal species are, for the most part, holding their own thanks to restrictions on hunting and a system of nature reserves and protected areas that encompass some 25% of Israel's land. However, protected areas are hardly a panacea for biodiversity loss. Many are quite small and isolated and can therefore offer only limited protection for endangered species. Moreover, many of the reserves in the south are also used for military exercises. Sometimes this overlap works to nature's advantage because civilian visitors are allowed in only on weekends and holidays, but the soldiers, tanks and jets cause significant disruption, especially for mammals.

Wildflowers

The hillsides of Israel and the Palestinian Territories are carpeted with yellow, orange, red, pink, purple and white wildflowers from about January to March (later at higher elevations, eg on Mt Hermon). The anemones and cyclamens of the Be'eri Forest in the northern Negev and the Beit Keshet forest near Nazareth are particularly astonishing. Irises can be found on Mt Gilboa, and native orchids in the Jerusalem Hills.

During the 1960s, Israel's first-ever environmental campaign succeeded in persuading Israelis to refrain from picking wildflowers, an act that remains illegal.

Water, Source of All Life

In the arid Middle East, no resource is more precious than water – without it humans, animals and plants quite simply cannot survive. That's why King Hezekiah (8th century BCE) put so much effort into building a tunnel to ensure Jerusalem's water supply in time of siege, and why similar technology was employed by the Israelites at Tel Hatzor (9th century BCE); both sites are open to the public. And that's why in Palestinian–Israeli peace negotiations, most scenarios have left the three most difficult issues for last: Jerusalem, the fate of Palestinian refugees and...water.

As soon as Israel declared independence, it began to plan the transport of water from the Galilee, with its relatively plentiful rainfall, to the dryer south. By the 1960s, thanks to the reservoirs, tunnels and open canals of the 130km National Water Carrier – visible as you drive through the Lower Galilee – prodigious quantities of water were being piped to central Israel and the Negev Desert.

In *The Natural History of the Bible* (2007), Daniel Hillel, a world-renowned soil physicist and water management expert (he was one of the creators of drip irrigation), examines the influence of local ecology on the people and world of the Scriptures.

ENVIRONMENT WILDFLOWERS

ANIMALS OF THE BIBLE

An initiative known as Hai-Bar (literally 'wildlife') has, since 1968, taken on the challenge of reintroducing animal species that appear in the Bible but later became extinct in the Holy Land.

The Hai-Bar program's modus operandi has been to bring together a small number of animals from other parts of the region and breed them in captivity until their offspring can gradually be reintroduced to their natural habitats. In a parallel initiative, birds of prey, their populations ravaged by pesticides, have also been bred and returned to the wild.

While some zoologists question the historical accuracy of a few of the selected mammal species, the Hai-Bar program has largely been a success. Starting with the Asian wild ass, which appears in Isaiah's prophesies, a variety of endangered animals have been quietly reintroduced to the country's open spaces. A small group of Persian fallow deer was secretly airlifted from Iran in 1978 on the last El Al flight out of Tehran before Khomeini's revolution; these shy animals have taken hold in the Galilee reserve of Akhziv and in the hills west of Jerusalem. The Arabian oryx, whose straight parallel horns, viewed from the side, gave Crusaders the impression that they were unicorns, are also back.

The two Hai-Bar breeding and reacclimation centres – one at Yotvata in the Arava, the other on Mt Carmel, near Haifa – are being downsized, having completed most of their planned reintroductions, but are still well worth a visit for fans of Middle Eastern mammals.

A BILLION BIRDS A YEAR

Twice a year, 500 million birds from an unbelievable 283 species migrate through Israel and the Palestinian Territories: in the fall as they head south from Europe and northwestern Asia to wintering grounds in Africa; and in the spring as they return to their summer breeding grounds.

Most migrating birds prefer to fly over land, where they can conserve energy by catching thermals. As a result, the Mediterranean and Caspian Seas end up funnelling huge numbers of Africa-bound birds to Israel's Mediterranean coast and the Jordan Valley (the Syrian-African Rift Valley), turning the latter into the largest avian fly-way in the world – some describe it as a 'superhighway' for birds.

Having so many birds flying through a narrow corridor along the eastern edge of Israel and the Palestinian Territories creates some of the world's most outstanding opportunities for birdwatching. Websites worth a look include the following:

Israel Birding Portal (www.birds.org.il) – details on Israel's six main birding centres.

Agamon HaHula (www.agamon-hula.co.il) – these reconstituted wetlands in the Upper Galilee are so popular with migrating cranes that some stay all winter.

Lotan Nature & Bird Reserve (www.kibbutzlotan.com) – Kibbutz Lotan offers migrating birds a lush sanctuary in the heart of the Arava desert.

International Birding & Research Center (www.eilat-birds.org) – an old garbage dump near Eilat has been turned into a salt marsh where exhausted birds can refuel.

But water was still in short supply – today, rain supplies only about half of Israel's needs. It was this chronic shortfall that inspired Israeli researchers to invent modern drip irrigation, now a common sight in fields around the world, and that led to the construction of infrastructure that allows almost 90% of Israel's waste water to be recycled for use in agriculture.

Since 2005 Israel has built five enormous reverse-osmosis desalinisation plants along the Mediterranean coast that will soon supply 40% of Israel's drinking-quality water – and use some 10% of the country's electricity. For the first time in the history of the Middle East, water is no longer a zero-sum game. In the mid-1960s, clashes between Israel and Syria over water rights almost led to war, and Israel has disagreements over water both with Jordan, which shares water rights to the Jordan River, and with the Palestinians, who accuse Israel of taking the lion's share of West Bank water. Plentiful desalinated water – at a cost of about US 60 cents per 1000 litres – may defuse a key source of regional tension and even create opportunities for Arab–Israeli political and economic cooperation, in addition to freeing everyone from dependence on unreliable rainfall and aquifers threatened by seawater infiltration (Gaza's groundwater is already severely compromised by high levels of salinity, fertilisers and sewage).

Israeli scientists have also tried to find less costly ways to maximise water use. The ancients – especially the Nabataeans – developed sophisticated techniques to channel rare desert cloudbursts in ways that made agriculture possible even in the arid central Negev. Near the ruins of ancient Avdat, researchers at the Even-Ari Research Station began working in the 1960s to rediscover Nabataean techniques of terracing and water storage.

Tel Aviv has had remarkable success in convincing city residents to cycle rather than drive, thanks in part to two decades of grassroots activism by the Israel Bicycle Association (www.bike.org.il). The city now has some 120km of dedicated bike paths.

Wetlands Conservation

During the 1950s – a period of unbounded faith in the ability of technology to bring 'progress' – the Hula wetlands in the northeastern

Galilee were drained to create farmland, destroying hugely important bird habitats and a key nutrient sink for the Sea of Galilee basin. The diversion of spring water and winter run-off for agriculture, industry and home use has degraded the aquatic habitats of many of Israel and the Palestinian Territories' streams and rivers, including the Jordan, a situation made worse by sewage run-off from Palestinian cities in the West Bank.

But not all is bleak for Israel's wetlands. Parts of the Hula swamps have been restored, and the Alexander River (www.restorationplanning. com/alex.html), 13km south of Caesarea, has been cleaned up and re-habilitated. In 2003 the latter project won the prestigious Thiess International Riverprize, awarded by the Australia-based International River Foundation (www.riverfoundation.org.au).

Is the Dead Sea Dying?

Because of pumping from the Jordan River, its tributaries and the Sea of Galilee by Israel, Jordan and Syria, the amount of water flowing annually into the Dead Sea is one billion cubic metres (over 90%) less than it would be naturally. As a result, evaporation is causing the sea to shrink rapidly, with the water level dropping some 1.2m per year – the surface area is now just 70% of what it was two decades ago. Thousands of sink-holes have appeared around the shoreline, posing a safety hazard and threatening both agriculture and tourist sites.

Proposals to refill the Dead Sea with seawater have been floating around for years. One idea calls for bringing in water from the Mediterranean through a 'Med–Dead Canal', while another proposes a 'Red–Dead Canal' from the Red Sea. The difference in altitude (over 400m) could be used to generate hydroelectricity and produce desalinated water.

In 2013 an agreement was signed by Israel, the Palestinian Authority and Jordan to build a 110km-long canal through Jordan that would deliver 100 million cubic metres of water to the Dead Sea and desalinate a similar quantity of water at a plant in Aqaba. Environmentalists are concerned about the impact on the Dead Sea of introducing seawater carrying a different mix of minerals as well as living organisms.

Conflict with Israel, fuel shortages and intra-Palestinian political rivalries have shut down Gaza's sewage treatment system. As a result, some of Gaza's streets are awash with human excrement, and 100,000 cubic metres of raw sewage pour into the Mediterranean every day.

The Perils of Development

The population of Israel and the Palestinian Territories has grown by more than a million people each and every decade since 1948, making today's population roughly seven times larger than it was seven decades ago. Over the same period Israel, initially a poor developing nation, has grown into a prosperous Western economy. The country's industrialisation, construction boom and enthusiasm for highways have generated pollution and sprawl comparable to those in the West – but because of Israel's small size, environmental ramifications are often felt more acutely. While Israel has been a world leader in water management, it has fallen far behind in other areas.

Air pollution in many Israeli and Palestinian cities is worse than almost anywhere in Europe, and periodically reaches dangerous levels. On the solar energy front, little has improved since a 1970s building code required that all Israeli apartments and homes install passive solar panels to heat water. Local waste management is surprisingly underdeveloped, with recycling rates well below those in Western Europe. Burial of rubbish at inexpensive municipal landfills is the default option, despite the dwindling reserves of available real estate. (Maybe policymakers just want to be generous to future archaeologists...)

Sprawl has also emerged as a serious problem, as more affluence has generated inefficient land-use patterns. In the past, most Israelis lived

The Israel Nature & Parks Authority (www.parks.org.il) administers most of Israel's national parks and nature reserves. Save money by buying a six-park 'Green Card' for 110NIS or an all-park card for 150NIS, both valid for 14 days.

ONLINE ENVIRONMENTAL RESOURCES

For more information on the state of the environment – and what's being done about it – in Israel and the Palestinian Territories, check out the websites of the following environmental organisations:

Adam Teva v'Din (www.adamteva.org.il) – Israel's premier environmental advocacy organisation plays hardball in the courts, suing polluters and lethargic government agencies.

Applied Research Institute of Jerusalem (www.arij.org) – an independent Palestinian research and advocacy organisation.

Arava Institute for Environmental Studies (www.arava.org) – a teaching and research centre that brings Israelis, Palestinians and Jordanians to Kibbutz Ketura near Eilat.

Friends of the Earth Middle East (www.foeme.org) – promotes cooperation between Israeli, Palestinian and Jordanian environmentalists.

Israeli Ministry of Environmental Protection (www.sviva.gov.il) – an increasingly powerful government ministry responsible for environmental regulation and enforcement.

Life & Environment – The Israeli Union of Environmental NGOs (www.sviva.net) – umbrella organisation for more than 130 Israeli environmental groups.

Palestine Wildlife Society (www.wildlife-pal.org) – an educational and research NGO focusing on nature conservation.

Palestinian Ministry of Environmental Affairs (www.mena.gov.ps) – charged with environmental regulation and education.

Society for the Protection of Nature in Israel (www.natureisrael.org) – Israel's oldest and largest environmental organisation.

in apartment buildings, but their aspirations to move 'up and out' into 'villas' (single-family homes) have led to a proliferation of low-density communities based on a two-cars-per-family lifestyle. Open spaces have given way to roads and suburbs. Environmentalists have fought hard to stop this trend, but with only isolated success. However, a campaign to curb construction near beaches has produced dramatic results: laws now protect the coastline, banning most construction within 300m of the water line and guaranteeing public access to all beaches.

Israel's environmental movement has grown bolder and more powerful in recent years. At the local government level, 'green' parties have begun to find a constituency.

Survival Guide

Safe Travel

Is it safe? This is a question friends and family are likely to ask when you announce your plans to travel to Israel and/or the Palestinian Territories. The answer will always depend on current events, and can change within the space of a few days. The one certainty is that it's always a good idea to pay attention to advice from your country's foreign affairs department or ministry. You should also ask questions of any contacts you may have in this part of the world before you head here.

Travel Advisories & Information

A number of government websites offer travel advisories and information on current hot spots. Be sure to register your travel plans with your country's foreign affairs department or ministry so that they can email you

security updates and advice if necessary. The best way to register is online.

Australian Department of Foreign Affairs (www.smartraveller.gov.au)

British Foreign Office (www.gov.uk/foreign-travel-advice)

Canadian Department of Foreign Affairs (http://travel.gc.ca)

US State Department (http://travel.state.gov)

Security Measures in Israel

Israel has some of the most stringent security policies in the world. Streets, highways, markets and public facilities can be cordoned off on the basis of intelligence (eg regarding a possible suicide bombing) and abandoned shopping bags, backpacks

and parcels are picked up by bomb squad robots and blown up. Vehicles can be pulled over by the military and inspected for weapons or fugitives, especially near checkpoints. In recent years the number of terrorist attacks inside Israel has dropped (there were 128 in 2004 and just 10 in 2013), but it pays to remain vigilant about suspicious people or packages, especially when travelling by public transport.

When entering bus or rail terminals, shopping malls, supermarkets and other public venues, your bags may be searched or X-rayed. You may also be checked with a metal detector wand or asked 'Yesh lecha neshek?' ('Do you have a gun?'). It's amazing how quickly you'll get used to this.

In 2011 the Israel Defense Forces (IDF) deployed the Iron Dome (Kippat Barzel) mobile air defence system for the first time. Used to protect populated areas (especially cities such as Ashdod, Ashkelon, Be'er Sheva, Tel Aviv and Jerusalem), the system can intercept and destroy short-range rockets and artillery shells fired from distances of 4km (2.5 miles) to 70km (43 miles). It has proved to be highly effective and was utilised extensively and successfully during the 2014 Israel–Hamas conflict, intercepting and disabling 735 rockets fired from Gaza,

TRAFFIC ACCIDENTS

The number of traffic fatalities in Israel has fallen in recent years (303 traffic deaths in 2013 compared with an average of more than 600 per year in the 1990s) and the percentage of fatalities per population is considerably lower than in many other countries (3.3 fatalities per 100,000 inhabitants as opposed to Australia's 5.2 and the United States' 11.6). That said, driving here can be dangerous, particularly on rural roads and highways where drivers often speed and take risks when overtaking. Stick to speed limits and always drive defensively.

WHAT TO DO IN A MISSILE OR ROCKET ATTACK

If you hear an air-raid siren (a rising-and-falling tone) while in Israel, you should immediately head to the nearest Mamad (reinforced concrete room) or conventional bomb shelter and close all doors and windows. Depending on how far from the launch site in Gaza, southern Lebanon or Syria you are, and depending on what type of missile it is, you may have as little as 10 seconds to get ready for impact (in Tel Aviv, for instance, the warning time for a Gaza-launched missile is 90 seconds).

If you're in a building without a Mamad (only buildings constructed after the First Gulf War of 1991 have them), head to a room situated furthest from the direction of the threat with the smallest possible number of outside walls, windows and openings. (In Eilat, the threat will usually come from Sinai; in Tel Aviv, it will come from Gaza; and in the north, it will usually come from Lebanon.) Another option is to take shelter in an interior staircase or a corridor as far away from windows and doors as possible. If you're on the top floor of a building, descend two floors – but not all the way to the ground floor.

If you are outdoors or in a vehicle, enter the nearest building and follow the above instructions. If you're in an exposed area, lie on the ground face down away from your car and cover your head with your hands.

If there are no additional instructions (eg on the radio), you can exit the shelter or get back into your car after 10 minutes. Stay clear of any unidentified objects and notify the authorities if you see a rocket lying on the ground.

This advice applies year-round, not just when there is an active conflict. The website of Israel's Home Front Command, www.oref.org.il, has advice about what to do in a rocket, missile, chemical or biological weapon attack, plus training videos and a map of early warning alerts.

90% of the total number targeted at populated areas.

News in English

When travelling in this region, you should regularly check the media for news about possible safety and security risks.

The English edition of **Haaretz** (www.haaretz.com), Israel's left-of-centre newspaper, is sold at newsstands bundled with the **International Herald Tribune**. The right-of-centre **Jerusalem Post** (www.jpost.com) is also widely available. There's an English website affiliated with the Hebrew daily **Yediot Aharonot** (www.ynetnews.com). The bi-weekly **Jerusalem Report** (www.jpost.com/JerusalemReport/Home.aspx) analyses current affairs.

IBA World Service (www.iba.org.il/world) has 15-minute English radio bulletins daily at 6.30am, 12.30pm and 8.30pm (Jerusalem: 100.3 MHz, 100.5 MHz and 101.3 MHz; Tel Aviv: 100.5 MHz and 101.2 MHz; Galilee: 100.3 MHz, 101.3 MHz and 101.8 MHz; northern Negev: 101.8 MHz). The BBC World Service, broadcast from Cyprus, can be picked up on 1323 kHz AM/MW.

Israel TV's Channel 1 broadcasts nine minutes of English news at 4.50pm Sunday to Thursday. Cable and satellite packages almost always include BBC, CNN, Sky, Fox and other TV news channels.

Safe Travel in the West Bank

Travel in the West Bank is generally very safe. In the tradition of Arab hospitality, Palestinians are welcoming to tourists – like other regions that are not widely visited, tourists are often the object of curiosity, but visitors facing hostility in the West Bank is almost unheard of.

That said, the West Bank is under military occupation, and clashes between the Israeli military and Palestinian youths at checkpoints and in some of the more restive cities are common, particularly on Fridays and after major events, such as Palestinian funerals. Steer clear of protests and, as much as possible, areas where protests are common – these include a number of villages next to Israeli settlements in the Hebron Hills and, at times, Qalandia Checkpoint. Ask ahead at your hotel or hostel before travelling.

Here are a few tips for safe travel in the West Bank:

➡ Always carry your passport. You will not need it when entering the West Bank but you will need it, as well as your loose-leaf Israeli visa, to leave.

➡ Don't wander into the refugee camps on your own. Go with a local guide.

➡ If you wear any outward signs of Judaism, you may be mistaken for an Israeli settler (settlers are deeply resented by most Palestinians).

➡ Always avoid areas where demonstrations are being staged. Do not under any circumstances photograph Palestinian protestors (or, indeed, Israeli soldiers) without their express consent.

➡ Travel during daylight hours. Poor road signage, roadblocks and checkpoints make the West Bank disorienting enough in the daytime; travelling after dark will only add to the confusion.

➡ Use caution when approaching road blocks and checkpoints – Israeli soldiers are on high alert at all times, and causing unnecessary anxiety could lead to all sorts of problems and confrontations. Remember: they have no idea that you're just a curious visitor.

Political Protests

Israel is a democracy, where political protests are a legally protected right. But residents of West Bank areas administered by the Israeli army (ie under military rule) aren't protected by those same rights. This means that harsh measures – including truncheons, tear gas, stun grenades and rubber bullets – are often used against Palestinian protesters and the supporting Israelis who sometimes join them at demonstrations. Be warned that if you show up at a protest rally, even just to watch,

you stop being an innocent outsider and become a participant in the conflict.

Demonstrations can also get out of hand in Israel. This is particularly the case when ultra-Orthodox Jews clash with police in places such as the Mea She'arim neighbourhood in Jerusalem or the city of Beit Shemesh. There have also been situations when members of extreme right-wing groups have assaulted left-wing activists at demonstrations in support of territorial compromise or against the Jewish settlements.

Temple Mount/Al-Haram ash-Sharif in Jerusalem's Old City is a major flashpoint for demonstrations. Although Jordan has administrative control of this holy site, the Israelis are in charge of security and sometimes deny Muslim men under the age of 45 access to the compound (and hence to the Al-Aqsa Mosque) when the security situation is judged to be unsettled. This can trigger violent demonstrations in the Old City's Muslim Quarter, around Damascus Gate and in East Jerusalem, particularly on Fridays after noon prayers. It's best to avoid these areas when the political situation is tense.

In order to keep the peace, the Israeli security forces also deny Jews the right to pray in the compound, something that infuriates those of an ultra-nationalistic persuasion and has led to violent

confrontations between security forces and demonstrators in the past.

Minefields

Some parts of Israel and the Palestinian Territories – particularly along the Jordanian border and around the periphery of the Golan Heights – are still sown with anti-personnel mines. Fortunately, known mined areas are indicated in pink on topographical maps and are fenced with barbed wire sporting dangling red (or rust) triangles and/or yellow and red 'Danger Mines!' signs.

When hiking, don't stray from marked trails and never climb over or through a barbed-wire fence. In the Jordan Valley and the Arava, flash floods sometimes wash away old mines, depositing them outside the boundaries of known minefields – wherever you are, never, *ever* touch anything that looks like it might be an old artillery shell, grenade or mine.

If you find yourself in a mined area, retrace your steps only if you can clearly see your footprints. If not, stay where you are and call for help. If someone is injured in a minefield, do not rush in to assist even if they are crying out for help – instead, find someone who knows how to enter a mined area safely.

Directory A–Z

Accommodation

Both Israel and the Palestinian Territories offer accommodation options for every budget and style of travel. In Israel, expect prices – though not always standards – on a par with Western Europe. The West Bank is quite a bit cheaper, with many of the best options clustered in Ramallah and Bethlehem.

ISRAEL

Accommodation prices vary enormously with the day of the week and the season.

Weekday rates generally run from Saturday or Sunday night through Wednesday or Thursday night.

Weekend rates apply on Friday and sometimes Thursday (many Israelis don't work on Friday) and/or Saturday night.

High-season pricing is in force during July and August in most parts of the country. The exceptions: extremely hot areas such as the Dead Sea and the Sea of Galilee.

High-high-season prices occur on Jewish holidays such as Rosh HaShanah, Shavu'ot and the week-long

Passover and Sukkot festivals, especially in popular getaways such as the Galilee, the Golan Heights and Eilat. At these times, book well in advance.

Accommodation prices given in shekels include Israel's value added tax (VAT) of 18%, which foreign tourists do not have to pay, so most places (though not some B&Bs) charge non-Israelis significantly less than their shekel prices. Prices given in US dollar prices, and those generated by hotel booking websites, do not include VAT so Israeli citizens will find an extra 18% tacked on at checkout.

PALESTINIAN TERRITORIES

Room prices remain fairly constant year-round, the exception being in Bethlehem, where rates rise around Christmas and Easter. Book well ahead if you're planning on travel at these times.

B&Bs (Tzimmerim)

The most common form of accommodation in the Upper Galilee and Golan is the *tzimmer* (or *zimmer*). No one really knows how the German

word for 'room' came to symbolise for Israelis all that's idyllic about a cabin in the country, though the term may have been inspired by the 'Zimmer frei' signs you often see at German guesthouses. Prices are generally upper-midrange or higher. It's not always possible to check in late at night.

A *tzimmer* is often a room or cabin in a rural area with rustic, varnished-pine decor, satellite TV, a kitchenette and – in more luxurious units – a spa bath. Some places serve great breakfasts but others offer beds without breakfast.

To find a *tzimmer*, keep an eye out for signs on the street or check the following websites:

➜ www.zimmeril.com

➜ www.israel-tours-hotel.com

➜ www.weekend.co.il (in Hebrew)

➜ www.zimmer.co.il (in Hebrew)

Camping

If you're on a tight budget, staying in a tent (or at least a sleeping bag) is a great way to save some serious shekels.

Camping is forbidden inside nature reserves but various public and private bodies run inexpensive camping sites (www.campingil.co.il) at about 100 places around the country, including 22 operated by the **Israel Nature & Parks Authority** (1222 3639; www.parks.org.il) next

BOOK YOUR STAY ONLINE

For more accommodation reviews by Lonely Planet authors, check out http://lonelyplanet.com/hotels/. You'll find independent reviews, as well as recommendations on the best places to stay. Best of all, you can book online.

to nature reserves. Some are equipped with shade roofs (so you don't need a tent), lighting, toilets, showers and barbecue pits. In Hebrew, ask for a *chenyon laila* or an *orchan laila*.

Camping is particularly popular on the shores of the Sea of Galilee. Some organised beaches – offering toilet facilities, a decent shower block and security – charge per person admission fees, but others are free if you arrive on foot (visitors with wheels pay a per car fee).

In the West Bank camping should be avoided because of general security concerns.

Hostels & Field Schools

Almost three dozen independent hostels and guesthouses belong to Israel Hostels (www.hostels-israel. com), whose members offer dorm beds for 100NIS, good-value doubles and unmatched opportunities to meet other travellers.

Israel's 19 official Hostelling International (HI) hostels and guesthouses – significantly upgraded since the days of no-frills dorms and timer-activated communal showers – offer spotless, institutional rooms that are ideal for families, and also offer copious breakfasts. For details, check out the website of the Israel Youth Hostels Association, www. iyha.org.il/eng.

The **Society for the Protection of Nature in Israel** (SPNI; ☎ 057 200 3030; www.

natureisrael.org) runs nine field schools *(beit sefer sadeh)* in areas of high ecological value. Offering basic but serviceable accommodation, they're popular with school groups and families. Book well ahead, especially during school vacation periods.

In Jerusalem, pilgrims' hostels run by religious organisations serve mainly, but not exclusively, religious travellers. As you would expect, they lack the party atmosphere of some independent hostels but offer solid value and are a secure way to stay in the Old City. Accommodation designed for pilgrims can also be found in Nazareth and Bethlehem and around the Sea of Galilee.

Hotels

Israel's hotels and guesthouses range from gorgeous to grim; most belong to chains. Generally speaking, hotel prices are highest in Tel Aviv, Jerusalem and Eilat.

Israeli hotels are famous for their generous buffet breakfasts. Although most hotel restaurants serve only kosher food, they remain open on Shabbat and Jewish holidays.

In the Palestinian Territories, most of the tourist-class hotels are in Ramallah and Bethlehem, though there are a few proper hotels elsewhere in the West Bank. An excellent hotel booking website is www.palestine hotels.com.

Guesthouses are plentiful in the Palestinian Territories and make a good-value alternative to hotels or hostels. Bethlehem, in particular, has some attractive, atmospheric possibilities. Another option is a homestay – the Hospitality Club (www. hospitalityclub.org) has a number of Palestinian members offering travellers a bed for the night.

Kibbutz Guesthouses

Capitalising on their beautiful, usually rural locations, quite a few kibbutzim offer midrange guesthouse accommodation. Often constructed in the socialist era but significantly upgraded since, these establishments allow access to kibbutz facilities (including the swimming pool), have a laid-back vibe and serve deliciously fresh kibbutz-style breakfasts. Prices are sometimes as low as 350NIS for a double without breakfast. For details and reservations, check out the **Kibbutz Hotels Chain** (☎ 03-560 8118; www.kibbutz.co.il).

Activities

Archaeological Digs

For details on archaeological digs that welcome paying volunteers, check out these websites:

Biblical Archaeology Society (http://digs.bib-arch. org/digs)

Hebrew University of Jerusalem (http://archae ology.huji.ac.il/news/excava tions.asp)

Israeli Foreign Ministry (www.mfa.gov.il) Search for 'archaeological excavations'.

Birdwatching

The Mediterranean coast, the Hula Valley and the Eilat area are some of the world's foremost venues for birding; for details, see p394. Gatherings of twitchers (birdwatchers) include the Hula Valley Bird

---

SLEEPING PRICE CATEGORIES

The following prices are for double rooms with breakfast on weekends and in the high (but not 'high-high', ie holiday) seasons.

PRICE RANGE	ISRAEL	PALESTINIAN TERRITORIES
Budget ($)	less than 350NIS	less than 260NIS
Midrange ($$)	350NIS to 600NIS	260NIS to 400NIS
Top End ($$$)	more than 600NIS	more than 400NIS

Festival (www.hulabirdfestival.org) and the Eilat Bird Festival (www.eilatbirdsfestival.com).

Cycling

Mountain biking has become hugely popular in Israel in recent years, especially among hi-tech yuppies with SUVs (a stereotype but not an untrue one). Many cycling trails go through forests managed by the Jewish National Fund (www.kkl.org.il); for details, click 'Cycling Routes' on its website. Shvil Net (www.shvilnet.co.il) publishes Hebrew-language cycling guides that include detailed topographical maps.

Races are regularly held in locales such as the Dead Sea; many are sponsored by the Israel Cycling Federation (www.israelcycling.org.il). There is also a variety of annual long-distance rides, such as the Arava Institute & Hazon Israel Ride (www.hazon.org/israel-ride/arava-institute-hazon-israel-ride) and the ALYN Hospital International Charity Bike Ride (www.alynride.org). Israel Spokes (www.israelspokes.com) is a cycling organisation that runs group rides. Popular Hebrew-only cycling forums, great for finding local clubs, group rides and equipment, include Shvoong (www.shvoong.co.il), Groopy (http://groopy.co.il) and Harim (www.harim.co.il).

Companies and cycling groups that organise rides and tours around Israel:

Cyclenix (www.cyclenix.com)

EcoBike Cycling Vacations (www.ecobike.co.il)

Genesis Cycling (www.genesiscycling.com)

Israel Cycling Tours (www.israelcycling.com)

Israel Pedals (www.israelpedals.co.il)

SK Bike Tours (www.skbike.co.il)

Urban cycling is highly developed in Tel Aviv thanks to 120km of dedicated bike paths and lanes. For details on getting around by bicycle, see p413.

For information on cycling and group rides in the West Bank, contact Bike Palestine (www.bikepalestine.com).

Hiking

With its unbelievably diverse terrain – ranging from the alpine slopes of Mt Hermon to the parched wadis (river beds) of the Negev – and almost 10,000km of marked trails, Israel offers some truly superb hiking. The country gets little or no precipitation for at least half the year so Israelis can plan outings without having to worry about getting rained on – and, because water is so precious, they love nothing more than to spend a summer's day sloshing through a spring-fed stream shaded by lush vegetation. Whenever you hit the trails, don't forget to bring a hat and plenty of water, and plan your day so you can make it back before dark.

At many national parks and nature reserves (www.parks.org.il), basic walking maps with English text are handed out when you pay your admission fee. In other areas, the best maps to have – in part because they indicate the precise boundaries of minefields and live-fire zones used for army training – are the 1:50,000-scale topographical maps produced by the Society for the Protection of Nature in Israel (SPNI), sold at bookshops, SPNI field schools and some nature reserves.

The website www.tiuli.com, run by Lametayel, Israel's largest camping equipment store, has details in English on the hiking options around the country (the Hebrew website is much more extensive). The SPNI's Mokedteva (www.mokedteva.co.il) has up-to-date information in Hebrew on weather, hiking routes, trail difficulty, trail closures and special events.

Popular long-distance trails (from north to south):

Israel National Trail (Shvil Yisra'el; www.israelnationaltrail.com) Rambles for 940km through Israel's least-populated and most-scenic areas, from Kibbutz Dan in the north to Taba on the Red Sea. Trail blazes are orange, blue and white.

Sea-to-Sea Hike (Masa MiYam l'Yam; www.seatoseatrail.com) A 70km route from the Mediterranean (Achziv Beach) to the Sea of Galilee (near Ginnosar) via Mt Meron and Amud Stream. Takes three to five days.

Jesus Trail (www.jesustrail.com) A 65km route from Nazareth's Church of the Annunciation to Capernaum, on the Sea of Galilee. Passes through Christian, Jewish, Muslim, Bedouin and Druze communities.

Gospel Trail (www.goisrael.com) The Israeli Ministry of Tourism's 63km-long version of the Jesus Trail runs from Nazareth's Mt Precipice to Capernaum, avoiding built-up areas.

Sea of Galilee Circuit (Shvil Sovev Kineret, Kinneret Trail) Circumnavigates the Sea of Galilee. Of the planned 60km, 45km have so far been marked with white-purple-white trail blazes.

Nativity Trail Stretches 160km from Nazareth to Bethlehem, mostly through the beautiful landscapes of the northern West Bank. Must be done with a guide – for details, contact Hijazi Travel (http://hijazih.wordpress.com), Walk Palestine (www.walkpalestine.com) or Green Olive Tours (www.toursinenglish.com).

Abraham Path (Masar Ibrahim al-Khalil; www.masaribrahim.ps) It may be many years before this planned trans–Middle Eastern walking trail is fully operational, but one section that's already open goes from Nabus via Jericho to Hebron.

Jerusalem Trail (www.jerusalemtrail.com) A 42km circuit that connects the Israel National Trail with Jerusalem, meandering through the Jerusalem Hills and around the Old City.

On the West Bank, for security reasons it's generally not a good idea to wander around the countryside unaccompanied. Consult local organisations such as Walk Palestine (www.walkpalestine.com) to find a guide and for up-to-date information on areas considered safe; Jericho and environs are usually a good bet. You might want to pick up a copy of *Walking Palestine* (www.walkingpalestine.org) by Stefan Szepesi or *Walking in Palestine* by Tony Howard and Di Taylor.

Scuba Diving

The Red Sea has some of the world's most spectacular and species-rich coral reefs. Good value scuba courses and dive packages are available in Eilat, but the underwater life is a lot more dazzling across the border in Sinai – however, the US, the UK and Australia recommend avoiding all travel to Sinai, except by air to Sharm el-Sheikh. The waters of the Mediterranean aren't nearly as colourful but at places such as Caesarea you can explore Atlantis-like ancient ruins.

Windsurfing

Windsurfer Gal Fridman won Israel's only ever Olympic gold medal at the 2004 Athens games, so it comes as no surprise that the country offers world-class windsurfing conditions. Popular venues include the Mediterranean coast, the Red Sea and even the Sea of Galilee.

Customs Regulations

Israel allows travellers 18 and over to import duty-free up to 1L of spirits and 2L of wine, 250mL of perfume, 250g of tobacco products (200 cigarettes) and gifts worth no more than US$200. Pets such as dogs, cats and parrots can be brought into Israel but require submitting advance paperwork to the Ministry of Agriculture.

Bringing drugs, drug paraphernalia, mace (self-defense tear gas), laser jammers (to confuse police-operated laser speed guns), fresh meat and pornography is prohibited.

Dangers & Annoyances

Theft is no more and no less of a problem in Israel and the Palestinian Territories than in any other country, so take the usual precautions: don't leave valuables in your vehicle or hotel room, and keep important documents and cash in a money belt. In hostels, check your most valuable belongings and documents into the front-desk safe. On intercity buses, it's fine to stow large bags in the luggage hold but keep valuables with you. Pickpockets have been known to lurk in crowded tourist spots and busy markets so keep alert and stay aware of what's happening around you. Bike theft is rampant so use a massive, reinforced steel chain lock (not a cable), and never leave an expensive bike on the street overnight.

Discount Cards

A Hostelling International (HI) card is useful for discounts at official HI hostels. An International Student Identity Card (ISIC) doesn't get anywhere near as many discounts as it once did – none, for instance, are available on public transport.

Some museums and sights offer discounts to senior citizens, though to qualify you may not only need to be senior but also a citizen.

If you're visiting lots of the national parks and historical sites run by the Israel Nature & Parks Authority (www.parks.org.il), you can save by purchasing a Green Card, valid for 14 days, that gets you into all INPA sites for just 150NIS (a six-park version costs 110NIS). With membership in the Israel Society for the Protection of Nature in Israel (www.natureisrael.org) you'll get discounts on accommodation at field schools and outings.

Electricity

220V/50Hz

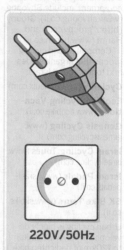

220V/50Hz

Embassies & Consulates

Jerusalem may be Israel's capital, but unresolved political issues dating to 1948 have led most diplomatic missions to set up shop in or near Tel Aviv. A few countries maintain consulates in Jerusalem, Haifa and/or Eilat.

Most diplomatic missions are open in the morning from Monday to Thursday or Friday; some are also open in the afternoon.

Australian Embassy (✆03-693 5000; www.israel.embassy.gov.au; 28th fl, Discount Bank Tower, 23 Yehuda HaLevi St, 6513601 Tel Aviv)

Canadian Embassy (✆03-636 3300; www.canadainternational.gc.ca/israel; 3/5 Nirim St, 6706038 Tel Aviv)

Egyptian Embassy (www.egyptembassy.net) Eilat (✆08-637 6882; 68 Afrouni St; ◷9-11am Sun-Thu); Tel Aviv (✆03-546 4151; 54 Basel St, 6274429; ◷9-11am Sun-Tue) In Eilat, deliver your passport, application and one passport-size photo in the morning and pick up the visa around 2pm the same day. In Tel Aviv the process may take a few days.

French Embassy Jerusalem (✆02-629 8500; www.consulfrance-jerusalem.org; 5 Paul Émile Botta St, 9410905); Tel Aviv (✆03-520 8500; www.ambafrance-il.org; 112 Herbert Samuel Esplanade, 6357231)

German Embassy (✆03-693 1313; www.tel-aviv.diplo.de; 19th fl, 3 Daniel Frisch St, 6473104 Tel Aviv)

Irish Embassy (✆03-696 4166; www.embassyofireland.co.il; 17th fl, 3 Daniel Frisch St, 6473104 Tel Aviv)

Jordanian Embassy (✆03-751 7722; 10th fl, 14 Abba Hillel St, 5250607 Ramat Gan) You can apply in the morning and pick your visa up around 2pm the same day; bring one passport-size photo. Linked to adjacent Tel Aviv by various buses that serve Petach Tikva, including Dan bus 66.

Netherlands Embassy (✆03-754 0777; http://israel.nlembassy.org; 13th fl, 14 Abba Hillel St, 5250607 Ramat Gan)

New Zealand Embassy (✆03-695 1869; www.mfat.govt.nz; 3 Daniel Frisch St, 6473104 Tel Aviv)

Turkish Embassy (✆03-524 1101; 202 HaYarkon St, 6340507 Tel Aviv) Consulate in Jerusalem (✆02-591 0555; http://jerusalem.cg.mfa.gov.tr; 87 Nablus Rd, Sheikh Jerrah, 9720826).

UK Embassy Jerusalem (✆02-541 4100; www.ukinjerusalem.fco.gov.uk; 15 Nashashibi St, Sheikh Jarrah, 9720415); Tel Aviv (✆03-725 1222; www.ukinisrael.fco.gov.uk; 192 HaYarkon St, 6340502)

US Embassy Haifa (✆04-853 1470; 26 Ben-Gurion Ave, 350232); Jerusalem (✆02-630 4000; http://jerusalem.usconsulate.gov; 14 David Flusser, Arnona, 9378322); Tel Aviv (✆03-519 7475; http://israel.usembassy.gov; 71 HaYarkon St, 6343229)

Food

Two useful websites listing thousands of restaurants, cafes and bars all over Israel:

➡ www.restaurants-in-israel.co.il

➡ www.restaurants.co.il

Gay & Lesbian Travellers

Israel has a very lively gay scene. Named 'Best City of 2011' in a worldwide poll of the readers of GayCities (www.gaycities.com), Tel Aviv has plenty of rainbow-coloured flags, a huge Gay Pride Parade and plenty of hang-outs. Haifa and Jerusalem have smaller gay communities. The resort town of Eilat is gay friendly, although the scene is mostly Israeli tourists. Most local organisations offering support, information, contacts and events are based in Tel Aviv and Jerusalem.

Orthodox Judaism, Islam and almost all of the Holy Land's Christian churches adamantly oppose homosexuality so it's appropriate to be circumspect in religious neighbourhoods. There are no laws in Israel against homosexuality. Israel does not have gay marriage but does recognise gay and lesbian marriages performed abroad.

Homosexuality and gay culture are very much taboo in the Palestinian Territories, and hundreds of gay Palestinians, fearing they'll be killed by their families, have taken refuge in Israel. To better understand the difficult plight of gay and lesbian Palestinians, check out:

➡ www.globalgayz.com/middle-east/palestine

➡ www.aswatgroup.org/en

EATING PRICE CATEGORIES

The price of a restaurant's average main dish determines which price category it's in.

PRICE RANGE	ISRAEL	PALESTINIAN TERRITORIES
Budget ($)	less than 35NIS	less than 35NIS
Midrange ($$)	35NIS to 70NIS	35NIS to 55NIS
Top End ($$$)	more than 70NIS	more than 55NIS

Insurance

It's always a good idea to take out a travel insurance policy before leaving home. In addition to the usual coverage for sickness (visiting an emergency room/casualty ward can be expensive) and theft, make sure that your coverage is appropriate for your specific needs. For instance, if you plan to scuba dive, skydive or ski, make sure your policy covers these activities. Almost all policies exclude liabilities caused by 'acts of war'.

Worldwide travellers' coverage is available online at www.lonelyplanet.com/travel-insurance.

Even as a tourist, it's possible to get pretty complete medical coverage at reasonable rates through one of Israel's excellent HMOs provided you'll be staying for at least three to six months. For details, drop by one of the offices of these organisations:

Maccabi Healthcare Services (☑073-260 6619; www.maccabi4u.co.il) Look for details on its Well-Come program.

Me'uchedet (☑077-270 3756; www.meuhedet.co.il) Provides coverage under its Foreign Members Plan.

Internet Access

Wi-fi hot spots can be found all over Israel (eg in almost all cafes and many restaurants) and in quite a few places in the Palestinian Territories. In Israel, wi-fi is also available on many intercity buses and trains, though it's rather slow. The city of Tel Aviv offers free wi-fi in dozens of public spaces all over the city. HI youth hostels and more than a few fancy hotels charge for both wi-fi and the use of internet computers; at ILH hostels and B&Bs and in midrange hotels, wi-fi is usually free.

Legal Matters

In Israel, smoking is banned in all enclosed public spaces; violators – or the owners of the place where scofflaws light up – can face on-the-spot fines.

The police have been known to arrest people for having minute quantities of drugs in their possession, despite official policy being more lenient.

Visitors to Israel – unlike Israeli citizens – are not allowed to proselytise. Religion is a sensitive matter here so sharing your faith's 'good news' too enthusiastically can lead to angering locals and complications with the police.

In the West Bank, Palestinian police are not permitted to arrest tourists but can detain a tourist before turning them over to the Israeli security forces.

If you're arrested, there's little your embassy can do for you while the legal process plays itself out, other than sending a low-ranking diplomat to visit you.

Maps

Tourist office maps, when available, tend to be rudimentary. Excellent road maps of Israel and the Palestinian Territories are published by a Tel Aviv–based company called Mapa (www.mapa.co.il/maps) and sold at all bookshops; its website has a detailed Hebrew-language map of the whole country. The databases used by Google Maps and GPS-based navigational devices are not as developed as in most Western countries.

For hikers, the Society for the Protection of Nature in Israel (www.natureisrael.org), known in Hebrew as HaChevra I'Haganat HaTeva, publishes a series of 20 1:50,000-scale topographical trail maps (mapot simun shvilim), available only in He-

brew. Not only do they indicate nature reserves (shown in green with the name in purple) and all marked hiking trails, but they also show areas used by the Israel Defence Forces (IDF) for live-fire military exercises (shitchei esh; indicated in pink) and the location of old minefields (sdot mokshim; in pink with a border of red triangles). The maps are 87NIS if purchased directly from the SPNI (eg at field schools) and are also available at bookshops; waterproof versions may cost a bit more.

Money

ATMs

ATMs are widespread, and Visa, MasterCard and, increasingly, American Express and Diners cards are accepted almost everywhere. Most – but not all – ATMs in Israel and the West Bank do Visa and MasterCard cash advances.

To prevent your debit or credit card issuer from suspecting fraud and blocking your account, let them know when you'll be in Israel and/or the Palestinian Territories.

Cash

Israel's official currency is the Israeli New Shekel (NIS or ILS), usually referred to as the shekel (shkalim in the plural).

The shekel is divided into 100 agorot. Coins come in denominations of 10 and 50 agorot (marked ½ shekel) and one, two and five NIS; notes come in denominations of 10, 20, 50, 100 and 200NIS.

Foreign tourists are entitled to a VAT refund on items worth a total of at least 400NIS purchased from certain Israeli shops (look for a sticker reading 'tax refund for tourists' in the window). Purchases must be sealed in partially transparent plastic and accompanied by a tax-refund invoice (a standard receipt will not suffice). Claim your refund – subject to a handling fee of up to 15% – when you exit the country by air or land. At Ben-Gurion airport, the refund desk is in the Check-In Hall; tax officials must see your purchases so take care of refund formalities before going through security.

The Palestinian Territories do not have their own currency. Rather, they use Israeli shekels and, to a lesser degree, Jordanian dinars and US dollars.

Moneychangers

Israeli banks charge a hefty commission so the best exchange deals are usually available at post office branches able to handle foreign currency and from independent exchange bureaus, neither of which charge commissions.

Tipping

Until recently, tipping wasn't an issue in Israel, but these days waiters expect a tip of 10% to 15% or more – in cash, not by credit card – depending on the level of service and how fancy the place is (the pricier the joint, the higher the percentage). Except for groups, restaurant bills almost never include service – if in doubt, ask. Israeli waiters generally pool their tips and share them with kitchen staff. In the Palestinian Territories, tipping in restaurants is not the norm, except in touristy places, so waiters will be grateful for any gratuity.

In hotels, it's a nice touch to leave 10NIS to 20NIS a night for housekeeping staff.

Taxi drivers in both Israel and the Palestinian Territories do not expect tips.

Travellers Cheques & Wire Transfers

Travellers cheques – used these days by almost no one – can be changed at most banks but charges can be as high as 20NIS per cheque. You're much better off at a post office branch that handles foreign currency or at a no-commission exchange bureau.

Post offices offer Western Union international money-transfer services.

Opening Hours

Opening hours in Israel are generally as follows:

ATMs Generally 24 hours a day, seven days a week (may be closed on Shabbat in Orthodox Jewish areas).

Banks Most are open from 8.30am to sometime between

ON THE SEVENTH DAY THOU SHALT REST

The Jewish Sabbath, known in Hebrew as Shabbat, begins 18 minutes (36 minutes in Jerusalem) before sundown on Friday and lasts until an hour after sundown on Saturday (technically, until three stars can be seen in the heavens, according to Jewish law). In mostly Orthodox neighbourhoods (eg much of Jerusalem), the arrival of Shabbat is marked with a siren.

Halacha (Jewish law) prohibits the conduct of business on Shabbat, but in many Jewish-majority areas of Israel, including West Jerusalem and Tel Aviv, 'status-quo' agreements allow restaurants, places of entertainment (theatres, cinemas, discos, bars), museums and small groceries – but not retail shops or full-size supermarkets – to stay open on Shabbat.

On land owned by kibbutzim (eg Kibbutz Shefayim) and in parts of Tel Aviv (eg in the Namal/Port area), boutiques and shops sell things on Shabbat, using non-Jewish staff to avoid fines from the Ministry of Labor and Social Affairs, which – to avoid employing Jews on the Sabbath – sends out only non-Jewish (usually Druze) inspectors!

In general, Israel's public transport does not run on Shabbat. Exceptions: certain bus lines in the religiously mixed city of Haifa that have been running seven days a week since the time of the British Mandate; some long-distance intercity buses, eg to Eilat; and bus lines that serve mainly non-Jewish towns. However, many intercity service taxi lines do run on the Sabbath, as do regular taxis.

In predominantly Muslim areas (East Jerusalem, Akko's Old City, parts of Jaffa, the West Bank and Gaza) many businesses are closed on Friday but remain open on Saturday. In mainly Christian areas (eg Haifa's Wadi Nisnas, Nazareth, Bethlehem and the Armenian and Christian quarters of Jerusalem's Old City), businesses are usually closed on Sunday.

National parks, nature reserves and most museums are open seven days a week but close an hour or two earlier on Friday afternoon. Christian religious sites may be closed on Sunday morning, while mosques are often closed to visitors on Friday.

LEFT LUGGAGE OFFICES

Because of security concerns, left-luggage services are few and far between in Israel. However, there are now luggage lockers (lokerim) in the central bus stations in Jerusalem, Tel Aviv, Be'er Sheva and Hof HaCarmel (Haifa); and Ben-Gurion airport has a short-term baggage storage service (open 8am to 9.45pm Sunday to Thursday and 8am to 2.45pm Friday) in the Kerem parking garage. Other than that, pretty much your only option is to stash your stuff at your hotel.

12.30pm and 2pm Monday to Thursday, plus a couple of afternoons a week, from 3pm or 4pm until as late as 6.30pm. Many branches are open on Sunday, and some also open on Friday morning.

Bars and pubs Hours are highly variable, but many – especially in Tel Aviv – are open until the wee hours. Thursday and Friday are the biggest nights out.

Clubs and discos The trendiest boogie joints don't open their doors until after midnight, closing around dawn. In Tel Aviv and Eilat most operate seven days a week, while in Haifa and Jerusalem they tend to open only on weekends (ie Thursday and Friday nights).

Post offices Generally from 8am to 12.30pm or 1pm Sunday to Thursday, with many reopening from 3.30pm to 6pm on certain days; main branches tend to dispense with the siesta. Friday hours are 8am to noon. Expect earlier closing times during the Passover and Sukkot holidays and in July and August.

Restaurants Hours are highly variable, with some establishments winding down in mid-afternoon (eg hummus shops) and others serving hot dishes until well after midnight. A few upmarket establishments close between lunch and dinner. Virtually all kosher restaurants are closed on Shabbat (Friday night and Saturday) and Jewish holidays. During Ramadan, almost all restaurants in Muslim areas, except those in hotels, are closed during daylight hours.

Shopping malls Generally from 9.30am or 10am to 9.30pm or 10pm Sunday to Thursday and until 2pm or 3pm on Friday and the eves of Jewish holidays.

Shops Usually from 9am to 6pm or later Sunday to Thursday and until 2pm or 3pm on Friday and the eves of Jewish holidays.

Post

Sent with Israel Post (www.israelpost.co.il), letters and postcards to North America and Australasia take seven to 10 days to arrive; to Europe it's a bit less. Incoming mail takes three or four days from Europe and around a week from other places; packages are much slower. A domestic letter weighing up to 50gm costs 2NIS. Internationally, letters and postcards cost 3.80NIS to Europe and 5.60NIS to North America or Australia.

For express service, options include DHL (www.dhl.co.il) and UPS (www.ups.com); Israel Post's EMS (Express Mail Service) is cheaper but slower and not as reliable.

Telephone

Costs

Domestic land-line-to-land-line calls are cheap, but – depending on the company and call plan involved – calling a mobile phone from a land line or another mobile can cost 0.80NIS a minute or

more. Be careful when you use the phone in your hotel room – hotels often charge exorbitant rates.

Mobile Phones

Although overseas cell-phones and smartphones work in Israel (on gadgets that can handle 900/1800 MHz), roaming charges can be ruinous. Fortunately, Israel's various mobile phone operators (the market was opened to competition in 2012), including old-timers Orange (www.orange.co.il), Pelefone (www.pelephone.co.il) and Cellcom (www.cellcom.co.il), and newcomers Hot Mobile (www.hotmobile.co.il) and Golan Telecom (www.golantelecom.co.il), offer pay-as-you-go SIM cards as well as cheap monthly plans with a variety of data options. A number of online companies sell Israeli SIMs internationally.

Mobile phone numbers start with ☎05 plus a third digit. When calling a local land line from a mobile phone, always dial the area code.

If you are near Israel's borders (especially with Jordan), you may discover that your mobile phone has switched to a Jordanian network. Manually switch your gadget back to your Israeli network or you may clock up pricey roaming charges.

Phone Codes

Israel's country code is ☎972; the Palestinian Territories use both ☎972 and ☎970. To call from abroad, dial your international access code followed by the country code, the local or cellphone area code (minus the zero) and the subscriber number.

Several competing companies, each with their own three-digit international access code, offer remarkably cheap (as little as 0.05NIS a minute) international direct-dial rates from Israel, including 012 Smile (www.012.net), Netvision (http://netvision.cell-com.co.il), Bezeq International-al (www.bezeqint.net), Golan Telecom (www.golantelecom.co.il) and Hot Mobile (www.hotmobile.co.il). Some companies require that you sign up in advance, others bill you through your phone plan.

Phonecards

Prepaid local and international calls can be made using a variety of phonecards, sold at post offices, lottery kiosks and newsstands.

Time

For most of the year, Israel and the Palestinian Territories are two hours later than GMT/UTC, seven hours later than New York, 10 hours later than San Francisco and eight or nine hours earlier than Melbourne. But because Israel, the Palestinian Authority and Hamas-ruled Gaza sometimes go on and/or off daylight savings time (summer time) on slightly different dates than the US, Europe and – to maximise confusion – each other, these times can shift by up to one hour.

As of 2014, Israel goes on and off daylight savings time on almost the same dates – in very late March and very late October – as Europe.

Tourist Information

Nearly every major Israeli city has a tourist office offering brochures and maps; some also organise city walking tours. The only tourist office in the Palestinian Territories is in Bethlehem.

Useful websites include:

➡ **www.goisrael.com** – Israel's Ministry of Tourism.

➡ **www.igoogledisrael.com** – tips on travelling and living in Israel.

➡ **www.parks.org.il** – Israel Nature & Parks Authority.

➡ **www.sirajcenter.org** – an NGO that sponsors cross-cultural and community tourism in Palestine.

➡ **www.travelpalestine.ps** – Palestinian Ministry of Tourism & Antiquities.

➡ **www.travelujah.com** – comprehensive information for Christian travellers.

➡ **www.visitpalestine.ps** – excellent Ramallah-based travel website.

Travellers with Disabilities

In Israel, access to public amenities for people with disabilities, including those in wheelchairs, is approaching the levels of Western Europe and North America. Almost all hotels and HI hostels are required to have one or more rooms outfitted for wheelchair users, and many tourist attractions, including museums, archaeological sites and beaches, are wheelchair accessible to a significant degree. Quite a few nature reserves offer trails designed for wheelchairs (see www.parks.org.il and www.kkl.org.il), with new ones being added each year. Restaurants are a mixed bag because few have fully wheelchair-accessible bathrooms. Kerb ramps for wheelchairs are widespread.

For details on accessibility in Israel, check out the website of Access Israel, www.aisrael.org. **Yad Sarah Organisation** (📞02-644 4444; www.yadsarah.org; 124 Herzl Blvd, Jerusalem) lends wheelchairs, crutches and other mobility aids free of charge (deposit required).

The Palestinian Territories are less well equipped and getting around is made more difficult by IDF checkpoints, which often have to be crossed on foot and sometimes require moving over and around barriers.

Visas

Israel

Israel no longer stamps tourists' passports (though it retains the right to do so). Instead, visitors are given a small loose-leaf entry card to serve as proof of lawful entry. It's easy to lose but try not to as it's your only proof that you're in the country legally.

We've heard reports of Israeli authorities at Allenby/King Hussein Bridge and Ben-Gurion airport issuing 'Palestinian Authority Only' entry permits to travellers with family or personal connections in the West Bank, making it difficult or impossible to get past the IDF roadblocks that regulate traffic from the West Bank into Israel, including Jerusalem. Conversely, authorities at the airport have been known to require that some travellers sign a form declaring that they will not enter the Palestinian Authority without permission from Israeli authorities.

Students require a student (A/2) visa; kibbutz volunteers must arrange, through their host organisation, a volunteer's (B/4) visa.

ON-ARRIVAL TOURIST VISAS

In general, Western visitors to Israel and the Palestinian Territories are issued free on-arrival tourist (B/2) visas by Israel. For specifics on who qualifies, visit www.mfa.gov.il (click on 'Consular Services' and then 'Visas'). Your passport must be valid for at least six months from the date of entry. Officials can demand to see proof of sufficient funds and/or an onward or return ticket but rarely do so.

On-arrival visas are usually valid for 90 days. But some travellers, such as those entering by land from Egypt or Jordan, may be given just 30 days or even two weeks – it's up to the discretion of

OVERSEAS ISRAELIS & PALESTINIANS

According to the US State Department, the Israeli government regards the foreign-born children of Israelis as Israeli citizens and therefore requires them to enter and exit Israel using an Israeli passport and to comply with the country's military draft laws; and it treats Palestinians born in the West Bank or Gaza – and, in some cases, their children and grandchildren – as Palestinian nationals who must exit and enter using a Palestinian passport, regardless of whether they hold a foreign passport. For details, see www.travel. state.gov – type 'Israel' under 'Learn About Your Destination', then expand the 'Entry, Exit & Visa Requirements' tab.

Unless they receive special advance authorisation, persons considered by Israel to be Palestinian nationals are required to enter and exit the country via Allenby–King Hussein Bridge rather than, for instance, Ben-Gurion airport. Conversely, persons considered Israeli citizens can use any Israeli airport or land crossing *except* Allenby–King Hussein Bridge.

---

the border control official. If there is any indication that you are coming to participate in pro-Palestinian protests, plan to engage in missionary activity or are seeking illegal employment, you may find yourself on the next flight home.

VISA EXTENSIONS

To extend a tourist (B/2) visa, you have a couple of options:

➡ Do a 'visa run' to Egypt, Jordan or overseas. This might get you an additional three months – or just one. Ask other travellers for the latest low-down.

➡ Apply to extend your visa (90NIS). Extensions are granted by the **Population & Immigration Authority** (☎3450; www.piba.gov.il; ⊙generally 8am-noon Sun-Tue & Thu), part of the Ministry of the Interior, whose offices include bureaus in Jerusalem (1 Shlomzion HaMalka St), Tel Aviv (Kiryat HaMamshala, 125 Menachem Begin Rd) and Eilat (2nd fl, HaKenyon HaAdom, HaTemarim Blvd). Bring a passport valid for at least six months beyond the requested extension period, a recent photo, a letter explaining why you want/need an extension (plus documentation), and evidence of sufficient funds

for the extended stay. Offices in smaller towns are often easier and faster to deal with. If you would qualify for an *oleh* (immigrant) visa under Israel's Law of Return – ie you have at least one Jewish grandparent or have converted to Judaism and have documentation demonstrating this – it's easy to extend your tourist visa for as long as you'd like, or even become an Israeli citizen.

You can be fined if you overstay your visa. Travellers who overstay by just a few days report no hassles or fines but it's best not to risk it.

Jordan

Visitors from most Western countries are eligible to receive single-entry, extendable, two-week visas at the following places:

➡ The Jordan River–Sheikh Hussein crossing (visa costs JD40), 30km south of the Sea of Galilee.

➡ The Yitzhak Rabin–Wadi Araba crossing (visa is free), a few kilometres north of Eilat and Aqaba.

Note: on-arrival visas are *not* available at the Allenby–King Hussein Bridge crossing.

Contact a Jordanian embassy or consulate (abroad or in Ramat Gan, near Tel

Aviv) for a visa in any of the following cases:

➡ You want to enter Jordan via Allenby–King Hussein Bridge.

➡ You need a multiple-entry visa.

➡ At-the-border visas are not available to people of your nationality.

Single/double/multiple entry visas, valid for two/three/six months from date of issue, cost a hefty JD40/60/120.

Note: if you crossed into the West Bank and/or Israel through Allenby–King Hussein Bridge *and* re-enter Jordan the same way, you do not need to apply for a new Jordanian visa, provided you return while your Jordanian visa or its extension is still valid. Remember to keep the stamped exit slip and present it on returning.

Volunteering

Israel and the Palestinian Territories abound with volunteer opportunities. In Israel these are often on archaeological digs, at ILH hostels or environmental organisations, while in the Palestinian Territories they often involve helping the many NGOs working to improve everyday life for Palestinians. These websites list a selection of organisations that arrange volunteer placements: The National Council for Volunteering in Israel (www.ivolunteer. org.il), Israel Hostels (www. hostels-israel.com/ volunteer-in-a-hostel) and Medical Aid for Palestinians (www.map-uk.org).

If you're between 18 and 35, it's also possible to volunteer on a traditional kibbutz (p318) in Israel. Volunteers interested in a taste of the lifestyle at these communal agricultural centres can expect to spend two to six months helping with manual labour, which could include anything from gardening to washing up or milking cows. Food and accommodation are provided and sometimes a small weekly allowance. For more information, visit www. kibbutz.org.il/eng or read about one Brit's personal experience at www.kibbutz-volunteer.com.

Weights & Measures

Israel, the West Bank and Gaza all follow the international metric system of weights and measures.

Women Travellers

Female travellers will generally feel as safe and comfortable in Israel and the Palestinian Territories as they would in any Western country. Thus, you should take the same sensible precautions as you do back home – for instance, don't hitchhike or hike by yourself, and avoid dark and deserted alleyways, lanes and paths. On some beaches foreign women may attract unwanted attention.

When you plan your day, keep in mind local expectations regarding modest attire. While tight-fitting, revealing outfits are common in urban centres such as Tel Aviv, they are inappropriate in more conservative parts of Israel and the West Bank, and are likely to be met with overt hostility in Gaza and in ultra-Orthodox Jewish neighbourhoods such as Me'a She'arim in Jerusalem. When visiting conservative areas and when visiting all religious sites – Jewish, Muslim, Christian, Druze and Baha'i – you should wear clothing that covers your knees and shoulders. In Muslim and Christian areas, long trousers are OK, but in some Jewish areas – and at all Jewish holy sites – only a long skirt is acceptable.

It's a good idea to carry a shawl or scarf with you at all times. You will need this to cover your head and shoulders when visiting Muslim holy sites (mosques, tombs and the Temple Mount), and it can come in handy if your definition of modest attire doesn't align with that of the caretaker in charge of a religious site.

In buses and sheruts, a woman sitting next to an ultra-Orthodox Jewish man may make him uncomfortable. Depending on how you look at it, that's either his problem or a local sensitivity you should respect.

Work

Travellers used to be able to turn up in Tel Aviv and find casual work in bars and restaurants but these days the pickings are thin. One option in that city might be to enquire at guesthouses and restaurants near the beach.

Working legally requires a permit from the Ministry of the Interior and, as in North America or Western Europe, these aren't easy to get – with one exception. If you would qualify for an *oleh* (immigrant) visa under the Law of Return – ie if you have at least one Jewish parent or grandparent and have documents to prove it – you can arrange a working visa with relative ease.

If you do find work and discover that you have been cheated by your employer, you can get free advice from **Kav LaOved Worker's Hotline** (☑03-688 3766; www.kavlaoved.org.il; 4th fl, 75 Nachalat Binyamin St, Tel Aviv); see its website for the times English-speaking staff are on hand.

Transport

GETTING THERE & AWAY

Israel has peace treaties with Egypt and Jordan so it's easy to combine a visit to Israel and the Palestinian Territories with a trip to Petra and/ or to the Red Sea coast of Sinai (although at press time, Western governments were recommending against travel to Sinai for security reasons).

Flights and tours can be booked online at www.lonelyplanet.com/bookings.

Air

Airports

Israel's main gateway is **Ben-Gurion International Airport** (TLV; ☑arrivals & departures 03-972 3333; www.iaa.gov.il), 50km northwest of Jerusalem and 18km southeast of central Tel Aviv. Ultramodern Terminal 3 handles about 14 million passengers a year. For up-to-the-minute details on arrivals and de-

partures, go to the airport's English website and click 'On-Line Flights' at the top.

A handful of flights from Europe, most of them charters, touch down at **Ovda airport** (VDA; ☑1 700 705 022; www.iaa.gov.il/Rashat/en-US/Airports/Ovda), 60km north of Eilat. Should Ben-Gurion airport have to close, Ovda serves as a back-up (so does Larnaca, Cyprus).

Israeli airport security is very tight so international travellers should check in at least three hours prior to their flight – when flying both to and from Israel.

Airlines

Israel's privatised flag carrier, **El Al** (LY; ☑03-977 1111; www.elal.co.il), has direct flights to several dozen cities in Western and Eastern Europe, as well as long-haul services to New York (Kennedy), Newark, Toronto, Los Angeles, Johannesburg, Mumbai, Bangkok, Hong Kong and Beijing; some flights to Asian destinations are codeshares.

The company was privatised in 2005, leading to a significant improvement in service, though it is not a member of any of the three global airline alliances (Star Alliance, One-World and Skyteam). Sun D'Or (www.sundor.co.il) is El Al's charter subsidiary.

Known for having the tightest security in the business, El Al's aircraft – like those of other Israeli airlines – are reportedly equipped with technology to foil heat-seeking anti-aircraft missiles.

Some of the cheapest flights from North America to Tel Aviv are offered by Air Canada via Toronto and US Airways via Philadelphia. A variety of European carriers offer trans-Atlantic services with a stopover in their hub city, making it easy to combine travel from North America to Israel and the Palestinian Territories with a visit to cities such as London, Paris, Frankfurt, Amsterdam, Rome or Istanbul.

Almost all the major European airlines have flights to

CLIMATE CHANGE & TRAVEL

Every form of transport that relies on carbon-based fuel generates CO_2, the main cause of human-induced climate change. Modern travel is dependent on aeroplanes, which might use less fuel per kilometre per person than most cars but travel much greater distances. The altitude at which aircraft emit gases (including CO_2) and particles also contributes to their climate change impact. Many websites offer 'carbon calculators' that allow people to estimate the carbon emissions generated by their journey and, for those who wish to do so, to offset the impact of the greenhouse gases emitted with contributions to portfolios of climate-friendly initiatives throughout the world. Lonely Planet offsets the carbon footprint of all staff and author travel.

Tel Aviv. Budget and charter airlines that link Tel Aviv with Europe but may not pop up on air-ticket search engines include the following:

Air Baltic (www.airbaltic.com)

Air Berlin (www.airberlin.com)

Air Méditerranée (www.air-mediterranee.fr)

Arkia (www.arkia.com)

Brussels Airlines (www.brusselsairlines.com)

easyJet (www.easyjet.com)

Enter Air (www.enterair.pl)

Germanwings (www.germanwings.com)

Israir (www.israirairlines.com)

Jetairfly (www.jetairfly.com)

Meridiana (www.meridiana.it)

Niki (flyNiki; www.flyniki.com)

Norwegian (www.norwegian.com)

Smartwings (www.smartwings.net)

TUI (www.tuifly.com)

Vueling (www.vueling.com)

The only Middle Eastern cities with direct air links to Tel Aviv are Amman, served by Royal Jordanian (www.rj.com); Cairo, served by Air Sinai (a low-profile but astonishingly expensive subsidiary of Egyptair); and Istanbul, served by Turkish Airlines (www.turkishairlines.com).

El Al has nonstop flights – some of them codeshares (eg with Thai) – to/from eastern Asia, as does Korean Air (www.koreanair.com). But the cheapest way to get to/from South, Southeast and East Asia is often via Istanbul on Turkish Airways, via Addis Ababa on Ethiopian Airlines, or via Amman on carriers such as Royal Jordanian, Qatar Airways (with a stopover in Doha), Emirates (via Dubai) and Etihad (via Abu Dhabi).

Tickets

Good deals to/from Israel are sometimes available from **ISSTA** (☎03-777 7777; www.issta.com; 109 Ben Yehuda St, Tel Aviv), the Israeli student travel agency, which has branches around the country.

Daka 90 (☎073-390 9090; www.daka90.co.il), whose name means 'at the last minute', sometimes advertises very inexpensive flights, including one way.

Many Israeli backpackers on their way to South, Southeast or East Asia, or Australia book through **FLYeast** (☎09-970 0400; www.flyeast.co.il), which specialises in inexpensive flights via Amman and then Doha, Dubai or Abu Dhabi (yes, Israelis are allowed to transit through those hubs). You can either fly the Tel Aviv–Amman leg or – to save a bit of cash – take a chartered bus.

Land

For details on land travel to/from Jordan and Egypt, see p30.

Sea

There are no longer passenger ferry services from Haifa to Limassol, Cyprus.

GETTING AROUND

Israel has an efficient and relatively inexpensive public transport system, with buses going everywhere and trains connecting the main cities.

The West Bank is served by local buses that link the cities with East Jerusalem, and by a plethora of shared and private taxis.

Air

Seven days a week, flights to Eilat from Tel Aviv's Sde Dov airport (set to close in 2016), Ben-Gurion airport's domestic terminal and Haifa are handled by Arkia (www.arkia.com) and Israir (www.israirairlines.com).

Deals are often available online, with one-way tickets sometimes going for as little as US$25 to or from Ben-Gurion – the price of a bus ticket!

Bicycle

Cycling is a great way to get around Israel. The distances between cities, villages, nature reserves and archaeological sites are relatively short; many highways have wide shoulders (though drivers can politely be described as erratic, and cycling is forbidden on some major intercity routes); and there is a growing number of off-road bike trails and scenic byways. Biking is also a great way to meet people and experience the country at ground level. Best of all, it's free and environmentally friendly.

The main drawback to cycling in Israel, other than the risk of being run over, is the heat. Always set off as early in the day as possible and carry plenty of water. Choose your route carefully: while the coastal plain is flat enough, the Upper Galilee, the Golan and the Dead Sea region have lots of steep hills, and the Negev Desert and the Jordan Valley can be mercilessly hot. One of the best one-day bike trips is around the Sea of Galilee (bikes can be hired in Tiberias).

Bicycles can be taken on intercity buses for no charge and are allowed on all trains – including those serving Ben-Gurion airport – *except* during rush hour (6am to 9am and 3pm to 7pm) Sunday to Thursday and on Saturday evening (there's no rush hour on Friday and the eves of Jewish holidays so all trains are bike-friendly then). Folding bikes can travel with you inside buses and can be taken on all trains.

Some bike shops in Israel will rent out bikes by the week, and may agree to buy a bike back from you if you purchase it new from their shop. You'll find plenty of bike shops in Tel Aviv (eg along HaHashmona'im St), Jerusalem, Haifa and other cities; the two largest chains are **Rosen & Meents** (☑1-599 501 090; www.rosen-meents. co.il) and **Matzman & Merutz** (☑03-562 6789; www. matzman-merutz.co.il). Bike hire isn't really an option in the Palestinian Territories but if you have a bike there shouldn't be a problem bringing it through the checkpoints.

Some airlines allow you to bring along your bicycle for a reasonable fee while others charge a small fortune so check before you book.

Bus

Israel

Almost every town, village and kibbutz has bus service at least a few times a day – except, that is, from Friday afternoon until Saturday in the late afternoon or evening, when the vast majority of intercity lines don't run at all (exceptions include services to Eilat and Majdal Shams).

Sample one-way fares include:

➜ Jerusalem to Tel Aviv – 19NIS

➜ Tel Aviv to Kiryat Shmona – 49.50NIS

➜ Tel Aviv to Eilat – 82NIS

Tickets are sold at bus station ticket windows and by bus drivers; exact change is not needed. Return tickets, available on a few lines (eg to Eilat), cost 15% less than two one-way tickets.

Most discounts are available only if you have a rechargeable Rav-Kav smartcard, which comes in two versions: personalised (*ishi*), which has your picture on it and requires filling out an application; and anonymous (*anonimi*), which is sold at stations (5NIS) and by drivers (10NIS) and is transferable but qualifies you for only limited discounts. The good news is that both get you 20% off all fares; the bad news is that at present, you need a separate Rav-Kav account for each bus company (a single card can hold up to eight accounts).

Israel no longer has a bus duopoly (the Egged and Dan cooperatives used to divide the country between them). Rather, there are now about 20 companies, including Egged and Dan, that compete for routes in Ministry of Transport tenders. The **Public Transportation Info Center** (☑1 900 72 1111; www. bus.co.il), a snap to use once you figure it out, provides

details in English on all bus companies' routes, times and prices. Smartphone apps for Android and iPhones can be downloaded from the website. To get information via SMS (text message), send a question (in Hebrew) beginning with the word *otobus* to ☑4949.

Bus companies you're likely to run across:

Afikim (☑6686, 052 999 6686; www.afikim-t.co.il)

Dan (☑03-639 4444; www. dan.co.il)

Egged (☑2800, 03-694 8888; www.egged.co.il)

Kavim (☑072-258 8787; www. kavim-t.co.il)

Metropoline (☑073-210 0422, 5900; www.metropoline. com)

Nateev Express (☑3553, 1-599 559 559; www.nateevex-press.com)

Nazareth Tourism & Transport (NTT; ☑1 599 559 559; www.ntt-buses.com)

Rama (☑3254, 04-696 4025; www.golanbus.co.il)

The only bus tickets that need to be (or can be) ordered in advance are Egged tickets to/from Eilat, which can be reserved up to 14 days ahead via www.egged.co.il, by smartphone app or by phone (dial ☑2800 or ☑03-694 8888). Note: the system may only accept Israeli credit cards; PayPal may also be an option.

West Bank

In East Jerusalem and the West Bank, a number of small, Arab-run bus companies provide public transport. Unlike their counterparts in Israel, they operate right through the weekend.

Car & Motorcycle

To drive a vehicle in Israel and the Palestinian Territories, all you need is your regular driving licence; an international driving licence is not required.

DRIVING ON SHABBAT

According to most interpretations of Halacha (Jewish law), driving a motor vehicle violates the sanctity of Shabbat (the Sabbath), in part by contravening prohibitions against lighting fire and travelling more than 2000 cubits. As a result, certain streets, neighbourhoods and villages populated almost exclusively by Orthodox and ultra-Orthodox Jews are closed to traffic from sundown on Friday until an hour after sundown on Saturday, as well as on many Jewish holidays. If you come upon a street blocked by a barrier, don't drive around it or you may find yourself facing angry locals or even having stones thrown at you.

By tradition (though not law), no one in Jewish areas of Israel – except for emergency services – drives a motor vehicle on Yom Kippur.

Israel's automobile association is known as **Memsi** (02-625 9711; www.memsi.co.il; 31 Ben Yehuda St, Jerusalem).

Car Hire/Rental

Having your own wheels lets you travel at your own pace, stay in out-of-the-way B&Bs, get lost along back roads and – if necessary – cover a lot of ground in a short amount of time. It doesn't make much sense to have a car in Jerusalem or Tel Aviv – parking can be a big hassle – but it's a great idea in hilly Haifa and in the Galilee, Golan and Negev, where many towns and villages are served by just a handful of buses a day.

Israel's biggest concentration of rental agencies is along Tel Aviv's HaYarkon St (one block in from the beach), but most companies have offices around the country, including the following:

Avis (www.avis.co.il)

Budget (www.budget.co.il)

Cal Auto (www.calauto.co.il)

Eldan (www.eldan.co.il) The only company with an office in Kiryat Shmona.

Green Peace (www.greenpeace.co.il) Based in East Jerusalem; pickup possible at Allenby Bridge.

Hertz (www.hertz.co.il) The only company with a Dead Sea office.

Car hire with insurance and unlimited kilometres costs as little as 140NIS per day, US$200 per week or US$600 per month (the incredibly cheap prices advertised online don't include insurance). Israelis, unlike tourists, have to pay VAT/sales tax (18%). Significant discounts are available online, eg through the sort of websites that sell aeroplane tickets. Remember that gasoline/petrol costs about US$2 per litre/US$7.60 per US gallon.

There's a surcharge for airport pick up (Budget charges US$27.50). If you get parking or traffic tickets, the rental company may forward them to you, including a handling fee of 60NIS. Some companies require that renters be at least 25 years old.

Read the fine print on your insurance contract carefully, especially regarding the excess (deductible), which can be US$400 or more – though for an additional fee (eg US$18) you can reduce that to zero. Some credit cards give cardholders free CDW (collision damage waver) coverage but you may still have to purchase liability (3rd-party) insurance – check with your card issuer. Even insurance policies sold by rental companies don't usually cover damage to the car's undercarriage or tyres.

Note that rental agencies generally forbid you to take their cars into parts of the West Bank defined in the Oslo Accords as Areas A and B – **Dallah** (02-627 9725; www.dallahrentacar.com) and Goodluck (www.good-luckcars.com) are notable exceptions. It's no problem, though, driving on Rte 1 from Jerusalem to the Dead Sea or Rte 90 from the Dead Sea to the Sea of Galilee.

In Tel Aviv and its inner suburbs, Car2Go (www.car2go.co.il) hires out cars by the hour, charging 140NIS for an annual membership plus 20NIS per hour (180NIS per day) and 2NIS per kilometre (1NIS per kilometre after the first 50km).

Road Conditions

Most Israeli roads are in pretty good shape but the newer ones, built to the latest safety standards, are safest. A visible minority of Israeli drivers are aggressive and/or unpredictable so drive carefully – and defensively – at all times.

North–south highways are designated by even numbers, while east–west routes have odd numbers; in general,

numbers rise as you go south-to-north and west-to-east. Thus, Rte 2 runs along the Mediterranean coast while Rte 90 hugs the country's eastern border with Jordan; Israel's northernmost road, almost on the Lebanese border, is Rte 99. Rte 1, an exception to this sequencing, links Tel Aviv with Jerusalem and the Dead Sea.

Israel has three toll roads:

➡ **Rte 6** (Kvish Shesh; www.kvish6.co.il) Runs up the centre of the country for 140km. Bills for tolls – up to 33NIS – are sent to car owners on the basis of a national database of licence plate numbers.

➡ **Carmel Tunnels** (www.carmeltunnels.co.il; one/two sections 7.50/14.90NIS) Runs under Mt Carmel south of Haifa. Payment can be made in cash or by credit card.

➡ **Fast Lane** (Nativ Mahir; www.fastlane.co.il) A 13km express lane from Ben-Gurion Airport to Tel Aviv. Tariffs vary based on traffic conditions – the worse it is, the more you pay.

In the West Bank, the highways reserved for Jewish settlers are usually modern and quick but on other roads traffic is often held up by donkey carts, traffic jams and army checkpoints.

Road Rules

Vehicles drive on the right-hand side of the road in Israel and the Palestinian Territories; seatbelts are required at all times. Unless you have a hands-free set, using a mobile phone while driving is illegal and subject to a fine of 1000NIS.

Israeli road signs are marked in English, Hebrew and (usually) Arabic; be prepared for some quirky transliterations. The best road maps are produced by Mapa (www.mapa.co.il/maps) and are available at all bookshops.

From November to March, car headlights must be

turned on whenever you're driving on an intercity road.

Israeli police cars always have their blue (sometimes red-and-blue) lights flashing, so seeing police lights in your rear-view mirror doesn't mean you're in trouble (if you are, they'll make that clear with a loudhailer).

Hitching

Although hitching was once a common way of getting around Israel, recent reports of violent crime, including kidnapping, make this a risky business and we do not recommend it. Women should not hitch without male companions and all travellers should be cautious about the cars they get into. The local method of soliciting a lift is simply to point an index finger at the road. Hitching is still most common in the Upper Galilee and Golan regions.

Local Transport

Bicycle

Bike paths have been going up in cities all over Israel but the most developed network is in Tel Aviv, which has a municipal bike rental program called Tel-O-Fun (www. tel-o-fun.co.il).

Bus

Local buses reach every corner of major cities but if you don't read Hebrew it can be a challenge to figure out the bus routes – just ask locals or any passing bus driver.

Taxi

Taking a 'special' (*speshel;* ie nonshared) taxi can be very convenient but, at times, a bit of a hassle because some unscrupulous drivers overcharge tourists. The best way to avoid getting ripped off is to sound like a confident old hand as you give the street address, including a cross street. It's almost always to your advantage to use the

meter (by law the driver has to put it on if you ask); make sure it is reset to the flag-fall price after you get in. A trip across town in Jerusalem or Tel Aviv should cost about 30NIS to 50NIS.

Meter fall is 12.30NIS (10.50NIS in Eilat). Tariff 2 (25% more expensive than Tariff 1) applies between 9pm and 5.30am and on Shabbat and Jewish holidays. Wait time costs 94NIS per hour. Legitimate surcharges include the following:

➡ Pick-up at Ben-Gurion airport – 5NIS

➡ Piece of full-size luggage – 4.40NIS

➡ Third and fourth passengers – 4.90NIS each

➡ Phone order – 5.20NIS

Many Israelis now use the mobile phone app GetTaxi (www.gettaxi.co.il), available in Android and iPhone versions, to order and pay for taxis in all parts of Israel (except Eilat). Uber launched in Israel in 2014.

Taxi drivers do not expect tips, but in the absence of a rip-off attempt, it's fine to leave a shekel or two in change.

Sherut (Shared Taxi)

To Israelis it's a *sherut* (sheh-*root*) while Palestinians call it a *service* (pronounced ser-*vees*), but whatever name you use, shared taxis are a useful way to get around. These vehicles, often 13-seat minivans, operate on a fixed route for a fixed price, like a bus except that they don't have pre-set stops. If you don't know the fare, ask your fellow passengers.

Sheruts (Hebrew plural: *moni'ot sherut* – the word *sherutim* means 'bathrooms'!) are generally quicker than buses. They begin their runs from a recognised taxi rank and leave only when they're full so you may have to hang around for a while,

though rarely more than 20 minutes. You can get out anywhere you like but will probably have to pay the full fare to the final destination. Many sheruts operate 24/7 and are the only means of public transport in Israel on Shabbat and Jewish holidays, eg between Tel Aviv and Jerusalem. Prices are the same or lower than buses except on Shabbat, when they rise slightly.

On the West Bank, shared taxis are plentiful and can take the form of chugging old Mercedes cars as well as minibuses. They can often be found near main town squares, eg in Ramallah. Regular sheruts link Nazareth with Jenin.

Tours

Tours are great if you're short on time or if you have a special interest – those run by the Society for the Protection of Nature in Israel, for example, are terrific for nature enthusiasts.

On the West Bank, a tour can be a good way of both getting oriented and staying safe.

Israel

Society for the Protection of Nature in Israel (SPNI; ☑057 200 3030; www. teva.org.il) Runs highly regarded nature hikes (eg to see spring wildflowers) suitable for the whole family; they are mainly for Israelis so tour guides speak Hebrew – but SPNI outings are a good way to meet locals. Only the Hebrew website lists trips.

Abraham Hostel (☑02-566 0045; www.abrahamtours. com) Runs excellent day tours of Jerusalem, the West Bank (including Bethlehem, Nablus and a 'dual-narrative tour' of Hebron), the Dead Sea, Masada, Haifa, the Galilee and the Golan. Also goes to Petra.

Bein Harim Tours (☑03-542 2000; www.beinharim.co.il) Custom tours around Israel and trips to Petra.

Touring Israel (☎077-450 3900; www.touringisrael. com) Tailor-made, top-end trips around Israel.

United Tours (☎03-617 3333; www.unitedtours.co.il) Large operator with one- and two-day trips all over the country.

Palestinian Territories

Green Olive Tours (☎03-721 9540; www.greenolivetours. com) Offers a wide variety of highly political but insightful day trips and multiday tours in both the West Bank and Israel.

Hijazi Travel (☎059 952 3844; http://hijazih.wordpress. com) Owner Hijazi Eid specialises in West Bank hiking and trekking, as well as city tours.

Alternative Tourism Group (☎02-277 2151; www. atg.ps) Culture, religion and politics, as well as walks along the Nazareth-to-Bethlehem Nativity Trail.

Abu Hassan Alternative Tours (☎052 286 4205; www. alternativetours.ps) Offers both 'political' and 'touristic' day trips.

Train

Israel Railways (☎5770, 077-232 4000; www.rail. co.il) runs a comfortable and convenient network of passenger rail services; details on departure times are also available from the **Public Transportation Info Center** (☎1 900 72 1111; www. bus.co.il). Trains do not run from mid-afternoon Friday until after sundown on Saturday. Return tickets are 10% cheaper than two one-way tickets; children aged five to 10 get a 20% discount. Unlike buses, Israel's rail system is wheelchair accessible.

Israel Railway's oldest line, inaugurated in 1892 and famously scenic, links three Tel Aviv stations with southern Jerusalem (23.50NIS, 1½ hours). The system's heavily

used main line runs along the coast at least twice an hour, affording fine views of the Mediterranean as it links Tel Aviv with the following locations:

➡ Haifa (32NIS, one hour)
➡ Akko (41.50NIS, 1½ hours)
➡ Nahariya (46.50NIS, 1½ hours)

Other useful services from Tel Aviv:

➡ Ben-Gurion airport (16NIS, 18 minutes, at least hourly 24 hours a day except Shabbat)
➡ Be'er Sheva (31.50NIS, 1½ hours, hourly)

Construction is underway on a US$2 billion high-speed rail link that will cut the travel time between Tel Aviv and Jerusalem to 30 minutes, with a stop on the way at Ben-Gurion airport; the planned completion date is 2017. Another new high-speed line is scheduled to link Haifa with Beit She'an (60km) in 2016.

Health

While it's never nice to be injured or become sick while you're travelling, you can at least take some comfort in the knowledge that Israel has world-class medical facilities. Those available in the Palestinian Territories are not quite as advanced, but you can rest assured that in an emergency a hospital in Israel is never too far away.

While standards of health are high in Israel, there are several location-specific conditions for travellers to be aware of, particularly dehydration, heat exhaustion and sunburn.

Before You Go

It's usually a good idea to consult a government travel health website before departure.

Australia (www.smartraveller. gov.au)

Canada (www.hc-sc.gc.ca/ hl-vs/travel-voyage/index-eng. php)

UK (www.doh.gov.uk)

USA (wwwnc.cdc.gov/travel) Search for the booklet *Health Information for International Travel* ('Yellow Book').

World Health Organization (www.who.int/ith/en) You can download the book *International Travel & Health*.

MD Travel Health (www. mdtravelhealth.com) Provides country-by-country travel health recommendations.

In Israel & the Palestinian Territories

Availability & Cost of Health Care

Israel has first-rate state-funded hospitals across the country, plus a number of private hospitals and clinics. For a list of hospitals, see www.science. co.il/hospitals.asp. Large cities in the Palestinian Territories have reasonable hospital facilities, but these can be crowded or short on supplies.

Pharmacies *(beit merkachat)* in Israel are a common sight on city streets; pharmacists speak English and can give advice about what medicine to take if you describe your problem. In cities, at least one pharmacy is always on call *(beit merkachat toran)* – phone ☏106 (the local municipal hotline) for details, or check out the links at www.online-israel.info/search-internet/ health/city (in Hebrew). Some branches of Super Pharm are open 24 hours. In the Palestinian Territories, medicine may be expired so check the date.

If you require any prescribed medication, take enough from home to get you through your trip and bring a copy of the prescription details in case you need a refill. Note: Israeli pharmacies can accept only prescriptions issued by Israeli doctors.

Private dental clinics are found everywhere from suburban streets to shopping malls. Standards of dental care are high, but keep in mind that your travel insurance will not usually cover you for anything other than emergency dental treatment.

Infectious Diseases

LEISHMANIASIS

Spread through the bite of an infected sandfly, leishmaniasis – endemic to Israel and the Palestinian Territories – can cause a slowly growing skin lump or ulcer. It may develop into a serious life-threatening fever, usually accompanied by anaemia and weight loss. Infected dogs and animals such as rock rabbits (hyraxes or dassies) are also carriers of the infection. Sandfly bites should be avoided whenever possible.

MIDDLE EAST RESPIRATORY SYNDROME

Since 2012, cases of MERS (Middle East Respiratory Syndrome) have been confirmed in the Arabian Peninsula, Jordan and Lebanon but not at this stage in Israel and the Palestinian Territories. Symptoms of MERS include fever, coughing and shortness of breath; the illness is spread through close contact, meaning most people are not at risk. Almost one-third of those with confirmed cases of MERS have died, though most of those people had an underlying medical condition. For more details, see www.cdc.gov/coronavirus/mers.

RABIES

Rabies is rare but present in Israel and the Palestinian Territories so avoid contact with stray dogs and wild animals such as foxes.

Spread through bites or licks on broken skin from an infected animal, rabies is fatal. Animal handlers should be vaccinated, as should those travelling to remote areas where a reliable source of post-bite vaccine is not available within 24 hours. Three injections are needed over a month. If you have not been vaccinated, you will need a course of five injections starting within 24 hours or as soon as possible after the injury. Vaccination does not provide you with immunity; it merely buys you more time to seek appropriate medical help.

Traveller's Diarrhoea

Traveller's diarrhoea can occur with a simple change of diet, so even though Israeli food and water are generally healthy you may get an upset stomach simply because your body is not accustomed to the new foods – it may take a few days to adjust. Keep in mind that in summer outdoor food spoils quickly, so this is a good time to avoid hole-in-the-wall shwarma and falafel joints because hummus goes bad quickly. (Eating hummus in an indoor restaurant is likely to be safer.) Be even more careful in the Palestinian Territories.

If you develop diarrhoea, be sure to drink plenty of fluids, preferably an oral rehydration solution containing salt and sugar. A few loose stools don't require treatment, but if you start

having more than four or five stools a day you should start taking an antibiotic (usually a quinolone drug) and an antidiarrhoeal agent (such as loperamide). If diarrhoea is bloody, persists for more than 72 hours, or is accompanied by fever, shaking chills or severe abdominal pain, you should seek medical attention.

Environmental Hazards

HEAT ILLNESS

Heat exhaustion is one of the most common ailments among travellers in Israel and the Palestinian Territories. This occurs following heavy sweating and excessive fluid loss with inadequate replacement of fluids and salt. It is particularly common in hot climates when taking unaccustomed exercise before full acclimatisation. Symptoms include headache, dizziness and tiredness. Dehydration is already happening by the time you feel thirsty – aim to drink enough water that you produce pale, diluted urine. The treatment for heat exhaustion consists of replacing fluid with water or fruit juice or both, and cooling by cold water and fans. The treatment of the salt-loss component consists of salty fluids as in soup or broth, and adding a little more table salt to foods than usual.

Heat stroke is much more serious. This occurs when the body's heat-regulating mechanism breaks down. An excessive rise in body temperature leads to the cessation of sweating, to irrational and hyperactive behaviour, and eventually to loss of consciousness and death. Rapid cooling by spraying the body with water and fanning is an ideal treatment. Emergency fluid and electrolyte replacement by intravenous drip is usually also required.

INSECT BITES & STINGS

Mosquitoes may not carry malaria but can cause irrita-

tion and infected bites. Using DEET-based insect repellents will prevent bites. Mosquitoes also spread dengue fever.

Bees and wasps cause real problems only to those with a severe allergy (anaphylaxis). If you have a severe allergy to bee or wasp stings you should carry an adrenaline injection or similar.

Sandflies are located around the Mediterranean beaches. They usually cause only a nasty itchy bite, but can carry a rare skin disorder called cutaneous leishmaniasis. Bites may be prevented by using DEET-based repellents.

The number of jellyfish has been increasing over the years, thanks to overfishing in the Mediterranean (fish eat jellyfish, and in the absence of predators the jellyfish have boomed). A jellyfish sting is irritating, but in most cases it wears off in about 10 or 15 minutes. A particularly strong sting (or a sting to the face or genitals) requires an evaluation by a physician.

Scorpions are frequently found in arid or dry climates. They can cause a painful bite that is rarely life threatening.

Bedbugs are occasionally found in hostels and cheap hotels. They lead to very itchy, lumpy bites. Spraying the mattress with an appropriate insect killer will

IF YOU REQUIRE MEDICAL CARE

For emergency first aid or evacuation by ambulance to a hospital in Israel, call the country's national emergency medical service, **Magen David Adom** (✆101), on any phone. Magen David Adom stations also provide after-hours first aid.

In the West Bank and Gaza, Palestinian hospitals can take care of most health problems but for anything serious, you're better off transferring to an Israeli hospital such as one of the two Hadassah Hospital campuses in Jerusalem.

For less urgent matters, you can do one of the following:

➡ Ask at your hotel for a nearby physician's office.

➡ Check the list of doctors on the website of the US Embassy (http://israel.usembassy.gov/consular/acs/doctors.html).

➡ In the Jerusalem area, contact **Terem Emergency Medical Centers** (✆1 599 520 520; www.terem.com) or the **Family Medical Center – Wolfson** (✆02-561 0297; http://fmcwolfson.com).

➡ In Tel Aviv, contact **Tel Aviv Doctor** (✆054 941 4243, toll-free 1-800-201 999; www.telaviv-doctor.com; Room 106, 35 Basel St, Basel Heights Medical Centre; ⊙daily).

If you become seriously ill, you may want to contact your embassy or consulate.

do a good job of getting rid of them.

Scabies are also sometimes found in cheap accommodation. These tiny mites live in the skin, particularly between the fingers. They cause an intensely itchy rash. Scabies are easily treated with lotion available from pharmacies; people who you come into contact with also need treating as they may become asymptomatic carriers.

SNAKE BITES

The vast majority of the snakes that live in Israel and the Palestinian Territories are not poisonous – but some, such as the Palestine viper (*tzefa; Vipera palaestinae*), are. Do not walk barefoot or stick your hand into holes or cracks.

If bitten by a snake, do not panic. Half of people bitten by venomous snakes are not actually injected with poison (envenomed). Immobilise the bitten limb with a splint (eg a stick) and apply a bandage over the site with firm pressure, similar to a bandage over a sprain. Do not apply a tourniquet, or cut or suck the bite. Get the victim to medical help as soon as possible so that antivenin can be given if necessary.

WATER

Tap water is safe to drink in Israel but sometimes has an unpleasant taste (in some areas it is slightly saline) so many Israelis use filters or spring water dispensers at home. Bottled water is available everywhere. Do not drink water from rivers or lakes as it may contain bacteria or viruses that can cause diarrhoea or vomiting.

Language

HEBREW

Hebrew is the national language of Israel, with seven to eight million speakers worldwide. It's written from right to left in its own alphabet.

Read our coloured pronunciation guides as if they were English and you'll be understood. Most sounds have equivalents in English. Note that a is pronounced as 'ah', ai as in 'aisle', e as in 'bet', i as the 'ea' in 'heat', o as 'oh' and u as the 'oo' in 'boot'. Both kh (like the 'ch' in the Scottish *loch*) and r (similar to the French 'r') are guttural sounds, pronounced at the back of the throat. The apostrophe (') indicates the glottal stop (like the pause in the middle of 'uh-oh'). The stressed syllables are indicated with italics.

Basics

Hello.	שלום.	sha·*lom*
Goodbye.	להתראות.	le·hit·ra·*ot*
Yes.	כן.	ken
No.	לא.	lo
Please.	בבקשה.	be·va·ka·*sha*
Thank you.	תודה.	to·*da*
Excuse me./ Sorry.	סליחה.	sli·*kha*

WANT MORE?

For in-depth language information and handy phrases, check out Lonely Planet's *Middle East Phrasebook*. You'll find it at **shop.lonelyplanet.com**, or you can buy Lonely Planet's iPhone phrasebooks at the Apple App Store.

How are you?

מה נשמע? ma nish·*ma*

Fine, thanks. And you?

טוב, תודה. tov to·*da*
ואתה/את? ve·a·*ta*/ve·*at* (m/f)

What's your name?

איך קוראים לך? ekh kor·*im* le·*kha*/lakh (m/f)

My name is ...

שמי ... shmi ...

Do you speak English?

אתה מדבר אנגלית? a·*ta* me·da·*ber* ang·*lit* (m)
את מדברת אנגלית? at me·da·*be*·ret ang·*lit* (f)

I don't understand.

אני לא מבין/מבינה. a·*ni* lo me·*vin*/me·vi·*na* (m/f)

Accommodation

Where's a ...?	?... איפה	e·fo ...
campsite	אתר הקמפינג	a·*tar* ha·*kemp*·ing
guesthouse	בית ההרחה	bet ha·'a·ra·kha
hotel	בית המלון	bet ma·*lon*
youth hostel	אכסניית הנוער	akh·sa·ni·*yat* no·*ar*
Do you have a ... room?	יש לך חדר ...?	yesh le·*kha*/lakh khe·*der* ... (m/f)
single	ליחיד	le·ya·*khid*
double	זוגי	zu·*gi*

How much is it per ...?	כמה זה עולה ל ...?	ka·ma ze o·le le ...
night	לילה	*lai*·la
person	אדם	a·*dam*

NUMBERS

1	אחת	a·khat
2	שתיים	shta·yim
3	שלוש	sha·losh
4	ארבע	ar·ba
5	חמש	kha·mesh
6	שש	shesh
7	שבע	she·va
8	שמונה	shmo·ne
9	תשע	te·sha
10	עשר	e·ser
100	מאה	me·a
1000	אלף	e·lef

Note that English numerals are used in modern Hebrew text.

Eating & Drinking

Can you recommend a ...?	אתה יכול להמליץ על ...?	a·ta ya·khol le·ham·lits al ... (m)
	את יכולה להמליץ על ...?	at ye·cho·la le·ham·lits al ... (f)
cafe	בית קפה	bet ka·fe
restaurant	מסעדה	mis·a·da

What would you recommend?
מה אתה ממליץ? ma a·ta mam·lits (m)
מה את ממליצה? ma at mam·li·tsa (f)

What's the local speciality?
מה המאכל המקומי? ma ha·ma·'a·khal ha·me·ko·mi

Do you have vegetarian food?
יש לכם אוכל צמחוני? yesh la·khem o·khel tsim·kho·ni

I'd like the ..., please.	אני צריך/ צריכה את ..., בבקשה.	a·ni tsa·rikh/ tsri·kha et ... be·va·ka·sha (m/f)
bill	החשבון	ha·khesh·bon
menu	התפריט	ha·taf·rit

Emergencies

Help!	הצילו!	ha·tsi·lu
Go away!	לך מפה!	lekh mi·po

Call ...!	תתקשר ל ...!	tit·ka·sher le ...
a doctor	רופא	ro·fe/ro·fa (m/f)
the police	משטרה	mish·ta·ra

I'm lost.
אני אבוד. a·ni a·vud (m)
אני אבודה. a·ni a·vu·da (f)

Where are the toilets?
איפה השירותים? e·fo ha·she·ru·tim

I'm sick.
אני חולה. a·ni kho·le/kho·la (m/f)

Shopping & Services

I'm looking for ...
אני מחפש ... a·ni me·kha·pes ... (m)
אני מחפשת ... a·ni me·kha·pe·set ... (f)

Can I look at it?
אפשר להסתכל על זה? ef·shar le·his·ta·kel al ze

Do you have any others?
יש לך אחרים? yesh le·kha/lakh a·khe·rim (m/f)

How much is it?
כמה זה עולה? ka·ma ze o·le

That's too expensive.
זה יקר מדי. ze ya·kar mi·dai

There's a mistake in the bill.
יש טעות בחשבון. yesh ta·ut ba·khesh·bon

Where's an ATM?
איפה יש כספומט? e·fo yesh kas·po·mat

Transport & Directions

Is this the ... to (Haifa)?	האם זה ... זאת ה ... ל(חיפה)?	ha·im ze/ zot ha ... le·(khai·fa) (m/f)
boat	אונייה	o·ni·ya (f)
bus	אוטובוס	o·to·bus (m)
plane	מטוס	ma·tos (m)
train	רכבת	ra·ke·vet (f)

What time's the ... bus?	באיזו שעה האוטובוס ה ...?	be·e·zo sha·a ha·o·to·bus ha ...
first	ראשון	ri·shon
last	אחרון	a·kha·ron

SIGNS – HEBREW

Entrance	כניסה
Exit	יציאה
Open	פתוח
Closed	סגור
Information	מודיעין
Prohibited	אסור
Toilets	שירותים
Men	גברים
Women	נשים

One ... ticket, please.	كرتيس	kar·tis
	أحد ...	e·khad ...
	بوكشة.	be·va·ka·sha
one-way	לכיוון אחד	le·ki·vun e·khad
return	הלוך ושוב	ha·lokh va·shov

How much is it to ...?

כמה זה ל ...؟ ka·ma ze le ...

Please take me to (this address).

תיקח/תיקחי אותי ti·kakh/tik·khi o·ti
(לכתובת הזאת) (lak·to·vet ha·zot)
בוקשה. be·va·ka·sha (m/f)

Where's the (market)?

איפה ה (שוק)؟ e·fo ha (shuk)

Can you show me (on the map)?

אתה/את a·ta/at
יכול/יכולה להראות ya·khol/ye·kho·la le·har·ot
לי (על המפה)؟ li (al ha·ma·pa) (m/f)

What's the address?

מה הכתובת؟ ma hak·to·vet

ARABIC

The type of Arabic spoken in the Palestinian Territories (and provided in this section) is known as Levantine Arabic. Note that there are significant differences between this colloquial language and the MSA (Modern Standard Arabic), which is the official written language in the Arab world, used in schools, administration and the media. Arabic is written from right to left in Arabic script.

In our pronunciation guides a is pronounced as in 'act', aa as the 'a' in 'father', ae as the 'ai' in 'air', aw as in 'law', ay as in 'say', e as in 'bet', ee as in 'see', i as in 'hit', oo as in 'zoo', u as in 'put', gh is a guttural sound (like the Parisian French 'r'), r is trilled, dh is pronounced as the 'th' in 'that', th as in 'thin' and kh as the 'ch' in the Scottish loch. The apostrophe (') indicates the glottal stop (like the pause in the middle of 'uh-oh').

Basics

Hello.	مرحبا.	mar·ha·ba
Goodbye.	خاطرك.	khaa·trak (m)
	خاطرك.	khaa·trik (f)
Yes.	ايه.	'eeh
No.	لا.	laa
Please.	اذا بتريد.	'i·za bit·reed (m)
	اذا بتريدي.	'i·za bit·ree·dee (f)
Thank you.	شكراً.	shuk·ran
Excuse me.	عفواً.	'af·wan
Sorry.	آسف.	'aa·sif (m)
	آسفة.	'aas·fe (f)

How are you?

كيفك؟/كيفك؟ ki·fak/ki·fik (m/f)

NUMBERS

1	١	واحد	waa·hed
2	٢	اثنين	'it·nayn
3	٣	ثلاثة	ta·laa·te
4	٤	اربع	'ar·ba'
5	٥	خمسة	kham·se
6	٦	ستة	sit·te
7	٧	سبعة	sab·'a
8	٨	ثمانية	ta·maa·ne
9	٩	تسعة	tis·'a
10	١٠	عشرة	'ash·ra
100	١٠٠	مية	mi·'e
1000	١٠٠٠	الف	'elf

Note that Arabic numerals, unlike letters, are written from left to right.

Fine, thanks. And you?

منيح/منيحة mneeh/mnee·ha (m/f)
وأنت/أنتي؟ oo 'ent/'en·tee (m/f)

What's your name?

شو اسمك؟ shoo 'es·mak (m)
شو اسمك؟ shoo 'es·mik (f)

My name is ...

اسمي ... ... 'es·mee ...

Do you speak English?

بتحكي إنكليزي؟ btah·kee ing·lee·zee

I don't understand.

ما فهمت. maa fa·he·met

Accommodation

Where's a ...?	وين ...؟	wen ...
campsite	مخيّم	mu·khay·yam
guesthouse	بيت الضيوف	bayt id·du·yoof
hotel	فندق	fun·du'
youth hostel	فندق شباب	fun·du' sha·baab

Do you have a ... room?	في عندكن غرفة ...؟	fee 'ind·kun ghur·fe ...
single	بتخت منفرد	bi·takht mun·fa·rid
double	بتخت مزدوج	bi·takht muz·daw·wej

How much is it per ...?	قديش هقه؟	'ad·deesh li·...
night	ليلة	lay·le
person	شخص	shakhs

SIGNS – ARABIC

Entrance	مدخل
Exit	مخرج
Open	مفتوح
Closed	مغلق
Information	معلومات
Prohibited	ممنوع
Toilets	دورات المياه
Men	الرجال
Women	النساء

Eating & Drinking

Can you recommend a ...?	بتوصي بـ...؟	bit·waa·see bi·...
cafe	مقهى	ma'·ha
restaurant	مطعم	mat·am

What would you recommend?
بشو بتوصي؟ bi·shoo btoo·see

What's the local speciality?
شو الوجبة الخاصة؟ shoo il·waj·be il·khaa·se

Do you have vegetarian food?
في عندكن fee 'ind·kun
طعام نباتي؟ ta·'aam na·baa·tee

I'd like the ..., please.	بدي ...، لو سمحت.	bid·dee ... law sa·maht
bill	الحساب	il·hi·saab
menu	قائمة الطعام	'ae·'i·met it·ta·'aam

Emergencies

Help!
ساعدني! saa·'id·nee (m)
ساعديني! saa·'i·dee·nee (f)

Go away! (to a man/woman)
روح!/ rooh/
روحي! roo·hee

Call ...!	اتصل بـ...!	'it·ta·sil bi·...
a doctor	دكتور	duk·toor
the police	الشرطة	ish·shur·ta

I'm lost.
أنا ضائع. 'a·na daa·'i' (m)
أنا ضائعة. 'a·na daa·'i·'e (f)

Where are the toilets?
وين الحمامات؟ wen il·ham·maa·maat

I'm sick.
أنا مريض. 'a·na ma·reed (m)
أنا مريضة. 'a·na ma·ree·de (f)

Shopping & Services

I'm looking for ...
بدور عن ... bi·daw·wer 'an ...

Can I look at it?
ورجني ياه؟ war·ji·nee yaah (m)
ورجيني ياه؟ war·jee·nee yaah (f)

Do you have any others?
في عندكن غيرها؟ fee 'ind·kun ghay·ru

How much is it?
قديش هقه؟ 'ad·deesh ha'·'u

That's too expensive.
هيدا غالي اكتير. ha·da ghaa·lee 'ik·teer

There's a mistake in the bill.
في خطأ بالحساب. fee kha·ta' bil·hi·saab

Where's an ATM?
وين جهاز الصرافة؟ wen je·haez is·sa·raa·fe

Transport & Directions

Is this the ... to (Petra)?	هذا الـ... لـ(بيترا)؟	ha·da il·... la·(bee·tra)
boat	سفينة	sfee·ne
bus	باص	baas
plane	طائرة	taa·'i·re
train	قطار	'i·taar

What time's the ... bus?	أمتى الباص الـ...؟	'em·ta il·baas il·...
first	اول	'aw·wel
last	اخر	'aa·khir

One ... ticket, please.	تذكرة ... اذا بتريد	taz·ki·re ... 'i·za bit·reed
one-way	ذهاب	za·haab
return	ذهاب واياب	za·haab oo 'ee·yaab

How much is it to ...?
قديش الاجرة لـ...؟ 'ad·deesh il·'uj·re la ...

Please take me to (this address).
اوصلني عند 'oo·sal·nee 'ind
(هيدا العنوان). (ha·da il·'un·waan)

Where's the (market)?
وين الـ(سوق)؟ wen il·(soo')

Can you show me (on the map)?
بتورجني btwar·ji·nee
(عالخريطة)؟ ('al·kha·ree·te)

What's the address?
شو العنوان؟ shoo il·'un·waan

GLOSSARY

The language origin of non-English terms is noted in brackets: Hebrew (H) and Arabic (A). Singular and plural is noted as (s) and (pl) while masculine and feminine terms are noted as (mas) and (fem).

ablaq (A) – in architecture, alternating bands of light and dark stone

abu (A) – father (of), often used as part of a name; see also *umm*

agorot (H) – smallest unit of the shekel; 1 shekel = 100 agorot

ain (A) – water spring or source; also *ein*

al (A) – the definite article, 'the'; also spelled 'el-' or with the L replaced by the letter that follows it, eg ash-sharif

aliya (H) – immigration to Israel (literally 'going up')

b'seder (H) – OK

bab (A) – door, gate

bakashot (H) – a cycle of petitionary prayers sung in synagogues that follow some Sephardic rites (eg those from Aleppo, Syria) in the early hours of Shabbat during the winter months

be'er (H) – well

beit knesset (H) – synagogue

beit merkachat (H) – pharmacy

beit/beth (H) – house

bimah (H) – central platform in a synagogue

bir (A) – well

burj (A) – fortress or tower

caravanserai (A) – see *khan*

daf (A) – tambourine

derekh (H) – street or road

ein (H) – spring

Eretz Yisra'el (H) – the Land of Israel

Eretz Yisra'el HaShlema (H) – the Greater Land of Israel, a term once used by the Jewish settler movement to refer to the territory that they believe God promised the People of

Israel (includes the West Bank and the Golan Heights and, for some, Gaza)

gadol (H) – big

gan (H) – garden or park

Haganah (H) – literally 'defence'; the Jewish underground army during the British Mandate; the forerunner of the modern-day Israel Defense Forces (IDF)

hajj (A) – annual Muslim pilgrimage to Mecca

Hamas (A) – Harakat al-Muqaama al-Islamiya; militant Islamic organisation that aims to create an Islamic state in the pre-1948 territory of Palestine

hammam (A) – public bathhouse

har (H) – mountain

haraam (A) – literally 'forbidden'; holy sanctuary

Hared/Harediya/Haredim/Harediyot (H, mas s/fem s/mas pl/fem pl) – an ultra-Orthodox Jew, a member of either a Hasidic group or one of the groups opposed to Hasidism, known as Litvaks ('Lithuanians') or 'Misnagdim' ('opponents')

Hasid/Hasidim (H, mas s/mas pl) – member of an ultra-Orthodox group with mystical tendencies founded in Poland in the 18th century by the Ba'al Shem Tov

hazzanut (H) – Jewish liturgical singing

Hebrew Bible – the Old Testament

Hezbollah (A) – Iranian-backed Shiite political party and militia active in Lebanon

hof (H) – beach

hurva (H) – ruin

IDF – Israel Defense Forces; the national army

iftar (A) – the daily, dusk breaking-of-the-fast feast during Ramadan

intifada (A) – literally 'shaking off'; term Palestinians use to describe an uprising against Israel; the First Intifada lasted

from 1987 to 1990. The Second Intifada lasted from 2001 to 2005

Islam (A) – literally 'voluntary surrender to the will of God (Allah)'; the religion of the vast majority of Palestinian people

isra'a' (A) – the 'Night Journey' of the Prophet Mohammed from Mecca to Jerusalem

juhhal (A) – literally 'the ignorant'; members of the Druze community who are not *uqqal*

kafr (A) – village

kashrut (H) – religious dietary laws, ie the rules of keeping *kosher*

katan (H) – small

keffiyeh (A) – the black-and-white chequered Palestinian Arab headscarf

ketuba (H) – Jewish wedding contract

kfar – village

khan (A) – also called a *caravanserai*, a travellers' inn usually constructed on main trade routes, with accommodation on the 1st floor and stables and storage on the ground floor around a central courtyard

khirbet (A) – ruins (of)

kibbutz/kibbutzim (H, s/pl) – a communal settlement run cooperatively by its members; kibbutzim, once based solely on farming, are now involved in a wide range of industries; see also *moshav*

kibbutznik (H) – member of a *kibbutz*

kikar (H) – square; roundabout

kippa/kippot (H, s/pl) – skull-cap worn by observant Jewish men (and among reform and conservative Jews, sometimes by women); known in Yiddish as a *yarmulke*

Klezmer (H) – traditional music of Eastern European Jews, often described as traditional Jewish soul music

Knesset (H) – Israeli Parliament

Koran (A) – see *Quran*

kosher (H) – food prepared according to Jewish dietary law; see also *kashrut*

ma'ayan (H) – spring, pool

madrassa (A) – theological school, especially one associated with a mosque

majdal (A) – tower

makhtesh (H) – erosion cirque

matkot (H) – Israeli beach tennis

menorah (H) – a seven-branched candelabrum that adorned the ancient Temple in Jerusalem and has been a Jewish symbol ever since; it is now the official symbol of the State of Israel

mi'raj (A) – the Prophet Mohammed's ascent from Jerusalem to Heaven

midrahov (H) – pedestrian mall

mihrab (A) – prayer niche in a mosque, indicating the direction of Mecca

mikveh (H) – Jewish ritual immersion bath

minaret (A) – the tower of a mosque; from which the call to prayer is traditionally sung

mitzvah (H) – a commandment or obligation; a good deed

Mizrahi/Mizrahim (H, s/pl) – a Jew from one of the Middle East Jewish communities, eg from one of the Islamic countries such as Morocco, Yemen or Iraq; this term is often used interchangeably with Sephardi, though technically only the descendants of Jews expelled from Spain are Sephardim

moshav/moshavim (H, s/pl) – cooperative settlement, with a mix of private and collective housing and economic activity; see also *kibbutz*

moshavnik (H) – a member of a moshav

muqarna (A) – corbel; architectural decorative devices resembling stalactites

nahal (H) – river

Naqba (A) – literally the 'Catastrophe'; this is what the Palestinians call the 1948 Arab–Israeli War

nargileh (A) – water pipe; see also *sheesha*

ney (A) – flute

oleh/olah/olim/olot (H, s mas/s fem/pl mas/pl fem) – immigrant

PA – Palestinian Authority

PFLP – Popular Front for the Liberation of Palestine

PLO – Palestine Liberation Organisation

PNC – Palestinian National Council, ruling body of the PLO

Quran (A) – the holy book of Islam

ras (A) – headland

refusenik (H) – originally a Jew in the Soviet Union who was denied permission to emigrate to Israel; sometimes used today to refer to Israelis who refuse to serve in the IDF in the West Bank

rehov (H) – street

ribat (A, H) – pilgrim hostel or hospice

sabil (A) – public drinking fountain

sabra (H) – literally 'prickly pear'; native-born Israeli

servees (A) – term used for small bus or service taxi in the Palestinian Territories, see also *sherut*

settler – a term for Israelis who have created new communities on territory captured from Jordan, Egypt and Syria during the 1967 Six Day War; the Hebrew word for settler is *mitnachel*

sha'ar (H) – gate

shabab (A) – literally, 'youths'; young Palestinians who formed the backbone of the intifadas by confronting the IDF and throwing stones

Shabbat (H) – the Jewish Sabbath observed from sundown on Friday evening to an hour after sundown on Saturday

shalom (H) – peace; hello; goodbye

Shari'a (A) – Muslim law

Shechina (H) – divine presence

sheesha (A) – water pipe, term used in Egypt; see also *nargileh*

sheikh (A) – learned or old man

shekel/sh'kalim (H, s/pl) – Israeli monetary unit

Shema (H) – Judaism's central statement of belief in the oneness of God

sherut (H) – shared taxi, service taxi; Israeli minivans that operate on fixed routes, in or between cities; see also *servees*

shiva (H) – ritual week-long period of mourning for first-degree relatives

shofar (H) – ram's horn traditionally blown on Rosh HaShana and Yom Kippur

shtetl (H) – small, traditional Eastern European Jewish village

sukkah/sukkot (H, s/pl) – small dwellings built during the feast of Sukkot

taboun (H) – a clay oven

tel (H) – a hill; in archaeology, a mound built up as successive cities were built and destroyed on the same site

Torah (H) – the Five Books of Moses, ie the first five books of the Hebrew Bible (the Old Testament); also called the Pentateuch

Tzahal (H) – Hebrew acronym for the Israel Defense Forces (IDF)

tzimmer (H) – literally 'room' in German; B&B or holiday-cabin accommodation; also spelled 'zimmer'

tzitzit (H) – white tassels worn by orthodox Jewish men, attached to the four corners of a square undergarment; also the knotted fringes on the prayer shawl

ulpan/ulpanim (H, s/pl) – language school

umm (A) – mother (of); feminine equivalent of *abu*

UNRWA – UN Relief & Works Agency for Palestine Refugees

uqqal (A) – the wise; the select inner core of the Druze community; see also *juhhal*

wadi (A) – river that's dry except during downpours

WZO – World Zionist Organisation

ya'ar (H) – forest

yad (H) – hand; memorial

yeshiva/yeshivot (H, s/pl) – Jewish religious seminary or school

zimmer (H) – see *tzimmer*

Behind the Scenes

SEND US YOUR FEEDBACK

We love to hear from travellers – your comments keep us on our toes and help make our books better. Our well-travelled team reads every word on what you loved or loathed about this book. Although we cannot reply individually to your submissions, we always guarantee that your feedback goes straight to the appropriate authors, in time for the next edition. Each person who sends us information is thanked in the next edition – the most useful submissions are rewarded with a selection of digital PDF chapters.

Visit **lonelyplanet.com/contact** to submit your updates and suggestions or to ask for help. Our award-winning website also features inspirational travel stories, news and discussions.

Note: We may edit, reproduce and incorporate your comments in Lonely Planet products such as guidebooks, websites and digital products, so let us know if you don't want your comments reproduced or your name acknowledged. For a copy of our privacy policy visit lonelyplanet.com/privacy.

OUR READERS

Many thanks to the travellers who used the last edition and wrote to us with helpful hints, useful advice and interesting anecdotes:

Ana van Es, Jilles van Dam, Mahmoud Muna, Margaux Thierrée, Naomi Jenkins, Neal Hirst, Teresa Lampropoulos.

AUTHOR THANKS
Daniel Robinson

Special thanks to (north to south): Talal (Mt Hermon); Clery (Metulla); Irit Steinberg (Hula Nature Reserve); Meni Tzuberi (Katzrin); Chanoch (Yehudiyya); Ido Shaked (Gamla); Doron (Bikta b'Kadita); Riki & Dov Ruckenstein and Moshe Tov Kreps (Tzfat); Tal Ben David (Rosh Pina); Etha & Erwin Frenkel (Korazim); Lilach (Majrase); Mariana Bravo (Magdala); Nissim Mazig (Kursi); Moshe Ohz (Tiberias); Ayala & Ofer Markman, Roni Barziv and Mira Lugasi (Haifa); Egi (Hammat Gader); Maoz Yinon, Linda Hallel, Sami Jabali & Silke, Emile Emran, Abed and Abu Ayyad of the White Mosque, and Tariq Bsoul of Nazarene Transport & Tourism (Nazareth); Vered (Belvoir); Sarinah Kalb and Leo, Bella and Shoshana (Tel Aviv); Noam (Ein Feshkha); Michal and Sivan (Ein Gedi Nature Reserve); Shai (Ein Gedi Field School); Kfir

(Masada); Sarah (Ein Bokek tourist office); Asaf Madmony (Ne'ot HaKikar); and, most especially, my wife, Rachel, and son, Yair, for their unwavering support, understanding and patience.

Orlando Crowcroft

I would like to thank the staff and volunteers at the Cinema Guest House and the Freedom Theatre in Jenin for their insights and advice on their city – past, present and future. Yazeed Abu Khdeir in Jerusalem, my fixer and friend and a partner on West Bank road trips too numerous to mention. Layla Torres in Bethlehem. All the staff at Area D Hostel in Ramallah and International Friends Youth Hostel in Nablus; my homes away from home during the research of this book. Hazem Balousha and Heidi Levine, who looked after me in Gaza. Lastly every West Bank taxi driver, coffee seller or shopkeeper who went out of their way to put me on the right path when I pulled up and begged directions in broken Arabic.

Virginia Maxwell

Many thanks to Peter Handsaker and Pat Yale, who accompanied me on two research trips to Israel for this job, as well as to my expert co-author Daniel Robinson and to locals Mira Marcus, Oren Mor, Yael Biedermann, Maoz Inon, Yaron Burgin, Naomi Dvora, Gal Mor, Lee Balot, Yoash Limon and Omer from the Overstay.

Jenny Walker

Returning to Petra is always a great pleasure, not just on account of the spectacular ancient city, but also because the people of Wadi Musa and Umm Sayoun live up to their reputation for 'heart and wit'. Thanks as ever to all Jordanian friends who have helped over the years of engagement with this chapter and to my beloved husband, Sam Owen, who accompanied and supported as ever during research and write-up.

ACKNOWLEDGEMENTS

Climate map data adapted from Peel MC, Finlayson BL & McMahon TA (2007) 'Updated World Map of the Köppen-Geiger Climate Classification', *Hydrology and Earth System Sciences*, 11, 1633–44.

Cover photograph: Hisham's Palace, West Bank, Vdovin Ivan/Alamy.

Illustrations: pp50-1 by Javier Zarracina; pp338-9 by Michael Weldon.

THIS BOOK

This 8th edition of Lonely Planet's *Israel & the Palestinian Territories* guidebook was researched and written by Daniel Robinson (coordinating author), Orlando Crowcroft, Virginia Maxwell and Jenny Walker. The previous edition was written by Daniel Robinson (coordinat-ing author), Michael Kohn, Dan Savery Raz and Jenny Walker. This guidebook was produced by the following:

Destination Editor Helen Elfer

Product Editors Kate Chapman, Samantha Forge

Book Designer Cam Ashley

Assisting Editors Sarah Bailey, Katie Connolly, Melanie Dankel, Kate Evans, Kirsten Rawlings

Cover Researcher Naomi Parker

Thanks to Elizabeth Jones, Kate Kiely, Ilana Kosky, Anne Mason, Kate Mathews, Claire Naylor, Karyn Noble, Katie O'Connell, Lonely Planet Cartography, Samantha Tyson

Index

Map Legend

Sights

- Beach
- Bird Sanctuary
- Buddhist
- Castle/Palace
- Christian
- Confucian
- Hindu
- Islamic
- Jain
- Jewish
- Monument
- Museum/Gallery/Historic Building
- Ruin
- Shinto
- Sikh
- Taoist
- Winery/Vineyard
- Zoo/Wildlife Sanctuary
- Other Sight

Activities, Courses & Tours

- Bodysurfing
- Diving
- Canoeing/Kayaking
- Course/Tour
- Sento Hot Baths/Onsen
- Skiing
- Snorkelling
- Surfing
- Swimming/Pool
- Walking
- Windsurfing
- Other Activity

Sleeping

- Sleeping
- Camping

Eating

- Eating

Drinking & Nightlife

- Drinking & Nightlife
- Cafe

Entertainment

- Entertainment

Shopping

- Shopping

Information

- Bank
- Embassy/Consulate
- Hospital/Medical
- Internet
- Police
- Post Office
- Telephone
- Toilet
- Tourist Information
- Other Information

Geographic

- Beach
- Hut/Shelter
- Lighthouse
- Lookout
- Mountain/Volcano
- Oasis
- Park
- Pass
- Picnic Area
- Waterfall

Population

- Capital (National)
- Capital (State/Province)
- City/Large Town
- Town/Village

Transport

- Airport
- Border crossing
- Bus
- Cable car/Funicular
- Cycling
- Ferry
- Metro station
- Monorail
- Parking
- Petrol station
- Subway station
- Taxi
- Train station/Railway
- Tram
- Underground station
- Other Transport

Note: Not all symbols displayed above appear on the maps in this book

Routes

- Tollway
- Freeway
- Primary
- Secondary
- Tertiary
- Lane
- Unsealed road
- Road under construction
- Plaza/Mall
- Steps
- Tunnel
- Pedestrian overpass
- Walking Tour
- Walking Tour detour
- Path/Walking Trail

Boundaries

- International
- State/Province
- Disputed
- Regional/Suburb
- Marine Park
- Cliff
- Wall

Hydrography

- River, Creek
- Intermittent River
- Canal
- Water
- Dry/Salt/Intermittent Lake
- Reef

Areas

- Airport/Runway
- Beach/Desert
- Cemetery (Christian)
- Cemetery (Other)
- Glacier
- Mudflat
- Park/Forest
- Sight (Building)
- Sportsground
- Swamp/Mangrove

OUR STORY

A beat-up old car, a few dollars in the pocket and a sense of adventure. In 1972 that's all Tony and Maureen Wheeler needed for the trip of a lifetime – across Europe and Asia overland to Australia. It took several months, and at the end – broke but inspired – they sat at their kitchen table writing and stapling together their first travel guide, *Across Asia on the Cheap*. Within a week they'd sold 1500 copies. Lonely Planet was born.

Today, Lonely Planet has offices in Franklin, London, Melbourne, Oakland, Beijing and Delhi, with more than 600 staff and writers. We share Tony's belief that 'a great guidebook should do three things: inform, educate and amuse'.

OUR WRITERS

Daniel Robinson

Coordinating Author; Haifa & the North Coast, Lower Galilee & Sea of Galilee, Upper Galilee & Golan, The Dead Sea Brought up near San Francisco and Chicago, Daniel spent part of his childhood in Jerusalem, a bit of his youth at Kibbutz Lotan and many years in Tel Aviv, where he worked on a PhD in late Ottoman history, covered suicide bombings for the Associated Press, and helped lead the local Critical Mass campaign for bike paths. A Lonely Planet author since 1989, he holds a BA in Near Eastern Studies from Princeton and an MA in Jewish History from Tel Aviv University. His favourite activities in Israel include cycling Tel Aviv's historic avenues, hiking the wadis of Ein Gedi, and birdwatching in the Hula and Arava Valleys.

Read more about Daniel at https://auth.lonelyplanet.com/profiles/daniel_robinson

Orlando Crowcroft

West Bank, The Gaza Strip Orlando Crowcroft has spent the bulk of his career so far reporting from the Middle East, including Egypt, the Gulf and the Kurdish region of Iraq. His first trip to the West Bank was to attend a football tournament in 2012, when a surprise Palestinian win in Hebron against Tunisia triggered a pitch invasion – and a love affair with the West Bank. In 2014 he was based in Tel Aviv and Jerusalem as a stringer for the Guardian and the National, covering Israel, the West Bank and Gaza during the summer war between Hamas and Israel.

Virginia Maxwell

Jerusalem, Tel Aviv, The Negev Although based in Australia, Virginia spends much of her year researching guidebooks in the Mediterranean region. The author of guidebooks to Italy, Spain, Turkey, Morocco, Egypt, Syria, Lebanon, Iran and the United Arab Emirates, she knows Mediterranean Europe and the Middle East well and adores both regions for their culture, history, architecture, art and food. This is her first time covering Israel & the Palestinian Territories for Lonely Planet. Virginia also wrote the Safe Travel section.

Jenny Walker

Petra Jenny Walker has written widely on the Middle East in many Lonely Planet publications and is a member of the British Guild of Travel Writers. She has a long academic engagement in the region (dissertation on Doughty and Lawrence, MPhil thesis from Oxford University on the perception of the Arabic Orient and current PhD studies at NTU) and is currently Associate Dean at Caledonian University College of Engineering in Oman. She has travelled in 110 countries from Panama to Mongolia.

Published by Lonely Planet Publications Pty Ltd
ABN 36 005 607 983
8th edition – October 2015
ISBN 978 1 76034 276 0
© Lonely Planet 2015   Photographs © as indicated 2015
10 9 8 7 6 5 4 3 2 1
Printed in China